THE GREENWOOD ENCYCLOPEDIA OF

African American Literature

THE GREENWOOD ENCYCLOPEDIA OF
African American Literature

VOLUME III

I–N

Edited by

Hans Ostrom and J. David Macey, Jr.

GREENWOOD PRESS
Westport, Connecticut • London

Library of Congress Cataloging-in-Publication Data

The Greenwood encyclopedia of African American literature / edited by Hans Ostrom and J. David Macey, Jr.
    p.   cm.
    Includes bibliographical references.
    ISBN 0–313–32972–9 (set : alk. paper)—ISBN 0–313–32973–7 (v. 1 : alk. paper)—
    ISBN 0–313–32974–5 (v. 2 : alk. paper)—ISBN 0–313–32975–3 (v. 3 : alk. paper)—
    ISBN 0–313–32976–1 (v. 4 : alk. paper)—ISBN 0–313–32977–X (v. 5 : alk. paper)   1. American
    literature—African American authors—Encyclopedias.   2. African Americans—Intellectual life—
    Encyclopedias.   3. African Americans in literature—Encyclopedias.   I. Ostrom, Hans A.
    II. Macey, J. David.
    PS153.N5G73   2005
    810.9'896073—dc22   2005013679

British Library Cataloguing in Publication Data is available.

This book is included in the *African American Experience* database from Greenwood Electronic Media.
For more information, visit www.africanamericanexperience.com.

Library of Congress Catalog Card Number: 2005013679
ISBN: 0–313–32972–9 (set)
        0–313–32973–7 (vol. I)
        0–313–32974–5 (vol. II)
        0–313–32975–3 (vol. III)
        0–313–32976–1 (vol. IV)
        0–313–32977–X (vol. V)

First published in 2005

Greenwood Press, 88 Post Road West, Westport, CT 06881
An imprint of Greenwood Publishing Group, Inc.
www.greenwood.com

Printed in the United States of America

The paper used in this book complies with the
Permanent Paper Standard issued by the National
Information Standards Organization (Z39.48–1984).

10 9 8 7 6 5 4 3 2 1

CONTENTS

LIST OF ENTRIES

Johnson, Freddie Lee, III (born 1958)

Johnson, Georgia Douglas (1886–1966)

Johnson, Guy (born 1945)

Johnson, Helene (1906–1995)

Johnson, Jack (1878–1946)

Johnson, James P[rice] (1894–1955)

Johnson, James Weldon (1871–1938)

Johnson, Mat (born 1970)

Johnson Publishing Company (1942–present)

Johnson-Coleman, Lorraine (born 1962)

Johnson-Hodge, Margaret

Jones, Edward P. (born 1950)

Jones, Edward Smyth (1881–?)

Jones, Gayl (born 1949)

Jones, Laurence C. (1884–1975)

Jones, Patricia Spears (born 1955)

Jones, Sarah (born 1974)

Jones, Solomon (born 1967)

Jones-Meadows, Karen

Jordan, Barbara Charline (1936–1996)

Jordan, June (1936–2002)

Jordan, Michael Jeffrey (born 1963)

Journal of Black Poetry (1966–1973)

Joyce, Joyce Ann (born 1949)

Just Us Books (1988–present)

Kai, Nubia (born 1948)

Karenga, Maulana (born 1941)

Kaufman, Bob (1926–1986)

Keats, Ezra Jack (1919–1983)

Keckley, Elizabeth (c. 1818–1907)

Keene, John R., Jr. (born 1965)

Kelley, Norman (born 1954)

Kelley, William Melvin (born 1937)

Kelley-Hawkins, Emma Dunham (1863–1938)

Kenan, Randall Garrett (born 1963)

Kennedy, Adrienne (born 1931)

Killens, John Oliver (1916–1987)

Kincaid, Jamaica (born 1949)

King, Martin Luther, Jr. (1929–1968)

King, Woodie, Jr. (born 1937)

Kitchen Table: Women of Color Press (1981–present)

Kitt, Sandra (born 1947)

Knight, Etheridge (1931–1991)

Knopf, Alfred A. (1892–1984)

Kocher, Ruth Ellen (born 1965)

Komunyakaa, Yusef (born 1947)

Kool Moe Dee (born 1963)

Kweli, Talib (born 1975)

Labor

Ladd, Florence (born 1932)

Lamar, Jake (born 1961)

Lane, Pinkie Gordon (born 1923)

Langston, John Mercer (1829–1897)

Langston Hughes Society (1981–present)

Lanusse, Armand (1812–1867)

Larsen, Nella (1891–1964)

Last Poets, The

Lattany, Kristin Hunter (born 1931)

LaValle, Victor (born 1972)

Lawrence, Jacob (1917–2000)

Leadbelly [Ledbetter, Huddie] (1889–1949)

Lee, Andrea (born 1953)

Lee, Helen Elaine (born 1959)

Lee, Jarena (1783–?)

Lee, Spike (born 1957)

Lesbian Literature

Lester, Julius (born 1939)

Lewis, Theophilus (1891–1974)

Lincoln, C[harles] Eric (1924–2000)

Literary Canon

TOPICAL LIST OF ENTRIES

The following list of entries, organized according to topical categories, includes a complete list of author entries and provides a comprehensive overview of the *Encyclopdedia*'s coverage of the literary, critical, historical, cultural, and regional contexts of African American literature. Please consult the Index for assistance in locating discussions of specific literary texts and other topics.

Athletes and Sports

Ali, Muhammad (born 1942)

Basketball

Campanella, Roy (1921–1993)

Carter, Rubin "Hurricane" (born 1937)

Johnson, Jack (1878–1946)

Jordan, Michael Jeffrey (born 1963)

Louis, Joe (1914–1981)

Mays, Willie Howard, Jr. (born 1931)

Robinson, Jackie [Jack Roosevelt] (1919–1972)

Authors

Abernathy, Ralph David (1926–1990)

Adams, Jenoyne (born 1972)

Adoff, Arnold (born 1935)

Ai (born 1947)

Albert, Octavia Victoria Rogers (1853–1889)

Aldridge, Ira (1807–1867)

Alers, Rochelle (born 1943)

Alexander, Elizabeth (born 1962)

Alexander, Lewis (1900–1945)

Allen, Jeffrey Renard (born 1962)

Allen, Richard (1760–1831)

Allen, Samuel Washington (born 1917)

Allison, Hughes (1908–c. 1974)

Als, Hilton (born 1961)

Amos, Robyn (born 1971)

Anderson, Garland (1886–1939)

Anderson, Mignon Holland (born 1945)

Cotter, Joseph Seamon, Sr. (1861–1949)

Cowdery, Mae V. (1909–1953)

Craft, William (1824–1900) and Ellen Smith Craft (1826–1891)

Crafts, Hannah

Crouch, Stanley (born 1945)

Crummell, Alexander (1819–1898)

Cruse, Harold Wright (born 1916)

Cullen, Countee (1903–1946)

Cuney-Hare, Maud (1874–1936)

Dandridge, Raymond Garfield (1882–1930)

Danner, Margaret Esse Taylor (1915–1984)

Danticat, Edwidge (born 1969)

Darden, Christopher (born 1957)

Dash, Julie (born 1952)

davenport, doris (born 1949)

Davis, Angela Y. (born 1944)

Davis, Bridgett M. (born 1960)

Davis, Daniel Webster (1862–1913)

Davis, Frank Marshall (1905–1987)

Davis, Thulani N. (born 1949)

Dean, Phillip Hayes (born 1937)

DeBerry, Virginia (born c. 1962) and Donna Grant (born c. 1963)

Delaney, Lucy A. (c. 1828–?)

Delany, Martin R. (1812–1885)

Delany, Samuel R. (born 1942)

DeLoach, Nora (1940–2001)

Demby, William (born 1922)

Dent, Thomas Covington (1932–1998)

Derricotte, Toi (born 1941)

Dett, R[obert] Nathaniel (1882–1943)

Detter, Thomas P. (c. 1826–?)

DeVeaux, Alexis (born 1948)

Dickerson, Debra J. (born 1959)

Dickey, Eric Jerome (born 1961)

Dillon, Leo (born 1933) and Diane Dillon (born 1933)

Dixon, Melvin (1950–1992)

Dodson, Howard (born 1939)

Dodson, Owen (1914–1983)

Dorr, David F. (1827/1828–1872)

Douglass, Frederick (1818–1895)

Dove, Rita (born 1952)

Drake, David (c. 1800–c. 1870)

Drumgoold, Kate (c. 1858–?)

Du Bois, W.E.B. (1868–1963)

Duckett, Larry (1953–2001)

Due, Tananarive (born 1966)

Duke, Lynne (born 1956)

Dumas, Henry (1934–1968)

Dunbar, Paul Laurence (1872–1906)

Dunbar-Nelson, Alice Moore (1875–1935)

Duncan, Thelma Myrtle (born 1902)

Dunham, Katherine (born 1909)

Durem, Ray (1915–1963)

Durham, David Anthony (born 1969)

Dyson, Michael Eric (born 1958)

Eady, Cornelius (born 1954)

Edmonds, S[heppard] Randolph (1900–1983)

Edwards, Grace F[rederica] (born c. 1943)

Edwards, Junius (born 1929)

Edwards, Louis (born 1962)

Elam, Patricia (born c. 1971)

Elaw, Zilpha (c. 1790–?)

Elder, Lonne, III (1927–1996)

Elizabeth (1766–1866)

Ellis, Erika (born 1965)

Tyree, Omar (born 1969)

Ulen, Eisa Nefertari (born 1968)

Van Der Zee, James (1886–1983)

Vashon, George Boyer (1824–1878)

Verdelle, A. J. (born 1960)

Vernon, Olympia (born 1973)

Vroman, Mary Elizabeth (1923–1967)

Wade-Gayles, Gloria Jean (born 1938)

Walker, Alice (born 1944)

Walker, Blair S. (born 1955)

Walker, David (1785–1830)

Walker, Joseph A. (1935–2003)

Walker, Margaret Abigail (1915–1998)

Walker, Persia (born 1957)

Walker, Rebecca (born 1969)

Wallace, Michele Faith (born 1952)

Walrond, Eric D[erwent] (1898–1966)

Walter, Mildred Pitts (born 1922)

Walton, Anthony (born 1960)

Waniek, Marilyn Nelson. *See* Nelson, Marilyn

Ward, Douglas Turner (born 1930)

Ward, Jerry Washington, Jr. (born 1943)

Ward, [James] Theodore (Ted) (1902–1983)

Washington, Booker T. (1856–1915)

Washington, Mary Helen (born 1941)

Washington, Teresa N. (born 1971)

Waters, Ethel (1896–1977)

Weatherly, Tom (born 1942)

Weaver, Afaa Michael (born 1951)

Webb, Frank J. (c. 1828–c. 1894)

Webb, Mary (1828–1859)

Weber, Carl (born 1970)

Wesley, Dorothy Burnett Porter (1905–1995)

Wesley, Valerie Wilson (born 1947)

West, Cheryl L. (born 1965)

West, Dorothy (1907–1998)

Wheatley, Phillis (c. 1753–1784)

Whipper, William (1804–1876)

White, Edgar Nkosi (born 1947)

White, Paulette Childress (born 1948)

Whitehead, Colson (born 1969)

Whitfield, James Monroe (1822–1871)

Whitfield, Van (born c. 1964)

Whitman, Albery Allson (1851–1901)

Wideman, John Edgar (born 1941)

Wilkins, Roy (1901–1981)

Wilks, Talvin Winston (born 1961)

Williams, Bert (1874–1922)

Williams, Crystal (born 1970)

Williams, Edward Christopher (1871–1929)

Williams, George Washington (1849–1891)

Williams, John A. (born 1925)

Williams, Samm-Art (born 1946)

Williams, Sherley Anne (1944–1999)

Williams-Garcia, Rita (born 1957)

Wilson, August (born 1945)

Wilson, Edward Everett (1867–1952)

Wilson, Ernest James, Jr. (1920–1990)

Wilson, Francis H. (Frank) (1886–1956)

Wilson, Harriet E. (c. 1827–c. 1863)

Winbush, Raymond (born 1948)

Wolfe, George C. (born 1954)

Woods, Paula L. (born 1953)

Woodson, Jacqueline (born 1964)

Wright, Bil (born c. 1974)

Wright, Charles H. (born 1918)

Wright, Charles S. (born 1932)

Wright, Courtni Crump (born 1950)

Historical and Cultural Figures

Literary Movements, Schools, and Organizations

Music and Musicians

I

Iceberg Slim (1918–1992) (also known as Robert Beck; born Robert Lee Maupin). Novelist. Sometimes referred to as "America's pimp laureate," Robert Lee Maupin was born August 4, 1918, the son of a hotel chef, in **Chicago, Illinois**. He is more widely recognized by the names Iceberg Slim or Robert Beck, but especially the former. The story of Iceberg Slim's hard life is as powerful as any of his fiction. His father abandoned his family just after he was born; his mother later remarried. The happiness that followed was short-lived; his mother fell in love with a street hustler and his stepfather died the following year. An event that had manifold effects on the young Maupin was the hustler's horrific beating of his mother (followed by the man's disappearance) on his fourteenth birthday. This image of his suffering mother entrenched in him a hardness and a bitterness that is visible both in his life on the streets and in his writing. Upon graduating from high school with extremely high marks, Maupin won a scholarship to the Tuskegee Institute. He was already drawn to the life of the streets, however. During his second year in college, he began pimping and bootlegging liquor. After he was caught, and while in prison, he changed his name to Iceberg Slim, a moniker representing his ice-cold emotions. In Chicago, during the 1940s and 1950s, he became essentially the king of pimps, possessing stables of prostitutes. Around this time, he became addicted to heroin and cocaine, but got clean after his third stretch in prison. Upon his release in the 1960s, he moved to **Los Angeles, California,** to pursue a normal life and took up writing, changing his name to Robert Beck. Beck was his mother's last name at the time. His books all describe the rage existing in the heart, soul, and daily life of the Black man, with special emphasis being placed on the sex and violence that come along with it. He felt his life was the result of being in a torture chamber behind America's happy façade of democracy and justice. He had been an inmate and a victim of this system, and it was up to him to construct a new, literary life for himself. He died on April 28, 1992, at the age of seventy-three.

Two of his best-known works, *Pimp: The Story of My Life* (1967) and *The Naked Soul of Iceberg Slim* (1971), are the autobiographical chronicles of his criminal career. *Trick Baby* (1967) is the story of Johnny O'Brien, aka "White Folks," the son of a Black prostitute and a White "john." His light skin allows him to pass for White, but he refuses to do so because of his Black consciousness (*see* **passing**). He uses his ability to pass and his knowledge of the con to scam White people. The story was first related to Beck by one of his prison cellmates. *Trick Baby* was made into a film by Universal Pictures in 1973 (and is sometimes called *Double Con*) and is extremely representative of the **blaxploitation** sub-genre of cinema. The studio bought the rights to *Pimp* after the success of *The Godfather*, but because of its controversial subject matter, the project was put on indefinite hold. *Mama Black Widow* (1969) follows the fortunes of a Southern African American family during the migration to the North, while focusing on the **coming of age** of Chicago drag queen Otis Tilson in the 1930s and 1940s. His other books included *Airtight Willie & Me* (1979), *Death Wish* (1976), *Doom Fox* (1998), and *Long White Con* (1977) (a sequel to *Trick Baby*). The books of Iceberg Slim (with the exception of *Doom Fox*) were all published in the 1960s and 1970s and influenced the **rap** artists of the 1980s and 1990s, particularly Ice-T, who took his name in tribute to "the greatest hustler of all time."

A theme that runs throughout the work of Iceberg Slim is the importance of Black identity and Black consciousness. He was a vociferous supporter of the **Black Panther Party**, and his use of street slang has been celebrated as one of the most identifying characteristics in the genre. His ear for the underworld is absolutely unsurpassed. His work, along with that of **Donald Goines, Chester Himes**, and **Clarence Cooper, Jr.**, gives readers an unusual amount of insight into the pain and struggle found in the ghettoes of the United States.

Resources: Iceberg Slim: *Airtight Willie & Me* (New York: Holloway House, 1996); *Death Wish* (New York: Holloway House, 1996); *Doom Fox* (New York: Grove, 1998); *The Long White Con* (New York: Holloway House, 1988); *Mama Black Widow* (New York: Holloway House, 1996); *The Naked Soul of Iceberg Slim* (by Robert Beck) (New York: Holloway House, 2000); *Pimp: The Story of My Life* (New York: Holloway House, 1987); *Trick Baby* (New York: Holloway House, 1996); Peter A. Muckley, *Iceberg Slim: Life as Art* (Pittsburgh, PA: Dorrance, 2003).

Marc Leverette

Internet. *See* **E-Zines, E-News, E-Journals, and E-Collections.**

J

Jackson, Angela (born 1951). Poet, novelist, short story writer, and playwright. Jackson is perhaps best known for her work as a poet. She was born in Greenville, Mississippi, but moved from **the South** to **Chicago, Illinois**, as a child. Her work is infused with both Southern and Midwestern influences. Jackson remained in Chicago and attended college at Northwestern University. In 1970, during the **Black Arts Movement**, Jackson became involved in Chicago's Organization of Black American Culture (**OBAC**), whose goal was to advance the conscious development and articulation of a Black aesthetic. Studying with the poet **Haki Madhubuti**, who was also a member of the workshop, Jackson began to perform her poetry and soon had a reputation as a talented poet and writer. In 1976 Jackson became coordinator of OBAC. She has acknowledged her time in the organization as the greatest influence on her writing.

Much of Jackson's work focuses on identity, family, spirituality, and love. Her style is tied to the African American oral tradition, and it is filled with language that is thick with metaphor and simile, rhythm and sound. Her words convey a tonality rich with a musicality and inflection that express an urban sensibility. Jackson also employs **signifying**, which relies on the indirect use of words, thereby altering the meaning of the word. This technique is especially evident in the poem "The Village Woman and the Swinging Guests (of Tarzan and Jane)."

In 1974 Jackson published her first collection of poetry, *Voodoo/Love Magic*, which was followed by *The Greenville Club* in 1977. Jackson has also found success as a playwright. In the late 1970s she began to adapt her poetry for the stage, and in 1978 the Chicago Showcase Theatre produced her play *Witness!*

In 1980 the Parkway Community House Theatre produced *Shango Diaspora: An African-American Myth of Womanhood and Love*, and in 1984 it produced *When the Wind Blows*.

Jackson has received many honors and awards, including being a representative at the United States 2nd World Festival of Black and African Arts and Culture (FESTAC) in 1977 and the Shelley Memorial Award of the Poetry Society of America.

Resources: Trudier Harris and Thadious M. Davis, eds., *Dictionary of Literary Biography*, vol. 41, *Afro-American Poets Since 1955* (Detroit: Gale Research Co., 1985); Angela Jackson: *And All These Roads Be Luminous* (Chicago: TriQuarterly Books/ Northwestern University Press, 1998); *Dark Legs and Silk Kisses: The Beatitudes of the Spinners* (Evanston, IL: TriQuarterly Books/Northwestern University Press, 1993); *The Greenville Club* (Chicago: Obahouse Press, 1977); *Solo in Boxcar Third Floor E.* (Chicago: Obahouse Press, 1985); *Voodoo/Love Magic* (Chicago: Third World Press, 1974); Scott Peacock, ed., *Contemporary Authors*, vol. 176 (Farmington Hills, MI: Gale Group, 1999).

Cameron Christine Clark

Jackson, Brian Keith (born 1967). Novelist and playwright. Brian Keith Jackson, one of the most critically acclaimed members of a younger generation of American writers, was born in **New Orleans, Louisiana**. After receiving his B.A. from Northeast Louisiana University (now the University of Louisiana at Monroe) in 1990, he moved to New York City, where he was a stand-up comic and actor. He became a playwright in order to correct the images of African American men in the theater, movies, and the media. His plays were performed at various New York venues, such as La Mama Experimental Theatre Club, **Nuyorican Poets Café**, and Theater for the New City.

Jackson, who has written for *Nylon*, *Paper*, *The London Observer*, and *Vibe*, has garnered international as well as national attention since the publication of his debut novel, *The View from Here* (1997). Published in a French edition as *Vu d'ici* (2001) and acknowledged as a best-seller in South Africa, *The View from Here* focuses on African American family life in **the South**. Jackson's other novels are *Walking Through Mirrors* (1998) and *The Queen of Harlem* (2002). In all three novels, African American protagonists are confronted with issues of identity. Excerpts from Jackson's novels have appeared in anthologies such as *Shade* (1996), edited by Bruce Morrow and Charles H. Rowell, and *Gumbo: A Celebration of African American Writing* (2002), edited by **Marita Golden** and **E. Lynn Harris**. *The View from Here* has received the Literary Award for First Novelist from the Black Caucus of the American Library Association, and *The Queen of Harlem* has been cited by *Black Issues Book Review* as one of the best books of 2002. Additional recognition of Jackson's literary talents include the Middle-Atlantic Writers Association's Distinguished Writers Award (2002) and fellowships from Art Matters, the Jerome Foundation, and the Millay Colony for the Arts.

Although he has been compared with such celebrated authors as **John Edgar Wideman**, **Alice Walker**, **Toni Morrison**, and Truman Capote, and has achieved popular culture status with his selection as one of *People* magazine's Top 50 Bachelors (2002), Brian Keith Jackson remains focused on presenting the diversity of the African American experience in print.

Resources: "Brian Keith Jackson," *People*, June 24, 2002, p. 107; "Class Act," *New York*, Apr. 22, 2002, p. 146; Marita Golden and E. Lynn Harris, eds., *Gumbo: A Celebration of African American Writing* (New York: Harlem Moon, 2002); Brian Keith Jackson: *The Queen of Harlem* (New York: Doubleday, 2002); *The View from Here* (New York: Pocket Books, 1997); *Walking Through Mirrors* (New York: Atria, 1998); "Uptown Boy," *Paper*, June–July 2002, 34.

Linda M. Carter

Jackson, Elaine (born 1943). Playwright, actor, and professor. Jackson is best known for her first play, *Toe Jam* (1971), which is, in part, about unique predicaments faced by African American women, especially actors, in the theater. It was published in the landmark collection *Black Drama Anthology* (1971), edited by **Woodie King, Jr.**, and **Ron Milner**. The anthology also included plays by **Amiri Baraka**, **Loften Mitchell**, **Ben Caldwell**, **Phillip Hayes Dean**, and **Ed Bullins**. Jackson thus is among the African American dramatists whose careers emerged during the **Black Arts Movement**. She was born and grew up in **Detroit, Michigan**, and attended Wayne State University. She became an actor and moved to California, but also appeared in plays Off-Broadway in New York City. Jackson's play *Cockfight*, concerning a troubled marriage, was produced in 1976, followed by *Paper Dolls* (1979), which, like *Toe Jam*, concerns African American actors. *Paper Dolls* was published in the anthology *Nine Plays by Black Women* (1986). *Birth Rites* (1987) concerns mother–daughter relationships. Jackson has won a National Endowment for the Arts award and a Rockefeller Foundation award, both for playwriting. She has taught at Wayne State University, as well as at Lake Forest College, outside **Chicago, Illinois**.

Resources: "*Cockfight*," *The New Yorker*, Oct. 31, 1977, pp. 116–117; Rosemary K. Curb, "'Goin' Through Changes': Mother–Daughter Confrontations in Three Recent Plays by Young Black Women," *Kentucky Folklore Record* 25 (1979), 96–102; Elaine Jackson: *Paper Dolls*, in *Nine Plays by Black Women*, ed. Margaret B. Wilkerson (New York: New American Library, 1986), 347–423; *Toe Jam*, in *Black Drama Anthology*, ed. Woodie King, Jr., and Ron Milner (New York: New American Library, 1971), 592–671; Yolanda M. Manora, "Jackson, Elaine," in *The Oxford Companion to African American Literature*, ed. William L. Andrews, Frances Smith Foster, and Trudier Harris (New York: Oxford University Press, 1997), 391–392; Barbara Molette, "They Speak. Who Listens? Black Women Playwrights," *Black World* 25, no. 6 (1976), 28–34; Larry Neal, "The Black Arts Movement," *Drama Review* 12, no. 4 (1968), 29–39; Bernard L. Peterson, Jr., *Contemporary Black American Playwrights and Their Plays: A Bio-graphical Directory and Dramatic Index* (Westport, CT: Greenwood Press, 1988), 266.

Hans Ostrom

Jackson, George Lester (1941–1971). Prison activist and autobiographer. Jackson's memoirs provided radical critique of American society during turbulent 1960s and early 1970s. Jackson was born September 23, 1941, in **Chicago, Illinois**. His father was a postal worker and his mother was extremely protective of her son, rarely allowing him to leave the house during his early childhood years. During his adolescence, however, Jackson was often in trouble with the law.

His father moved the family to **Los Angeles, California**, in 1956, but the change in location failed to halt Jackson's criminal activity. Jackson joined a street gang called the Capones. After spending time at the Paso Robles youth facility north of Los Angeles, Jackson was arrested at age nineteen for a gas station robbery that netted only $71. On the advice of his attorney, and assuming he would receive lenient treatment, Jackson pleaded guilty. Due to his previous offenses, however, he was given an indefinite term of from one year to life in prison.

In 1960, Jackson entered the California prison system, where he would remain for the rest of his life. At Soledad Prison, Jackson challenged institutional rules and regulations; consequently, authorities transferred him to San Quentin Prison. During his tenure at San Quentin, he was influenced by an older inmate, W. L. Nolen, who introduced him to the political writings of Karl Marx and Mao Tse-Tung (*see* **Marxism**). Jackson and Nolen established the Black Guerrilla Family, a revolutionary organization which asserted that African Americans should seek the overthrow of an American capitalist system that perpetuated racism and the economic exploitation of the Black underclass.

Jackson maintained that he was repeatedly denied parole because of his political activities. In 1968, he was returned to Soledad, where he continued to call for revolution and served as a prison organizer for the **Black Panther Party**. In 1970, three Black Soledad prisoners were shot and killed by a White guard. In response, another White guard was murdered, and the authorities blamed Jackson and two other inmates, who became known as the Soledad Brothers. Many critics of the prison system, such as **Angela Y. Davis**, believed that the inmates were being framed, and Jackson fanned these flames with the publication of *Soledad Brother*, a collection of his prison letters that quickly became a best seller. In an effort to express solidarity with his older brother, Jonathan Jackson was killed on August 7, 1970, during an attempt to take over a California courthouse and free three prisoners.

While awaiting trial for the murder of the Soledad guard, Jackson was transferred back to San Quentin in the summer of 1971. There he completed his second book of essays and letters, *Blood in My Eye*, in which he called for a racial civil war in America and predicted his own death. Only a week after the book was completed, Jackson was shot and killed on August 21, 1971, while allegedly attempting to escape from San Quentin. Authorities maintain that Jackson's lawyer, Stephen Bingham, slipped the inmate a gun, while Jackson's supporters assert that the prisoner was murdered for his political activities.

Bingham was later acquitted of the charges. While Jackson's call for revolution was not realized, his writings well demonstrate the radical racial politics of the 1960s. (*See* **Prison Literature**.)

Resources: George Jackson: *Blood in My Eye* (New York: Random House, 1972); *Soledad Brother: The Prison Letters of George Jackson* (New York: Coward-McCann, 1970); Paul Liberatore, *The Road to Hell* (New York: Atlantic Monthly Press, 1996); Eric Mann, *Comrade George* (Cambridge, MA: Hovey Street Press, 1972); Min S. Yee, *The Melancholy History of Soledad Prison* (New York: Harper's Magazine Press, 1973).

Ron Briley

Jackson, Jesse L[ouis] (born 1941). Human rights activist, minister, presidential candidate, and author. Well-known for his activism and captivating speeches, Jesse L. Jackson has also made important contributions to the African American literary tradition. Born in South Carolina, Jackson attended the University of Illinois on a football scholarship. Because of racism, he transferred to North Carolina Agricultural and Technical College, a predominantly Black school. He was elected student body president, and president of the North Carolina Intercollegiate Council on Human Rights. In 1963, he "led a ten-month demonstration that included marches, sit-ins, and boycotts at area establishments where African American patrons were unwelcome" (Williams, 599). In 1964, he received a bachelor's degree in sociology, and served as field representative for the Congress of Racial Equality (CORE), an organization created "to integrate restaurants and other public places" (Altman, 57). Finally, in 1964, President Lyndon B. Johnson signed the Civil Rights Act of 1964 to "[outlaw] discrimination on the basis of race, color, sex, religion, or national origin in public accommodations" (Altman, 49).

A year later, Jackson attended the Chicago Theological Seminary on a Rockefeller grant. While at a march in Selma, Alabama, Jackson met **Martin Luther King, Jr**. In 1966, Jackson joined the Southern Christian Leadership Conference (SCLC). The SCLC had been founded in 1957 by Martin Luther King, Jr., **Ralph David Abernathy**, and others "to help coordinate the growing civil rights movement . . . and to encourage nonviolent, direct-action operations directed toward ending discrimination and segregation" (Altman, 236). King appointed Jackson head of Operation Breadbasket, a program "designed to increase the economic power of African Americans" (Beckner, 106). Jackson was with King when the latter was assassinated in **Memphis, Tennessee**, in 1968.

Jackson continued to be a significant and powerful figure throughout the 1970s and beyond. Resigning from his position with the SCLC in 1971, he founded Operation PUSH (People United to Save Humanity). This program was designed not only for African Americans, but for all impoverished and oppressed people around the world (Williams, 600). Jackson established several successful programs within PUSH, such as PUSH for Excellence, PUSH Commercial Division, and PUSH Ministers Division.

Jesse Jackson surrounded by marchers carrying signs advocating support for the Hawkins-Humphrey Bill for full employment. Courtesy of the Library of Congress.

In the 1980s, Jackson was instrumental in the release of hostages in the Middle East. In 1984 and 1988, he ran for president of the United States, the third African American to do so, following **Frederick Douglass** and **Shirley Chisolm**. In 1986, he founded the National Rainbow Coalition, "to act as a political arm of Operation PUSH" (Williams, 601). His other pursuits include writing a syndicated newspaper column, hosting a round table discussion group airing on cable television, and publishing books.

Jackson's books include *Legal Lynching: Racism, Injustice, and the Death Penalty* (1996), *It's About the Money!* (1999), and *Legal Lynching: The Death Penalty and America's Future* (2001). In the *Legal Lynching* books, Jackson, in collaboration with his son, Congressman Jesse L. Jackson, Jr., and Bruce Shapiro, exposes the history and flaws of the death penalty. He also presents an urgent plea to eliminate capital punishment, because it "fails to deliver on the most basic premises of fairness and justice" (Jackson et al., 8). In *It's About the Money!*, Jackson and his son provide a step-by-step guide to financial empowerment.

Resources: Susan Altman: *The Encyclopedia of African American Heritage* (New York: Facts on File, 1997); *Extraordinary African-Americans* (New York: Children's Press, 2001); Chrisanne Beckner, *100 African-Americans Who Shaped American History* (San Mateo, CA: Bluewood Books, 1996); *Campaign '96* (Educational Video Group, 1996); Marshall Frady, *Jesse: The Life and Pilgrimage of Jesse Jackson* (New York: Random House, 1996); Henry Louis Gates, Jr., and Cornel West, *The African-American Century: How Black Americans Have Shaped Our Country* (New York: Free

Press, 2000); *Great Speeches*, vol. 7 (Educational Video Group, 1991); James Haskins, *I Am Somebody! A Biography of Jesse Jackson* (Hillside, NJ: Enslow, 1992); Jesse L. Jackson, Sr., with Jesse L. Jackson, Jr. *Legal Lynching: Racism, Injustice, and the Death Penalty* (New York: Marlowe, 1996); Jesse L. Jackson, Sr., and Jesse L. Jackson, Jr., with Mary Gotschall, *It's About the Money!* (New York: Times Business, 2000); Jesse Jackson, Sr., Jesse L. Jackson, Jr., and Bruce Shapiro, *Legal Lynching: The Death Penalty and America's Future* (New York: New Press, 2001); *Jesse Jackson: Civil Rights Leader and Politician* (Schlessinger Video Productions, 1992); Bradley Steffens and Dan Woog, *Jesse Jackson* (San Diego: Lucent Books, 2000); Nicole L. Bailey Williams, "Jesse L. Jackson," in *Notable Black American Men*, ed. Jessie Carney Smith (Detroit: Gale Research, 1998).

Gladys L. Knight

Jackson, Mae (born 1946). Poet, fiction writer, playwright, activist, and educator. In 1970, Jackson was awarded the Conrad Kent Rivers Third Memorial Award for her poetry collection *Can I Poet with You?* (1969). Jackson's collection marked her as a member of the **Black Arts Movement**, which emerged in the mid-1960s and was led, in part, by a New York City cohort of artists and poets, including Jackson's friend and mentor **Nikki Giovanni**, as well as by **Amiri Baraka** (then known as LeRoi Jones), **Larry Neal**, **Sonia Sanchez**, **Ben Caldwell**, and others. Their work expressed outrage at the continuing disenfranchisement for African Americans despite the victories of the **Civil Rights Movement**. Jackson located the revolutionary in personal relationships and showcased African American artists in the American scene. In the 1970s and early 1980s, her poems appeared in *Black Creation*, *Black Scholar*, **Negro Digest** and **Journal of Black Poetry**, as well as in the anthologies *Black Out Loud* and *The Poetry of Black America*, both compiled by **Arnold Adoff**. Her short fiction has appeared in *Essence* (Lindberg). In the later 1980s and 1990s, Jackson collaborated as a playwright with the Negro Ensemble Company, taught creative writing workshops in New York City prisons, contributed to the online *Jinn Magazine* (through the Pacific News Service), and was a feature poet in the "Celebrating Literary Brooklyn" series, part of the Langston Hughes Centenary Event. In 1993, Jackson received the Josephine Shaw Lowell Community Service Award in recognition of her contributions to impoverished communities. Jackson remains an active volunteer in her community and is the director of Children Without Walls, an arts program for the children of women in prison (Nemy).

Resources: Arnold Adoff, comp.: *Black Out Loud: An Anthology of Modern Poems by Black Americans* (New York: Atheneum, 1970); *The Poetry of Black America: Anthology of the 20th Century* (New York: Harper & Row, 1973); *Contemporary Authors Online* (Detroit: The Gale Group, 2001), http://galenet.gale.com; Mae Jackson, *Can I Poet with You?* (Detroit: Broadside Press, 1969, 1972); Kathryne V. Lindberg, "Mae Jackson," in *The Oxford Companion to African American Literature*, eds. William L.Andrews, Frances Smith Foster, and Trudier Harris (New York: Oxford University Press, 1997), 392–393; Enid Nemy, "Chronicle," *New York Times*, Mar. 18, 1993,

p. B8; *Selected Black American Authors: An Illustrated Bio-bibliography*, comp. by James A. Page (Boston: G. K. Hall, 1977).

Michelle LaFrance

Jackson, Mattie J. (c. 1846–?). Autobiographer and escaped slave. Mattie J. Jackson's inspiriting life story of family, **slavery**, abuses, resistance, escape and freedom is described in *The Story of Mattie J. Jackson* (1866). Her story was written and arranged by Lucy Schuyler Thompson, Jackson's stepmother. Jackson longed to be educated and to become a historian who would reveal her story of slavery. Her narrative begins with her unnamed great-grandfather, who was captured from an unknown country in Africa and later enslaved in the state of New York. Jackson published her story partly to benefit the newly emancipated and to earn money that would enable her to get an education.

Mattie Jane Jackson was born in Missouri around 1846 to Ellen Turner and Westly Jackson, both slaves. The Jacksons had three daughters. Westly Jackson, after being sold further away, escaped to freedom with his wife's help and blessing. Ellen Jackson Turner attempted an escape with Mattie and her sister, but they were unsuccessful. As slaves, the family was subject to many physical and mental abuses. Ellen Turner Jackson Brown (she wed another man) took every opportunity to encourage her children to escape slavery.

Mattie Jackson escaped to freedom in Indianapolis, Indiana. Her sister also managed to escape, but the family was unable to locate her subsequently. After more than forty-three years of **slavery** and oppression, Mattie's mother escaped bondage with her son. The day after Ellen found Mattie in Indianapolis, they moved to **St. Louis, Missouri**.

To facilitate her escape from slavery, Mattie took her wages ($25.00) from her master's purse. After her escape she demonstrated her ability to write when she sent her former master a thank-you letter for her wages.

Resources: William L. Andrews, ed.: "Introduction," in *Six Women's Slave Narratives* (New York: Oxford University Press, 1988), xxix–xli; *To Tell a Free Story: The First Century of Afro-American Autobiography, 1760–1865* (Urbana: University of Illinois Press, 1986); Joanne M. Braxton, *Black Women Writing Autobiography: A Tradition Within a Tradition* (Philadelphia: Temple University Press, 1989); L. S. Thompson, *The Story of Mattie J. Jackson; A True Story* (1866), in *Six Women's Slave Narratives*, intro. William L. Andrews (New York: Oxford University Press, 1988).

Regina V. Jones

Jackson, Monica. Novelist. Jackson began writing romance novels after she attended a writing workshop and then faced a long period of recovery from surgery. But despite the commercial success of a number of her novels, her writing has not provided her with a great deal of financial security. As a single mother, she has found it necessary to continue to work a "regular" job. Trained as a registered nurse, she continues to work part-time at the Menninger Foundation, a highly regarded psychiatric facility.

Jackson may be best known for her series of novels featuring the Eastmans, an African American family whose passionate attachments are typically connected in some way to broader issues in contemporary African American life. Among her novels are *Heart's Desire* (1998), *A Magical Moment* (1999), *The Look of Love* (1999), *Never Too Late for Love* (2000), and *Too Hot to Handle* (2001).

Among novelists in the **romance** genre, Jackson is also noteworthy for her interest in the paranormal. In *A Magical Moment* and *In My Dreams* (2004), women with preternatural powers avenge the victims of abuse. Jackson has contributed a more wryly humorous story in this general vein to the anthology *Dark Thirst* (2004). It concerns a plus-sized woman who finds an alternative to dieting in being a vampire.

Jackson has also contributed short fiction to the anthology *A Whole Lotta Love* (2004), which includes romantic stories involving plus-sized women, and is one of the four authors who have produced the more widely reviewed collaborative novel *The Sistahood of Shopaholics* (2003).

Resources: Leslie Esdaile, Monica Jackson, Reon Laudat, and Niqui Stanhope Griffin, *The Sistahood of Shopoholics* (New York: St. Martin's, 2003); Monica Jackson: *Heart's Desire* (New York: Kensington, 1998); *In My Dreams* (New York: Kensington/ Dafina, 2004); *The Look of Love* (Washington, DC: Arabesque/BET, 1999); *Love's Celebration* (New York: Kensington, 1998); *A Magical Moment* (Washington, DC: BET, 1999); *Midnight Blue* (New York: Kensington, 1997); *Never Too Late for Love* (Washington, DC: Maidstone/BET, 2000); *Too Hot to Handle* (Washington, DC: BET, 2001); Kalyn Johnson, "Review of *The Sistahood of Shopaholics*," *Black Issues Book Review* 5, no. 6 (Nov./Dec. 2003), 51.

Martin Kich

Jackson, Murray E. (1926–2002). Poet, educator, and politician. A former member of the Wayne State University board of governors, Murray Jackson was born in **Philadelphia, Pennsylvania**, and grew up in **Detroit, Michigan**, where he attended the public schools. After serving in the U.S. Navy, he completed his bachelor's and master's degrees in humanities, specializing in classics, at Wayne State University.

Jackson taught courses in poetry at the Center for the Study of Higher Education and the College of Education at the University of Michigan. After his retirement from teaching in 1992, he often mentored students from diverse backgrounds. He was especially instrumental in helping students from low-income families to succeed in higher education.

Jackson's collections of poetry include *Watermelon Rinds and Cherry Pits* (1991) and *Woodland Sketches: Scenes from Childhood* (1990). A major contributor to the anthology *Paradise Valley Days* (1998), Jackson also published poems in *New Poems from the Third Coast* (2000) and numerous other journals and anthologies. *Bobweaving Detroit* (2004) is a collection of his selected poems. On the dust jacket of the book, a comment by **Arnold Rampersad** of Stanford University reads: "Grounded in the city that Murray Jackson knew so well and clearly loved so much, [these poems] move almost effortlessly from the urban particulars of one man's life, expressed with tenderness, humility, honesty, and intelligence, to some of the deepest questions we can pose about living and loving, struggling and enduring, prevailing." Also on the dust jacket, **Houston A. Baker, Jr.**, of Duke University states: "These resonant poems bob and weave in graceful, dedicated rhythms of urban black public life and dark communal wisdom, to execute the most remarkable ballet of the inner passions, lyrical evocations of natural and peopled worlds where the soul eternally discovers wonder, desire, elegant beauty and love."

As an established poet, Jackson conducted poetry seminars and workshops for students in the Freshman Seminar Program at the University of Michigan, and "Poetry and the City, from Augustine to St. Antoine Street" in the College of Education at Wayne State University. A resident poet for the Detroit Public Library, he convened poetry workshops for the *Writers' Voice* and *Inside/Out* newsletters. He occasionally held poetry sessions in convalescent homes, senior citizen buildings, public schools, and several other venues such as the Harold Washington Library and Dartmouth College.

Besides his educational and creative endeavors, Jackson was active in the community. After serving on the board of trustees of Wayne County Community College, he became the college's first President. He served on several City of Detroit commissions, and he became the first executive director of the Detroit Council of the Arts in 1975.

A member of the American Association of University Professors, Jackson was an advocate for youth, serving on several boards, such as the Detroit Council for Youth Services and the Student Advocacy Center. He received an Honorary Doctor of Humane Letters degree from the board of governors at Wayne State University. He was also appointed governor emeritus and set up an endowed scholarship in his name.

Resources: Detroit Black Writers Guild, *Paradise Valley Days* (Detroit: Black Writers Guild, 1998); Murray Jackson: *Bobweaving Detroit: The Selected Poems of Murray Jackson*, ed. Ted Pearson and Kathryne V. Lindberg (Detroit: Wayne State University Press, 2004); *Watermelon Rinds and Cherry Pits* (Detroit: Broadside Press, 1991); *Woodland Sketches: Scenes from Childhood* (Ypsilanti, MI: X-Press Productions, 1990).

Ella Davis

Jackson, Rebecca Cox (1796–1871). Preacher and autobiographer. All but unknown prior to the rediscovery and publication of her fiery autobiographical narrative, Jackson was an itinerant evangelist and early Black Shaker.

Born free in Horntown, Pennsylvania, Jackson, whose, parents died young, lived with her grandmother and then her brother, Joseph Cox, during her youth. Joseph Cox, a tanner, also ministered to the congregation at Bethel African Methodist Zion Church in **Philadelphia, Pennsylvania**, and was a noted evangelist in his own right. She married Samuel S. Jackson prior to 1830, but the childless couple continued to live with Joseph Cox, with Rebecca working as a seamstress and caring for Joseph's children.

Jackson experienced a religious awakening in 1830, during a tremendous thunderstorm; this scene opens her narrative. She became active in small prayer groups and then in public preaching. Her **gender**—and her assertion that celibacy was required for the holy—made her a controversial figure, and she left her family to become an itinerant preacher.

In the 1840s, Jackson joined a community of Shakers at Watervliet, New York, and it was here that she seems to have met her lifetime companion, Rebecca Perot. Jackson and Perot lived in the Shaker community, usually the only African Americans among the seventy or so residents, until July 1851, when they traveled to Philadelphia. Jackson resumed preaching, attempted to share the beliefs of Shaker founder Ann Lee with African Americans, and experimented with spiritualism. She and Perot returned briefly to Watervliet in the late 1850s and secured the community's blessing to found a Shaker "family" in Philadelphia.

The size and character of Jackson's Philadelphia Shaker community remain unclear. Jackson and Perot were probably seen as outsiders by most Philadelphia Blacks, not only because they were women but also because their beliefs were far from more established groups such as the AME Church. They seem to have supported themselves mainly as domestics. The 1860 census lists them as live-in servants of a White auctioneer, and the 1870 census lists the two sharing a small residence—with Perot as a cook for a family and Jackson, by then ailing and aged, as "keeping house." Still, there were Black Shakers in Philadelphia at the turn of the twentieth century who seem to be traceable to Jackson and Perot, who took the name Rebecca Jackson on Jackson's death. Jackson's narrative was never published in her lifetime but has been recognized since as an important text in the study of nineteenth-century African American spirituality.

Resources: Jean McMahon Humez, "Jackson, Rebecca Cox," in *Black Women in America*, ed. Darlene Clark Hine (Brooklyn, NY: Carlson, 1993), vol. 1, 626–627; Rebecca Cox Jackson, *Gifts of Power: The Writings of Rebecca Cox Jackson*, ed. Jean McMahon Humez (Amherst: University of Massachusetts Press, 1981); Daniel A. Payne, *History of the African Methodist Episcopal Church* (Nashville, TN: AME Sunday School Union, 1891).

Eric Gardner

Jackson, Sheneska (born 1970). Novelist. Sheneska Jackson grew up in South Central **Los Angeles, California**. After she completed a degree in journalism at California State University at Northridge, she could not find work as a reporter, so for three years she supported herself by working as a medical secretary. She eventually channeled her interest in writing in a new direction, and the result reads much like the archetypal Hollywood success story. Her workday started at 7:30, but each morning she would rise at 3:00 A.M. to work for four hours on what would become her first novel. When she sent the manuscript to an agent, he agreed to represent her, and within two days, he had secured a $200,000 contract for two novels from Simon and

Schuster. Literally overnight, Jackson's prospects were almost completely transformed, and she now teaches creative writing in the UCLA extension program.

Jackson's first novel, *Caught Up in the Rapture* (1996), is a somewhat unusual initiation story. The protagonist, a pop singer named Jazmine Deems, is twenty-six years old when the novel opens, but she has always been sheltered by her overprotective father, a preacher. When Jazmine secures her first record contract, it offers her a first full taste of independence, but being self-reliant means that she has to learn how to deal with a record company executive with a serious cocaine habit and with her new boyfriend, a rapper with dangerous gang affiliations.

In Jackson's second novel, *Li'l Mama's Rules* (1997), the main character is a self-controlled teacher. The title refers to the "rules" by which she governs her emotional life, but they have not prepared her to deal with the news that she is HIV-positive. The title of Jackson's third novel, *Blessings* (1998), refers to a beauty shop in which a group of women gather, trying to make sense out of the dilemmas that define their lives and out of the ironies that emerge from the mix of their experiences.

Resources: Thomas J. Brady, "From Dead-end Job to One-way Success," *Philadelphia Inquirer*, June 8, 1997, p. Q2; Sheneska Jackson: *Blessings* (New York: Simon and Schuster, 1998); *Caught Up in the Rapture* (New York: Simon and Schuster, 1996); *Li'l Mama's Rules* (New York: Simon and Schuster, 1997); "Rookie's Rapture," *People*, June 10, 1996, p. 125.

Martin Kich

Jackson-Opoku, Sandra (born 1953). Poet, novelist, scriptwriter, and journalist. Jackson-Opoku was born and reared in **Chicago, Illinois**. After studying at Chicago's Columbia College for three years, Jackson attended the University of Massachusetts as a Peabody scholar, earning a B.A. in Afro-American Studies in 1976. Her education also includes an American Film Institute certificate in creation for television.

Jackson-Opoku's first publication was a book of poetry, *My East Is in My Limbs* (1978). In 1982, she authored the novel *The Tender Mending* with Lia Sanders. This work was awarded a National Endowment for the Arts fellowship in fiction, which Jackson-Opoku used to write *The River Where Blood Is Born* (1997), a family saga concerning the trials faced by a group of African and African American women over two centuries. The book sprang in part from journals Jackson-Opoku wrote when she was an exchange student in Nigeria in the mid-1970s. The novel won the Black Caucus of the American Library Association Award for Fiction in 1998. Jackson-Opoku also received the Coordinating Council of Literary Magazines–General Electric Fiction Award for Younger Writers, and a Ragdale Foundation U.S.–Africa Writers fellowship. In 1997, her play *Affirming the Tradition, Transcending the Condition* was produced by ETA, a creative arts foundation in Chicago. Her most recent novel is *Hot Johnny (and the Women Who Loved Him)*, published in 2001.

Jackson-Opoku currently teaches at Chicago State University and also works as a freelance journalist, a travel columnist, and a television script-writer. In addition to writing, she owns a small communications consulting firm in Chicago that provides editorial, scriptwriting, and corporate communications services.

Resources: Sandra Jackson-Opoku: *Affirming the Tradition, Transcending the Condition* (n.p., 1997); "Ancestors: In Praise of the Imperishable," in *The Woman That I Am: The Literature and Culture of Contemporary Women of Color*, ed. D. Soyini Madison (New York: St. Martin's Press, 1994); *Hot Johnny (and the Women Who Loved Him)* (New York: Ballantine, 2001); *My East Is in My Limbs* (n.p., 1978); *The River Where Blood Is Born* (New York: One World/Ballantine, 1997); Sandra Jackson-Opoku with Lia Sanders, *The Tender Mending* (New York: Dell, 1982); Cara Jepsen, "In Print: A Bad Man Is Good to Find," *Chicago Reader*, Feb. 23, 2001, p. 14; Roger Noel, "She Knows Rivers," *AFRIQUE*, Sept. 1997, 5; Denise I. O'Neal, "Who's the Real Hot Johnny?" *Chicago Sun-Times*, Feb. 4, 2001, p. 14; Jalyne R. Strong, "How 'The River' Was Born," *AFRIQUE*, Sept. 1997, 9.

Esther L. Jones

Jacobs, Harriet Ann (1813–1897). Ex-slave, author of a **slave narrative**, and activist on behalf of the emancipated Southern slaves. Jacobs's narrative, *Incidents in the Life of a Slave Girl. Written by Herself* (1861), marks a significant moment and turning point in nineteenth-century African American literature. As the literary critic **William L. Andrews** has stated, her book, along with the *Narrative* (1845) of **Frederick Douglass**, represents the apex of the slave narrative genre. It incorporates elements of early American literature such as the Indian captivity narrative, **prison literature**, the **novel**, the tragic mulatta tale, and the Puritan jeremiad, while simultaneously introducing crucial aspects of Southern slave culture—**sermons**, **spirituals**, folk traditions— to create a uniquely African American text.

Very few female ex-slaves in the eighteenth and nineteenth centuries possessed the funds, time, patronage, and facility to publish narratives of their lives in **slavery**. Even when they did, quite often they emulated Louisa Picquet or Silvia Dubois by dictating to or conducting interviews with White (usually male) editors, who then transcribed these accounts with considerable editorial license that served their own religious, political, or educational purposes. Fewer still were slave narratives such as *Running a Thousand Miles for Freedom; or, The Escape of William and Ellen Craft from Slavery* (1860), in which, as several critics have suggested, the married authors **Ellen and William Craft** collaborated, even though William's voice dominates. Some literary productions even masqueraded as female slaves' narratives when they had not been written by African Americans at all, such as the sensational *Autobiography of a Female Slave* (1857), penned by the White Kentucky slaveholder Martha Griffith Browne (Mattie Griffith), who had inherited and then liberated her "property," moved north, and befriended abolitionists before emigrating to Europe to revive her failing health.

Incidents in the Life of a Slave Girl therefore carries additional importance because it inserts a rare, first-person, ex-slave woman's voice into the African American literary tradition, thereby introducing a stunning and detailed examination of traumas that slave women exclusively experienced: rape, sexual harassment, the jealousies of the mistress, and forced couplings with other male slaves. With its written indictment of the "peculiar institution," Jacobs's book thus complements the public oral testimonies of **Sojourner Truth, Maria W. Stewart, Frances Ellen Watkins Harper, Sarah Parker Remond, Harriet Tubman, Mary Webb**, Ellen Craft, and other literate and unlettered African American women preaching and lecturing in the United States, England, and Europe before the **Civil War**. Jacobs's life, begun "among the lowly" Southern slaves (Stowe, title page to *Uncle Tom*) and completed in the nation's capital, where she died after working for the newly freed men and women, testifies to the personal and political collaborations that characterized antislavery activism, and later the movements for suffrage, the cessation of racial violence, and African Americans' economic and social enfranchisement.

Jacobs uses pseudonyms in her autobiography (she calls herself "Linda," for example) to protect vulnerable friends and families still living in **the South**. It is due to the exhaustive scholarship of the historian and literary critic Jean Fagan Yellin that we not only can authenticate Jacobs's story, but also can identify the real men and women she fictionalizes. Jacobs was born in bondage in Edenton, North Carolina, to mulatto parents. Her father (Elijah) was an itinerant slave carpenter, and her mother (Delilah) also a slave. She and her brother John enjoyed a sheltered and happy childhood until their mother died in 1819 and, at six years of age, she realized her status as a slave and began chores for her White mistress (Margaret Horniblow). Nevertheless, her owner was a kind one who defied the slave codes in order to instruct Jacobs in reading and writing, and she furthermore encouraged Jacobs's interest in Christianity, trained her to sew, and provided liberal time for her to visit with her principled and assertive free grandmother Martha (Molly Horniblow).

When her kind mistress died (Jacobs's father passed on shortly thereafter), Jacobs was bequeathed in 1825 to the three-year-old daughter of the Flints (Dr. James Norcom, Jr., and his wife, Maria), who became her tormenters. Although her new master was a respected community member and pious churchgoer, out of public view he starved, whipped, and abused his slaves. In particular, he tortured the adolescent Jacobs with whispered sexual innuendoes and his persistent resolve to make her his mistress. Flint's jealous wife suspected her husband's attraction but, in the context of **slavery**, where the adultery of slave masters and the rape of slave women was an everyday reality that polite society ignored, she took out her anger and frustration on Jacobs.

In a bid to gain control of her own body and to assert her will over that of her cruel master, Jacobs became the lover of a wealthy White man whom she calls Mr. Sands (Maj. Samuel Tredwell Sawyer), and they had two children, Ben (Joseph) and Ellen (Louisa). She then escaped the Flint household and hid in woods, swamps, and safe houses until finally returning to her free grandmother's attic, where she remained for the next seven years. With Jacobs's son and daughter now much at risk for sale by Dr. Flint (in slavery, the condition of a child followed that of the mother), Sands reneged on his promise to free them but arranged them to work for relatives up north. Meanwhile, Jacobs wrote letters to Dr. Flint as if her flight to freedom had succeeded.

When Jacobs fled her attic prison in 1842, she found work in New York City as a nanny in the household of the author Nathaniel Parker Willis and his wife, Cornelia, and reunited with her daughter, her brother (who had also escaped and become an abolitionist), and later her son, now a sailor. Flint's relatives, however, tracked her down and came north to reclaim her and her children with the support of the 1850 Fugitive Slave Law. Cornelia Willis ended this situation by initiating a fund-raising effort and eventually purchasing Jacobs's freedom.

Jacobs's letters about slavery in the *New York Tribune* caught the attention of the abolitionist press and galvanized her decision to write a full-fledged book. The activist Lydia Maria Child edited the manuscript on matters of grammar and style, and helped guide it through the publishing process. Jacobs's collaborations with Child and her book's explicit attempts to feminize the evils of slavery underscored the effectiveness of arguments linking the bondage of African American women to the legal, religious, and cultural mores restricting the lives of White middle-class wives and mothers. The publication of *Incidents* in British and American editions links it to **Phillis Wheatley**'s *Poems on Various Subjects, Religious and Moral* (1773) and the autobiographies of such former slaves such as Douglass and **William Wells Brown**, as well as literary works by White abolitionists such as Stowe and John Greenleaf Whittier, to demonstrate the importance of transatlantic alliances in engineering the social reforms of the age. Finally, Jacobs established forms and themes for African American women's **autobiography** that would be emulated and transformed by late nineteenth-century memoirists such as **Elizabeth Keckley**, and that would resonate in the fiction of **Toni Morrison**, **Sherley Anne Williams**, **Octavia E. Butler**, and others giving voice in the twentieth century to the humanity of enslaved women.

Resources: William L. Andrews, *To Tell a Free Story: The First Century of Afro-American Autobiography, 1760–1865* (Urbana: University of Illinois Press, 1986); Charles T. Davis and Henry Louis Gates Jr., eds., *The Slave's Narrative* (New York: Oxford University Press, 1985); Frances Smith Foster: *Witnessing Slavery: The Development of Ante-Bellum Slave Narratives* (Westport, CT: Greenwood Press, 1979); *Written by Herself: Literary Production by African American Women, 1746–1892* (Bloomington: Indiana University Press, 1993); Deborah M. Garfield and Rafia Zafar, eds., *Harriet Jacobs and Incidents in the Life of a Slave Girl: New Critical Essays* (New York: Cambridge University Press, 1996); James C. Hall, ed., *Approaches to Teaching Narrative of the Life of Frederick Douglass* (New York: Modern Language Association, 1999); Harriet Jacobs, *Incidents in the Life of a Slave Girl*, by Linda Brent (pseudonym), ed. L. Marie Child (New York: Harcourt Brace Jovanovich, 1973); Deborah E.

McDowell and Arnold Rampersad, eds., *Slavery in the Literary Imagination* (Baltimore: Johns Hopkins University Press, 1989); John Sekora and Darwin T. Turner, eds., *The Art of Slave Narrative: Original Essays in Criticism and Theory* (Macomb: Western Illinois University Press, 1982); Harriet Beecher Stowe, *Uncle Tom's Cabin, or, Life Among the Lowly* (Boston: John P. Jewett, 1852); Jean Fagan Yellin, *Harriet Jacobs: A Life* (New York: BasicCivitas Books, 2004).

Barbara McCaskill

James, Darius (born c. 1969). Novelist, nonfiction writer, and performance poet. A native of the Lower East Side of New York City, James has been associated with the Poetry Project at St. Mark's Church in the East Village and with the broader avant-pop cultural movement identified with the area. After living for several years in Montreal, where he honed performance art pieces at alternative clubs, James returned to New York, where he created a sensation in the 1990s with two books, *Negrophobia* (1992) and *That's Blax-ploitation!* (1995). He parlayed the attention garnered by the books into a stint as contributing editor of the quarterly book supplement of the weekly *New York Press*, and began to find a broader interest in his articles and reviews at some mainstream, as well as alternative, periodicals. In the late 1990s, he emigrated to Berlin, where he has become a prominent figure on the radical cultural scene.

In *Negrophobia: An Urban Parable: A Novel* (1992), James has combined elements of the film script, the comic book, and performance art in a book that might not be recognizable as a novel except that his second subtitle announces that it is, indeed, a work in that genre. It is worth noting that the elements drawn from performance art have enabled him to perform parts of the book to great effect on stage. As Ann Diamond noted in her review in the *Montreal Gazette*, James has been influenced by **Chester Himes, Ishmael Reed, hip-hop** culture, and the spoken-word poetry scene. He also works in the radical political tradition of **Eldridge Cleaver,** H. Rap Brown, and others whose vision of contemporary American society has been apocalyptic.

Negrophobia resists summary as much as any novel by William Burroughs. Its premise is that a racially prejudiced White girl from a privileged background, with the improbable name of Bubbles Brazil, provokes an African American maid to put a dark spell on her. This spell suddenly drops the girl into the depths of an urban nightmare so unremittingly bleak and dreadful that James's excursions into brutal surrealism seem almost a reprieve. Some critics have dismissed the book as an excessive self-indulgence, but others have found it too fiercely iconoclastic to dismiss. Even the cover of the book has provoked controversy, leading various interest groups to accuse the publisher of both racism and reverse racism.

That's Blaxploitation! has had a more mainstream appeal. Using the **blax-ploitation** films of the 1970s as a starting point, James explores the ways in which commodified culture has the potential, paradoxically, both to debase and to invigorate the cultural awareness of its target audience. The book has been widely cited in subsequent studies of African American culture, American popular culture, and film history.

Resources: Michael J. Agovino, "Next Up," *Esquire*, Aug. 1997, p. 32; Christian Haye, "Darius James," *BOMB* 40 (Spring 1992), 12–14; Andrew Hultkrans, "Review of *That's Blaxplotation!*," *Artforum International* 34 (Summer 1996), 12–13; Dunkor Imani, "Bring on Da Funk," *Black Issues Book Review* 2 (Nov./Dec. 2000), 26–27; Darius James: *Froggie Chocolates' Christmas Eve/Froggie Chocolates Weihnachtsabend* (Berlin: Verbrecher, 2003); *Negrophobia: An Urban Parable: A Novel* (Secaucus, NJ: Carol Publishing Group, 1992); *That's Blaxplotation! Roots of the Baadasssss 'Tude (Rated X by an All-Whyte Jury)* (New York: St. Martin's Griffin, 1995); Gene Seymour, "Racial Myth and Pop Culture," *The Nation*, Aug. 12/19, 1996, pp. 34–36.

Martin Kich

James, Kelvin Christopher (born c. 1945). Novelist. Born in Port of Spain, Trinidad, James completed a B.S. at the University of the West Indies in 1967. After working as a high school science teacher for a year, he emigrated to the United States. From 1973 to 1979, he worked as a medical technologist at Harlem Hospital in New York City. At the same time, he did graduate work at Columbia University, completing an M.A. in 1975, an M.S. in 1976, and an Ed.D. in 1978. He has continued to reside in **Harlem, New York**, and has worked primarily as a freelance writer. He has received a New York Foundation for the Arts fellowship in fiction.

The stories in James's *Jumping Ship* (1992) are divided into three sections. The first group, set on an unnamed Caribbean island, emphasize the disparity between the conception of the Caribbean as a paradise and the hard realities that its impoverished peoples face on a daily basis. The second group is set on borders, where the gains and costs of migration are pointedly in evidence. The stories in the third group have urban American settings and explore the narrow margins between hope, rage, and despair in neighborhoods characterized by crowded desolation.

James's first novel, *Secrets* (1993), is set in the Caribbean and focuses on the relationship between a teenaged girl named Uxann and her father. Very studious and determined to win her father's approval, Uxann is distraught when she learns that her father is having an extramarital relationship with her best friend. The situation goes from bad to much worse when father and daughter become separately inebriated and he subsequently mistakes Uxann for his lover. The geographic and social details of the setting are rendered vividly, and the story is framed in mythic elements. As a result, the story, which might easily have descended into a chronicle of sordidness, has some of the fateful resonance associated with classical Greek tragedies. The novel was a finalist for a National Book Critics Circle Award.

Despite James's efforts to give it mythic overtones, *A Fling with a Demon Lover* (1996) is a more conventional macabre thriller. A thirty-eight-year-old teacher named Sassala Jack thinks that a fling with Ciam, a twenty-three-year-old Caribbean immigrant, is a harmless diversion from her demanding job and studies and from her monotonous home life. But as she unexpectedly becomes more involved with Ciam, she is justifiably, increasingly uneasy about how little she really knows about him.

James contributed the essay "Fractals of a Grander Pattern" to **Elizabeth Núñez** and Brenda M. Greene's collection *Defining Ourselves: Black Writers in the 90s* (1999). A selection of his work was chosen for inclusion in **Gloria Naylor**'s *Children of the Night: The Best Short Stories by Black Writers, 1967 to the Present* (1995). His short stories, articles, and reviews have appeared in such periodicals as *American Letters, Between C&D, BOMB, Callaloo, Les Jungles d'Amérique, The Literary Review,* and *Massachusetts Review.*

Resources: William Grimes, "The Black Writer Vis-à-vis the World," *New York Times,* Mar. 25, 1996, p. C11; Heather Hathaway, "Review of *Jumping Ship*," *African American Review* 29 (Winter 1995), 695; Kelvin Christopher James: *A Fling with a Demon Lover* (New York: HarperCollins, 1996); *Jumping Ship and Other Stories* (New York: Random House, 1992); *Secrets* (New York: Random House, 1993); Tom Piazza, "Review of *Jumping Ship*," *New York Times Book Review,* Oct. 25, 1992, p. 20; "Secrets in the Garden," *American Visions* 9 (Feb./Mar. 1994), 11–12.

Martin Kich

Jazz. Jazz is a musical form initially created and most significantly innovated by African Americans, yet is culturally comprehensive in its synthesis of diverse influences. In simplistic terms, the music fuses, on one hand, a rhythmic sensibility (emphasizing polymeter, implied beats, rhythmic conflict) and a set of performative qualities (including call-and-response, tonal variations, and improvisation) inherited from various West African music, with a harmonic sense (and instrumentation) drawn from so-called Western classical and band music. While definitions like this are inevitably too basic and ultimately unsatisfactory in describing the music's intricate origins and complex integration of elements, one might safely assert that jazz is a music that emerges out of American diversity. A form inaugurated by African American musicians in **the South**, particularly around **New Orleans, Louisiana**, jazz exploits the confluence of cultural styles unique to the United States. Though still relatively new, jazz has already enjoyed a dynamic history since its birth around the turn of the twentieth century. Initially viewed by some as a scandalous music for its ties to the red-light district of New Orleans, the music has achieved widespread critical acceptance over its first century. Indeed, jazz is now frequently celebrated as "America's classical music," and venerated in Public Broadcasting System documentaries, repertory concerts, and academic curricula. As an influential African American artistic product, jazz has been a signal marker of Black American artistic genius, and a forceful argument for the centrality of African American expressivity in the development of a recognizably American culture.

Clarence Major suggests that the etymology of the word "jazz" can be traced back as far as the 1620s. He further suggests that "jazz" is "very likely a modern word for *jaja* (Bantu), which means to dance, to play music; early variants are 'Jas,' 'jass,' and 'jassy'" (Major, 255).

On a social level, jazz has been a significant medium for Black protest and ironic engagement with mainstream discourses, as well as the quintessential aesthetic manifestation of American democratic possibility. Jazz is a largely improvised music that depends on the individual soloist's ability to negotiate convention and innovation, tradition and novelty. This dynamic is apparent whenever a jazz musician plays an earlier musical form such as the **blues**, or trades solo passages with a fellow improviser on the bandstand, or offers a new rendition of a song made famous by an earlier giant in the pantheon such as Louis Armstrong or Charlie Parker. (*See* **Gillespie, Dizzy, Charlie Parker, and Thelonious Monk**.) Each of these examples reveals how jazz, as **Ralph Ellison** argues, "is an art of individual assertion within and against the group. Each true jazz moment... springs from a contest in which each artist challenges all the rest; each solo flight, or improvisation, represents... a definition of his identity as individual, as member of the collectivity and as a link in the chain of tradition" (266–267). This characteristic tension in jazz between a search for individualism and the preservation of community is central to an understanding of its importance for African Americans in both historical and literary contexts. As Eric Porter suggests, from the early twentieth century, when jazz emerged nationally amid black migration and urbanization, the music was, for African Americans, "a business enterprise and a set of institutional relationships, a focal point for political and social debate, a vehicle for individual and communal identity formation, and, eventually, an idea" (6). On a strictly literary level, **Henry Louis Gates, Jr.** argues that jazz, in its endless allusiveness and improvisational freeplay, offers a model for intertextuality in African American literature. The music's signature practice of repetition and formal revision is, in Gates's theory of **signifying**, the signal trope in the definition of an African American literary tradition. Gates writes, "There are so many examples of Signifyin(g) in jazz that one could write a formal history of its development on this basis alone" (63).

In the 1920s, jazz was important to **Harlem Renaissance** debates about the potential for race advancement through African American cultural achievement. **Langston Hughes**, perhaps most famously, championed the new music as an expression of African American collective memory and cultural distinctiveness, a form that Hughes suggested both recorded and redressed the difficulties of being Black in the United States. "[J]azz to me," Hughes writes in "The Negro Artist and the Racial Mountain" (1926), "is one of the inherent expressions of Negro life in America: the eternal tom-tom beating in the Negro soul—the tom-tom of revolt against weariness in a white world, a world of subway trains and work, work, work; the tom-tom of joy and laughter, and pain swallowed in a smile" (58). But as Hughes also notes in the essay, jazz, at that early stage in its history, was already an object of derision for the Black bourgeoisie. Anxious over the music's place within the overt sexuality of contemporary nightclub culture, or apprehensive over the way jazz was marketed and consumed within the cult of primitivism, the African American middle class devalued the music's significance through a conspiracy of silence.

Louis Armstrong conducting his band, 1937. The NBC microphone appears in the foreground. Courtesy of the Library of Congress.

As Richard A. Long notes, "nowhere in **Crisis**," the official magazine of the **NAACP**, "even during the high days of the jazz age, do we find [the editor, **W.E.B.**] **Du Bois** mentioning [early jazz musicians Louis] Armstrong, or [Duke] Ellington . . . or Fletcher Henderson" (130). If, as Du Bois had argued in "Criteria of Negro Art," "all Art is propaganda," and Black art specifically should be centered on the "propagandistic" revision of the Black image in the white imagination, then perhaps Louis Armstrong's clowning about barbecue on the record "King of the Zulus," or Duke Ellington's performing "Echoes of the Jungle" amid the feather-clad chorus girls at the Cotton Club, were perilously reminiscent of the iconography the Harlem intelligentsia hoped to reconfigure (514). Thus, even as jazz was amassing immense national popularity among both Black and White listeners, many prominent African American intellectuals were reluctant to endorse its importance without reservation. (*See* **Ellington, Edward Kennedy "Duke".**)

Through the 1930s, jazz emerged as America's popular music in the form of big band **swing**. With mainstream acceptance and mass consumer appeal, however, swing became the province of "Whiteness" in a market flooded by White bandleaders such as Benny Goodman, Glenn Miller, and Artie Shaw. These White musicians commanded more marketing money and lucrative bookings than their Black counterparts. Though some established black artists, such as Armstrong, Ellington, and **William "Count" Basie**, were still financially secure within a music industry that enforced segregation's systemic inequality, younger African American jazz musicians confronted limited market potential.

In the face of these strictures, emerging Black jazz musicians in the 1940s, such as Charlie Parker and Dizzy Gillespie began to reimagine the sound of jazz in after-hours jam sessions. Moving jazz away from the big band and back to its small-group origins, and directing the improviser's vocabulary from a mainly tonal approach to radical chromaticism, these young innovators gave birth to a radically new style: modern jazz or bebop. As Scott DeVeaux suggests, "Bebop was . . . an attempt to reconstitute jazz—or more precisely, the specialized idiom of the improvising virtuoso—in such a way as to give its Black creators the greatest professional autonomy *within* the marketplace" (27). Though economic interests may have stimulated bebop's origins, historians have argued that the music's emergence was inextricable from a more assertive push for civil rights among African Americans in the 1940s. Eric Lott, for instance, argues that the music's birth must necessarily be viewed in historical context, alongside events such as the contribution of Black auto workers in the UAW's efforts to unionize the Ford Motor Corporation; the desegregation of defense plants under the leadership of **A. Philip Randolph**; the founding of the Congress of Racial Equality in 1942; and **race riots** in **Los Angeles, California**, **Detroit, Michigan**, New York, and other cities (Lott, 457–458). "Bebop," Lott writes, "was intricately if indirectly related to the militancy of the moment. Militancy and music were undergirded by the same social facts; the music attempted to resolve at the level of style what the militancy fought in the streets" (459).

At the peak of the **Civil Rights Movement** in the 1950s and 1960s, black jazz artists used the music to voice protest against enduring racial inequalities, and to pay homage to African American political leaders. One of the most forceful jazz anthems from the period is Charles Mingus's "Original Faubus Fables," recorded in 1960 for an independent label, Candid Records. The composition had originally appeared on Mingus's 1959 Columbia Records release, *Mingus Ah Um*, as "Fables of Faubus," but the larger label balked at the song's lyric and insisted it be recorded as an instrumental. On the later record, Mingus restored the words to the composition, offering a satirical assault on Arkansas governor Orville Faubus's notorious pro-segregation stance in the late 1950s, mocking him as "sick and ridiculous" for opposing school integration, and booing the Ku Klux Klan.

Drummer Max Roach's 1960 album, *We Insist! Freedom Now Suite*, also recorded for Candid Records, is similarly uncompromising in its remonstration, offering an essential expression of protest for its recognition of racial inequality in transhistorical and international terms. Roach's suite includes the segments "Driva' Man," which remembers the brutality of White overseers during **slavery**; "Tears for Johannesburg," which laments South African apartheid; and the incendiary, "Triptych: Prayer/Protest/Piece," a tour de force that features a searing vocal performance by Roach's wife, Abbey Lincoln. The album is also notable for its cover, which features a photo of African American protesters seated at a segregated lunch counter in Greensboro, North Carolina. The prodigious tenor saxophonist John Coltrane also offered numerous socially meaningful musical statements during this period. Coltrane's 1963 anthem, "Alabama," for instance, was composed in response to the Sixteenth Street Baptist Church bombing earlier that year in Birmingham, and modeled after **Martin Luther King**'s elegiac sermon for the four girls who died in the tragedy. The saxophonist also registered his support for King's life and work in the 1966 musical tribute, "Reverend King." Coltrane's fellow saxophonist, Archie Shepp, pays similar tribute to **Malcolm X** on his 1965 album, *Fire Music*, which features the composition "Malcolm, Malcolm, Semper Malcolm." Shepp was among the most politically outspoken free jazz artists of the 1960s.

Free jazz, a postbebop style, had originated chiefly out of the work of the saxophonist Ornette Coleman, and emphasized a move from way the rigidity of earlier improvising conventions. Free jazz dismissed song form and set chord structures in an attempt to liberate the improviser from established patterns. Many free jazz musicians openly endorsed the black nationalist politics of the **Black Power** movement in the late 1960s, and conceived of their music as necessarily related. Shepp, for example, insisted that "it is precisely because of the emerging identity of the Negro that jazz is beginning to take on a unique character," and argued that "the new black expression [would] play a tremendous part in the shaping of the new ethic" (Wilmer, *Jazz People*, 158). Amid these currents, the free jazz pianist Cecil Taylor urged Black musicians to dissociate themselves from the predominantly White music industry, calling for a mass boycott of jazz clubs, record companies, trade papers, and federated unions. Free jazz musicians also articulated black nationalist rhetoric in performative terms. Valerie Wilmer summarizes: "As black nationalism developed following the Civil Rights struggle, becoming visible in the adoption of African and Islamic customs, names and dress, so the music broadened to contain obvious references to the strands that had been woven into the fabric of contemporary jazz" (*Serious*, 27–28). These obvious suggestions included free jazz musicians' integration of "non-Western" instruments, frequent references to Africa in the titles of compositions, and the wearing of colorful African robes onstage.

Since the late 1970s, mainstream jazz has entered what many identify as a neoclassical period, dominated by a new generation of musicians conversant with earlier styles and markedly reverent in their consideration of the past. The most famous and influential of these musicians is the trumpeter and composer Wynton Marsalis. Marsalis's critical and commercial success has no doubt had some bearing on the fidelity with which many younger jazz musicians have revisited older jazz styles since the mid-1980s. Off the bandstand, Marsalis has been a dominant force in directing the music's canonization: since 1991 he has been the artistic director of New York's Jazz at Lincoln Center program, and he is a major onscreen presence in filmmaker Ken Burns's nineteen-hour documentary *Jazz*, which aired on PBS in 2001. In these capacities Marsalis has argued that jazz is a disciplined tradition on a par with the most demanding of other artforms, and primarily a product of African American musicianship. These assertions counter the disdain and misunderstanding with which the music was greeted earlier in its history, and work to establish the music as the one of the most enduring Black American contributions to American national culture. (*See* **Blues Poetry**; **Jazz in Literature**; **Performance Poetry**.)

Resources: Amiri Baraka, *Black Music* (New York: Morrow, 1967); John Miller Chernoff, *African Rhythm and African Sensibility* (Chicago: University of Chicago Press, 1979); Scott DeVeaux, *The Birth of Bebop: A Social and Music History* (Berkeley: University of California Press, 1997); W.E.B. Du Bois, "Criteria of Negro Art" (1926), in *W.E.B. Du Bois: A Reader*, ed. David Levering Lewis (New York: Holt, 1995), 516–520; Ralph Ellison, "The Charlie Christian Story" (1958), in *The Collected Essays of Ralph Ellison*, ed. John F. Callahan (New York: Modern Library, 1995), 266–272; Walter C. Farrell, and Patricia A. Johnson, "Poetic Interpretations of Urban Black Folk Culture: Langston Hughes and the 'Bebop' Era," *MELUS* 8, no. 3 (Fall 1981), 57–72; Floyd, Samuel A., Jr.: "African Roots of Jazz," in *The Oxford Companion to Jazz*, ed. Bill Kirchner (New York: Oxford University Press, 2000), 7–16; *The Power of Black Music: Interpreting Its History from Africa to the United States* (New York: Oxford University Press, 1995); Henry Louis Gates, Jr., *The Signifying Monkey: A Theory of African-American Literary Criticism* (New York: Oxford University Press, 1988); Ted Gioia, *The History of Jazz* (New York: Oxford University Press, 1997); Langston Hughes, "The Negro Artist and the Racial Mountain" (1926), in *Within the Circle: An Anthology of African American Literary Criticism from the Harlem Renaissance to the Present*, ed. Angelyn Mitchell (Durham, NC: Duke University Press, 1994), 55–59; Richard A. Long, "Interactions Between Writers and Music During the Harlem Renaissance," in *Black Music in the Harlem Renaissance*, ed. Samuel A. Floyd, Jr. (Westport, CT: Greenwood Press, 1990), 129–37. Eric Lott, "Double V, Double Time: Bebop's Politics of Style" (1988), in *The Jazz Cadence of American Culture*, ed. Robert G. O'Meally (New York: Columbia University Press, 1998), 456–468; Leonard Lyons, *The 101 Best Jazz Albums: A History of Jazz on Records* (New York: Morrow, 1980); Clarence Major, *Juba to Jive: A Dictionary of African-American Slang* (New York: Penguin, 1994); Leroy Ostransky, *The Anatomy of Jazz* (Seattle: University of Washington Press, 1964); Eric Porter, *What Is This Thing Called Jazz?: African American Musicians as Artists, Critics and Activists* (Berkeley: University of California Press, 2002); Mark Tucker, ed., *The Duke Ellington Reader* (New York: Oxford University Press, 1993); Valerie Wilmer: *As Serious as Your Life: John Coltrane and Beyond* (1977; London: Serpent's Tail, 1992); *Jazz People* (1977; New York: DaCapo, 1991).

Michael Borshuk

Jazz in Literature. As a label, "jazz" encompasses such a wide array of music and ideas that coming up with a suitable definition can be a daunting task. Certainly there is the music, including (sometimes overlapping categories, and overlapping figures such as Miles Davis) the following "schools": New Orleans (King Oliver, Louis Armstrong, Jelly Roll Morton), early New York and

Chicago styles (Fletcher Henderson, Earl Hines, Bix Beiderbecke), swing (**Edward Kennedy "Duke" Ellington, William "Count" Basie, Billie Holiday**, Ella Fitzgerald), big band (Gerald Wilson, Miles Davis-Gil Evans), bop (**Charlie Parker, Dizzy Gillespie** [*see* **Gillespie, Dizzy, Charlie Parker, and Thelonious Monk**], Bud Powell), hard bop (Wes Montgomery, Clifford Brown, Art Blakey), West Coast/cool (Miles Davis, Chet Baker, Lennie Tristano), soul jazz (Cannonball Adderley, Jimmy Smith), free jazz (Ornette Coleman, Cecil Taylor, John Coltrane), fusion (Miles Davis, Tony Williams, Herbie Hancock), chamber jazz and third stream (Gunther Schuller, John Lewis), avant-garde (Anthony Braxton, John Zorn), Latin jazz (Machito, Tito Puente, Mongo Santamaria), smooth jazz (Al Jarreau, Anita Baker, Grover Washington), and neotraditional jazz (Wynton Marsalis, Marcus Roberts). These various styles, developed and practiced in various locations in sometimes overlapping time periods linked to modernization, migratory patterns, sociopolitical developments, and phonograph recording distribution and media airplay, include some of the most important and influential music made in the world in the twentieth century. They also reflect the importance accorded to improvisation and individual expression in jazz, emphasizing the primacy of finding one's own voice in a world that seeks to suppress it or deny it, or insist on uniform and undifferentiated expression. Certainly, as people continue to work within these various "schools" and attempt to develop new directions, jazz players doubtless will continue to make major contributions to the field of music.

Additionally, the term "jazz" is sometimes also used as an all-encompassing reference to African American music of the twentieth century, including the **blues**—which is often seen as a primary source for jazz—rhythm and blues, and soul music. This is because these African American musical genres have a variety of characteristics in common, such as strong rhythmic emphasis, syncopation, blue notes, and improvisation, and as such can be seen as distinctly related genres. In this sense, "jazz" can also be used to refer to the impulse to do in other media what jazz does in music, especially related to the important elements of improvisation, both individual and group, polyrhythmic and percussive emphases, and the quest for freedom that is frequently seen as a central element of jazz. In African American literature, some of the most important figures in the field—**Langston Hughes, Sterling A. Brown, Claude McKay, Gwendolyn Brooks, Robert Hayden, Melvin Tolson, Richard Wright, Ralph Ellison, James Baldwin, Amiri Baraka, Angela Y. Davis, Larry Neal, Sonia Sanchez, Ntozake Shange, Michael S. Harper**, and **Toni Morrison** among them—have added their voices to the chorus of jazz performers who have been so central to African American (and American) culture since its inception. (The list of non-African American writers who have employed jazz in their works—including Carl Sandburg, William Carlos Williams, F. Scott Fitzgerald, **Carl Van Vechten**, Robert Lowell, Allen Ginsberg, Jack Kerouac, John Clellon Holmes, Eudora Welty, Robert Creeley, Muriel Rukeyser, and many others—is equally long.)

Jazz music has distinct ties to the West African culture from which the bulk of the slaves brought to America in the North Atlantic slave trade were taken. Such elements as polyrhythms, call-and-response patterns, syncopation, blue notes, percussive performance techniques, and vocal and instrumental straining, growling, and buzzing effects are all traceable to West Africa, as is the idea that music serves an important communal function that is present in various aspects of everyday life. **Alice Walker** references this notion as reflected on American soil in her short story "Everyday Use," which portrays both the daily spiritual and practical uses of art, in this case quilting, in opposition to the notion of art for art's sake. The predominance of polyrhythms in individual musical performances may in fact reflect the notion that a community is made up of a variety of ideas, personalities, and styles that can nonetheless still coalesce into a unified whole. During the eighteenth and nineteenth centuries, these techniques and ideas were reflected in various African American musical genres such as **spirituals** and jubilees, work songs, field hollers, and game songs, all of which served important individual and communal functions in **slavery** and postslavery societies.

In the post-**Reconstruction** era, **ragtime** (Scott Joplin, James Scott), blues, and eventually jazz began to emerge from the music of earlier eras to express the desires, aspirations, and frustrations, and to serve the needs, of new generations of African Americans confronting a Jim Crow "freedom" that offered some possibilities and progress, though they were frustrated by social and political manifestations of attitudes held over from slavery times. Somewhere around the turn of the twentieth century in **New Orleans, Louisiana**—a city with a long tradition of African American musical performance, such as performances at Congo Square beginning in 1817 and in the important red-light Storyville district in the early twentieth century—elements of the blues and ragtime genres began to merge with the techniques and instrumentation of Black and **Creole** brass bands, which blended African and European characteristics in bands such as those led by James Reese Europe, to bring the music we know as jazz into existence.

Though the first jazz recordings were made by a White group—the Original Dixieland Jazz Band—in 1917, since its inception most of the important developments in jazz have come from musicians from the African American communities that created it, though there have been some talented and important white players (Bix Beiderbecke, Django Reinhardt, Lennie Tristano) as well. Thus, jazz has often served as a metaphor for indigenous Black creativity, technique, and style—for Black genius resistant in many ways to the domination of a European artistic aesthetic, though it is clear that jazz is not untouched by European components. Jazz's wild popularity in the 1920s—it gave the era its name, "The Jazz Age"—its mainstreaming in the 1930s with the dominance of swing and boogie-woogie, its capturing of the restless, frenetic pace of postwar, post-Hiroshima America, and its centrality in expressing the anger and spirituality of the Black aesthetic—all this reflects the expressive flexibility of jazz and its continued relevance to African American and American culture. By celebrating Black roots, Black culture, and the possibilities of the individual Black voice in relation to them, it has remained central not only as a musical form but also as a resource for African American artists in other media, especially literature.

How does the reader tell when the jazz influence is present in a work of literature? There can be some obvious hints. For example, the work may be called jazz, as in **Bob Kaufman**'s "Bagel Shop Jazz," or "O-JAZZ-O War Memoir: Jazz, Don't Listen to It at Your Own Risk," or Toni Morrison's *Jazz*. It may refer to places where jazz is performed, as in Langston Hughes's "Jam Session," **Thulani N. Davis**'s "CT at the Five Spot," or **Wanda Coleman**'s "In a Jazz Club He Comes on a Ghost." It may mention characteristics of jazz music, such as Langston Hughes's "Flatted Fifths" or **Carolyn M. Rodgers**'s "We Dance like Ella Riffs." It may mention jazz performers, real (**Michael S. Harper**'s "Dear John, Dear Coltrane" or **Sarah Webster Fabio**'s "For Louis Armstrong, a Ju-Ju") or imagined (James Baldwin's "Sonny's Blues"). Just as the title of **August Wilson**'s play *Ma Rainey's Black Bottom* refers also to a song recorded by Ma Rainey, so **Al Young**'s "Body and Soul" and "Lester Leaps In" refer to two famous jazz vehicles, and Carolyn M. Rodgers' "Written for Love of an Ascension—Coltrane" references a John Coltrane composition. The work may refer to a type of jazz, such as **Xam Wilson Cartiér**'s *Be-Bop, Re-Bop*. And the work may refer to or imply the etymology or meaning of jazz related to West Africa languages, sexual potency (as in **Nella Larsen**'s *Quicksand*), or the dynamics of style. Of course, writers may combine the influence of jazz with other literary elements as well: Ralph Ellison combines elements of Modernism picked up from T. S. Eliot and James Joyce with the appreciation of Louis Armstrong in *Invisible Man*, and **Ted Joans** combines jazz and surrealism in poems such as "Jazz Me Surreally Do." All of these ways make it obvious that the jazz tradition should serve as a context for understanding the work in which it is used, and invite or force the reader to enter the jazz world in order to grasp the social, political, aesthetic, and spiritual implications and meanings of jazz, not only for the individual work but also for the reader, the culture, the country, and the world.

It can be difficult to pin down in concrete terms the variety of subtle ways that material from the oral tradition influences the written tradition, especially if the material is not verbal. There are, of course, singers in the jazz tradition, but instrumentalists have predominated. How, then, do nonverbal sounds influence the writing of words? The answer lies in the dominant characteristics of jazz with regard to aesthetic and technique. For example, the rhythms of various kinds of jazz (and other African American music), including the frequent use of polyrhythms (combining various rhythmic patterns), along with the employment of syncopation (playing before or after the normally accented beat) and rough or stretched intonations, can be reflected in the scat singing (Louis Armstrong, Ella Fitzgerald) and vocalese (Eddie Jefferson, Jon Hendricks) of jazz. These can in turn also influence the word rhythms, textures, and structures of the writer seeking to capture the spirit of those rhythms. Thus, when Ralph Ellison's character Peter Wheatstraw (partially based on blues singer William Bunch, known on records as Peetie Wheatstraw) introduces himself to Ellison's protagonist in *Invisible Man*, his highly rhythmic and syncopated folk speech captures the rhythms of African American vernacular music, and his highly colorful manner is compared to the sounds and/or movements of a bear, rooster, and a dog, all of which turn up in titles and lyrics in the jazz tradition, reflecting the sometimes rough-hewn quality of the music. Langston Hughes makes use of the "hip" language (daddy-o, jive, dig) and rhythms of jazz and blues in many of his poems, and structures his entire volume *Montage of a Dream Deferred* using the poly-rhythms and syncopation of bop to unify his multipoem, multivoiced portrait of a complex, dynamic, shifting **Harlem, New York**, as a contemporary community in transition.

Additionally, both **Ann Lane Petry**'s *The Street* and Toni Morrison's *Jazz* have been interpreted as using shifts in chronology, pacing, and emphasis or accent in a jazzlike way. Always looking for ways to reflect the unity and power of African American culture, Langston Hughes, in his experimental volume *Ask Your Mama*, combines elements of jazz, blues, **gospel music**, the dozens, and other African American musical materials to confront American society about its own rapacity and hypocrisy. The reader can even see in Amiri Baraka's stage direction in *Great Goodness of Life* a reflection of the value of the jazz performer in awakening African Americans to their plight and to strategies for resistance. A confused Court Royal, who is being inter-rogated by an unseen "voice of the judge," is described as "jerk[ing] his head like he's suddenly heard Albert Ayler," a free jazz musician whose highly original sound, manner of improvisation, and use of folk motifs in his work provide an example of the attempt of performers in the jazz tradition to shock people out of the Euro-conventional and move them to rethink their notions of what art, society, and life are and are supposed to be. This is, of course, a sound that can be frightening as well, as Larry Neal relates in *The Glorious Monster in the Bell of the Horn*, though it can also be warmly passionate and rewarding as well. It is also important to acknowledge that a variety of African American writers have embraced the importance of oral performance to their work, emphasizing not only readings of their work but also recording their work to musical accompaniment, beginning with Langston Hughes and en-compassing recordings by authors such as Sterling A. Brown, Sarah Webster Fabio, Michael S. Harper, Amiri Baraka, and **Ishmael Reed**.

In the twentieth century, and into the twenty-first, jazz has been, and will continue to be, a major force as a musical genre. It exerts a powerful influence on writers who seek to connect to an indigenous African American art form that acknowledges the importance of African roots and the African American community; exalts originality of voice and idea, improvisation, and freedom of expression; and at its best exemplifies the concept of unity out of diversity (E Pluribus Unum) that confronts the failures of the American democratic experiment, providing a wellspring of possibilities. In language, tone, rhythm, structure, aesthetic, and philosophy, it offers alternatives to the writer of African American, as well as American (and even world) literature (see the Czech writer Josef Škvorecky's "Eine Kleine Jazzmusik," for example). As outlined in important critical works such as Larry Neal's "Any Day Now: Black Art and Black Liberation," Ralph Ellison's writings on jazz, **Sherley Anne Williams**'s "The Blues Roots of Contemporary Afro-American Poetry," **Houston A. Baker, Jr.**'s *Blues, Ideology, and Afro-American Literature*, as well as Leroi Jones/Amiri Baraka's *Blues People* and *Black Music*—and evident in a great amount of African American literature produced from a multitude of perspectives of time, place, aesthetic, and philosophy—jazz is a major force in African American literature.

Resources: Primary Sources: Richard N. Albert, *From Blues to Bop: A Collection of Jazz Fiction* (Baton Rouge: Louisiana State University Press, 1990); Amiri Baraka, *New Music—New Poetry* (India Navigation LP 1048); Marcela Breton, ed., *Hot and Cool: Jazz Short Stories* (New York: Plume, 1990); Jayne Cortez, *Taking the Blues Back Home* (PGD Verve LP 31918); Sascha Feinstein and Yusef Komunyakaa, eds.: *The Jazz Poetry Anthology*, vol. 1 (Bloomington: Indiana University Press, 1991); *The Second Set*, vol. 2 of *Jazz Poetry Anthology* (Bloomington: Indiana University Press, 1996); Langston Hughes, *The Weary Blues with Langston Hughes* (Verve CD 841 660-2); Ted Joans, *Jazz Poems* (S Press LP 451); Art Lange and Nathaniel Mackey, eds., *Moment's Notice: Jazz in Poetry and Prose* (Minneapolis, MN: Coffee House Press, 1993); Ishmael Reed, *Conjure* (American Clave LP 1006). **Secondary Sources:** Sascha Feinstein: *Bibliographic Guide to Jazz Poetry* (Westport, CT: Greenwood Press, 1998); *Jazz Poetry: From the 1920s to the Present* (Westport, CT: Greenwood Press, 1997); William J. Harris, *The Poetry and Poetics of Amiri Baraka* (Columbia: University of Missouri Press, 1985); Michael Jarrett, *Drifting on a Read: Jazz as a Model for Writing* (Albany: State University of New York Press, 1999); A. Yemisi Jimoh, *Spiritual, Blues, and Jazz People in African American Fiction* (Knoxville: University of Tennessee Press, 2002); Robert G. O'Meally, ed.: *The Jazz Cadence of American Culture* (New York: Columbia University Press, 1998); and *Living with Music: Ralph Ellison's Jazz Writings* (New York: Modern Library, 2001); Alan J. Rice, "Finger Snapping to Train Dancing and Back Again: The Development of Jazz Style in African American Prose," *Yearbook of English Studies* 24 (1994), 105–116; Steven C. Tracy: "The Blues Novel," in *The Cambridge Companion to the African American Novel*, ed. Maryemma Graham (Cambridge: Cambridge University Press, 2004); *Langston Hughes and the Blues* (Urbana: University of Illinois Press, 1988); Steven C. Tracy, ed., *Write Me a Few of Your Lines: A Blues Reader* (Amherst: University of Massachusetts Press, 1999); Craig Hansen Werner, *Playing the Changes: From Afro-Modernism to the Jazz Impulse* (Urbana: University of Illinois Press, 1994).

Steven C. Tracy

Jeffers, Lance (1919–1985). Poet, short story writer, novelist, and educator. Born in Fremont, Nebraska, Jeffers was raised by his grandfather, a medical doctor, in Stromberg, Nebraska. Jeffers' grandfather is the subject of the title poem, "Grandsire," in Jeffers's *Grandsire* (1974). His grandfather died in May

1929, and Jeffers moved, at the age of ten, to **San Francisco, California**, to live with his mother, Dorothy, and his stepfather, Forrest Jeffers, the maintenance man in a White apartment building. Jeffers's mother continued to teach him classical piano, which he had begun to study at the age of five in Nebraska; as a teenager, he turned to **jazz** and became an accomplished jazz pianist (Dorsey). After attending several colleges and serving in the U.S. Army (1942–1946), Jeffers earned a B.A. and an M.A. from Columbia University. Beginning in 1951, he taught at several universities including Texas A&M, California State University at Long Beach, and North Carolina State University, where he became a full professor and taught from 1974 until his death.

Jeffers published one novel, *Witherspoon*, in 1983 and contributed stories, poems, and articles to a number of literary magazines and anthologies, but he is best known for his poetry. His collections include *My Blackness Is the Beauty of This Land, When I Know the Power of My Black Hand, O Africa, Where I Baked My Bread*, and *Grandsire*. According to David F. Dorsey, Jr., "Lance Jeffers' poetry is an important and striking expression of black contemporary poetics. Yet, because it is so unique, it offers interesting evidence for the flexibility and potentials of a communal aesthetic. It is even more important, however, as a unique and passionate reflection of Black life in the United States." Jeffers believed in the need to persevere in the fight against racial injustice and in the significance of Black poetry in the struggle. He once wrote that "the future of black poetry lies on two foundation stones: (1) continued rage and protest, continued vehement criticism of oppression and the oppressor and American society, and (2) careful analysis of blackfolk.... We will be the masters of our destiny—and our poetry will help to sweep the way" (King). Jeffers's poems continue to be included in such anthologies as *In Search of Color Everywhere: A Collection of African-American Poetry* (1994) and *The Second Set*, vol. 2 of *The Jazz Poetry Anthology* (2004).

Resources: David F. Dorsey, Jr., "Jeffers, Lance," in *Dictionary of Literary Biography*, vol. 41, *Afro-American Poets since 1955*, ed. Trudier Harris and Thadious M. Davis (Detroit: Gale, 1985); Lance Jeffers: *Grandsire* (Detroit: Lotus, 1979); *My Blackness Is the Beauty of This Land* (Detroit: Broadside, 1970); *O Africa, Where I Baked My Bread* (Detroit: Lotus, 1977); *When I Know the Power of My Black Hand* (Detroit: Broadside, 1974); *Witherspoon* (Atlanta: G. A. Flippin, 1983); Woodie King, Jr., ed., *The Forerunners: Black Poets in America* (Washington, DC: Howard University Press, 1975); Ann Shockley and Sue P. Chandler, *Living Black American Authors* (New York: Bowker, 1973).

Deborah Brown

Jefferson, (Blind) Lemon (1893–1929) (also known as Deacon L. J. Bates). **Blues** singer. Blind Lemon Jefferson, the first commercially successful country-blues musician, is acknowledged as a seminal figure in the development of blues and **jazz**. His recordings in the 1920s helped popularize African American music among Whites and memorialized early twentieth-century Black culture of **the South**. Contemporary folk, **gospel music**, rock 'n' roll, **soul**, and even **rap**

music owe a debt to Jefferson's creativity, as does poetry that partakes of the blues tradition (*see* **Blues Poetry**).

Jefferson was born near Wortham, a hamlet south of Dallas, **Texas**. He may not have been completely blind at birth or even as an adult, for he wore clear glasses and is reported to have been able to navigate unfamiliar areas with some success. In 1917 Jefferson moved to Dallas, where he met and collaborated with prominent blues musicians such as Huddie Ledbetter (also known as **Leadbelly**). Jefferson died in **Chicago, Illinois**, under unexplained circumstances, in 1929.

Like most early blues singers, much of Jefferson's repertoire consisted of traditional material adapted to his own style, often improvised for audiences on the spot. When he did write original songs, the erotically charged lyrics of many of them both propelled his sales and agitated moralists. Jefferson also recorded **spirituals**, including "I Want to Be like Jesus in My Heart," under the pseudonym Deacon L. J. Bates. The raw energy of Jefferson's high, slightly whiny voice could produce startlingly evocative effects. Among his best-loved recordings are "Match Box Blues," "That Black Snake Moan," "Hangman's Blues," and "See That My Grave Is Kept Clean." Paul Oliver writes of Blind Lemon's cultural importance: "Blues singers of the stature of Blind Lemon Jefferson became the new black folk heroes through the recording medium. . . . [The] record industry brought the blues into countless homes, made the names of singers familiar in households; their music was shared for dancing and entertainment by countless thousands who might never see or hear them personally, and the content of the blues lyrics spoke for the black masses" (Oliver, *Story*, 108).

Resources: William Barlow, *"Looking Up at Down": The Emergence of Blues Culture* (Philadelphia: Temple University Press, 1989); Samuel Barclay Charters, *The Country Blues* (New York: Da Capo Press, 1975); William R. Ferris, *Blues from the Delta* (New York: Da Capo Press, 1988); Blind Lemon Jefferson: *The Best of Blind Lemon Jefferson* (CD) (Yazoo, 2000); *Blind Lemon Jefferson: The Complete 94 Classic Sides Remastered* (CD) (Jsp Records, 2003); Paul Oliver, *The Story of the Blues: The Making of Black Music* (London: Pimlico, 1997); *Yonder Come the Blues: The Evolution of a Genre* (New York: Cambridge University Press, 2001); *The Story of the Blues: From Blind Lemon Jefferson to B.B. King* (DVD) (Music Video Distributors, 2004); Robert L. Uzzell, *Blind Lemon Jefferson: His Life, His Death, and His Legacy* (Austin, TX: Eakin Press, 2002).

Geoff Hamilton

Jefferson, Roland S. (born 1939). Novelist and filmmaker. Born in **Washington, D.C.**, to a drama professor and a judge, Jefferson moved with his family to **Los Angeles, California**, when he was five years old. He completed a B.A. at the University of Southern California in 1961 and an M.D. at Howard University in 1965. He served in the Air Force, including a tour in Vietnam, from 1969 to 1971. He has subsequently lived in Los Angeles, where he has maintained a practice as a forensic psychiatrist while intermittently writing novels and making films.

The author of five novels published over almost three decades, Jefferson has sought to combine the conventions of the thriller genre with the social relevance of more "serious" fiction. His first and best-known novel, *The School on 103rd Street* (1976), is set during the tumultuous years following the assassination of **Martin Luther King, Jr.** Its protagonist is a Watts physician who discovers a sinister government conspiracy to suppress any possibility of a Black revolt.

A Card for the Players (1978) describes the intricate details of a scheme to steal a fortune in Las Vegas that, paradoxically, involves losing a fortune at the gaming tables. *559 to Damascus* (1986) concerns a terrorist plot to acquire and use nuclear weapons. *Damaged Goods* (2003) combines elements of the caper novel, the prison novel, and the romantic triangle and, in the process, bridges the conventions of the noir tradition and aspects of **hip-hop** culture.

Jefferson's articles and reviews have appeared in a wide variety of periodicals and newspapers. Most notably, he contributed the article "Black Graffiti: Image and Implications" to *Black Scholar* (1976).

Jefferson has written and directed the films *Angel Dust: The Wack Attack, Disco 9000, Pacific Inferno,* and *Perfume.* In 1979, he was inducted into the Black Filmmakers Hall of Fame.

Resources: Hal Hinson, "Movies: Long Whiff of Cheap Perfume," *Washington Post,* Mar. 5, 1991, p. B2; Roland F. Jefferson: *A Card for the Players* (Los Angeles: New Bedford, 1978); *Cocaine Fever* (Los Angeles: Holloway House, 1982); *Damaged Goods* (Los Angeles: Milligan, 2003); *559 to Damascus* (Los Angeles: New Bedford, 1986); *The School on 103rd Street* (New York: Vantage, 1976; Norton, 1997), also as *The Secret Below 103rd Street* (Los Angeles: Holloway House, 1983); Bridgette A. Lacy, "Review of *The School on 103rd Street*," *Washington Post Book World,* Nov. 23, 1997, p. X11.

Martin Kich

Jeffries, Tamara Yvette (born 1964). Poet, short story writer, nonfiction writer, and magazine editor. Tamara Jeffries has published short stories, poetry, and creative nonfiction, and is perhaps most widely known for her extensive work in magazine publishing. She first gained national recognition in 1991, when her story "Little Anderson" won first prize in the *Essence* magazine short story contest, which resulted in publication of the story and a $2,000 prize. Jeffries was born in Danville, Virginia, on October 5, 1964, to Frank Jeffries, Jr., and Barbara Gwynn Jeffries, both teachers. After graduating from Hampton University in 1987, with a degree in mass media arts, Jeffries began her career in magazines at the now defunct Whittle Communications in Knoxville, Tennessee. She later moved to **Atlanta, Georgia**, where she did editorial and writing work for a college marketing firm. While in Atlanta, she also worked for the Nexus Contemporary Art Center and Hammond House, both arts organizations, doing publicity, writing, and arts programming. At this time she also published articles about health and culture for a variety of Atlanta-based publications.

The focus of Jeffries's career returned to journalism after she moved to **Philadelphia, Pennsylvania**, in 1995. She took a job as managing editor at *HealthQuest* magazine, eventually becoming editor in chief. From there she was hired as health editor at *Essence* in January 2000. She was promoted to features editor and then to her current position of executive editor. In addition to her magazine work, she completed an M.F.A. in creative nonfiction at Goucher College in **Baltimore, Maryland**, in 2001. That year she married Sinclair Towe, whom she had met in the early 1990s, when she was living in Atlanta.

Since the 1991 publication of "Little Anderson," Jeffries has had short stories anthologized in several books: "Orphan," in *In the Tradition: An Anthology of Young Black Writers* (1992), "Black Tea," in *Voices of the Exiled* (1994), and "The Call," in *Tenderheaded: A Comb-Bending Collection of Hair Stories* (2001). She has had additional stories, poems, personal essays, and articles published in the *Cleveland Plain Dealer Sunday Magazine*, *Catalyst* magazine, the *International Review of African American Art*, and *Essence*.

Resources: Tamara Jeffries: "Black Tea," in *Voices of the Xiled: A Generation Speaks for Itself*, ed. Michael Wexler and John Hulme (New York: Doubleday, 1994), 144–146; "The Call," in *Tenderheaded: A Comb-Bending Collection of Hair Stories*, ed. Juliette Harris and Pamela Johnson (New York: Pocket Books, 2001); "Going Under: Artists on the Healing Power of Artmaking," *International Review of African American Art* 16, no. 4 (2000), 2–15; "In a Mission: A Writer Muses on Living in an Altered Space," *Cleveland Plain Dealer Sunday Magazine*, Aug. 30, 1998, p. 18; "Orphan," in *In the Tradition: An Anthology of Young Black Writers*, ed. Kevin Powell and Ras Baraka (New York: Writers and Readers, 1992), 338–343; Stephen Talty, "The Death of Coercion," in his *Mulatto America: At the Crossroads of Black and White Culture—A Social History* (New York: HarperCollins, 2003), 263.

Shelley Martin

Jenkins, Beverly Hunter (born 1951). Novelist. A prolific writer of contemporary African American historical romances, Jenkins has been described on the dust jackets of her novels as "headed for superstar status." A literary descendant of historical romance writers **Frances E. W. Harper** and **Pauline E. Hopkins**, Jenkins accurately renders Black women engaging in **race, gender**, and class struggles as they aspire to nineteenth-century public posts.

A native of **Detroit, Michigan**, and one of seven children born to Cornelius Hunter (teacher) and Delores Hunter (administrative assistant), Jenkins acquired from her mother an appreciation of African American history ignored by the textbooks in the Detroit public schools that she attended. Assessing the reason why few people are familiar with black history from 1865 until 1965, Jenkins observes, "History books have a tendency to say we [African Americans] didn't exist. . . . It's always black folks come to America, black folks were slaves, black folks were freed in 1865. Then we disappeared. History picks us up again rioting in 1965. But what happened for those 100 years?" (Decker, 139).

Jenkins answers her own question in the eleven novels she has published, all of which revisit nineteenth-century America and fill in the gaps that history books have ignored. Her black heroines assert themselves publicly as teacher in *Night Song* (1994), physician in *Vivid* (1995), abolitionist in *Indigo* (1996), newspaper reporter in *Topaz* (1997), contraband relief worker at a Union Army, **Civil War** camp and orphanage proprietor in *Through the Storm* (1998), cattle rancher in *The Taming of Jessi Rose* (1999), banker in *Always and Forever* (2000), tavern owner in *Before the Dawn* (2001) and gambler-turned-mail-order bride in *A Chance at Love* (2002). *Belle and the Beau* (2002) and *Josephine and the Soldier* (2003) are romance novels for teenage readers. Her most recent novel, *The Edge of Midnight*, was released in 2004.

Jenkins started writing in the fourth grade as newspaper editor at Jones Elementary. She pursued a degree in English at Michigan State University in 1974 but did not graduate. Married with two children, Jenkins is also a lay preacher in the Episcopal Church.

Resources: Rita B. Dandridge, *Black Women's Activism: Reading African American Women's Historical Romances* (New York: Peter Lang, 2004); Ed Decker, "Beverly Jenkins," in *Contemporary Black Biography*, vol. 14, ed. Mpho L. Mabunda and Shirelle Phelps (Detroit: Gale Research, 1997), 138–140; Beverly Jenkins: *Always and Forever* (New York: Avon, 2000); *Before the Dawn* (New York: Avon, 2001); *Belle and the Beau* (New York: Avon, 2002); *A Chance at Love* (New York: Avon, 2002); *Indigo* (New York: Avon, 1996); *Josephine and the Soldier* (New York: Avon, 2003); *Night Song* (New York: Avon, 1994); *The Taming of Jessi Rose* (New York: Avon, 1999); *Through the Storm* (New York: Avon, 1998); *Topaz* (New York: Avon, 1997); *Vivid* (New York: Avon, 1995).

Rita B. Dandridge

Joans, Ted (1928–2003). Poet, musician, visual artist, and raconteur. One of the few African Americans associated with the **Beat Movement**, Joans had a long, varied career that spanned various art forms (jazz poetry, spoken word, music, painting, collage, prose), movements (Beat, Pan-Africanism, **Black Power**, Surrealism), and locations (New York City, London, Tangiers, **Paris, France**, Timbuktu, Vancouver, Canada). Joans's body of work is remarkable for its combinations of these seemingly disparate categories.

Ted Joans was born Theodore Jones on July 4, 1928, in Cairo, Illinois. In 1951, after earning a bachelor's degree in fine arts at Indiana University, he moved to Greenwich Village in New York City, where he quickly fell in with the other poets, painters, and bohemians of the Beat Generation. His apartment became a well-known gathering place at which his compatriots such as LeRoi Jones (**Amiri Baraka**), Jack Kerouac, Allen Ginsberg, and the painter Bob Thompson could often be found. Joans is often linked with some of the more storied cultural events associated with the Beats. When the legendary saxophonist Charlie "Bird" Parker died in 1955, it was allegedly Joans, Parker's friend and former roommate, who began the graffiti "Bird Lives!" that appeared on walls around New York. (*See* **Gillespie, Dizzy, Charlie Parker,** and **Thelonious Monk**.) Joans was also the prototype for the photographer Fred McDarrah's "Rent-a-Beatnik" enterprise through which well-off suburbanites could rent a "hip" individual (often complete with beret) to attend their parties and read poetry.

Discussions of Joans often reference two of his more famous sayings: "Jazz is my religion" (also the title of a poem) and "surrealism is my point of view." These two inspirations form a thread that runs throughout all of Joans's work from *Beat Poems* (1957) and *Funky Jazz Poems* (1959) to his last two volumes, *Teducation: Selected Poems 1949–1999* and *Our Thang* (2001), a collaboration with his companion, the artist Laura Corsiglia. Joans's poetic style can be described as a combination of colloquial speech, declamatory statements, surrealistic wordplay, and free-flowing improvisation reminiscent of a jazz solo.

Langston Hughes and André Breton were two of Joans's major influences and literary mentors. Hughes's poetry about ordinary African Americans in the rhythms of **blues** and **jazz** had been a force in Joans's life since the age of ten. Established as the dean of Black poetry by the time Joans arrived in New York, Hughes admired Joans's jazz poetry and provided him with encouragement, support, and inspiration. In 1962 Joans exiled himself to Mali partially due to American racism. However, he and Hughes continued a long, fruitful correspondence. Poems such as "Passed on Blues: Homage to a Poet" and "Ted Joans on Langston Hughes" attest to Hughes's significance and Joans's admiration and affection for the elder poet. Joans's association with the surrealist master André Breton began with a letter he wrote to the French artist in which Joans, as an isolated surrealist, announced his desire to join an international surrealist movement. Joans made such an impression that Breton once pronounced him the only African American surrealist. His debt to Breton is evident in poems such as "Sure Really," "Surreally Hungry," "Nadja Rendevous," and "Sanctified Rhino."

Joans's poetic output during the middle to later 1960s reflected a deeper engagement with the politics and culture of the Black world. His best-known volumes during that period are *Black Pow-Wow: Jazz Poems* (1969), *Afrodisia: Old and New Poems* (1969), and *A Black Manifesto in Jazz Poetry and Prose* (1971). These poems often express an anger that reflects his engagement with the worldwide cries of "Black Power." Joans's range now extended to include poems for African and African American leaders such as **Malcolm X** ("My Ace of Spades"), Patrice Lumumba ("Lumumba Lives Lumumba Lives!"), **Stokely Carmichael** ("S.C. Threw S.C. into the Railroad Yard"), and Kwame Nkrumah ("Pan African"). He had not, however, abandoned his previous themes. Adamant that the lives of Black people all over the globe consisted of more than just politics, these wide-ranging texts mix jazz, eroticism, surrealism, art, and humor in with his political concerns.

Joans continued his journeys over the years that followed, writing, performing, painting, and publishing all over the world. It is impossible to quantify the effect that Joans's creative and social energies had on the communities with which he was associated. He maintained a vast circle of creative and political associations. Fellow poets attest to Joans's significance, yet he has generally been excluded from the major Beat and African American literary anthologies. Although never inactive, he enjoyed a reemergence of sorts onto the American literary scene with the publication of *Teducation* (1999), a collection of his selected poems. In addition, recent critical reevaluations of the Beat Generation and interest in the "Black Beats" (including Joans, the **San Francisco, California**, poet **Bob Kaufman**, and LeRoi Jones/Amiri Baraka) are beginning to rectify his absence from literary histories. Joans died in Vancouver, British Columbia in 2003.

Resources: Primary Sources: Ted Joans: *The Aardvark-Watcher = Der Erdferkelforscher* (Berlin: Literarisches Colloquium Berlin, 1980); *Afrodisia: Old and New Poems* (New York: Hill & Wang, 1971); *All of Ted Joans and No More: Poems and Collages* (New York: Excelsior Press, 1960); *Beat Poems* (New York: Deretchin, 1957); *A Black Manifesto in Jazz Poetry and Prose* (New York: Hill & Wang, 1971); *Black Pow-Wow: Jazz Poems* (New York: Hill & Wang, 1969); *Double Trouble* (Paris: Editions Bleu Outremer, 1992); *Funky Jazz Poems* (New York: Rhino Review, 1959); *The Hipsters* (New York: Corinth, 1961); *Our Thang* (Victoria, BC: Ekstasis Press, 2001); *Teducation: Selected Poems, 1949–1999* (Minneapolis, MN: Coffee House Press, 1999).

Secondary Sources: Michel Fabre, "Ted Joans: Surrealist Griot," in his *From Harlem to Paris: Black American Writers in France, 1840–1980* (Urbana: University of Illinois Press, 1991), 309–323; Skip [Henry Louis] Gates [Jr.], "Ted Joans: Tri-Continental Poet," *Transition* 48 (1975), 4–12; A. Robert Lee: "Black Beat: Performing Ted Joans," in *Reconstructing the Beats*, ed. Jennie Skerl (New York: Palgrave, 2004), 117–132; "The Black Beats: The Signifying Poetry of LeRoi Jones/Amiri Baraka, Ted Joans and Bob Kaufman," in his *Designs of Blackness: Mappings in the Literature and Culture of Afro-America* (Sterling, VA: Pluto Press, 1998); Gerald Nicosia, "Gerald Nicosia Talks with Ted Joans," in *The Beat Vision: A Primary Source Book*, ed. Arthur Knight and Kit Knight (New York: Paragon House, 1987).

Amor Kohli

Joe, Yolanda (born 1962). Mystery novelist, juvenile writer, novelist, and television and radio newswriter and producer. Yolanda Joe is the author of nine novels, six of which have become national best-sellers. Her writing style has frequently been called "high-spirited" and "heartwarming" by reviewers, and is often complimented for its blend of vivid lyricism with fast-paced wit. Joe's work is difficult to characterize because each novel covers distinct territory. Her first published murder mystery, *Falling Leaves of Ivy* (1992), explored as a sidebar the difficulties of friendships across racial and class lines. *My Fine Lady* (2004) is Joe's updating of the popular musical *My Fair Lady*—complete with a heroine who raps. *The Hatwearer's Lesson* explores issues of adultery, intergenerational love, and self-love.

Yolanda Joe attended an all-Black public high school in **Chicago, Illinois**. She was the first in her family to attend college, receiving several academic scholarships to attend Yale and the Columbia School of Journalism. Following graduation, Joe worked as a newswriter for CBS in Chicago and produced radio and television news broadcasts. She cites **Zora Neale Hurston, J. California Cooper,** and **Nikki Giovanni** as the authors who have served as her primary inspirations, but also frequently notes her grandmother's encouragement as quintessential to her development as a professional and a writer (*Yolanda Joe Home Page*). The pen name Ardella Garland is used by Joe to honor her maternal great-grandmother, who wished to be a writer. (*See* **Crime and Mystery Fiction.**)

Resources: Yolanda Joe: *Bebe's By Golly Wow* (New York: Doubleday, 1998); *Details at Ten* (writing as Ardella Garland) (New York: Pocket Books, 2002); *Falling Leaves of Ivy* (Stamford, CT: Longmeadow Press, 1992); *The Hatwearer's Lesson* (New York: Dutton, 2003); *He Say, She Say* (New York: Doubleday, 1997); *Hit Time* (writing as Ardella Garland) (New York: Simon and Schuster, 2002); *My Fine Lady* (New York: Dutton, 2004); *This Just In* (New York: Doubleday, 2000); *Video Cowboys* (New York: Simon and Schuster, 2005); *Yolanda Joe Home Page*, http://www.yolandajoe.com.

Michelle LaFrance

John the Conqueror. Trickster, folk hero, and folk term. John the Conqueror is a major **trickster** figure in American slave **folklore**. The trickster, a common figure in West African stories, often took the form of a seemingly weak and powerless animal or human who, more often then not, outwitted a menacing antagonist or prevailed in an impossible situation.

These tales made the great leap across the Atlantic when, in the 1600s, countless West Africans were brought to **the South** as slaves to work on the plantations. Though the White plantation owners forbade them to read or write, the slaves continued their oral traditions, whether in the field or in the seclusion of the slave quarters. Away from the watchful eye of the slave master, Blacks created John. Later participants in the folklore tradition would refer to him as John the Conqueror, High John, or High John the Conqueror. In these tales, John was a slave like themselves. He was intelligent and hardworking (when it served his purpose). John also knew how to survive. He knew the spoken and unspoken codes of life on the plantation. He used subterfuge to steal his master's choice pigs. He appeared foolish to evade hard **labor** and floggings. John usually, though not always, outwitted Old Master. Nevertheless, most John tales ended with humor and provided the slaves with laughter, hope, and instructions on how to survive life on the plantation.

Folklorists such as J. Mason Brewer and **Zora Neale Hurston** pioneered the collection, documentation, and publication of the John tales. These stories reveal much about the character, perceptions, and experiences of slaves. They also have helped establish John as a significant icon in the African American literary tradition.

John the Conqueror, High John, and High John the Conqueror are also names that refer to a **conjuring** root. In *Mules and Men* (1935), Hurston deals not only with High John the folk hero, but also High John the root. This root is used to ward off evil and attract good fortune in **voodoo** practices. The use of High John, the root, is an occasional theme in the **blues** and literary tradition (Yronwode).

Resources: Roger D. Abrahams, ed., *Afro-American Folktales* (New York: Pantheon Books, 1985); John W. Blassingame, *The Slave Community: Plantation Life in the Antebellum South* (New York: Oxford University Press, 1972); B. A. Botkin, ed., *Lay My Burden Down: A Folk History of Slavery* (Chicago: University of Chicago Press, 1945); J. Mason Brewer, *American Negro Folklore* (Chicago: Quadrangle, 1968); Darlene Clark Hine, William C. Hine, and Stanley Harrold, *The African American Odyssey* (Upper Saddle River, NJ: Prentice-Hall, 2000); Langston Hughes and Arna W. Bontemps, eds., *The Book of Negro Folklore* (New York: Dodd, Mead, 1958); Zora Neale Hurston: "High John the Conqueror," *American Mercury* 57 (1943), 450–458; *Mules and Men* (Philadelphia: Lippincott, 1935); Carol S. Taylor Johnson, "High John the Conqueror," in *The Oxford Companion to African American Literature* (New York: Oxford University Press, 1997); Steve Sanfield, *The Adventures of High John the Conqueror* (New York: Orchard Books, 1989); Henry D. Spalding, ed., *Encyclopedia of Black Folklore and Humor* (Middle Village, NY: Jonathan David, 1972); John W. Wilson, *High John the Conqueror* (New York: Macmillan, 1948); Catherine Yronwode, "John the Conqueror" (2003), *Lucky Mojo*, http://209.96.136.38/johntheconqueror .html.

Gladys L. Knight

Johnson, Amelia E. (1859–1922). Novelist, poet, and publisher. The author of *Clarence and Corinne; or, God's Way* (1890), Johnson was simultaneously the first woman author and the first African American author published by the American Baptist Publication Society. *Clarence and Corinne* was the first Sunday school book published by an African American author. Johnson's full name was Amelia Etta Hall Johnson, but she published under the name Mrs. A. E. Johnson. She published two other novels, *The Hazeley Family* (1894) and *Martina Meridian, or What Is My Motive?* (1901). Both novels were used in Sunday schools to encourage ethical behavior and teach morality.

Johnson (then named Amelia E. Hall) was educated in Ontario, Canada, and began writing poetry at a young age. In 1874, she moved to **Baltimore, Maryland**, the native home of her parents, where she became a teacher ("Amelia E. Johnson," 731–732). In 1877, she married Rev. Harvey Johnson, a pastor at the Union Baptist Church in Baltimore ("The Reunion," 162). Throughout her adulthood, she wrote children's stories for the *National Baptist* and originated "The Children Corner" column in the *Sower and Reaper*. She was also published in *Baptist Messenger*, *Our Women and Children* magazine, and *American Baptist*. In later years, she edited the literary magazines *Joy* (1887), which contained short stories, poems and articles for African American women, and *Ivy* (1888), which contained African American history written to encourage reading ("The Reunion," 163). She died on March 29, 1922.

Resources: "Amelia E. Johnson," in *Black Firsts: 4,000 Ground-Breaking and Pioneering Historical Events*, ed. Jessie Carney Smith, 2nd rev. and enl. ed. (Detroit: Visible

Ink Press, 2003), 731–732; Blyden Jackson, *A History of Afro-American Literature*, vol. 1, *The Long Beginning, 1746–1895* (Baton Rouge: Louisiana State University Press, 1989); Amelia E. Johnson: *Clarence and Corinne; or God's Way* (Oxford: Oxford University Press, 1988); *The Hazeley Family* (Oxford: Oxford University Press, 1988); "The Reunion" (excerpt from *Clarence and Corinne*), in *Afro-American Women Writers 1746–1933*, ed. Ann Allen Shockley (Boston: G. K. Hall, 1988), 162–170.

Kimberly P. Draggoo

Johnson, Angela (born 1961). Children's writer, poet, and novelist. Johnson is known for realistically depicting African American youth and their families living everyday lives. In high school, Johnson wrote primarily punk poetry that she kept to herself (Pendergast and Pendergast). While attending Kent State University in Ohio, her writing continued to be a solitary occupation—Johnson steered clear of the university's literary magazine, for example. She left college and spent a couple of years in Volunteers in Service to America (VISTA) before deciding to become a full-time writer. In contrast to the traditional stories, **folktales**, and nostalgia pieces that were popular in children's writing at the time Johnson first began publishing, her stories focus on the daily moments and events of typical families. From *Tell Me a Story, Mama* (1989) to *The First Part Last* (2003), Johnson's characters face common difficulties, have ordinary struggles, and overcome those struggles through the support of their families, their communities, and their own inner strength. Several themes recur in Johnson's writing. Her stories are often generational, involving youth, their parents, and their grandparents or other members of their extended families. Plots of her narratives are frequently nonlinear. *Toning the Sweep* (1993), the book for which Johnson won her first Coretta Scott King Award, recounts the story not only of fourteen-year-old Emily, but also the stories of her mother and her Grandmama Ola. The stories are recounted by all three females, and they include the 1964 **lynching** of Emily's grandfather, Grandmama Ola's struggle with cancer, and her relocation to Cleveland. Johnson's most recent work, *The First Part Last* (2003), travels backward and forward through time as it recounts the story of Bobby, a sixteen-year-old single father struggling to raise his infant daughter, and explores Bobby's relationship with his girlfriend Nia as well as the response of their parents to the news of the pregnancy.

Johnson's books deal with difficult topics, such as mental illness (*Humming Whispers*, 1992), single parenting (*Songs of Faith*, 1998), the **Civil Rights Movement** (*Toning the Sweep*, 1993), and grief. Her characters rely on their inner strength and the support of their community to survive in spite of their problems. A prolific writer, Johnson has published nearly three dozen books since 1989. Johnson writes across genres, and her works include picture books (such as *Tell Me a Story, Mama* [1989], *Do Like Kyla* [1990], *Julius* [1993], *Daddy Calls Me Man* [1997], and *I Dream of Trains* [2003]), young-adult novels (*Toning the Sweep, Humming Whispers Heaven* [1998], *Songs of Faith* [1998], *Looking for Red* [2002], *Just Like Josh Gibson* [2004], and *The First Part Last*), short stories (*Gone from Home: Short Takes* [1998]), and poems (*The Other Side: Shorter Poems* [1998]). (*See* **Children's Literature**.)

Throughout her career, Johnson's writing has received critical acclaim for its poetic, spare nature. Her first book, *Tell Me a Story, Mama*, received a Best Books citation from the *School Library Journal*. *When I Am Old with You* (1990) earned the writer the Ezra Jack Keats New Writer Award. Johnson is a three-time winner of the Coretta Scott King Award (for *Toning the Sweep*, *Heaven*, and *The First Part Last*) and has twice received the Coretta Scott King Honor Award (*The Other Side: Shorter Poems*, *When I Am Old with You*). *Toning the Sweep* also received the Best Books citation of the *School Library Journal*. In 2003, Johnson became the third young-adult novelist ever to receive a prestigious MacArthur fellowship. In 2004, *The First Part Last* was awarded the Michael L. Printz Award for Excellence in Young Adult Literature.

Resources: "Angela Johnson," in *Contemporary Authors Online* (Detroit: Gale Group, 2001), http://galenet.gale.com; Lucille H. Gregory, "Angela Johnson," in *Twentieth-Century Children's Writers*, 4th ed., ed. Laura Standley Berger (Detroit: St. James Press, 1995); Angela Johnson: *The First Part Last* (New York: Simon and Schuster, 2003); *Humming Whispers* (1992; repr. New York: Orchard, 1995); *Tell Me a Story, Mama* (1989; repr. New York: Orchard, 1992); *Toning the Sweep* (New York: Scholastic, 1993); *When I Am Old with You* (New York: Orchard, 1990); Sarah Pendergast and Tom Pendergast, "Angela Johnson," in *St. James Guide to Children's Writers*, 5th ed. (Detroit: St. James Press, 1999).

Heidi Hauser Green

Johnson, Charles R. (born 1948). Novelist, short story writer, cartoonist, screenwriter, professor, and literary critic. Charles Richard Johnson began his artistic career as an illustrator and cartoonist; barely into his twenties, he created, coproduced, and hosted *Charlie's Pad* (1970–1980), a PBS instructional series on the finer points of cartooning. His graduate work with the American writer and critic John Gardner, however, inspired him to take up "moral fiction" as a mode of artistic and intellectual production. Today Johnson is known primarily for his cross-genre narrative craft, which reflects an imaginative synthesis of Buddhism, Western philosophy, and African American history and **folklore**.

Born in Evanston, Illinois, in 1948, Johnson has enjoyed professional success in a variety of cultural media. He received his bachelor's and master's degrees from Southern Illinois University in 1971 and 1973, respectively. Johnson went on to study phenomenology and literary aesthetics at the State University of New York at Stony Brook, where his Ph.D. was backdated from 1999 to 1988 to coincide with the publication of his dissertation on the existential dimensions of contemporary Black literature, *Being and Race*. Long situated in the U.S. academy, Johnson has been the S. Wilson and Grace M. Pollock Professor of Creative Writing at the University of Washington since 1990. In 1998 Johnson won the prestigious MacArthur Fellowship, or "genius grant," and in 2002 he received the American Academy of Arts and Letters

Award for Literature. He has worked extensively in television, collaborating most recently with Patricia Smith on *Africans in America* (1998), a PBS documentary series about the tragedies and legacies of U.S. **slavery**.

Johnson's fiction articulates Black historical and cultural experience with philosophical inquiry. His first novel, *Faith and the Good Thing* (1974), follows a Southern Black girl's quest for the "good thing," the spiritual meaning of life, in the face of poverty and sexual violence in **Chicago, Illinois**; his second, *Oxherding Tale* (1982), refigures the "classic" **slave narrative**, such as **Frederick Douglass**'s (1845), in terms of the Buddhist parable "Ten Ox-Herding Tales." Critics have noted the philosophical didacticism of these novels, and it was not until *Middle Passage* (1990), which won the National Book Award, that Johnson solidified his reputation as a major American writer who deploys message and form with aplomb. In *Middle Passage*, the freed slave Rutherford Calhoun stows away on the slave ship *Republic* to avoid marital and financial debts in **New Orleans, Louisiana**. But a divisive rebellion finds Rutherford caught between loyalty to his White crewmates and sympathy for the cargo, which consists of bonded men from an African tribe of wizards called the Allmuseri. Resolution of the crisis hinges on how Rutherford negotiates each group's competing claims to freedom, personhood, and justice. The tribesmen, who also figure in *Oxherding* and the story collection *The Sorcerer's Apprentice* (1986), represent for Johnson an understanding of the human condition that combines folk wisdom and spiritual practice with philosophical idealism and utopianism.

Dreamer (1998) is Johnson's celebrated allegory of man's capacity to achieve enlightened self-consciousness. The setting here is the **Civil Rights Movement** and the final years of Dr. **Martin Luther King, Jr.**'s life. Johnson grants King a doppelgänger, Chaym, foregrounding a kind of dialectics of revolution. The resolve that the spiritual and political leader evinces in negotiating protest and power, insurgent demands and commitment to nonviolence, is characteristic of Johnson's conflict-driven yet ultimately holistic philosophical-aesthetic oeuvre. (*See* **Middle Passage**; **Utopian Literature**.)

Resources: **Primary Sources:** Charles R. Johnson: *Being and Race: Black Writing Since 1970* (Bloomington: Indiana University Press, 1988); *Dreamer: A Novel* (New York: Scribner's 1998); *Faith and the Good Thing* (New York: Viking, 1974); *Middle Passage* (New York: Atheneum, 1990); *Oxherding Tale* (Bloomington: Indiana University Press, 1982); *The Sorcerer's Apprentice: Tales and Conjurations* (New York: Atheneum, 1986); *Soulcatcher and Other Stories* (San Diego: Harcourt, 2001); *Turning the Wheel: Essays on Buddhism and Writing* (New York: Scribner's 2003). **Secondary Sources:** Rudolph P. Byrd, ed., *I Call Myself an Artist: Writings by and about Charles Johnson* (Bloomington: Indiana University Press, 1999); Jonathan Little: *Charles Johnson's Spiritual Imagination* (Columbia: University of Missouri Press, 1997); "Erasing the Buddha," *Contemporary Literature* 44, no. 4 (Winter 2003), 743–747; Jim McWilliams, ed., *Passing the Three Gates: Interviews with Charles Johnson*, ed. Jim McWilliams (Seattle: University of Washington Press, 2004); William R. Nash, *Charles Johnson's Fiction* (Urbana: University of Illinois Press, 2003); Hans Ostrom,

"Middle Passage: African-American Saga in the Running for National Book Award," *Soundlife* (Sunday suppl.), *Tacoma News Tribune*, Nov. 13, 1990, pp. SL 6–7.

Kinohi Nishikawa

Johnson, Charles Spurgeon (1893–1956). Editor, sociologist, professor, social activist, and college president. Born in Bristol, Virginia, Charles S. Johnson graduated with a B.A. in sociology from Virginia Union University in 1916. Under the tutelage of the sociologist Robert E. Park, Johnson earned a Ph.B. (Bachelor of Philosophy) from the University of Chicago in 1917. It was here that Johnson met many of the nation's leading philanthropists, including the oil magnate John D. Rockefeller and the Sears Roebuck tycoon Julius Rosenwald. In 1921 he moved to New York City to direct research and edit the magazine **Opportunity** for the National Urban League. In *Opportunity*, Johnson published short stories and poems by Black authors and sponsored monthly literary contests. Among the writers he published were **Langston Hughes**, **Zora Neale Hurston**, and **Countee Cullen**. A key figure in the **Harlem Renaissance**, Johnson used his connections within the White philanthropic community to garner support for Black literature. Blyden Jackson, Johnson's colleague at Fisk University, credited him with helping to launch the careers of such literary luminaries as Zora Neale Hurston, **Arna Bontemps**, and **James Weldon Johnson**. Many historians, including David Levering Lewis, view Johnson's March 21, 1924, Civic Club dinner in New York City as the most significant promotional event of the Renaissance. He invited more than 300 guests, including **Alain Locke**, James Weldon Johnson, **W.E.B. Du Bois**, **Jessie Redman Fauset**, and Albert Barnes. The event helped numerous Black writers and poets to find mainstream venues for their work.

Continuing his support of literary efforts, Johnson edited *Ebony and Topaz*, a collection of poems and short stories by participants in the Renaissance, in 1927. The anthology included work by Alain Locke, **Alice Moore Dunbar-Nelson**, Arna Bontemps, and Langston Hughes. In 1928, as the Harlem Renaissance faded, Johnson returned to **the South** to take a position in the Social Science Department at Fisk University, eventually becoming the institution's president in 1946. His prominence drew

Charles S. Johnson, 1948. Courtesy of the Library of Congress.

867

national and international attention to Fisk, and he recruited **Sterling A. Brown**, **Edward Franklin Frazier**, James Weldon Johnson, Arna Bontemps, and Aaron Douglas to the faculty. While at Fisk, Johnson published many books, including *Shadow of the Plantation* (1934), *The Negro College Graduate* (1938), and *Growing up in the Black Belt* (1941). Johnson died of a heart attack in 1956.

Resources: Patrick J. Gilpin and Marybeth Gasman, *Charles S. Johnson: Leadership Behind the Veil in the Age of Jim Crow* (Albany: State University of New York Press, 2003); Charles S. Johnson: *Growing Up in the Black Belt* (1941; New York: Schocken Books, 1967); *The Negro College Graduate* (1938; New York: Negro Universities Press, 1969); *Shadow of the Plantation* (Chicago: University of Chicago Press, 1934); Charles S. Johnson, ed., *Ebony and Topaz* (New York: Opportunity/National Urban League, 1927); David Levering Lewis, *When Harlem Was in Vogue* (New York: Knopf, 1981); Richard Robbins, *Sidelines Activist: Charles S. Johnson and the Struggle for Civil Rights* (Jackson: University Press of Mississippi, 1996).

Marybeth Gasman

Johnson, Doris (born 1937). Novelist. Johnson is a highly successful writer of **romance novels**. Born in Jersey City, New Jersey, she began writing seriously at a mature age: her first novel, *Love Unveiled*, was published by Genesis Press in 1996. *Love Unveiled* (written under the pseudonym Gloria Greene) is a conventional romance novel featuring an improbably rich, Virginia-based family of Black supermodels, high fashion photographers, and a millionaire boyfriend. The story develops in hotel suites, limousines, and restaurants in New York City and **Paris, France**. The heroine, Julia Hart, falls in love with the millionaire, Bradman Coleman, but has to struggle against his preoccupation with business matters and his irrational, Othello-like proneness to destructive jealousy. Of course, all hurdles are overcome by the end of the novel, and Brad and Julia become entwined emotionally and sexually.

Johnson's subsequent novels—all published by Arabesque Books under Johnson's own name—follow a similar format. The most intriguing novel is *Precious Heart* (2000). In this work, Johnson—a New York Community College graduate in sociology—brings substantial social anxieties to the fore. The leading female, Diamond Drew, struggles to accept her recently deceased mother's decision to donate her organs to another stricken woman. Romance novels nearly always feature an older female character who urges the young leads to overcome apprehension, prejudice, and shyness. In *Love Unveiled*, Bradman's former mother-in-law, Helen Stevenson, takes this role, insisting that Bradman forget about his late wife's infidelities, and catch Julia while he can. This character type in *Precious Heart*, Peaches Ferguson, arouses interest because her role is to plead with Diamond to forget her worries about the "violation" of her late mother's body—an unusual departure from the usual "Go get him, girl!" advice of such characters. However, the romance element of *Precious Heart* is, as ever, wholly conventional. A relation of the woman who was saved by receiving a transplant from Diamond's mother, Steven Rumford, writes to Diamond, expressing his gratitude. Diamond disdains his sentiments. The reader, correctly, guesses that the novel will then narrate a troubled love story between Diamond and Steven, one that will end in marriage.

Johnson has become a prolific author; since the late 1990s, she has published at the rate of just over one novel a year. Her romance novels are invariably reviewed with great favor by the industry's "bible," *Romantic Times*.

Resources: Doris Johnson: "Homepage," http://doris-johnson.com; *Love Unveiled* (published under the pseudonym Gloria Greene) (Columbus, MS: Genesis, 1996); *Precious Heart* (New York: Arabesque, 2000); Lora McDonald, "Interview with Doris Johnson," The Romance Reader Connection, http://theromancereadersconnection.com/aotm/authorofthemonthjohnsondoris.html.

Kevin DeOrnellas

Johnson, Fenton (1888–1958). Poet, editor, and activist. Fenton Johnson contributed to the promotion of African American letters in the **Chicago Renaissance** (1900–1920) and was a transitional figure from the Romantic tradition to the modern period of African American poetics. Born on May 7, 1888, to Elijah H. and Jessie Taylor Johnson, Johnson was raised in an upper-middle-class environment on the South Side of **Chicago, Illinois**. He was educated in the Chicago public school system and then attended the University of Chicago and Northwestern University. Upon graduation, he left for the University of Kentucky at Louisville to teach, but when the experience proved to be financially challenging, he returned home to pursue his literary interests.

Johnson wrote several plays for Robert Mott's Pekin Theatre, a popular concert hall and nightclub in Chicago. Although the titles of Johnson's plays have not been identified, reviews of the theater's high standard for the quality of its productions seem to suggest that his works had merit. During this time, Johnson published his first volume of poetry, *A Little Dreaming* (1913). The poems in this first collection are written in traditional verse forms and in the style of **Paul Laurence Dunbar**. Most of the poems in this book concern love and intimate relationships.

Soon after the publication of this work, Johnson left Chicago to attend the Pulitzer School of Journalism at Columbia University, where he wrote several articles for the Eastern Press Association and the *New York News*. He also published two more volumes of poetry: *Visions of the Dusk* (1915) and *Songs of the Soil* (1916). These collections are markedly different in style from the first collection. In these books Johnson experiments with verse forms and writes in **free verse**. Many poems in these books focus on the plight of the working class and on life in an urban ghetto. The urban realism of these poems, as well as the tone of disillusionment and bitterness, suggest a move toward Modernist poetry. These poems also incorporate folk material, as well as the diction and language of common people.

In 1916, Johnson returned to Chicago to focus on his journalistic career. With support from his Uncle Jesse Binga, a banker, he formed the *Champion* magazine. Even though the *Champion* magazine was modeled after **W.E.B.**

Du Bois's *The Crisis*, it lasted for only eight issues. Soon after the publication of the last issue, Johnson produced another magazine, *The Favorite*. Published between 1918 and 1921, this magazine presented stories about the African American working class.

During this time, Johnson also devoted some of his energies to social reform. He organized the Reconciliation Movement to deal specifically with how working-class African Americans were treated by the justice system. He used his magazine as an instrument of propaganda to "impress upon the world that it is not a disgrace to be a Negro, but a privilege" (6). In one of his most anthologized poems, "Tired," he expresses the sentiment of those he represented: He is tired of working and building up someone else's civilization.

In 1920, Johnson published a collection of short stories, *Tales of Darkest America* (1920), and a collection of essays, *For the Highest Good* (1920). He also continued to write poetry for local and national periodicals. Editors such as Harriet Monroe and **Arna Bontemps** included him in their literary projects. In 1930, Bontemps invited Johnson to work at the Chicago bureau of the **Federal Writers' Project**. Here, Johnson must have imparted his wisdom to other writers such as **Frank Marshall Davis**, **Willard Motley**, and **Richard Wright**. Johnson may have also influenced **Langston Hughes**, who was in Chicago during the 1930s.

Although Johnson's writing career had diminished by the mid-1930s, his influence on modern poetics is important. He is often credited with being the first African American poet to make use of the free verse form in his poetry. Although Johnson did not directly align himself with the poets of the **Harlem Renaissance**, he did demonstrate the importance of valuing one's own culture, and throughout the remainder of his life he championed causes to promote African American arts and letters.

Resources: Primary Sources: Fenton Johnson: *For the Highest Good* (Chicago: Favorite Magazine, 1920); *A Little Dreaming* (Chicago: Peterson, 1913); *Songs of the Soil* (New York: Fenton Johnson, 1916); *Tales of Darkest America* (Chicago: Favorite Magazine, 1920); *Visions of the Dusk* (New York: Fenton Johnson, 1915). Secondary Sources: Robert Baksa, *Three Portraits: For Male Low Voice with Piano to Prose Poems of Fenton Johnson* (New York: Composers Library Editions, 1996); James P. Hutchinson, "Fenton Johnson: Pilgrim of the Dusk," *Studies in Black Literature* 7 (Autumn 1976), 14–15; Shirley Lumpkin, "Fenton Johnson," in *Dictionary of Literary Biography*, vol. 45, *American Poets, 1880–1945*, ed. Peter Quatermain (Detroit: Gale Research, 1986); Lorenzo Thomas, "Fenton Johnson: The High Cost of Militance," in his *Extraordinary Measures: Afrocentric Modernism and Twentieth-Century American Poetry* (Tuscaloosa: University of Alabama Press, 2000), 11–44; Lisa Woolley, "Fenton Johnson and Marita Bonner: From Chicago Renaissance to Chicago Renaissance," in her *American Voices of the Chicago Renaissance* (DeKalb: Northern Illinois University Press, 2000), 120–146; Hammett Worthington-Smith, "Fenton Johnson," in *Dictionary of Literary Biography*, vol. 50, *Afro-American Writers Before the Harlem Renaissance*, ed. Trudier Harris (Detroit: Gale Research, 1986).

Mary Hricko

Johnson, Freddie Lee, III (born 1958). Novelist. Johnson has been hailed as a male counterpart to novelist **Terry McMillan** because his novels deal with modern African American issues. Many problems that his characters encounter, however, are universal. Further, his descriptive, flowing prose is so compelling that the reader is quickly drawn into the plots regardless of questions of ethnicity or **gender**. The serious themes that undergird his two novels, *Bittersweet* and *A Man Finds His Way*, fall into two categories: (1) a refutation of the stereotype of the shiftless, irresponsible Black male and (2) the importance of faith, specifically Christianity, in getting through life in one piece. Although his characters are flawed, and their situations are sometimes raw, God ultimately, always, wins. *Bittersweet*, Johnson's first novel, presents the struggles of three completely different brothers: a hardened street thug, a sorely tempted minister, and a hardworking corporate man struggling through a divorce. Ostensibly, the story is about "women troubles," but it is also as much about their love for one another and the bonds that hold families together (Spratling, 2002). *A Man Finds His Way* features a divorced history professor warring against bigotry in the Black as well as in the White community and dealing with his son's problems, specifically an accusation of rape. In both books, concern about children is paramount. Women are powerful but peripheral characters who cause pain as well as pleasure. Although there is plenty of sensuality, each hero eventually pursues "the good woman."

At this writing, Johnson is a professor of history at Hope College. Before going into academia, he worked in the corporate world and served in the U.S. Marines. These experiences give his work a sturdiness and a ring of truth, so that the reader easily identifies with the conflicts the characters face. His third novel, *Other Men's Wives*, was published in 2005.

Resources: Debbie Bogenschutz, "Review of *Bittersweet* by Freddie Lee Johnson," *Library Journal*, Nov. 15, 2001; Freddie Lee Johnson: *Bittersweet* (New York: One World, 2002); *A Man Finds His Way* (New York: One World/Ballantine, 2003); Dawn R. Reeves, "Review of *Bittersweet* by Freddie Lee Johnson," *RAWSISTAZ*, http://www.therawreviewers.com/TRR/Reviews/Bittersweet.htm; "Review of *Bittersweet*, by Freddie Lee Johnson," *Publishers Weekly*, Dec. 10, 2001; "Review of *Bittersweet* by Freddie Lee Johnson," *PMA Literary and Film Management*, http://www/pmalitfilm.com/2001.html; "Review of *A Man Finds His Way* by Freddie Lee Johnson," *Bookreporter*, http://www.bookreporter.com/reviews/035445988.asp; Cassandra Spratling, "Brotherly Love," review of *Bittersweet*, *Detroit Free Press*, Jan. 13, 2002; Ahmad Wright, "Review of *Bittersweet* by Freddie Lee Johnson," *Black Issues Book Review*, Jan. 1, 2002.

Mary Hanford Bruce

Johnson, Georgia Douglas (1886–1966). Poet and playwright. A highly prolific poet, playwright, and short story writer, Johnson is widely recognized as one of "the most productive artists of the Harlem Renaissance" and "one of the first African American female poets to achieve a national reputation" (Donlon, 23).

Born Georgia Blanche Douglas Camp on September 10, 1886, Johnson spent her childhood and adolescence in Rome, Georgia, and **Atlanta, Georgia**. The daughter of Laura Douglas and George Camp, she graduated from Atlanta University's Normal School in 1893. Following her graduation, Johnson accepted a teaching position in Marietta, Georgia, which she held until 1902, when she enrolled in the Oberlin Conservatory of Music and the Cleveland College of Music, where she studied composition, piano, and violin.

On September 28, 1903, she married Henry Lincoln Johnson, and in 1910, the couple moved to 1461 S Street N.W. in **Washington, D.C.** The house, where Johnson resided for more than fifty years, became home to "one of the greatest literary salons of the Harlem Renaissance" (Honey). Throughout much of the 1920s, Johnson hosted a weekly Saturday Nighters' Club, which was attended by such acclaimed writers of the **New Negro** Renaissance (later the **Harlem Renaissance**) as **Jean Toomer, Langston Hughes, Angelina Weld Grimké**, and **Alice Moore Dunbar-Nelson**.

Between 1926 and 1932, Johnson wrote "Homely Philosophy," a weekly newspaper column that was syndicated by twenty publications. During this same time, she gained attention for her dramatic work, writing one-act plays that were produced by little theater groups. *Blue Blood*, a play about the rape of Black women by White men, was produced by the Krigwa Players in 1926, and the following year earned an honorable mention in **Opportunity** magazine's contest. That same year, *Plumes*, a folk tragedy about Black funeral rites, won first prize in the contest. Although *Blue Blood* and *Plumes* are arguably Johnson's best-known plays, she also wrote several **lynching** plays—*Sunday Morning in the South* (1926), *Safe* (1929), and *Blue-Eyed Black Boy* (1930)—and two historical dramas about runaway slaves—*Frederick Douglass* (1935) and *William and Ellen Craft* (1935).

Despite her successes as a dramatist, Johnson is best known for her work as a poet. She published her first poems—"Gossamer," "Fame," and "My Little One"—in **The Crisis** magazine in 1916 and, over the course of her long and prolific career, wrote four volumes of poetry: *The Heart of a Woman* (1918), *Bronze* (1922), *An Autumn Love Cycle* (1928), and *Share My World* (1962).

Although quite prolific in the early part of her career, Johnson became less so after the death of her husband on September 10, 1925. With two sons, both of whom she put through college, and a household to support, Johnson accepted a job with the U.S. Department of Labor as commissioner of conciliation, which left her little time to pursue writing. Johnson's writing also was compromised by her inability to secure fellowship money. Still, during this time, she continued to produce a few poems, short stories (at times writing under the pseudonym Paul Tremain), plays, and her newspaper column.

In 1965, Johnson was awarded an honorary doctorate by Atlanta University. One year later, on May 14, 1966, she died of a stroke.

Resources: Addell Austin Anderson, "Georgia Douglas Johnson," in *American Playwrights, 1880–1945: A Research and Production Sourcebook*, ed. William W. Demastes (Westport, CT: Greenwood Press, 1995), 224–229; Jocelyn Hazelwood Donlon, "Georgia Douglas Johnson," in *Black Women in America*, vol. 1, ed. Darlene Clark Hine (Brooklyn, NY: Carlson, 1993), 640–642; Winona Fletcher, "Georgia Douglas Johnson," in *Dictionary of Literary Biography*, vol. 51, ed. Thadious Davis and Trudier Harris (Detroit: Gale Research, 1987), 153–164; Christy Gavin, ed., *African-American Women Playwrights: A Research Guide* (New York: Garland, 1999); "Georgia Douglas Johnson," in *The Black Renaissance in Washington*, D.C., June 20, 2003, D.C. Library, http://www.dclibrary.org/blkren/bios/johnsongd.html; Maureen Honey, "Georgia Douglas Johnson's Life and Career," *Department of English: Modern American Poetry*, UIUC, Aug. 3, 2003, http://www.english.uiuc.edu/maps/poets/g_l/Douglas-johnson/life.htm; Georgia Douglas Johnson: *An Autumn Love Cycle* (New York: Harold Vinal, 1928); "Blue Blood," in *Fifty More Contemporary One-Act Plays*, ed. Frank Shay (New York: Appleton, 1938); "Blue-Eyed Black Boy," in *Wines in the Wilderness: Plays by African American Women from the Harlem Renaissance to the Present*, ed. Elizabeth Brown-Guillory (Westport, CT: Greenwood Press, 1990); *Bronze: A Book of Verse* (Boston: Brimmer, 1922); *The Heart of a Woman and Other Poems* (Boston: Cornhill, 1918); "Let Me Not Lose My Dream," "Old Black Men," "Black Woman," "The Heart of a Woman," and "I Want to Die While You Love Me," in *The Portable Harlem Renaissance Reader*, ed. David Levering Lewis (New York: Viking, 1994), 273–276; "Plumes," in *Plays of Negro Life: A Source Book of Native American Drama*, ed. Alain Locke and Montgomery Gregory (New York: Harper and Brothers, 1927); "Safe," in *Wines in the Wilderness: Plays by African American Women from the Harlem Renaissance to the Present*, ed. Elizabeth Brown-Guillory (Westport, CT: Greenwood Press, 1990); *The Selected Works of Georgia Douglas Johnson* (New York: G. K. Hall, 1997); "A Sunday Morning in the South," in *Black Theatre, U.S.A.: Forty-five Plays by Black American Playwrights, 1847–1974*, ed. James V. Hatch and Ted Shine (New York: Free Press, 1974); Elizabeth McHenry, *Forgotten Readers: Recovering the Lost History of African American Literary Societies* (Durham, NC: Duke University Press, 2002); Yvonne Shafer, *American Women Playwrights, 1900–1950* (New York: Peter Lang, 1995); Ann Trapasso, "Georgia Douglas Johnson," in *Notable Black American Women*, ed. Jessie Carney Smith, Book 1 (Detroit: Gale, 1992), 578–584.

Heath A. Diehl

Johnson, Guy (born 1945). Novelist. The only son of **Maya Angelou**, Guy Johnson has published two adventure novels that, combined, offer a sweeping fictional glance of the struggles of African Americans in the twentieth century. Following in the footsteps of African American detective novelists, including **Chester Himes** and **Walter Mosley**, Johnson creates heroes who are not afraid to kill their enemies and who are determined to protect their honor, family, and friends.

Set in the early twentieth century, Johnson's debut novel, *Standing at the Scratch Line* (1998), begins in **New Orleans, Louisiana**, when LeRoi "King"

Tremain is forced to flee after he mistakenly kills two white deputies while trying to protect his family from the DuMonts, with whom the Tremain family has been feuding for generations. A member of the "colored" 369th Battalion, he fights racism as well as the Germans in France during **World War I**. On his return, he becomes wealthy from Prohibition, and he continues to protect his family as he fights the mob in **Harlem, New York**, the Ku Klux Klan in Louisiana, and politicians in a Black township in Oklahoma.

Set in 1982, Johnson's sprawling sequel, *Echoes of a Distant Summer* (2002), focuses on King Tremain's grandson, Jackson St. Clair Tremain. Long estranged from his legendary grandfather, he is summoned to his deathbed in Mexico. Before he can inherit his grandfather's $50 million fortune, he must continue the feud with the DuMont family of Louisiana, now aligned with the San Francisco mafia. Jackson discovers he is truly King's grandson.

The two novels successfully combine Black machismo heroism with the narratives of a sprawling family saga. Both novels incorporate love interests for the heroes, but women are secondary to the all-male world of honor, violence, justice, and power. Johnson currently lives in Oakland, California, with his wife and son.

Resources: Guy Johnson: *Echoes of a Distant Summer* (New York: Random House, 2002); *Standing at the Scratch Line* (New York: Random House, 1998).

Ymitri Jayasundera

Johnson, Helene (1906–1995). Poet. Johnson was one of the most accomplished poets of the **Harlem Renaissance**, but she never published even one book of her own. Her gift was recognized in the 1920s by other writers, most notably **Countee Cullen**, who anthologized eight of her most characteristic works in *Caroling Dusk* (1927). Yet Johnson, who was noted for being shy and retiring, chose not to pursue poetry as a career, and was, aside from a few poems appearing in the journal *Challenge: A Literary Quarterly* (edited by **Dorothy West**) in the mid-1930s, virtually unheard from after the peak years of the Harlem Renaissance. In sum, she left a body of published work whose colorful exuberance and youthful vitality are made all the more poignant by their short duration. While Verner Mitchell's collection of her work reveals that Johnson did continue to write a few poems in late middle age, in the 1930s she became Mrs. William Warner Hubbell, a wife and mother, and dropped out of the literary scene in which she shone so brightly for such a short time.

Johnson was an only child, born in **Boston, Massachusetts**, to parents who separated soon after her birth. With her cousin Dorothy West, she attended Boston's Lafayette School, the Martin School, and the Girls Latin School, and they honed their literary skills with writing courses at Boston University and joined the Saturday Evening Quill Club, a Black writers' salon. In 1927, the cousins moved to New York City, befriended **Zora Neale Hurston**, attended Columbia University's Extension Division, and were swept up in the creative energy and artistic efflorescence of **Harlem, New York**. Even before moving to New York, Johnson, then age eighteen, had the confidence to submit "Trees at Night" to *Opportunity* magazine. This, her first published poem, won honorable mention at the Urban League's first annual literary awards ceremony in May 1925. It is as if her talent sprang fully formed at its inception. "Trees at Night" exemplifies Johnson's intensely visual, image-focused poetry, drawing inspiration from heightened representations of nature. Other works from the mid-1920s, such as "Night," "Metamorphism," "Magula," and "A Southern Road," similarly emphasize intense renditions of the external world's gorgeous, almost overwhelming sensuality.

Johnson was also a forceful social critic in a significant number of her thirty-four published works. The very early "My Race" (1925) contrasts the outward appearance of African Americans as carefree—a palatable stereotype—with her people's inner hunger for fulfillment which is just becoming formed. "The Road" (also from 1925) ostensibly praises the homely beauty of a road, but also compares its beauty to that of the oppressed people of her race: both are trodden down but eternally resilient. "Poem" (1927) expresses intense pride in being African American, colloquially linking Harlem's popular culture to its African roots in a jazzy, jagged rhythm.

While her most characteristic poems are cast in free verse, Johnson also favored the **sonnet** in works such as "Sonnet to a Negro in Harlem" (1927), "A Missionary Brings a Young Native to America" (1928), and "Invocation" (1929). Carefully wrought, Johnson's sonnets are a testament to her ability to craft controlled forms containing an almost riotous sensuality or simmering social critique. Johnson's small, bejeweled body of work revealed an outsized talent whose energy exemplified the Harlem Renaissance. (*See* **Jazz Poetry**; **Literary Societies**.)

Resources: Helene Johnson, "My Race," "A Southern Road," "Sonnet to a Negro in Harlem," and "Poem," in *The Portable Harlem Renaissance Reader*, ed. David Levering Lewis (New York: Viking, 1994), 276–277; Verner Mitchell, ed., *Waiting for Love: Helene Johnson, Poet of the Harlem Renaissance* (Amherst: University of Massachusetts Press, 2000); Raymond Patterson, "Helene Johnson," in *Dictionary of Literary Biography*, vol. 51, ed. Thadious Davis and Trudier Harris (Detroit: Gale, 1987), 164–167.

David A. Boxwell

Johnson, Jack (1878–1946). Professional boxer. The first Black heavyweight champion boxer, Jack Johnson was an important figure in African American culture and literature, thrilling Black audiences with his athletic talent and flouting of White society.

Johnson was born March 31, 1878, in Galveston, **Texas**. Dropping out of school after the fifth grade, he worked in the cotton fields and as a stevedore. He acquired his fighting skills through participation in the notorious "battle royals," in which blindfolded African American youth punched themselves senseless for the benefit of White audiences. In 1897, Johnson began his career as a professional boxer, and by 1903 he was the "colored" heavyweight champion. He defeated White champion Tommy Burns on December 26, 1908, in Sydney, Australia, thus becoming the first Black heavyweight champion. In the next year Johnson defended his title against five White challengers. In an effort to find a "great White hope" who would dethrone the talented and brazen Johnson, former champion Jim Jeffries was lured out of retirement. On July 4, 1910, in Reno, Nevada, Johnson dominated Jeffries, setting off national celebrations in the Black community and **race riots** in some areas of the country.

Outside the boxing ring, Johnson stirred controversy for his relationships with a number of White women. In May 1913, he was convicted for violating the Mann Act, which made it a felony to transport women across state lines for immoral purposes. To avoid prison, Johnson fled the country. He defended his title three times in Europe, but in 1919 he was beaten in a Havana, Cuba, bout by Jess Willard. Many boxing historians believe that Johnson, desperate for money, intentionally lost the fight.

In 1920, Johnson returned to the United States and served nine months in Leavenworth Prison. After his incarceration, he earned his living through boxing exhibitions, vaudeville acts, and a stint with Hubert's Museum in New York City. He was killed in an automobile accident on June 10, 1946, near Raleigh, North Carolina. Johnson was a charter inductee into the Boxing Hall of Fame in 1954.

Johnson's bravado was well captured in his autobiography *Jack Johnson in the Ring and Out* (1927). The important role played by Johnson in Black culture and **folklore** is well established in the writings of such notable figures as **W.E.B. Du Bois, Booker T. Washington, James Weldon Johnson, Richard Wright**, and **Ralph Ellison**. The brutality of the battle royals from which Johnson emerged is well captured in Ellison's *Invisible Man* (1952), while in *Along This Way* (1933) James Weldon Johnson found the boxer to be talented but lacking as a tragic hero. The 1968 play *The Great White Hope* by Howard Sackler, and a subsequent 1970 film directed by Martin Ritt, dramatized Johnson's life in the fictional character of Jack Jefferson. The life and career of Jack Johnson continue to fascinate with efforts to overturn his federal conviction attracting prominent intellectuals and sports figures.

Resources: Jervis Anderson, "Black Heavies," *American Scholar* 47 (1978), 387–395; J. Gerald Early, *The Culture of Bruising: Essays on Prizefighting, Literature, and Modern American Culture* (Hopewell, NJ: Ecco, 1994); Al-Tony Gilmore, *Bad Nigger!: The National Impact of Jack Johnson* (Port Washington, NY: Kennikat Press, 1975); Jack Johnson, *Jack Johnson: In the Ring and Out* (London: Proteus Publishing, 1977); Lawrence W. Levine, *Black Culture and Black Consciousness: Afro-American Folk Thought from Slavery to Freedom* (New York: Oxford University Press, 1977); Randy Roberts, *Papa Jack: Jack Johnson and the Era of White Hopes* (New York: Free Press, 1983); William H. Wiggins, "Jack Johnson as Bad Nigger: The Folklore of His Life," *Black Scholar* 2 (Jan. 1971), 4–19.

Ron Briley

Johnson, James P[rice] (1894–1955). Composer and pianist. Though often neglected in musical histories, Johnson figures as a major pianist of the **Harlem, New York**, stride school, as a writer of scores for musical shows, and as a composer of symphonic works. His influence on the development of **jazz** piano equals that of Scott Joplin, Jelly Roll Morton, Thomas "Fats" Waller, **Edward Kennedy "Duke" Ellington, William "Count" Basie**, Art Tatum, and Thelonious Monk (*see* **Gillespie, Dizzy, Charlie Parker, and Thelonious Monk**). In recent years, literary scholars and cultural historians have focused on the stage productions of the **Harlem Renaissance** and have begun to determine the significance of jazz and Black musical theater as more than marginalia to the politics and philosophies of **"New Negro"** intellectuals. Critics such as **W.E.B. Du Bois** and **Alain Locke** favored political advocacy, cultural self-determination, and "high art" over popular entertainment, but today Johnson is regarded a central contributor to African American culture.

Johnson was born in New Brunswick, New Jersey. His family moved to New York City in 1908, where the teenager learned to play the popular tunes and mastered the **ragtime** techniques that were the rage in the 1900s and 1910s. Johnson soon became fascinated with the music and flashy lifestyle of celebrated pianists (called "ticklers") such as Richard "Abba Labba" McLean and Luckyeth "Lucky" Roberts. The country dances, marches, church hymns, and folk songs Johnson had encountered at home as a child, regular attendance at the New York Symphony concerts, and music lessons from his teacher Bruno Gianinni complemented Johnson's early exposure to music.

Johnson recorded piano rolls for the Aeolian Company in 1916 and later for QRS. In 1921, Black Swan released his first record, "Harlem Strut," followed later that year by "Carolina Strut" and "Keep Off the Grass." Other Johnson staples are "If I Could Be with You" (1927/1944), "Old Fashioned Love" (1924/1939), and "The Mule Walk" (1938). He was Harlem's leading stride pianist, and his performances at rent parties often climaxed in "cutting contests," musical duels with Fats Waller and Willie "The Lion" Smith that left audiences in a frenzy.

Harlem stride piano strongly emphasized rhythm and syncopation, which Johnson fused with elements of European classical music. As Johnson describes the New York music scene, pianists "had to get orchestral effects, sound harmonies, chords and all the techniques of European concert pianists who were playing all over the city. New York developed the orchestral piano—full, round, big, widespread chords and tenths—a heavy bass moving against the right hand" (Davin, 170). The music combined the formal requirements of ragtime and classical music with the vocalization of the **blues** and the swing feel and improvisation of jazz.

Prime features of Harlem stride were its fast tempo and the delegation of radically different tasks for the right and left hands. In the words of Stanley Dance: "Alternating a chord in the middle of the keyboard with a single note, octave, or tenths in the lower register, [Johnson's] powerful left hand produced an exciting drive and momentum. Against this was set a stimulating treble part, executed in that grace and dexterity which had been the ragtime tickler's pride" (Ellington and Dance, 324) and which included improvised melodic lines. In "Imitator's Rag" (no recording exists), Johnson boasted to have played "Dixie" with his right hand and "The Star Spangled Banner" with his left at the same time.

Johnson also wrote the scores to several musical shows. Many theatrical productions in the 1920s included music and lyrics by Black writers and sported all-Black casts. *Plantation Days* (1923), *Runnin' Wild* (1923), and *Keep Shufflin'* (1928), a collaboration with Waller, capitalized on the "Negro vogue" and reached Black and White audiences alike. *Runnin' Wild* introduced the defining dance of the decade, the Charleston, and the emblematic song of the decade, "Charleston." "Skiddle-De-Skow" (from the 1929 musical *Messin' Around*) fused blues tonalities and stride rhythms with experimental harmonies. Recording with the great **Bessie Smith** and **Ethel Waters**, and playing on the soundtrack to Smith's film *St. Louis Blues* (1929), Johnson was able to further his reputation among record buyers and music fans throughout the country.

Johnson moved away from musical theater in the 1930s and devoted his energies to more ambitious compositions. *Harlem Symphony* (1932), *American Symphonic Suite*, the piano concerto *Jassamine* (1934, 1945, 1947), and *Yamakraw: A Negro Rhapsody* (performed at Carnegie Hall in 1928 with Waller as soloist) indicated his intention to write concert music. During his lifetime, Johnson's extended compositions never reached popular acclaim. They did, however, provide the inspiration for Duke Ellington's forays into the genre, most notably *Black, Brown, and Beige* (1945). The folk opera *De Organizer*, to which **Langston Hughes** contributed the libretto, was performed once at Carnegie Hall, but most of the musical scores from it have been lost (Ostrom; Rouder). Johnson suffered a partial stroke in 1940 but kept on recording, performing, and composing (he completed a show titled *Sugar Hill* in 1949) until a second stroke in 1951 ended his career. He died in 1955.

Resources: Scott E. Brown and Robert Hilbert, *James P. Johnson: A Case of Mistaken Identity* (Metuchen, NJ: Scarecrow, 1986); Tom Davin, "Conversations with James P. Johnson," (1959–1960), repr. in *Ragtime: Its History, Composers, and Music*, ed. John Edward Hasse (New York: Schirmer, 1985), 166–177; Duke Ellington and Stanley Dance, "James P. Johnson/*Father of the Stride Piano*," liner notes (1962), repr. in *Setting the Tempo: Fifty Years of Great Jazz Liner Notes*, ed. Tom Piazza (New York: Anchor, 1996), 320–326; Samuel A. Floyd, Jr., ed., *Black Music in the Harlem Renaissance* (1990; repr. Knoxville: University of Tennessee Press, 1993); Ted Gioia, *The History of Jazz* (New York: Oxford University Press, 1997); Richard Hadlock, *Jazz Masters of the Twenties* (1965; repr. New York: Collier Books, 1974); Max Harrison, "James P. Johnson," in *Reading Jazz*, ed. Robert Gottlieb (New York: Pantheon, 1996), 845–850; James P. Johnson: *Father of the Stride Piano* (rec. 1921–1939; Columbia, 1962); *James P. Johnson: King of Stride Piano* (Giants of Jazz, 1998); and *The Original James P. Johnson 1942–1945* (Smithsonian Folkways, 1996); Hans Ostrom, *A Langston Hughes Encyclopedia* (Westport, CT: Greenwood Press, 2002), 189, 291–292;

Willa Rouder, "James P. Johnson," in *The New Grove Dictionary of American Music*, ed. H. Wiley Hitchcock and Stanley Sadie (New York: Grove's Dictionaries of Music, 1986), vol. 2, 580–581; Gunther Schuller, *Early Jazz: Its Roots and Musical Development* (New York: Oxford University Press, 1968); Jon Michael Spencer, *The New Negroes and Their Music* (Knoxville: University of Tennessee Press, 1997).

Daniel T. Stein

Johnson, James Weldon (1871–1938). Poet, novelist, essayist, editor, lyricist, teacher, and civil rights leader. In the course of his life James Weldon Johnson was a teacher, a lyricist for a theatrical act, a school principal, an attorney, a newspaper editor and publisher, a diplomat, a poet and novelist, an executive of a civil rights organization, and a professor of literature. This astounding range of achievement was engendered by parents who were both freeborn before the **Civil War**, his father James in Virginia, his mother, Helen Dillet, of French and Haitian descent, in the Bahamas. James was the head-waiter at Jacksonville, Florida's, premier hotel; Helen was a teacher at the local school for African Americans. James William Johnson (he changed his middle name to Weldon in 1913) was born in Jacksonville on June 17, 1871. From his father young James seems to have learned confidence in his ability to succeed, while his mother taught him and his younger brother, John Rosemond, drawing, piano, and poetry.

When he was seventeen, Johnson spent the summer as secretary to Thomas Osmond Summers, a White Jacksonville physician who provided him, he notes in his **autobiography** *Along This Way* (1933), with his "model of all that a man and a gentleman should be." Dr. Summers was a late Victorian nonconformist: a research scientist who worked for the public good, a sophisticated reader, a poet, an atheist, and an antiracist. He took Johnson to **Washington, D.C.**, and New York City, and they shared ship cabins and hotel rooms as equals. He fostered Johnson's intellectual and artistic development, recommending and discussing books and commenting on the young man's first poems. This influence seems to have set the seal on Johnson's lifelong dual focus on public service and the private pleasures of art.

Johnson graduated from Atlanta University in 1894, having long since determined to be a writer. At Atlanta University he also learned how to be a "race man"; the ethical question of how graduates would be "of service to the race" after graduation was a lively topic of discussion among students and faculty. Johnson's first job was as principal of the elementary school where his mother had taught; he soon added a secondary curriculum, developing the first high school for Blacks in the state of Florida. For a year he served the Stanton School while also developing and editing a daily newspaper, which folded in 1896. Johnson studied law privately and became the first African American to be admitted to the Florida bar. For several years he practiced law, ran the Stanton School and spent the summers in New York City, writing theater songs with his brother and Bob Cole. It was the heyday of **ragtime**. American popular culture was awash with authentic images and sounds related to

African Americans and demeaning White minstrel show versions of them. Cole and Johnson Brothers (James never performed on stage) was a highly successful act. James found ways to make his lyrics, usually written in dialect, encompass authentic emotions and not merely repeat the stereotypes of Negro laziness, ignorance, and sensuality. His and his brother J. Rosemond's best work, in songs such as "The Congo Love Song" and "Under the Bamboo Tree," connect African American life to universal elements such as love, wistfulness, and verbal play. They saw themselves as refining and poeticizing the potent raw material of African American culture rather than recycling conventional situations and imagery from the minstrel tradition (*see* **Minstrelsy**).

Johnson's best-known collaboration with his brother was in the creation of "Lift Every Voice and Sing." Composed for a Lincoln's Birthday celebration in Jacksonville in 1900, the song was widely distributed throughout **the South** and was later adopted as the unofficial anthem of the National Association for the Advancement of Colored People (**NAACP**) and for African Americans in general.

> Lift every voice and sing,
> Till earth and heaven ring,
> Ring with harmonies of liberty.
> Let our rejoicing rise
> High as the listening skies,
> Let it resound loud as the rolling sea.
> Sing a song full of the faith that the dark past has taught us,
> Sing a song full of the hope that the present has brought us.
> Facing the rising sun of our new day begun,
> Let us march on till victory is won.

Despite his personal agnosticism, Johnson was able to connect here with the African American masses' confidence in the future based on religious faith.

In 1902 Johnson resigned the principalship and moved permanently to New York City, where he continued to work in the theater. He wrote dialect verse in the manner of his friend **Paul Laurence Dunbar** as well as dramatic monologues influenced by Robert Browning and **ballads** reminiscent of Rudyard Kipling. When not traveling with the act, he took classes at Columbia University with Brander Matthews, a writer and theater scholar and, like Dr. Summers, a man free of virulent racial prejudice. Johnson was fluent in Spanish, and Matthews called upon this knowledge in their studies of European **drama**. Matthews became a friend and mentor who offered Johnson advice on his new project, a **novel**. Johnson left Cole and Johnson Brothers in 1905, took the diplomatic service exams, and, through the influence of Matthews and **Booker T. Washington**, was appointed U.S. consul in Puerto Cabello, Venezuela, in the summer of 1906. He worked on the novel here and completed it before his second posting, to Corinto, Nicaragua, in 1909, to which he brought his new wife, Grace Nail. *The Autobiography of an Ex-Colored Man* was published anonymously in 1912 because Johnson felt that the book would not be accepted if it were known that the author was not telling a personal life story.

Johnson's only novel is a masterpiece of irony. Narrated by its nameless subject, an African American pale enough to pass for White, the novel presents a complex version of the dilemma of middle-class African Americans: how to choose between communal, race-conscious public service and individual, assimilationist personal safety and comfort. The ex-colored man is the illegitimate son of a White Southerner and an almost White African American woman. Brought up in Connecticut, the narrator does not have a Black identity until it is forced on him at school. Thereafter, he struggles to overcome the stereotypes of identity that limit and shame him.

Although Johnson allows the narrator considerable psychological self-analysis, the deepest narrative structure is the ex-colored man's unreliability. He presents his story in a voice of self-assurance, but the reader realizes that despite his measured, analytic tone, he does not really know himself. The reader arrives at different assessments of his actions than the narrator means to convey. The ex-colored man is, from earliest childhood, self-protective. He works hard to avoid emotional discomfort. In every situation that calls for him to assert his African American identity, to acknowledge his membership in the race (or take responsibility for not doing so) he takes the coward's self-protective way out. When his trunk and money are stolen on his way to Atlanta University, he does not register for college but takes a job in a cigar factory, where he learns about **race**, color caste, and social class. He concludes with chacteristic selfishness:

James Weldon Johnson, c. 1910. Courtesy of the Library of Congress.

> I can realize more fully than I could years ago that the position of the advanced element of the colored race is often very trying. They are the ones among the blacks who carry the entire weight of the race question; it worries the others very little. (p. 60)

When the cigar factory closes, the ex-colored man goes to New York City, where he learns to play ragtime piano in a nighttime world of drinking, gambling, interracial sexuality, and violence. He is befriended by a cultured White gentleman, a millionaire who takes him to Europe, but who also functions as a demonic tempter, urging the narrator to abandon his efforts to be race conscious. This mentor, unlike Johnson's Dr. Summers, is self-absorbed and cynical. He sees the racial situation as an evil, but a force "like the physical and chemical forces" that cannot be overcome. The narrator does not accept the man's advice to stay in Europe, but returns home, fearing that he will, as the tempter suggests, waste his life "amidst the poverty and ignorance, the hopeless struggle of the black people of the United States."

Back in Georgia, the ex-colored man studies Black folk expression, but then witnesses a **lynching** and is shaken by the ferocity and brutality of the Whites and the impotence of the Blacks. He flees to New York, abandoning his plans to compose music based on folk themes, **spirituals** and ragtime, once again avoiding the psychological pain of identity. In New York he decides on **passing** permanently, and is successful in business and in love, courting and marrying a White woman who keeps his secret even from their children. At the end it becomes clear that the ex-colored man has exhibited unconscious moral weakness in the face of every racial challenge. "The practical joke on society" that he announced at the beginning of the narrative has turned out to be a not very funny joke on him.

After leaving the consular service, Johnson returned to New York and began to write editorials for the *New York Age*, a weekly African American newspaper. His column dealt with foreign and domestic politics as well as culture and racial uplift. Johnson's commitment to racial improvement evidenced in these articles brought him to the attention of the fledgling NAACP (founded in 1909), which hired him as its field secretary in 1916. On the artistic front, Johnson translated the libretto of Spanish composer Enrique Granados's opera *Goyescas* for its Metropolitan opera premiere in 1915, and in 1917 he published a collection of his poetry, *Fifty Years and Other Poems*.

Johnson's early poems—some written as far back as his college years—fall into three groups. One set is composed of poems such as the **sonnet** "Mother Night," belonging to the tradition of nineteenth-century Romantic and Victorian verse. These sonnets and ballads are conventional stuff, with themes of lost love, untimely death, and mawkish humor. A second group is made up of poems on racial themes. The best work in the collection, poems such as "The White Witch," "Brothers," and "O Black and Unknown Bards," makes effective use of traditional forms (sonnet, ghost ballad, dramatic dialogue, etc.). The third group is **dialect poetry**; most of them make use of the dramatic monologue form favored by Dunbar. Most are not as rich or as effectively humorous as Dunbar's best, though some—"An Explanation," for example—are acutely observed comments on African American speech practices and performance folkways.

In 1920 Johnson was promoted to secretary (chief executive officer) of the NAACP, a position he held until retirement in 1930. Using his skills as attorney, public speaker, and mediator, he effectively led the organization into the forefront on civil rights issues such as the campaign to enact federal legislation against **lynching**. Johnson was also active as a writer and editor during this opening decade of the Harlem Renaissance. In 1922 he published a landmark anthology, *The Book of American Negro Poetry*, including a long historical and critical introduction that praises African American poetic production as proof of African American intellectual equality; an important, significantly revised second edition appeared in 1931. With his brother, who had gone on to a distinguished career in music, Johnson published *The Book of American Negro Spirituals* in 1925 and a second volume in 1926. His preface to the first of these texts delineates Johnson's ideas about folk creativity; in *The Second Book of American Negro Spirituals* he develops the ways the spirituals had helped change the image of African Americans from "beggar at the gates of the nation" to a powerful creative force.

Johnson's major work of this period is *God's Trombones: Seven Negro Sermons in Verse*, published in 1927, with illustrations by the noted Harlem Renaissance painter Aaron Douglas. Begun in 1917, these seven poems represent Johnson's maturation as a modern poet. The poems are dramatic monologues, minidramas reflecting Johnson's reading of Browning and his study with Matthews, but they are couched in Whitmanian **free verse** rather than in the tight, rhyming forms he had previously favored. Moreover, they capture the rhetorical creativity of African American preachers without recourse to dialect, and show the connections between religious emotion and the African American community's desire for political and social freedom.

Johnson's major artistic contribution to the Harlem Renaissance validated the Negro folk preacher as subject and as artist, refuting many popular culture images of an infantile Black Christianity. *God's Trombones* is loving and respectful of the performative power, vivid imagination, and verbal skill of the people's traditional leaders.

Johnson worked hard throughout the 1920s to promote the **New Negro** or **Harlem Renaissance**, and is considered one of its presiding spirits, along with **W.E.B. Du Bois** and **Alain Locke**. He wrote essays including "Race Prejudice and the Negro Artist" and "The Dilemma of the Negro Author" for mainstream magazines, bringing home the message that the new, brilliant African American art and literature proved the full and complete humanity of African Americans. In 1930 he published *Black Manhattan*, a history of New York that focused on the African American presence in the performing arts. In the latter part of the book, Johnson presented a memoir of his own time as a member of the theatrical world of turn-of-the-century New York, and concludes that Black artists in literature, art, and theater are "going far towards smashing the stereotypes" and "reshaping public sentiment and opinion." While the book pays little attention to the economic situation of the ordinary person in the city's growing ghettos, it is Johnson's broadest expansion of his ideas about how talented individuals can affect the development of the race.

Johnson retired from the NAACP in 1930, took a position teaching at Fisk University, and began work on his autobiography, which he published in 1933 as *Along This Way*. The book is thorough, comprehensive, and informative, but unemotional. Johnson presents himself as never expressing rage, anger, or misery; his life, as presented here, is entirely under his control. He suppresses a few items, such as his ties to the Booker T. Washington political machine and his early support for the 1915 American occupation of **Haiti**.

In 1934, now comfortably settled into a routine of teaching one term at Fisk and one term in the New York University School of Education, Johnson published *Negro Americans: What Now?* After reviewing the community's institutional strengths—the churches, fraternities, the Black press, and the NAACP—Johnson emphasizes education, both formal and informal, as a key to advancement of the race and offers advice on developing businesses, cracking unions, and maximizing the power of the Black vote. Turning from advice to inspiration, he offers a credo in defense of spiritual integrity:

I WILL NOT ALLOW ONE PREJUDICED PERSON OR ONE MILLION OR ONE HUNDRED MILLION TO BLIGHT MY LIFE. I WILL NOT LET PREJUDICE OR ANY OF ITS ATTENDANT HUMILIATIONS AND INJUSTICES BEAR ME DOWN TO SPIRITUAL DEFEAT. MY INNER LIFE IS MINE, AND I SHALL DEFEND AND MAINTAIN ITS INTEGRITY AGAINST ALL THE POWERS OF HELL. (103)

Johnson's last book, *Saint Peter Relates an Incident* (1935), brought together that longish poem, published privately in 1930, with a few other new works and selected poems from *Fifty Years*. "St Peter Relates an Incident of the Resurrection Day" is one of Johnson's most amusing efforts, joining a Byronic verse pattern and mock heroic manner, a bit of African American folkloric "**signifying**" about the color of the Unknown Soldier and a traditional literary folk fantasy of heaven and the afterlife.

Just after his sixty-seventh birthday, Johnson died in an automobile accident while on vacation in Maine with his wife, who survived. A quintessential "race man," he had given his racial community a lifetime of service and found time to create, in the *Autobiography* and *God's Trombones*, some enduring literature.

Resources: Primary Sources: James Weldon Johnson: *Along This Way: The Autobiography of James Weldon Johnson* (New York: Viking, 1933); *The Autobiography of an Ex-Colored Man* (1912; New York: Knopf, 1927); *Black Manhattan* (1930; repr. New York: Da Capo, 1991); *Complete Poems*, ed. Sondra Kathryn Wilson (New York: Penguin, 2000); *Fifty Years and Other Poems* (Boston: Cornhill, 1917); *God's Trombones: Seven Negro Sermons in Verse* (New York: Viking, 1927); *Saint Peter Relates an Incident* (New York: Viking, 1935); *Writings* (New York: Library of America, 2004); James Weldon Johnson, ed., *The Book of American Negro Poetry* (New York: Harcourt, Brace, 1922; rev. ed., New York: Harcourt Brace, 1931); *The Book of American Negro Spirituals* (New York: Viking, 1925); *The Books of American Negro Spirituals, Including the Book of American Negro Spirituals and The Second Book of Negro Spirituals* (New York: Da Capo Press, 1977), with John Rosamond Johnson. **Secondary Sources:** Anne

Carroll, "Art, Literature, and the Harlem Renaissance: The Messages of God's Trombones," *College Literature* 29, no. 3 (Summer 2002), 57–82; Robert E. Fleming, *James Weldon Johnson* (Boston: Twayne, 1987); Henry Louis Gates, Jr., and Cornel West, *The African American Century: How Black Americans Have Shaped Our Country* (New York: Free Press, 2000); Eugene Levy, *James Weldon Johnson: Black Leader, Black Voice* (Chicago: University of Chicago Press, 1973); Louis Hill Pratt, "James Weldon Johnson (1871–1938)," in *African American Authors, 1745–1945: A Bio-Bibliographical Critical Sourcebook*, ed. Emmanuel S. Nelson (Westport, CT: Greenwood Press, 2000), 297–305; Cristina L. Ruotolo, "James Weldon Johnson and the Autobiography of an Ex-Colored Musician," *American Literature* 72, no. 2 (June 2000), 249–274; Jennifer L. Schulz, "Restaging the Racial Contract: James Weldon Johnson's Signatory Strategies," *American Literature* 74, no. 1 (Mar. 2002), 31–58; Salim Washington, "Of Black Bards, Known and Unknown: Music as Racial Metaphor in James Weldon Johnson's *The Autobiography of an Ex-Colored Man*," *Callaloo* 25, no. 1 (Winter 2002), 233–256.

Joseph T. Skerrett, Jr.

Johnson, Mat (born 1970). Novelist. Johnson has published two novels that have been critically well received, *Drop* (2000) and *Hunting in Harlem* (2003). He was born in **Philadelphia, Pennsylvania**, the son of an Irish American father and an African American mother. His parents divorced when he was five, and he spent part of his childhood in the care of social workers ("Mat Johnson"). By his own account, he performed poorly in public schools but managed to get accepted into a state college and then spent a year studying abroad at the University of Wales in Swansea ("Mat Johnson"). Upon his return, he enrolled at Earlham College in Richmond, Indiana, where he thrived and became involved with the Black Student Union. After his senior year, he was awarded a Thomas J. Watson Fellowship, which allowed him to study and travel for a year in Europe. When he returned, he enrolled in Columbia University's M.F.A. program in creative writing. After earning an M.F.A., Johnson was employed as a copywriter by the Music Television Network (MTV) in New York City, and he lived in **Harlem, New York**, an experience he found energizing ("Mat Johnson"). His first novel, *Drop*, is semiautobiographical and traces the journey of Chris Jones from Philadelphia to Europe to New York and back to Philadelphia. His second novel, *Hunting in Harlem*, is, as the title suggests, set in Harlem and is a thriller laced with comedy. It involves former convicted felons and the highly complex real-estate industry in 21st-century Harlem. Johnson lives with his wife and child in Philadelphia.

Resources: Mat Johnson: *Drop* (New York: Bloomsbury Books, 2000); *Hunting in Harlem* (New York: Bloomsbury Books, 2003); "Mat Johnson," *Bloomsbury.com*, http://www.bloomsburymagazine.com/Authors/default.asp?id=154§=2.

Hans Ostrom

Johnson Publishing Company (1942–present). Publisher. Since 1942, this company has provided continuous popular media coverage of the African

American experience through a variety of publications. The company also has sought to encourage and cultivate literature by sponsoring short story contents, reviewing books by African American authors, and discussing the life events of contemporary African American authors in a way not seen or covered in the popular media. Thus, the largest Black-owned publishing company in America has served an essential function in informing African Americans about the lives of other African Americans in several formats across its various publications. According to its Web site, the company began in 1942 in **Chicago, Illinois**. John H. Johnson had a difficult time finding information about African Americans in White-owned and -published magazines. Only a college student at the time, he borrowed against his mother's furniture to start the publication of **Negro Digest**—a forerunner of *Jet* magazine. The main publication of the company, **Ebony**, was started in 1945. Touted as the African American equivalent of *Life* magazine, *Ebony* provided coverage of African American life across the United States as it had never been seen before. The four-color presentation of African Americans doubtless contributed toward the rise of Black uplift at this time—the publication of such a magazine proving that African American life was worthy to be seen in that way. Like *Life*, *Ebony* started as a weekly publication and went to monthly publication in the 1970s. *Ebony* is a sponsor of the Fashion Fair, a fund-raising fashion show tour featuring African American models, and is also a place to advertise other African American-produced products. Among the products advertised and touted in the magazine is the Fashion Fair cosmetic line, started in the 1960's by Johnson's wife, Eunice, to provide cosmetics for the Fashion Fair models when they couldn't find any makeup to suit their skin tones.

Jet magazine was started in 1965 as an inexpensive digest magazine on African American life. Within its pages, readers can find coverage on celebrities, as well as read about high-profile African American political figures from across the country. The magazine also covers weddings and other life events of ordinary African Americans. With the inclusion of "regular" people in its pages, Johnson's overarching belief of allowing African Americans to see themselves in the media continues to be fulfilled.

Johnson Publishing took on the job of providing products to African Americans that were hard to find. This was how Fashion Fair cosmetics developed and how Supreme Beauty Products was established. Also, at a time when no one was publishing African American books, Johnson Publishing started its own book division, publishing texts of African American history, including Lerone Bennett's landmark work *Before the Mayflower* (1969). The publication of these texts and the manufacture of these products again contributed to the uplift of the African American community.

After his daughter, Linda Johnson Rice, graduated from Northwestern University's Kellogg Graduate School of Management, John Johnson stepped aside for her to take over as president and chief operating officer. In 2002, she took over as CEO. With the passing of the business to his daughter in 1987,

John H. Johnson, chairman and publisher of the Johnson Publishing Company, poses with his daughter, president and CEO Linda Johnson Rice, at a celebration of the company's fiftieth anniversary in 1992. The company, located in Chicago, publishes *Ebony* and *Jet* magazines. AP/Wide World Photo.

Johnson created the circumstances by which the Johnson Family Publishing Company could continue well into the twenty-first century.

Resources: *Johnson Publishing Company*, http://www.fatherherry.org/BlackPress/johnson.htm; *Johnson Publishing Company*, http://www.hoovers.com/free/co/factsheet.xhtml?COID=40251; *Linda Johnson Rice*, http://www.infoplease.com/ipa/A0880191.html.

Piper G. Huguley-Riggins

Johnson-Coleman, Lorraine (born 1962). Storyteller and author. Lorraine Johnson-Coleman combines the Southern tradition of storytelling and her African American heritage to create stories that capture the essence, wisdom, and history of everyday life in the rural **South**. Johnson-Coleman was born and raised in New York City (Queens); her mother was a schoolteacher and her father a preacher, and both were from Southern backgrounds. Johnson-Coleman attended Queens College, receiving degrees in economics and English. Before publishing her first book, *Just Plain Folks* (1997), she worked as a consultant and advocate for the realistic portrayal of African American heritage in museums, local historical sites, and other venues. Johnson-Coleman entered storytelling after receiving positive feedback on her talks about African American heritage. After giving several such talks, she decided to collect her stories into a book.

Johnson-Coleman cites the storytelling and dialogue of **Zora Neale Hurston** and the critical and the commercial success of **Walter Mosley** as influences on her career as storyteller and author. She has performed at the annual Zora Neale Hurston Festival of the Arts and Humanities in Eatonville, Florida. Robert E. Hemenway, Hurston's biographer, has compared her work to Hurston's (Summer, 42). Johnson-Coleman has conducted writing workshops, has been featured in state literary festivals, and has guest-lectured for the University of Georgia system. Her interview on National Public Radio upon the publication of *Just Plain Folks* led to regular spots on NPR's *Morning Edition* as well as a thirteen-part series, *Just Plain Folks*, for *NPR Playhouse*. The audio book of *Just Plain Folks* won a Listen Up Award from *Publishers Weekly* as one of the best audio books of 1998.

Just Plain Folks is a collection of short stories based on stories told by family and friends in Johnson-Coleman's ancestral community of Farmville, North Carolina, as well as stories she collected from other rural Southern communities. The collection describes family reunions and characters such as Miz Lullabel Lee, who succeeded in sowing discord among a family when the Devil failed. Johnson-Coleman includes an "Afterthought" after each story, placing the tale in cultural context. In "An Afterword" to *Just Plain Folks*, she explains, "It [writing the collection] meant going back to some basic wisdom that is getting increasingly difficult to find, but once recorded is certainly worthy of praise. For me, the significance of my work is the ability to give voice to those very truths, and I have tried to do just that" (163). Johnson-Coleman's second book, *Larissa's Breadbook* (2001), depicts the multicultural heritage of the South in a combination of stories and recipes. Johnson-Coleman features her daughter, Larissa, as a character who helps ten women at a senior center prepare bread for her middle school's bake sale. While helping the women, Larissa learns about various cultures and recipes of the South, including African American, Cherokee, Scotch-Irish, Jewish, Italian, and Mexican. Johnson-Coleman created the women's stories, but she collected the recipes from family members and others across the country. In *Talking Mules and Other Folks: A Fable* (2001) Johnson-Coleman returns to Farmville, North Carolina, to chronicle a year in the community through the eyes of the animals of Tin Tub Place.

Resources: Primary Sources: Lorraine Johnson-Coleman: *Just Plain Folks: Original Tales of Living, Loving, Longing and Learning as Told by a Perfectly Ordinary, Quite Commonly Sensible, and Absolutely Awe-inspiring, Colored Woman* (Columbia, SC: Summerhouse, 1997); *Larissa's Breadbook: Baking Bread & Telling Tales with Women of the American South* (Nashville, TN: Rutledge Hill, 2001); *Talking Mules and Other Folks: A Fable* (Athens, GA: Hill Street, 2001). **Secondary Sources:** "Culturalist & Author Redefines Black History," *Tennessee Tribune*, Feb. 26, 1998, pp. 25+; Tasha Curtis, "Back to the Black Writing Renaissance," *Los Angeles Sentinel*, Mar. 17, 1999, pp. B4+; Bob Edwards, "Interview with Lorraine Johnson-Coleman," *Morning Edition*, NPR, June 12, 2001; "Lorraine Johnson-Coleman," in *Contemporary Authors*, vol. 180 (Detroit: Gale, 2000), 212–213; Bob Summer, "An African American Sampler from Three Southern Presses," *Publishers Weekly*, Dec. 8, 1997, p. 42.

Heather Martin

Johnson-Hodge, Margaret. Novelist. Born and raised in Jamaica, New York, Johnson-Hodge has more recently lived in **Atlanta, Georgia**. Although her works have typically been categorized as **romance novels**, they are notable for her attention to the psychology of the characters and for how they address serious themes.

Her first novel, *The Real Deal* (1998), began as a story that she wrote at the age of twelve. Treating an interracial relationship, the novel realistically depicts the constraints on the romantic possibilities for two fairly ordinary people who become acquainted in the workplace. Beyond the difference in race, the characters seem mismatched in terms of their perspectives, interests, and personalities. Nevertheless, they share a genuine interest in one another that may not cancel out their differences but does ultimately outweigh them. Johnson-Hodge addresses the issue of what defines romantic attachment if, for most people, the perfect match is not a possibility.

A New Day (1999) has a much more provocative premise. It focuses on a single mother who, in effect, prostitutes herself with her ex-husband in order to ensure his continued financial support of their daughter. The novel was included five times on *Mosaic* magazine's "What's Hot Top Five Fiction List." In *Butterscotch Blues* (2000), Johnson-Hodge treats the ramifications of the AIDS epidemic, exploring strains on a developing relationship when the man tests positive for HIV. *Some Sunday* (2001) is a sequel.

With a good deal of psychological interest, *Warm Hands* (2000) relates the story of a young woman who is lucky enough to be dumped by a self-absorbed loser and then to find romance with a professionally successful and emotionally caring man who becomes her fiancé. But shortly before their wedding day, she impulsively has one last fling with her former boyfriend and wrecks her relationship with her husband-to-be.

True Lies (2002) focuses on a man who remains in a bad marriage for the sake of his daughter but becomes involved in an extramarital relationship that only further complicates their lives. *A Journey to Here* (2003) centers on a nearly twenty-year marriage that has gradually gone stale. When the wife's old boyfriend suddenly reappears, wanting to restart their relationship, the marriage experiences a crisis that will either reinvigorate it or wreck it.

Resources: S. Shange Amani, "Review of *Butterscotch Blues*," *Black Issues Book Review* 2 (Sept./Oct. 2000), 25; Margaret Johnson-Hodge: *Butterscotch Blues* (New York: St. Martin's, 2000); *A Journey to Here* (New York: Dafina, 2003); *A New Day* (New York: St. Martin's, 1999); *The Real Deal* (New York: St. Martin's, 1998); *Some Sunday* (New York: Dafina, 2001); *True Lies* (New York: Dafina, 2002); *Warm Hands* (New York: St. Martin's, 2000).

Martin Kich

Jones, Edward P. (born 1950). Novelist and short story writer. Jones is best known as the Pulitzer-Prize winning author of *The Known World* (2003), a novel about an African American slave owner and plantation owner in Virginia in 1855. Jones was born and grew up in **Washington, D.C.**, the son of working-class parents. He earned his B.A. from Holy Cross College and an M.A. from the University of Virginia. His first book, a collection of short stories titled *Lost in the City* (1992), was nominated for a National Book Award. Jones has also won a Pen/Hemingway Award and a grant from the Lannan Foundation. With regard to *The Known World*, he has said that he first heard of African American slave ownership while he was in college, but did not consider writing fiction about the subject until much later (Hannaham). Of the relatively understated language in the novel, he has said, "I guess my sense is that **slavery** has emotions that come with it and I didn't need to overlay that with my own sense of 'neon language,' as I call it. I wanted to lay out the story in a very quiet manner. I felt that what people were going through in the novel was emotion enough and that the story would provide that" (Hannaham). Critic Carol Burns has observed, "Edward P. Jones's writing is deceivingly simple. His sharp, direct sentences belie the complexity of the characters he creates, such as the 'Young Lions' of his clear-eyed story from *Lost in the City*" (Burns). Although *The Known World* may be categorized as a work of **historical fiction** and is anchored in the fact that some slave owners were Black, Jones stresses the imaginative nature of the story, saying that it is "98 per cent fiction" and suggesting that the book focuses on the emotional and dramatic qualities of the topic rather than literal historical accuracy (Burns). In addition to writing, Jones appears regularly at colleges, literary festivals, and writers' conferences.

Resources: Carol Burns, "Off the Page: Edward P. Jones," *Washingtonpost.com*, Oct. 30, 2003, http://www.washingtonpost.com/wpdyn/articles/A11797-2003Oct24.html;

James Hannaham, "The Africana QA: Novelist Edward P. Jones," *Africana: Gateway to the Black World*, Nov. 19, 2003; http://www.africana.com/articles/qa/bk20031125 epjones.asp; Edward P. Jones: *Edward P. Jones*, http://www.harpercollins.com/author-intro/index.asp?authorid=5002; *The Known World* (New York: Amistad, 2003); *Lost in the City* (New York: Morrow, 1992).

Hans Ostrom

Jones, Edward Smyth (1881–?). Poet. Jones, born in Natchez, Mississippi, lived most of his adult life in Louisville, Kentucky, and Cambridge, Massachusetts. Desiring to attend Harvard University, he walked hundreds of miles from Kentucky to Massachusetts without any prior living arrangements or financial means. Upon his arrival, he slept on the grounds and was arrested for vagrancy. His first published poem, "Harvard Square," stems from that arrest; it received tremendous critical praise and enough public support to secure his quick release from jail. Harvard officials, in response, gave him a position on the custodial staff and allowed him to pursue his studies during his nonworking hours.

Jones continued to write poetry and published three collections in as many years. Few of his works are extant; however, what is available demonstrates his attention to poetic technique and formal verse. He eschewed writing in dialect, unlike his contemporary **Paul Laurence Dunbar**, whose **dialect poetry** often overshadowed his poems written in standard verse. Jones's first collection, *The Rose That Bloometh in My Heart and Other Poems* (1908), consists of romantic verse. The second, *Our Greater Louisville: Souvenir Poem* (1908), chronicles the tensions in Kentucky during the Black Patch War, a feud between merchants and consumers of tobacco, whose falling price spawned a buyer's market. Jones recognized the economic and historical consequences of the Black Patch War as a consequence of Kentucky's one-crop economy. His third volume, *The Sylvan Cabin; A Centenary Ode on the Birth of Lincoln and Other Poems* (1911), celebrates fellow Kentuckian, Abraham Lincoln, whose humble beginnings and opposition to **slavery** in the signing of the Emancipation Proclamation had endeared him to African Americans since the **Civil War**.

One of the poems included in *The Sylvan Cabin*, "A Song of Thanks," has become a widely popular recitation during the Thanksgiving holiday, and was included in **James Weldon Johnson**'s watershed anthology from the **Harlem Renaissance** period, *The Book of American Negro Poetry* (1922). The poem is a litany of small but significant gifts of nature and adeptly adheres to Johnson's call against the humor and pathos of dialect in poetry. Written in Standard English, "A Song of Thanks" is reminiscent of work by the British Romantic poets, including William Wordsworth, who often wrote about **nature**, and thus was an obvious choice to include in Johnson's anthology, cementing not only Jones's place in literary history but also celebrating the burgeoning development of the African American belletristic tradition.

Resources: James Weldon Johnson, ed. *The Book of American Negro Poetry* (New York: Harcourt, Brace, 1922); Edward Smyth Jones: *The Rose That Bloometh in My*

Heart (Louisville, KY: 1908); *Our Greater Louisville: Souvenir Poem* (Louisville, KY: n.p., 1908); *The Sylvan Cabin: A Centenary Ode on the Birth of Lincoln* (San Francisco: Sunset, 1915).

Candice Love Jackson

Jones, Gayl (born 1949). Fiction writer, poet, playwright, professor, and literary critic. Born in Lexington, Kentucky, Gayl Jones was creatively precocious, writing her first short story at the age of seven. Writing was a family affair: her grandmother, Amanda Wilson, wrote plays for church productions, and her mother, Lucille, was a fiction writer who wrote and read stories for her children. In a 1982 interview, Jones said that if her mother had not read to her as a child, she probably would never have thought of writing ("About My Work"). After high school, where her teachers described her as brilliant but painfully shy, Jones left **the South** to attend Connecticut College, where she earned a B.A. in English in 1971. By 1973, she had earned her M.A. in creative writing at Brown University and had seen her first play, *Chile Woman*, produced. In 1975, she earned her doctorate in creative writing at Brown and published *Corregidora*, her first novel. Jones's creative writing teacher, the poet **Michael S. Harper**, had given the manuscript to **Toni Morrison**, who edited both it and Jones's second novel *Eva's Man* (1976) for Random House.

Beginning what has become a lifelong exploration of both the physical and the psychological scars of **slavery**, Jones employs a compelling narrator in *Corregidora* in the figure of **blues** singer Ursa Corregidora. Wrestling with the painful complexities of her marriage, Ursa testifies to the impact of slavery, and the impact of its sexual legacy, on three generations of females. Amid the brutality, Ursa works out a mode of healing. She seems driven, as one critic suggests, by the mantra "Tell your story, or the master's story stands" (Burns). With the publication of this novel, lauded by **Darryl Pinckney** in *The New Republic* as "a small, fiercely concentrated story, harsh and perfectly told," Jones was hailed as a major new literary talent by such writers as John Updike and **James Baldwin**.

Jones further explored her preoccupation with psychological obsession, contradiction, and trauma, and what she calls the "blues relationship" between the sexes, in *Eva's Man*. This almost surreal work is told from the perspective of Eva Medina Canada, a victim of physical and sexual abuse, who ends up institutionalized for a disturbing act of murder and dismemberment by way of dental castration. Jones has described *Eva's Man* as "a horror story," "a kind of dream or nightmare" she felt compelled to transcribe. Jones's fascination with voices—with *how* things are said and not just with *what* is said—is paramount in all of her works. Beyond the pervasive influence of the blues, she is especially drawn to writers whose narratives are somehow connected to the oral tradition, from Chaucer, Cervantes, Ernest Hemingway, **Ralph Ellison**, and James Joyce, to Margaret Laurence, **Jean Toomer**, Gabriel García Márquez, Toni Morrison, and **Zora Neale Hurston**.

Jones was an assistant professor of English and Afro-American and African Studies at the University of Michigan from the late 1970s to the early 1980s, at which point she and her husband left the United States until 1988 because of legal problems. Her dramatic resignation from her post came by way of a letter addressed to the university, a copy of which was sent to President Ronald Reagan. The letter bluntly read, "I reject your lying, racist shit." During her years at Michigan, Jones published *White Rat* (1977), an eclectic medley of short stories, mostly set in rural Kentucky, that capture an African American **vernacular**, explore a variety of sexual issues and experiences, and address the politics of speech and silence. In Michigan, Jones also produced two volumes of poetry—*Song for Anninho* (1981) and *The Hermit-Woman* (1983).

Despite her gift for writing stark, evocative poetry, Jones considers herself primarily a fiction writer whose poems are but "little fictions" that foreground character and action. *Song for Anninho* is a retrospectively told, haunting **prose poem** dedicated to Jones's husband, Robert Higgins. The politically active Higgins, a former student at the University of Michigan, later assumed her surname. In this poignant love story between Almeyda and Anninho, two escaped slaves in seventeenth-century Brazil, Jones successfully moves beyond the "blues relationships" of her earlier published fiction and crafts a vision of love as the ultimate healing agent for physical and psychic abuse. *The Hermit-Woman* is a series of poems that illustrate love's mixed potential of danger and a promise. *Xarque and Other Poems* followed in 1985, while Jones was living abroad. A sequel to *Song for Anninho*, *Xarque* is set in mid-eighteenth-century Brazil and fuses past and present in a narrative spoken by Almeyda's granddaughter, Euclida.

Liberating Voices: Oral Tradition in African American Literature (1991) is Jones's only book of literary criticism to date. It offers a theoretical examination of the relationship between the African American oral and literary traditions. After a decade of living privately in Lexington, Kentucky, Jones published *The Healing* in 1998, a provocative meditation on healing as recounted from the unique perspective of Harlan Jane Eagleton, a larger-than-life former hairdresser, gambler, and rock-star manager-turned-faith healer. Advertised by Beacon Press as the book that convinced it to publish fiction for the first time in its 150-year history, *The Healing* was a finalist for the National Book Award. Its critical success was tragically overshadowed by the suicide that year of Jones's husband, Robert Higgins, during a police standoff at their home. *Mosquito* (1999), her most sprawling work of fiction to date, was published the following year. This imaginative political novel follows African American truck driver Sojourner Jane Nadine Johnson, a.k.a. Mosquito, as she travels through the American Southwest involved with a new scheme designed to help illegal Mexican immigrants.

Since the publication of *Corregidora* in 1975, Jones's works have drawn negative criticism on two principal counts—their excessive graphic violence and their lack of "positive **race** images." The latter claim is based on her purportedly negative images of Black men and her sexualized descriptions of Black women. On both counts, Jones's works may be defended as realistically conveying, in the lives of both her male and female characters, the public and private impact of slavery in the Americas. While she has noted the difficulties in dealing with Black female sexuality and admits to feeling extremely "double conscious" when treating the subject, she has said she will not provide "positive race images" at the expense of imaginative reality (Rowell). Jones remains a reclusive resident of Lexington, Kentucky. She rarely gives readings or interviews.

Resources: David Burns, "Scar Tissue: The Painful Beauty of Gayl Jones's *Corregidora*," www.db.vg/scartissue.html; Carol Margaret Davison, "'Love 'em and Lynch 'em': The Castration Motif in Gayl Jones's *Eva's Man*," *African American Review* 29 (1995), 393–410; Gayl Jones, "About My Work," in *Black Women Writers (1950–1980): A Critical Evaluation*, ed. Mari Evans (Garden City, NY: Anchor Books, 1984), 233–235; Charles H. Rowell, "An Interview with Gayl Jones," *Callaloo* 5 (1982), 32–53; Jerry W. Ward, Jr., "Escape from Trublem: The Fiction of Gayl Jones," *Callaloo* 5 (1982), 95–104.

Carol Margaret Davison

Jones, Laurence C. (1884–1975). Educator and writer. Laurence C. Jones is considered a pioneer of African American education in **the South**. He was born in 1884 to working-class parents in St. Joseph, Missouri. His father's position in the Pacific Hotel in St. Joseph allowed the Jones family to live modestly but comfortably, and the series of odd jobs that Jones held secured him a reputation for being industrious and hardworking. He attended grammar school in his hometown and began high school there as well, but, restless and eager, he boarded a train headed for Boston in 1898. He got only as far as Rock Island, Illinois, however, and, under the care of his uncle, Jones finished high school in Marshalltown, Iowa. In 1903 he enrolled at the University of Iowa, where he was influenced by John Ruskin's writings on political economy and **Booker T. Washington's** autobiography, *Up from Slavery*. After graduating in 1907, Jones traveled to Hot Springs, Arkansas, that summer. Although he had been offered a teaching position at Tuskegee, Jones accepted a position at the Utica Institute in Utica, Mississippi, and taught there until 1909.

The poverty that Jones encountered in the South so distressed him that he decided to open the Piney Woods Country Life School in Piney Woods, Mississippi, in 1909. From its modest beginnings with two students seated under a cedar tree, the school gradually realized Jones's belief in the efficacy of hard work and Christian living. Jones consistently sought contributions from wealthy donors, and with these funds the school grew from forty to fifteen hundred acres, with its students performing all of the school's daily operations and constructing its campus. Known as the "Booker T. Washington of Mississippi," Jones was invited in 1919 to help standardize the curriculum of African-American high schools, and he supported talented graduates of Piney

Woods by lending them money to attend college. In 1929 Jones was influential in encouraging the Mississippi State Department of the Blind to establish a school for the blind at Piney Woods, and it remained there until 1950, when the Mississippi School for the Blind opened in Jackson.

In December 1954, Jones appeared on the television program *This Is Your Life*, and the stories told about him and his school prompted donations totaling more than $700,000 from all over the country. Rejecting countless offers from other state and educational institutions, Jones remained at Piney Woods his entire career. His publications include *Piney Woods and Its Story* (1922), *The Spirit of Piney Woods* (1926), a series of Sunday evening talks delivered to his students, and *The Bottom Rail* (1935), which examined race relations in Mississippi from 1910 to 1935. Jones died in 1975.

Resources: Laurence C. Jones: *The Bottom Rail* (New York: Fleming H. Revell, 1935); *Piney Woods and Its Story* (New York: Fleming H. Revell, 1922); *The Spirit of Piney Woods* (New York: Fleming H. Revell, 1931); Leslie Harper Purcell, *Miracle in Mississippi: Laurence C. Jones of Piney Woods* (New York: Comet, 1956).

Philip J. Kowalski

Jones, Patricia Spears (born 1955). Poet and playwright. Jones is a versatile writer whose works address multicultural themes. She was born in Forest City, Arkansas, and graduated from Rhodes College, in **Memphis, Tennessee**, in 1973, with a degree in communications. She moved to New York City soon after, and worked as the program coordinator for St. Marks Poetry Project for many years, as well as at a number of arts organizations; more recently, she has been director of planning and development at the New Museum of Contemporary Art. Her first book of poems, *The Weather That Kills*, was published in 1995, and her poems have been anthologized in Scribner's *Best American Poetry 2000* (edited by Rita Dove); *Ordinary Women* (1978), which she also edited with Sara Miles, Sandra Maria Esteves, and Fay Chiang; *Black Sister* (1982); *Homegirls: A Black Feminist Anthology* (1983); *Sisterfire: Black Womanist Fiction and Poetry* (1994), *Aloud: Voices from the Nuyorican Poets Café* (1994); and *Poetry After 9/11: An Anthology of New York Poets* (2002).

Jones is also a playwright and has worked collaboratively with performance artists Lenora Champagne and Cindy Carr, in *Women in Research*, and with composer Jed Distler at the Non Sequitur Festival in 2000. Her play *Mother*, which premiered in New York in 1994, is a dazzling display of political agit-prop, noted the *New York Times*, laced with anger and irony. Yet much of her verse concerns intimate female bonds or subtle rites of passage. She writes of an exotic taxi ride across the Hudson River in "What I Will Miss Is Kissing in Cabs" and comments on those little devils that rally "we shefolk fast before sunrise" in "Pump." She offers advice to the lovelorn as well, in "Sapphire": "yes, you can live on martinis and chocolate!"—but for how long, one wonders.

Resources: Miguel Algarín and Bob Holman, eds., *Aloud: Voices from the Nuyorican Poets Café* (New York: Owl Books, 1994); Rita Dove, ed., *Best American Poetry 2000* (New York: Turtleback Books, 2000); Dennis Loy Johnson and Valerie Merians, eds.,

Poetry After 9/11: An Anthology of New York Poets (Hoboken, NJ: Melville House, 2002); Patricia Spears Jones, *The Weather That Kills: Poems* (Minneapolis, MN: Coffee House Press, 1995); Sarah Miles, Patricia Jones, Sandra Esteves, and Fay Chiang, eds., *Ordinary Women* (New York: Ordinary Women, 1978); Charlotte Watson Sherman, ed., *Sisterfire: Black Womanist Fiction and Poetry* (New York: HarperPerennial, 1994); Barbara Smith, ed., *Homegirls: A Black Feminist Anthology* (New York: Kitchen Table/Women of Color Press, 1983); Erlene Stetson, ed., *Black Sister: Poetry by Black American Women, 1746–1980* (Bloomington: Indiana University Press, 1981).

Josh Gosciak

Jones, Sarah (born 1974). Poet, playwright, and actor. Jones attended Bryn Mawr College in Pennsylvania on a Mellon scholarship for minorities. She is of African American and Caribbean European descent, and explores human rights, racism, and **feminism** through the various characters she portrays in her solo performances. These productions have attracted global attention along with accolades from local critics, women's groups, and sold-out audiences. In 1997, Jones won the **Nuyorican Poets Café**'s Poetry Slam. *Surface Transit* opened in 1998 and won the HBO Aspen Comedy Arts Festival Best One-Person Show category in 2000. In *Women Can't Wait!*, Jones portrays eight women characters from around the world who are oppressed by laws that violate their human rights. This production, written specifically for Equality Now, was performed at the United Nations International Conference on Women's Rights and enjoyed sold-out runs in New York. Jones's *Waking the American Dream* focuses on the immigrant experience and was commissioned by the National Immigrants Forum; it is the forerunner to her most recent work, *bridge & tunnel*. She appeared in **Spike Lee**'s film *Bamboozled* in 2000 and in Eve Ensler's *The Vagina Monologues* off-Broadway.

In 2004, Jones premiered her work *bridge & tunnel* in New York's Greenwich Village with Meryl Streep as one of the producers. She successfully sued the Federal Communications Commission for banning her poem "Your Revolution," a response to the misogynistic lyrics of many **rap** songs, from the airwaves. She stated, "I'm mainly inspired by the way we've been 'hoodwinked and bamboozled' as Malcolm X would say—as a society, and frankly globally—by images out there, the stereotypes, the ridiculous notions of who's who."

Jones has received a number of honors, including a Helen Hayes Award, a Drama Desk nomination, and an Obie Award for *bridge & tunnel* in 2004. She has performed at the Kennedy Center for the Performing Arts, and at the Berkeley Repertory, as well as in India and Nepal. She has received grants for her activist art from the Ford Foundation, the Kellogg Foundation, and others.

Resources: Jennifer Block, "Sarah Jones Can't Wait," *Ms.*, Oct.–Nov. 2000, 82–84; Sarah Jones: *bridge & tunnel: A Trip Through American Identity in Eight Voices* (Los Angeles: Three Rivers Press, 2004); home page, http://www.sarahjonesonline.com/bio/bio/html; 2004 Obies, http://www.villagevoice.com/obies/2004winners.shtml.

Joan F. McCarty

Jones, Solomon (born 1967). Novelist and journalist. A well-known journalist and a novelist with a growing reputation, Jones was born and raised in **Philadelphia, Pennsylvania**. He attended Temple University for a year and a half before dropping out because of a drug addiction. For several years, he lived on the streets or in homeless shelters. Never giving up entirely on his dream of being a writer, he began to contribute to *Shelter News and Views*, a newsletter published by the Ridge Avenue Homeless Shelter, and then to the *Philadelphia Tribune*.

After overcoming his addiction, Jones returned to Temple to complete a degree in journalism. While pursuing his studies, he began contributing to the *Philadelphia Inquirer*, *Philadelphia Weekly*, and *Philadelphia* magazine, as well as the *Tribune*. His main source of income was, however, a full-time position as a desk attendant at a condominium complex. This job involved a good deal of "dead" time, and Jones took advantage of it by writing the early drafts of what would become his first novel, *Pipe Dream* (2001). Like his two subsequent novels, *Pipe Dream* combines the hard-boiled style with a progressive political slant. It centers on a group of drug addicts who are being hunted by the police for a murder they did not commit.

The Bridge (2003) focuses on a police detective who returns to the public housing projects where he grew up in order to find the missing child of an old friend. In some ways, the daily life in the projects provides reminders of his own past, but in other ways it has become something completely foreign to his experience. Thus, on a number of levels, his sense of place and identity is tested.

Ride or Die (2004) is a contemporary reworking of the Romeo and Juliet story. In this instance, the star-crossed young lovers are the son of a local drug lord and the daughter of a minister who has become one of the leading social activists in the community. *Keeping Up with the Jones* (2004) is a collection of Jones's columns and essays, providing a wry commentary on the paradoxes and ironies of daily life.

Despite all of his recent success, Jones has demonstrated his continuing commitment to helping those who are still grappling with the problems he has overcome. He serves on the boards of the Philadelphia Committee to End Homelessness and the Calvary Association for the Empowerment of Families and Youth.

Resources: Patrick Henry Bass, "The Mix: Books," *Essence*, July 2001, 50–51; Anthony C. Davis, "Review of *Pipe Dream*," *Black Issues Book Review* 3 (July/Aug. 2001), 32; Solomon Jones: *The Bridge* (New York: St. Martin's/Minotaur, 2003); *Keeping Up with the Jones* (Philadelphia: Sola, 2004); *Pipe Dream* (New York: Villard/Strivers Row, 2001); *Ride or Die* (New York: St. Martin's/Minotaur, 2004); Barbara Sutton, "Review of *Pipe Dream*," *New York Times Book Review*, July 29, 2001, p. 16.

Martin Kich

Jones-Meadows, Karen. Playwright. Educated as a teacher, Karen Jones-Meadows taught for three years in the **Boston, Massachusetts**, public schools and for another year in North Carolina before she committed herself to playwriting. She had been writing poems in which she had so believably captured the voices of certain speakers that some readers had encouraged her to try her hand at writing plays.

The title character in Jones-Meadows's first play, *Henrietta* (1985), is a bag lady whose characterization is sympathetic without sacrificing credibility. The play is set on a city street and concerns her developing acquaintance with a young African American man who often passes her on his way to and from his high-paying job. Staged initially by the Negro Ensemble Company, the play was a great success and established Jones-Meadows as an important new voice in the American theater. Jones-Meadows's only published play, *Henrietta* has been included in **Woodie King, Jr.**'s, *The National Black Drama Anthology* (1995).

Jones-Meadows's most widely produced play has been *Harriet's Return*, in which she chronicles **Harriet Tubman**'s development of the **Underground Railroad** while personalizing the characterization with insights into her family life and her state of mind. Jones-Meadows has earned kudos for her own performances in the lead role in productions staged at community and university theaters throughout the United States. She has also directed a number of productions of her play *Sala Cinderella*, which reframes the fairytale as an African folk tale.

Jones-Meadows's other plays include *Brandon's Bounty*, *The Challenge*, *Crystals*, *Rounding off Time*, *Shower of Tears*, *The Stars of Urban Life*, and *Tapman*. After living in New Jersey for more than a decade, Jones-Meadows moved to Placitas, New Mexico. In addition to writing new plays, she has increasingly been offered opportunities to write screenplays and teleplays. She continues to give workshops throughout the country.

Resources: Laura Andrews, "Heroine Harriet Tubman Shown as Romantic Figure," *New York Amsterdam News*, Apr. 15, 1995, p. 23; John Beaufort, "Gusto and Unpretentiousness from the Negro Ensemble Company," *New York Times*, Feb. 4, 1985, Arts and Leisure, p. 32; Mel Gussow, "Stage: *Tapman*, with Moses Gunn," *New York Times*, Mar. 1, 1988, p. C 17; Edith Oliver: "Off Broadway," *The New Yorker*, Feb. 4, 1985, pp. 92–93; and "The Theater: Colloquy," *The New Yorker*, Mar. 14, 1988, pp. 80–81.

Martin Kich

Jordan, Barbara Charline (1936–1996). Lawyer, politician, educator, autobiographer, and educational writer. Jordan is known for having been an inspiring orator, for her role in the investigation of the Watergate Scandal of the early 1970s, and for her intelligent nonfiction writing. A native Texan, Jordan graduated magna cum laude from Texas Southern University in 1956, and in 1959, she received a law degree from Boston University. Shortly thereafter, she began her law practice and worked as an administrative assistant for a judge in Harris County, **Texas**. Jordan's political career began when she organized one of Houston's voting drives to support John F. Kennedy as the

Democratic Party's presidential candidate in the 1960. She ran for the Texas House of Representatives in 1962 and 1964, but was unsuccessful both times. In 1966, however, she was elected to the Texas Senate, becoming the first African American woman elected to the Texas Senate and the first African American to serve since 1883. After six years in the Texas Senate, Jordan ran for the U.S. House of Representatives. She was elected in 1972, the first African American woman elected to Congress from **the South**.

After taking her seat, Jordan was appointed to the House Judiciary Committee. She received national attention in 1974, when the House Judiciary Committee's hearings on the impeachment of President Richard M. Nixon were televised nationwide. Her great oratorical skill and legal knowledge enabled Jordan to articulately express to the public the severity of the allegations. As more unfavorable information was revealed, Jordan voted for the articles of impeachment. Nixon resigned on August 9, 1974, before the House Judiciary Committee came to a final decision. Jordan achieved national recognition again in 1976 when she became the first African American woman to deliver the keynote address at the Democratic National Convention. She remained in Congress until 1978 and then returned to Texas to teach political ethics at the University of Texas at Austin.

In 1979, Jordan wrote of her numerous accomplishments in her **autobiography**, *Barbara Jordan: A Self-Portrait*: advocating environmental reform; promoting greater assistance for minorities, the impoverished, and the elderly; supporting the Equal Rights Amendment; sponsoring reforms to increase workers' compensation; and extending the Voting Rights Act of 1965 to include Mexican Americans in the Southwest. Jordan also wrote the research report *Local Government Election Systems* (1984) with Terrell Blodgett and *The Great Society: A Twenty-Year Critique* (1986), a collection of political articles edited by Elspeth Rostow. Despite her absence from Congress, Jordan was still politically active. The Democratic Convention chose her as the keynote speaker in 1992, and she was appointed to chair the U.S. Commission on Immigration Reform in 1993. The following year, she received the Medal of Freedom, the nation's highest civilian honor. After being diagnosed with leukemia in 1995, Jordan died in 1996 from viral pneumonia, a complication of leukemia.

Resources: Barbara A. Holmes, *A Private Woman in Public Spaces: Barbara Jordan's Speeches on Ethics, Public Religion, and Law* (Harrisburg, PA: Trinity Press International, 2000); Barbara Jordan and Shelby Hearon, *Barbara Jordan: A Self Portrait* (Garden City, NY: Doubleday, 1979); Barbara Jordan and Elspeth Rostow, eds., *The Great Society: A Twenty Year Critique* (Austin, TX: Lyndon Baines Johnson Library, 1986); James Mendelsohn, *Barbara Jordan: Getting Things Done* (Brookfield, CT: Twenty-first Century Books, 2000); Sandra Parham, ed., *Barbara C. Jordan: Selected Speeches* (Washington DC: Howard University Press, 1999); Mary Beth Rogers, *Barbara Jordan: American Hero* (New York: Bantam, 1998).

Dorsía Smith Silva

Jordan, June (1936–2002). Poet, activist, essayist, novelist, memoirist, playwright, and academic. Jordan, born in **Harlem, New York**, to West Indian immigrants, spent much of her early years in the impoverished Bedford-Stuyvesant section of **Brooklyn, New York**, and eventually settled in Berkeley, California. Her immigrant heritage and the multicultural communities in which she lived often served as the subject matter for her essays and other work on America and democracy. Jordan attended Barnard College from 1953 to 1955 and 1956 to 1957, earning a B.A., as well as the University of Chicago (1955–1956). She taught at various universities, including the City University of New York, Connecticut College, and Sarah Lawrence College, before directing the poetry center and creative writing program while a tenured professor of English at the State University of New York at Stony Brook (1974–1985). In 1986 Jordan began lecturing in the University of California, Berkeley, English Department, and eventually became a professor of African American and Women's Studies. At Berkeley, Jordan developed her popular course "Poetry for the People," from which student poems were collected into an anthology in 1995. Jordan refused to segregate teaching, activism, writing, and living in her quest to develop a "people's poetry" and to make the American dream of pluralism and democracy a reality. Jordan's honors include a National Book Award nomination, grants from the Rockefeller Foundation and the National Endowment for the Arts, and a National Association of Black Journalists award. She is remembered as much for her writing as she is for her political commitments to valuing diversity in all its manifestations: nationality, sexuality, **gender**, language, **race**, geography, class, and ideology.

In her **autobiography**, Jordan recounts her father's abusive lessons that she must always be on guard both physically and mentally, teaching her that she must be a "soldier" ready to fight for her life in a world where even the safest spaces may hide danger. While she was growing up, Jordan's father engaged her in a rigorous program of memorizing long passages from the Bible as well as from canonical Western texts such as those of William Shakespeare and Edgar Allen Poe. Much of Jordan's creative work endeavors to offer a literary tradition where people of color are not marginalized by an all-White canon. Jordan became a poet at the age of seven when she composed lines on pavement around her neighborhood. In 1951, her sophomore year, Jordan transferred from prestigious Midwood High to the Northern School for Girls in Massachusetts (on a scholarship). At both schools, she was one of the first African Americans to attend. In her autobiography, Jordan reports, "I was the 'only' one...I felt outnumbered. I was surrounded by 'them.' And there was no 'we.' There was only 'me.' I didn't like it" (2002, 248–249). Her career is marked by attempts to build the diverse community she found lacking in many parts of the United States. In her third collection of essays, *Technical Difficulties: African-American Notes on the State of the Union* (1992), Jordan presents Park Slope, Brooklyn, as a model multiracial community. And in the essay "Waking Up in the Middle of Some American Dreams," she describes such a community as the true manifestation of American democracy. Jordan explains, "*Demos*, as in democratic, as in a democratic state, means people, not person" (1992, 19).

After leaving Brooklyn, Jordan married Michael Meyer in 1955, gave birth to her only son, Christopher David Meyer, in 1958, and divorced her husband in 1965. During this time Jordan also worked on a film chronicling urban Black life, collected fellow poets' work into anthologies, and researched a biography on the pioneering activist Fannie Lou Hamer (1972). Much of her early work was published alongside that of other African American women writers gaining recognition in the 1970s through the **Black Arts Movement** and an emergent feminist movement. Throughout her career, Jordan continued to direct much of her energy and work toward Black women, including poems and essays dedicated to her colleagues and foremothers Fannie Lou Hamer, **Ntozake Shange**, **Alice Walker**, and **Phillis Wheatley**.

Throughout her career, Jordan remained committed to placing African American experience and **vernacular** at the center of her work. Her most noted contribution to African American literature is her consistent advocacy and inventive use of Black English in her writing, teaching, and political debates. Jordan's first novel, *His Own Where* (1971), is written in the voice of a narrator speaking in Black English, a language common to the predominantly Black and immigrant Brooklyn neighborhood of her childhood. Jordan also wrote much of her poetry in Black English, especially her poems about the character DeLiza, as in "Sometimes DeLiza" from her collection *Naming Our Destiny* (1989): "Sometimes DeLiza/she forget about location/and she wondering what to do/to make she Black self/just a little more/conspicuous" (203). Along with **James Baldwin** and **Amiri Baraka**, in the 1970s through the 1990s Jordan was a key public voice defending Black English as a viable language in the classroom and in society during fierce English-only and anti-affirmative action movements in the United States, especially in California. Over the course of her career, Jordan's prose, too, increasingly assumed the poetic and dialogic forms that reflected the actual speech of the immigrant and multicultural communities that her essays address.

Jordan's initial fame in the 1970s was also due in large part to emerging feminist movements (*see* **Feminism/Black Feminism**) that valued creative work for its ability to bring the diverse personal experiences of women into public arenas. Jordan's poetry in the 1970s is especially valued for a personal politics that places Black women's experiences at the center of political analysis. In "Poem About My Rights," from *Passion* (1980), Jordan directly connects the speaker's experience of rape with the invasion of Namibia by South Africa. Her efforts to value the experiences and voices of marginalized people earned her recognition as an important political voice as well as one of the most important African American women poets of the later twentieth century, especially with her much anthologized poems "What Would I Do White?," from *Things That I Do in the Dark* (1977); "1977: Poem for Miss Fannie Lou Hamer," from *Passion* (1980), and "From Sea to Shining Sea," from *Living Room* (1985). Jordan also published celebratory love poetry alongside her explicitly political poetry, especially in the later collections *Haruko: Love Poetry* (1994) and *Kissing God Goodbye* (1997).

Jordan's legacy as an intellectual is as important as her legacy as a poet. In 1981, Jordan became one of the first African American women to publish a book-length collection of essays. In *Civil Wars* (1981) and in her four subsequent essay collections and regular columns in *The Progressive*, Jordan helped define the category "political essays" by writing about key political events and controversies as an African American woman deeply committed to democracy, justice, and global solidarity. Just before her death, she published a retrospective collection of new and selected essays in *Some of Us Did Not Die* (2002). In her work, Jordan is always aware of her voice as a "Black spokesperson" addressing audiences divided along multiple lines including race, gender, and ideology (McPhail). Jordan offers her audience "righteous rage" as a response to injustice in poems and essays about apartheid in Soweto, Nelson Mandela's imprisonment and freedom, U.S. activities in Nicaragua, Bernard Goetz's racially motivated violence, presidential policies that disproportionately impact poor people and people of color, anti-affirmative action referenda, and many other headline political events. Jordan's creative work is deeply grounded in her activism regarding civil rights, the **Vietnam War**, South African apartheid, Palestine, Nicaragua, Lebanon, the **Gulf War**, bisexual identity, and terrorism. At the same time that she celebrates the lofty goals of democracy, she rigorously seeks out and values the voices of displaced peoples. For Jordan, poetry was both a place of, and a means toward, justice. Like **Richard Wright**, Jordan conceives of poetry itself as a "blueprint" for activism, especially in her Poetry for the People project (Muller).

When Jordan died in 2002, after a long battle with cancer that began in the 1970s, her death was noted by a diverse range of writers, activists, students, and scholars. Rather than mourning, many marked Jordan's passing with tributes in which writers came together, often in long poetry readings like those from her course in "Poetry for the People," to continue her project of giving voice to the people—all people—and in making poetry a powerful agent of political protest and change. In her tribute to Jordan's activist poetics, **Angela Y. Davis** described Jordan's legacy thus: "There was always joy in her rage. Politics was her life; collective pain, as well as collective resistance, was always something she felt in a deeply personal way" (Davis, 1). (*See also* **Protest Literature**.)

Resources: Primary Sources: June Jordan: *Affirmative Acts: Political Essays* (New York: Anchor, 1998); *Civil Wars* (Boston: Beacon Press, 1981); *Dry Victories* (New York: Holt, Rinehart, and Winston, 1972); *Fannie Lou Hamer* (New York: Crowell, 1972); *Haruko: Love Poems* (New York: High Risk Books, 1994); *His Own Where* (New York: Crowell, 1971); *I Was Looking at the Ceiling and Then I Saw the Sky* (New York: Scribner's, 1995); *Kimako's Story* (Boston: Houghton Mifflin, 1981); *Kissing God Goodbye: Poems, 1991–1997* (New York: Anchor, 1997); *Living Room: New Poems* (New York: Thunder's Mouth, 1985); *Moving Towards Home: Political Essays* (London: Virago, 1989); *Naming Our Destiny: New and Selected Poems* (New York: Thunder's

Mouth, 1989); *New Days: Poems of Exile and Return* (New York: Crowell, 1974); *New Life: New Room* (New York: Crowell, 1975); *On Call: Political Essays* (Boston: South End Press, 1985); *Passion: New Poems, 1977–1980* (Boston: Beacon Press, 1980); *Soldier: A Poet's Childhood* (New York: Basic Civitas Books, 2000); *Some Changes* (New York: Dutton, 1971); *Some of Us Did Not Die: New and Selected Essays of June Jordan* (New York: Basic Civitas Books, 2002); *Soulscript: Afro-American Poetry* (Garden City, NY: Doubleday, 1970); *Technical Difficulties: African-American Notes on the State of the Union* (New York: Pantheon, 1992); *Things That I Do in the Dark: Selected Poetry* (Boston: Beacon Press, 1977); *The Voice of the Children* (New York: Holt, Rinehart and Winston, 1970); *Who Look at Me* (New York: Crowell, 1969); **Secondary Sources:** Carol Boyce Davies, *Black Women, Writing and Identity: Migrations of the Subject* (New York: Routledge, 1994); Angela Davis, "Tribute to June Jordan," *Meridians* 3, no. 2 (2003), 1–2; Peter Erickson, "Putting Her Life on the Line: The Poetry of June Jordan," *Hurricane Alice: A Feminist Quarterly* 7, no. 1–2 (Winter–Spring 1990), 4–5; Agnes Moreland Jackson, "June Jordan," in instructor's guide to *Heath Anthology of American Literature*, Paul Lanter, ed., vol. 2, 4th ed. (Boston: Houghton Mifflin, 2002); Lauren Muller et al., eds., *June Jordan's Poetry for the People: A Revolutionary Blueprint* (New York: Routledge, 1995); Scott MacPhail, "June Jordan and the New Black Intellectuals," *African American Review* 33, no. 1 (Spring 1999), 57–71.

Brian J. Norman

Jordan, Michael Jeffrey (born 1963). Basketball player, entrepreneur, and autobiographer. Considered one of the best players and fiercest competitors in the history of the National Basketball Association (NBA), Jordan has earned hundreds of millions of dollars in product endorsements. He is known by various nicknames, including Air Jordan, Mike, MJ, His Airness, and #23 or 23 (his jersey number in college and the NBA). Born to upper-middle class parents in **Brooklyn, New York**, Jordan accompanied his family when they returned to North Carolina in the mid-1960s. He attended Laney High School in Wilmington, where he failed to make the varsity boy's basketball team his sophomore year. He quickly improved, and played well enough to gain a scholarship from the University of North Carolina, where he played three seasons. He was named National College Player of the Year in 1984. That year the Chicago Bulls picked him third in the NBA draft. He played fifteen seasons in the NBA, thirteen for the Chicago Bulls, who won six NBA Championships (1991–1993 and 1996–1998). He retired in 2003 with many league records and awards. He represented the United States twice in the Olympics, in 1984 and 1992, winning gold metals both times. Jordan has remained involved in professional basketball as an executive, and he frequently mentions future ownership of an NBA team.

Jordan started a major trend in high fees for endorsements by professional athletes when he negotiated a $250,000 per year contract with Nike in 1984. The contract also included royalties for items on which his name or the associated stylized image of his form flying to the basket for a slam dunk appeared. (The highly athletic, "flying" style arguably began with the play of

Julius Erving approximately a decade earlier, but Jordan popularized it enormously.) This part of the agreement earned him a great deal of money once the "Air Jordan" brand spread from shoes to items such as clothing and duffel bags. He used his growing public image, which he scrupulously maintained, to acquire further endorsement deals with McDonald's, Coca-Cola, Gatorade, Hanes, and other companies (LaFeber). He has lent his name or image to car dealerships, a clothing line, and a brand of men's cologne. In 1995 Jordan starred in the live-action/cartoon film *Space Jam* alongside Bugs Bunny, and *Like Mike* (2002), a film about a teenage boy who finds a pair of Jordan's shoes that give him miraculous basketball skills, drew on Jordan's celebrity.

Although respected for his basketball prowess, Jordan has been a controversial figure at times, criticized for his reluctance to become involved in political or explicitly racial causes, and for having his body used as an ambivalent image of the African American male. **Michael Eric Dyson** sees the image as a conflicting but instructive one: "the symbolic carrier of racial and cultural desires to fly beyond limits and obstacles" (74). **bell hooks** calls the image the "quintessential symbol of the fetishized eroticized black male body of spectacle" (134). **John Edgar Wideman** describes Americans' fascination with Jordan's image as a "modern, media-driven, vicarious, virtual possession of a black body better than buying a slave, . . . you could choose to appropriate and identify with only those black body parts you desired" (*Hoop*, 41). **Eloise Greenfield** has written a children's book titled *For the Love of the Game: Michael Jordan and Me* (1999). In 1998 Jordan, with Mark Vancil, published the **autobiography** *For the Love of the Game: My Story*.

Resources: Greg Ahrenhoerster, "(Don't) Be the Ball: Or, What Michael Jordan-Wannabes Can Learn from Ralph Ellison," *Aethlon: The Journal of Sport Literature* 18, no. 1–2 (Fall 2000–Spring 2001), 21–27; Michael Eric Dyson, "Be Like Mike? Michael Jordan and the Pedagogy of Desire," in his *Reflecting Black: African-American Cultural Criticism* (Minneapolis: University of Minnesota Press, 1993), 64–75; Eloise Greenfield, *For the Love of the Game: Michael Jordan and Me* (New York: Harper-Trophy, 1999); David Halberstam, *Playing for Keeps: Michael Jordan and the World He Made* (New York: Random House, 1999); bell hooks, "Feminism Inside: Toward a Black Body Politic," in *Black Male: Representations of Masculinity in Contemporary American Art*, ed. Thelma Golden (New York: Whitney Museum, 1994), 127–140; Michael Jordan, *For the Love of the Game: My Story*, ed. Mark Vancil (New York: Crown, 1998); Walter LaFeber, *Michael Jordan and the New Global Capitalism* (New York: Norton, 1999); John Edgar Wideman: *Hoop Roots: Playground Basketball, Love, and Race* (Boston: Houghton Mifflin, 2001); and "Michael Jordan Leaps the Great Divide," *Esquire*, Nov. 1990, pp. 138+.

Ian W. Wilson

Journal of Black Poetry (1966–1973). Literary magazine. The *Journal of Black Poetry* was one of many revolutionary little magazines that emerged during the **Black Arts Movement** (1965–1976), a period in which the arts community developed an aesthetic tradition rooted in **Black Power**. ("Little magazine" is a term used to describe literary magazines of relatively small circulation.) The violence of the 1960s, marked by assassinations and widespread urban riots, served as a catalyst for change. There was a discernible shift from civil rights and integration to a more radical, separatist philosophy. Political activists such as **Stokely Carmichael** urged African Americans to "define their own goals, to lead their own organizations, and to reject the racist institutions and values of American society" (Dulaney, 54–55). Black writers and intellectuals responded by developing "a new literary politics, an aesthetics of separatism" (Johnson and Johnson, 164). Many established their own publishing ventures and founded Afrocentric magazines as a means of expressing distinct Black voices largely excluded from Western culture. (*see* **Afrocentricity**.)

Joe Goncalves, poetry editor of *Black Dialogue*, developed the idea for the *Journal of Black Poetry* when he received more poems than he could publish. His aim was to create a poetry forum exclusively for Black writers for "black people everywhere." The inaugural issue appeared in the spring of 1966 as a "small magazine with mimeographed pages and a lithographed cover" (Salaam). **Larry Neal** hailed the *Journal of Black Poetry* as "the first and most important" literary publication of the Black Arts Movement, while **Hoyt Fuller**, the influential editor of **Negro Digest**, recommended that the journal receive "the immediate and enthusiastic support of everyone who loves poetry and is concerned about supporting black writers" (Johnson and Johnson, 187).

Although the editorial policy of the *Journal of Black Poetry* was considered eclectic, it published works that "spoke in loud tones of racial matters" (Johnson and Johnson, 196). Numerous poems filled its pages, with as many as 40 to 50 in a single issue. Contributions by new poets appeared alongside well-known authors, such as **Gwendolyn Brooks**, Don L. Lee (later known as **Haki R. Madhubuti**), and **Sonia Sanchez** (Daniel, 217). The writing was expressive and improvisational, patterned after **jazz** music and Black speech. Poets rejected traditional lyrical conventions and explored "free verse, typographical stylistics; irreverent, often scatological diction; and linguistic experimentation" (Gabbon). From time to time, the journal published special issues with guest editors. Among them were **Clarence Major**, Larry Neal, and **Dudley Randall**.

While the focus of the journal was poetry, it also featured reviews, literary criticism, news, and illustrations. Readers might find articles such as "Coltrane's music . . . 'The Death of Yakub,' 'The Fire Must be Permitted to Burn Full Up' (literary criticism), and 'Black Arts Mexico' (Marvin X)" (Redmond, 562). Discussions of the Black aesthetic appeared on a regular basis. **Amiri Baraka** (then known as LeRoi Jones), one of the acknowledged main leaders of the Black Arts Movement, wrote influential essays that shaped the direction of Black literature based on new aesthetic principles.

Like most literary magazines of its time, the *Journal of Black Poetry* did not have a strong subscriber base or sufficient advertising revenue. It ceased publication in the summer of 1973, after nineteen issues. The following year

Goncalves began *Kitabu Cha Jua*, "the book of the sun." It was short-lived, with only two annual issues published. (*See* **Free Verse**; **Poetics**; **Prose Poem**.)

Resources: Walter C. Daniel, *Black Journals of the United States* (Westport, CT: Greenwood Press, 1982); W. Marvin Dulaney, "Black Power," in *Encyclopedia of African-American Civil Rights: From Emancipation to the Present*, ed. Charles D. Lowery and John F. Marszlek (New York: Greenwood Press, 1992); Joanne V. Gabbon, *Furious Flower: A Revolution in African American Poetry*, http://www.jmu.edu/furious-flower/poetry.htm; Abby Arthur Johnson and Ronald Maberry Johnson, *Propaganda and Aesthetics: The Literary Politics of Afro-American Magazines in the Twentieth Century* (Amherst: University of Massachusetts Press, 1979); Eugene Redmond, "Stridency and the Sword: Literary and Cultural Emphasis in Afro-American Magazines," in *The Little Magazine in America: A Modern Documentary History*, ed. Elliott Anderson and Mary Kinzie (Yonkers, NY: Pushcart, 1978); Kaluma ya Salaam, "Historical Overviews of the Black Arts Movement," in *Modern American Poetry* (New York: Oxford University Press, 1997); http://www.english.uiuc.edu/maps/blackarts/historical.htm.

Lori Ricigliano

Joyce, Joyce Ann (born 1949). Scholar and literary critic. Joyce is an Afrocentric literary critic and scholar. Her critical work presupposes the centrality of the African experience and aesthetic in the analysis of African American literature (*see* **Afrocentricity**).

Joyce was born in Valdosta, Georgia, in 1949 to Henry Joyce, Jr., a truck driver, and Edna Freelove Joyce, a cotton mill worker. She married journalist Walter Gholson III in 1989 and they have one child, Malik.

Joyce was one of the first African Americans to attend Valdosta State College, where she earned her B.A. in English in 1970. She received an M.A. in English from the University of Georgia in 1972 and a Ph.D. in American literature from the University of Georgia in 1979.

Joyce has had a long and distinguished career as an academic. From 1972 to 1974 and 1978 to 1979, she was an instructor of English at Valdosta State College, where she was one of the first African American faculty members. She served as an assistant/associate professor of English at the University of Maryland, College Park, from 1979 to 1989; as professor of English at the University of Nebraska, Lincoln, from 1989 to 1992; and as professor at Chicago State University from 1992 to 1997. At Chicago she also served as associate director of the Gwendolyn Brooks Center for Black Literature and Creative Writing (1995), and later as coordinator and chairperson of the Black American Studies Department (1996–1997). Joyce served as chairperson of the African-American Studies Department at Temple University from 1997 to 2001. Since 2001, she has been a professor in the Women's Studies Department at Temple University.

Joyce has received significant recognition for her work. She was a Ford Foundation fellow from 1970 to 1973. She received the George Kent Award for Literary Criticism in 1993, the Distinguished Alumnus Award from Valdosta State University in 1994, and the American Book Award for Literary Criticism in 1995.

Joyce's scholarly work ranges from literary anthologies to extended critiques of specific authors to book-length treatments of literary theory. Joyce coedited *The New Cavalcade* (1991, 1992), an updated version of an influential anthology of African American writing, *Cavalcade* (1971), edited by Charles Nichols, **Arthur P. Davis**, and **J. Saunders Redding**. *The New Cavalcade* is composed of more than 300 selections by more than 150 authors, and includes short stories, novels, essays, autobiographical pieces, and poems. Joyce has also provided extensive critiques of selected African American authors, including **Richard Wright** and **Sonia Sanchez**.

In *Warriors, Conjurers and Priests: Defining African-Centered Literary Criticism* (1994), Joyce calls for an understanding of African American literature through an appreciation of and grounding in African and African American history and culture. *Warriors, Conjurers and Priests* is a political work as well as a critical one—Joyce criticizes the dominant use of traditional European-centered literary theory and aesthetic standards to assess African American literature. By insisting on an African-centered (or Black aesthetic) basis for the critical evaluation of African American works, Joyce emphasizes the social nature of assessing texts and the larger cultural and political apparatus surrounding both author and audience. She argues for the recognition of the importance of intellectual and artistic traditions emanating from the African continent and their influence on American literature.

Resources: Joyce Ann Joyce: *Ijala: Sonia Sanchez and the African Poetic Tradition* (Chicago: Third World Press, 1996); *Richard Wright's Art of Tragedy* (Iowa City: University of Iowa Press, 1986); *Warriors, Conjurers and Priests: Defining African-Centered Literary Criticism* (Chicago: Third World Press, 1994); Joyce Ann Joyce, Arthur P. Davis, and J. Saunders Redding, eds.: *The New Cavalcade: African American Writing from 1760 to the Present*, 2 vols. (Washington, DC: Howard University Press, 1991–1992); *Selected African American Writing from 1760 to 1910* (New York: Bantam Books, 1996); Charles H. Nichols, Arthur P. Davis, and Saunders Redding, *Cavalcade: Negro American Writing from 1760 to the Present* (Boston: Houghton Mifflin, 1971).

Kimberly Black-Parker

Just Us Books (1988–present). Publisher of **children's literature**. Before 1988, Cheryl Hudson and Wade Hudson were frustrated over how little reading material for African American children was available in bookstores. Their dissatisfaction with the children's book market sparked the idea to create their own publishing company, committed to African American children. In 1988, they established Just Us Books in East Orange, New Jersey.

Wade Hudson, founding chief executive officer of the company, grew up in Mansfield, Louisiana, during the early 1950s and 1960s, in the midst of racial segregation and discrimination. "Mansfield had to be as segregated a town as any place in the United States back then" ("Wade Hudson"). After attending Southern University in the late 1960s and early 1970s, he worked as a news reporter, sportswriter, and public relations specialist, and offered his skills to several civil rights organizations in Baton Rouge, Louisiana. Hudson has authored and edited a variety of children's books, establishing Just Us Books as a leader in culturally diverse children's literature. *Afro-Bets ABC*; *Afro-Bets 123*; *Afro-Bets Book of Black Heroes From A to Z*; *How Sweet the Sound: African-American Songs for Children*; and *I'm Gonna Be* are just a few of the many books from Just Us Books. Wade and Cheryl Hudson agree that the need for African American children to see themselves in storybooks as heroes and heroines is essential in building prestige and self-esteem. "We thought about the words of **Langston Hughes** in an essay entitled, 'The Negro Artist and the Racial Mountain,'" writes Cheryl. "'We young Negro artists who create now intend to express our individual dark skinned selves without fear of shame'" (quoted in "Wade Hudson").

"The need for African American children's books is not just to advance cultural awareness for African Americans families, but also alert white families in America to the vast literary landscape of culturally diverse reading material," writes Wade Hudson ("Wade Hudson"). Over the years Just Us Books has proven its commitment to literary excellence and innovated story content. Both Wade and Cheryl Hudson insist that their product stay true to the African American traditions of good storytelling so apparent during the **Harlem Renaissance** in works by **Zora Neal Hurston**, Langston Hughes, and **Gwendolyn Bennett**. Maintaining a literary trail blazed by some of America's finest African American writer's ensures Just Us Books a vibrant reading audience.

Resources: Wade Hudson and Cheryl Hudson, eds., *How Sweet the Sound: African-American Songs for Children* (Orange, NJ: Just Us Books, 1995); Wade Hudson and Valerie Wilson Wesley, *Afro-Bets Book of Black Heroes from A to Z: An Introduction to Important Black Achievers for Young Readers* (Orange, NJ: Just Us Books, 1988); "Wade Hudson," in *Metropolis Found: New York Is Book Country 25th Anniversary Collection* (New York: New York Is Book Country, 2003).

Robert H. Miller

K

Kai, Nubia (born 1948). Poet, playwright, novelist, and children's writer. In the African American literary tradition of activist writers, Kai uses writing as a vehicle for heightened spiritual consciousness, community development, and socioeconomic and political liberation. She blends her devotion to the cultures and history of African people throughout the world with an aesthetic influenced by **jazz** and rhythm and **blues,** and a commitment to art that addresses the concerns and aspirations of everyday lives. An examination of Kai's life reveals a prolific writer, teacher, community worker, drug rehabilitation counselor, scholar, radio producer and commentator, actor, accomplished musician, and world traveler. Her diverse interests have been pursued simultaneously, as if each pursuit fed the other and nurtured her overall understanding of art and life.

Born on July 30, 1948, in **Detroit, Michigan,** Kai is the eldest of three siblings. Her parents, Olga Walls and Clifford Steele, Jr., instilled in her a love for performance, knowledge, and community. Mrs. Steele recited the poetry of **Langston Hughes** and **Paul Laurence Dunbar** to her children. Kai was especially affected by this. Inspired to write at an early age, she was also influenced by the British Romantics, by **Dudley Randall,** and by **Margaret Esse Taylor Danner**. Kai's oeuvre reflects an ongoing interest in emotion, immediacy, and movement—attributes she associates with poetry. Poetry was the doorway to theater and fiction. Kai cites the dramas of **Amiri Baraka, Ed Bullins, Alice Childress,** and **Douglas Turner Ward** as models for her plays, which have been staged throughout the United States. Her fiction includes an unpublished **historical novel**. Life in Detroit, the dynamics of the human rights struggle, and the work of African American musicians—particularly

John Coltrane, **Sun Ra**, Ornette Coleman, and Nina Simone—helped to clarify the direction of Kai's artistic endeavors. The visual artists Elizabeth Catlett and **Jacob Lawrence** also served as guides to her aesthetic.

In 1974, Kai earned a bachelor's degree in anthropology and African American Studies from Wayne State University in Detroit. She also received a Tompkins Award in Fiction and Drama. This award was the first of many honors, including two fellowships from the National Endowment for the Arts (1986, 1992). From 1975 to 1977, she produced more than eighty programs for *Seminar in Black*, a public radio series. This work led to other mass-media projects. In Detroit, she cofounded the Crescent Poets, who linked their work to the political agendas of the **Black Panther Party** and the Republic of New Afrika, and conducted readings in bars and nightclubs. Kai also cofounded The Storytellers, Inc., which performed **folktales** during the early 1980s. In 1989, Kai moved to **Washington, D.C.**, where she became a very active member of the arts scene. In 1991, she wrote *The Sweetest Berry on the Bush*, a collection of fables and **folktales** for children. Kai received her master's degree in African literature and languages from the University of Wisconsin–Madison in 1997, and her doctorate in African Studies from Howard University in 2004.

Resources: Nubia Kai: *Peace of My Mind* (Detroit: Pamoja Press, 1975); *Solos* (Detroit: Lotus Press, 1988); *The Sweetest Berry on the Bush* (Chicago: Third World Press, 1993); Woodie King, Jr., ed.: *The National Black Drama Anthology: Eleven Plays from America's Leading African-American Theaters* (New York: Applause Theatre Books, 1995), 149–199; *New Plays for the Black Theatre* (Chicago: Third World Press, 1989), 153–194; Naomi Long Madgett, ed., *Adam of Ife: Black Women in Praise of Black Men* (Detroit: Lotus, 1992), 48, 121, 131, 183; Daphne Williams Ntiri, ed., *Roots and Blossoms: African American Plays for Today* (Troy, MI: Bedford, 1991), 207–267.

Monifa Love Asante

Karenga, Maulana (born 1941). Scholar, philosopher, and activist. Karenga is recognized as one of the most important figures in contemporary African American political, cultural, and intellectual movements. He is best known for his involvement in the **Black Power** movement of the 1960s. His contribution to the formation of **Black Studies** as an academic discipline and his influence on artists of the **Black Arts Movement** places him in the vanguard of African American scholars.

Karenga first became involved in the political struggles of the 1960s as a student at Los Angeles City College and UCLA, where he was a leader in campus politics. The Watts revolt of 1965 spurred him to join the Black Freedom Movement (later known as the Black Power movement). Influenced by the Pan-African philosophies of nationalist leaders such as **Malcolm X** and Kwame Nkrumah, Karenga began to formulate his own theory of cultural revolution as an essential component of the liberation struggles of African people. He founded the Organization Us in 1965, an association devoted to social and cultural change, in order to advance his philosophy of *Kawaida*. The main premise of *Kawaida* is that the fundamental crisis affecting African Americans is a crisis in culture resulting from Western cultural hegemony. The communitarian value system of the *Nguzo Saba* (The Seven Principles) is a central part of *Kawaida* philosophy and serves as the core of the Pan-African holiday of Kwanzaa.

Kawaida's significance as a corrective philosophy is evident from its impact on writers such as **Amiri Baraka** and **Haki Madhubuti** during the Black Arts Movement. Their attempts to articulate a definitive Black aesthetic rooted in a national Black cultural consciousness is clearly located in the *Kawaida* tradition. In his essay "Black Cultural Nationalism," Karenga explains the relationship between art and people. He states, "Black art must be for the people, by the people and from the people. That is to say, it must be functional, collective and committing. . . . Black art, like everything else in the Black community, must respond positively to the reality of revolution" (1971, 33).

Kawaida acted as a precursor to the emergence of Black psychology and **Afrocentricity** in the 1970s and 1980s, and Karenga remains a vital force in the activist-intellectual tradition of African culture as professor and chair of the Department of Black Studies at California State University at Long Beach, director of the *Kawaida* Institute of Pan-African Studies, and national chairman of Organization Us. His *Introduction to Black Studies* (2000), first published in 1982, has become a seminal text in the discipline. In 1995 Karenga was selected to write the official mission statement of the historic Million Man March/Day of Absence. And with the publication of works such as *Selections from the Husia: Sacred Wisdom of Ancient Egypt* (1984) and *Odu Ifa: The Ethical Teachings* (1999), Karenga demonstrates his ongoing commitment to the study of classical African culture and the reconstruction of ancient traditions in an effort to advance a moral and ethical framework of empowerment and liberation for the contemporary African community.

Resources: Geoffrey Jahwara Giddings, *Contemporary Afrocentric Scholarship: Toward a Functional Cultural Philosophy* (Lewiston, NY: Edwin Mellen, 2003); Maulana Karenga: "Black Cultural Nationalism," in *The Black Aesthetic*, comp. Addison Gayle, Jr. (Garden City, NY: Doubleday, 1971), 33; *Kawaida: A Communitarian African Philosophy* (Los Angeles: University of Sankore Press, 2000); *Kwanzaa: A Celebration of Family, Community, and Culture* (Los Angeles: University of Sankore Press, 1998).

Stephanie M. Yarbough

Kaufman, Bob (1926–1986). Poet and performance artist. Bob Kaufman was a political and social critic and a major poet of the Black Consciousness movement who began writing before the prominence of Black Consciousness and the **Black Arts Movement** of the 1960s. He was a favorite of **Langston Hughes**, who published Kaufman's poems in several Black poetry anthologies, and became a living legend to Black poets. Kaufman is considered a major figure in the **Beat Movement** and is an important figure in twentieth-century African American literature and American poetry, though he did not fully receive this status until after his death from emphysema in 1986. "He wasn't just political, he was metaphysical, psychological, surrealist, and enlightened, extending his care into the whole of society of poetry, seeing that as revolution" (*Cranial Guitar*, 7). Kaufman did not keep diaries or journals, did not publish literary **essays** or reviews, and did not maintain correspondence. He was encouraged to begin writing down his poetry by his wife, Eileen Singe Kaufman. Kaufman's works include *Abomunist Manifesto* (1959), *Second April* (1959), *Does the Secret Mind Whisper?* (1960), *Solitudes Crowded with Loneliness* (1965), *Golden Sardine* (1967), *Watch My Tracks* (1971), *Ancient Rain* (1981), and *Cranial Guitar: Selected Poems by Bob Kaufman* (1996). He also founded a poetry magazine, *Beatitude*, with William J. Margolis.

Kaufman's poetry addresses the complexities of human and civil rights in a post–**World War II** America and as a response to **McCarthyism**. His work reflects his refusal to be categorized by cultural and societal identifiers: "he was and was not black, Jew, Beatnik, hetero/homosexual, American, African, Buddhist, junkie, drunk, jailbird, jazz poet, musician, minstrel, 'Abomunist'" (Nielsen, 167). His work indicates some influence by such Modernist artistic movements as Dadaism, Futurism, and **Surrealism**. Kaufman's poetry was experimental in form; he used a variety of formal and informal poetic conventions sparked by his connections to **jazz**; a jazz aficionado, Kaufman used jazz to blur racial and class lines and a Surrealist approach to poetry based on his awareness of "paradox and discontinuity," bebop, and Black speech patterns and on his desire to acknowledge and critique some of the political and social issues and injustices present in American culture. His "elusive and allusive writings" and outright refusal to conform to a model American lifestyle were his methods of addressing these conflicts; Kaufman "critiques the subtle rules and punishments that, as he knew them, enforce American bourgeois values of race, class, sexuality, and rationality" (Andrews et al., 239).

Kaufman was born in **New Orleans, Louisiana**, to an African American/ Jewish Pullman porter and a black schoolteacher from a **Creole** family of Martinique. He was one of thirteen children, and his mother exposed him to books and reading at a young age. Kaufman was educated in the New Orleans public school system until he left and became a merchant seaman. He was involved in the National Maritime Union and the Progressive Party. He lived in New York City until he married his wife, Eileen, and settled in **San Francisco, California**. Kaufman then lived in both San Francisco's North Beach District and New York City's Greenwich Village. Known "as a silent and wiry Blackman, [he] walked the streets of San Francisco's North Beach District by day and night," looking like a panhandler or a madman. Kaufman performed his poetry on the street and in cafés. He was called "the Black Rimbaud" because he perpetuated the "French tradition of a poet as outsider, madman, outcast" and spent time in France among some of the original Surrealists. He was arrested thirty-six times in one year, and in 1959 his political work caused him to be blacklisted. Exposed to police brutality, Kaufman was often denied his civil rights. He also dealt with alcoholism, drug addiction, incarceration, and electroshock therapy. He understood human suffering and "recorded both with humor and pathos the pain of society's victims" (Andrews et al., 239).

Resources: William L. Andrews, Frances Smith Foster, and Trudier Harris, eds., *The Concise Oxford Companion to African American Literature* (New York: Oxford University Press, 2001); Lee Bartlett, ed., *The Beats: Essays in Criticism* (Jefferson, NC: McFarland, 1981); Neeli Cherkovski, *Whitman's Wild Children: Portraits of Twelve Poets* (South Royalton, VT: Steerforth Press, 1999); *Dictionary of Literary Biography*, vol. 41, *Afro-American Poets Since 1955*, ed. Trudier Harris and Thadious Davis (Detroit: Gale Group, 1985), 196–202; Bob Kaufman: *The Ancient Rain: Poems, 1956–78* (New York: New Directions, 1981); *Cranial Guitar: Selected Poems by Bob Kaufman*, ed. Gerald Nicosia (Minneapolis, MN: Coffee House Press, 1996); *Solitudes Crowded with Loneliness* (New York: New Directions, 1965); Aldon Lynn Nielsen, *Reading Race in American Poetry: An Area of Act* (Urbana: University of Illinois Press, 2000).

Allia A. Matta

Keats, Ezra Jack (1919–1983). Illustrator and author of children's picture books. Although Keats is White and grew up in a Jewish neighborhood, he is best known for his sensitive depictions of minority children and his distinctive use of collage in his illustrations of his numerous picture books. Keats's artistic talents, evident at an early age, were encouraged by his Polish immigrant parents, who provided him with art supplies during his childhood. However, they also sought to discourage him from basing a career on his talents, for they could not see Keats supporting himself in adulthood with art. During the **Great Depression**, he put his art to work with the Works Progress Administration (WPA), painting murals and later working as a comic book illustrator. After creating camouflage patterns for the Air Corps during **World War II**, Keats became an illustrator for various authors; his first book was *Jubilant for Sure* (1954) by Elisabeth Hubbard Lansing. He went on to illustrate fifty-four books.

While illustrating for others, Keats recognized a lack of minority characters in children's books, and decided he wanted that to change. His first book published as both author and illustrator was *My Dog Is Lost!* (1960), which featured a Puerto Rican boy. His second book, *The Snowy Day* (1962), introduced an African American character named Peter, and won the prestigious Caldecott Medal in 1963. It was illustrated using one of his favorite artistic media, collage. Keats went on to write more books featuring Peter, including *Whistle for Willie* (1964), *Peter's Chair* (1967), *A Letter for Amy* (1968), and *Goggles!* (1969). He also wrote a series based on a child named Louie that included *Louie* (1975) and *Louie's Search* (1980). He eventually wrote and/or illustrated more than eighty-five books; several of his works have been adapted for short films and other media for school-age children.

In addition to writing some of the earliest nonstereotypical depictions of diversity, Keats established a foundation that presents awards to promising writers with fewer than six published children's books. These books must reflect the tradition of Keats's writing: multicultural, strong family relationships, universal qualities, and appeal to children younger than nine years old. The first winner of the Keats book award in 1986 was *The Patchwork Quilt*, written by Valerie Flournoy and illustrated by Jerry Pinkney.

Praise for Keats's works tends to focus on the universal nature of his themes and his depiction of minority characters without attempting to write ethnic books. Although he intentionally depicted African American children in inner-city settings, he portrays the ethnicity without resorting to stereotype. He simply shows children as they go through their daily life. Along with his stories, his illustrations, especially the mixed-media collages, also receive recognition and praise. Keats's works realistically reflect the grim reality of urban living while presenting the innocent joy and hope that he saw as a universal quality in all children.

Resources: Primary Sources: Ezra Jack Keats: illustrator, *Jubilant for Sure*, by Elisabeth Hubbard Lansing (New York: Crowell, 1954); *Goggles!* (New York: Macmillan, 1969); *A Letter for Amy* (New York: Harper & Row, 1968); *Louie* (New York: Greenwillow, 1975); *Louie's Search* (New York: Four Winds, 1980); author and illustrator, *My Dog Is Lost* (New York: Cronwell, 1960); *Peter's Chair* (New York: Harper & Row, 1967); *The Snowy Day* (New York: Viking, 1962); and *Whistle for Willie* (New York: Viking, 1964). **Secondary Sources:** Brian Alderson, *Ezra Jack Keats: Artist and Picture-Book Maker* (Gretna, LA: Pelican, 1994); Dean Engel and Florence B. Freedman, *Ezra Jack Keats: A Biography with Illustrations* (New York: Silver Moon, 1995); Richard Seiter, "Ezra Jack Keats," in *Dictionary of Literary Biography*, vol. 61, *American Writers for Children Since 1960: Poets, Illustrators, and Nonfiction Authors*, Glenn Estes, ed. (Detroit: Gale, 1987), 116–125; Gerard Senick and Alan Hedblad, eds., *Children's Literature Review*, vol. 35 (Detroit: Gale, 1995), 82–143.

Susie Scifres Kuilan

Keckley, Elizabeth (c. 1818–1907). Seamstress and author. Most of the details of Keckley's life come from her **autobiography** and sole literary work, *Behind the Scenes; or, Thirty Years a Slave and Four Years in the White House* (1868). She was born near Dinwinddie Court House, Virginia, about 1818 (based on evidence from her autobiography, however, Foster surmises Keckley was born in 1824 [xix]). Both Keckley and her mother, Agnes, were owned by Armistead Burwell. Her father, George Pleasant, also a slave, lived on another plantation, and saw his wife and daughter infrequently (Foster, xix). When Elizabeth was eight, Pleasant's owner sent him to Tennessee, and neither Agnes nor Elizabeth saw him again. At fourteen, Elizabeth was sent to work for Burwell's son and his wife, and moved to North Carolina with them four years later. Soon thereafter, she bore a son, George, to a White man. Keckley moved back to Virginia to live with Burwell's daughter, Anne, and her husband, Hugh Garland. Eventually, they all moved west to **St. Louis, Missouri**. Although hesitant at first, Garland eventually allowed Keckley to purchase her freedom in 1855 for $1,200, a sum she raised through loans from friends and her work as a seamstress.

She married James Keckley in 1852 but separated from him after eight difficult years. In 1860, she moved to **Washington, D.C.**, to pursue a career as a dressmaker and acquired several notable clients, including Mrs. Jefferson Davis, which eventually led to her position as Mary Todd Lincoln's "seamstress, nurse, spiritual advisor, and friend" (Foster, xxx). Keckley's son was killed in the **Civil War**, and she published her autobiography, *Behind the Scenes*, three years later. Her decision to reveal the details of the "Old Clothes Scandal," in which Mrs. Lincoln attempted to sell her clothes and jewelry to pay thousands of dollars in clothing debts, garnered largely hostile reactions and effectively ended her friendship with Lincoln. Unable to revive her business following the reception of her book, Keckley gradually withdrew from public life. She died on May 28, 1907.

Keckley's *Behind the Scenes* is notable for its innovation in form and resistance to categorization. An autobiographical hybrid, it combines the conventions of sentimental fiction, the American dream, the **slave narrative**, the memoir, and social criticism (Foster, x–xii, xv). She gives just three chapters to her life as a slave, and devotes the rest of the book to the four years she spent in Washington. Also remarkable is her focus on the lives of Abraham and Mary Todd Lincoln rather than on details of her personal life. Yet Foster argues that White House memoirs and exposés were quite popular at the time of the book's publication (xlviii), and that the book's negative reception has as much to do with Keckley's **race** and **gender** as with its content. In the twentieth century, *Behind the Scenes* is cited in all the major studies of Mary Todd Lincoln and is regarded as an accurate source of historical information. But the book's "insights into nineteenth-century African Americans" and its "rare behind-the-scenes view of the formal and informal networks that African Americans established among themselves and within the larger mid-nineteenth-century culture" constitute its real importance (Foster, lxiii–lxiv). In recent years, critics have explored the complexity of Keckley's autobiographical persona and the book's narrative structure. Xiomara Santamarina considers the significance of **labor** in *Behind the Scenes*, arguing that it is "about a specific black woman's production and circulation of social value."

Resources: Frances Smith Foster, "Historical Introduction," in *Behind the Scenes: Thirty Years a Slave, and Four Years in the White House* (Urbana: University of Illinois Press, 2001), ix–lxvii; Elizabeth Keckley, *Behind the Scenes; or, Thirty Years a Slave and Four Years in the White House*, ed. Frances Smith Foster (Urbana: University of Illinois Press, 2001); Xiomara Santamarina, "Behind the Scenes of Black Labor: Elizabeth Keckley and the Scandal of Publicity," *Feminist Studies* 28 (Fall 2002), 514–538; Carolyn Sorisio, "Unmasking the Genteel Performer: Elizabeth Keckley's 'Behind the Scenes' and the Politics of Public Wrath," *African American Review* 34 (Spring 2000), 19–39.

Rebecca R. Saulsbury

Keene, John R., Jr. (born 1965). Novelist. Born in **St. Louis, Missouri**, Keene completed a B.A. at Harvard University and an M.F.A. at New York University. He has been a graduate fellow of Cave Canem and a longtime member of the Dark Room Writers Collective. His writing has been supported with fellowships or grants from Bread Loaf, the Massachusetts Arts Foundation, the New York Times Foundation, and Yaddo. He has held the Simon Blattner Visiting Professorship at Northwestern University and has taught at the University of Virginia and Brown University. He has presented courses in fiction writing, cross-genre writing, African American and diasporic writing, and literature in translation. While at Virginia, he served as the managing editor of **Callaloo**.

Keene's first book is *Annotations* (1995), an autobiographical novel about growing up as a gay African American in St. Louis. But unlike most autobiographical novels, *Annotations* is very experimental in its form and style. Reviewers have emphasized its poetic compression of expression and its jazz-like improvisations, not just with its striking, descriptive language but also with its characters and events. An amalgamation of genres rendered in a singular, lyrical voice, the novel has been compared to **Jean Toomer**'s *Cane*. Moreover, although Keene's novel is stylistically and tonally very different from Harry Crews's *A Childhood: A Biography of a Place*, it might also be described as a novel "of a place." Keene has cited the Guyanese novelist Wilson Harris and the poet Wallace Stevens as literary influences. For *Annotations*, Keene received the Critics Choice Award from the *San Francisco Review of Books*; the novel was also named one of the top twenty-five fiction books of 1995 by *Publishers Weekly*.

Keene's achievements have been recognized with a number of other honors, including the AGNI/John Cheever Prize, a Critics' Choice Award, the 2001 SOLO Poetry Prize, and a citation from the Fund for Poetry. His work has been nominated for four Pushcart Prizes. Selections of his work have been chosen for inclusion in **Kevin Powell**'s *Step into a World: A Global Anthology of the New Black Literature* (2000) and in *Best Gay American Fiction* (1997). His poems and short stories have appeared in such periodicals as *AA Review, African-American Review, Bay Windows, Bridge, Code, Fence, Hambone, Harvard Gay and Lesbian Review, James White Review, Kenyon Review, Nocturnes,* and *Ploughshares*. He has also contributed reviews to the *Washington Post Book World*. (*See* **Gay Literature**.)

Resources: Brian Evenson, "Review of Annotations," *Review of Contemporary Fiction* 16 (Spring 1996), 149–150; Philip Gambone, "Review of Annotations," *New York Times Book Review*, Dec. 17, 1995, p. 22; John R. Keene, Jr., *Annotations* (New York: New Directions, 1995).

Martin Kich

Kelley, Norman (born 1954). Journalist and novelist. A resident of **Brooklyn, New York**, Norman Kelley is a freelance writer whose work has appeared in a variety of newspapers, periodicals, and online publications. He has also produced segments for New York radio. He has gained a reputation as a controversial social commentator and has established himself as the author of unusual **crime and mystery fiction**.

Kelley has edited and contributed to the essay collection *R&B, Rhythm and Business: The Political Economy of Black Music* (2002). The book presents the case that African Americans have been underrepresented on the business side of the music industry, given the degree to which African American performers have creatively transformed American music and culture. As a result, the tremendous revenue produced by the industry has not greatly enriched individual African Americans or, by extension, African American communities. The book garnered a great deal of attention because its publication coincided with Michael Jackson's much-publicized charges that he had been mistreated and cheated by the racist management of his record label.

Ironically, one of Jackson's most vociferous supporters on the issue was Al Sharpton, who receives unflattering scrutiny in Kelley's *The Head Negro in Charge Syndrome: The Dead End of Black Politics* (2004). Kelley argues that African American political leaders have shifted the emphasis too much from "protest to politics" and that they have sacrificed the meaningful symbolism of a common cause to the pursuit of photo opportunities that enhance their personal celebrity but have little broader effect on their constituencies. One of Kelley's most often cited political articles is "Memoirs of a Revolutionist," an essay-review of **Stokely Carmichael**'s *Ready for Revolution: The Life and Struggles of Stokely Carmichael* that appeared in *The Nation* in the fall of 2003.

Kelley's mystery novels—*Black Heat* (1997), *The Big Mango* (2000), and *A Phat Death* (2002)—feature Nina Halligan, an African American private investigator who had been an assistant district attorney and is now an adjunct professor of political science. Although she has a terse, tough manner reminiscent of Mickey Spillane's detective Mike Hammer, Halligan is also shrewdly intellectual and has a lesbian best friend. Kelley's novels are unusual for their incorporation of a great deal of political, social, and cultural commentary. *A Phat Death* fictionally complements *R&B: Rhythm and Business* by treating the corruption and violent competition in the **hip-hop** music scene.

Resources: Karen Holt, "Fiction's Fresh Beats: Streetwise Fiction Turns a Corner, with a Fistful of Novels about the Hip-Hop Music Scene," *Publishers' Weekly*, Sept. 8, 2003, p. 19; Norman Kelley: *Black Heat* (New York: Cool Grove, 1997); *The Head Negro in Charge Syndrome: The Dead End of Black Politics* (New York: Nation Books, 2004); *The Big Mango* (New York: Akashic, 2000); *A Phat Death* (New York: Amistad, 2002); *R&B, Rhythm and Business: The Political Economy of Black Music* (New York: Akashic, 2002).

Martin Kich

Kelley, William Melvin (born 1937). Novelist and short story writer. William Melvin Kelley is a major figure among writers in the **Black Arts Movement**, the generation succeeding **Richard Wright**, **Ralph Ellison**, and **James Baldwin**; his work combines Ellison's literary inventiveness, Wright's racial indignation, and Baldwin's insights into urban culture. Born in New York City, where his father edited the African American weekly newspaper, **The Amsterdam News**, Kelley was educated at the Fieldston School and Harvard University. At Harvard, he studied with the novelist John Hawkes, who encouraged his interest in writing and introduced him to experimental forms in fiction. After publishing his first short story in 1959, Kelley left college to pursue the life of a professional writer.

His first novel, *A Different Drummer* (1962), combines Kelley's interest in the mythic and his admiration of William Faulkner to tell the story of Tucker

Caliban, great-grandson of a legendary forebear known as "the African," a sharecropper in an imaginary Southern state who poisons his fields, burns his farm, and abandons his land as a protest against racial and economic oppression. His action inspirits the Black folk, and there ensues a mass exodus of Blacks from the state, to the consternation of the Whites, for whom the departed Blacks had provided not only cheap **labor** but also a defining counteridentity. Told through a series of White narrators, the novel reflects Kelley's appreciation of Faulkner's fictional Yoknapatawpha County, Mississippi, with its overlapping narratives that connect myth, legend, and history and Black and White characters representing the entangled racial and economic strata of Southern society.

Dancers on the Shore (1964) is a collection of sixteen short stories that feature three families introduced in *A Different Drummer* (and who reappear in later works): the White and Black descendants of Confederate general Dewey Willson, the middle-class Dunfords, and the working-class Bedlows. The themes of these stories summarize Kelley's driving concern with interracial relations, both sexual and economic, and with class and identity relations within African American communities. In "The Only Man on Liberty Street," for example, a little girl comes to understand that the White man who visits her mother once or twice a week is her father. When the father defies community conventions and leaves his White wife to live with the child's mother, the Whites rally behind the vengeful wife, threatening physical harm to the little girl and forcing the father to return to his wife. The stories embody Kelley's concern to "help repair the damage done to the soul of the Negro in the past three centuries" (Wright).

William Melvin Kelley, 1963. Courtesy of the Library of Congress.

A Drop of Patience, Kelley's second novel, was published in 1965. It tells the story of Ludlow Washington, a blind **jazz** musician who is destroyed by his discovery that he has been exploited by the people he trusted to manage his career, even by the White woman he loved, and by his discovery that blindness—Kelley's metaphor for African American vulnerability—is after all, a meaningful deficit. Ludlow's recovery results in his abandoning his jazz career and finding work and community in a church that needs a musician. The novel reflects Kelley's feeling that artists are not likely to be properly appreciated in the context of American racial oppression, and that building African American community is more important than vain individual achievements.

dem (1967) marks a significant departure from Kelley's earlier fiction. His protagonist, Mitchell Pierce, is a middle-class White man, an advertising executive in New York City, and most of the action through the first three parts of the novel involves White characters only. A darkly comic **satire**, *dem* shows Mitchell as a narcissistic victim of White American delusions about reality, including **race** and sexuality. Mitchell falls in love with a character on a TV soap opera and cannot distinguish the actress, whom he stalks and beds, from the performance. He is casually prejudiced against Asians and Jews, and fires his Black housekeeper because he believes she must be stealing from him. When his wife gives birth to twins, one White and one Black, Mitchell goes to Harlem to search for Cooley, the Black twin's father. His quest is a nighttime journey into an underworld where his racial and sexual identities become uncertain, unstable. Mitchell is duped into using his cuckolder, the **trickster** Calvin Coolidge Johnson, as his "detective" in the search for the baby's father. Mitchell is a rather unsympathetic character, and though we see the action of the novel exclusively from his point of view, it is clear that he is meted out not cruel and undeserved punishment, but rather what seems appropriate retributive justice for the damage done to the soul of the **Negro**.

In *Dunfords Travels Everywheres* (1970), his last novel to date, Kelley uses dreamscapes and Joycean language play as well as Faulknerian invention of place to tell the story of Chig Dunford, an African American college student traveling in an imaginary European country with a group of five White American friends. Chig's educated but racially unaware adventures are contrasted with those of his double, Carlyle Bedlow, at home in **Harlem, New York**. Like Joyce's twins Shem and Shaun in *Finnegans Wake*, Chig and Carlyle are contrasting aspects of a single identity, in this case aspects of African American political, cultural, and racial consciousness. Chig is naïve, sleeping, and dreaming; Carlyle is wide-awake, streetwise, and militant. While Chig pursues a presumedly White woman, arousing the racial resentment of his "liberal" White traveling companions, Carlyle agrees to seduce a Black Harlem dentist's wife for pay, then changes sides in true trickster fashion. While Chig returns to the United States on a steamship that he believes is also transporting slaves, Carlyle engages in a struggle with the devil to save the soul of his friend Hondo. When they meet in a Harlem tavern, Chig still cannot acknowledge their brotherhood, and is sent for further satiric dream lessons on the contrasting mythic heritages of Black and White Americans. Much of the narrative is presented in a dense (indeed, often impenetrable) play with dream distortions of language, persons, and events, but careful reading is rewarded with jokes, ironies, and transformations that delight and impress.

Kelley held fellowships from the John Hay Whitney Foundation and the National Institute of Arts and Letters during the 1960s. He taught at the New School University and the State University of New York at Geneseo, lived abroad, and taught again at Sarah Lawrence College. Kelley is an exemplary figure of the Black Arts Movement, embodying the struggle to be both an individual artist presenting individualized characters rather than symbols and types, and at the same time creating literature that proceeds from African American culture and meets the African American community's need to understand its racial enemies, suppress its internal demons, and celebrate its neglected greatness.

Resources: Bernard Bell, *The Afro-American Novel and Its Tradition* (Amherst: University of Massachusetts Press, 1987); Darryl Dickson Carr, *African American Satire: The Sacredly Profane Novel* (Columbia: University of Missouri Press, 2001); William Melvin Kelley: *Dancers on the Shore* (Garden City, NY: Doubleday, 1964); *dem* (Garden City, NY: Doubleday, 1967); *A Different Drummer* (Garden City, NY: Doubleday, 1962); *A Drop of Patience* (Garden City, NY: Doubleday, 1965); *Dunfords Travels Everywheres* (Garden City, NY: Doubleday, 1970); John S. Wright, "Foreword," in William Melvin Kelley, *dem* (Minneapolis, MN: Coffee House Press, 2000), ix–xliv.

Joseph T. Skerrett, Jr.

Kelley-Hawkins, Emma Dunham (1863–1938). Novelist. Long thought of as one of the earliest Black novelists, Kelley-Hawkins may not, according to recent discoveries, have been African American.

According to those discoveries—made separately by Holly Jackson and Katherine Flynn—Kelly-Hawkins was born in Dennis, Massachusetts (on Cape Cod), to mariner Issac D. Kelley and his wife Gabrielia; all of the family are noted as "white" in several census records. Emma D. Kelley married Benjamin A. Hawkins in 1893, and the couple had two daughters, Gala and Megda. They settled near Providence, Rhode Island, and Kelley-Hawkins died there and was buried in Moshassuck Cemetery in Central Falls.

Both of Kelley-Hawkins's novels, *Megda* and *Four Girls at Cottage City*, are spiritual bildungsromans that show female characters growing closer to a deeply Baptist conception of God, and both treat **race** only indirectly, when at all (while many of the characters, for example, have **"White"** features, race is almost never labeled). Both books are set in Cottage City, Massachusetts, an area on Martha's Vineyard that was later renamed Oak Bluffs and that had a reputation as a vacation spot for the African American elite by the early part of the twentieth century (although just how early is a matter of some debate).

When *Megda* was published in 1891, Kelley-Hawkins included a frontispiece photograph of what appears to be a young, light-skinned African American woman with a facsimile signature below. Though the novel carries a byline of "Forget-Me-Not," beneath this byline—and in the facsimile signature—the name "Emma Dunham Kelley" appears. By the publication of her second novel in 1895, she had dispensed with the pseudonym and listed herself as "Emma D. Kelley-Hawkins." Though the Providence-based Continental Printing Company issued the first edition of *Four Girls*, the **Boston, Massachusetts**, publisher James H. Earle published editions of both books (*Megda* in 1891 and 1892, and *Four Girls* in 1898); he is also listed in the copyright for *Megda*. Earle published a range of faith-centered books, including an edition of **Frances Ellen Watkins Harper**'s *Iola Leroy*.

Probably building from the photograph in *Megda* and the associations with Cottage City and James Earle, Maxwell Whiteman included Kelley-Hawkins in his 1955 *A Century of Fiction by American Negroes, 1853–1952*, and she was later listed in several bibliographies of Black writers—culminating in the inclusion of her novels in the Schomburg Library of Nineteenth-Century Black Women Writers (1988). Since then, Kelley-Hawkins, though not yet the subject of a detailed study, has been treated by several scholars of early African American literature. These critics' analyses and the discoveries by Jackson and Flynn will undoubtedly be tested and debated as scholars reconsider Kelley-Hawkins and her work.

Resources: Holly Jackson, "A Case of Mistaken Identity," *Boston Globe*, Feb. 20, 2005; Emma Dunham Kelley, *Megda*, ed. Molly Hite (1891; repr. New York: Oxford University Press, 1988); Emma Dunham Kelley-Hawkins, *Four Girls at Cottage City*, ed. Deborah E. McDowell (1898; repr. New York: Oxford University Press, 1988); David Mehegan, "Correcting a case of Mistaken Identity," *Boston Globe*, Mar. 5, 2005, refers to Flynn's forthcoming work.

Eric Gardner

Kenan, Randall Garrett (born 1963). Novelist, short story writer, essayist, and biographer. In his introductory essay to a republication of *The Souls of Black Folk*, by **W.E.B. Du Bois**, Kenan lists the writers whose masterpieces of twentieth-century African American literature have been influenced by Du Bois (**Richard Wright, Ralph Ellison, James Baldwin, Toni Morrison**). He could very well have included his own name. Many critical interpretations and literary reviews of Kenan's writing note a connection between his work and these writers, especially Baldwin and Morrison. Like Morrison, Kenan moved to New York City and worked in the publishing industry after finishing college, and like Baldwin, he struggled to reconcile his homosexuality with his religious upbringing. With a novel, a collection of short stories, a biography, and a hybrid piece that is part travel journal and part book-length essay, Kenan has earned a place for himself alongside these other literary masters.

Not long after entering the University of North Carolina (UNC) at Chapel Hill, Kenan, a physics major, began to devote more attention to what had been just a hobby or diversion for him: the written word. He had been a fan of **science fiction** while growing up, but his interest in other types of literature was somewhat limited. Kenan notes in his book *Walking on Water* (1999) that a member of the English faculty at UNC, Max Steele, led him to a greater appreciation of a literature, including "the work of James Baldwin and Richard Wright and **Alice Walker** and Toni Morrison," as well as Shakespeare and others (615). Besides fostering a love of reading others' writing, Steele stimulated Kenan's interest in developing his own writing. Kenan eventually changed his major to English and graduated from UNC with honors in creative writing.

Additionally, Steele pointed out to Kenan that his "background was rich and fecund and just made to be written about" (*Walking*, 615). Given his first two books, Kenan seems to have taken this last bit of advice to heart.

Kenan's first book, the novel *A Visitation of Spirits* (1989), is set in Tims Creek, a fictionalized version of Chinquapin, North Carolina, the community where Kenan grew up. This novel has two plots: one is the story of Jimmy Greene, the minister of a Black church and a school principal, who witnesses his cousin's suicide; the other is the story of the cousin, Horace Cross. The novel opens with Horace, a Black, gay teenager, summoning a demon in a Satanic ritual, in hopes that he might be turned into a bird. Horace has been brought to this point by not fitting into the community or measuring up to the expectations of his family. *A Visitation of Spirits* illustrates, through flashbacks of Horace's brief life, the insidiousness of racism and homophobia. The bookish Horace is ill at ease among the young Black boys at his school when they become interested in sports and girls. The circle of White boys he hangs around with seems to associate with him as an act of teenage rebellion and not out of any sense of true friendship. And among his own family and church, he is alienated, finding no way to square their religious fundamentalism with his homosexuality.

This story of a Black, teenage boy grappling with a religious community and uncomfortable within his own family obviously resonated with James Baldwin's *Go Tell It on the Mountain* (1953). The numerous comparisons that critics have made between the two works are, therefore, understandable. Other critical interpretations, though, make convincing claims about the book's relationship to Baldwin's novels *Giovanni's Room* (1956) and *Another Country* (1962). However, Kenan himself pointed out in a 1993 interview that he and Baldwin were "writing about different worlds" (Hunt, 415). Not only is there the difference of some thirty-six years—years in America and the world at large that were culturally and historically quite significant—but Kenan's Southern, rural, middle-class background is not the same as Baldwin's "impoverished, urban, Northern experience" (Hunt, 415).

The character of Jimmy Greene appears, albeit rather remotely, in Kenan's collection of short stories, *Let the Dead Bury Their Dead and Other Stories* (1992). The title story, "Let the Dead Bury Their Dead," is purportedly Jimmy Greene's compiled history of Tims Creek, from its earliest origins as a settlement of escaped slaves, a "Maroon Society." Besides runaway slaves, the town's history includes sorcery, zombies, and an all-consuming fire from Heaven. These sorts of supernatural elements appear in other stories in the collection. "Clarence and The Dead" is about a preschool-aged boy who communes with ghosts and frightens the townsfolk with his uncanny predictions. The protagonist of "Things of This World" befriends a stranger who could be death or an angel or something else entirely. And "Tell Me, Tell Me" recounts how the ghost of a little Black boy haunts the widow of the White racist who murdered him. Kenan's short story "Now Why Come That Is?" appeared in a special edition of *Callaloo* in 1998; it is the tale of man tormented by a spectral hog. Such fantastic aspects in his fiction have served as the basis for many critics' comparison of

Kenan's work with Morrison's, but it has also elicited analogies of Kenan with **Gloria Naylor** and Gabriel García Márquez.

The deployment of the fantastic and supernatural to convey truths, however, is not the totality of Kenan's focus. The short story "This Far," from *Let the Dead Bury Their Dead*, is a well-researched, but fictional, account of **Booker T. Washington** visiting Tims Creek. Kenan's skill at conducting research, as demonstrated in this story, reappears in his informative and readable young-adult biography *James Baldwin* (1994). Kenan has also turned his penchant for research to geography and demographics in his encyclopedic work *Walking on Water*, a study of African American life across the United States. In line with Du Bois, *Walking on Water* and the essay from Norman Mauskopf's book of photographs, *A Time Not Here* (1996), ruminate on Blackness and what it means to be African American. (*See* **Gay Literature; Queer Theory.**)

Resources: Primary Sources: Randall Kenan: "Introduction," in *The Souls of Black Folk*, by W.E.B. Du Bois (New York: Signet Classics, 1995); *James Baldwin* (New York: Chelsea House, 1994); *Let the Dead Bury Their Dead and Other Stories* (New York: Harcourt, Brace Jovanovich, 1992); "Now Why Come That Is?" *Callaloo* 21, no. 1 (1998), 119–132; "That Eternal Burning," in *A Time Not Here*, by Norman Mauskopf (Santa Fe, NM: Twin Palms, 1996); *A Visitation of Spirits* (New York: Grove, 1989); *Walking on Water: Black American Lives at the Turn of the Twenty-first Century* (New York: Knopf, 1999). **Secondary Sources:** Doris Betts, "Randall Garrett Kenan: Myth and Reality in Tims Creek," in *Southern Writers at Century's End*, ed. Jeffrey J. Folks and James A. Perkins (Lexington: University Press of Kentucky, 1997), 9–20; Trudier Harris, "Southern Voices, Southern Tales: Randall Kenan's 'Clarence *and* The Dead,'" in her *The Power of the Porch: The Storyteller's Craft in Zora Neale Hurston, Gloria Naylor, and Randall Kenan* (Athens: University of Georgia Press, 1996), 105–136; Sharon Patricia Holland, "(Pro)Creating Imaginative Spaces and Other Queer Acts: Randall Kenan's *A Visitation of Spirits* and Its Revival of James Baldwin's Absent Black Gay Man in *Giovanni's Room*," in *James Baldwin Now*, ed. Dwight A. McBride (New York: New York University Press, 1999), 265–288; V. Hunt, "A Conversation with Randall Kenan," *African American Review* 29, no. 3 (1995), 411–420; Sheila Smith McKoy, "Rescuing the Black Homosexual Lambs: Randall Kenan and the Reconstruction of Southern Gay Masculinity," in *Contemporary Black Men's Fiction and Drama*, ed. Keith Clark (Urbana: University of Illinois Press, 2001), 15–36; Robert McRuer, "Queer Locations/Queer Transformations," in his *The Queer Renaissance: Contemporary American Literature and the Reinvention of Lesbian and Gay Identities* (New York: New York University Press, 1997), 69–115.

Timothy K. Nixon

Kennedy, Adrienne (born 1931). Playwright and educator. Kennedy is a widely acclaimed playwright. She is the daughter of Cornell and Etta Hawkins and was born in **Pittsburgh, Pennsylvania**, in 1931. Kennedy grew up in an integrated neighborhood in Cleveland, Ohio, and received her B.A. from Ohio State University in 1952. She experienced the stark contrast between her positive childhood experience in an integrated neighborhood and the negative effects of racism, most visibly demonstrated by the unrest in the early years of government-mandated racial integration, while a student at Ohio State University, and it continues to shape her concerns as a playwright. In 1953 Kennedy married Joseph C. Kennedy; they had two sons. In 1954 Kennedy entered Columbia University to study creative writing. She went on to study and write with the American Theatre Wing (1958) and Edward Albee at the Circle-in-the-Square School (1962). Kennedy continues to write and teach, and has taught at universities ranging from Princeton and Yale to the University of California at Berkeley and at Davis.

Kennedy's work came of age during the **Black Arts Movement**, and her plays represent a commitment to issues of **race** and Blackness within the context of the United States. However, her plays are also concerned with global issues of race and power. From her Obie-winning play, *Funny House of a Negro* (produced in 1962), to her experimental and fragmented memoir, *People Who Led to My Plays* (1987), Kennedy's writing is most often categorized as Surrealist. The plots of her works are often secondary to the poetic and symbolic imagery they produce. Linear storytelling is not necessarily Kennedy's concern, as is most recently demonstrated by *People Who Led to My Plays*, a collection of images woven together by stream-of-consciousness story fragments. (*See* **Surrealism**.)

Adrienne Kennedy, 1964. Courtesy of the Library of Congress.

Kennedy's most famous play, *Funny House of a Negro*, which was begun and finished while she was traveling through Europe and Africa during 1960 and 1961, tells the fractured story of a young girl, Negro-Sarah, who is visited by spirits as seemingly disparate as Queen Victoria, Jesus, and the African leader Patrice Lumumba. The work explores issues of sexual and physical violence, race, and **gender** through a series of hauntings and conflicts experienced by Sarah during a sort of waking nightmare-dream. The ideas of motherhood, fatherhood, rape, salvation, and power are represented throughout *Funny House*, and other of Kennedy's work, and point to the complicated nature of a racialized American identity.

Kennedy's plays have been produced in major theaters all over the world, ranging from London's Royal Court Theatre and the National Theatre to New York's Joseph Papp Public Theatre. Kennedy attempts to push the boundaries of form as well as of Black and American identity. Her plays and other writings represent the violence resulting from the clash of **race**, **gender**, and culture in the United States. Her plays include *The Owl Answers* (1963), *A Rat's Mass* (1966), *The*

Lennon Play: In His Own Write (1968), *Lesson in a Dead Language* (1968), *A Beast's Story* (1969), *An Evening with Dead Essex* (1973), *A Movie Star Has to Stare in Black and White* (1976), *She Talks to Beethoven* (1989), *Sleep Deprivation Chamber* (1996), and *Ohio State Murders* (1990).

In 1980 Kennedy wrote two children's plays, *Black Children's Days* and *Lancashire Lad*. She also has written a memoir, *People Who Led to My Plays* (1987), and a novella, *Deadly Triplets* (1990).

Resources: Adrienne Kennedy: *Adrienne Kennedy in One Act* (Minneapolis: University of Minnesota Press, 1988); *The Adrienne Kennedy Reader*, ed. Werner Sollors (Minneapolis: University of Minnesota Press, 2001); *Deadly Triplets: A Theatre Mystery and Journal* (Minneapolis: University of Minnesota Press, 1990); *People Who Led to My Plays* (New York: Knopf, 1987); *Sleep Deprivation Chamber: A Theatre Piece* (New York: Theatre Communications Group, 1996); Jacqueline Wood, "Weight of the Mask: Parody and the Heritage of Minstrelsy in Adrienne Kennedy's *Funny House of a Negro*," *Journal of Dramatic Theory and Criticism* 17, no. 2 (Spring 2003), 5–24.

Eve Dunbar

Killens, John Oliver (1916–1987). Novelist, essayist, and college professor. John Oliver Killens, twice nominated for the Pulitzer Prize in fiction, was born in Macon, Georgia. He attended Edward Waters College, Morris Brown College, Atlanta University, Howard University, Robert H. Terrell Law School, Columbia University, and New York University. Killens worked at the National Labor Relations Board (NLRB) in **Washington, D.C.** (1936–1942), served in the U.S. Army's Pacific Amphibian Forces (1942–1946), and resumed working for the NLRB in **Brooklyn, New York** (1946). For two years, Killens attempted to organize workers for the Congress of Industrial Organizations (CIO). In 1950 he cofounded and became the first chair of the Harlem Writers Guild, a forum where a number of African American authors who later gained prominence read drafts of their works. From 1954 to 1970 Killens, who participated in the 1955 Montgomery bus boycott, was active in the **Civil Rights Movement**. A lecturer at various colleges and universities, he was writer-in-residence at Fisk University (1965–1968), Howard University (1971–1972), and Medgar Evers College of the City University of New York (1981–1987), where a chair was established in his name and where the National Black Writers Conference, founded by Killens and **Elizabeth Nunez**, has been held since 1986 (Macon; Wiggins).

Killens is best known for his six novels: *Youngblood* (1954); *And Then We Heard the Thunder* (1963), which was nominated for a Pulitzer Prize; *'Sippi* (1967); *Slaves* (1969); *The Cotillion or One Good Bull Is Half the Herd* (1971), which was also nominated for a Pulitzer Prize; and *The Great Black Russian: A Novel on the Life and Times of Alexander Pushkin* (1989). Killens's additional publications include *Black Man's Burden* (1965), a collection of essays; *Black Southern Voices* (1992), an anthology edited with **Jerry W. Ward**, Jr.; short stories; plays; screenplays; and young-adult books. Among Killens's honors are awards from the Harlem Writers Guild (1978), the Middle Atlantic Writers Association (1984), and the Before Columbus Foundation (1986).

Resources: Arthur P. Davis, J. Saunders Redding, and Joyce Ann Joyce, eds., *The New Cavalcade: African American Writing from 1760 to the Present*, vol. 2 (Washington, DC: Howard University Press, 1992), 28–29; Wanda Macon, "John O. Killens," in *The Oxford Companion to African American Literature*, ed. William L. Andrews, Frances Smith Foster, and Trudier Harris (New York: Oxford University Press, 1997), 419–420; Sharon Malinowski, ed., *Black Writers: A Selection of Sketches from Contemporary Authors*, 2nd ed. (Detroit: Gale, 1994), 347–351; Ann Allen Shockley and Sue P. Chandler, *Living Black American Authors: A Biographical Directory* (New York: Bowker, 1973), 89; William H. Wiggins, Jr., "John Oliver Killens," in *Dictionary of Literary Biography*, vol. 33, *Afro-American Fiction Writers after 1955*, ed. Thadious M. Davis and Trudier Harris (Detroit: Gale, 1984), 144–152.

Linda M. Carter

Kincaid, Jamaica (born 1949). Novelist, short story writer, and essayist. Jamaica Kincaid is best known for writing about her native West Indies island of Antigua in novels, short stories, and essays. She was born Elaine Potter Richardson on May 25, 1949, in Saint John's, the capital of Antigua, then a British colony. Her stepfather, a carpenter, was significantly older than her mother, Annie Richards. Her grandmother, a Carib Indian who practiced obeah, a form of worship involving sorcery and magic, was influential in Kincaid's early years. After Kincaid was nine years old, her mother gave birth to three boys. These births meant that Kincaid was no longer the sole focus of her mother's attention, and they also added to the strain of their family's already impoverished life. It was during this time that Kincaid turned to reading books for companionship, but reading only served to emphasize her poverty and her subjection under White rule. At the first opportunity, Kincaid moved to New York City, where she worked initially as a nanny. She severed all ties with her homeland, including her family, by not reading or responding to their letters and not leaving a forwarding address. Even though her works all focused on her native land or people from there, she did not go home for more than nineteen years, by which time she was already a famous writer.

While working as a nanny, Kincaid went to school, worked in a variety of jobs, and changed her name to Jamaica Kincaid. After several years of working with others and developing relationships within the literary community, she became a regular contributor to *The New Yorker*. These contributions led to many of her full-length publications. At one point after moving to the United States, Kincaid attended college but quickly discovered that she was not academically prepared for the rigors of university courses. For her work, however, she was awarded honorary degrees from Williams College, Long Island University, Colgate University, Amherst College, and Bard College. For Kincaid, writing became her salvation and her liberation—a fact evident in her works, stated by her, and noted by her critics.

Kincaid's **coming-of-age** writing explores the nature of growing up with a government education being provided by a colonial power and the ensuing separation when the female protagonist leaves her native land and her mother in a search for an identity separate from them both. Within her explorations, we see the links between colonial powers and patriarchy, and the several ways these powers influence a woman's identity, sexuality, and mode of living. In Kincaid's writing, mothers earn their daughters' long-lasting resentment by serving as the teacher and police of the cultural norms. Relationships with father figures appear less frequently but tend be somewhat problematic because Kincaid depicts these men as having less influence and being weaker than the women. Most critics acknowledge that Kincaid pays little attention to men in her works, and that she chooses instead to focus on women, especially on mother–daughter relationships.

Most of Kincaid's works are highly regarded for their poetical language and for poignantly depicting the colonial nature of her native Antigua. Although her writing tends to be autobiographical, her themes allow these works to transcend her **autobiography** and become more universal. These themes include the mother–daughter relationships, native islanders' reaction to urban America, and a woman's search for identity. Also, prominent are her depictions of racial inequality and White rule over predominantly Black populations of Caribbean islands, such as Antigua.

Her first book, *At the Bottom of the River* (1983), is a collection of short stories and short memoir pieces that focuses on the mother–daughter theme. As in many of her works, Kincaid develops the theme by focusing on the wonderful nature of day-to-day life. One story in this work is "Girl," a short piece that balances on a thin line between poetry and prose as it portrays the commands a mother gives to her daughter through the course of ordinary life. Other stories within this collection, such as "The Letter from Home," also focus on day-to-day life. Many critics label the entire work as long **prose poetry** and review it favorably. The book brought Kincaid the Morton Dauwen Zabel Award of the American Academy and Institute of Arts and Letters in 1983.

Kincaid's first novel, *Annie John* (1985), is a series of interrelated short stories and is autobiographical in nature. Like *At the Bottom of the River*, *Annie John* focuses on the relationship between the protagonist and her mother as it develops in day-to-day life. The protagonist of this coming-of-age novel is attempting to establish her identity as separate from her mother, and she facilitates this separation by emigrating to England. Unlike most bildungsromans, which focus on the future by eschewing the past, *Annie John*, written as a flashback, is more concerned at looking into the past with nostalgia.

Kincaid's next full-length work, *A Small Place* (1988), is a somewhat satirical analysis of European and American exploitation of Antigua, especially by tourists, and the corruption of those in power in Antigua. She makes pointed connections between earlier White rule and the current state of affairs for the Black population by linking the current corruption to the past colonial rule. She points to the irony of people who live in run-down homes and drive a taxi for a living—a taxi that happens to be a luxury Japanese vehicle, fueled with leaded gasoline. This example is just one in a string of contradictions and ironies that parallel the history of Antigua as it attempts to escape colonial, White rule.

Jamaica Kincaid, 1997. Taro Yamasaki/Time Life Pictures/ Getty Images.

A common theme in Kincaid's works is the relationship between women—a theme that she revisits in *Lucy* (1990). This novel was previously published in serial form in *The New Yorker*. While *Annie John* and *Lucy* have different characters, *Annie John* ends with Annie's last day on Antigua before emigrating, and *Lucy* begins with Lucy's first day in the United States. This apparent linkage leads many critics to view the two novels as the halves of one whole. In this novel, the protagonist Lucy engages in numerous liaisons with various men as a way of exploring her sexuality, but also as a way to deflect her true feelings for her mother. On one hand, Lucy, much like Kincaid, wants a relationship with her mother, yet she also continually rejects any overtures by her mother and has to deal with the long-term separation from her mother and her homeland. We learn that Lucy rejects her mother partially because her mother puts greater hopes and expectations on Lucy's younger male siblings. Lucy also discovers that escape from her native land does not provide the happiness that she expected.

Kincaid shifts her setting to Dominica, a different Caribbean island from her previous works, in *Autobiography of My Mother* (1996). Once again, however, she focuses on the alienation between a daughter, Xuela, and her mother. In this novel, however, the mother, herself left motherless when her mother abandoned her, dies giving birth to Xuela. Xuela, who has chosen to remain childless, breaks the cycle of motherless daughters. This work was a finalist for the National Book Critics Circle Award for fiction and a finalist for the PEN Faulkner Award, and won the Boston Book Review Fisk Fiction Prize.

My Brother (1997) is a memoir that deviates from her normal works in that it does not focus on her mother, mother/daughter relationships, or any relationship between women. Rather, this book explores her brother's battle with and eventual death from AIDS. Just as Kincaid's relationship with her mother was strained, so Kincaid never had a strong relationship with her brother, yet she is willing to explore her feelings for him and his illness with tenderness in this work. This work was nominated for the National Book Award.

Kincaid's works explore the connections between mothers and daughters, including the rebellions, the strong feelings, and the fear and desire for separation. Many critics who praise her use of symbolism, poetic language, and imagery view the way she treats these subjects as metaphors for the relationship between colonizers and colonized (Kester-Shelton). Her focus on domestic activities seems to be a way for her to explore social concerns. Critics praise the authentic voices of her characters, including their pain of attempting to grow up in a world that is not always idyllic. She depicts the insider's perspective of growing up in Antigua with an overbearing mother who attempts to instill in her daughter all the cultural norms that tend to perpetuate inequalities of **race**, **gender**, and sexuality.

Kincaid's first in-depth exploration of her feelings toward her biological father is depicted in *Mr. Potter* (2002), as she once again takes pages from her life and presents them in a fictional format. Mr. Potter is an illiterate taxi driver in Antigua—one similar to those discussed at length in *A Small Place*. The narrator of this novel is one of Mr. Potter's numerous illegitimate daughters—daughters he never acknowledges. While ostensibly a story of Mr. Potter, the novel focuses more on Mr. Potter's lack of paternal acknowledgment and the narrator's disillusionment at their nonexistent relationship. She repeats throughout the novel that Mr. Potter is her father, as if repeating it often enough will make it more of an emotional reality than merely a biological reality.

In 1989, Kincaid collaborated with artist Eric Fischl to create a children's book called *Annie, Gwen, Lilly, Pam, and Tulip*, a story of five young girls as they grow up. In 2001, Kincaid collected some of her early essays from *The New Yorker* into a book titled *Talk Stories* (2001). She coedited the 1995 *Best American Essays*. She wrote an introduction to a book of photographs titled *Generations of Women: In Their Own Words* (1998), which explores the nature of mother–daughter bonds. She also wrote a series of articles for *The New Yorker* about various aspects of gardening, especially referring to her own garden in Vermont. These essays were later published in *My Garden (Book)* (1999), and as in her other works, Kincaid explores the idea of colonization using gardens as a metaphor. Her other books on gardening and gardens include *Poetics of Place* (1998) and an edited volume titled *My Favorite Plant: Writers and Gardeners on the Plants They Love* (1998).

In addition to appearing in *The New Yorker*, Kincaids's short stories and essays have been published in such magazines as *Harper's*, *Rolling Stone*, and *The Paris Review*. Kincaid also won the Lila Wallace-Reader's Digest Fund annual writer's award for 1992. Kincaid currently lives in Vermont and is married to composer Allen Shawn. They have two children.

Resources: Primary Sources: Jamaica Kincaid: *Annie, Gwen, Lilly, Pam, and Tulip* (New York: Knopf, 1989); *Annie John* (New York: Farrar, Straus, and Giroux, 1985); *At the Bottom of the River* (New York: Farrar, Straus, and Giroux, 1983); *Autobiography of My Mother* (New York: Farrar, Straus, and Giroux, 1996); "Introduction," in *Generations of Women: In Their Own Words*, ed. Mariana Cook (Collingdale, PA: Diane, 1998); *Lucy* (New York: Farrar, Straus, and Giroux, 1990); *Mr. Potter* (New York: Farrar, Straus, and Giroux, 2002); *My Brother* (New York: Farrar, Straus, and Giroux, 1997); *My Garden (Book)* (New York: Farrar, Straus, and Giroux, 1999); *My Favorite Tool* (New York: Farrar, Straus, and Giroux, 2005); *A Small Place* (New York: Farrar, Straus, and Giroux, 1988); *Talk Stories* (New York: Farrar, Straus, and Giroux, 2001); Jamaica Kincaid, ed., *My Favorite Plant: Writers and Gardeners on the Plants They Love* (New York: Farrar, Straus, and Giroux, 1998); Jamaica Kincaid and Robert Atwan, eds., *Best American Essays* (New York: Houghton, 1995); Jamaica Kincaid and Lynn Geesaman, *Poetics of Place* (New York: Umbrage, 1998). **Secondary Sources:** Jana Evans Braziel, "Daffodils, Rhizomes, Migrations: Narrative Coming of Age in the Diasporic Writings of Edwidge Danticat and Jamaica Kincaid," *Meridians: Feminism, Race, Transnationalism* 3, no. 2 (2003), 110–131; C. E. Clark, ed., *Concise Dictionary of American Literary Biography, Supplement: Modern Writers, 1900–1998* (Detroit: Gale, 1998); *Contemporary Black Biography*, vol. 4 (Detroit: Gale, 1993); *Contemporary Literary Criticism*, vol. 43 (Detroit: Gale, 1987); Kevin S. Hile and E. A. Des Chenes, eds., *Authors and Artists for Young Adults*, vol. 13 (Detroit: Gale, 1994); Gary E. Holcomb, "Travels of a Transnational Slut: Sexual Migration in Kincaid's *Lucy*," *Critique: Studies in Contemporary Fiction* 44, no. 3 (Spring 2003), 295–312; Pamela Kester-Shelton, ed., *Feminist Writers* (Detroit: St. James Press, 1996); Josh Lauer and Neil Schlager, eds., *Contemporary Novelists*, 7th ed. (Detroit: St. James Press, 2001); Tom Pendergast and Sara Pendergast, eds., *St. James Guide to Young Adult Writers*, 2nd ed. (Detroit: St. James Press, 1999); Jessie Carney Smith, ed., *Notable Black American Women*, vol. 1 (Detroit: Gale, 1992).

Susie Scifres Kuilan

King, Martin Luther, Jr. (1929–1968). Baptist minister, author, and civil rights activist. Martin Luther King, Jr., was the most renowned leader of the **Civil Rights Movement** in the United States during the 1950s and 1960s. He is known for his eloquent speeches and **sermons** delivered in a style heavily influenced by prophetic books of the Old Testament. His doctrine of brotherly love and nonviolent, direct action against racism—inspired by the teachings of Jesus, Henry David Thoreau, Mohandas K. Gandhi, and liberal Protestant theologians—was crucial to winning full citizenship rights for Blacks as well as other groups of racial minorities.

King was born and raised in Sweet Auburn, a Black middle-class neighborhood in **Atlanta, Georgia**, on January 15, 1929. His father, Michael (later Martin Luther) King, Sr., was pastor of the Ebenezer Baptist Church, a Black congregation founded by his maternal grandfather; his mother, Alberta Williams King, was the choir director of the church as well as a schoolteacher. King was educated at David T. Howard Elementary School, Atlanta University Laboratory School, and Booker T. Washington High School. After finishing his junior year at Booker T. Washington, King entered Morehouse College in Atlanta as a gifted student, earning his B.A. degree in sociology in 1948. While attending Morehouse, he was ordained as a Baptist minister. In the fall of the same year, King entered Crozer Theological Seminary in Chester, Pennsylvania, where he learned liberal Protestant theology and the Gandhian philosophy of nonviolence. After receiving a Bachelor of Divinity from Crozer in 1951, he began doctoral study in theology at Boston University. While living in **Boston, Massachusetts**, King met and married Coretta Scott, a Marion, Alabama, native and a student at the New England Conservatory of Music. The couple had four children. In 1954, a year before he received a Ph.D. in systematic theology, King was installed as pastor of the Dexter Avenue Baptist Church in Montgomery, Alabama.

By the time King and his family settled in Montgomery, Southern Blacks were simmering with rage against racial discrimination. King first became involved in civil rights activism through the boycott of the Montgomery bus system by Blacks. The National Association for the Advancement of Colored People (**NAACP**) elected King the leader of the Montgomery Improvement Association (MIA), which carried out the bus boycott. In his first civil rights speech, delivered to 7000 Blacks at Holt Street Baptist Church, King declared, "There comes a time when people get tired of being trampled over by the iron feet of oppression." He added, however, that the fight for racial equality would be carried out through nonviolent means. The yearlong boycott of city buses was met by harassment, arrests, attacks, and intimidation by the police and White supremacists; King's home was bombed on January 30, 1956. Finally, on November 13, the U.S. Supreme Court declared segregation of public buses unconstitutional; on December 21, the Montgomery buses were desegregated. The bus boycott represented the first large-scale use of nonviolent resistance against racial discrimination in American history, making King a national hero for the oppressed—a moral voice, seasoned with Christian love, fighting for social justice.

In January 1957, King and other Black leaders formed the Southern Christian Leadership Conference (SCLC), a ministerial organization aimed at coordinating local civil rights groups in **the South**. The SCLC was instrumental in pressuring the federal government and Congress to pass the Civil Rights Act and the Voting Rights Act. As the first president of the SCLC, King delivered hundreds of speeches and consulted with other civil rights leaders across the country. In 1957, he received the Spingarn Medal, awarded annually by the NAACP to a distinguished American Negro.

In 1960, King and his family relocated from Montgomery to Atlanta, where he took the associate pastorate at his father's church. Under King's leadership, the SCLC gave its support to hundreds of Blacks in Greensboro, North Carolina, who were holding sit-ins at lunch counters. Later that year, King and thirty-three young people were arrested at one such sit-in at an Atlanta department store. He was released from prison, but only through the intervention of Democratic presidential candidate John F. Kennedy. King next supported, without much success, the 1961 Albany, Georgia, movement for voter registration, desegregation of public places, and equal employment opportunity, among other causes. Local Black groups rioted, defying King's plea to use peaceful means to end racial discrimination. (*See* **Race Riots**.)

In April 1963, King led a large-scale civil rights campaign in Birmingham, an uprising featuring peaceful marches by thousands of Blacks. More than 4,000 demonstrators were put in jail. As 2,500 more youths marched through the streets, they were brutally suppressed by police who used fire hoses, German shepherds, tear gas, and clubs. King was arrested, jailed, and held in solitary confinement. On April 16, he wrote "Letter from Birmingham Jail" to White

Martin Luther King, Jr., at a press conference in 1964. Courtesy of the Library of Congress.

ministers who had opposed his campaign. He contended that unjust laws were unworthy of obedience and that nonviolent, direct action was intended to "create such a crisis and foster such a tension that a community which has constantly refused to negotiate is forced to confront the issue." Police brutality, which bolstered the national outcry to end racial segregation in the South, led President Kennedy to propose an extensive civil rights bill in Congress. In August, King and other civil rights leaders orchestrated a march on **Washington, D.C.**—the largest civil rights protest in U.S. history—to draw national and international attention to racial problems in the United States and pressure Congress to pass Kennedy's bill. It was at this march that King delivered the famous speech "I Have a Dream" to more than 200,000 civil rights supporters of various races who had gathered around the Lincoln Memorial. He addressed the crowd, "I have a dream that my four little children will one day live in a nation where they will not be judged by the color of their skin, but by the content of their character." (*See* **Essay**.)

The year 1964 saw the historic passage of the Civil Rights Act. Signed by President Lyndon B. Johnson, it outlawed segregation of public accommodations and guaranteed equal opportunity in employment, education, and federal programs. In the summer, the SCLC supported CORE (Congress of Racial Equality) in its massive voter registration campaign for the Freedom Summer. In the same year, King was received two honors. In January, he was chosen by *Time* magazine as Man of the Year, and in December, he received the Nobel Peace Prize for advancing racial justice in the United States.

Having seen the passage of the Civil Rights Acts, King devoted more time and attention to securing federal voting rights for Blacks. In February 1965, he was arrested and briefly jailed while leading, alongside John Lewis, a "stand-in" at the Dallas County Courthouse in Selma, Alabama. After a Black man named Jimmy Lee Jackson was killed by a state trooper, King led a protest march with hundreds of religious people including Catholic priests and nuns, Protestant clergymen, and rabbis. Police responded with nightsticks and tear gas, fatally injuring Rev. James Reeb. After "Bloody Sunday," the day when police brutality reached its peak, more than 3,000 protesters marched from Selma to Montgomery. With the state capitol building as backdrop, King delivered a speech to a crowd of more than 20,000 people. The violence in Selma forced President Lyndon B. Johnson to seek passage of the Voting Rights Act. Approved by Congress, it was signed into law on August 6.

King's stature as the most revered civil rights leader began to diminish as the nation became increasingly preoccupied with the **Vietnam War**. Starting in early January 1966, King openly opposed U.S. military action in Vietnam, which he maintained was dishonorable and morally unjustifiable. War expenditures, he believed, would be better used for alleviating the plight of poor Blacks. In his "Beyond Vietnam" speech, delivered at Riverside Church in New York City on April 4, King called the United States "the greatest purveyor of violence in the world today." His antiwar stance alienated many fellow civil rights leaders as well as government figures, including President Johnson and J. Edgar Hoover, head of the FBI.

King's stature also diminished as militant Black leaders, especially those in Northern cities, began to question the effectiveness of his nonviolent civil protests. Accusing him of being too cautious, they resorted to violence in protest against Black poverty in ghettoes. The August 1965 rioting in the Watts district of **Los Angeles, California**, served as a prime example. At the beginning of 1966, King launched a massive protest in **Chicago, Illinois**—the first major civil rights campaign outside **the South**. Marchers demanded abolition of racial discrimination in housing, employment, and schooling. King also established Operation Breadbasket to promote job opportunities for Blacks. Except for Operation Breadbasket, however, King's Chicago campaign resulted largely in unfulfilled promises.

On November 27, 1967, King announced the "Poor People's Campaign," a multiracial, nonviolent mass march to be held in Washington, D.C. Its aim was to demand elimination of all forms of barriers to economic freedom for the impoverished. It also called for the funding of a $12-billion "Economic Bill of Rights." While organizing this campaign, King accepted a request by sanitation workers in **Memphis, Tennessee**, to support their strike. He flew to Memphis and delivered a speech, "I've Been to the Mountaintop," at Mason Temple on April 3, 1968. In this prophetic address, King compared himself to Moses, who led his people out of slavery in Egypt but was not allowed by God to enter Canaan. The following day, while standing on the balcony of the Lorraine Motel, he was assassinated by a sniper. More than 10,000 people gathered outside the Ebenezer Baptist Church in Atlanta, where his funeral was held. James Earl Ray, a White sanitation worker, was charged with the murder. He pleaded guilty on March 10, 1969, and was sentenced to ninety-nine years in prison. (*See* **Abernathy, Ralph David.**)

During his life as a civil rights leader, King wrote five books elucidating his philosophy of nonviolent protest: *Stride Toward Freedom: The Montgomery Story* (1958), a memoir in which he recollected the Montgomery bus boycott and theorized nonviolent civil disobedience; *Strength to Love* (1963), a collection of sermons expounding on civil protests founded upon the principle of Christian charity; *Why We Can't Wait* (1964), in which he recounts the experiences in Birmingham and contends that all Americans are morally obligated to act to improve race relations; *Where Do We Go from Here: Chaos or Community?* (1967), containing his reflections on the future of the civil rights movement; and *The Trumpet of Conscience* (1968), a collection of five speeches including "Youth and Action" and "Nonviolence and Social Change."

A towering symbol of peaceful resistance, King has become a legendary figure in modern American history. In 1977, he was posthumously awarded the Presidential Medal of Freedom for his nonviolent struggle for the rights of Blacks. In October 1980, the Martin Luther King, Jr., National Historic Site was established in Atlanta, and in 1983, Congress designated the third Monday in January, beginning in 1986, as a national holiday in honor of his birth. In 1996, Congress established the Selma-to-Montgomery National Historic Trail under the National Trails System Act. In addition to all this, numerous streets, highways, and schools across the United States bear the name of King.

Resources: John J. Ansbro, *Martin Luther King, Jr.* (Maryknoll, NY: Orbis, 1982); Lewis V. Baldwin, *There Is a Balm in Gilead: The Cultural Roots of Martin Luther King, Jr.* (Minneapolis, MN: Fortress Press, 1991); Taylor Branch, *Parting the Waters: America in the King Years 1954–1963* (New York: Simon and Schuster, 1988); Richard L. Deats, *Martin Luther King, Jr.* (New York: New City Press, 1999); David J. Garrow, *Bearing the Cross: Martin Luther King, Jr., and the Southern Christian Leadership Conference, 1955–1968* (New York: Morrow, 1986); Martin Luther King, Jr.: *Strength to Love* (New York: Harper & Row, 1963); *Stride Toward Freedom: The Montgomery Story* (New York: Harper & Row, 1958); *The Trumpet of Conscience* (New York: Harper & Row, 1968); *Where Do We Go from Here: Chaos or Community?* (New York: Harper & Row, 1967); *Why We Can't Wait* (New York: Harper & Row, 1964); Flip Schulke and Penelope O. McPhee, *King Remembered* (New York: Norton, 1986); Stephen B. Oates, *Let the Trumpet Sound: The Life of Martin Luther King, Jr.* (New York: Harper & Row, 1982).

John J. Han

King, Woodie, Jr. (born 1937). Director, playwright, producer, and editor. Referred to by Peter Bailey as the "Renaissance man of black theatre" (Peterson, 294), Woodie King has provided African American theater artists and audiences with viable African American theatrical productions by writing, producing, and directing plays, as well as by editing several anthologies of African American drama. King was born in Baldwin Springs, Alabama, but moved to Mobile, Alabama, when he was a young boy. After his parents' separation when he was five years old, he moved with his mother to **Detroit, Michigan**. He attended Cass Technical High School, and in 1958 he was awarded a scholarship to attend Will-O-Way School of the Theatre, from which he graduated in 1961 with a B.A. degree. Beginning in 1960, King wrote drama reviews for the *Detroit Tribune*, as well as a few short stories that were published in **Negro Digest** in August 1962 and June 1963. King spent two years at Wayne State University, where he did postgraduate work in theater. While there, King cofounded the Concept East Theatre with **Ron Milner** in order to provide African American students with opportunities to play roles for which they were often overlooked in the university's theatrical productions.

The Concept East Theatre staged plays by such playwrights as **Ed Bullins**, Edward Albee, Ron Milner, and **Amiri Baraka** (formerly LeRoi Jones). In 1964, King won a John Hay Whitney fellowship to study directing and theater administration under Lloyd Richards and Wynn Handman at the American Place Theatre. This was a great opportunity for King, and he had five of his plays staged while there. In 1965, King became cultural arts director of Mobilization for Youth, "an antipoverty program . . . [which] . . . produced plays, dances, and films" (Vallillo, 172). King's friend **Langston Hughes** encouraged him to adapt Hughes's first collection of poems, *The Weary Blues*, for the stage, which he did successfully in 1966. A year later, King adapted Hughes's poems on the character Jesse B. Simple for the stage, under the title *Just Simple*, and he directed a "theatre vignette" by Hughes, "Mother and Child," in 1965, off-Broadway (Ostrom).

During the late 1960s and the 1970s, King expanded his horizons to documentary filmmaking, producing his first film, *The Game*, in 1968; it won an award at the Venice Film Festival. His 1970 documentary film, *Right On!* received an International Film Critics Award, and in 1978, King wrote, directed, and produced the film *Black Theatre: The Making of a Movement*. Besides his filmmaking projects, King continued to work in the theater during this time, producing four one-act plays by **Ben Caldwell**, Ron Milner, Ed Bullins, and Amiri Baraka called *A Black Quartet* in 1969. He also founded his own theater in 1970—New Federal Theatre—which continues to be a space for the staging of African American drama. In 1980, King wrote a book titled *Black Theatre, Present Conditions*, and throughout the 1970s and into the 1990s, he has edited several anthologies of plays, poetry, and fiction. He has also written many critical essays and articles on the theater for numerous African American and mainstream publications. (*See* **Drama**.)

Resources: Primary Sources: Woodie King, Jr., *Black Theatre, Present Condition* (New York: National Black Theatre Touring Circuit, 1981); Woodie King, Jr., ed.: *Black Short Story Anthology* (New York: Columbia University Press, 1972); *Black Spirits: New Black Poets in America* (New York: Random House, 1972); *The Forerunners: Black Poets in America* (Washington, DC: Howard University Press, 1975); *The National Black Drama Anthology: Eleven Plays from America's Leading African-American Theaters* (New York: Applause Books, 1995); *New Plays from the Black Theatre* (Chicago: Third World Press, 1989); *Voices of Color: Scenes and Monologues from the Black American Theatre* (New York: Applause Books, 1993); Woodie King, Jr., and Ron Milner, eds., *Black Drama Anthology* (New York: Columbia University Press, 1972). **Secondary Sources:** Kenya Dilday, "Woodie King, Jr.," in *Encyclopedia of African American Culture and History*, vol. 3, ed. Jack Salzman, David Lionel Smith, and Cornel West (New York: Macmillan Library Reference, 1996); Hans Ostrom, *A Langston Hughes Encyclopedia* (Westport, CT: Greenwood Press, 2002), 259; Bernard Peterson, *Contemporary Black American Playwrights and Their Plays: A Biographical Directory and Dramatic Index* (Westport, CT: Greenwood Press, 1988); Stephen M. Vallillo, "Woodie King, Jr.," in

Dictionary of Literary Biography, vol. 38, *Afro-American Writers After 1955: Dramatists and Prose Writers* (Detroit: Gale Research, 1985).

Ama S. Wattley

Kitchen Table: Women of Color Press (1981–present). Feminist publishing company. Founded by **Barbara Smith** and **Audre Lorde**, Kitchen Table: Women of Color Press was the first press devoted to the publication and promotion of literary and critical works by women of color. It was founded with the intent to combat the relative invisibility of and the silencing of minority perspectives both by the culture at large and by mainstream publishing houses in the United States. Based in lesbian-feminist politics and committed to work that explores women's/lesbian history and experience, Kitchen Table sought to create a space where issues central to women and minorities would be heard and explored. Kitchen Table gave women of color a venue through which they could describe, identify, and explore issues of **race**, class, sexuality, politics, and experience. The work that Kitchen Table has published, and continues to publish, profoundly shapes the practice of Women's Studies, lesbian studies, and contemporary literature and feminism. (*See* **Lesbian Literature**.)

The press has produced fifteen award-winning titles, including *Home Girls: A Black Feminist Anthology*, edited by Barbara Smith (1983); *This Bridge Called My Back: Writings by Radical Women of Color*, edited by Cherríe Moraga and Gloria Anzaldúa (1983); and *Cuentos: Stories by Latinas*, edited by Alma Gómez, Cherríe Moraga, and Mariana Romo-Carmona (1983). Kitchen Table's publications defined new issues, such as racism and homophobia in the women's movement; multiple levels of oppression faced by women of color; and the intersections of religion, race, and sexuality. Importantly, they reexamined old issues from new perspectives, asking new questions and forcing new responses and action. They opened up a discussion that continues today and made the concerns of women of color central not only to the women's movement but also to lesbian-feminism, queer politics, and third-wave feminism.

The mission of Kitchen Table reflects the lifelong work of its two founders, Barbara Smith and Audre Lorde. Born in 1934 in New York City, Audre Lorde was a lifelong writer, activist, and educator. She fought on all fronts and forged links among her identities as an African American, a woman, and a lesbian. Her involvement with Kitchen Table reflects her struggle to fight injustice in all its forms. Lorde's many publications include her autobiographical novel *Zami: A New Spelling of My Name* (1982), *Sister Outsider* (1984), and *Need: A Chorale for Black Women's Voices* (1990). She died in 1992 of breast cancer.

Like Lorde, Barbara Smith examines the intersection of race, class, sexuality, and **gender**. She is a writer, activist, scholar, and publisher and her groundbreaking work in African American lesbian history and experience has given voice to a historically silenced population. Today, Smith continues to confront racism, sexism, and homophobia while creating a space for women of color and for lesbians. She is the author of numerous essays, stories, lectures, and works of criticism, as well as the editor of three major essay collections about Black women: *Conditions: Five, the Black Women's Issue* (1979); *All the Women Are White, All the Men Are Black, But Some of us Are Brave: Black Women's Studies* (with Gloria T. Hull and Patricia Bell Scott; 1982); and *Home Girls: A Black Feminist Anthology* (1983; 2nd ed., 2000).

Resources: Mila D. Aguilar, *Comrade Is as Precious as a Rice Seedling: Poems*, intro. Audre Lorde (Latham, NY: Kitchen Table: Women of Color Press, 1984); Cheryl Clarke, *Narratives: Poems in the Tradition of Black Women* (Latham, NY: Kitchen Table: Women of Color Press, 1983); Alma Gomez, Cherríe Moraga, and Mariana Romo-Carmona, eds., *Cuentos: Stories by Latinas* (Latham, NY: Kitchen Table: Women of Color Press, 1983); Gloria T. Hull, *Healing Heart: Poems, 1973–1988* (Latham, NY: Kitchen Table: Women of Color Press, 1989); Audre Lorde, *I Am Your Sister: Black Women Organizing Across Sexualities* (Latham, NY: Kitchen Table: Women of Color Press, 1985); Cherríe Moraga and Gloria Anzaldúa, eds., *This Bridge Called My Back: Writings by Radical Women of Color* (Latham, NY: Kitchen Table: Women of Color Press, 1983); Barbara Omolade, *It's a Family Affair: The Real Lives of Black Single Mothers* (Latham, NY: Kitchen Table: Women of Color Press, 1986); Barbara Smith, ed., *Home Girls: A Black Feminist Anthology* (Latham, NY: Kitchen Table: Women of Color Press, 1983); Mitsuye Yamada, *Desert Run: Poems and Stories* (Latham, NY: Kitchen Table: Women of Color Press, 1988); Hisaye Yamamoto, *Seventeen Syllables and Other Stories*, intro. King-Kok Cheung (Latham, NY: Kitchen Table: Women of Color Press, 1988).

Melissa A. Rigney

Kitt, Sandra (born 1947). Novelist. Sandra Kitt is a popular author of **romance novels** and the first African American author to be published by Harlequin, arguably the preeminent publisher of romance fiction. She has written more than twenty novels and has been nominated for an **NAACP** Image Award in Fiction; many of her novels have been listed on regional best-seller lists. *Significant Others* (1996) was named by the online bookseller Amazon.com as one of the top twenty-five romances of the last century. One of her novels has been optioned for film, and she has written children's books and screenplays, as well as articles and reviews for museum and library journals. Born in New York City, she received a M.F.A. from the City University of New York. She was previously a graphic designer and freelance illustrator, as well as an information specialist in astronomy and astrophysics at the American Museum of Natural History in New York City and manager of library services at the Richard S. Perkin Library of the Hayden Planetarium. She has exhibited her work throughout the United States, designed greeting cards for UNICEF, and illustrated books for the science writer Isaac Asimov. She is a frequent lecturer and panelist at conventions, and teaches courses in publishing and basic fiction writing.

Resources: Sandra Kitt: *Between Friends* (New York: Signet, 1998); *Close Encounters* (New York: Signet, 2000); *The Color of Love* (New York: Signet, 1995); *Family Affairs* (New York: Signet, 1999); *She's the One* (New York: Signet, 2001); *Sincerely* (New York: BET Books, 2000); *Suddenly* (New York: BET Books, 2001).

Saundra K. Liggins

Knight, Etheridge (1931–1991). Poet, prisoner, "toast" maker, and teacher. Born in Corinth, Mississippi, Knight abandoned school by the ninth grade, joined the Army by the age of sixteen, and was discharged ten years later, when dependencies on alcohol and drugs led him to prison for the offense of purse snatching in 1960. While Knight gained notoriety for urban "toasts" (oral improvisations of poems and narratives rooted in nineteenth-century African storytelling traditions) long before his incarceration, it was not until he was serving time at the Indiana State Prison that he began his illustrious career as a "prison poet" (see **Prison Literature**). He was often visited by major literary figures such as **Gwendolyn Brooks**, and was supported by members of the **Black Arts Movement**, such as his first wife, **Sonia Sanchez**.

For eight years, Knight wrote poetry in prison. The release of his first published collection, *Poems from Prison* (1968), roughly coincided with his release from prison. The poem "The Idea of Ancestry" from that collection suggests that personal freedoms can prevail in the bleakest of circumstances. The book also includes poems that indict the American prison system, such as "For Freckle-Faced Gerald" and "Hard Rock Returns to Prison from the Hospital of the Criminal Insane." The latter is one of Knight's best-known poems. The character "Hard Rock" is presented as the one Black man in prison who stands up to oppression and racism. In the poem, prison administrators decide to perform a makeshift lobotomy on Hard Rock, and he is stripped of the strength, the identity, and the self-determination that characterized him. In this regard the poem is comparable to Ken Kesey's *One Flew over the Cuckoo's Nest* (1962), in which the rebellious Randall Patrick McMurphy suffers the same fate as Hard Rock.

The publication of *Black Voices from Prison* (1970), an anthology he edited and contributed to, reinforced Knight's reputation as a political, even revolutionary, poet. His **blues**-inspired verse links him with major writers such as **Richard Wright** and **Langston Hughes**. The critic Frank Magill suggests that Knight's poetry reflects a practice common to African American literature—paying respect to elders and familial ancestors (Magill, 419). In addition to being compared to major literary figures such as Walt Whitman and **Sterling A. Brown**, Knight won the respect of his peers while holding teaching positions (from 1969 to 1972) at the University of Pittsburgh, the University of Hartford, and Lincoln University in Pennsylvania.

Knight continued to struggle with addictions, checking himself in and out of drug-dependency treatment centers, and going through a divorce with Sanchez. However, within a two-year span Knight was remarried, awarded a National Endowment for the Arts grant (1972), nominated for the National Book Award and the Pulitzer Prize (1973), and awarded a Guggenheim fellowship (1974). Along with **Amiri Baraka** and **Haki Madhubuti**, Knight, who successfully experimented with African-based rhythms, blues idioms and **jazz**, was one of the most inspirational figures to join the Black Arts Movement. Knight's impulse to establish connections in social and literary communities would reveal itself in *Belly Song and Other Poems* (1973). Reflecting his belief that prison and family leave uniquely indelible marks, Knight's fourth major collection, *Born of a Woman* (1980), pays homage to the essential female figures in his life. By this time, Knight had divorced his second wife, Mary Ann McAnally, and was married to his third wife, Charlene Blackburn. A poem such as "The Stretching of the Belly" (dedicated to Blackburn) compares a woman's stretch marks to a man's battle scars. Many of the poems that appear in both *Belly Song* and *Born of a Woman* have been recognized by critics such as Patricia L. Hill for resurrecting instrumental devices from the blues (Hill, 21). Citing Knight's "Hard Rock Returns to Prison from the Hospital for the Criminal Insane" as a quintessential example of prison poetry, H. Bruce Franklin states: "In the immediate background of contemporary Black prison poetry is the body of work songs developed by Black convicts on chain gangs and prison farms" (254).

Critics such as Hill and Franklin have also noted the ways that Knight's poetic works actively demonstrate the connection between slave songs, urban toasts, and contemporary **rap** music. Knight was an editor of the magazine *Motive*, as well as a contributing editor for the journal *New Letters*. After winning the Shelley Memorial Award from the Poetry Society of America in 1985, Knight published his most comprehensive collection, *The Essential Etheridge Knight* (1986), which won the 1987 American Book Award. Knight earned his bachelor's degree in American poetry and criminal justice from Martin Center University in 1990. He died from lung cancer on March 10, 1991.

Resources: H. Bruce Franklin, *Prison Literature in America: The Victim as Criminal and Artist* (New York: Oxford University Press, 1989); Patricia L. Hill, "'Blues for a Mississippi Black Boy': Etheridge Knight's Craft in the Black Oral Tradition," *Mississippi Quarterly* 36, no. 1 (Winter 1982–1983), 21–34; Etheridge Knight: *Belly Song and Other Poems* (Detroit: Broadside Press, 1973); *Black Voices from Prison* (New York: Pathfinder Press, 1970); *Born of a Woman* (Boston: Houghton Mifflin, 1980); *The Essential Etheridge Knight* (Pittsburgh, PA: University of Pittsburgh Press, 1986); *Poems from Prison* (Detroit: Broadside Press, 1968); Frank N. Magill, "The Poetry of Etheridge Knight," in *Masterpieces of African-American Literature*, ed. Frank N. Magill (New York: HarperCollins, 1992), 419–422.

Stephen M. Steck

Knopf, Alfred A. (1892–1984). Publisher. Alfred Abraham Knopf is widely considered one of the most important figures in the history of book publishing, and the publishing firm of Knopf and its affiliates remain, collectively, a prestigious, influential publishing house. He believed in blending book art and craftsmanship with works of literature to create a new standard in the literary world. In addition to starting his own publishing company, Knopf was personally responsible for publishing the works of the most influential writers of the twentieth century. Knopf was born on September 12, 1892, in New York City, to Samuel and Ida Knopf. He attended Columbia College and originally intended to become a lawyer, with his sights set on Harvard Law School. While at Columbia, however, Knopf became intrigued by literature and the world of publishing. His first position in the publishing industry was as a clerk in the accounting department of Doubleday, and he quickly ascended through the ranks, holding positions in manufacturing, advertising, and sales.

Ultimately, Knopf began working in the editorial department at Doubleday and specifically requested to publicize the books of the British novelist Joseph Conrad, whom he had met in England during the summer of 1912. Knopf came up with the unique idea of reissuing Conrad's works, eleven in all, in a series under one common imprint. Two years later, he decided to start his own publishing firm. He established his office in a building owned by his father and, armed with $5,000 and a plethora of ideas about how to make books beautifully, Knopf set about making his mark in the world of publishing.

Blanche Wolf, a young woman he had met while a student at Columbia, became Knopf's assistant and, in 1916, his wife. They shared a love of books and a fascination with the borzoi, a Russian wolfhound that originated in the seventeenth century—a cross between an Arabian greyhound and a thick-coated Russian breed. The borzoi became the insignia of Alfred A. Knopf, Inc., and appears on the title pages and spines of most Knopf books. From the beginning, Knopf infused his work with the ideal of excellence. He and his wife were involved in every aspect of publishing, from working directly with writers, reviewing manuscripts, and designing books to advertising and actual production. Knopf is quoted as saying, in an early catalog, that he "loved books physically."

The first title published under the Knopf imprint was a translation of four plays written by Emile Augier, a nineteenth-century French dramatist whose work focused on bourgeois domesticity, realism, and **satire**. The book was printed with orange and blue binding and a Cheltenham typeface. After Knopf's first success, his firm quickly became renowned for the range of type-faces it used. Each Knopf book contains a detailed colophon, an inscription at the end of a book giving facts about its publication, including the typographical design. Early works published by Knopf included those by Thomas Mann, T. S. Eliot, Max Beerbohm, Willa Cather, and Clarence Day. Between 1924 and 1934, Knopf also published *The American Mercury*, a monthly magazine edited by H. L. Mencken, a prominent journalist and political commentator as well as Knopf's mentor.

Blanche Knopf was an equal partner in all things, and many of her successes involved publishing notable works during the **Harlem Renaissance**. For example, the firm of Knopf published the following books by **Langston Hughes**: *The Weary Blues* (1926), *The Dream Keeper* (1932), *Fine Clothes to the Jew* (1927), *Fields of Wonder* (1947), *Not Without Laughter* (1930), *One-Way Ticket* (1949), *Ask Your Mama* (1961), *Selected Poems of Langston Hughes* (1959), and *The Panther and the Lash* (1967), the latter the last collection of poetry by Hughes published in his lifetime. Throughout her time as a publisher, Blanche Knopf remained committed to introducing the American public to African American literature.

Often Knopf chose titles that would prove profitable in the long term, through continuing sales, as evidenced by the firm's all-time best-seller, Kahlil

Gibran's *The Prophet*, which has sold more than 2 million copies. Gibran was one of the most influential Arabic-language writers of the early twentieth century. The work of this artist, poet, and philosopher has since been translated into more than twenty languages.

Other writers published by Knopf include E. M. Forster, D. H. Lawrence, Jean-Paul Sartre, Albert Camus, Sigmund Feud, Franz Kafka, John Updike, Langston Hughes, **Nella Larsen**, John Cheever, André Gide, Barbara Tuchman, Dashiell Hammett, and, more recently, **Ernest James Gaines**, Michael Ondaatje, Elie Wiesel, James Ellroy, V. S. Naipul, Anne Tyler, and **Toni Morrison**. Twenty-one Knopf authors have been honored with the Nobel Prize; twenty-nine have won the National Book Award; forty-nine have received the Pulitzer Prize; and twenty-five have won the National Book Critics Circle Award. The stable of Knopf writers represented an international and cosmopolitan section of the literary world, and Knopf books were easily characterized as some of the most important books of their time.

Knopf publishes poetry, fiction, and cookbooks, and in 1991 it launched Everyman's Library, a series of literary classics reissued in affordable, hardbound editions. Other endeavors have included a series of travel guides and nature guides. Beginning in 1920, Knopf kept in regular correspondence with readers via hardbound chapbooks, first *The Borzoi*, then *The Borzoi Quarterly*, and finally *The Borzoi Reader*.

In April 1960, Alfred A. Knopf, Inc., merged with Random House, which is now the largest English-language trade book publisher in the world. Knopf retained significant autonomy and chairmanship of the company's board of directors. Both Knopf and his wife also held seats on the board of directors of Random House. Throughout his lengthy career, Knopf published thousands of titles, and his imprint continues at Random House, publishing more than 100 titles a year. Beyond publishing, Knopf was passionate about conservation. In his lifetime, he served on the boards of several conservation societies, including the Advisory Board on National Parks, Historic Sites, Buildings and Monuments. Blanche Knopf died in 1966. Knopf survived her for eighteen years, and died on August 11, 1984. Many of the Knopfs' records have been archived at the University of Texas at Austin—an extensive collection documenting the daily activities of the publishing firm.

Resources: Stephen Carter, *The Emperor of Ocean Park* (New York: Knopf, 2002); Ernest J. Gaines, *A Lesson Before Dying* (New York: Knopf, 1993); Langston Hughes, *Selected Poems of Langston Hughes* (New York: Knopf, 1959, 1993); Nella Larsen: *Passing* (New York: Knopf, 1929); *Quicksand* (New York: Knopf, 1928); Toni Morrison: *Beloved* (New York: Knopf, 1987); *Paradise* (New York: Knopf, 1998); *Song of Solomon* (New York: Knopf, 1977).

Roxane Gay

Kocher, Ruth Ellen (born 1965). Poet. Ruth Ellen Kocher is the author of three poetry volumes: *One Girl Babylon* (2003), *When the Moon Knows You're Wandering* (2002), which received the Green Rose Prize; and *Desdemona's Fire*

(1999), winner of the **Naomi Long Madgett** Award. Her poetry has appeared in numerous journals and anthologies and in the Academy of American Poets' permanent Poetry Exhibit (poets.org). Her work has been translated into Persian in the Iranian literary magazine *She'r*.

Kocher spent most of her childhood and adolescence in a housing project in Wilkes-Barre, Pennsylvania. Her first collection, *Desdemona's Fire*, opens with "Poem to a Jazz Man," which—like many of Kocher's poems—interweaves explorations of biracial identity with remembrances of childhood in Pennsylvania. The speaker of this poem is a daughter who imagines her absent father's seduction of her mother, thereby forging a connection with the father she never knew. Kocher repeatedly exploits the tensions between fiction and reality through retellings of classic tales in literature and mythology. Frequently disturbing, sometimes violent, her poems explore ways in which language becomes a tool to work through fear or make peace with haunting memories.

At Pennsylvania State University, where Kocher earned a B.A. in English, she was influenced by the poet Bruce Weigl. She won fellowships from the Bucknell Seminar for Younger Poets and from Cave Canem. Kocher received her M.F.A. in creative writing from Arizona State University, where the poet Norman Dubie encouraged her to find not only what is beautiful in language but also what is unexpected. Kocher also cites as poetic influences Louise Glück, **Audre Lorde**, and Theodore Roethke. After earning a Ph.D. in English at Arizona State, Kocher now teaches creative writing and African American literature at the University of Missouri in **St. Louis**.

Resources: Vanessa Holford Diana, "I Have Lied Again to Get the Story Right: An Interview with Ruth Ellen Kocher," in *Voices of America: Interviews with American Writers* (Cadiz: Aduana Vieja, 2004); Ruth Ellen Kocher: *Desdemona's Fire* (Detroit: Lotus Press, 1999); *One Girl Babylon* (Kalamazoo, MI: New Issues Press, 2003); *When the Moon Knows You're Wandering* (Kalamazoo, MI: New Issues Press, 2002).

Vanessa Holford Diana

Komunyakaa, Yusef (born 1947). Poet. Komunyakaa's poetry reflects his childhood in the racially charged rural **South**, reveals his enthusiasm for **jazz** and literature, and illustrates his experiences as a Black soldier in the **Vietnam War**. Komunyakaa was born and raised in Bogalusa, Louisiana, the youngest of five children. Born James Willie Brown, Komunyakaa legally reclaimed the name Komunyakaa, the surname of his grandparents, who arrived in the United States as stowaways on a ship from Trinidad (Hedges, B2). As a child, Komunyakaa was a self-described daydreamer, spending much of his time either outdoors observing nature or working with his father, a finishing carpenter, whom he describes as a "black Calvinist" and who believed that hard **labor** and endurance led to freedom (*Conversation with Toi Derricotte*). Komunyakaa credits his methodical work with his father as a poetic influence during his childhood. Other early influences, evident in his poetry, include **jazz** and **blues**, which resonated from his mother's wooden radio, and the Bible, which he read twice through to absorb its rhythm (Conley).

Shortly after graduating from high school in 1965, Komunyakaa joined the military and was quickly sent to fight in the Vietnam War. While there, he was an information specialist and, later, editor of *The Southern Cross*, a military newspaper. After his tour of duty, Komunyakaa was awarded the Bronze Star and left the military. At this point in his life, Komunyakaa had written only one poem, a 100-stanza piece in honor of his high school graduating class. He wrote no poetry in Vietnam, though he took with him Hayden Carruth's *The Voice That Is Great Within Us* and Donald Allen's *The New American Poetry* (Lehman).

Yusef Komunyakaa, 1998. James Keyser/Time Life Pictures/Getty Images.

Upon returning to the United States, Komunyakaa pursued a bachelor's degree in English and sociology at the University of Colorado. While there, he took a creative writing class, and he has not stopped writing since. After graduating in 1975, Komunyakaa went on to Colorado State University, where he earned his M.A. in 1979, and then to the University of California at Irvine to pursue an M.F.A. in creative writing, which he received in 1980. During this time Komunyakaa published his first two books of poetry, *Dedications and Other Dark Horses* (1977) and *Lost in the Bonewheel Factory* (1979). Shortly after joining the faculty of the University of New Orleans, Komunyakaa caught the attention of reviewers by publishing *Copacetic* (1984), a collection of jazz-inspired pieces modeled after works by **Langston Hughes** and **Amiri Baraka** (Gwynn, 176).

From **New Orleans, Louisiana**, Komunyakaa traveled north to teach English at Indiana University from 1985 to 1996. While there, he produced some of his most memorable works, including *I Apologize for the Eyes in My Head* (1986), which alludes to his experiences in Vietnam and which won the San Francisco Poetry Center Award, and the critically acclaimed *Dien Cai Dau* (1988), "crazy" in Vietnamese, a full-blown resurrection of Komunyakaa's wartime experiences. *Magic City* (1992), which reflects on his childhood and early manhood, followed. Komunyakaa's *Neon Vernacular* (1993), a compilation of both new and old poetry, was awarded the Pulitzer Prize for poetry, the Kingsley Tufts Award for poetry, and the William Faulkner Prize in 1994.

In 1996, Komunyakaa left Indiana University and held one-year lectureships at the University of California and Washington University. Today, he is a professor of the Council of Humanities and Creative Writing at Princeton University. Since moving to the East Coast, Komunyakaa has published several more books of poems, including *Thieves of Paradise* (1998), *Talking Dirty to the Gods* (2000), *Pleasure Dome: New and Collected Poems, 1975–1999* (2001), and

Scandalize My Name (2002). His most recent work, *Taboo: The Wishbone Trilogy, Part One* (2004), has been described as a "personalized interior mosaic of black history and culture" where myth meets reality (Muratori, 66).

Komunyakaa credits a variety of poets, writers, and genres for inspiring and influencing his works. The first poem he committed to memory was Edgar Allan Poe's "Annabel Lee." Other poetic influences include **Robert Hayden**, Elizabeth Bishop, **James Weldon Johnson**, Ralph Tennyson, Shakespeare, and the **Harlem Renaissance** writers (Lehman). Komunyakaa also studied T. S. Eliot, Ezra Pound, Paul Celan, Aimé Césarie, Baudelaire, the French Surrealists, **Jean Toomer**, **Bob Kaufman**, **Helene Johnson**, and **Amiri Baraka** (Conley). Komunyakaa urges aspiring writers not only to read great literary works, but to be well educated in other fields of knowledge, including science, psychology, anthropology, and history (Lehman).

Resources: **Primary Sources:** Yusef Komunyakaa: *Copacetic* (Middletown, CT: Wesleyan University Press, 1984); *I Apologize for the Eyes in My Head* (Middletown, CT: Wesleyan University Press, 1986); *Lost in the Bonewheel Factory* (Amherst, MA: Lynx House Press, 1979); *Magic City* (Middletown, CT: Weselyan University Press, 1992); *Neon Vernacular: New and Selected Poems* (Middletown, CT: Wesleyan University Press, 1993); *Pleasure Dome: New and Collected Poems* (Middletown, CT: Weselyan University Press, 2001); *Princeton University Creative Writing Program Faculty 1997–1998*, http://www.princeton.edu/-visarts/Yusef1.htm; *Taboo: The Wishbone Trilogy, Part One* (New York: Farrar, 2004); *Talking Dirty to the Gods* (New York: Farrar, Straus, and Giroux, 2000); *Thieves of Paradise* (Middletown, CT: Wesleyan University Press, 1998). **Secondary Sources:** Susan Conley, "About Yusef Komunyakaa," *Ploughshares: The Literary Journal at Emerson College*, http://www.pshares.org/issues/article.cfm?prmArticleid=4251 (May 4, 2005); Toi Derricotte, "Review of *Copacetic, I Apologize for the Eyes in My Head, Dien Cau Dau*, and *Neon Vernacular*, by Yusef Komunyakaa," *Kenyon Review* 15, no. 4 (1993), 217, 222; R. S. Gwynn, ed., *Dictionary of Literary Biography*, vol. 120, *American Poets Since World War II*, 3rd ser. (Detroit: Gale Research, 1992); Chris Hedges, "A Poet of Suffering, Endurance and Healing," *New York Times*, July 8, 2004, metro ed., p. B2; David Lehman, "Interview with Yusef Komunyakaa" (Nov. 10, 1999), http://www.cortlandreview.com/features/millennium/index.html; Thomas F. Marvin, "Komunyakaa's FACING IT," *Explicator* 61, no. 4 (2003), 242–245; Fred Muratori, "Review of *Taboo: The Wishbone Trilogy, Part One*, by Yusef Komunyakaa," *Library Journal*, Sept. 15, 2004, p. 66; "Yusef Komunyakaa," Academy of American Poets, http://www.poets.org/poets/poets.cfm?prmID:23; "Yusef Komunyakaa," University of Central Oklahoma Literature Resource Center (July 11, 2001), http://galenet.galegroup.com; *Yusef Komunyakaa in Conversation with Toi Derricotte* (Santa Fe, NM: Lannan Foundation, 1999).

Julie Claggett

Kool Moe Dee (born 1963). Rap and **hip-hop** artist. Kool Moe Dee is considered a pioneer of **rap** music. Born Mohandas Dewese in **Harlem, New York**, he displayed an early fondness for rhyme in the books of Dr. Seuss and the poetry of **Muhammad Ali**. He showed his rap beginnings at house parties in Harlem, where he grabbed the microphone to demonstrate his ability to compose rhymes. With bandmates L.A. Sunshine and Special K, he formed the Treacherous Three in high school, one of the first hip-hop groups. Together they released popular singles such as "Yes We Can-Can" and "Feel the Heartbeat." Dee launched a solo career when new artists such as Run DMC diminished his band's popularity. In 1986, after completing a degree in communications at the State University of New York at Old Westbury, he released (with Teddy Riley) the hit single "Go See the Doctor," a song about AIDS. His fellow rappers lauded this creation of a classic "old school" rap single. Kool Moe Dee's music is described by one reviewer as having "no gimmicky segues, no fussy overproduction and none of that muddled, mealy-mouthed banter that many younger rappers try to pass off as rhyme" (Morgan). He is well known for his feud with fellow rapper LL Kool J; the two fired lyrical salvos at one another in their compositions. Kool Moe Dee was the first rapper to perform at the Grammy Awards, as the result of 1989's "Knowledge Is King." He was also vocal in his opposition to misogynistic language in rap. In 2003, Dee authored a book titled *There's a God on the Mic: The True 50 Greatest MCs*. In addition to his music and writing, he has numerous minor film and television credits.

Resources: Nelson George, *Buppies, B-Boys, Baps, & Bohos* (Cambridge, MA: Da Capo Press, 2001); Kool Moe Dee, *There's a God on the Mic: The True 50 Greatest MCs* (New York: Thunder's Mouth Press, 2003); "Kool Moe Dee," in *The Virgin Encyclopedia of Popular Music*, ed. Colin Larkin (London: Virgin/Muze, 1997); Joan L. Morgan, "Record Brief" *New York Times*, July 21, 1991, H25; Angela Spence Nelson, "Theology in the Hip-Hop of Public Enemy and Kool Moe Dee," in *The Emergence of Black and the Emergence of Rap*, ed. Jon Michael Spencer (Durham, NC: Duke University Press, 1991), 51–59; Frank Tortorici, "Kool Moe Dee," VH1.com (Aug. 8, 1999), http://www.vh1.com/artists/news/516476/08071999/kool_moe_dee.jhtml.

Mark Wadman

Kweli, Talib (born 1975). Hip-hop artist and social activist. Born in Flatbush, **Brooklyn, New York**, Talib Kweli is considered hip-hop's "conscious son." His original given name was Talib Kweli Greene. Growing up in a household where both parents were professors, Talib Kweli (Arabic for "student of truth") gained a tremendous amount of knowledge from reading and writing short stories, plays, and poetry. This writing eventually helped him create **hip-hop** lyrics. "Hip-hop became a way for me to write and be cool; it gave me a language to speak to my peers," he recalls. In 1997 Kweli released his first single, "Fortified Love," under the name Reflection Eternal. The following year he and his childhood friend Mos Def teamed up to create the group Black Star. Through their music, the hip-hop tandem addressed issues of social consciousness and love within the African American community. An expression of that love was evident when Kweli and Mos Def purchased Brooklyn's oldest

Black-owned bookstore, Nkiru Books, which is now Nkiru Center for Education and Culture, a nonprofit organization promoting literacy and multicultural awareness for people of color.

In 1999 Kweli once again was moved to action, collaborating on a hip-hop album that protested the murder of Amadou Diallo, an African immigrant shot forty-one times by New York City police officers. His first solo compact disk, *Quality*, premiered in 2002. *Quality* proved to be a personal and intelligently crafted album, displaying his lyrical dexterity as well as his vision for freedom and peace. Kweli believes *Quality* was about him growing as a man and as an artist. He also believes that artists should have a sense of responsibility, artistic and social (Wallace). Kweli's second CD, *Beautiful Struggle*, appeared in 2004.

Resources: Talib Kweli: *Beautiful Struggle* (compact disc) (New York: Rawkus, 2004); *Quality* (compact disc) (Los Angeles: MCA, 2002); Earnest M. Wallace, personal interview with Talib Kweli (electronic mail), Sept. 15, 2004.

Earnest M. Wallace

L

Labor. The French philosopher Jean-Paul Sartre wrote, "man may be born a slave . . . or a feudal baron, or a proletarian. But what never varies are the necessities of being in the world, of having to labor and to die there" (303). In other words, no matter whether we are poor or rich, powerful or not, each one of us must be born, we must die, and, in between, we must labor. Labor, in other words, is, along with birth and death, a universally shared experience among all persons. But if work is a central component of identity for every individual, it is even more so for African Americans, whose history is founded on their ancestors having been involuntarily captured and imported as laborers to build America. **Slavery** is the ultimate example not just of labor but of compulsory labor. But in discussing labor as a universal limitation that every person must encounter in some way, Sartre goes on to write that "every human purpose presents itself as an attempt either to surpass these limitations, or to widen them, or else to deny or to accommodate oneself to them" (304). In other words, we can welcome labor as a part of our identity, or we can try to resist it because of the way it limits our identity. From past days of **slavery** to more contemporary times of **affirmative action** debates, each of these responses to labor has been an important theme explored in the literature of African American writers.

African American work songs and **folktales** are full of imaginary characters who represent different responses to the painful labors required by slavery. Because slavery is all about compulsory work, it is not surprising that many stereotypes of African Americans are also about work—either being able to work incredibly hard and long, like **John Henry**, or being lazy and tricky, like Brer Rabbit. We can see that John Henry's identity as a man is shaped by his ability to work hard, even harder and longer than a machine: "John Henry said to his captain,/A man ain't nothin' but a man,/But before I'll let dat steam drill beat me down,/I'll die wid my hammer in my hand" (Gates and McKay, 46). Labor is so important to him that he would rather die than quit. But the trickster Brer Rabbit would rather do anything than work: "Brer Rabbit got tired about three minutes after he started [clearing new ground], but he couldn't say anything if he didn't want to hear the other animals calling him lazy" (Gates and McKay, 119). Women, like men, also had to confront the "necessity of labor" and were also, like men, caught between two stereotypes of being a hard worker and looking to get something for free. **Margaret Abigail Walker**'s 1937 poem "For My People" tells us her enslaved ancestors' labors included "washing ironing cooking scrub/bing sewing mending hoeing plowing digging planting pruning/ patching" (Gates and McKay, 1572): the length of her list gives us an idea of just how much work was performed by women during slavery. One of the folktales collected by novelist and anthropologist **Zora Neale Hurston** explains "Why the Sister in Black Works Hardest": the Black sister moved the bundle dropped by God because neither the White mistress, "ole massa," nor the slave man would, and because she foolishly believed "there's nearly always something good in great big boxes," she opened it up only to find that "it was full of hard work" (Gates and McKay, 111). We begin to see, then, that most folktales recognize and discuss the importance of labor—either performing it or escaping it.

While work songs and folktales were circulated orally within the African American community itself, published **slave narratives** designed to circulate through the White community as a means of abolishing slavery tend to emphasize the capacity of African Americans to work hard. Sometimes the hard work is celebrated as a means of stepping toward freedom and independence, but sometimes it is presented as sheer drudgery that serves no constructive purpose. In perhaps the best-known slave narrative, **Frederick Douglass** writes, "It was a step toward freedom to be allowed to bear the responsibility of a freeman, and I was determined to hold on upon it. I bent myself to the work of making money." When his owner no longer allowed Douglass to make contracts for his own labor, Douglass writes that "instead of seeking work, as I had been accustomed to do previously to hiring my time, I spent the whole week without the performance of a single stroke of work. I did this in retaliation" (Gates and McKay, 359). Douglass realized that his skilled labor was a source of power for his master, and so he learned to control that power and to use it for his own journey to freedom. Likewise, in **Harriet Ann Jacobs**'s slave narrative *Incidents in the Life of a Slave Girl* (1861), we learn that Harriet's grandmother worked so hard selling baked goods that she was able to accumulate the substantial sums of money required to buy many of her family members' freedom (Gates and McKay, 210).

But for other slaves who told their stories, hard labor was no guarantee of freedom or respect. **Sojourner Truth** knew that her hard work in the fields in some ways handicapped her ability to be respected as woman: "I have plowed, and planted, and gathered into barns, and no man could head me—and ar'n't I a woman? I could work as much and eat as much as a man (when I could get it), and bear de lash as well—and ar'n't I a woman?" (Gates and McKay, 200). Frado, the heroine of *Our Nig* (1859), labors and serves and toils throughout her entire life for little in return except a broken body. For some, labor can be redemptive; for others, it seems to only punish.

As the legal system of plantation slavery gave way to sharecropping, and as great numbers of Southern African Americans moved north to seek work in the factories vacated by White men called to fight **World War I**, images of work in African American literature became more psychologically potent, whether the labor was welcomed or not. Early in the twentieth century, the African American intellectuals **Booker T. Washington** and **W.E.B. Du Bois** acknowledged the centrality of work to the formation of African American character and destiny, but disagreed about its consequences. Crediting his own success to the work ethic he was able to demonstrate as a school custodian, Washington nonetheless was sensitive to the ways the legacy of slavery complicated attitudes about labor: "The whole machinery of slavery was so constructed as to cause labour, as a rule, to be looked upon as a badge of degradation, of inferiority. Hence labour was something that both races on the slave plantation sought to escape" (Gates and McKay, 497).

In his famous "Atlanta Exposition Address" (1895), however, Washington urges White businessmen to hire African American laborers rather than draw from the new waves of European immigrants whose backgrounds would make them more likely to join unions, assuring them that African Americans would be grateful for the work even while they remained satisfied with social separation. In Sartre's language, this might be seen as a stand that argues for "accommodating" oneself to certain limitations, since Washington urged that African Americans be trained as manual laborers rather than for positions of leadership. On the other hand, Du Bois argues in *Souls of Black Folk* that to train African Americans only as manual laborers was a continued means of oppression; instead, he argued for the development of "a **talented tenth**" who could lead the African American people toward greater economic development and therefore justice. For Du Bois, it was education, not labor, that would deliver his community away from the despairing legacy of slavery and toward "the greater ideals of the American Republic" (Gates and McKay, 617–619).

Many subsequent twentieth-century writers have continued to explore the relationship between African Americans and labor, and most seem to focus on expressing the psychological damage of Booker T. Washington's emphasis on "the dignity of common labor." When the protagonist of **Richard Wright**'s novel *Native Son* (1940) realizes he will not be allowed to train as a pilot, he instead takes a job as chauffeur to a wealthy White family. His physical and psychological discomfort during his job interview is severe: we feel the painful oppression under which he suffers as he can find no place to put his hands, his body, or even his eyes. He is nearly paralyzed with fear and hatred that will soon explode. **Ralph Ellison**'s protagonist in *Invisible Man* (1952) begins his journey north full of Washington-like confidence that he will find a fulfilling job; he soon finds himself working at a paint factory where he is much despised and nearly killed by the only other African American, old Mr. Brockway, who yells upon seeing him, "Union!...I knowed you belonged to that bunch of trouble-making foreigners! I knowed it! Git out! Git out of my basement!...You two-bit, trouble-making union louse!"

Langston Hughes's poetry often expresses empathy for working people and their condition. Jesse B. Simple of Hughes's "Simple" stories and Alberta K. Johnson of the "Madam" poems are both working-class individuals. In the 1930s, Hughes's poetry reflected his interest in Marxist and socialist ideas. This poetry includes "Ballads [sic] of Lenin," "Chant for Tom Mooney," "Good Morning Revolution," "One More 'S' in the U.S.A.," "Revolution," and "Song of the Revolution" (Ostrom). Hughes also wrote plays with labor-related themes (Duffy) and, with **James P. Johnson**, he collaborated on the "**blues** opera" *De Organizer*.

The psychological pressures and spiritual alienation that arise in many stories about modern factory work are expressed by **Ann Lane Petry** in her 1946 story "Like a Winding Sheet" (Gates and McKay, 1478) as she shows how a happy couple whose home had been a safe haven from work is destroyed through domestic abuse after the husband's White female boss has called him a "nigger" on the factory floor. Petry's novel *The Street*, also from 1946, and **Sarah Elizabeth Wright**'s *This Child's Gonna Live* (1969) both make clear the way children can be preyed upon when one or both of their parents are compelled to work far from home. But there are, of course, many positive images of the empowering qualities of labor when it is performed for the right reasons under the right conditions. Many of the short stories published in magazines such as *The Crisis* and *Opportunity* during the 1930s show how African Americans working together can transform their lives; **Alice Walker**'s Celie from *The Color Purple* (1982) labors over her sewing machine to make "folkspants"; **John Edgar Wideman**'s *Brothers and Keepers* (1984), like **James Baldwin**'s "Sonny's Blues" (1957), considers the ways that middle-class jobs such as teaching and writing can lift some people out of the ghetto life that is characterized by deep generational patterns of unemployment.

The inherent unfairness of some folks being able to escape compulsory labor while others cannot is best illustrated in the many literary representations of "the flying Africans," those who "rose on the air. They flew in a flock that was black against the heavenly blue...they went so high. Way above the plantation, way over slavery land. Say they flew away to *Free-dom*....They say that the children of the ones who could not fly told their children. And now, me, I have told it to you" (Hamilton 171–172). (*See* **Marxism**.)

Resources: Primary Sources: Ralph Ellison, *Invisible Man* (1952; repr. New York: Vintage Books, 1989); Henry Louis Gates, Jr., and Nellie Y. McKay, eds., *Norton Anthology of African American Literature* (New York: Norton, 1996); Virginia Hamilton, *The People Could Fly: American Black Folktales* (1985; repr. New York: Knopf, 1993);

Jean Paul Sartre, "Existentialism Is a Humanism," in *Existentialism from Dostoevsky to Sartre*, ed. Walter Kaufmann (Cleveland and New York: Meridian–World, 1956), 287–311; Richard Wright, *Native Son* (1940; repr. New York: HarperPerennial, 1993); Sarah E. Wright, *This Child's Gonna Live* (1969; repr. New York: Feminist Press, 2002). **Secondary Sources:** American Social History Project, *Who Built America? Working People and the Nation's Economy, Politics, Culture and Society*, 2 vols. (New York: Pantheon, 1989–1992); Teresa L. Amott and Julie A. Matthaei, *Race, Gender and Work: A Multicultural Economic History of Women in the United States* (Boston: South End Press, 1991); Susan Duffy, ed., *The Political Plays of Langston Hughes* (Carbondale: Southern Illinois University Press, 2000); Alferdteen Harrison, ed., *Black Exodus: The Great Migration from the American South* (Jackson: University Press of Mississippi, 1991); Hans Ostrom, *A Langston Hughes Encyclopedia* (Westport, CT: Greenwood Press, 2002), 229, 233, 356–358; Howard Zinn, *A People's History of the United States* (New York: HarperPerennial, 1990).

Jennifer Campbell

Ladd, Florence (born 1932). Novelist, nonfiction writer, psychologist, teacher, administrator, and social critic. Ladd has achieved acclaim as a writer of both nonfiction and fiction. The daughter of teachers, Ladd was raised in **Washington, D.C.** She became interested in psychology after typing term papers for her mother. In 1953, Ladd graduated from Howard University with a psychology degree and completed graduate work in 1958, receiving a Ph.D. in social psychology from the University of Rochester. She gained her first teaching experience at Simmons College. After her husband received a Fulbright scholarship, Ladd followed him to Turkey and taught at Robert College and the American College for Girls in Istanbul. She returned to the United States in 1965 and began teaching at Harvard University's Graduate School of Education and the Graduate School of Design, positions that allowed her to pursue her interest in psychology and environmental studies. She has also taught at the Massachusetts Institute of Technology and at Wellesley College, where she was employed as dean of students, and became the director of the Mary Ingraham Bunting Institute at Radcliffe College, the center of advanced studies for women, in 1989.

For a brief period, Ladd was a research consultant with the Institute of International Education's South African Education Program, and served as a liaison to the United Nations as a result of her employment at Oxfam America. She was a trustee of the National Council for Research on Women, has been an overseer of the Museum of Fine Arts in **Boston, Massachusetts**, and is currently a trustee of Hampshire College. She held fellowships at the Bunting Institute and at the W.E.B. Du Bois Institute, and was a resident fellow at the MacDowell Colony. In 1998, she taught fiction writing at the Women's Institute for Continuing Education in **Paris, France**.

Much of Ladd's writing centers on social justice and activism, feminist principles, and a sense of community and relationships. Florence Ladd published her first novel, *Sarah's Psalm*, in 1996. It received the Literary Award for

Best Fiction from the Black Caucus of the American Library Association. *Sarah's Psalm* speaks on the relevance of cross-continental relationships, most specifically those between African American women and their counterparts in Africa. The novel delves into the difficulty of a woman combining her love of career and her respect for her marriage. Ladd's nonfiction has been published in several anthologies, including *A Stranger in the Village* and *Dutiful Daughters*, and she coauthored *Different Strokes: Pathways to Maturity in the Boston Ghetto* (1979).

Resources: Yvonne Crittenden, "A Mystical Journey to Africa," *Canoe* (Sept. 29, 1996), http://www.jdeq.com/JamBooksReviewsS/sarahpsalm_ladd.html; *The Feminist Sexual Ethics Project*, Brandeis University, http://www.brandeis.edu/projects/fse/Pages/board1.html; "Florence Ladd: Biography," *History Makers*, http://www.thehistorymakers.com/biography.asp?bioindex=444&category=educationMakers; Jean Gould, ed., *Dutiful Daughters: Caring for Our Parents as They Grow Old* (Seattle, WA: Seal Press, 1999); Farah J. Griffin and Cheryl J. Fish, eds., *A Stranger in the Village: Two Centuries of African American Travel Writing* (Boston: Beacon Press, 1998); Florence Ladd, *Sarah's Psalm* (New York: Scribner's, 1996); Florence Ladd et al., *Different Strokes: Pathways to Maturity in the Boston Ghetto* (Boulder, CO: Westview Press, 1976); Wilma Slaight, "Florence Ladd," Wellesley College, http://www.wellesley.edu/Anniversary/ladd.html.

Anne Marie Fowler

Lamar, Jake (born 1961). Novelist, journalist, teacher, and editor. A New York native, Lamar graduated cum laude from Harvard University. Within six months of graduating, he was hired at *Time* magazine (Wells). He served as a staff writer and associate editor at *Time*, and contributed to the "Milestones" and "Nation" sections of the publication between 1983 and 1989; he also contributed to *Esquire*, the *New York Times*, and *Details*. Upon leaving *Time*, Lamar published his first work, *Bourgeois Blues* (1991), a memoir that deals with Lamar's personal struggle to find his own racial and social identity as a middle-class Black man. He then moved to Ann Arbor, Michigan, for financial reasons, and began his first novel, *The Last Integrationist* (1996). In 1992, Lamar was awarded the Lyndhurst Prize, a three-year grant for his work *Bourgeois Blues*. The award enabled Lamar to relocate to **Paris, France**, in 1993, and he still resides there.

Besides *Bourgeois Blues* and *The Last Integrationist*, Lamar's literary works include *Close to the Bone* (1998); *If 6 Were 9* (2001), also published in French as *Le Chaméleon Noir*; and *Rendezvous Eighteenth* (2003). Inspired primarily by the works and life of **James Baldwin**, Lamar has attempted to assess the effects of American race relations in both mainstream novels and mystery or thriller books (Wells). Characters in Lamar's novels typically face challenges in defining their racial or social identities as they struggle to escape politically or socially charged scandals in America or Paris. Lamar currently teaches History of African-American Music and Culture at the École Polytechnique in Paris, works as a freelance writer, and is working on his fifth book, based on minor characters from *Rendezvous Eighteenth*.

Resources: Jake Lamar: *Bourgeois Blues* (New York: Summit Books, 1991); *Close to the Bone* (New York: Crown, 1998); *If 6 Were 9* (New York: Crown, 2001), also in French as *Le Chaméléon Noir* (Paris: Rivages, 2001); *The Last Integrationist* (New York: Crown, 1996); *Rendezvous Eighteenth* (New York: Minotaur, 2003); Monique Wells, "The Africana Profile: Novelist Jake Lamar" (Apr. 27, 2004), Africana.com, http://www .africana.com/articles/daily/bk20040427lamar.asp.

Allison Bennett

Lane, Pinkie Gordon (born 1923). Poet, scholar, and teacher. Lane's numerous literary achievements include being nominated for a Pulitzer Prize in 1979 for her book *Mystic Female* and being the first African American woman to receive a Ph.D. at Louisiana State University in 1967. A native of **Philadelphia, Pennsylvania**, Lane moved to **Atlanta, Georgia**, in 1945 to attend Spelman College on a four-year scholarship. In 1949, she graduated magna cum laude with a bachelor's degree in English and married Ulysses Simpson Lane. Over the next seven years she taught public school in Florida and Georgia and went on to earn a master's degree from Atlanta University in 1956, after which she moved with her husband to Baton Rouge, Louisiana. She taught from 1957 to 1959 at Leland College in Baker, Louisiana, before taking a job at Southern University, where she eventually became a full professor and was appointed director of the English Department, a position she held from 1974 until her retirement in 1986.

Lane's early interest in creative writing focused on fiction. After she was introduced to the poetry of **Gwendolyn Brooks** in the early 1960s, Lane moved toward writing poetry. Her first published poem, "This Treasured Book," appeared in **Phylon**, a periodical published by Atlanta University, in 1961. Other poems have been published in such periodicals as **Callaloo**, *Southern Review*, *Ms.*, **Black American Literature Forum**, and *African American Review*. Her first book of poetry was titled *Wind Thoughts* (1972). It was followed by *The Mystic Female* (1978), *I Never Scream: New and Selected Poems* (1985), *Girl at the Window* (1991), and *Elegy for Etheridge* (2000).

Lane's work has appeared in numerous anthologies, and she has served as editor or contributing editor for several periodicals and collections. In addition to the Pulitzer nomination, she won an Image Award from the **NAACP**, a National Award for Achievement in Poetry from the **College Language Association**, a Black Caucus of National Council of Teachers of English Award of Recognition for Artistic Achievement, and a Middle Atlantic Writers Association Creative Achievement Award, among others. She served as Louisiana's first African American poet laureate from 1989 to 1992, as visiting distinguished professor at the University of Northern Iowa from 1993 to 1994, and as DuPont Scholar at Bridgewater College in 1994.

Resources: Primary Sources: Ann Dobie, *An Anthology of Contemporary Louisiana Poets* (Baton Rouge: Louisiana State University Press, 1998); Pinkie Gordon Lane: *Elegy for Etheridge* (Baton Rouge: Louisiana State University Press, 2000); *Girl at the Window: Poems* (Baton Rouge: Louisiana State University Press, 1991); *I Never*

Scream: New and Selected Poems (Detroit: Lotus Press, 1985); *A Literary Profile to 1977* (Baton Rouge: P. G. Lane, 1977); *The Mystic Female* (Fort Smith, AR: South and West, 1978); *Poems to My Father* (Baton Rouge: Pinkie Gordon Lane, 1972); *Songs to the Dialysis Machine* (Baton Rouge: Pinkie Gordon Lane, 1972); *Wind Thoughts* (Fort Smith, AR: South and West, 1972). **Secondary Sources:** Violet Harrington Bryan, "Evocations of Place and Culture in the Works of Four Contemporary Black Louisiana Writers: Brenda Marie Osbey, Sybil Kein, Elizabeth Brown-Guillory, and Pinkie Gordon Lane," *Louisiana Literature* 4 (Fall 1987), 49–60; Stephen Henderson, *Understanding the New Black Poetry: Black Speech and Black Music as Poetic References* (New York: Morrow, 1973); "Pinkie Gordon Lane," *Biography Resource Center* (2004), http://galenet .galegroup.com.servlet/BioRC; Kalumu ya Salaam, ed., *Word Up: Black Poetry of the 80s from the Deep South* (Atlanta: Beans and Brown Rice, 1990).

Shelley Martin

Langston, John Mercer (1829–1897). Activist, lecturer, and autobiographer. A figure more important to African American history than literature, Langston nonetheless published an important **autobiography** and several speeches.

The son of a wealthy White planter, Ralph Quarles, and of Lucy Jane Langston, a slave of mixed ethnicity whom Quarles had emancipated in 1806, Langston was born in Louisa County, Virginia. Both of his parents died when he was young, and his older brothers took him to Ohio, where he lived with William Gooch, a friend of his father's, between 1834 and 1839. When the Gooch family moved to Missouri, a court determined that both Langston's person and a sizable inheritance from his father would be threatened in a slave state. For the next five years, he boarded with several different families in Ohio. He received his A.B. degree from Oberlin College in 1849 and hoped to study law, but he was refused admission to law school. Instead, he returned to Oberlin, and graduated from its theology program in 1853.

Instead of the ministry, though, Langston chose local politics. He read law with Philemon Bliss, and in 1854 he became the first African American to be admitted to the Ohio bar. The next year, he became the first African American elected official, winning election as the township clerk of Brownhelm, the population of which was mostly White. For more than a decade, Langston was a force in Oberlin-area politics and made a name for himself as both a lawyer and an abolitionist. In the 1860s, he helped to recruit African American troops for the **Civil War**, and he was elected president of the newly founded National Equal Rights League. During **Reconstruction**, he lectured nationally for equal rights and gained a national reputation in the Republican Party. Some of these lectures were published individually as pamphlets, and in 1883 he issued a collection of lectures, *Freedom and Citizenship*.

Langston moved to **Washington, D.C.**, where he founded Howard University's law department in 1869; eventually he would serve as the university's acting president, but was denied the presidency by university trustees. He held positions on the District of Columbia's Board of Health (1871–1878), as minister to **Haiti** (1877–1885), and as president of the all-Black Virginia

Normal and Collegiate Institute in Petersburg (1885–1887). He ran for Congress after Democrats in the area forced him out of the Institute presidency. The election results were hotly contested, and Langston ended up only serving a few months of his term, as the first African American congressman from Virginia. Returning to Washington, he continued to practice law and lecture. In 1894, Langston published his autobiography, *From the Virginia Plantation to the National Capitol.*

Langston's family retained a prominent national position. Charles, his older brother, was the husband of Langston Hughes's grandmother, Mary Leary. (Mary Leary's first husband, Sheridan Leary, had been killed in **John Brown**'s raid on Harper's Ferry in 1859.) **Langston Hughes** was, therefore, Langston's grand-nephew.

The town of Langston, **Oklahoma**, is named after Langston, as is Langston University, located in the town. (*See* **Abolitionist Movement**.)

Resources: William Cheek and Aimee Lee Cheek: "John Mercer Langston," in *Black Leaders of the Nineteenth Century*, ed. Leon Litwack and August Meier (Urbana: University of Illinois Press, 1988), 102–126; *John Mercer Langston and the Fight for Black Freedom, 1829–1865* (Urbana: University of Illinois Press, 1989);

John Mercer Langston, c. 1870. Courtesy of the Library of Congress.

Hans Ostrom, *A Langston Hughes Encyclopedia* (Westport, CT: Greenwood Press, 2002).

Eric Gardner

Langston Hughes Society (1981–present). The Langston Hughes Society is the first scholarly association named in honor of an African American writer. It is a national association of scholars, teachers, creative and performing artists, students, and lay persons who promote the life and legacy of **Langston Hughes**. The first African American to make his living solely by his pen, Hughes wrote in every genre, with the possible exception of formal literary criticism. Throughout his four decades of literary creativity that is virtually unrivaled in American letters, Hughes wrote poetry, **drama**, **autobiography**, history, fiction, prose comedy, and juvenile literature. He edited anthologies, wrote libretti, perfected the Black **gospel** song-play, and collaborated on translations. Hughes wrote more than fifty books.

The formation of the Langston Hughes Society occurred in three stages. First, the Langston Hughes Study Conference in Joplin, Missouri (Hughes's birthplace), on March 13–14, 1981, served as the catalyst for the society. Sponsored by Missouri Southern State College and funded by the Missouri Committee for the Humanities, the conference attempted to assess the status of Langston

Hughes in contemporary American literature and attracted scholars from across the country as well as students and the general public.

Second, the founding meeting of the society was held in the **Baltimore, Maryland**, home of Therman and Lillian O'Daniel on June 26, 1981, the date Hughes received the **NAACP** Springarn Medal in 1960. O'Daniel edited the widely read collection of essays *Langston Hughes: Black Genius*, and he first expressed the idea to form the Langston Hughes Society. George Bass (Providence, Rhode Island), Faith D. Berry (McLean, Virginia), Alice A. Deck (Grinnell, Iowa), Akiba Sullivan Harper (Atlanta, Georgia), Therman O'Daniel, and Eloise Y. Spicer (Woodrow Wilson High School, Washington, D.C.) launched the Langston Hughes Society.

Third, in October 1981, the six founding members, with a statement on the purpose and membership of the Society, met in Atlanta at the home of Millicent Dobbs Jordan, who had known Langston Hughes while he was a visiting teacher in the Atlanta University Center. Initial officers of the society were Richard K. Barksdale, University of Illinois (president); Millicent Dobbs Jordan, Spelman College (vice president); Alice A. Deck, Grinnell College (secretary-treasurer); Therman B. O'Daniel, Morgan State University (editor); and George Houston Bass, Brown University (executor/trustee of the Langston Hughes estate and executive editor). Presidents of the Society have included Richard K. Barksdale, University of Illinois (1981–1983); **R. Baxter Miller**, University of Tennessee (1984–1990); Ruthe T. Sheffey, Morgan State University (1990–1992); Akiba Sullivan Harper, Spelman College (1992–1998); Leonard A. Slade, Jr., State University of New York at Albany (1998–2000); and **Dolan Hubbard**, Morgan State University (2000–present).

The Langston Hughes Review, the official publication of the Langston Hughes Society, was first published in 1982. Its editors have included Therman B. O'Daniel, Morgan State University (1982–1983); Charles H. Nichols and Berry Beckman, Brown University (1984), George Houston Bass, Brown University (1985–1989); Amrijit Singh, Rhode Island College (1990–1991); and Thadious Davis, Brown University (1992). Corporate editors have been Dorothy Denniston, **Michael S. Harper**, **Michael E. Dyson**, and Elmo Terry Morgan, Brown University (1983); R. Baxter Miller, University of Georgia (1994–1995); Dolan Hubbard, University of Georgia (1995–1998); and Valerie Babb, University of Georgia (1999–present). The Society welcomes scholars and laypersons who are interested in promoting the legacy of Langston Hughes.

Resources: Faith Berry, "The Universality of Langston Hughes," *Langston Hughes Review* 1, no. 2 (Fall 1982), 1–10; Alice A. Deck, "The Langston Hughes Society: Its Inaugural Year," *Langston Hughes Review* 1, no. 2 (Fall 1982), 27–28; Dolan Hubbard, "Langston Hughes Society," in *Organizing Black America: An Encyclopedia of African American Associations*, ed. Nina Mjagkij (New York: Garland, 2001), 299–300; R. Baxter Miller, "Langston Hughes," in *Dictionary of Literary Biography*, vol. 51, *Afro-American Writers from the Harlem Renaissance to 1940*, eds. Trudier Harris and

Thadious M. Davis (Detroit: Gale Research, 1987), 112–133; Web page, http://www
.langstonhughessociety.org.

Dolan Hubbard

Lanusse, Armand (1812–1867). Poet, editor, short story writer, and educator. A native of **New Orleans, Louisiana**, Lanusse, a French **Creole**, was a
major contributor to the literary arts in francophone Louisiana during the
1840s whose writing reflected an affiliation with French Romanticism.
Though Lanusse is most recognized as a poet, in 1843 he published a short
story, "Un Mariage de Conscience" (A Marriage of Conscience) in *L'Album
Littéraire, Journal des Jeunes Gens, Amateurs de Litterature!*, a monthly review of
Creole writing in Louisiana. Though the journal was short-lived, its purpose
influenced Lanusse, who in 1845 edited *Les Cenelles*, the first anthology of
poetry written by people of color in the United States. Its title, roughly
translated as "hawthorn fruit" (an indigenous fruit of Louisiana), sought to
capture the place of free men of color (*gens de couleur libre*) in a society divided
between free Whites and a majority enslaved Black population. In addition to
writing the dedication and introduction to the collection of eighty-five poems,
Lanusse contributed eighteen poems. Though the collection is noteworthy for
its place in Black writing in the United States, the poems in the collection are
at times most noted for their lack of engagement in Black racial identity,
challenges to **slavery**, and calls for Black liberation. Therefore, the poetry in
Les Cenelles differs significantly from works of other nineteenth-century Black
writers, including such figures as **Jupiter Hammon, George Moses Horton**,
and **Frances Ellen Watkins Harper**, to name a few.

In this regard, Régine Latortue and Gleason R. W. Adams write, "Trapped
between races, between classes, and between cultures, the Louisiana Creoles could
not or would not confront the problems and conflicts that blacks, no matter how
elevated, experienced" ("Preface," *Les Cenelles*, xiii). Despite these limitations,
Lanusse is still considered as having at least vaguely confronted the system of
plaçage in two of his poems, "Epigramme" and "To Elora." While the poems are
considered "modest" in quality, some of the anthology's contributors garnered
critical acclaim during their era, including **Victor Séjour**, who enjoyed temporary
prominence as one of the most prolific and celebrated playwrights working in
Paris, France. While it is uncertain whether Lanusse ever resided in Paris, both
Séjour and Pierre Dalcour, another contributor to the collection, were contemporaries of Alexandre Dumas Père and Victor Hugo. Following his literary
career, Lanusse was an educator and school principal at the Catholic School for
Indigent Orphans of Color in New Orleans. Here, in his education experiences,
Lanusse is considered as most likely having made his most substantial contribu-
tion to Black life. He died in New Orleans in 1867.

Resources: Edward Maceo Coleman, ed., *Creole Voices: Poems in French by Free Men
of Color, First Published in 1845. A Centennial Edition* (Washington, DC: Associated
Publishers, 1945); Michel Fabre, "The New Orleans Connection," in his *From Harlem*

to Paris: Black American Writers in France, 1840–1980 (Urbana: University of Illinois Press, 1991), 9–21; Blyden Jackson, "Early Abolitionist Poets," in his A History of Afro-American Literature, vol. 1, The Long Beginning, 1746–1895 (Baton Rouge: Louisiana State University Press, 1989), 225–234; John Maxwell Jones, Jr., "The Pre-Civil War Period (1800–1860)," in Slavery and Race in Nineteenth-Century Louisiana-French Literature (Camden, NJ: published by the Author, 1978), 10–57; Armand Lanusse, "Un Mariage de Conscience," L'Album Littéraire, Journal des Jeunes Gens, Amateurs de Litteraire! (1843); Armand Lanusse, ed., Les Cenelles. Choix de Poésies Indigènes (New Orleans: H. Lauve, 1845); Régine Latortue and Gleason R. W. Adams, trans., Les Cenelles. A Collection of Poems by Creole Writers of the Early Nineteenth Century (Boston: G. K. Hall, 1979).

Robin Goldman Vander

Larsen, Nella (1891–1964). Novelist. Known for her work during the **Harlem Renaissance**, Larsen wrote about the politically charged subjects of racial identity and White privilege as well as the social roles and expectations for women in the 1920s. She obscured many of the details of her personal life, which may have been a statement about her privacy or the desire to move between both Black and White cultures. Born in **Chicago, Illinois**, to Mary Hanson Walker, who was Danish, and Peter Walker, who was of West Indian descent, Larsen would not know family life with her parents. Shortly after her birth, her parents separated and her mother married another Dane, Peter Larsen. Soon after Larsen's mother remarried, she gave birth to another daughter. Many scholars speculate that the young Nella may have had a difficult childhood and a tense relationship with her stepfather, since she was the only "non-White" member of her immediate family. This struggle to identify herself as either Black or White, and the social constrictions placed on African Americans, would become a recurring theme throughout her life and her writing.

Regardless of these tensions, Larsen received an excellent education. She attended public schools in Chicago until 1907, when her stepfather enrolled her in Fisk University Normal School. She then attended Fisk University in **Nashville, Tennessee**, from 1909 to 1910. Then she decided to finish her education in Denmark, and audited classes at the University of Copenhagen for two years. Upon returning to the United States, she attended nursing school at Lincoln Hospital in New York City. After graduating from nursing school, she spent a brief time at the Tuskegee Institute, helping to train other nurses and serving as head nurse at John Andrew Memorial Hospital. However, Larsen soon returned to New York, and from 1916 to 1921 she worked as a nurse for both Lincoln Hospital and the Department of Health. During this time she met and married a physicist, Elmer S. Imes.

Shortly after her marriage, Nella Larsen Imes, as she was known, began making the acquaintance of men and women involved in the growing arts movement later known as the Harlem Renaissance. The well-educated Larsen had been interested in writing and began trying to publish her work. One of her particular interests was **children's literature**. **Jessie Redmon Fauset**, another significant female writer of the Harlem Renaissance, was the editor of *The Brownies' Book*, a children's magazine founded by Fauset with **W.E.B Du Bois** and Augustus Dill. The magazine was created with the goal of reducing the stigma many African American children felt about being black. Larsen became a published author for the first time in *The Brownies' Book* by writing two articles about Danish children's games.

As Larsen's interest in literature and the growing Harlem Renaissance increased, she decided to quit her job as a nurse. In 1921 she took a position at the public library in **Harlem, New York**, first working as a library assistant and eventually as the children's librarian. She also attended Columbia University to pursue a degree in library science. This immersion in the literary and arts community of Harlem fueled Larsen's desire to become a full-fledged writer. As she attended school, she immersed herself in writing and worked on

Undated portrait of Nella Larsen. Yale Collection of American Literature, Beinecke Rare Book and Manuscript Library.

several pieces of short fiction that were published under the pen name Allen Semi, which is Nella Imes spelled backward. She was also busy working on what would eventually become her first novel, *Quicksand*. She stayed at the library in Harlem until September 1926, when her first short story, "Correspondence," was published in **Opportunity**. She felt ready to pursue a full-time career in writing.

As the wife of a prominent physicist and with a love of literature and the arts, Larsen had the social prominence to become acquainted with many of the important writers of the Harlem Renaissance. She had already developed a relationship with Jessie Fauset in the early 1920s, and she also came to know **Langston Hughes**, **Carl Van Vechten**, and **Jean Toomer**, who shared her interest in writing about the often difficult situation of being caught between Black and White life and culture. Her association with some of these significant writers helped her land a publishing contract with **Alfred A. Knopf**, one of the most notable and influential publishers of the time.

In 1928, *Quicksand* was published to critical acclaim and won the bronze medal from the Harmon Foundation. *Quicksand*'s heroine is Helga Crane, a woman who struggles with her identity as the daughter of a Danish mother and a Black father, and is then raised by her mother and a cruel White stepfather. The intelligent, yet troubled, Helga moves to **the South**, teaching at an all-Black school, only to find that she feels out of place because of her fair complexion. She continues to move about in search of a place she can call home; her travels take her to Harlem and even Denmark. After what seems to be a nervous breakdown, she decides to marry a Black, Southern man whom she knew from her time as a teacher. Living in a rural Southern community and becoming a mother weighs down Helga and makes her feel as if she is sinking in quicksand. She falls deeper and deeper into a depression. Certainly, Helga Crane's story echoed many of Larsen's own experiences. However, the novel is more than autobiographical fiction, for it serves as a commentary on issues of race and the conventions of women's sexuality.

Larsen's second novel, *Passing* (1929), tackled many of the same issues as its predecessor. However, *Passing* dealt more specifically with the issues of **race** and the practice of **passing**. The novel follows the lives of its two main characters, Clare Kendry and Irene Redfield. As a light-skinned Black woman, Clare escapes poverty by successfully passing as a White woman. She marries a wealthy White man, who thinks she is White, and lives the life of a New York socialite. Clare's childhood friend, Irene, has married a successful Black doctor. When the friends reunite, Clare finds she is attracted to Irene's husband and pursues a relationship with him. Feeling threatened, Irene reveals the truth of Clare's racial heritage to her husband. In a climactic ending to the story, Clare falls out of a window before her husband can confront her about the truth. Having a much more dramatic storyline than *Quicksand*, *Passing* deals directly with the problematic practice of passing that many African American men and women felt pressured to do during this era. As a commentary on both the narrowness of the Black bourgeois and the sometimes shifting color line, Larsen's novel was politically and socially significant in both African American and White communities at the time of its publication.

The publications of *Quicksand* and *Passing* sealed Nella Larsen as a significant literary figure not only in the Harlem Renaissance but also in the first half of the twentieth century. As the first African American woman to win a Guggenheim fellowship for creative writing, she was a critically acclaimed and celebrated writer. However, her career was cut short by scandal. In the same year she won the Guggenheim, she published the short story "Sanctuary" in *Forum* magazine. The story is about a man who seeks refuge at a friend's mother's house after shooting someone. As the story unfolds, the man comes to realize that the person he has shot is the friend whose mother has given him sanctuary. Although it was a powerful story, it was quickly compared with a story published in the early 1920s, and Larsen was accused of plagiarism. She was able to prove her innocence of such accusations and even published a follow-up essay in *Forum*, "The Author's Explanation." However, the public sting of the accusations all but ended her career. With the money from the Guggenheim, she tried to escape the humiliation caused by the allegations and traveled to Europe to work on her next novel. It was subsequently turned down by Knopf.

By 1933, Larsen began experiencing marital problems, and because of her notoriety, she suffered through a divorce that was sensationalized in the press, including rumors of infidelity and attempted suicide. After her divorce, Larsen kept to herself and desperately sought privacy. Using her full married name, she lived as Nella Larsen Imes, cutting off connections with her literary friends and ending her career as a writer. She returned to nursing and lived and worked in obscurity in New York City until her death in 1964.

Resources: Hazel Carby, "The Quicksands of Representation," in her *Reconstructing Womanhood: The Emergence of the Afro-American Woman Novelist* (Oxford: Oxford University Press, 1987); Barbara Christian, *Black Women Novelists: The Development of a Tradition, 1892–1976* (Westport, CT: Greenwood Press, 1980); Thadious Davis, *Nella Larsen, Novelist of the Harlem Renaissance: A Woman's Life Unveiled* (Baton Rouge: Louisiana State University Press, 1994); Nella Larsen, *Quicksand* and *Passing*, ed. Deborah McDowell (New Brunswick, NJ: Rutgers University Press, 1986); Charles R. Larson, *Invisible Darkness: Jean Toomer and Nella Larsen* (Iowa City: University of Iowa Press, 1993); Jacquelyn McLendon, *The Politics of Color in the Fiction of Jessie Fauset and Nella Larsen* (Charlottesville: University Press of Virginia, 1995).

Melissa Hamilton Hayes

Last Poets, The. Poets, musicians, and activists. On May 19, 1968, three young poets, David Nelson, **Abiodun Oyewole**, and Gylan Kain, walked on stage in Mount Morris Park in **Harlem, New York** (now **Marcus Garvey Park**). It was **Malcolm X** Day. They had come with hundreds of others to honor the memory of Malcolm X on his forty-third birthday. The moment they took the stage, the history of American music changed forever.

To appreciate the significance of The Last Poets, it is necessary to imagine the political and social climate of the times. By 1968, hopefulness in Black communities was fading. Lyndon Johnson's Great Society program was undermined by the high cost of the **Vietnam War. Martin Luther King, Jr.**, had been assassinated on April 4, and Robert F. Kennedy would suffer the same fate on June 6. The country was spiraling into chaos fueled by racism, poverty, and violence. There were riots in eleven cities after King's assassination. The community felt deeply betrayed by the White political establishment. Without its most powerful and prominent leaders, there seemed to be a political and cultural void in the Black community (D'Ambrosio, 1).

Enter the Last Poets, pioneers of **hip-hop**. The impact of their first performance was explosive. It sent shock waves of rhythm and rebellion rippling across generations. But they needed a name to symbolize the hope and commitment they wanted to communicate. David Nelson read a poem by a South African poet, "Towards a Walk in the Sun." The last line reads: "The only poem you will hear will be the spear point pivoted in the punctured marrow of the villain." Nelson amended it to read: "Therefore, we are the 'last poets' of the world" (Mills, G1). This apocalyptic vision became part of the message of the Last Poets. They also sang about the beauty of Black people: all the shades from yellow and beige to black, with a love as "sweet as scuppernong wine."

The Last Poets were deeply influenced by the **Black Arts Movement**, whose purpose was African American liberation. Because of their militant message they earned the title "bards of Black pride and revolution." In retrospect, the roots of **rap** music can be traced back to the late 1960s and the birth of The Last Poets. Militant messages decrying the state of society and African Americans were first vocalized by The Last Poets, the purveyors of sharp, insightful street poetry that, combined with African percussive rhythms, laid the groundwork for future rap artists.

The Last Poets released several albums during their career. The first two, "Last Poets" and "This is Madness," are considered classics, not just because of the originality of the music but also because of the powerful compositions, which articulated the feelings of an oppressed people. When first released, these albums found success on both the R&B and pop charts. With little promotion or marketing, they quickly sold over a million copies (D'Ambrosio, 2).

Unfortunately, during this period the group experienced irreparable conflicts that destroyed their unity. The change in personnel was considerable: Don Babatunde joined in 1991; Umar Bin Hassan joined in 1969, left in 1972, rejoined in 1973, and left in 1979; Sulieman El-Hadi joined in 1972 and died in 1995; Jalal joined in 1969; Gylan Kain left in 1969; Felipe Luciano joined in 1968 and left in 1969; David Nelson left in 1968; Nilija died in 1981; and Abiodun Oyewole left in 1969.

Throughout the 1970s and 1980s, Jalal and El-Hadi recorded as The Last Poets. They also released *Vibes from the Scribes: Selected Poems*. In 1995, The Last Poets, featuring Abiodun Oyewole and Umar Bin Hassan, released "Holy Terror." Guest musicians included Bootsy Collins, George Clinton, and Grand Master Melle Mel.

Oyewole and Hassan are now the principal members of The Last Poets. In 1996, they released *On a Mission: Selected Poems and a History of the Last Poets*, and are still determined to deliver their message: "We're no more godfathers of the spoken word than the man in the moon; it comes in a package from the motherland. But we accept that there is work out there that we can do. People need to see a focal point, a beacon, and we don't have no problem with shining, we don't walk away from the fight."

Resources: Antonio D'Ambrosio, "Soundtrack to Struggle: The Last Poets Are Still Making Music About What Is Happening in the Streets, Using the Language of Streets," *Colorlines* 6, no. 4 (Winter 2003–2004); Katie Davis and Laura Sydell, "The Last Poets Are Seen as Fathers of Rap," *All Things Considered*, National Public Radio (Aug. 1, 1993); David Gonzalez, "A Poet Warns About a Waste of Black Rage," *New York Times*, Sept. 18, 1996, p. B1; The Last Poets: *Chastisement* (London: Charly, 1972), CD; *1st Album* (New York: Verese Records, 2002), CD; *Holy Terror* (New York: Rykodisc, 1995), CD; *Vibes from the Scribes: Selected Poems* (Trenton, NJ: Africa World Press, 1992); *Real Rap* (London: Recall Records, 1999), CD; *This Is Madness* (New York: Douglass, 1971); *Time Has Come* (Los Angeles: Polygram, 1997); Last Poets, with Kain, *Poetry Is Black* (New York: Collectables, 2002); David Mills, "The Last Poets: Their Radical Past, Their Hopeful Future, Their Broken Voice," *Washington Post*, Dec. 12, 1993, p. G1; Abiodun Oyewole and Umar Bin Hassan, *The Last Poets on a Mission: Selected Poems and a History of The Last Poets* (New York: Henry

Holt, 1996); Theresa Stern and John Grady, "The Last Poets: Abiodun Oyewole Interview," http://www.furious.com/perfect/lastpoets/html.

John Greer Hall

Lattany, Kristin Hunter (born 1931). Novelist, children's writer, journalist, screenwriter, documentary writer, elementary school teacher, and professor. Lattany is known as a remarkably versatile writer. Born in **Philadelphia, Pennsylvania**, she is the daughter of George Lorenzo Hunter, a school principal and U.S. Army colonel, and Mabel Eggleston Hunter, a pharmacist and schoolteacher. Lattany received her B.S. in education from the University of Pennsylvania in 1951. She accepted a position as a third-grade teacher but resigned before the academic year was complete in order to pursue her love of writing. She held jobs as a copywriter, an information officer for the city of Philadelphia, and a health services director at Temple University. For twenty-three years, she was an English professor at the University of Pennsylvania, retiring in 1995. Her first and best-received book, *God Bless the Child* (1964), was the work that set the tone for many of her later works. Her most successful piece of work, *The Landlord* (1966), was a direct opposite to the tragedy of her first work and one that sought to define new promise in the slums. United Artists released a movie adaptation of the novel, for which Lattany wrote the screenplay. The humor and comic style of this work prompted her to move into **children's literature**. *The Soul Brothers and Sister Lou* (1970) was Lattany's first piece of young-adult literature, for which she won the National Council on Interracial Books for the Children Award. In it, Lattany focuses on escape from the ghetto through music. The sequel, *Lou in the Limelight*, was released in 1981. Her novel *Kinfolks* (1996) enhanced her reputation further. Her most recent work, *Do unto Others* (2000), speaks to **Afrocentricity**, or the spirit of African pride and resiliency.

Lattany writes about identity amid conflict; growing up in hostile surroundings; the search for value and direction; community struggle; and the intricacy of intracultural and intercultural relationships. She exhibits the strength of both youths and females in their ability to rise against poverty and negativity. Her young-adult and children's books offer alternatives to living in the ghetto, and she effectively demonstrates her ability to compose **protest literature** while rallying for positive change. Lattany's numerous awards include the Moonstone Black Writing Celebration Lifetime Achievement Award (1996), the Christopher Award (1974), the Book Festival Award (1973), the Lewis Carroll Award (1971), and the Philadelphia Athenaeum Award (1960), among others, for her writing and her media expertise. Her work has been widely translated.

Resources: LaToya Chisholm, Bernadette Davis, and Sheena Stanley, "Kristin Hunter Lattany," in *Voices from the Gaps: Women Writers of Color* (Dec. 20, 2001), http://voices.cla.umn.edu/vg/Bios/entries/lattany_kristin_hunter.html; Kristin Hunter Lattany: *Do unto Others* (New York: One World/Ballantine, 2000); *God Bless the Child* (1964; repr. Washington, DC: Howard University Press, 1986); *Kinfolks* (New

York: Ballantine, 1996); *Lou in the Limelight* (New York: Scribner's, 1981); *The Soul Brothers and Sister Lou* (New York: Avon, 1970); Sondra O'Neale, "Kristin Hunter," *Afro-American Fiction Writers After 1955*, ed. Thadious Davis and Tradier Harris (Detroit: Gale, 1984); Rennie Stinson, "Kristin Hunter," in *Contemporary African American Novelists*, ed. Emmanuel Nelson (Westport, CT: Greenwood Press, 1999).

Anne Marie Fowler

LaValle, Victor (born 1972). Novelist and short story writer. Raised in Flushing and Rosedale in Queens, New York, by his mother and grandmother, who were natives of Uganda, LaValle draws on his urban childhood and the many cultures he observed as he crafts his fiction. He began writing after three years studying English at Cornell University, but this change had nothing to do with the school. LaValle gained weight in his teens and began to isolate himself, and these habits went with him to college in 1990. When he stopped attending class in his junior year, LaValle was dismissed from Cornell, but remained in Ithaca and also traveled. He describes this time as one when he had lost touch with reality but refused to see doctors, afraid of a family medical history dotted with schizophrenia and bipolar disorder (Parker). LaValle wrote his way back to balance, drawing on his youth in Queens and dynamics of friendships in his community. After he finished his bachelor's degree at Cornell in 1995, he enrolled in the M.F.A. program in creative writing at Columbia University. There, LaValle's writing developed further, as did his sensibilities as a writer. He helped found the Our Word/Writers of Color discussion forum, where students talk about books by writers of color, and worked on developing the stories that became both his master's thesis and first book, *Slapboxing with Jesus*. This collection of stories, primarily **coming-of-age** stories from urban cultures, was published in 1999. In addition to recognition by Kirkus Review and others as a remarkable new voice, LaValle won the PEN Open Book Award for Writers of Color for his collection.

Having finished graduate work at Columbia in 1998, LaValle spent the time between graduation and the publication of *Slapboxing* as a fellow at the Provincetown Arts Center in Provincetown, Massachusetts. Well known as an artist colony, "P-town" provides eight-month fellowships to talented, developing writers, and LaValle was officially among its 1998–1999 fellows. LaValle's second book, a novel titled *The Ecstatic* (2002), extends beyond his awareness of youthful friendship in the urban world and tells the story of a troubled young man, Anthony. Anthony's story parallels LaValle's own young life and wrestles with the ways families come together and are torn apart. Published in 2002, *The Ecstatic* was a finalist in 2003 for both the PEN/Faulkner Award and the Hurston/Wright Legacy Award. However, most of LaValle's time as a writer has been spent amassing a list of teaching credits that show both his desire to share his craft and a consciousness of his roots. LaValle taught at the Bank Street School (with Writers in the Schools) and the Bronx Council for the Arts before joining the creative writing faculty at Columbia. He spent the summer of 2004 teaching in the Voices of Our Nations Arts Foundation workshops for young writers of color and then traveled to Oakland, California, to teach graduate classes as a Distinguished Visiting Writer at Mills College.

Resources: Victor LaValle: *The Ecstatic* (New York: Crown, 2002); *Slapboxing with Jesus: Stories* (New York: Vintage, 1999); Lonnae O'Neal Parker, "From Fat to Phat: An Author's Happy Ending," *Washington Post*, Dec. 3, 2002, pp. C1–C2; Kevin Powell, ed., *Step into a World: A Global Anthology of New Black Literature* (New York: John Wiley, 2000).

Monica F. Jacobe

Lawrence, Jacob (1917–2000). Painter. Born in Atlantic City, New Jersey, Jacob Lawrence became one of the most influential, experimental, and prolific African American painters of the twentieth century. Growing up in Black neighborhoods, he witnessed firsthand the creativity of African Americans, their struggle and impassioned will to survive in the face of persecution. Despite having received no formal training in the arts, Lawrence benefited from government organizations such as after-school art clubs run in **Harlem, New York**, by Augusta Savage and Charles Alston and funded by the Works Progress Administration. Lawrence's artistic inspiration came from the African American world around him; the decorated homes of local families were his art galleries. The inspiration he drew from the love of color in a community frequently torn apart by despair not only mirrored the innovative techniques of earlier European masters, such as Vincent Van Gogh, who were committed to the imagination as a panacea for pain, but also had a deep impact upon his choice of form and content. Lawrence documented both his determination to paint the lives of everyday African Americans with dignity and respect and his experimentation with a juxtaposition of color to create emotional depth and an accessible symbolic language of the utmost immediacy. His interest in ordinary people invites comparison between his visual art and the poetry, fiction, and **drama** of **Langston Hughes**.

Lawrence lent dramatic power and an evocative rawness to his subject matter in one of his epic series, *Migration of the Negro*, by a repeated use of the color red—in the clothes of Black men, women and children; in the homemade quilts and artifacts decorating otherwise bare rooms; in the newspapers telling of hope in the North; and in the brutal **race riots** caused by conflict between White workers and Black immigrants. Given the widespread prejudices in the mainstream American arts toward African Americans, Lawrence exhorted Black artists to teach White audiences and patrons "to respect and to recognize the intellectual capacity of Black artists." Although his work was firmly rooted in the experiences of African Americans, he voiced the universal struggles of humanity. Thus, he produced paintings devoted not only to Black history and civil rights but also to **World War II**, Hiroshima, and American history in general. His influences were as diverse as Western artists (the Dutch Realist tradition and Goya, among others), Mexican muralists (Diego Riviera et al.), ancient Egyptian murals, and African American artists of the early twentieth century (Henry Tanner, **Romare Bearden**, Horace Pippin, et al.).

Although he shared many affinities with Social Realism, Lawrence remained committed to aesthetic experimentation throughout his career. His dabbling with abstraction, synthetic and analytic cubism, and the nonfigurative represented his determination to break the accepted boundaries for Black artistic expression. Nevertheless, Lawrence returned repeatedly to Black history for his inspiration, especially to those he considered Black heroes, such as Toussaint L'Ouverture, **Frederick Douglass**, and **Harriet Tubman**. The paintings of Jacob Lawrence dramatize the diversity of American life but also re-create a lost Black past for contemporary audiences.

Resources: Patricia Hills, "Jacob Lawrence as Pictorial Griot," *American Art* 7, no. 1 (1993), 41–59; Peter T. Nesbett and Michelle DuBois, eds., *Over the Line: The Art and Life of Jacob Lawrence* (Seattle: University of Washington Press, 2000); Ellen Harkins Wheat, *Jacob Lawrence: American Painter* (Seattle: University of Washington Press, 1986).

Celeste-Marie Bernier

Leadbelly [Ledbetter, Huddie] (1889–1949). Folk and **blues** singer. Leadbelly is considered a major influence on American folk, blues, **jazz**, and popular music. His enormous repertoire of songs and moving interpretations—boomed out with the accompaniment of a twelve-string guitar—helped to popularize and preserve African American music and folk traditions.

Born Huddie Ledbetter near Mooringsport, Louisiana, Leadbelly became legendary not only for his music but also for his trouble with the law. He spent one term in jail for assault, and three terms in prison for murder, assault with intent to murder, and felonious assault. While in Louisiana's Angola Penitentiary, Leadbelly was discovered by John and Alan Lomax, who were recording African American work songs, field hollers, **ballads**, and **spirituals** in **the South**. The Lomaxes eventually published a landmark collection of the singer's work, *Negro Folk Songs as Sung by Leadbelly* (1936), which played a key role in introducing Black southern folk music to a White audience. In the 1940s Leadbelly worked regularly as a nightclub singer and radio performer, though he failed to achieve large-scale commercial success or financial security during his lifetime. On December 9, 1949, Leadbelly died of Lou Gehrig's disease.

Among Leadbelly's most admired songs are his distinctive adaptations of "Midnight Special" and "Goodnight, Irene," which became popular hits by other artists after his death. Leadbelly is remembered as a dazzling live performer with a genius for extemporizing. As Charles Wolfe and Kip Lornell explain, "Part of the showmanship that fascinated audiences was Leadbelly's ability to improvise songs on the spot and to create odd, funny, rhyming introductions and explanations. Some of these resemble the **rap** music of the present day, a style that Leadbelly would have been right at home with; both forms have their roots in the 'patter' songs of early songsters like Henry Thomas, and the toasts and dozens of black narrative folklore" (Wolfe and Lornell, 242). Leadbelly also helped pioneer the emerging genre of the protest

Bunk Johnson, Leadbelly, George Lewis, and Alcide Pavageau playing at the Stuyvesant Casino in New York, c. 1946. Courtesy of the Library of Congress.

song in the 1930s, writing "The Bourgeois Blues," "The Scottsboro Boys Shall Not Die," and "We're Gonna Tear Hitler Down." These songs are similar to the poetry of protest that **Langston Hughes** wrote in the 1930s and early 1940s. (*See* **Protest Literature**.)

Resources: Moses Asch and Alan Lomax, eds., *The Leadbelly Songbook: The Ballads, Blues, and Folksongs of Huddie Ledbetter* (New York: Oak Publications, 1962); William Barlow, *"Looking Up at Down": The Emergence of Blues Culture* (Philadelphia: Temple University Press, 1989); Lawrence Cohn, *Leadbelly, The Library of Congress Recordings* (Elektra, 1966); Richard M. Garvin and Edmond G. Addeo, *The Midnight Special: The Legend of Leadbelly* (New York: B. Geis, 1971); Adam Gussow, *Seems like Murder Here: Southern Violence and the Blues Tradition* (Chicago: University of Chicago Press, 2002); Leadbelly: *Best of Leadbelly* (CD) (Cleopatra, 2000); *Bourgeois Blues* (CD) (Smithsonian Folkways, 1997); *Shout On* (CD) (Smithsonian Folkways, 1998); *Where Did You Sleep Last Night?* (CD) (Smithsonian Folkways, 1996); John Lomax and Alan Lomax, *Negro Folk Songs as Sung by Lead Belly* (New York: Macmillan, 1936); Paul Oliver: *The Story of the Blues: The Making of Black Music* (London: Pimlico, 1997); and *Yonder Come the Blues: The Evolution of a Genre* (New York: Cambridge University Press, 2001); Charles Wolfe and Kip Lornell, *The Life and Legend of Leadbelly* (New York: Da Capo Press, 1999).

Geoff Hamilton

Lee, Andrea (born 1953). Novelist, nonfiction writer, and travel writer. Andrea Lee is a fiction and nonfiction author whose work generally focuses on the Black, middle- and upper-middle-class experience in the United States and abroad. Her main characters are often expatriate women who are actively seeking to rebel against the overt racial politics of the **Civil Rights Movement**

and African American tradition. Some critics have responded with disappointment that Lee has not taken a more visible stance on racial subjugation, while others have applauded Lee's tacit movement away from **race** as the determining—or overdetermining—characteristic of non-White characters.

Lee was born in **Philadelphia, Pennsylvania**, and currently lives in Torino, Italy, with her husband and two children. She attended the Baldwin School of Bryn Mawr College, and received her bachelor's and master's degrees from Harvard University. Her first novel, *Russian Journal*, is an account of her ten-month stay in the Soviet Union in 1978 while her husband studied on fellowship in Moscow and Leningrad. In 1981, *Russian Journal* was nominated for the American Book Award for general nonfiction. Lee's second novel, *Sarah Phillips*, was released in 1984 and received the 1984 Jean Stein Award from the American Academy and Institute of Arts and Letters. Lee served as a staff writer for *The New Yorker* magazine. Her fiction and nonfiction pieces have appeared in the *New York Times Magazine*, the *New York Times Book Review*, *Vogue*, *Time*, and *The Oxford American*. (*See* **Travel Writing**.)

Resources: "A Conversation with Andrea Lee," http://www.randomhouse.com/boldtype/0902/lee/interview.html; Andrea Lee: *Interesting Women: Stories* (New York: Random House, 2002); *Russian Journal* (New York: Random House, 1981); *Sarah Phillips* (New York: Random House, 1984); Christopher Lehmann-Haupt, "A Review of *Sarah Phillips*," *New York Times*, Dec. 6, 1984, p. C22.

Michelle LaFrance

Lee, Helen Elaine (born 1959). Novelist and short story author. A native of **Detroit, Michigan**, Lee grew up in a household that loved literature and storytelling (Rowell). Her father was a lawyer who graduated from Harvard Law School, and her mother is a professor of comparative literature. Lee believes this enriching background later helped her to become a prominent author in lesbian and African American literature (Hammonds). Lee originally did not set out to become a novelist. She graduated magna cum laude from Harvard College, earned a law degree from Harvard Law School in 1985, and subsequently worked as a lawyer for the next nine years in **Chicago, Illinois**, and **Washington, D.C.** Eventually, Lee realized that she was better suited to be a novelist. She published her first book, *The Serpent's Gift*, in 1994. This novel explores the effects of domestic violence and the loss of a loved one that creates a strong bond between two families. For this book Lee won the American Library Association Black Caucus First Novelist Award. In 1999, she published her second acclaimed book, *Water Marked*. *Water Marked* focuses on the relationship between two estranged adult sisters who discovered that their father did not commit suicide, as they had believed.

Lee's short stories and other works have appeared in anthologies including *Ancestral House: The Black Short Story in the Americas and Europe* (1995), *Afrekete: An Anthology of Black Lesbian Writing* (1995), *The Bluelight Corner: Black Women Writing on Passion, Sex, and Romantic Love* (1999), *Black like Us: A Century of Lesbian, Gay, and Bisexual African American Fiction* (2002), and

Shaking the Tree: A Collection of New Fiction and Memoir by Black Women (2003). Lee is is a regular contributor to **Callaloo**.

Not only does Lee deal with sexuality in her work; she also seamlessly writes about issues such as racism, family relationships, history, loss, and redemption with regard to African American life. Besides writing, Lee has a flourishing career in academia. She currently lives in **Boston, Massachusetts**, and is an assistant professor of creative writing in the Massachusetts Institute of Technology Writing and Humanistic Studies Program. Because of the variety of issues she writes about, Lee's fictional works are an important asset for **lesbian literature**, and for literature in general.

Resources: Evelyn M. Hammonds, "Talking with Helen Elaine Lee," *Radcliffe Quarterly*, Fall 1999; Helen Elaine Lee: "Goodbye to the House," *Callaloo* 24, no. 4 (2001), 1083–1101; *Serpent's Gift* (New York: Atheneum, 1994); *Water Marked* (New York: Scribner's, 1999); Charles H. Rowell, "An Interview with Helen Elaine Lee," *Callaloo* 23, no. 1 (2000), 139–150.

Devona Mallory

Lee, Jarena (1783–?). Autobiographer and itinerant preacher. Born free in Cape May, New Jersey, Lee was the first African American woman to write a detailed account of her own life, *The Life and Religious Experience of Jarena Lee* (1836), and she was the first African American woman to receive official sanction from church authorities to preach. Beginning her narrative with the traditional "I was born," she proceeds to tell of her life prior to coming to God, saying of her upbringing, "my parents being wholly ignorant of the knowledge of God, had not therefore instructed me in any degree in this matter." In 1811, Lee married Joseph Lee, a pastor, with whom she had two children.

Several years later, Jarena Lee heard the voice of God, telling her to preach the Gospel. In her narrative she responds by saying, "No one will believe me," to which God replies, "Preach the Gospel; I will put words in your mouth, and will turn your enemies to become your friends." She resisted the call during her marriage, but after her husband died in 1818, she began to follow and sought to preach. In her narrative Lee recounts being rebuffed by Rev. **Richard Allen**, founder and bishop of the African Methodist Episcopal Church, disrupting the narrative to state: "O how careful we ought to be, lest through our by-laws of church government and discipline, we bring into disrepute even the word of life. For as unseemly as it may appear now-a-days for a woman to preach, it should be remembered that nothing is impossible with God." Resisting for eight years, Lee is finally compelled to preach when, while attending the Bethel church, a visiting minister loses the spirit, causing Lee to jump to his aid and preach. She feared expulsion from the church, but Rev. Richard Allen addressed the congregation, informing them of her earlier call and stating that he now believed it. In 1836, Lee published a shorter account of her life, and in 1849 she rewrote it to include her struggles with the church, titled *Religious Experience and Journal of Mrs. Jarena Lee, Giving an Account of Her Call to Preach the Gospel*. After 1849 there are no further records of Jarena

Lee's life. Her **autobiography** is included in anthologies edited by Andrews and Houchins.

Resources: William Andrews, ed., *Sisters of the Spirit: Three Black Women's Autobiographies of the Nineteenth Century* (Bloomington: Indiana University Press, 1986); Sue E. Houchins, ed., *Spiritual Narratives* (New York: Oxford University Press, 1988).

Pamela Ralston

Lee, Spike (born 1957). Film director, screenwriter, nonfiction writer, and children's author. Although known mostly for his bold and controversial films, Spike Lee has also made his mark in African American literature. His written works, like his films, expose issues relevant to contemporary African Americans, as well his concerns and experiences as one of few African American filmmakers. Born Shelton Jackson Lee in 1957, Lee was raised in **Brooklyn, New York**. His mother, Jacquelyn, was an art teacher at a White private school. His father, Bill, was a **jazz** musician. His parents supplemented their children's learning with African American literature, museums, plays, and concerts. Lee's formal education includes a degree in mass communications from Morehouse College, an all-Black college for men, and a master's degree in filmmaking from New York University.

Out of these experiences, Lee has created a number of films, many of which were successful but often critically labeled as radical. Prominent themes include racism, crime, and color discrimination, and his films often feature an all-Black cast. In the 1986 comedy *She's Gotta Have It*, Lee portrays a female protagonist who must decide among three eligible men. In *School Daze* (1988), Lee pits light-skinned elite Blacks against dark-skinned rural Blacks in order to explore color discrimination within African American communities. *Do the Right Thing* (1989) concerns explosive racial tensions that erupt during a sweltering summer in New York. A man's love of music, rather than racism, is at the heart of *Mo' Better Blues* (1990). Lee probes the complexities of interracial love relationships in *Jungle Fever* (1991) and the epic life of a criminal-turned-Muslim committed to bettering the lives of African Americans in *Malcolm X* (1992). *Crooklyn* (1994) is a semiautobiographical movie based on Lee's childhood. Lee explores crime in *Clockers* (1995); the life of a phone-sex operator in *Girl 6* (1996); the transformation of a busload of African American men en route to the historic Million Man March (1995) in *Get On the Bus* (1996); the deaths of four African American girls in a church bombing in *4 Little Girls* (1997); and exploitation in professional basketball in *He Got Game* (1998). In 1999, Lee directed his first all-White movie, about a serial killer, in *Summer of Sam*. Lee also directed *Bamboozled* (2000), *The Original Kings of Comedy* (2000), and a series on **Huey P. Newton** (2001), a cofounder of the **Black Panther Party**.

Lee has documented many of his trials as an African American filmmaker in a predominantly White industry and provides numerous insights on the behind-the-scenes happenings of several films in books, including *Spike Lee's Gotta Have It: Inside Guerrilla Filmmaking* (1987), *Uplift the Race: The*

Construction of "School Daze" (1988), Do the Right Thing: A Spike Lee Joint (1989), and By Any Means Necessary: The Trials and Tribulations of the Making of "Malcolm X" (1992). In Uplift the Race, Lee explains how many of the historical Black colleges were outraged by the focus on color discrimination in School Daze. In By Any Means Necessary, Lee discusses the changes he made in the Malcolm X script originally written by **James Baldwin**.

Best Seat in the House: A Basketball Memoir (1997) plots basketball's climb to "the big-money sports spectacular it is today," and Lee's personal ascension from nosebleed blue seats and aspiring filmmaker to courtside seats and world-renowned film director (Best Seat in the House, front flap). In 2002, Lee joined the ranks of African American celebrities such as **Bill Cosby**, Will Smith, **Toni Morrison**, and **Maya Angelou** when he authored with his wife, Tonya Lewis Lee, the children's book Please, Baby, Please.

Resources: Primary Sources: Books: Spike Lee, Spike Lee's Gotta Have It: Inside Guerrilla Filmmaking (New York: Simon and Schuster, 1987); Spike Lee with Lisa Jones: Do the Right Thing: A Spike Lee Joint (New York: Fireside, 1989); Mo' Better Blues (New York: Simon and Schuster, 1990); Uplift the Race: The Construction of "School Daze" (New York: Simon and Schuster, 1988); Spike Lee and Tonya Lewis Lee, Please, Baby, Please (New York: Simon and Schuster, 2002), Spike Lee with Ralph Wiley: Best Seat in the House: A Basketball Memoir (New York: Crown, 1997); By Any Means Necessary: The Trials and Tribulations of the Making of "Malcolm X" (New York: Hyperion, 1992). Films: Spike Lee, dir.: Bamboozled (New Line Cinema, 2000); Clockers (Universal Pictures, 1995); Crooklyn (Universal Pictures, 1994); Do the Right Thing (Universal Pictures, 1989); 4 Little Girls (HBO [documentary], 1997); Get on the Bus (Columbia Pictures, 1996); Girl 6 (Twentieth Century Fox, 1996); He Got Game (Buena Vista Pictures, 1998); A Huey P. Newton Story (PBS, 2001); Jungle Fever (Universal Pictures, 1991); Malcolm X (Warner Bros., 1992); Mo' Better Blues (Universal Pictures, 1990); The Original Kings of Comedy (Paramount Pictures, 2000); School Daze (Columbia Pictures, 1988); She's Gotta Have It (Island Pictures, 1986); Summer of Sam (Buena Vista Pictures, 1999). **Secondary Sources:** Biography Resource Center, Tacoma Public Library, Tacoma, WA, http://galenet.galegroup.com/servlet/BioRC; Cynthia Fuchs, ed., Spike Lee: Interviews (Jackson: University Press of Mississippi, 2002); "Spike Lee," in Contemporary Black Biography, vol. 19 (Detroit: Gale, 1998).

Gladys L. Knight

Lesbian Literature. African American lesbian literature changed the shape of American literary history by celebrating previously ignored writers as well as illuminating and resisting the triply oppressive intersection of racism, sexism, and homophobia silencing the voices of African American lesbians. Although the presence of lesbian themes appeared in late nineteenth- and early twentieth-century diaries and poems by writers such as **Alice Moore Dunbar-Nelson** and **Angelina Weld Grimké**, literary critics did not begin to pay serious attention to lesbian literature until the 1970s. As a result of the progress made by feminist and civil rights advocates in the 1960s, lesbian, feminist, and African American writers and scholars were better equipped to address the topic of lesbian literature and defend its importance in the 1970s. Additionally, the positive affirmation of African American culture and art provided by the **Black Power** movement and the **Black Arts Movement** influenced the emerging recognition of African American lesbian writers; at the same time, the lesbian tradition developed in reaction to the sexism and homophobia often associated with those movements.

Author and scholar **Barbara Smith** sounded the clarion call for the establishment of an African American women's tradition in her revolutionary essay "Toward a Black Feminist Criticism" (1977), originally published in the journal *Conditions*, a forum for the words of many other African American lesbian writers. In this often reprinted essay, Smith claimed, "All segments of the literary world—whether establishment, progressive, Black, female, or lesbian—do not know, or at least act as if they do not know, that Black women writers and Black lesbian writers exist" (157). Smith attributed the belated recognition of African American lesbian literature to the lack of interest, and to racism and homophobia on the part of both publishing houses and, ironically, those who would have seemed most likely to support lesbian writers: Euro-American feminists, lesbians, and "the Black community as well, which is at least as homophobic" (172).

In reaction, Smith advocated an approach that acknowledged the existence of an identifiable African American women's literary tradition. She encouraged her readers to recognize how this tradition defied both African American rights advocates and Euro-American feminists by refusing to prioritize either **race** or **gender** as a singular oppression to be fought. Instead, she argued that African American women's literature, and lesbian literature in particular, demonstrated how race and gender function in tandem as oppressive forces in mainstream America. To develop this thesis, Smith offered a controversial lesbian reading of **Toni Morrison**'s *Sula*. Smith argued that the close bond between Sula and Nel, though never consummated sexually, could be read as a lesbian relationship if one considered lesbianism synonymous with the marginalization of women and their resistance to Euro-American and African American patriarchal power. In this regard, Smith expanded on the ideas of other African American lesbian critics such as Wilmette Brown. The continued questioning of what it means to be lesbian is one of the most significant contributions of African American lesbian literature.

Lesbian literature has gained increasing attention since the 1970s. Critics began to search for and explore often hidden references to same-sex desire in earlier works by African American women. In *Color, Sex and Poetry: Three Women Writers of the Harlem Renaissance* (1987), poet and critic **Akasha [Gloria T.] Hull** called attention to Angelina Weld Grimké's unpublished love poetry to other women and Alice Moore Dunbar Nelson's diary narration of her affair with Fay Johnson Robinson. Hull emphasized the fact that none of their lesbian-centered works were published during their lifetimes. Critics also reexplored the relationship between the characters Clare Kendry and Irene

Redfield in **Nella Larsen**'s novel *Passing* (1929) as a representation of lesbian desire. Because the African American lesbian has historically been silenced or ignored by so many other social voices, the reclaiming of both unpublished and ignored texts has significantly corrected the American **literary canon**.

The 1970s likewise witnessed the publication of several landmark collections of poetry, fiction, and memoir. Writer and activist **Pat Parker** followed years of public poetry readings in support of lesbian women with her first collection, *Child of Myself* (1972), printed by the lesbian press she helped establish, Women's Press Collective. The poems in *Child of Myself* demonstrate the themes that characterize Parker's later work, such as race and class struggle, and lesbian resistance to compulsory heterosexuality. Stylistically, Parker made use of the African American **vernacular** and call-and-response traditions in her poetry to construct a bridge between lesbian experience and African American community.

The critic, author, and activist **Audre Lorde** published "Martha," her first poem to openly explore lesbian themes, in her second volume of poetry, *Cables to Rage* (1970), thereby launching one of the most extensive bodies of work to focus on African American lesbian themes as well as **nature**, place, family, cancer, **feminism**, and ethnic identity. Whereas Parker incorporated African American vernacular into her poetry, Lorde made use of female mythic figures from West African oral traditions to blend her voice with an international African women's tradition. In an interview with Charles Rowell published in **Callaloo** a year before her death, Lorde identified herself as "a Black, Lesbian, Feminist, warrior, poet, mother doing my work" (92). She inspired other African American women and lesbians to name themselves and create positive self-identities, and she expressed how her poetry and essays were not only encouragements of self-definition but also calls to social action: "I want my poems—I want all of my work—to engage, and to empower people to speak, to strengthen themselves into who they most want and need to be and then to act, to do what needs being done" (94). Lorde was an ardent lesbian rights activist who spoke at the first national march for Gay and Lesbian Liberation in **Washington, D.C.**, in 1979; she also cofounded **Kitchen Table: Women of Color Press**, which has since published important works by both heterosexual and homosexual women.

Lesbian fiction also made strides in the 1970s. **Ann Allen Shockley** published the first avowedly lesbian African American novel, *Loving Her* (1974), the story of a singer, Renay, who falls in love with an affluent Euro-American woman, leaves her abusive husband, and raises her daughter on her own. Aside from its revolutionary focus on same-sex desire, *Loving Her* confronted the controversial subjects of interracial relationships and parenting by homosexuals. Shockley was also the first African American woman to publish a short story collection centered on lesbian characters: *The Black and White of It* (1980). In spite of reviewers, including other African American lesbians such as **Jewelle Gomez**, who labeled Shockley's later work as shallow, unliterary, or too preoccupied with Euro-American characters, her fiction significantly contributed to the African American lesbian tradition in a decade that also gave rise to the poetry and plays of **June Jordan** and the establishment of *Azalea*, a magazine for Third World lesbians.

In the 1980s and 1990s, a number of new writers appeared in print and further diversified the stylistic, social, and political scope of lesbian literature. The poet, novelist, and critic Jewelle Gomez self-published her first collection of poems, *The Lipstick Papers* (1980). In her first novel, *The Gilda Stories* (1991), Gomez expanded the African American literary tradition of re-inventing popular myths; she revised the classic vampire tale to explore 200 years of African American history from a lesbian perspective. In both *The Gilda Stories* and essays, Gomez has called attention to the creative possibilities of **science fiction** and fantasy genres. Cherry Muhanji's debut novel, *Her* (1990), explored the bonds between women and the homophobia of **Detroit, Michigan**, in the 1960s. The **jazz**-inspired anthems in the poetry of Cheryl Clarke and the interracial relationships at the center of **Becky Birtha**'s fiction further evidence the diverse preoccupations and accomplishments of lesbian writers.

These writers have identified themselves publicly as lesbians and addressed how their sexuality influences their poems, stories, and memoirs; however, many writers who do not identify as lesbians have also contributed to the body of lesbian literature. **Alice Walker**'s portrayal of the love affair between Celie and Shug Avery in *The Color Purple* (1982) is arguably the most widely read account of an African American lesbian relationship. The love affair between Lorraine and Teresa is just one of the many complex experiences shared by the seven women characters of **Gloria Naylor**'s *The Women of Brewster Place* (1982). In **Ntozake Shange**'s novel *Sassafrass, Cypress and Indigo* (1982), Cypress dances with a lesbian collective and begins an affair with another dancer; as in Naylor's novel, Shange's story explores the relationship between lesbianism and many other issues affecting women, such as **Black Nationalism**, domestic abuse, and pregnancy.

The African American lesbian literary tradition continues to thrive, and it has inspired numerous anthologies, journals, and writer's organizations. Many of these, such as *This Bridge Called My Back: Writings by Radical Women of Color* (1981), exhibit how lesbian writers have embraced a multicultural community and united to resist a host of economic, political, and social problems. Edited by Barbara Smith, *Home Girls: A Black Feminist Anthology* (1983) includes poems, fiction, and essays by lesbian authors including Audre Lorde, Angelina Weld Grimké, Julie Carter, and Donna Allegra. Other noteworthy anthologies include *Black Like Us: A Century of Lesbian, Gay, and Bisexual African American Fiction* (2002); *Afrekete: An Anthology of Black Lesbian Writing* (1995); and *Does Your Mama Know? An Anthology of Black Lesbian Coming Out Stories* (1997), published by the African American lesbian publisher **Redbone Press**. *Aché*, a journal for African American lesbians, publishes literature, political essays, and art. These anthologies and organizations demonstrate that African American lesbian literature continues to command recognition of and acceptance for lesbian voices in literature and society; however, it also searches for a safe, self-affirming, positive cultural space—a community of its own where women can know and love and support other women. Becky Birtha's poem "My Next Lover" demonstrates the realization of this hope as the speaker does not wish, but declares, "My next lover will never give up on us" (140).

Resources: Becky Birtha, *The Forbidden Poems* (Seattle, WA: Seal Press, 1991); Devon W. Carbado et al., eds., *Black Like Us: A Century of Lesbian, Gay, and Bisexual African American Fiction* (San Francisco: Cleis Press, 2002); Jewelle Gomez, *The Gilda Stories: A Novel* (Ithaca, NY: Firebrand Books, 1991); Gloria T. Hull, *Color, Sex, and Poetry: Three Women Writers of the Harlem Renaissance* (Bloomington: Indiana University Press, 1987); Audre Lorde, *Cables to Rage* (Detroit: Broadside Press, 1970); Catherine E. McKinley and L. Joyce Delaney, eds., *Afrekete: An Anthology of Black Lesbian Writing* (New York: Anchor Books, 1995); Lisa C. Moore, ed., *Does Your Mama Know? An Anthology of Black Lesbian Coming Out Stories* (Decatur, GA: Redbone Press, 1998); Cherríe Moraga and Gloria Anzaldúa, eds., *This Bridge Called My Back: Writings by Radical Women of Color* (Watertown, MA: Persephone Press, 1981); Cherry Muhanji, *Her* (San Francisco: Aunt Lute Books, 1990); Gloria Naylor, *The Women of Brewster Place* (New York: Viking, 1982); Pat Parker, *Child of Myself* (Oakland, CA: Women's Press Collective, 1972); Charles H. Rowell, "Above the Wind: An Interview with Audre Lorde," *Callaloo* 14, no. 1 (1991): 83–95; Ntozake Shange, *Sassafrass, Cypress and Indigo* (New York: St. Martin's Press, 1982); Barbara Smith, "Toward a Black Feminist Criticism," in *All the Women Are White, All the Blacks Are Men, but Some of Us Are Brave*, ed. Gloria T. Hull, Patricia Bell Scott, and Barbara Smith (Old Westbury, NY: Feminist Press, 1982); Alice Walker, *The Color Purple* (New York: Harcourt Brace Jovanovich, 1982).

Laura A. Hoffer

Lester, Julius (born 1939). Novelist, poet, children's writer, and nonfiction writer. Lester is a prolific, award-winning author of more than thirty books that include fiction, nonfiction, **folklore, children's literature**, and poetry. He has also had numerous essays and reviews published in the *New York Times*, the *Village Voice*, and *Dissent*. He was born in **St. Louis, Missouri**, but grew up in **Nashville, Tennessee**, during the 1940s and 1950s. He therefore experienced segregation and its debilitating effects firsthand. After graduating from Fisk University in 1960, with a Bachelor of Arts degree in English, Lester pursued many interests, including music, political activism, and writing. While working as a photographer for the Student Nonviolent Coordinating Committee in **Atlanta, Georgia**, in 1967, Lester discovered his ability to influence change through his writing. Published in 1968, *Look Out Whitey! Black Power's Gon' Get Your Mama* argued succinctly for a radical change in the institutions responsible for the marginalization of "black people."

Lester's decision to pursue a career as a writer actually began when he was a child listening to family members, as well as the older people in his community, tell stories about the perseverance, sacrifice, and survival of Africans and African Americans during **slavery**. Within the context of these textual formations, Lester was able to identify a dynamic form of resistance that was both humanizing and dignifying. What Lester recognized in the storytelling and folklore of his youth was a powerful tradition of remembering, one that claimed his ancestors' histories and identified them as having lived. Through this lens Lester has challenged his readers to rethink and reimagine the **drama** of American **slavery** as it was perceived and experienced by those individuals whose stories have been excluded from history.

Using this critical insight to understand the changes occurring in America and the revolutionary discourse being advanced during the 1960s, Lester began to contest institutionalized notions of racial inferiority and the nihilist pathology African Americans were experiencing. In works such as *To Be a Slave* (1968), *Long Journey Home* (1972), and *Shining* (2003), and the contemporary retellings of stories such as *Uncle Remus: The Complete Tales* (1999) and *John Henry* (1994), Lester humanizes generations of African Americans overlooked and objectified. He speaks for those individuals whose social condition of slavery dictated their opportunities to experience themselves, their families, and true freedom.

Clearly, Lester's work seeks to claim lost histories while carrying forth the hopes and dreams of the African American "folk." His work passionately demonstrates a connectedness to the past that is necessary as we seek to reclaim the origins of the present self while making salient the truth for all to see.

Resources: Beth Brown, "A Comprehension of Time: Three Contemporary Black Authors Reflect," *Journal of Black Studies* 18, no. 1 (Sept. 1987), 109–115; Caren Dybek, "Black Literature for Adolescents," *The English Journal* 63, no. 1 (Jan. 1974), 64–67; Trudier Harris, "Genre," *Journal of American Folklore* 108 (Autumn 1995), 509–527; Julius Lester: *The Blues Singers: Ten Who Rocked the World* (New York: Jump at the Sun, 2001); *Long Journey Home: Stories from Black History* (1972; repr. New York: Puffin, 1998); *Look Out, Whitey! Black Power's Gon' Get Your Mama!* (1968; repr. New York: Grove, 1969); *Pharaoh's Daughter: A Novel of Ancient Egypt* (New York: HarperTrophy, 2002); *Shining* (San Diego: Silver Whistle, 2003); *To Be a Slave* (New York: Dial, 1968); *Why Heaven Is Far Away* (New York: Scholastic, 2002); Julius Lester and Rod Brown, *From Slave Ship to Freedom Road* (New York: Puffin Books, 1999); Julius Lester and Jerry Pinkney: *John Henry* (New York: Dial, 1994); *Uncle Remus: The Complete Tales* (New York: Dial, 1999); Wilfred D. Samuels, "And All our Wounds Forgiven," *African American Review* 31, no. 1 (Spring 1997), 176–182.

Pellom McDaniels III

Lewis, Theophilus (1891–1974). Journalist and drama/theater critic. Though one of the **Harlem Renaissance**'s more obscure figures—due to both the paucity and the brevity of his journalistic pieces—Theophilus Lewis's **drama** and theatrical criticism and reviews during this fascinating period form a significant contribution to African American literature. Appearing in **Charles Spurgeon Johnson**'s *Ebony and Topaz: A Collectanea* (1927) with works of such better known Harlem Renaissance writers as **Jessie Redmon Fauset, Langston**

Hughes, **Zora Neale Hurston, Countee Cullen**, and **Arna Botemps**, Lewis's "The Negro Actor's Deficit" is easily his most famous and representative work. Lewis's drama and theatrical criticism and reviews appeared in a variety of periodicals—particularly during his tenure as chief drama critic of *The Messenger* and drama/theater critic for the *Amsterdam News*, both Black newspapers.

During the 1920s and 1930s, Lewis's treatment of African American drama and theater in *The Messenger* and *Amsterdam News* thundered alongside the writings of **W.E.B. Du Bois, Alain Locke**, and **Wallace Thurman**, who were the more celebrated critics and reviewers of African American drama and theater. Du Bois would go on to play an instrumental role in giving literary birth to the careers of several up-and-coming Harlem Renaissance writers, while Lewis, Locke, and Thurman would later collaborate on Thurman's short-lived magazine, *Harlem: A Forum of Negro Life*. Lewis wrote a theater review for the periodical; Locke contributed an essay and Thurman, a book review.

Many of Lewis's drama/theatrical criticisms and reviews were very conservative, caustic, or moral in tone. Titles such as "The False Start of Negro Fiction," "The Frustration of Negro Art," and "Mr. Lewis Goes Puritan" allude to the often puritanical and iconoclastic nature of his writings. This is partly due to Lewis' bourgeoning religious interests.

Lewis, who converted to the Catholic faith and was baptized on August 23, 1939, published in a number of Catholic magazines, including *Catholic World* and *Interracial Review*, in the latter half of his career. He contributed a regular column to *Interracial Review* titled "Plays and a Point of View." The tone of such contributions necessarily limited the kind of liberality that other Harlem Renaissance critics and reviewers enjoyed when writing for strictly secular purposes.

In addition to drama and theatrical criticisms and reviews, Lewis wrote a number of book reviews, including one of **Richard Wright**'s *Native Son*, appearing in *Catholic World* in May 1941. The review argues: "The primary interest of *Native Son* is horror, one of the most fascinating themes of second-rate fiction. When the shocks and thrills cease, the interest flags and the sociological implications lose their force. The author deliberately makes Bigger Thomas a thoroughly worthless creature, an abnormal type who has no utility as a symbol of the consequences of race persecution. If the story had been written by a white author, both intellectuals and masses would denounce it as an attack on the race" ("The Saga of Bigger Thomas," 202).

Resources: Theophilus Lewis: "The Abbey Theatre Reviewed in Peace and Comfort," *America*, Aug. 1938, 442–443; "The False Start of Negro Fiction," *America*, Nov. 1937, 186–187; "The Frustration of Negro Art," *Interracial Review*, Apr. 1942, 58–60; "Mr. Lewis Goes Puritan," *America*, Mar. 1940, 664; "The Negro Actor's Deficit," in *Ebony and Topaz: A Collectanea*, ed. Charles S. Johnson (New York: Opportunity/ National Urban League, 1927); "The Negro Spirituals as Hymns of a People," *America*, Apr. 1939, 43–44; "The Saga of Bigger Thomas," *Catholic World*, May 1941, 202–206.

Brian L. Johnson

Lincoln, C[harles] Eric (1924–2000). Scholar of religion, novelist, poet, professor, and composer. Lincoln was an extremely versatile writer, producing works of fiction, history, social studies, and religion. He was born July 23, 1924, in the small Southern town of Athens, Alabama. He was raised by Less Charles Lincoln and Mattie Sowell Lincoln, his grandparents. Less Lincoln farmed three acres of land, and Mattie Lincoln worked as a laundress for the White residents of Athens. Even though both his grandparents worked, Lincoln claimed to have grown up "dirt poor" (*Durham Herald*). Lincoln once worked for a local dairy, delivering milk from 4:30 to 9:30 A.M. for 50 cents a week (*Durham Herald*).

Lincoln attended the Trinity School, which had been established in 1865 by the American Missionary Association; its goals were to train teachers to work in elementary high schools and to prepare young men and women to attend college. Lincoln graduated from Trinity in 1939, as valedictorian of his class, at the age of fourteen. After a short stay in **Chicago, Illinois**, Lincoln enrolled in LeMoyne College in **Memphis, Tennessee**. **World War II** interrupted Lincoln's studies, and after serving in the U.S. Navy, he returned to LeMoyne, where in 1947 he received a B.A. degree. By 1953, Lincoln had earned his M.A. degree from Fisk University in **Nashville, Tennessee**, and a B.D. degree from the University of Chicago. By 1960 Lincoln had received his M.Ed. and Ph.D. degrees from Boston University.

Lincoln spent the majority of his professional career in colleges and universities. He began his career in 1960 at Clark College in **Atlanta, Georgia**, as an assistant professor of religion and philosophy. By 1965 he had moved to Portland State College, where he served as professor of sociology, and in 1967 he became professor of sociology and religion at Union Theological Seminary in New York City. In 1973, he took an administrative position as chair of the Department of Religion at his alma mater, Fisk University. Lincoln ended his career at Duke University in Durham, North Carolina, where he served as professor of religion from 1976 to 1993. Lincoln received many honors during his illustrious career, including being named the William Ran Kenan, Jr., Distinguished Professor of Religion and Culture at Duke.

Lincoln was an accomplished writer who authored more than twenty scholarly books. These works included *The Black Muslims in America* (1961), *The Negro Pilgrimage in America* (1967), *Race, Religion, and the Continuing American Dilemma* (1984), and, with Lawrence H. Mamiya, *The Black Church in the African-American Experience* (1990). As a literary writer, Lincoln's most acclaimed books were a novel, *The Avenue, Clayton City* (1988), and his collected poems, *This Road Since Freedom* (1990), for which **Margaret Abigail Walker** wrote the introduction and **John Hope Franklin** wrote the epilogue. Lincoln's novel won the Lillian Smith Award and was praised by **Alex Haley** (*Greensboro News*). Lincoln also composed music, including the Alma Mater for Clark/Atlanta University and a Methodist hymn. On, May 14, 2000, Lincoln collapsed and died in his home in Durham, North Carolina, at the age of seventy-five. His papers are held at Woodruff Library, Atlanta University.

Resources: Primary Sources: C. Eric Lincoln: *The Avenue, Clayton City* (New York: Morrow, 1988); *The Black Muslims in America* (1961; Boston: Beacon Press, 1973); *The Negro Pilgrimage in America* (New York: Bantam Books, 1967); *Race, Religion, and the Continuing American Dilemma* (New York: Hill & Wang, 1984); *This Road Since Freedom: Collected Poems* (Durham, NC: Carolina Wren Press, 1990); C. Eric Lincoln Papers, Special Collections, Woodruff Library, Atlanta University; C. Eric Lincoln and Lawrence H. Mamiya, *The Black Church in the African-American Experience* (Durham, NC: Duke University Press, 1990). **Secondary Sources:** Alex Haley, interview with Lincoln, *Greensboro News and Record*, Apr. 22, 1988, sec. B; interview with Lincoln, *Durham Morning Herald*, Mar. 9, 1980, sec. B; Alton B. Pollard and Love H. Whelchel, Jr., eds., *How Long This Road: Race, Religion, and the Legacy of C. Eric Lincoln* (New York: Palgrave MacMillan, 2003).

Darryl B. Holloman

Literary Canon. A literary canon is best described as a collection of works that most accurately reveal and represent a culture. The word "canon" was first used in this way—to denote a collection of written works—in the 1300s by the Catholic Church, but since then it has been applied to any established collection of works in a given field. The concept of a single literary canon is fraught with difficulties because it exposes contradictions in individual and collective taste. Canonical texts may not always be popular, for example, and popular texts are excluded from many literary canons. Also, literary values depend upon a wide variety of social and historical circumstances. The academic literary canon consists of those texts valued by scholars, teachers, critics, and publishers, and it has been subject, at different times, to criticism for excluding influential popular literary texts, for excluding texts by women and/or ethnic minorities, and for otherwise being too narrow or inflexible. In the United States, debates about the literary canon reached a peak in the 1980s, partly because of the publication of E. D. Hirsch's *Cultural Literacy: What Every American Needs to Know* (1987), which tended to reassert traditional views of the literary canon and was viewed by some as a reaction against the inclusion of works by women, works by ethnic minorities, and other works once considered out of the mainstream. At that time, academics often spoke, perhaps somewhat melodramatically, of "a canon war" or "the culture wars" (Gates, *Loose Canons*; Jay, *American Literature and the Culture Wars*). **Feminist/ Black feminist literary criticism**, **multicultural theory**, and **queer theory**, in a variety of ways, attempt to demonstrate that choices concerning what should and should not be in a literary canon are much less objective than they may appear or are presumed to be, and are based on preexisting social and historical circumstances.

One of the principal questions in determining the African American literary canon involves issues of reception and valuation. How, in other words, was a work received not only by the masses but also by those individuals with the requisite cultural cachet to be perceived as arbiters of taste and value? The reception of **Claude McKay**'s *Home to Harlem* (1928) illustrates the tensions at work in the constitution of a canon of African American literature. The novel became the most successful commercial release by an African American writer up to its time. The masses heralded the text for its frank and unfettered portrayal of Black subjectivities. The Black intelligentsia, however, lambasted McKay's effort, rejecting its narrative as sensational, and critics accused McKay of relying too much on primitivism. In one of the more memorable critiques of McKay's work, **W.E.B. Du Bois** observed:

> For the most part [it] nauseates me, and after the dirtier parts of its filth I feel distinctly like taking a bath.... It looks as though McKay has set out to cater to that prurient demand on the part of white folk for a portrayal in Negroes of that utter licentiousness which convention holds white folk back from enjoying—if enjoying it can be labeled. (Stoff, 131)

Here Du Bois emphasizes the social context of McKay's novel, claims that the novel caters to White readers, and implies that such a work should not be part of an African American literary canon. Arguably, Du Bois's primary concern was legitimizing those texts that supported his notion of the **"Talented Tenth,"** the idea that an elite fraction of individuals within the African American community had the power, privilege, and prestige to speak and to make recommendations for—indeed, to represent—the entire community. During the **Harlem Renaissance**, **Wallace Thurman** and the other editors of the literary magazine *Fire!!* attempted to present literature that did not necessarily reflect Du Bois's point of view. The subtitle of the single-issue magazine, *Devoted to Younger Artists,* implicitly framed the disagreement in terms of different generations. Such disagreements about literary value are part of what makes literary movements such as the Harlem Renaissance and, later, the **Black Arts Movement** of the 1960s, vibrant, interesting, and influential.

The Norton Anthology of African American Literature offers a more recent illustration of the distinctions drawn between "popular" and "canonical" literature. Writing about the novelist **Terry McMillan**, the editors of the *Norton Anthology* note:

> To date McMillan's biggest success has been *Waiting to Exhale* (1992), her frank and occasionally hilarious treatment of four black women and their relationships with men: lovers, husbands, sons. An enormous best-seller, one that novelist Charles Johnson called "a tough love letter to black males everywhere," *Waiting to Exhale* became a successful movie in 1995, and McMillan moved even farther on her way to literary celebrityhood. (2572)

If *Waiting to Exhale* had such a momentous impact—if it is McMillan's "biggest success," "[a]n enormous best-seller," and "a successful movie," and if the novel has moved McMillan closer to "literary celebrityhood"—why do the editors not include an excerpt from the novel in the *Anthology*, a text that seeks to define and characterize the canon of African American literature? Why is one of McMillan's lesser-known short stories, "Quilting on the Rebound," included instead of *Waiting to Exhale*? These and various other kinds of questions arise when anthologies appear because most anthologies attempt to collect suppos-edly representative texts. At the same time, all anthologies are necessarily limited in scope, forcing editors to make choices about their particular version of a canon and inviting those choices to be questioned or supported by readers.

Many critics have called attention to the ways in which the construction of literary canons can exert a form of censorship. Barbara Herrnstein Smith, for example, examines the ways in which specific historical orthodoxies are elaborated and enforced by literary canons:

> The repeated inclusion of a particular work in literary anthologies not only promotes the value of that work but goes some distance toward creating its value, as does its repeated appearance on reading lists or its frequent citation or quotation by professors, scholars, and academic critics. For all those acts, at the least, have the effect of drawing the work into the orbit of attention of a population of potential readers; and by making it more accessible to the interests of those readers . . . they make it more likely both that the work will be experienced at all and also that it will be experienced as valuable. (29)

When one work is repeatedly invoked as a "canonical text," other, "non-canonical" works tend be swept under the rug. Smith comments on the po-litical nature of the canon:

> Since those with cultural power tend to be members of socially, economically, and politically established classes (or to serve them and identify their own interests with theirs), the texts that survive will tend to be those that appear to reflect and reinforce establishments ideologies. (34)

What is at stake in the construction of literary canons is the concept of valuation, what the theorist Pierre Bourdieu refers to as cultural capital. Bourdieu's conception involves the appreciation of cultural goods such as literary texts and the ways in which they acquire value and authority through the process of canonization (244).

The construction of a canon of African American literature is particularly complex because of the difficulties that early African American writers en-countered in publishing their work. In order to distribute their work, African American writers were often required to have amanuenses (individuals who would attest to their authorship) or imprimaturs (licenses to publish). Literary canons, which consist in large measure of printed texts, have difficulty ac-commodating or appropriately acknowledging the orality of so much of the African American literary tradition, especially early in that tradition. The variety of forms of expression within the African American literary canon helps to differentiate it from other canons. For example, **slave narratives,**

blues poetry, and speeches (by **Sojourner Truth** and **Frederick Douglass**, for instance) are considered to be legitimate elements of this canon.

The final selection in the voluminous *Norton Anthology of African American Literature* may signal the future of the African American literary canon. The *Anthology* concludes with a collection of poems by the gay male poet **Essex Hemphill**. Hemphill's inclusion shows how far attitudes toward the African American literary canon—as well as the canon itself—have changed, and that different approaches to reading literature, including feminist/Black feminist literary criticism, multicultural theory, and queer theory, influence choices about what ought to be reprinted and read. In a second edition of the *Norton Anthology of African American Literature*, appearing in 2004, some works have replaced others.

Literary canons differ in size, form, and purpose. For instance, one might refer to "the canon of American literature" and then consider what literary texts by African Americans belong in that canon (Hubbell). However, one could just as easily ask what texts by American writers should belong to the canon of English and American (or Anglo-American) literature. Just as legitimately, one might ask, in any given era, what texts belong in the African American literary canon. However, all literary canons, regardless of size, form, and purpose, are constantly in flux, so "*the* canon" creates an illusion of stability. For instance, in 1922, **James Weldon Johnson** edited the representative anthology *The Book of American Negro Poetry*, which helped to establish an emerging African American canon of poetry. Nine years later, he published a revised version in which some works and authors had been replaced by others, chiefly because effective new works and authors had, in the opinion of Johnson and others, come on the scene. In the second edition, Johnson was attempting to make his anthology reflect the growth and flux of literature. Because such growth and flux are perpetual, any concept of "the literary canon" will always be temporary.

Resources: Pierre Bourdieu, "The Forms of Capital," in *Handbook of Theory and Research for the Sociology of Education*, ed. John Richardson (Westport, CT: Greenwood Press, 1986), 241–258; Henry Louis Gates, Jr., *Loose Canons: Notes on the Culture Wars* (New York: Oxford University Press, 1992); Henry Louis Gates, Jr., and Nellie Y. McKay, eds., *The Norton Anthology of African American Literature* (New York: Norton, 1996; 2nd ed., 2004); E. D. Hirsch, Jr., *Cultural Literacy: What Every American Needs to Know* (Boston: Houghton Mifflin, 1987); Jay B. Hubbell, *Who Are the Major American Writers? A Study of the Changing Literary Canon* (Durham, NC: Duke University Press, 1972); Gregory S. Jay, *American Literature and the Culture Wars* (Ithaca, NY: Cornell University Press, 1997); James Weldon Johnson, ed., *The Book of American Negro Poetry* (New York: Harcourt, Brace, 1922; rev. ed., 1931); Claude McKay, *Home to Harlem* (1928; repr. Boston: Northeastern University Press, 1987); Terry McMillan, *Waiting to Exhale* (1992; repr. New York: Pocket Books, 1995); Barbara Herrnstein Smith, "Contingencies of Value: Alternative Perspectives for Critical Theory," in *Canons*, ed. Robert von Hallberg (Chicago: University of Chicago Press, 1984); Michael B. Stoff, "Claude McKay and the Cult of Primitivism," in

The Harlem Renaissance Remembered, ed. Arna Bontemps (New York: Dodd, Mead, 1972), 126–146; Wallace Thurman et al., eds., *Fire!! Devoted to Younger Negro Artists* (1928; facs. repr. New York: Fire Press, 1985).

Chris Bell

Literary Societies. Cultural and social organizations. For more than 200 years, African Americans have been gathering in public halls, churches, and homes to discuss the relationship between literature and their lives. Whether these gatherings are formally called literary societies, reading groups, or book clubs, they are often influenced by unique social circumstances and historical contexts. During the early 1800s, free Blacks in the North formed the first literary societies, believing that U.S. citizenship was linked to literacy, as exemplified in the creation and interpretation of written texts. Acting as "citizens," though they were denied this right, free Black Northerners were empowered by literacy activities that gave them access to a national public and allowed them to address the problems of democracy and the plight of all African Americans. David Walker's *Appeal* (1829), a controversial political pamphlet based on the Constitution and the Declaration of Independence, was a product of his affiliation with literary and civic organizations.

A relatively small but nonetheless well defined Black middle class that emerged after the **Civil War** created literary groups that continued this activist tradition. The groups often focused on topics concerning the progress of the race and sponsored public political lectures that appealed to larger Black audiences. In the early twentieth century, Black writers met in literary salons to share their work and to support one another in their literary careers. The **Harlem Renaissance** and the **Black Arts Movement** both inspired renewed interest in African American literature and produced texts such as **Nella Larsen**'s *Passing* (1929), **Wallace Thurman**'s *The Blacker the Berry* (1929), **Zora Neale Hurston**'s *Their Eyes Were Watching God* (1937) and **Amiri Baraka**'s *"Dutchman" and "The Slave"* (1964), as well as writings by **Larry Neal** and poetry by **Claude McKay**, **Langston Hughes**, **Nikki Giovanni**, and **Sonia Sanchez** that reading groups would discuss for years to come. Publishers large and small respond to the needs of a large Black reading audience today much as the early Black press did during the antebellum period. Books by Black writers are now more readily available than ever before in mainstream bookstores as well in specialty shops and online. In essence, the popularity of contemporary Black writers has spawned yet another "reading revolution" in African American communities and the creation of hundreds of reading groups.

Historians trace the development of literary societies to benevolent organizations of the late eighteenth century. In Northern urban areas, African Americans had established a kind of welfare system to combat poverty in their own communities. When they were denied general support and protection in American society, they formed mutual aid organizations to help those in financial need. Such early beginnings would influence the purpose of later literary societies, which focused on the development of a whole individual with moral values and educational aspirations. The fight for racial equality and citizenship waged by antislavery organizations were also important to the development of Black literary societies. Many Black abolitionists were also members of literary societies and supported their community through outreach programs. These factors led to the creation of cultural organizations that valued literacy as a hallmark of American citizenship, which free Blacks especially wanted to achieve. In fact, members of Black literary societies (as did the general public) during the Jacksonian era (1828–1840) equated literacy with democracy. According to Elizabeth McHenry, for free Blacks, "literacy was a key patriotic duty" (19). Free Blacks used reading, writing, and an appreciation for literature as tools to exercise their responsibilities as U.S. citizens.

With **slavery** in **the South** and pervasive racial prejudice against them in the North, free Blacks formed coalitions for self-improvement. The earliest literary societies were created in urban areas where Blacks had greater access to educational and economic opportunities. From about 1828 to around 1846, literary societies were formed in cities in Pennsylvania, New York, Massachusetts, Connecticut, Rhode Island, New Jersey, Ohio, and Michigan. Free Blacks in border states such as Maryland (in **Baltimore**) and in **Washington, D.C.**, also organized literary clubs. **Philadelphia, Pennsylvania**, as the city with the largest population of free Blacks and as the nucleus of abolitionist activities, had more literary societies than other locations. The Reading Room Society (1828), the Library Company of Colored Persons (1833), and the Female Literary Society (1831) were among the most prominent in Philadelphia (Porter, 556–564). These literary societies were formal, educational organizations that dealt with issues of oppression, racism, and discrimination. The members elected officers and formed committees to manage the societies as community organizations. Requirements for membership included paying fees to support the organizations' library acquisitions, operating their public reading rooms, or organizing public lecture forums. Many of these groups were either exclusively male or female, with a few catering to both sexes. Most important, their members subscribed wholeheartedly to the philosophy of racial uplift. They emphasized an individual's moral and intellectual development for the benefit of the entire race.

The political climate in the North was more favorable for the kind of Black nationalist agenda that literary societies supported with the aid of the Black press and abolitionists (*see* **Abolitionist Movement; Newspapers, African American**). Though communities of free Blacks existed throughout the South, they did not have a unifying means of communication to sustain a literacy movement similar to the one present among free Blacks in the North. Liberal periodicals such as *The Liberator, Freedom's Journal, The Colored American*, and **Frederick Douglass'** *The North Star* partnered with Black literary societies to disseminate reading materials and address political issues, as well as to advertise the activities of the literary societies. Based on their contents and their emphasis on literacy development, these publications played a major role in presenting a respectable Black cultural identity to the public. They served as "a medium of socialization" that provided models of behavior for their readers that the publishers believed were necessary to challenge negative racial stereotypes (McHenry, 90). "Developing literary character, the components of which included morality, self-discipline, intellectual curiosity, civic responsibility, and eloquence, was cast as both a private virtue and a civic duty: it benefited the individual, but it was essential for the common good as well" (McHenry, 100). As evidence of their refinement and intellectual identity, members of the literary societies often published poetry in these newspapers. These individuals also created poetry and other original writings to present at meetings for critical discussion. Those members who could read and write were encouraged to develop their oratorical skills. Illiterate Blacks who could not understand written language benefited from the shared oral literacy of others. Together, the periodicals and the literary groups conducted a widespread literacy campaign to educate the Black masses.

Scholars have not made any direct link between the antebellum literary societies, their post–Civil War counterparts, and contemporary African American reading groups and book clubs, but they have discovered significant evidence of the civic and social activities of the earliest literary societies, which are comparable with today's Black literary groups. With less of a political incentive and more emphasis on socializing, members of contemporary literary groups meet in more casual settings to discuss specific works by Black authors or others that concern topics related to African American culture. While members of early Black female literary societies considered their meetings as "mental feasts" that satisfied the intellect (Winch, 104–105), Black book clubs today try to satisfy the soul as well. For instance, gatherings of Black women literary groups such as The Go On Girl! Book Club, which has a Web site, are considered "sacred time, sister-bonding time," as members discuss books while enjoying food and camaraderie in the relaxing atmosphere of their homes (Greenwood, 82). Members of this club and others like it often discuss their personal lives and offer each other emotional support when needed.

Sometimes these clubs are also essential supportive networks for isolated Black professionals to help them cope with the transitions in a diverse workplace. The change in setting and purpose is reflected in the design of the organization as well. Many reading groups now have an informal governing structure. Members often delegate responsibilities for various projects. For instance, the role of a discussion leader and/or host for a gathering may alternate among the members. If a group decides to sponsor a cultural event such as an author's visit on a reading tour, to create a fund-raiser, or to do volunteer work, most members may participate in these activities and contribute to their success according to their individual resources. While the history of early literary societies is largely unknown, many contemporary organizations continue the tradition of the cultural dissemination of racial pride through their connections within the Black community.

The growth of African American reading groups has been aided by the development of technology in recent years. The Internet, for instance, has created online communities that promote the study of Black literature. Popular Web-based book clubs such as the African American Literature Book Club (www.aalbc.com) and booksellers such as Black Expressions.com provide the latest selections by Black writers, resources for aspiring and professional writers, chat rooms, and up-to-date coverage of literary events. Televised discussions of selections from **Oprah Winfrey**'s Book Club have made it probably the most successful literary group to date. The popular Black talk-show host created an interracial forum for discussion, but she often highlights the works of African American writers. What began among a select few Blacks in the nineteenth century has now spread globally with computers, and there seems to be no indication that the "reading revolution" among African Americans will end in this new millennium. (*See* **Women's Clubs**.)

Resources: Go-On Girl Book Club Web site, http://www.goongirl.org (2004); Monique Greenwood et al., "Our Reading Revolution," *Essence*, Apr. 1999, pp. 82–83; Elizabeth McHenry, *Forgotten Readers: Recovering the Lost History of African American Literary Societies* (Durham, NC: Duke University Press, 2002); Dorothy B. Porter, "The Organized Educational Activities of Negro Literary Societies, 1828–1846," *Journal of Negro Education*, Oct. 1936, pp. 555–576; Julie Winch, "'You Have Talents—Only Cultivate Them': Philadelphia's Black Female Literary Societies and the Abolitionist Crusade," in *The Abolitionist Sisterhood: Women's Political Culture in Antebellum America* (Ithaca, NY: Cornell University Press, 1994), 101–118.

Sherita L. Johnson

Livingston, Myrtle Smith (1902–1973). Playwright. Smith was born in Holly Grove, Arkansas, on May 8, 1902, to Samuel Isaac and Lula C. Hall Smith. She lived in Denver, Colorado, as a child and from 1920 to 1922 attended Howard University, where she studied pharmacology. She transferred to Colorado Teachers College in Greeley, where she finished her career as a student and began her life as a dance and theater artist. She founded a dance group, a hobby she honed and later taught once she became a faculty member at Lincoln University in Jefferson City, Missouri, in 1928. While on the faculty as the director of women's athletics and a physical education and dance instructor, she wrote and directed plays. She taught for forty-four years.

As a playwright, Livingston is known most for the play *For Unborn Children*, published in the July 1926 issue of **The Crisis** magazine. She was one of the first Black women playwrights who addressed the theme of interracial marriage. Her only published play delivered a clear message to the world: miscegenation has far-reaching consequences for both Blacks and Whites. The play revolves around a Black lawyer's controversial intent to marry the White woman he has fallen in love with, despite both his sister's and his grandmother's resistance. Livingston imbues the play with feelings of anger and betrayal as Leroy's sister, Marion, says: "What is to become of us when our men throw us down?" (Hatch and Shinee 1974, 188). In efforts to teach Leroy the severity of his choice, his grandmother discloses that his mother was White and could not continue in her role as mother due to extreme ostracism. Livingston shows society's viewpoint toward the idea of miscegenation not only through the opposition of the grandmother and sister, but also through the lynch mob that awaits Leroy at his front door.

Resources: James V. Hatch and Omanii Abdullah, eds., *Black Playwrights, 1823–1977: An Annotated Bibliography of Plays* (New York: Bowker, 1977), 148; James V. Hatch and Ted Shine, eds., *Black Theatre U.S.A.: Forty-five Plays by African Americans, 1847–1974* (New York: The Free Press, 1974), 188; Darlene Clark Hine, *Black Women in America: An Historical Encyclopedia,* vol. 1 (Brooklyn, NY: Carlson, 1993), 729; Myrtle Smith Livingston, *For Unborn Children,* in *The Crisis,* July 1926.

Brandon L. A. Hutchinson

Location Theory. Location theory is a literary theory conceived by the Afrocentric scholar Molefi Kete Asante, professor in the Department of African American Studies at Temple University (*see* **Afrocentricity**). It provides a framework for examining the historical and cultural consciousness of writers and critics from the African continent and in the **diaspora**, including African Americans. A key assumption of location theory is that all texts emerge from a particular cultural position. This assumption challenges traditional textual analysis, wherein European historiography and orientation are often assumed to be the universal position. Writers grounded or "located" in the proper cultural context generally produce texts that accurately reflect the African experience, Asante argues. He further suggests that writers produce texts that, in figurative terms, are "decapitated" or cut off from the history and culture of African people or "lynched" and "strung up" with Eurocentric signs, symbols, and motifs. Although these authors often possess literary skills, their cultural dislocation is evident in works that demonstrate little to no genuine historical or cultural knowledge.

Language, attitude, and direction are considered to be the main markers of an author's location, according to the theory. Language involves essentially the semantic analysis of words presented in a text. The overall concern of the Afrocentric critic is whether the language used to describe African people, culture, or history is liberating or oppressive. Liberating language corresponds to the beliefs and values of the people, and language that refers to Africans in pejorative terms is oppressive if the writer makes no attempt to interrogate the political meanings of such language. Terms such as "savage," "primitive," or "tribal," which merely reproduce the myths and stereotypes of African people and culture, are often used by Eurocentric writers and critics, regardless of racial or ethnic identity. The manner in which language is presented often reveals the author's attitude toward certain people, ideas, and situations, and provides clues to the direction or overall objective of the text. Whether the objective is to promote African agency and power or to maintain European cultural hegemony, a close examination of the language, attitude, and direction of a text can assist the critic in determining whether an author is ultimately located or dislocated within the Afrocentric paradigm. In his seminal essay "Locating a Text: Implications of Afrocentric Theory," Asante praises the work of African American writers such as **Henry Dumas** and **Charles H. Fuller, Jr.**, for addressing themes and issues relevant to the historical and cultural reality of African people.

Location theory provides an alternative to Eurocentric assumptions and objectives and is widely used by Afrocentric scholars. Although created as a method of analysis for African literature, it constructs a framework that can also be used to engage multicultural perspectives in literature as well as other forms of creative production, such as drama and film.

Resources: Molefi Kete Asante: *The Afrocentric Idea*, 2nd rev. and enl. ed. (Philadelphia: Temple University Press, 1998); "Locating a Text: Implications of Afrocentric Theory," in *The Afrocentric Paradigm*, ed. Ama Mazama (Trenton, NJ: Africa World Press, 2002); "Location Theory and African Aesthetics," in *The African Aesthetic: Keeper of the Traditions*, ed. Kariamu Welsh-Asante (Westport, CT: Greenwood Press, 1993).

Stephanie M. Yarbough

Locke, Alain LeRoy (1886–1954). Editor, philosopher, critic, and professor. Locke is widely considered to be a crucial figure in the development of early twentieth-century African American literature and intellectual life. He was born in **Philadelphia, Pennsylvania**, to middle-class parents; his father was Pliny Ishmael Locke, who had earned a law degree from Howard University and taught at the School of Pedagogy in Philadelphia. Locke went on to earn an undergraduate degree from Harvard University in 1907. Then he became the first African American to be awarded a Rhodes scholarship, which enabled him to take a degree in literature from Oxford University. He completed his formal education by returning to Harvard to complete a Ph.D. in philosophy in 1918. Like **W.E.B. Du Bois**, therefore, Locke brought considerable intellectual gravity to the **Harlem Renaissance**, the artistic and social movement of which the two were arguably the most important leaders.

Locke's influence on African American literature was exerted in a variety of areas. He edited the landmark anthology *The New Negro* (1925), which takes its title from the concept of the **New Negro,** which represented an ideal of economic, social, and artistic achievement and was closely connected to Du Bois's ideas about a **"Talented Tenth"** that would lead African Americans in the twentieth century. The anthology included works by **Langston Hughes, Claude McKay, Countee Cullen,** and **Jean Toomer,** among others. Locke also edited a special issue of the journal *Survey Graphic* in 1925 that featured the work of younger writers. In addition, he served as a go-between, helping to secure patronage for young writers. For example, he was a good friend of Mrs. Charlotte Osgood Mason, who supported the early careers of Langston Hughes and **Zora Neale Hurston**. Subsequently, Hughes and Mason parted ways over differing views about literature, a conflict that is reflected in Hughes's short story "The Blues I'm Playing," in which a female musician discovers she must break with her wealthy patron. Locke and Hurston more or less sided with Mrs. Mason with regard to the disagreement with Hughes, and this circumstance probably contributed to the subsequent feud between Hurston and Hughes, who had been collaborating on the play *Mule Bone* in 1930. (The "*Mule Bone* controversy" is detailed in an introduction to the 1991 edition of the play.) There is also some indication that Locke was sexually and romantically interested in both Hughes and Cullen (Rampersad).

In addition to adding intellectual weight and vision to the Harlem Renaissance, editing *The New Negro*, and editing *Survey Graphic*, Locke was a professor of philosophy at Howard University in **Washington, D.C.**, from 1918 to 1953, contributing significantly to the intellectual lives of numerous African Americans. He was absent from Howard University from 1925 to 1928 because the White president of the university suspended him for insubordination. Locke taught at Fisk University during those years, returning to Howard in 1929, as the Harlem Renaissance was winding down.

Alain Locke, 1926. Yale Collection of American Literature, Beinecke Rare Book and Manuscript Library.

Locke wrote book reviews, and an especially supportive one about Hughes's controversial volume of short stories, *The Ways of White Folks* (1934). In the review, Locke wrote: "These fourteen stories of Negro–white contacts told from the unusual angle of the Negro point of view are challenging to all who would understand the later phases of the race question as it takes on the new complications of contemporary social turmoil and class struggle" (565). Lewis notes that "Locke's role in the Harmon Foundation's decision to support African American painters [during the Harlem Renaissance] was crucial" (756).

Resources: Leonard Harris, ed., *The Critical Pragmatism of Alain Locke: A Reader on Value Theory* (Lanham, MD: Rowman & Littlefield, 1999); Zora Neale Hurston and Langston Hughes, *Mule Bone: A Comedy of Negro Life*, ed. George Houston Bass and Henry Louis Gates, Jr. (New York: HarperPerennial, 1991); David Levering Lewis, ed., *The Portable Harlem Renaissance Reader* (New York: Viking, 1994), 756; Russell J. Linneman, ed. *Alain Locke: Reflections on a Modern Renaissance Man* (Baton Rouge: Louisiana State University Press, 1982); Alain Locke, untitled review of *The Ways of White Folks*, by Langston Hughes, *Survey Graphic* 23 (Nov. 1934), 565; Alain Locke, ed., *The New Negro* (New York: Boni, 1925); Hans Ostrom, *A Langston Hughes Encyclopedia* (Westport, CT: Greenwood Press, 2002), 215–216; Arnold Rampersad, *The Life of Langston Hughes*, vol. 1, *1902–1941* (New York: Oxford University Press, 1986), 66–71.

Hans Ostrom

Lorde, Audre (1934–1992). Poet, essayist, activist, autobiographer, and nonfiction writer. Lorde is revered as one of the foremost African American women writers of the twentieth century. Her voluminous body of poetry, essays, and speeches; her theoretical foresight; and her riveting autobiographical writings have helped establish her reputation as one of the preeminent Black feminist thinkers and writers of our time. Self-described as a "black feminist lesbian mother warrior poet," Lorde continually refused to sever any one part of her identity from other aspects of her life that constituted her being and understanding of self. Her collective body of work makes clear that she was very committed to engaging issues surrounding racial, sexual, and class oppression. She was also determined to explore the meaning and treatment of difference in a society marred by prejudice and inequality. Many readers and writers have been inspired by her call to end oppressive silences and to seek justice and freedom for all members of society.

Lorde was born on February 18, 1934, in **Harlem, New York**, and grew up during the **Great Depression**. Her parents, Frederick Byron and Linda Belmar Lorde, were immigrants from Grenada who had planned to return to the West Indies until the Depression ended their hopes to do so. Audre Geraldine, the youngest of three daughters, was born tongue-tied and was considered legally blind because her nearsightedness was so acute. She learned how to talk as she learned how to read at the age of four. Even as a young child Lorde developed a fascination with language and words, so much so that she often spoke in poetry. It became a preferred mode of communication for her, and when she was unable to find poems that adequately described or expressed her feelings, she began to write her own. As she indicated in an interview with longtime friend and writer Adrienne Rich, "When someone said to me, 'How do you feel?' or 'What do you think?' or asked another direct question, I would recite a poem, and somewhere in that poem would be the feeling, the vital piece of information. It might be a line. It might be an image. The poem was my response" (*Sister Outsider*, 82). Her first poem was published in the magazine *Seventeen* when she was just seventeen years old, though by that time she had been writing poetry for several years.

The young Audre attended Catholic grammar schools in Manhattan before entering Hunter High School, places where she often felt like an outsider. She went on to receive her B.A. degree from Hunter College in 1959 and a master's in library science from Columbia University in 1961. Lorde supported herself as a student with jobs including medical clerk, factory worker, X-ray technician, social worker, and apprentice to a maker of stained-glass windows, experiences she details in her autobiographical writing. Following her graduation from Columbia, she was a librarian in New York public schools from 1961 through 1968. In 1962, Lorde married attorney Edward Ashley Rollins. They had two children, and divorced in 1970. Lorde became the head librarian at the Town School Library in New York City in 1966, and continued both her writing and her growing participation as an activist in the civil rights, antiwar, gay and lesbian, and feminist movements.

The year 1968 was an especially pivotal time for Lorde. She received a National Endowment for the Arts grant and became poet-in-residence at Tougaloo College in Mississippi. There she developed a real love for teaching and entered into relationships with other Black writers whom she had not experienced while participating in the Harlem Writers Guild, a writing group that made her feel as though she was tolerated rather than accepted as a writer. Her time at Tougaloo was also especially significant because it resulted in her meeting her longtime partner, Frances Clayton. Though she was there for only six weeks, her experiences in Mississippi were thus life-altering on many fronts. She realized that teaching and writing were vocations she not only wanted, but needed, to pursue; she shared an emotional connection with other writers and students for the first time, talking openly about poetry; she met someone who became her lifelong partner; and she received a copy of her first volume of poetry, *The First Cities*, published in 1968.

The First Cities, written on such themes as the nature of personal relationships and feelings, was the beginning of Lorde's very prolific published writing career. Her second volume of poetry, *Cables to Rage*, appeared in 1970, and focuses on such themes as love and parenting, the transcendence of birth, and the unfortunate reality of betrayal. Her third volume of poetry, *From a Land Where Other People Live* (1973), was nominated for a National Book Award. It signaled Lorde's growing exploration of oppression on a global scale even as it continued her investigation of the complexities of her identity; the nature of anger, love, and loneliness; and the importance of relationships.

Lorde's vision and voice as a poet continued to flourish in the wake of her first three publications. Her fourth volume of poetry, *New York Head Shop and Museum*, was released in 1974, and was followed by *Coal* in 1976, whose publication by Norton brought her a broader readership than she had previously experienced. Her most celebrated work, however, is likely her seventh volume of poetry, *The Black Unicorn* (1978), considered by many critics to be the literary masterpiece of her career as a writer. Its complex themes, surrounding motherhood, spirituality, pride, gender, and sexuality, emerge as she spans three centuries of the Black **diaspora** and seeks to reclaim African mythology. Her more recent poetry collections include *Chosen Poems, Old and New* (1982) and *Our Dead Behind Us* (1986). More than 300 of her poems have been brought together in *The Collected Poems of Audre Lorde* (1997), which offers its readers unparalleled access to her diverse body of poetry.

Though Lorde identified most with poetry as a writer, her presence in African American literature is certainly also marked by her prose, essays, speeches, and autobiographical writings. A frightening diagnosis of breast cancer led her to publish her first book-length prose collection, *The Cancer Journals*, in 1980. This moving and very personal text details her decision to undergo a mastectomy, her feelings surrounding (and refusal to wear) a prosthesis, her confrontation with death and her own mortality, the sustaining love of the women who surrounded her throughout her surgery and thereafter, and

Audre Lorde, c. 1975. Courtesy of the Library of Congress.

the power and rewards that can be found in what she terms "self-conscious living." It is a remarkable account of a woman openly confronting the silences surrounding an illness that affects millions of women across the globe, a woman who seeks to understand the implications of those silences more fully. As she puts it in the introduction to the text, "I am a post-mastectomy woman who believes our feelings need voice in order to be recognized, respected, and of use. I do not wish my anger and pain and fear about cancer to fossilize into yet another silence, nor to rob me of whatever strength can lie at the core of this experience, openly acknowledged and examined" (7). Lorde continued to write about issues surrounding cancer and her own battle with the illness in her 1988 collection *A Burst of Light*.

Lorde's prose writing continued with the publication of *Zami: A New Spelling of My Name* in 1982. Labeled a biomythography, this memoir draws from a combination of history, **autobiography**, poetry, and other creative elements to explore her childhood and upbringing, development as a writer, sexuality, and other pivotal moments and relationships in her life. Following the publication of *Zami*, many of Lorde's best-known essays and speeches were collected in *Sister Outsider* (1984). This collection reveals Lorde's unyielding exploration and examination of difference and the reactions that difference elicits, her belief that poetry is a necessity for women, her refusal to see herself apart from injustices that are experienced globally, and her ongoing investigations and theorizations of identity, sexuality, **feminism**, and oppression.

Lorde's accolades include two National Endowment for the Arts grants (1968 and 1981), two Creative Artists Public Service grants (1972 and 1976), a Broadside Poets Award (1975), an American Library Association Gay Caucus Book of the Year for *The Cancer Journals* (1981), a National Book Award for Prose (1989), a Borough of Manhattan President's Award for literary excellence (1987), and a Walt Whitman Citation of Merit as poet laureate of New York (1991). She was also cofounder, with **Barbara Smith**, of the **Kitchen Table: Women of Color Press**, and served as editor of the lesbian journal *Chrysalis*.

Lorde is likely best known, however, as a writer, speaker, and thinker who was deeply invested in the power and potential of words, and who used her vision and talent in the service of creating a more just world. Her writing continues to be widely taught in college classrooms nationwide, especially those centered on the areas of **gay literature** and **lesbian literature**, Women's Studies, contemporary poetry, and studies of race. Indeed, as many of her avid readers are well aware, Lorde's words have continued to live on well after her death. She was a writer who urged her readers to see themselves not only as agents in their own lives, but also as social members who were connected to all others and who had the power to foster or to work to eliminate social and political oppression. Her body of work continues to resound in those who share her commitment to and passion for justice, and who also seek to acknowledge and better understand those experiences shrouded in silence.

Resources: Primary Sources: Audre Lorde: *Between Ourselves* (Point Reyes, CA: Eidolon Editions, 1976); *The Black Unicorn* (New York: Norton, 1978); *A Burst of Light: Essays* (Ithaca, NY: Firebrand, 1988); *Cables to Rage* (London: Paul Breman, 1970); *The Cancer Journals* (1980; repr. San Francisco: Aunt Lute, 1997); *Chosen Poems, Old and New* (New York: Norton, 1982); *Coal* (New York: Norton, 1976); *The Collected Poems of Audre Lorde* (New York: Norton, 1997); *The First Cities* (New York: Poets Press, 1968); *From a Land Where Other People Live* (Detroit: Broadside Press, 1973); *I Am your Sister: Black Women Organizing Across Sexualities* (New York: Kitchen Table—Women of Color Press, 1985); *The Marvelous Arithmetics of Distance: Poems 1987–1992* (New York: Norton, 1993); *Need: A Chorale for Black Woman Voices* (Latham, NY: Kitchen Table—Women of Color Press, 1990); *New York Head Shop and Museum* (Detroit: Broadside Press, 1974); *Our Dead Behind Us: Poems* (New York: Norton, 1986); *Sister Outsider: Essays and Speeches* (Trumansburg, NY: Crossing Press, 1984); *Uses of the Erotic: The Erotic as Power*, Out and Out Pamphlet no. 3 (New York: Out and Out Books, 1978); *Undersong: Chosen Poems Old and New* (New York: Norton, 1992); *Zami: A New Spelling of My Name* (Watertown, MA: Persephone Press, 1982). **Secondary Sources:** Alexis DeVeaux, *Warrior Poet: A Biography of Audre Lorde* (New York: Norton, 2004); Barbara Christian, *Black Feminist Criticism: Perspectives on Black Women Writers* (New York: Pergamon, 1985); Gloria T. Hull, "Living on the Line: Audre Lorde and *Our Dead Behind Us*," in *Changing Our Own Words: Essays on Criticism, Theory, and Writing by Black Women*, ed. Cheryl A. Wall (New Brunswick, NJ: Rutgers University Press, 1989), 150–172; Claudia Tate, ed., *Black Women Writers at Work* (New York: Continuum, 1983).

Amanda Davis

Los Angeles, California. Approximately 11.25 percent of Los Angeles' 3.7 million residents are African American, but given the ever-increasing diversity in the city's population, African American cultural influence in the city has gradually eroded over the last quarter-century.

African Americans began to move to Los Angeles during the **Great Migration** out of the Deep South that occurred during the 1910s and 1920s. But the tremendous expansion of the city's industrial base during **World War II** greatly accelerated the growth of the city's African American population, as it did the city's total population. The new economic opportunities but persistent social and civil obstacles faced by African Americans during this period are powerfully depicted in **Chester Himes**'s novels *If He Hollers Let Him Go* (1945) and *Lonely Crusade* (1947). Himes had moved to Los Angeles hoping to find employment as a screenwriter with one of the film studios. The studios, however, did not hire African Americans into such positions, and Himes ended up working in the shipyards instead. The experience, in particular his mistreatment by fellow labor unionists because of his race, proved so disillusioning that he later emigrated to France. (*See* **Expatriate Writers**; **Paris, France**.)

The most well-known African American community of Los Angeles was Watts, a 2.5-square-mile district in the southeast of the city. Named for the real estate broker who developed it as a residential suburb for working-class families, Watts initially had an equal mix of Caucasian, Mexican American, and African American residents. **Arna Bontemps**, the poet and folklorist associated with the **Harlem Renaissance**, grew up in Watts before attending Pacific Union College. In the quarter-century following World War II, the African American population of Watts increased exponentially, and soon the district was almost entirely African American. In 1965, much of the commercial property in the district was destroyed in violent riots that erupted in response to inequities in the economic, educational, and political opportunities available to African Americans and in their treatment by law enforcement and the legal system.

Today, Watts is a largely Latino district, but the adjacent districts of South Central Los Angeles and Compton still have large African American populations. The Leimert Park neighborhood in the South Central district was long considered one of the largest and most stable middle-class African American neighborhoods in the United States. Like Watts, however, South Central Los Angeles and Compton have become economically depressed as much low-skilled industrial work has shifted to overseas plants. Dominated by gangs, the districts have come to be widely associated with the predatory violence and the drug-related culture of urban decay. In 1992, in the wake of the acquittal of the police officers being tried for beating Rodney King, South Central exploded in the largest riots the city had seen since those in Watts more than a quarter-century earlier. In the aftermath of the riots, many African Americans in the district relocated north to Antelope Valley or east to Inland Empire.

Of all of the African American writers currently connected in some way with Los Angeles, **Walter Mosley** is probably the most widely identified with the city. A native of Los Angeles, Mosley was educated at the City University of New York and has been a longtime New York resident. But in most of his novels, he has returned to Los Angeles as it was while he was growing up. Although he has produced work in several other genres, Mosley's career has been defined by his work in the mystery-detective genre. Indeed, Mosley has transcended the usual formulas of the genre and created an African American complement to the novels of Raymond Chandler, which have long provided the lens through which residents and outsiders alike have perceived the city. In Mosley's novels, however, readers are introduced not to some poetic underside of respectability, but rather to a truly gritty Los Angeles from which the manifestations of affluence are far removed, a Los Angeles of hard streets populated by hard characters for whom "romance" is not an illusory obsession but a truly dangerous delusion. (*See* **Crime and Mystery Fiction.**)

Mosley's equivalent to Philip Marlowe is Ezekial "Easy" Rawlins, a World War II veteran who becomes a sort of freelance private detective when he is laid off from an aircraft plant. With his sidekick, named Mouse, he investigates cases that are never as straightforward as they first seem. In *Devil in a Blue Dress* (1990) he is hired to track down a blonde who likes to hang out in Black jazz clubs but suddenly becomes very elusive. In *A Red Death* (1991) Easy buys some apartment buildings with stolen money and is then coerced by the IRS into cooperating with the FBI in their investigation of a union organizer whom they believe to be a communist operative. In *White Butterfly* (1992) Easy is hired to investigate the deaths of three young African American women, apparently the victims of a serial killer, and gets caught up in the politics of race when the killer's fourth victim is White and the notorious daughter of a prominent city official. Subsequent titles in the series have been *Black Betty* (1994), *A Little Yellow Dog* (1996), *Gone Fishin'* (1997), *Bad Boy Brawly Brown* (2002), and *Little Scarlet* (2004).

With the publication of *Always Outnumbered, Always Outgunned* (1998), Mosley introduced another series character. A collection of interconnected stories that have a novelistic unity, the book focuses on Socrates Fortlow, a recently released convict who has served twenty-seven years in an Indiana prison for rape and murder. After his release he relocates to Watts, where he gradually becomes a community activist. A subsequent Fortlow book has been *Walkin' the Dog* (1999).

Another notable mystery-detective novelist based in Los Angeles is **Gar Anthony Haywood**, whose series featuring ex–Los Angeles police officer Aaron Gunner has received a good deal of critical attention. Titles in the series have included *Fear of the Dark* (1988), *Not Long for This World* (1990), *You Can Die Trying* (1993), *It's Not a Pretty Sight* (1996), *When Last Seen Alive* (1997), and *All the Lucky Ones Are Dead* (1999).

Donald Goines, who was murdered in a Los Angeles hotel in 1974, was the most prolific African American author of crime "pulps" in the late 1960s and early 1970s. A former convict who had committed a variety of often violent crimes, Goines had a too-intimate knowledge of the hard milieu within which his characters lived and operated. A sort of literary equivalent to the **blaxploitation** films, his novels had titles such as *Black Gangster, Daddy Cool, Dopefiend, Inner City Hoodlum, Never Die Alone,* and *Whoreson.* In little more than a half-decade, Goines produced sixteen of these novels. Many were published by Holloway House, a Los Angeles publisher that has focused on what a reviewer for the *Washington Post* has described as an African American "literature of degradation." Although Holloway House claims that Goines's titles continue to sell well and altogether have sold several million copies, the publisher's most notorious and commercially successful offering has probably been the memoirs of the former pimp **Iceberg Slim**.

Even more controversial has been the effort of Marc Gerald's Syndicate Media Group to market noir novellas with gangsta rap CDs. The first offering in the series was *Street Sweeper*, by Ronin Ro, which features a hit man whose signature is that he makes his kills from city buses. Other titles in the series have included *The International* by Antoine Black, *XXL Money* by Roland Jefferson, and *Platinum* by Michael Gonzales. Civic and religious leaders in Los Angeles' gang-dominated neighborhoods have protested the pointed marketing of these packaged violent pulp novels and rap CDs to the very young men whom they are trying to persuade to abandon gang violence.

In contrast to these crime novelists, **Eric Jerome Dickey** has focused on the social and romantic relationships of middle-class African Americans in contemporary Los Angeles. Although not formally a "series," the novels are consistent in focus and intention. Since 1996, Dickey has published just about a novel per year, and his novels have proven to be increasingly popular. His first novel, *Sister, Sister* (1996), focuses on five sisters and explores how their closeness inevitably creates many complexities in their friendships and romantic relationships. Dickey's third novel, *Milk in My Coffee* (1998), depicts an interracial relationship. In his eighth novel, *Drive Me Crazy* (2004), he comes closest to Mosley's milieu. The protagonist is a chauffeur who has an affair with his boss's wife, agrees to kill his boss for a price, keeps the money without committing the murder, and then is stalked by the wife.

Currently a resident of Los Angeles, **Bebe Moore Campbell** was born in **Philadelphia, Pennsylvania**, and raised there and in North Carolina. Most of her work has been set in the Northeast or the South, but in her novel *Brothers and Sisters* (1994) she has explored the causes and effects of the riots that followed the Rodney King verdict. The protagonist is an African American woman working at a downtown bank who is both appalled and deeply moved by the riots. Her ambivalence toward the riots reflects her broader ambivalence about her place and the place of African Americans within American society.

A native of Pasadena and a graduate of Pasadena City College and UCLA, **Octavia Butler** has been the first African American woman to achieve broad recognition within the **science fiction** genre. She has received several Hugo and Nebula Awards. Best known for her "Patternists" series, which depicts a futuristic society managed by a race of telepaths, Butler has drawn directly on his work experience in Los Angeles in the novel *Kindred* (1979), in which the character Dana has many autobiographical aspects.

Born in West Los Angeles, **Paul Beatty** is a leading voice among the generation of African American writers now coming to prominence. His novels include the critically acclaimed *The White Boy Shuffle* (1996) and *Tuff* (2000). His collections of poetry include *Big Bank Take Little Bank* (1990) and *Joker, Joker, Deuce* (1993). Other young African American novelists with Los Angeles connections include **Jenoyne Adams** (*Resurrecting Mingus*, 2001), Nancy Rawles (*Love Like Gumbo*, 1997), Nina Revoyr (*Southland*, 2003), and John Ridley (*Stray Dogs*, 1997).

The most prominent African American poet based in Los Angeles has probably been **Wanda Coleman**. For her collection *Bathwater: Wine* (1999) she received the Lenore Marshall Poetry Prize, and her collection *Mercurochrome: New Poems* (2001) was a finalist for the National Book Award. Other African American poets with Los Angeles connections have included **Harryette Mullen**, Saundra Sharp, and Conney Williams. Los Angeles is also home to the well-known rap poet Medusa, the slam poet Sekou the Misfit, and the self-described "performance novelist" Heather Woodbury.

African American plays have been produced by a variety of theater companies in Los Angeles, from community to university to major commercial theaters. A number of theater companies in Los Angeles are devoted specifically to producing African American and other multiethnic plays. These include the Cornerstone Theater Company, the Robey Theater Company, the Towne Street Theater, the Unity Players Ensemble at the Stella Adler Theater, and the West Village Theater at the Robert Pitts Center.

June Jordan's play *I Was Looking at the Ceiling and Then I Saw the Sky* (1995) explores racial tensions and romantic conundrums that pointedly surface in the response to an earthquake in Los Angeles. **Anna Deavere Smith**'s *Twilight: Los Angeles, 1992: On the Road: A Search for American Character* (1993) is a work of "documentary theater," telling the story of the riots that follow the Rodney King verdict through the words of people who experienced those riots firsthand. After a peripatetic upbringing as an "army brat," **Suzan-Lori Parks** has settled in Los Angeles. The author of a number of experimental plays, Parks received the Pulitzer Prize for Drama in 2002 for her play *Topdog/Underdog*.

Resources: Jerry Cohen and William S. Murphy, *Burn, Baby, Burn! The Los Angeles Race Riot, August, 1965* (New York: Dutton, 1966); Robert Conot, *Rivers of Blood, Years of Darkness* (New York: Bantam, 1967); David M. Fine, *Imagining Los Angeles: A City in Fiction* (Albuquerque: University of New Mexico Press, 2000); David M. Fine, ed., *Los Angeles in Fiction: A Collection of Essays* (Albuquerque: University of New Mexico Press, 1995); Juliet Murphet, *Literature and Race in Los Angeles* (New York: Cambridge University Press, 2001); Charles E. Wilson, Jr., *Walter Mosley: A Critical Companion* (Westport, CT: Greenwood Press, 2003).

Martin Kich

Lotus Press (1972–present). Publisher. Established by **Naomi Long Madgett** and three supporters in **Detroit, Michigan**, Lotus Press has published more than eighty books of poetry to date. Although some of its early publications express sentiments and points of view in keeping with the **Black Arts Movement**, Lotus aimed to provide a creative space for an array of Black poetry of excellence regardless of political outlook. Its first publication was Madgett's *Pink Ladies in the Afternoon: New Poems, 1965–1971* (1972). In 1974 Madgett assumed full editorial and financial leadership of the press, often editing, printing, and distributing the titles at her own expense. Lotus Press's primary goal was to encourage Black poets by being a publisher that not only would showcase their work but also would ensure their longevity as writers. This goal was particularly crucial in the 1970s and early 1980s, when major publishing houses seldom released more a few poetry titles per year. Several of Lotus's poets, including Madgett, also published with **Dudley Randall's Broadside Press.** The two presses formed a support system for important African American writers in the 1970s, including Randall, **Margaret Abigail Walker,** and **Audre Lorde.** Lotus also played an important role in distributing and promoting the works of established poets, including **May Miller,** Herbert Woodward Martin, **Lance Jeffers, James Emanuel,** and **Houston A. Baker, Jr.** It also supported the early careers of new poets such as **Toi Derricotte, Paulette Childress White, Bill Harris,** Baraka Sele (Pamela Cobb), and Kiarri T-H. Cheatwood.

One of Lotus Press's most significant contributions has been in secondary education. Frustrated by the dismissal of Black poetry by White teachers, Madgett published *Deep Rivers—A Portfolio: 20 Contemporary Black American Poets* in 1978, a collection of highly visual poster-poems along with a teacher's guide that included suggestions on how such poetry could be integrated into English courses. *Deep Rivers,* which is still in print, was well received by the National Council of Teachers of English, which ordered several hundred copies and distributed them to schools across the United States.

Lotus Press has received much critical acclaim as one of the few small Black presses to enjoy more than three decades of continued success. It is also regarded as having played an ongoing role in opening up the **literary canon** to African American poets. Dudley Randall's poetry collection *A Litany of Friends* (1981) and the critically acclaimed *Adam of Ife: Black Women in Praise of Black Men* (1992), an anthology about African American men as perceived through the eyes of African American women, are but two examples of the excellence Lotus is known for. Madgett and the press have won many awards and honors, including the 1993 American Book Award. In 1993, Lotus temporarily turned over book distribution to Michigan State University Press, which also published titles by the first five winners of the Naomi Long Madgett Poetry Award for outstanding poetry by an African American. In 1998, Lotus Press resumed distribution and has since published winners of the yearly poetry award.

Resources: Melba Joyce Boyd and M. L. Liebler, eds., *Abandon Automobile: Detroit City Poetry 2001* (Detroit: Wayne State University Press, 2000); Lotus Press, *A Short History of Lotus Press* (Detroit: Lotus Press, 2004); Julius E. Thompson, *Dudley Randall, Broadside Press, and the Black Arts Movement in Detroit, 1960–1995* (Jefferson, NC: McFarland, 1999).

Dara N. Byrne

Louis, Joe (1914–1981). Prizefighter. Joe Louis (born Joseph Louis Barrow), the heavyweight champion of the world during the 1930s and 1940s, symbolized African American patriotism and pride during the **Great Depression** and **World War II.** His fighting skills and heroism made the boxer a significant subject in African American literature of the twentieth century.

Louis was born May 13, 1914, in Chambers County, Alabama, where the family struggled economically following the death of Louis's institutionalized father. The young Louis worked in the cotton fields and spent little time in school. In 1926, the family moved to **Detroit, Michigan**, seeking greater economic opportunity in the industrialized North. Louis again eschewed school, contributing to the family's income by delivering groceries.

The young man found a sense of direction in boxing in the Golden Gloves program, winning the heavyweight championship of Detroit in 1934. He fought his first professional fight on July 4, 1934, under the direction of the African American managers John Roxborough and Julian Black as well as the trainer Jack Blackburn, who became a father figure to Louis. The management team was concerned that Louis would not be able to attain a heavyweight championship if he followed the example of the previous Black champ, Jack Johnson, who was considered arrogant and threatening to Whites. Accordingly, Louis was forbidden to be photographed alone with White women, gloat over fallen opponents, and go to nightclubs alone.

Louis's first major fight was at Yankee Stadium in New York on July 25, 1935, against the Italian heavyweight Primo Carnera. The bout took on symbolic importance with the Italian invasion of Ethiopia, and Louis was a knockout winner in six rounds. With his reputation growing, Louis was scheduled to fight former champion Max Schmeling of Germany on June 19, 1936. He failed to train vigorously for the contest, and Schmeling was victorious with a knockout. Nazi Germany used the bout as propaganda regarding Negro inferiority and Aryan superiority.

A rededicated Louis followed up the Schmeling fight with seven impressive bouts that earned him a shot at the championship. On June 22, 1937, Louis defeated champion Jim Braddock, becoming at age twenty-three the youngest heavyweight champion in boxing history. Following two title defenses, he secured a rematch with Schmeling. With the political situation deteriorating in Europe, the fight gained considerable international attention. On June 22, 1938, Louis destroyed his German opponent in less than two minutes, smashing the concept of Aryan superiority. Louis, who had fought only White opponents, was already a hero to the Black community, but with the defeat of Schmeling, he attained a large following in the White community and emerged for many as America's champion.

Louis continued to defend his title over the next three years, then enlisted in the armed services on January 10, 1942. During the war, Louis was a symbol of democratic nationalism for the United States. He participated in numerous war bond activities and fought exhibitions to raise money for the war effort. The purses from Louis's title defenses in 1942 were donated to the Navy and Army Relief Funds. The downside to these patriotic endeavors was that Louis found himself in debt and behind on his taxes.

Following the war, Louis defended his title numerous times in order to recoup his finances. He retired in 1948 as the first undefeated heavyweight champion (the loss to Schmeling was before Louis attained his championship). However, financial considerations brought the "Brown Bomber" out of retirement until his October 26, 1951, defeat at the hands of Rocky Marciano. Still plagued by financial problems, Louis performed as a professional wrestler and boxing referee while suffering numerous business setbacks. He spent his final years as a "greeter" at a Las Vegas casino before succumbing to a heart attack on April 12, 1981. Although he was often overlooked by American society in his later years, his World War II service to the nation was recognized at his burial in Arlington National Cemetery with full military honors.

During the difficult days of the Great Depression and World War II, Louis was a hero who offered hope, dignity, and pride for Black Americans. He refused to succumb to the negative stereotypes of African Americans perpetuated by the popular culture of the era. Louis has figured in the work of such prominent African American writers as **Langston Hughes, Richard Wright, James Baldwin, Malcolm X, Maya Angelou, Chester Himes, Ernest James Gaines,** and **Amiri Baraka.**

Louis's victories over his White opponents were celebrated in the Black community during the 1930s. While Blacks poured into the streets of New York City to cheer his victory over Primo Carnera, celebrations in the rural South had to be more subdued. In *I Know Why the Caged Bird Sings*, Maya Angelou described rural Blacks crowding into her uncle's village store in order to listen to radio broadcasts of Louis's fights. Angelou writes that Louis was the race. If he faltered, "We were back in **slavery** and beyond help." But when Louis emerged triumphant, "It wouldn't do for a Black man and his family to be caught on a lonely country road on a night when Joe Louis had proved that we were the strongest people in the world." Richard Wright contended that Louis allowed Blacks to feel invincible, asserting, "From the symbol of Joe Louis Negroes took strength, and that moment all fear, all obstacles were wiped out, drowned." In his autobiography, Malcolm X observed, "Every Negro boy old enough to walk wanted to be the next Brown Bomber." In his second autobiography, *I Wonder as I Wander*, Langston Hughes discusses the symbolic importance of the Louis–Schmelling bouts, especially to African Americans.

Louis was cognizant of the heavy burden placed upon him by the Black community, observing in his **autobiography** that he was perceived as a "savior" who would "show them whites." It was a heavy burden to bear, but Louis was equal to the task of becoming a Black hero in White America.

Resources: Maya Angelou, *I Know Why the Caged Bird Sings* (New York: Random House, 1969), 110–115; Gerald Astor, *". . . And a Credit to His Race": The Hard Life and Times of Joseph Louis Barrow, a.k.a. Joe Louis* (New York: Saturday Review Press, 1974); Lenwood G. Davis, comp., *Joe Louis: A Bibliography of Articles, Books, Pamphlets, Records, and Archival Materials* (Westport, CT: Greenwood Press, 1983); Gerald Early, *The Culture of Bruising: Essays on Prizefighting, Literature, and Modern American Culture* (Hopewell, NJ: Ecco Press, 1994); Malcolm X and Alex Haley, *The Autobiography of Malcolm X* (New York: Grove Press, 1965), 23–24; Langston Hughes, "Prelude to Spain," in his *I Wonder as I Wander* (New York: Rinehart, 1956), 314–321; Lawrence W. Levine, *Black Culture and Black Consciousness: Afro-American Folk*

Thought from Slavery to Freedom (New York: Oxford University Press, 1977); Joe Louis with Edna Rust and Art Rust, Jr., *Joe Louis: My Life* (New York: Berkley Publishing, 1981); Donald McRae, *Heroes Without a Country: America's Betrayal of Joe Louis and Jessie Owens* (New York: HarperCollins, 2004); Chris Mead, *Champion: Joe Louis, Black Hero in White America* (New York: Scribner's, 1985); Barney Nagler, *Brown Bomber* (New York: World Publishing, 1972); Richard Wright, "Black Pride Popped Loose on the Day Joe Louis Won," *Detroit Free Press*, Apr. 13, 1981, pp. 1B, 3B.

Ron Briley

Love, Monifa A. (born 1955). Poet, novelist, and professor. Love's second book of poems, *Dreaming Underground*, won the 2003 **Naomi Long Madgett** Poetry Award from **Lotus Press** in **Detroit, Michigan.** Lotus Press also published her first volume, *Provisions* (1989), which she published under the name Monifa Atungaye. Love was born and grew up in **Washington, D.C.,** where she was among the first African American students to integrate the National Cathedral School for Girls (Ostrom, electronic-mail interview). She went on to graduate with honors from Princeton University, with a degree in anthropology and a certificate in African American Studies. Later she completed an M.A. and a Ph.D. in English at Florida State University.

Love's poetry and fiction are characterized in part by the use of many different voices and forms, including multiple characters, interior monologues, fictionalized letters, and fictionalized diary entries. Her work also displays a keen sense of African and African American history and of questions connected to **gender.** She is also deeply interested in circumstances leading to the imprisonment of so many African American males and what such problems suggest about American society in general.

Love's first published novel, *Freedom in the Dismal*, appeared in 1998. Of this novel, **Robert Farris Thompson** wrote, "The myriad gifts of Monifa Love ... all come together as she writes the Great American Novel. This is banner-like writing that waves like a flag over the nation within the nation within the continent." With her cousin, Evans D. Hopkins, Love collaborated on the essay "Deep-Rooted Cane: Consanguinity, Writing, and Genre" (1997). Love is Professor of English at Morgan State University in **Baltimore, Maryland,** where she coordinates the creative writing program and teaches creative writing and humanities.

Resources: Monifa A. Love: *Dreaming Underground* (Detroit: Lotus Press, 2003); *Freedom in the Dismal* (Kaneohe, HI: Plover Press, 1998); (as Monifa Atungaye) *Provisions* (Detroit: Lotus Press, 1989); Monifa A. Love and Evans D. Hopkins, "Deep-Rooted Cane: Consanguinity, Writing, and Genre," in *Genre and Writing: Issues, Arguments, Alternatives,* ed. Wendy Bishop and Hans Ostrom (Portsmouth, NH: Boynton-Cook/Heinemann, 1997), 81–90; Hans Ostrom, electronic-mail interview with Monifa A. Love, Dec. 14, 2004; Robert Farris Thompson, comment, back cover of Love's *Freedom in the Dismal.*

Hans Ostrom

Love, Nat (1854–1921). Autobiographical writer. Nat Love, author of *The Life and Adventures of Nat Love, Better Known in the Cattle Country as "Deadwood*

Dick," by Himself (1907), was the first Black man to document life in the "cattle country" of the United States. Born in a Tennessee slave cabin, he won some money at age fifteen in a horse raffle and set out for the "new" land of Kansas to work as a cowboy, walking partway and hitching rides the rest. Love had been hearing about the possibility of finding work as a cowboy and knew that this particular occupation was more open to African Americans than many others, so when he arrived in Dodge City, he approached a unit with Black cowboys and was hired immediately. Love became an excellent cowboy and marksman, and he was able to identify all the cattle brands in the entire West.

The first part of his book is strongly informed by the **slave narrative**, with Love recounting what it was like for him growing up "owned" by another person. The largest part of his **autobiography**, however, consists of numerous fantastic accounts, full of braggadocio, of his life as a cowboy, told in tall-tale fashion so that truth is hard to distinguish from fact. For example, he tells of being captured by Indians, killing many Indians, and being shot fourteen times but left relatively unharmed. He claims to have known Bat Materson, Billy the Kid, and the Jesse James gang, among other famous Wild West figures. He also tells how, in 1876, he won the title "Deadwood Dick" after showing phenomenal skill at a rodeo, winning all the top prizes. It is this title of which he seems most proud, referring to it a number of times as proof of his being set apart from other men.

The final section of his book discusses his finding work as a Pullman porter in 1890, after leaving the wild and free cowboy life for good. This latter phase of his life shows his movement into the comfortable Black middle class. Here Love sets another precedent: he becomes one of the first Blacks to depict himself in an autobiography as a successful, middle-class African American.

An independent spirit, strong will, and penchant for self-promotion characterize Love. He associated himself with the opportunities and wide-open spaces of the West, a land he saw as freely giving of its opportunities and riches—after all, wasn't he a former slave child who had become phenomenally successful as a cowboy and as a Wild West figure? In this way Love exemplifies the idea of the self-made man, the new American ideology of self-styled upward mobility through hard work and determination made popular by Horatio Alger after the middle of the nineteenth century.

Resources: Blake Allmendinger, "Deadwood Dick: The Black Cowboy as Cultural Timber," *Journal of American Culture* 16, no. 4 (Winter 1993), 79–89; Art Burton, *Black, Red, and Deadly* (Austin, TX: Eakin, 1991); Philip Durham and Everett L. Jones, *The Negro Cowboys* (Lincoln: University of Nebraska Press, 1965); William Loren Katz, *The Black West* (New York: Touchstone, 1987); Nat Love, *The Life and Adventures of Nat Love, Better Known in the Cattle Country as "Deadwood Dick"* (1970; Lincoln: University of Nebraska Press/Bison Books, 1995); Brackette F. Williams, "Introduction," in *The Life and Adventures of Nat Love* (Lincoln: University of Nebraska Press, 1995).

Stephanie Gordon

Lynching. In 1991, during the U.S. Senate's confirmation hearings of Supreme Court nominee Clarence Thomas, Thomas referred to the sensational media coverage of the allegations of sexual impropriety brought forward by Anita Hill as a "high-tech lynching." The immediate uproar that resulted from Thomas's controversial use of this image to describe his situation demonstrates the sustained power of lynching as a symbol in African American discourse and American society. (*See* **Lynching, History of.**)

In American literature generally and African American literature in particular, the lynching scene—in which individuals suffer grisly and lethal punishment for alleged crimes or cultural infractions by groups acting outside the law—has played a very significant role. Starting with **slave narratives**, newspaper accounts, and the events related in the early Black press, stories of deadly violence directed against Black people by Whites were frequent in the antebellum years. Indeed, in "I Was Born: Slave Narratives, Their Status as Autobiography and as Literature," James Olney asserts that these scenes of violence appeared to such a degree that they became one of the defining characteristics of the slave narrative genre. These early texts recorded acts of White-on-Black violence and murder as a means to evoke the cruelty of slave masters and the failure of the nation to uphold the ideals of freedom and justice stated in the U.S. Constitution. Lynching imagery, in these early texts, was evidence of both an American failure of justice and **slavery**'s dehumanizing effects on the lyncher and the lynched.

After the **Civil War** and the passage of the Fourteenth Amendment, which granted citizenship rights to Black people, incidents of lynching reached a statistical high point as hate groups, including the Ku Klux Klan, grew in number and influence. During this period from the **Reconstruction** through the turn of the twentieth century, American authors approached the representation of these horrific events from a variety of perspectives. For the White writer Thomas Dixon, whose 1905 novel *The Clansman* sold more than 100,000 copies, images of lynching were used to enhance an ideology of White supremacy. In her book *Race, Rape, and Lynching: The Red Record of American Literature, 1890–1912*, Sandra Gunning claims that literature written from this extreme viewpoint represented lynching as the final and most necessary means of controlling a Black population that had, in the view of Dixon and others, become rebellious and threatening since the end of slavery.

Although not all White writers took the same extreme position as Dixon, notable authors of the era, including figures such as Thomas Nelson Page and **Mark Twain**, used images of lynching that were less racist in nature but that, nevertheless, depended upon images of violence against Blacks as a means of articulating key aspects of White identity. This trend would continue well into the twentieth century, most evidently in authors such as William Faulkner, whose White characters in the story "A Dry September" are defined by their participation in or withdrawal from acts of violence against Blacks.

Turn-of-the-century texts by African American authors also covered a variety of approaches to lynching imagery. For instance, in **Ida B. Wells-Barnett**'s 1895 pamphlet, *A Red Record: Tabulated Statistics and Alleged Causes of Lynchings in the United States, 1892–1893–1894*, the author cites journalistic sources to show lynching as a densely symbolic effort to erase the Black presence from the American scene. In other works, such as **Booker T. Washington**'s 1901 **autobiography**, *Up from Slavery*, the author presents lynching as a rare occurrence that did not overly concern most Black people. Washington's problematic statement, though meant to quell the fears of the White benefactors he depended upon for the continued funding of Tuskeegee Institute and other important projects for Black advancement, contradict the university's own statistical analysis of lynching trends published in 1979.

Representations of lynching by Black writers have had their greatest impact in the areas of fiction, poetry, and drama. During the **Harlem Renaissance**, lynching or the fear of lynching was a frequent motivation for character actions. In **Rudolph Fisher**'s story "City of Refuge," for example, the main character flees to **Harlem, New York**, in order to escape a Southern lynch mob. Similarly, in **James Weldon Johnson**'s *Autobiography of an Ex-Colored Man*, the narrator's multilayered account of a lynching is in part responsible for his decision to abandon Blackness and pass as a White man. Frequently in works from this era, lynching appeared in the form of a sort of subliminal dread that was not always seen directly but that indicated the boundaries of Black engagement with the American dream.

Langston Hughes, a contemporary of Fisher's and Johnson's, wrote at least four poems about lynching: "Flight," "Lynching Song," "Silhouette," and "Song After Lynching." A key scene in both his short story "Father and Son" and his play *Mulatto* (which dramatizes the plot of "Father and Son") involves a threatened lynching (Ostrom, 223–224).

In other early representations of lynching in fiction by Black writers, such as **Sutton E. Griggs**'s *Imperium in Imperio* or **Charles Waddell Chesnutt**'s *The Marrow of Tradition*, the lynching scene is not central to the development of the plot in the story in which it occurs, but, because they graphically describe the lynching practice, these works began an emphasis on lynching's ritual aspects. In *Exorcising Blackness: Historical and Literary Lynching and Burning Rituals*, **Trudier Harris** explores literary accounts of the lynching ritual in great detail and notes the repetition of particular events, such as torture, immolation, the taking of trophies from the lynched body, and the importation of other Whites to serve as witnesses to the spectacular event.

A key assertion in Harris's argument states that for Black authors these ritualized accounts, particularly in their emphasis on the castration of the lynched individual, reveal anxieties over the emasculation of Black male identities within a racist American scene. Thus, lynching images are common in African American fiction that focus on young men **coming of age.** For example, in "The Coming of John," a short story from **W.E.B. Du Bois**'s *The Souls of Black Folk*, the main character, John, faces a lynch mob when his education and intellectual maturation lead him to a new understanding of his position in the racial hierarchy of the American South. When black coming-of-age narratives are associated with sexual maturity, the lynching scene is apt to play an even more powerful role, as demonstrated in **Richard Wright**'s short story "Big Boy Leaves Home." Here, though the crowd chasing Big Boy wants to lynch him primarily because he has killed a White man, Big Boy's predicament is initially caused when he and his friends are discovered, naked, by a White woman. Wright, like other Black writers, uses lynching imagery to insist that American racism does not allow Black males to achieve a state of manhood and, instead, forces them to remain forever as big boys.

As the twentieth century progressed, though recorded occurrences of actual lynching declined, events like the highly publicized 1955 murder of fourteen-year-old **Emmett Till** kept lynching in the foreground of the American imagination, and the lynch scene remained a frequent image in American literature. In these later representations, lynching imagery was to become more ambiguous, but no less important. In **Ralph Ellison**'s *Invisible Man*, for example, the narrator's hallucinated dream at the novel's conclusion depends upon lynching and castration imagery, but without the naturalist limitations on choice and opportunity characteristic of representations in Wright's work. Rather, Ellison's narrator uses the lynching scene as a means of establishing the clarity of his vision and his transcendence of the societal blindness that has rendered him invisible. Other representations of lynching after 1950 have been affected by the viewpoints of **Black nationalism**. In **Toni Morrison**'s *Song of Solomon*, for example, the character Guitar and others form the group Seven Days in response to incidents of White-on-Black violence. Here, although the lynching event is not represented, its effect is represented in Guitar's morally ambiguous militant perspective.

At the turn of the twenty-first century, lynching remains a powerful literary symbol. In contemporary literature, however, representations of the lynching scene have been influenced by the practices of **post-modernism**. **Paul Beatty**'s 1996 novel *The White Boy Shuffle* exemplifies this post-modern approach. In that work, Beatty's protagonist, Gunnar Kaufman, recalls the high school experiences of his father, who was forced to reenact the lynching of civil rights workers Andrew Goodman, Michael Schwerner, and James Cheney. Beatty's satiric approach to this historic event recontextualizes the lynching scene in a fashion that exemplifies new approaches to American history. His novel is indicative of the ways in which lynching imagery has developed and suggests its continuing, but transformed, role in American literature.

Sadly, contemporary American life has not run out of real lynching events to serve as the basis for literary representations. The 1998 murder of James Byrd—a forty-nine-year-old Black man living in Jasper, **Texas**—shows us that lynching has not disappeared from American society. Though these events have become rare, their symbolic impact has not waned. They will remain evocative images in American literature.

Resources: Sandra Gunning, *Race, Rape, and Lynching: The Red Record of American Literature, 1890–1912* (Bloomington: Indiana University Press, 1984); Trudier Harris, *Exorcising Blackness: Historical and Literary Lynching and Burning Rituals* (New

York: Oxford University Press, 1996); James Olney, "I Was Born: Slave Narratives, Their Status as Autobiography and as Literature," in *The Slave's Narrative*, ed. Charles T. Davis and Henry Louis Gates, Jr. (New York: Oxford University Press, 1985), 148–175; Hans Ostrom, *A Langston Hughes Encyclopedia* (Westport, CT: Greenwood Press, 2002), esp. "Lynching," 223–224.

Dennis Chester

Lynching, History of. Lynching is the unlawful execution, often by hanging, of an individual by a mob. In the decades between the end of **Reconstruction** in 1877 and the 1930s, lynchings were commonplace in **the South**. According to Stewart E. Tolnay and E. M. Beck, more than 2800 Americans—approximately 2500 of them African Americans—lost their lives to lynch mobs in the South between 1882 and 1930. The **NAACP**, surveying the period from 1889 to 1918 and covering all of the United States, places the figure at 3,224, including 691 white men, 11 white women, 2,472 African American men, and 50 African American women. In fact, lynchings occurred not just in the South but also in other states. Asante and Mattson indicate that between 1889 and 1918, for example, 24 lynchings were reported in Wyoming, 24 in Indiana, and 335 in **Texas**. Although there are examples of lynchings in America predating the end of Reconstruction and throughout the twentieth century, most lynchings occurred in the late nineteenth and early twentieth centuries. Although the practice of lynching was often defended as necessary to combat African American lawlessness and the threat of interracial sexual relations, lynching is more accurately characterized as a method of using murder to terrorize and control a subjugated population of African Americans in the post–**Civil War** era. Lynching has no basis in legitimate law.

Lynchings often became public spectacles: announced in advance, attended by a broad spectrum of society, and widely reported on in the press, complete with photographic evidence of brutalized bodies. Often lynchings were committed in public places—town squares or in front of courthouses—and photographic mementos of lynchings were available for purchase. Although the practice of lynching was often associated with the reign of terror led by the Ku Klux Klan—in both its Reconstruction and early twentieth-century variations—it was by no means limited to members of that notoriously racist and violent organization. More shockingly, lynchings often received quasi-public sanction, for members of law enforcement were often either complicit in allowing the release of prisoners for public lynchings or in their choice not to arrest and/or prosecute perpetrators of lynchings. Also deplorable are the reasons cited to justify lynchings; these included everything from adultery, vagrancy, and burglary to using obscene language and even voting for a candidate from the "wrong" political party (Tolnay and Beck).

Views on the history and etymology of the terms "lynch" and "lynch law" vary. James Cutler points to several possible origins of the terms: James Fitzstephen Lynch of Galway, Ireland, who executed his own son in 1493; the etymological origins of lynch in *to linch*, meaning to beat severely with a pliable instrument; Lynch's Creek, South Carolina, location of racial violence during Reconstruction; and Charles Lynch, for his administration of justice during the Revolutionary War. Despite the lack of certainty about the origins of the term "lynch," its earliest use in America can be dated positively to the first decades of the nineteenth century, and it has always been associated with summary execution by a mob.

The number of individuals lynched in a given year peaked in 1891 and 1892, with 194 and 226 lynchings in those years, respectively. Throughout the remainder of the nineteenth century, the total number of lynchings remained above 100 for each year. In the first decade of the twentieth century, at least fifty lynching were reported each year. In 1901, 1903, and 1908, the number exceeded 100 per year (Asante and Mattson; Tolnay and Beck). The vast majority of these lynchings are notable for their intense and ritualistic violence. Lynchings' victims were often dragged through the streets, verbally taunted, spit upon, whipped, beaten, cut, and branded before, during, and after the victim was killed by hanging or burning alive. Horrifically, parts of corpses such as fingers, toes, ears, and genitalia were sometimes collected as mementos of the occasion.

The crusade to end lynching in the United States began in the final decade of the nineteenth century and continued relatively unabated until the middle of the twentieth. During that time, organizations such as the Council on International Cooperation, the Young Women's Christian Association, the National Association of Colored Women, the United Negro Improvement Association, the National Citizens Rights Association, the National Equal Rights League, the American Civil Liberties Union, and others worked toward the eradication of lynching through programs of education, investigation, and publicity, as well as through advocacy for a federal antilynching statute. While activists such as **Ida B. Wells-Barnett** and organizations such as the NAACP and the Association of Southern Women for the Prevention of Lynching fought most valiantly for enactment of federal antilynching legislation, they were never successful. The antilynching crusade nevertheless paved the way for the **Civil Rights Movement**, and helped to establish the NAACP as a national force to be reckoned with in its pursuit of political and social justice.

Ida B. Wells-Barnett vocally and eloquently challenged the most prominent myth surrounding lynching—that most lynchings were justified in response to the rape of White women by Black men. She challenged this myth by investigating lynchings throughout the South and publicizing her findings. Her 1895 *On Lynchings* broadcast her findings to the world, showing that rape was seldom the charge for which Black men were lynched, and that the numerous lynchings of African American women directly challenged the alleged connection between rape and lynching. Moreover, Wells-Barnett argued that lynching was more accurately a mechanism for depriving African Americans of their constitutionally protected rights. Her book set the precedent for the antilynching campaigns that followed.

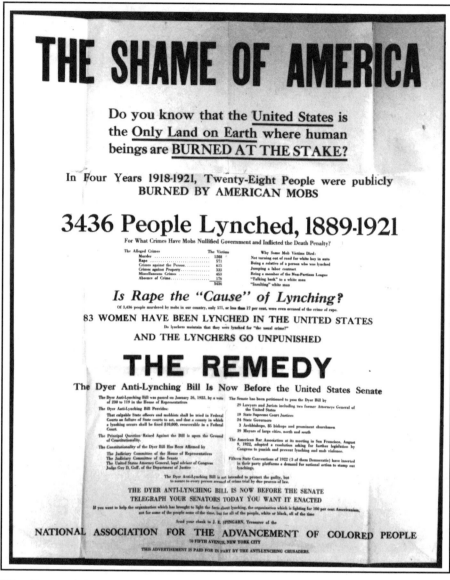

"The Shame of America"—NAACP flyer for Dyer's Anti-Lynching Bill, 1922–1923. Yale Collection of American Literature, Beinecke Rare Book and Manuscript Library.

When the NAACP was founded in 1909, a vigorous antilynching effort was already under way. However, because of the leadership of **James Weldon Johnson** and then of **Walter White** (whose 1929 *Rope & Faggot: A Biography of Judge Lynch* remains an indispensable account of lynching), trying to stop lynching became a primary focus of the organization. The NAACP hired Johnson in 1916, and by 1918 he had helped to launch a five-year attack on lynching. While this campaign included conferences, letter-writing campaigns, and countless editorials in the organization's publication **The Crisis**, the most visible

effort was in support of the Dyer bill—a piece of antilynching legislation introduced by Leonidas Dyer (a Republican from Missouri) in April 1918. Although
this bill and others like it—including the Costigan–Wagner bill in 1937—passed
the House of Representatives, no federal antilynching bill ever received Senate
approval. Between 1918 and 1923 and again between 1933 and 1937, a large
proportion of the NAACP's operating budget and its organizational efforts were
directed toward the crusade to end lynching.

Although America is long past the period in which "lynch law" was pervasive, lynchings can and do still occur with some frequency. (Wexler calls
a mob's murder of an African American couple in Georgia in 1946 "the last
mass-lynching in America.") Fortunately, widespread awareness of the unsup-
portable reasons behind "lynch law" and greater attention to the principle of
due process have meant that perpetrators of racial violence are more likely to be
apprehended and prosecuted for crimes ranging from kidnapping to inciting
violence to murder. Numerous likely reasons exist for the decline in lynchings
following the 1930s. Most of these are linked in some way to antilynching
activism. They include the intensified prosecution of lynch mobs, increased
African American migration to the North, greater tolerance of African
Americans in the South, mass media's attention to the topic, advances made by
the Civil Rights Movement, and the nation's preoccupation with the **Great
Depression** and **World War II**.

In addition to Wells-Barnett and White, other African American writers
have taken on the difficult subject of lynching in a variety of works. For example,
Paul Laurence Dunbar's poem "The Haunted Oak" concerns lynching, and
Claude McKay wrote a poem titled "The Lynching." **Jean Toomer**'s "Portrait in
Georgia," from *Cane*, dramatizes the fear instilled in African American men by
the specter of lynching. **Langston Hughes** represents lynching in the poems
"Flight," "Lynching Song," "Silhouette," and "Song After Lynching," as well
as in the short story "Father and Son," which concludes with a lynch mob
searching for the protagonist, Bert. Hughes used versions of the plot in "Father
and Son" in his play *Mulatto* and in an opera for which he wrote the libretto, *The
Barrier*. In addition, Billie Holliday's song "Strange Fruit" is, in part, about
lynching (Margolick and Als). (*See* **Lynching**; **Till, Emmett**.)

Resources: Molefi K. Asante and Mark Mattson, *The African-American Atlas: Black
History and Culture* (New York: Macmillan, 1998); Mark Curriden and Leroy Phillips,
*Contempt of Court: The Turn-of-the Century Lynching That Launched 100 Years of Fed-
eralism* (New York: Anchor, 2001); James Elbert Cutler, *Lynch-Law: An Investigation into
the History of Lynching in the United States* (Montclair, NJ: Patterson Smith, 1969); David
Margolick and Hilton Als, *Strange Fruit: The Biography of a Song* (New York: Ecco,
1991); National Association for the Advancement of Colored People, *Thirty Years of
Lynching in the United States: 1889–1918* (1919; repr. New York: Arno Press, 1969);
Stewart E. Tolnay and E. M. Beck, *A Festival of Violence: An Analysis of Southern
Lynchings, 1882–1930* (Urbana: University of Illinois Press, 1995); Ida B. Wells-
Barnett, *On Lynchings: Southern Horrors, A Red Record, Mob Rule in New Orleans* (New
York: Arno Press, 1969); Laura Wexler, *Fire in a Canebrake: The Last Mass Lynching in*

America (New York: Scribner's, 2003); Walter White, *Rope & Faggot: A Biography of Judge Lynch* (New York: Knopf, 1929); Stephen J. Whitfield, *A Death in the Delta: The Story of Emmett Till* (Baltimore: Johns Hopkins University Press, 1991); Robert L. Zangrando, *The NAACP Crusade Against Lynching, 1909–1950* (Philadelphia: Temple University Press, 1980).

Matthew R. Davis

Lyric Poetry. Considered the broadest category of poetry, a lyric is any relatively short poem that expresses the personal mood or perception of a single speaker, not necessarily the poet. (Originally the *lyric* poem was meant to be accompanied by a *lyre*, a stringed instrument.) Throughout its long history, African American literature has struggled creatively with such a categorization. Traditionally, lyric poetry (as opposed to dramatic or narrative/**epic poetry**) encompasses a wide variety of genres from the more common dramatic monologue, **sonnet**, **villanelle**, elegy, hymn, and ode to the aubade, **haiku**, and epithalamion (*see* **Formal Verse**). Due to the **vernacular** roots of African American literature, it might be argued that African American literature widens this category by including **spirituals** and **gospel**, work songs, **blues poetry**, and **jazz** poetics. With this emphasis on musicality in mind, much of the African American poetic tradition (particularly in the twentieth century) closely parallels the lyric's musical origins.

Still other African American poems further widen the lyric category by employing not a singular speaker ("I"), but a communal speaker ("we"). Communal speakers appear in African American lyric poetry from **Paul Laurence Dunbar**'s "We Wear the Mask" (1895) to **Gwendolyn Brooks**'s "We Real Cool" (1960). Similarly, in many poems, **Langston Hughes** uses the pronoun "I" to stand for a group of people, as in "The Negro Speaks of Rivers," so the singular pronoun represents a collective persona in this case (Ostrom, 77–78). Moreover, in keeping with the **signifying** nature of African American literature, African American lyric poetry often invokes its own ancestry. Many African American poets refer explicitly to earlier African American historical figures, poets, or artists; this tradition appears in poems such as **Robert Hayden**'s "A Letter from Phillis Wheatley" (1978), referring to one of the earliest known African American poets, and **Jayne Cortez**'s "How Long Has Trane Been Gone" (1969), referring both to an early twentieth-century blues lyric and to the jazz musician John Coltrane. To gain a more varied sense of development and periodization in African American poetry, readers might usefully consider the introductions to anthologies of African American poetry and literary criticism, such as those by **James Weldon Johnson**, Stephen Henderson, **Michael S. Harper**, and **Anthony Walton**.

Colonial and Antebellum Periods

Phillis Wheatley's *Poems on Various Subjects, Religious and Moral* (1773) was the first published volume of African American literature. Her collection includes hymns and odes dedicated to classical figures ("To Maecenas"). Some poems express admiration ("To S.M., a Young African Painter, on Seeing His Works"). Still other poems, dedicated to American figures, garnered the most contemporary recognition: "To His Excellency General Washington" and the elegy "On the Death of the Rev. Mr. George Whitefield." "On Being Brought from Africa to America" is a more personal meditation on **slavery** and the potential of Christian redemption. In subsequent critical debates the poem has been considered controversial for its heavy emphasis on Christian redemption of Wheatley's "sable race."

Recent interventions in African American literature have excavated other poets from this time period who often remain overlooked. These include **George Moses Horton**, **Jupiter Hammon**, **Lucy Terry**, and **James Monroe Whitfield**. Horton published three books of poetry: *The Hope of Liberty* (1829), *The Poetical Works of George M. Horton* (1845), and *Naked Genius* (1865). Like Wheatley's collection, Horton's collections contain very few references to slavery; the majority of these poems concern the more traditional lyric moods of grief and love, as well as religion. However, some consider his slavery poems, such as "On Hearing of the Intention of a Gentleman to Purchase the Poet's Freedom" and "The Slave's Complaint," his best work. Hammon's "An Evening Thought" and "An Address to Miss Phillis Wheatly" rely on the psalmlike structure of early Methodist hymns. Terry's "Bars Fight" (c. 1746, pub. 1855) is a ballad. The renown of Whitfield's collection *America and Other Poems* (1853) rests largely on the title poem, an ironic hymn to nationalism.

The Nineteenth Century

In the nineteenth century, African American poets gained a slightly broader audience and continued to work within traditional lyric forms. **Frances Ellen Watkins Harper**'s prolific literary production spanned several decades and covered several genres, including novels, essays, and poetry. During the nineteenth century, she published at least eight collections of poetry; during the decade after emancipation alone, she published three collections of poetry. Among Harper's known surviving collections, she is best known for *Poems on Miscellaneous Subjects* (1854); by 1874, this collection had undergone twenty editions. With the notable exception of *Moses: A Story of the Nile* (1869), an epic written in **free verse**, Harper typically wrote in rhyming quatrains of varying meters. Many of her poems disputed slavery outright, making her one of the founders of protest thematics in African American literature. Her poem "Eliza Harris" (1853), a direct response to *Uncle Tom's Cabin*, earned her immediate recognition when *The Liberator* published it. In poems such as "The Slave Mother" (1854) and "Bury Me in a Free Land" (1864), Harper used keenly sentimental rhetoric and dramatic monologues in order to rally her audience to the abolitionist cause. Other poems, such as "Songs for the People" (1895) and "An Appeal to My Country Women" (1900), appeal to a wider American audience, specifying humanitarian reasons for common cause or sisterhood.

While **Paul Laurence Dunbar** also wrote in Standard English, using lyric forms such as the ode and the hymn, his reputation rested largely on his lyric dialect poetry such as "When Malindy Sings," and "A Negro Love Song." As a result of this reputation, detractors have critiqued his poetry for perpetuating the "happy Negro" stereotype initiated by Southern White writers, while other anthologists of American literature have simply ignored his contributions to American poetry by omitting his poetry altogether. Dunbar's defenders have answered these critiques by emphasizing the White appetite for dialect poetry and concurrent disdain for Negro-authored poetry in Standard English. They have also noted the nuanced irony of "We Wear the Mask" and Dunbar's incisive exploration of "why the caged bird sings" in "Sympathy." Dunbar published several major collections, including *Oak and Ivy* (1893), *Majors and Minors* (1895), and *Lyrics of Lowly Life* (1896), the title of which referred to Wordsworth's *Lyrical Ballads*.

Other poets of this period include **Charlotte Forten Grimké, Angelina Weld Grimké, Alice Moore Dunbar-Nelson, Georgia Douglas Johnson, Benjamin Griffith Brawley,** and **William Stanley Braithwaite.** A prominent literary critic, Braithwaite also published poetry, leaning toward traditional forms such as rhyming quatrains ("The Watchers") and the octave ("The House of Falling Leaves"). (*See* **Narrative Poetry.**)

New Negro Renaissance

The poetry of the **New Negro** Renaissance, or the **Harlem Renaissance,** reveals an upsurge in racial consciousness and a turn away from sentimental apology or self-pity, and an emphasis on ancestry and self-awareness. While African American poets continued to use lyric poetry, these forms were now often infused with unapologetic anger and purposeful irony. The most prominent example of this infusion is **Claude McKay**'s collection *Harlem Shadows* (1922), generally thought to have inaugurated the Renaissance. McKay is particularly noted for using the sonnet as a form of protest. "If We Must Die" and "To The White Fiends" are two of McKay's famously militant sonnets. **Countee Cullen**'s sonnet "Yet Do I Marvel" explores the ironic situation of the Black artist in a racist society. By contrast, **Arna Bontemps**'s lyrics are known for their meditative, reflective qualities, often referring to reaping and sowing ("A Black Man Talks of Reaping") as a metaphor for the consequences of history.

Several poets of the Renaissance experimented with vernacular roots as well as "high poetic" forms. James Weldon Johnson's work exemplifies this combination. He wrote not only dialect poems ("Sence You Went Away,") but also the unofficial "Negro National Anthem" ("Lift Ev'ry Voice and Sing" [c. 1900, pub. 1921]). His landmark anthology, *A Book of American Negro Poetry* (1922), includes his own poetry as well as an incisive introductory essay covering the aesthetics of Negro poetics. **Jean Toomer**'s virtuoso novel *Cane* (1923) pays homage to Southern Negro culture and mourns the upheaval caused by the **Great Migration.** *Cane*'s modernist poetic experimentation includes not only prose and scripted dialogue, but also **prose poems** ("Karintha") and lyric poems ("Evening Song," "Song of the Son"). In a similar vein,

A group portrait of poets. Front row, left to right: Sterling Allen Brown, unidentified, Margaret Walker, Langston Hughes. Back row, left to right: Arna Wendell Bontemps, Melvin B. Tolson, President Jacob L. Reddix, Queen Dodson, and Robert C. Hayden, 1945. Courtesy of the Library of Congress.

Countee Cullen's poem "Heritage" asks "What is Africa to me?"—Africa's significance to African Americans forcibly removed from Africa.

Realism, Modernism, Naturalism

Continuing in the vein of ancestral invocation, other poets focused specifically on exploring the vernacular tradition of spirituals, work songs, **ballads**, and blues. Though Langston Hughes's career was launched during the New Negro Renaissance, his career spans several decades and several literary periods. One of his signature poems, "The Negro Speaks of Rivers," meditates on the place of the Negro across centuries, continents, and civilizations. Like Hughes, **Sterling A. Brown** experimented with the vernacular, writing dialect and folk poems that problematized the humor and pathos commonly associated with dialect verse. Publishing, along with other criticism and anthologies, several collections of his own poetry, Brown is known for creating the hybrid "blues ballad." The similarly multitalented poet and professor **Melvin B. Tolson** incorporated the communal speaker and the stridency of protest poetry with the musical terms for classical symphonic movements (e.g., "Allegro Moderato") in his most anthologized poem, "Dark Symphony."

Drawing partly on the momentum gained from the Renaissance, a few poets continued to experiment with traditional and vernacular forms during and after **World War II**. In her collection *For My People* (1942), **Margaret Abigail Walker** used the folk ballad in poems such as "Molly Means" and "Poppa Chicken" as well as the sonnet. The collection's title poem, which won the Yale University Younger Poet's Award, is a Whitmanesque sermon-anthem to her Black audiences. **Robert Hayden** is known more for his historical poems, such as "Middle Passage" (considered a hybrid of the lyric and narrative) (*see* **Middle Passage**). However, he also wrote ballads ("The Ballad of Nat Turner," "A Ballad of Remembrance") as well as introspective lyrics ("Those Winter Sundays," "A Plague of Starlings," "Ice Storm").

Though Gwendolyn Brooks won the Pulitzer Prize for her epic poem *Annie Allen* (1949), she also experimented with the elegy, sonnet, ballad, and lyric. In *A Street in Bronzeville* (1945), her sonnet sequence "Gay Chaps at the Bar" transforms the sonnet's traditional subject, love, into war (Pettis, 36). Throughout her long and distinguished career, Brooks signified on traditional poetic forms, yet also adapted the free verse stylings of the Black Aesthetic, or the **Black Arts Movement**.

The Black Arts Movement

Rather than depending on traditional lyric forms to be heard and accepted by a mainstream audience, as some of their poetic predecessors had, the poets of the Black Arts Movement celebrated innovative experimentation through free verse. They played with several elements, including spelling and phonetics, line breaks, and punctuation such as the slash to emphasize or create pauses. Yet several poets of the Black Arts Movement used and experimented with lyric forms as well. The title poem of **Amiri Baraka**'s *Preface to a Twenty Volume Suicide Note* (1961) is a lyric of despair. **Larry Neal**'s "For Our Women" (1968) celebrates the endurance and beauty of Black women. **Etheridge Knight**'s poignant collection *Poems from Prison* (1968) includes lyric meditations on the effects of imprisonment and liberation on identity and ancestry. **Nikki Giovanni**'s well-known lyrics of childhood, "Nikki-Rosa" (1968) and "Knoxville, Tennessee" (1968) appeared during this period. **Haki R. Madhubuti** (Don Lee)'s radically experimental poetics still retained the lyric's singular speaking voice in "a poem to complement other poems" (1969). Later, Black Arts performance poet **Sonia Sanchez** used the blues in *A Blues Book for Blue Black Magical Women* (1974), and love lyrics and haiku in her *Homegirls & Handgrenades* (1984). **June Jordan**'s "Poem About My Rights" (1980) highlights her transnational political consciousness, reaching from France to South Africa. As the poem's speaker puts it, "I am the history of the rejection of who I am."

Lyric Poetry Since 1975

Lyric poets who have published since (roughly) 1975 have continued to work with traditional, vernacular, ancestral, and experimental strands from the earlier parts of the twentieth century. The multiracial poet **Ai** has published six collections of dramatic monologues, inhabiting the viewpoints of public figures such as Senator Joseph McCarthy, Robert Oppenheimer, and John F. Kennedy. Jayne Cortez's jazz **poetics** concern not only musicians ("How Long Has Trane Been Gone," "Jazz Fan Looks Back") but also her African roots ("Adupe"). **Yusef Komunyakaa**'s extensive repertoire includes poems about his Vietnam military experience (*Dien Cai Dau* [1988]) as well as blues poems calling on past ancestry ("Trueblood Blues," referring to the character in *Invisible Man*, and "Elegy for Thelonious"). **Harryette Mullen** uses folk speech and quatrains in her collection *Muse & Drudge* (1995). Michael S. Harper's many accomplishments include blues elegies for jazz musicians, most notably in his collection *Dear John, Dear Coltrane* (1970) and "Last Affair: Bessie's Blues Song." Derek Walcott, winner of the 1992 Nobel Prize, writes lyrics across Caribbean, African, and African American traditions.

The lyrics of several contemporary Black female poets have involved and celebrated the Black female body. Many of **Lucille Clifton**'s best-known lyrics celebrate the Black female body ("homage to my hips," "homage to my hair"); her later poems include elegies for historical figures ("powell march 1991," "4/30/92 for rodney king"). **Colleen McElroy** also explores issues related to the body in her spare, warmly ironic lyric poems. **Audre Lorde** was lesbian, Black, activist, feminist, poet, memoirist, and essayist, and throughout her career struggled with the pigeonholing that these labels created. Her lyric poetry ranges from protest litanies ("A Litany for Survival") and personal lyrics of motherhood ("Now That I Am Forever with Child") to metaphorical celebrations of Blackness ("Coal"). **Rita Dove**, the second African American to win the Pulitzer Prize, credits the Black Arts Movement for paving the way to her artistic freedom. Her collection *Mother Love* (1995) uses both Italian and Shakespearean forms of the sonnet, but also transmutes these into another sonnet form altogether.

Though more known for their novels or memoirs, some writers have crossed genres into lyric poetry; **Ishmael Reed**'s "Dualism," **Sherley Anne Williams**'s "I Want Aretha to Set This to Music," and **Maya Angelou**'s "Phenomenal Woman" and "Still I Rise" are prominent examples.

Finally, among the newer generation of African American poets, **Elizabeth Alexander**, **Kevin Powell**, and **Ras Baraka** stand out as voices who expand on several strands of their African American poetic ancestry, including the lyric and the blues. Recent anthologies of new African American poetry are testament to the anthology's power to unearth new trends. *The Norton Anthology of African American Literature*'s inclusion of **rap** and **hip-hop** lyrics also points toward new directions in African American lyric poetry, and a further expansion of the definition of lyric poetry itself. (*See also* **Performance Poetry**.)

Resources: Fahamisha Patricia Brown, *Performing the Word: African American Poetry as Vernacular Culture* (New Brunswick, NJ: Rutgers University Press, 1999); William W. Cook, "The Black Arts Poets," in *Columbia History of American Poetry*, ed. Jay Parini (New York: Columbia University Press, 1993), 674–706; Joanne V. Gabbin, "Poetry," in *The Oxford Companion to African American Literature*, ed. William Andrews, Frances Smith Foster, and Trudier Harris (New York: Oxford University Press, 1997); Joanne V. Gabbin, ed., *The Furious Flowering of African American Poetry* (Charlottesville: University Press of Virginia, 1999); Henry Louis Gates, Jr., and Nellie Y. McKay, eds., *The Norton Anthology of African American Literature*, 2nd ed. (New York: Norton, 2004); Carolivia Herron, "Early African American Poetry," in *Columbia History of American Poetry*, ed. Jay Parini (New York: Columbia University Press, 1993), 23–32; Michael S. Harper and Anthony Walton, eds.: *Every Shut Eye Ain't Asleep: An Anthology of Poetry by African Americans Since 1945* (Boston: Little, Brown, 1994); and "Introduction," in *The Vintage Book of African American Poetry: 200 Years of Vision, Struggle, Power, Beauty, and Triumph from 50 Outstanding Poets*, ed. Michael S. Harper and Anthony Walton (New York: Vintage, 2000), xxiii–xxxiii; Stephen E. Henderson, *Understanding the New Black Poetry: Black Speech and Black Music as Poetic References* (New York: Morrow, 1973); James Weldon Johnson, *The Book of American Negro Poetry* (New York: Harcourt, Brace, 1922); E. Ethelbert Miller, ed.: *Beyond the Frontier: African American Poetry for the 21st Century* (Baltimore: Black Classic Press, 2002); and *In Search of Color Everywhere: A Collection of African-American Poetry* (New York: Stewart, Tabori, & Chang, 1994); Hans Ostrom, *A Langston Hughes Encyclopedia* (Westport, CT: Greenwood Press, 2002), esp. "Collective Persona," 77–78, and "Poetics," 306–308; Jay Parini, ed., *The Columbia History of American Poetry* (New York: Columbia University Press, 1993); Joyce Pettis, *African American Poets: Lives, Works, and Sources* (Westport, CT: Greenwood Press, 2002); Arnold Rampersad, "The Poetry of the Harlem Renaissance," in *Columbia History of American Poetry* (New York: Columbia University Press, 1993), 452–476.

Tamiko Nimura

M

Mackey, Nathaniel (born 1947). Poet, prose writer, essayist, and editor. Through his poetry, prose, criticism, and editing, Mackey has helped define and extend forms of innovation within African American literature. Born in Miami, Florida, in 1947, he received a B.A. from Princeton in 1969 and a Ph.D. in English and American literature from Stanford University in 1975. Since 1979 he has taught at the University of California, Santa Cruz. In addition to several chapbooks, he is the author of three books of poetry: *Eroding Witness* (1985), selected by **Michael S. Harper** for the National Poetry Series; *School of Udhra* (1993), and *Whatsaid Serif* (1998). Appearing in each are numbered installments of the open-ended "Song of the Andoumboulou," based in part on Dogon myths. In 1995 Mackey recorded *Strick*, a reading of "Song of the Andoumboulou 16–25" accompanied by percussion, reeds, and flutes. His ongoing prose series, *From a Broken Bottle Traces of Perfume Still Emanate*, is a collection of letters written by N., a jazz composer and multi-instrumentalist. The series includes *Bedouin Hornbook* (1986, 1997), *Djbot Baghostus's Run* (1993), and *Atet, A.D.* (2001).

Cross-cultural, intergeneric, and structurally complex, Mackey's writing draws on Pan-African mythology, improvisational **jazz**, and the formal innovations of twentieth-century American poetry and **poetics**. Addressing multiple relations of distance and connection, Mackey's poems drift through various physical, cultural, and musical landscapes. An eclectic writer, he lists his "aesthetic tendencies" as including "poetry in the Imagist/Objectivist tradition, African-American **modernism** and **post-modernism** from the **Harlem Renaissance** to the present, **surrealism**'s New World offshoots, the alternative U.S. writing represented by Donald Allen's anthology *The New American*

Poetry 1945–1960, Caribbean writing, ethnopoetics and jazz" ("Editing *Hambone*," 667–668). These interests are evident in Mackey's collection of critical essays titled *Discrepant Engagement: Dissonance, Cross-Culturality, and Experimental Writing* (1993, 2000), and they have also shaped his work as an editor. Since 1974 he has edited the influential magazine **Hambone**, publishing a diverse array of American and international writers. Among his other projects is the anthology (with Art Lange) *Moment's Notice: Jazz in Poetry and Prose* (1993). In 2000 *Callaloo* dedicated a special issue (23, no. 2) to his work.

Resources: Primary Sources: Art Lange and Nathaniel Mackey, eds., *Moment's Notice: Jazz in Poetry & Prose* (Minneapolis, MN: Coffee House Press, 1993); Nathaniel Mackey: *Atet, A.D.* (San Francisco: City Lights, 2001); *Bedouin Hornbook* (Los Angeles: Sun & Moon, 1997); *Discrepant Engagement: Dissonance, Cross-Culturality, and Experimental Writing* (1993; repr. Tuscaloosa: University of Alabama Press, 2000); *Djbot Baghostus's Run* (Los Angeles: Sun & Moon, 1993); "Editing *Hambone*," *Callaloo* 23, no. 2 (2000), 665–668; *Eroding Witness* (Urbana: University of Illinois Press, 1985); *Paracritical Hinge: Essays, Talks, Notes, Interviews* (Madison: University of Wisconsin Press, 2005); *School of Udhra* (San Francisco: City Lights, 1993); *Whatsaid Serif* (San Francisco: City Lights, 1998). **Secondary Sources:** Dimitri Anastasopoulos, "Resisting the Law: Nathaniel Mackey's *Djbot Baghostus's Run*," *Callaloo* 23, no. 2 (2000), 784–795; Brent Hayes Edwards, "Notes on Poetics Regarding Mackey's *Song*," *Callaloo* 23, no. 2 (2000), 572–591; Paul Naylor, "The 'Mired Sublime' of Nathaniel Mackey's *Song of the Andoumboulou*," *Postmodern Culture* 5, no. 3 (May 1995), http://www.iath.virginia.edu/pmc/contents.all.html; Aldon Lynn Nielsen, "N + 1: Before-the-Fact Reading in Nathaniel Mackey's Postcontemporary Music," *Callaloo* 23, no. 2 (2000), 796–806; Peter O'Leary, "Deep Trouble/Deep Treble: Nathaniel Mackey's Gnostic Rasp," *Callaloo* 23, no. 2 (2000), 516–537; Mark Scroggins, "Nathaniel Mackey," in *Dictionary of Literary Biography*, 5th ser., vol. 169, *American Poets Since World War II*, ed. Joseph Conte (Detroit: Gale, 1996), 179–191; Megan Simpson, "Trickster Poetics: Multiculturalism and Collectivity in Nathaniel Mackey's *Song of the Andoumboulou*," *MELUS* 28, no. 4 (Winter 2003), 35–54.

James Maynard

Madgett, Naomi Long (born 1923). Poet, editor, educator, and publisher. Madgett is an important contemporary African American poet and an enormously influential editor, publisher, creator, and proponent of contemporary African American poetic works. Her own published work has spanned over six decades.

Madgett was born in Norfolk, Virginia, in 1923—one of three children of a pastor and scholar, Rev. Clarence Marcellus Long, and Maude Selena Hilton Long, a homemaker and former teacher. The Long family moved to East Orange, New Jersey, when Madgett was two years old, when her father became pastor of Calvary Baptist Church. Madgett suffered the indignities of overt discrimination in her early years of schooling. Nevertheless, she experienced a loving and relatively secure childhood and family life that was neither materially affluent nor excessively deprived—no easy feat for any family during the **Great Depression**. The Longs moved to **St. Louis, Missouri**, in the late 1930s, when Madgett was in high school. Madgett attended a segregated high school, where she was supported and encouraged to write and to develop her art. Upon graduating in 1941, she published her first volume of poetry, *Songs to a Phantom Nightingale*. Madgett was seventeen years old.

Madgett attended Virginia State College for Negroes (now Virginia State University), her mother's alma mater, and graduated in 1945 with a bachelor's degree in English. Madgett's parents moved to New Rochelle, New York, during her college years, and Madgett started attending graduate school at New York University. She married Julian Fields Witherspoon in 1946 and moved to **Detroit, Michigan**, where she became a writer and copyreader for the African American newspaper *Michigan Chronicle*. Madgett gave birth to a daughter (the poet **Jill Witherspoon Boyer**) in 1947. Her marriage to Witherspoon ended, and Madgett then worked as a service representative for the Michigan Bell Telephone Company to support herself and child, and took night classes at what is now Wayne State University. She married William Harold Madgett in 1954 and gave birth to two sons, while also earning a teaching certificate and a master's degree in English at Wayne State University.

Madgett began teaching high school in Detroit in 1955 and taught for twelve years. During her tenure with the Detroit public schools, she introduced the first course offered in Afro-American literature. She published her second volume of poetry, *One and the Many*, in 1956. She divorced Madgett in 1960, though she retained his name. Madgett underwent artistic growth in the 1960s partly as a result of participation in a writer's workshop at Wayne State University. Her third volume of poetry, *Star by Star*, was published in 1965.

In 1968, Madgett began teaching English at Eastern Michigan University, where she eventually became a full professor. She earned her Ph.D. at the International Institute for Advanced Studies in 1980. She retired from Eastern Michigan in 1984 to devote herself to publishing and the development of her creative works.

Madgett and other investors established **Lotus Press** in 1972. She and her spouse, Leonard Patton Andrews, whom she married in 1972, took over Lotus Press and continued to publish poetry. For many years, Madgett personally subsidized the publication costs of Lotus's titles as well as performing all of the necessary functions to produce a text—manuscript selection, layout, editing, promotion, bookkeeping, and shipping. In 1980, Lotus became a nonprofit corporation. It has published more than seventy titles, many of which are still in print. Through Lotus, Madgett is responsible for the publication of works by of some of the most prominent contemporary African American writers, such as **Paulette Childress White**, **Toi Derricotte**, **Houston A. Baker, Jr.**, **Pinkie Gordon Lane**, and **Gayl Jones**.

Madgett has produced a significant and impressive body of work over the sixty-plus years she has been a commercially published author. Her poems have appeared in countless magazines and journals, and have been included in more than 100 anthologies and textbooks. Madgett's creative work was influenced by formal traditional European forms, such as those of the Romantic and Victorian poets. Major twentieth-century artistic and social movements, such as the **Harlem Renaissance** and the **Civil Rights Movement**, have also influenced her work. Madgett received encouragement for her work from the poets **Langston Hughes** and **Countee Cullen**.

Madgett's work has both engaged and transcended race. Unlike work produced during the influential **Black Arts Movement** of the 1970s, Madgett's poetry is not overtly polemical—her style emphasizes a subtler, yet nevertheless direct, engagement with social issues and themes in some of her work. Her poems are lyrical in style and many poems (such as in *One and the Many* and *Star by Star*) exhibit an effective use of imagery drawn from **nature**. Her words easily evoke mood and feeling, and create visceral images in the minds of their readers. Other frequent themes of her work include the exploration of family and kinship relations and the experience of human emotions. The library of Michigan State University holds a Lotus Press archive.

Resources: Primary Sources: Naomi Long Madgett: *Adam of Ife: Black Women in Praise of Black Men* (Detroit: Lotus Press, 1992); *Deep Rivers, a Portfolio: Twenty Contemporary Black American Poets* (Detroit: Lotus Press, 1978); *Exits and Entrances: New Poems* (Detroit: Lotus Press, 1978); *A Milestone Sampler: 15th Anniversary Anthology* (Detroit: Lotus Press, 1988); *Octavia and Other Poems* (Chicago: Third World Press, 1988); *One and the Many* (New York: Exposition, 1956); *Phantom Nightingale: Juvenilia: Poems, 1934–1943* (Detroit: Lotus Press, 1981); *Pink Ladies in the Afternoon: New Poems, 1965–1971* (Detroit: Lotus Press, 1972); *Remembrances of Spring: Collected Early Poems* (Detroit: Lotus Press, 1993); *Songs to a Phantom Nightingale* (New York: Fortuny's, 1941); *Star by Star: Poems* (Detroit: Harlo Press, 1965); *A Student's Guide to Creative Writing* (Detroit: Lotus Press, 1980). **Secondary Sources:** "Naomi Long Madgett," in *Contemporary Authors*, vol. 23 (Detroit: Gale, 1996); Thomasine Mosely Williams, "Handing Out Wings" (profile of Naomi Long Madgett), *About Time Magazine* (Sept./Oct. 1998), http://www.abouttimemag.com/sep98story2.html.

Kimberly Black-Parker

Madhubuti, Haki R. (Don L[uther] Lee) (born 1942). Poet, essayist, professor, and publisher. Madhubuti started **Third World Press** (TWP) with the assistance of **Carolyn M. Rodgers** and Johari Amini on September 20, 1967. TWP was an influential publisher of literature during the **Black Arts Movement**. In 1969, Madhubuti and Safisha (who later became his wife) started the Institute of Positive Education/New Concept School, and in 1998, the Betty Shabazz International Charter School. Madhubuti is the author of twenty-six books, Distinguished Professor at Chicago State University, and founder of the **Gwendolyn Brooks** Center for Black Literature and Creative Writing.

Madhubuti, whose original name was Don L. Lee, was born in Little Rock, Arkansas. He pursued undergraduate studies at several colleges in the **Chicago, Illinois**, area, and he also served in the U.S. Army from 1960 to 1963. He changed his name to Haki R. Madhubuti in the late 1960s. In 1984 he earned an M.F.A. in writing from the University of Iowa. His stature in the Black Arts Movement is unsurpassed, and since the 1960s he has remained a prolific poet, essayist, and community activist.

Celebrating its thirty-seventh anniversary in 2004, TWP is the oldest and longest running Black publishing house in America. In 1967, in his small basement apartment near 63rd and Ada streets on the South Side of Chicago, Madhubuti started TWP with a used mimeograph machine and $400 from a poetry reading. TWP has supported the tenets of **Black Power**, a theme of 1960s activism and of Madhubuti's own poetry, from *Think Black* (1967) to *Tough Notes* (2002). In the 1960s, Madhubuti, refusing to compromise his artistry, struck out on his own, selling his work from coast to coast and establishing a substantial following without being published by major publishers.

At first, poetry was the primary focus of TWP: Madhubuti, *Think Black* and *Black Pride* (1968); Johari Amini, *Black Essence* (1968), and **Sterling Plumpp**, *Portable Soul* (1969) were among the authors and books the press published early on. Through the 1970s and 1980s TWP added autobiography, fiction, nonfiction, **children's literature**, psychology, history, inspiration, politics, and culture to its lists. Black intellectuals such as Chancellor Williams, John Henrik Clarke, **Amiri Baraka**, **Woodie King, Jr.**, **Hoyt Fuller**, Ruby Dee, **Mari Evans**, Nathan Hare, and Frances Cress Welsing found a literary home at TWP. In the 1990s and at this writing, the Press publishes work by **Derrick Bell**, Vivian Gordon, Lily Golden, Fred L. Hord, **Kalamu ya Salaam**, Useni E. Perkins, George Kent, Keorapetse Kegositsile, **Geneva Smitherman**, Asa G. Hilliard, Acklyn Lynch, and, of course, Madhubuti. TWP's best-sellers are *The Isis Papers: The Keys to the Colors*, by Frances Cress Welsing; *The Destruction of Black Civilization: Great Issues of a Race from 4500 BC to 2000 AD*, by Chancellor Williams; *Wise, Why's, Y's*, by Amiri Baraka; *Blacks*, by Gwendolyn Brooks; *Afrolantica Legacies*, by Derrick Bell; and *Black Men, Obsolete, Single, Dangerous?*, by Madhubuti. Each of these volumes has sold 50,000 or more copies.

Switching her work to TWP, Gwendolyn Brooks, the first Black to receive a Pulitzer Prize for poetry, helped the Press to succeed, becoming godmother to Haki Madhubuti. His own mother was brutally killed when he was sixteen years old. TWP posthumously printed Brooks's *In Montgomery, and Other Poems* (2003).

As a poet, Madhubuti's first titles, *Think Black* and *Black Pride*, are representative of his whole corpus of writing. His poetry is original in its intensity, capturing the spirit and ethos of the 1960s. His entire body of poetry and nonfiction demonstrates the staying power of the Black Arts Movement. His early themes encouraged readers and listeners to destroy the word "n/Negro" and to adopt another racial classification. He was among the first writers to use the term "African American" in his work, as opposed to "Black" or **"Negro."** Other Black nationalist themes in his work include responsibility to family, to friends, and to political struggle. He is particularly adept at writing about Black maleness and how Black males should approach and appreciate Black women.

He writes about Black women from varied positions: as son, father, husband, lover, teacher, friend. And always he writes about Africa and how those of African descent should celebrate and critique the birthplace of humanity. In his poetry and essays Madhubuti does not simply glorify Blacks. He also chides, plays the dozens with, **signifies** on, and rebukes what he considers negative behavior that hurts the collective community of African Americans. For example, in a recent book, *Tough Notes*, he writes forcefully about rape and battery of women. Normally at the end of his books, he provides a bibliography to encourage his audience to read and study more about the issues he has creatively or journalistically offered. Writing is one of Haki Madhubuti's methods of advancing liberation.

Third World Press follows the model of the defunct **Broadside Press** founded by **Dudley Randal**l in 1965. Because of TWP's longevity, it now stands as a beacon for others interested in independent publishing. TWP, still located on Chicago's South Side, is a $1 million facility that employs twelve people. It is housed in a former Catholic school and church in the middle of a working-class neighborhood. In a separate wing, New Concept Preschool and the Betty Shabazz International Charter School instruct Black children from an African-centered curriculum. (*See* **Afrocentricity.**)

Madhubuti has supported Third World Press since its inception with part of his teaching salaries from Howard University and Chicago State University, never accepting royalty payments for his own work. Similarly, he bolsters his schools, New Concept (1972) and the Betty Shabazz International Charter School (1998). Both annually serve about 340 youngsters from preschool to eighth grade. New Concept is one of three independent Black educational institutions dating back at least twenty years.

As a poet, a publisher, a professor, and a school founder, Madhubuti has embodied the values of the Black Arts Movement in a variety of ways.

Resources: Haki R. Madhubuti: *Black Pride* (Chicago: Third World Press, 1968); *Don't Cry, Scream* (Chicago: Third World Press, 1992); *Enemies: The Clash of Races* (Chicago: Third World Press, 1978); *GroundWork: New and Selected Poems of Don L. Lee/Haki R. Madhubuti from 1966–1996* (Chicago: Third World Press, 1996); *Kwanzaa: A Progressive and Uplifting African American Holiday* (Chicago: Third World Press, 1985); *Run Toward Fear: New Poems and a Poet's Handbook* (Chicago: Third World Press, 2004); *Say That the River Turns: The Impact of Gwendolyn Brooks* (Chicago: Third World Press, 1987); Telephone interview with Regina Jennings, Feb. 2004; and *Think Black* (Detroit: Broodside Press, 1967); Mary A. Mitchell, "Afrocentric Educators Practice What They Teach," *Chicago Sun Times*, Sept. 14, 1997, p. 19; Patrick T. Reardon, "Poetic Justice: Success Hasn't Diminished Haki Madhubuti's Passion for the 'Struggle,'" *Chicago Tribune*, Aug. 10, 2000, sec. 5; Regina Jennings: "Cheikh Anta Diop, Malcolm X, and Haki Madhubuti: Claiming and Containing Black Language and Institutions," *Journal of Black Studies* 33 (Fall 2002), 126–144; "The Malcolm X Vision in the Poetics of Haki Madhubuti: Issues of Meleness and Memory," unpublished manuscript.

Regina Jennings

Magazines, Literary. The history of African American literary magazines extends back to the mid-nineteenth century, and reflects most major trends in Black literary and political thought. From its start, African American literature has negotiated the dual roles of creative expression and political advocacy, and the same can be said of the literary magazines that have helped make the literature public. African American literary magazines have provided a means for Black writers to develop independently of the White publishing industry, to explore distinctly Black ideologies and aesthetic movements, and to find a Black reading public.

Black literary journals were not generally distinguished from Black **newspapers** or abolitionist periodicals until the latter half of the nineteenth century and the abolition of **slavery** in 1865. Until this time, many antislavery publications, including *Colored American Magazine* (1837–1841), *Frederick Douglass' Paper* (1851–1859), and *Douglass's Monthly* (1859–1861), carried occasional literary works and works that would later be considered literary, such as **slave narratives**. These papers had a strong abolitionist bent, and while they included book reviews and occasional creative pieces, they were not clearly literary in scope. The first African American literary magazine was *The Anglo-African Magazine* (1859–1862), founded in New York by Thomas Hamilton. It contained a variety of news, general interest, abolitionist, and editorial pieces, as well as poetry, reviews, and short fiction. **Martin R. Delany**'s novel *Blake or the Huts of America* was published serially in the magazine, and **Frances Ellen Watkins Harper** contributed fiction, poetry, and essays. *The Anglo-African Magazine* was the first African American magazine to encourage the development of a Black American literary identity.

In the early twentieth century, Black literary magazines began to develop and flourish. The National Association for the Advancement of Colored People (**NAACP**)'s official journal, *The Crisis*, was founded in 1910 under the editorship of **W.E.B. Du Bois**, who became a major force in identifying and encouraging new Black writing talent for years to come.

In the 1920s, the **Harlem Renaissance** fostered a host of new literary journals. *Stylus*, the first African American literary journal to appear out of a Black college or university, was published at Howard University intermittently between 1916 and 1929. It featured writers such as **Zora Neale Hurston**, **Charles Waddell Chestnutt**, Du Bois, and **Alice Moore Dunbar-Nelson**. *Opportunity* (1923–1949), founded by **Charles Spurgeon Johnson**, published fiction, poetry, and book reviews. *Fire!!* (1926) was an ambitious journal that published a single issue, in November 1926. Its editorial board included **Wallace Thurman**, Zora Neale Hurston, **Langston Hughes**, and **Gwendolyn Bennett**. The journal's tone was radical and confrontational, and its production values were very high. Unfortunately, it was a financial disaster. The same editorial group followed up with *Harlem* (1928), which took a more sedate, conciliatory tone but was undermined by the financial crash of 1929.

In the **Great Depression** of the 1930s, artists and cultural workers of all types were beset by financial woes. Money troubles hit Black literary journals hard, because their financially solvent reading audience was usually smaller than that for White journals. At the same time, the **New Negro** literary movement of the 1920s found no obvious successor in the 1930s, apart from a dedicated group of Chicago artists who formed the core of the **Chicago Renaissance**. **Dorothy West** tried to encourage new Black writers with her journal *Challenge* (1934–1937), whose associate editor was the prominent and outspoken **Richard Wright**. Unfortunately, while *Challenge* published such notable authors as **Countee Cullen**, **Arna Bontemps**, Langston Hughes, **Pauli Murray**, **Helene Johnson**, and Harry T. Burleigh, West found that the overall quality of submissions was low. In 1938 West responded to criticisms from the Chicago school by handing editorship of the journal over to a group including Wright, Benjamin Appel, Valdemar Hill, **Sterling A. Brown**, **Owen Dodson**, and **Margaret Abigail Walker**. This group published one issue of *New Challenge* (1938), which took a more socially didactic, Communist tone than *Challenge* had. It also published Wright's influential essay "Blueprint for Negro Writing," which urged African American writers to use Social Realism as an aesthetic and political tool. (*See* **Marxism**.)

The 1940s and **World War II** saw the institution of several new Black literary journals, most with a less radical, more integrationist political tone. Many Black leaders became disillusioned with the organized Left during this period, and especially with communism. **Phylon** (founded 1940), a scholarly quarterly founded in **Atlanta, Georgia**, by Du Bois, was a consistent forum for new fiction and reviews. *Harlem Quarterly* (1949–1950) and *Negro Quarterly* (1942–1944) proved less stable, while *Negro Story* (1944–1946) developed, in its short life, a reputation for publishing Social Realist and leftist works by authors such as **Chester Himes** and **Ralph Ellison**.

The year 1950 saw the appearance of one of the longest-running and most popular African American literary magazines, **Negro Digest** (1942–1951, 1961–1970). Conceived of by its founder, **Hoyt Fuller**, as a Black *Reader's Digest*, *Negro Digest* included general-interest articles as well as literary works and reviews. In 1970 the magazine changed its name to *Black World* (1970–1976). In both incarnations, it maintained a highly comprehensive listing of African American cultural and literary news in its news and notes columns. Other journals of the 1950s included Casper Leroy Jordan's *Free Lance* (1953–1976), a Beat-focused magazine based in Cleveland, Ohio; *CLA Journal* (founded 1957), a scholarly journal supported by the Black-based **College Language Association** and edited by **Therman O'Daniel**; and the experimental *Yuden* (1958–1963?), founded in Greenwich Village by LeRoi Jones (later known as **Amiri Baraka**).

The 1960s was a period of intense social and creative activity in African American literary periodicals. Innumerable journals were founded, renamed, abandoned, and rediscovered during this period, while the battle for civil rights raged and the **Black Arts Movement** gained momentum. Key titles included *Liberator* (1961–1971), a Black nationalist journal edited by Daniel Watts and published by the Afro-American Research Institute in New York

City; **Black Dialogue** (1965–1972), edited by Arthur Sheridan and Edward Spriggs; and **Journal of Black Poetry** (1966–1973), edited by Joe Goncalves and a forum for new Black poetry with a nationalist bent. During this same period, *Negro American Literature Forum* (1967–1977) was founded; it later became **Black American Literature Forum** (1977–1992) and was adopted as the official journal of the Modern Language Association's Division on Black American Literature and Culture in 1983. In 1992 it was renamed *African American Review*.

Numerous other journals were founded in the fertile 1960s. **Nkombo** (1968–1974), was sponsored by the **Free Southern Theater**, and emphasized Black Southern writing; *Umbra* (founded 1963) created by **Thomas Covington Dent** and the Society of **Umbra**, linked the post-**Beat Movement** with new avant-garde writing; and *Transition* (founded 1961, intermittent) was founded in Uganda by an Indian scholar, Rajat Neogy. *Transition* was later taken over by the Nigerian writer Wole Soyinka and published in Ghana, and in 1991, it reemerged under the guidance of Aimé Césaire, Carlos Fuentes, **bell hooks**, **Toni Morrison**, and Soyinka, as the official publication of the W.E.B. Du Bois Institute at Harvard.

African American literary journals continued to emerge during the 1970s through to the present. Some of the most influential were **Callaloo** (founded 1976), edited by *Umbra*'s Dent; *Black World*; *Obsidian* (1975–1982, with subsequent versions in later years), and *Black Issues Book Review* (founded 1999). These and other modern African American literary magazines continue to connect Black writers with their audiences, to support new and independent voices, and to preserve African American literature for future generations.

Resources: Mary Fair Burks, "The First Black Literary Magazine in American Letters," *CLA Journal* 19 (1976), 318–321; Walter C. Daniel, "*Challenge Magazine:* An Experiment That Failed," *CLA Journal* 19 (1976), 494–503; Calvin Hernton, "Umbra: A Personal Recounting," *African American Review* 27 (1993), 579–584; Abby Arthur Johnson and Ronald Johnson: "Charting a New Course: African American Literary Politics Since 1976," in *The Black Columbiad: Defining Moments in African American Literature and Culture*, ed. Werner Sollors and Maria Diedrich (Cambridge, MA: Harvard University Press, 1994), 369–381; "Forgotten Pages: Black Literary Magazines in the 1920s," *Journal of American Studies* 8 (1974), 363–382; "Scholarly Journals and Literary Magazines," in *Oxford Companion to African-American Literature*, ed. William L. Andrews, Frances Smith Foster, and Trudier Harris (New York: Oxford University Press, 1997); Bill Mullen, "Popular Fronts: *Negro Story* Magazine and the African American Literary Response to World War II," *African American Review* 30 (1996), 5–15; Ronald Querry and Robert E. Fleming, "A Working Bibliography of Black Periodicals," *Studies in Black Literature* 3, no. 2 (1972), 31–36; Eugene Redmond, "Stridency and the Sword: Literary and Cultural Emphasis in Afro-American Magazines," *TriQuarterly* 43 (1978), 538–573; Jerry Ward, "Southern Black Aesthetics: The Case of *Nkombo* Magazine," *Mississippi Quarterly* 44, no. 2 (1991), 143–150.

Karen Munro

Major, Clarence (born 1936). Novelist, poet, essayist, lexicographer, and professor. Clarence Major is an important voice who established himself during the **Black Arts Movement** of the 1960s as an experimental writer and has created a prolific body of work since then. Born in **Atlanta, Georgia**, he moved to **Chicago, Illinois**, with his mother after his parents divorced, although he remained connected to **the South** through frequent visits to his father and relatives. He briefly attended the Art Institute of Chicago before joining the Air Force in 1955 and subsequently turning his primary artistic attentions to writing. In 1958, he founded his own journal, *Coercion*, which he published until 1961.

In 1969, Major edited an important anthology of poetry, *The New Black Poetry*, which brought together the work of writers developing a new Black aesthetic, such as **Ishmael Reed, Nikki Giovanni, Sonia Sanchez,** Don L. Lee **(Haki R. Madhubuti)**, and LeRoi Jones **(Amiri Baraka)**. Though the volume spoke of a new Black nationalist aesthetic, it drew freely from poems both more and less overt in their political content (*see* **Black Nationalism**). The following year, Major published the first important collection of his own poems, *Swallow the Lake*, which drew from poems he had printed in two smaller Coercion Press books, and other poems he had written.

Despite his considerable reputation as a poet, it is as an experimental fiction writer that Major has had the most impact. In 1969, Olympia Press, noted for supporting the work of Henry Miller and William S. Burroughs, brought out his first novel, *All-Night Visitors*. Unfortunately, the press cut roughly half the manuscript to emphasize the erotic content. As a result the work was open to criticism of being a stereotypical portrayal of a Black man and a series of one-dimensional women. The larger themes regarding the main character, Eli, get lost in a crush of images as he tries to comprehend the world around him, come through more clearly in the restored version (1998). Major's next novel, *NO* (1973), was a similarly fragmentary narrative of a young Black man; his third novel, *Reflex and Bone Structure* (1975), continued his experimentation with the fragmented narrative, but this time he comically played it against the form of a detective novel. However, the narrator assures the reader that he is extending reality, not simply describing it, and the novel ends with the narrator taking credit for the deaths of Cora and Dale, which the narrator concedes was no more than a device he himself set. *Emergency Exit* (1979) was Major's most experimental to date; the slender plot is about Allen Morris, a drug dealer who goes to visit his lover in Inlet, Connecticut. The novel carefully interrupts its narrative with such things as photographs, charts, some of Major's own paintings, dictionary definitions, and even, at one point, a page asking the reader, "how do you feel about it?"

Though Major continued writing in an experimental vein in *My Amputations* (1986), *Such Was the Season* (1987) marked a turn to more conventional narrative. A good deal of postmodern wit remains (one subplot involves a conspiracy to rig tomato prices), but at its core, this is a comic novel about one week in the life a Southern Black family matriarch, Annie Eliza, and her family. Similarly, though *Painted Turtle: Woman with Guitar* (1988) has an episodic construction, in contrast to his earlier works, this novel contains a more conventional narrative, though one still concerned with the nature of representation. Based on Major's extensive immersion in Zuni culture (as is his 1989 collection of poems, *Some Observations on a Stranger at Zuni in the Latter Part of the Century*), *Painted Turtle* tells the story of a Zuni woman who has been forced out of the tribe and now makes her living as a folksinger, singing in part about her Zuni background. Narrated by an American Indian who is trying to seduce Painted Turtle, the novel continues Major's reflections on the nature of narrative, while its focus away from the African American experience calls attention to the multicultural nature of his art.

This move toward more conventional but still impressionistic narrative continued eight years later in *Dirty Bird Blues* (1996), a **blues** novel about Manfred Banks, a blues musician in the 1950s who lives the life of a blues song. Likewise, though his 2003 novel, *One Flesh*, engages more plot threads than it ever cares to tie up, this story of an African American mixed-race artist and his love affair with a Chinese American poet returns Major to the concerns of multiculturalism and the problems of representation that he developed in his Zuni works.

Clarence Major has remained an important editorial presence in African American literature. In the 1990's, he published two anthologies, *Calling the Wind* (1993) and *The Garden Thrives* (1996), collections of, respectively, African American short fiction and African American poetry from the twentieth century. He also updated his earlier *Dictionary of Afro-American Slang* (1970) and expanded it, publishing it as *Juba to Jive: A Dictionary of African American Slang* (1994) (*see* **Slang**). Published at a time when Ebonics was a controversial educational issue, *Juba to Jive* was a conscious attempt to document the vitality of African American English. Additionally, Major has maintained an active career as a teacher in higher education. He has held positions at the State University of New York at Binghamton, Temple University, Howard University, and Sarah Lawrence University, and currently is Professor of English at the University of California at Davis.

In 1999, Major published an important collection of poems, *Configurations: New and Selected Poem, 1958–1998*, which culled poems from eight previous collections and added quite a few new ones. The poems concern painting, racism, sex, and travel, among an astonishing array of other topics. This collection allows the reader to chart Major's development as a writer, but also to see how some issues remain constant concerns for him. The poem "On the Nature of Perspective," for instance, begins, "Sometimes there is a point/ Without a point of view," which neatly summarizes the concern with subverting single-perspective narrative in his novel.

Resources: Primary Sources: Clarence Major: *Afterthoughts: Essays and Criticism* (Minneapolis, MN: Coffee House Press, 2000); *All-Night Visitors* (1969; repr. Boston: Northeastern University Press, 1998); *Configurations: New & Selected Poems 1958–1998* (Port Angeles, WA: Copper Canyon Press, 1998); *Dirty Bird Blues* (San Francisco: Mercury

House, 1996); *Emergency Exit* (New York: Fiction Collective, 1979); *Fun and Games: Short Fictions* (Duluth, MN: Holy Cow, 1990); *Juba to Jive: A Dictionary of African-American Slang* (New York: Penguin, 1994); *My Amputations* (New York: Fiction Collective, 1986); *NO* (New York: Emerson Hall, 1973); *Painted Turtle: Woman with Guitar* (Los Angeles: Sun and Moon, 1988); *Reflex and Bone Structure* (New York: Fiction Collective, 1975); *Some Observations of a Stranger at Zuni in the Latter Part of the Century* (Los Angeles: Sun and Moon, 1989); *Such Was the Season* (San Francisco: Mercury House, 1987); *Trips: A Memoir* (Minneapolis, MN: Coffee House Press, 2001). **Secondary Sources:** *African American Review* (spec. iss.) 28 (Spring 1994); Bernard W. Bell, *Clarence Major and His Art: Portraits of an African American Postmodernist* (Chapel Hill: University of North Carolina Press, 2001); Nancy Bunge, ed., *Conversations with Clarence Major* (Jackson: University Press of Mississippi, 2002); Keith Byerman, *Fingering the Jagged Grain: Tradition and Form in Recent Black Fictions* (Athens: University of Georgia Press, 1985).

Thomas J. Cassidy

Major, Marcus (born c. 1972). Novelist. Born into a military family at Fort Bragg, North Carolina, Major moved frequently with his family as he grew up, living in Maryland, Alabama, Wisconsin, Kentucky, and New Jersey. He completed a B.A. in English at Richard Stockton College in New Jersey and earned a teaching certification in African-American Studies. He subsequently taught at the elementary and middle-school levels in the Newark, New Jersey, school system.

A chance meeting with a former classmate reminded Major of the great enthusiasm that he had had for writing while in college. Almost immediately after this encounter, he began the first draft of what would become his first novel, *Good Peoples* (2000). The novel debuted at number 4 on the Blackboard best-seller list, was a main selection of the Black Expressions Book Club, and earned Major a place on Barnes & Noble's Discover Great New Writers list. His second novel, *4 Guys and Trouble* (2001), proved to be equally popular. It was also a main selection of the Black Expressions Book Club and made the *Essence* best-seller list. Indeed, the continuing popularity of Major's books is reflected in the fact that all of them have been reissued as paperbacks and as audiobooks.

In *Good Peoples*, Major adroitly chronicles the romance between an African American schoolteacher and a Cuban American lawyer in **Philadelphia, Pennsylvania**. Approaching thirty, both characters are old enough to be guarded about commitment and yet still young enough at heart to have somewhat idealized romantic expectations.

4 Guys and Trouble focuses on a group of four close friends with very individual personalities. At the point in their lives when they are becoming established professionally, they are grappling with their uncertainty over whether becoming more settled in their personal lives is the equivalent of settling for something less than what they might yet find in their relationships with women.

In *A Man Most Worthy* (2003), Major reworks a much-used romantic formula, focusing on an extraordinarily successful African American entrepreneur who, in attempting philanthropically to improve his old neighborhood in Newark, New Jersey, reconnects with a former lover who is now a school principal. Major avoids the most common, clichéd turns in this type of story by having the reunited pair confront the continuing significance of the issues that kept them from staying together in the first place.

A Family Affair (2004) is a sequel to *Good Peoples* in which the focal character, now happily married, deals with the disintegration of his parents' marriage and the unsettling behavior of a teenage niece, of whom he and his wife have temporarily assumed custody.

Major has also contributed *Got to Be Real* (2001), a collection of novellas on romantic themes, and to Jill Morgan's collection *Mothers and Sons: A Celebration in Memoirs, Stories, and Photographs* (2000).

Resources: Askhari Hodari, "Review of *Good Peoples*," *Black Issues Book Review* 2 (Mar./Apr. 2000), 18; Marcus Major: *A Family Affair* (New York: Dutton, 2004); *4 Guys and Trouble* (New York: Dutton, 2001); *Good Peoples* (New York: Dutton, 2000); *A Man Most Worthy* (New York: Dutton, 2003); Claudia Sarden, "Review of *A Family Affair*," *Black Issues Book Review* 6 (Jan./Feb. 2004), 53; Glenn Townes, "Review of *A Man Most Worthy*," *Black Issues Book Review* 5 (Jan./Feb. 2003), 32–33; Roger Waiters, "Review of *4 Guys in Trouble*," *Black Issues Book Review* 3 (May/June 2001), 20.

Martin Kich

Malcolm X (1925–1965). Political activist, religious leader, speechwriter, speaker, and memoirist. Born Malcolm Little in Omaha, Nebraska, Malcolm X was one of the most influential leaders of his time. His writings, speeches, and thinking continue to exert a powerful influence on Black politics today. He was one of eight children born to Baptist minister Earl Little and homemaker Louise Little. Because of his ardent support for Black Nationalist leader **Marcus Garvey**, Earl Little received death threats from White supremacist groups. These threats forced the Little family to relocate twice before Malcolm X's fourth birthday. In 1929, the Little home in Lansing, Michigan, burned to the ground. Two years later, the elder Little was found dead on the Lansing trolley tracks under suspicious circumstances. Although the police ruled both incidents as accidents, the Little family believed the White supremacist group The Black Legion was responsible. This was only the beginning of the Little family's tragedies, however. As a result of the many stresses placed upon her by the loss of her husband and being the sole caretaker of a large brood of children, Malcolm X's mother had a mental collapse. She subsequently went into a mental institution. The children were then parceled out to foster homes and orphanages, some of them ending up in White homes.

In spite of having a difficult early life, Little was an attractive, precocious child and an excellent student, working hard and participating in many school activities. He was also eager to please and inclined to overlook racist slights.

However, a turning point came when, in speaking to a teacher, he expressed a desire to become a lawyer. The teacher, a White man, made a cruelly racist comment about how that goal was unrealistic. This comment caused Malcolm X to lose interest in his studies, and he subsequently dropped out of school. He moved around the Northeast and got involved in petty crimes. In 1946 he was arrested and convicted on burglary charges, and was sentenced to ten years in prison.

While in prison, due to his brother's influence, Malcolm converted to the Black Muslim faith and began reading the Koran. A highly controversial religious group, the **Nation of Islam** professed a profound suspicion of Whites, tending to believe that the White man's world and Christian faith were inherently evil. They also instilled racial pride in Blacks, arguing for the tenets of **Black Nationalism**. It was at this time that Malcolm X changed his last name to "X," a common practice among Nation of Islam converts because they believed their family names to have originated with White slave owners.

While in prison, Malcolm X showed many leadership qualities, reading classics in the prison library and leading a prison debating team. After serving seven years of his ten-year sentence, he was paroled. He went to the head-quarters of the Nation of Islam in **Chicago, Illinois**; met the group's leader, Elijah Muhammad; and became his devoted follower.

Brilliant, charismatic, and a spectacular, inflammatory orator, Malcolm X quickly rose through the ranks. He was soon appointed a minister and national spokesman for the Nation of Islam. He helped establish new mosques in **Detroit, Michigan**, and **Harlem, New York**, and used many forms of media to get the Nation of Islam's message across. Because of his drive and conviction, membership in the Nation of Islam swelled dramatically in the years 1952 to 1963. It was not long before his fame eclipsed that of his mentor, Elijah Mohammed.

Malcolm X was strongly opposed to **Martin Luther King**'s belief in non-violent action and peaceful protest. Instead, he believed violence was an option in cases involving self-protection. Furthermore, he soundly renounced both integration and notions of racial equality, calling instead for a separation of Blacks from mainstream society and emphasizing Black independence and self-sufficiency. In spite of his charisma and growing numbers of followers, his approach was rejected by many civil rights leaders. Furthermore, his bitter criticism of civil rights leaders who advocated integration alienated many of them, and some of them considered him to be a fanatic.

After remaining celibate as a single man according to the strict doctrines of Islam, Malcolm X married Betty Shabazz in 1958. In 1961 he founded *Muhammad Speaks*, the official publication of the Nation of Islam movement. Then the tensions between Malcolm X and Elijah Muhammad began to heighten, due to the former's enormous popularity and the revelation that Elijah Muhammad had been having affairs with numerous women in his or-ganization and fathering children by some of them. This was an especially bitter blow to Malcolm X, who lived strictly according to the Muslim faith. He began to show more and more signs of independence from the Nation of Islam, clearly preferring, for example, active political engagement, although doing so was contrary to Elijah Muhammad's teachings. When Elijah Muhammad publicly silenced Malcolm X after John F. Kennedy's assassination for saying that the President's "chickens had come home to roost," Malcolm X became even more alienated from Elijah Mohammed. Furthermore, he got wind of rumors that his spiritual mentor had been plotting to have him assassinated. Although it was impossible to know whether these rumors were true, Malcolm X decided to leave the Nation of Islam and begin his own sect. He also began employing bodyguards around the clock because he was getting numerous death threats, just as his father had.

In 1964 Malcolm X founded the Moslem Mosque, Inc. He also made a life-transforming trip to Mecca at that time, which caused him to modify his views on the innate evil of Whites. As a result, he began espousing a doctrine of the brotherhood of man. In October of that year he also reaffirmed his conversion to orthodox Islam. The death threats continued against him, however. His home was firebombed on February 14, 1965; and on February 21, 1965, Malcolm X, just thirty-nine years old, was assassinated at a speaking engagement at the Audubon Ballroom in New York City. The killers shot him fifteen times at close range. After a funeral with hundreds in attendance, he was buried in Ferncliff Cemetery in Hartsdale, New York. In March 1966, his three assassins, all members of the Nation of Islam, were convicted of first-degree murder.

Malcolm X, 1964. Courtesy of the Library of Congress.

Prior to his death, Malcolm X had collaborated with **Alex Haley** on his life story, *The Autobiography of Malcolm X* (1965). The memoir, based primarily on interviews Haley had done with Malcolm X, is now recognized as a classic of African American **autobiography**. It was widely distributed after his death and became a battle cry for civil rights for many Black youth. Given Malcolm X's early loss of his parents, his poverty-stricken childhood, the enormous obstacles he overcame, and his radical change from hoodlum to religious and ideological leader, the book speaks to all Americans, regardless of race, because it depicts his growing awareness of the world around him and his need for self-respect and action. Largely because of renewed interest in this autobiography and because of **Spike Lee**'s 1992 film *Malcolm X*, Malcolm X is now viewed as a man who stood on the principles of Black self-help, racial pride, and world brotherhood, instead of as a hate-filled fanatic. *The Autobiography of Malcolm X* is still widely read today, often taught in America's public schools, colleges, and universities.

Resources: Roger Barr, *Malcolm X* (San Diego: Lucent, 1994); George Breitman, ed., *By Any Means Necessary: Speeches, Interview, and a Letter, by Malcolm X* (New York: Pathfinder Press, 1970); John Henrik Clarke, *Malcolm X: The Man and His Times* (Trenton, NJ: Africa World Press, 1990); Louis A. DeCaro, Jr., *On the Side of My People: A Religious Life of Malcolm X* (New York: New York University Press, 1996); Michael Eric Dyson, *Making Malcolm: The Myth and Meaning of Malcolm X* (New York: Oxford University Press, 1995); Michael Friedly, *Malcolm X: The Assassination* (New York: Ballantine, 1995); Peter Goldman, *The Death and Life of Malcolm X* (New York: Harper & Row, 1973); Malcolm X and Alex Haley, *The Autobiography of Malcolm X* (New York: Grove Press, 1965); Bruce Perry, *Malcolm* (Barrytown, NY: Station Hill, 1991); William W. Sales, Jr., *From Civil Rights to Black Liberation: Malcolm X and the Organization of Afro-American Unity* (Boston: South End, 1994); William Strickland, *Malcolm X: Make It Plain* (New York: Viking, 1994); Eugene Victor Wolfenstein, *The Victims of Democracy: Malcolm X and the Black Revolution* (New York: Guilford, 1993).

Stephanie Gordon

Mallette, Gloria (born 1953). Novelist. Gloria Mallette was born in Gadsden, Alabama. When she was two and a half years old, her mother died, and her father decided to move the family, which included five children, to New York City. There his sister assumed most of the responsibility for raising Mallette and her siblings.

Mallette attended college for several years, taking courses primarily in the liberal arts. She subsequently worked as an office manager and executive assistant in fund-raising for the Brooklyn Museum of Art and Brooklyn College, and as the Federal Perkins Loan coordinator at Medgar Evers College. Although she has described the jobs themselves as interesting and challenging, she never enjoyed working for someone else. Since her late teens, she had entertained the idea that she could become a writer, and in the early 1990s, she decided to make a serious effort at realizing that ambition.

Her first novel, *When We Practice to Deceive* (1995), was published as a mass-market paperback. A courtroom drama with a great deal of psychological interest, the novel focuses on the opposing attorneys, both of whom are African American women but one of whom has been "**passing**" for White.

Despite her success in placing her first novel, Mallette had a great deal of difficulty in finding a publisher for her second. After five years of peddling the manuscript, she decided to self-publish *Shades of Jade*. Her self-marketing was successful enough to sell more than 13,000 copies, and she secured a contract with Random House that allowed her to write full-time.

Shades of Jade (2000) focuses on a professionally successful African American woman who is very cynical about marriage and as an alternative carries on simultaneous relationships with four married men. Thus, when she begins to receive anonymous threats over the telephone, she is not sure which of her adulterous relationships has been discovered. In a somewhat contrived irony, when she tries to hide herself to escape the outraged wife who has now begun to stalk her, she finally finds a single man to whom she is attracted.

In *Promises to Keep* (2002), Mallette skillfully blends elements of the crime story and the family drama. Given custody of his daughter, Meika, because her mother is a crack addict, Troy Kirkwood moves back into his parents' home. Shortly afterward, he mysteriously disappears and is found murdered in a park. His brother is determined to find the killer but, like the police, he has very few leads. In the midst of this family's grief and all of the unanswered questions about the murder, Meika's mother reappears and demands custody of her daughter. (*See* **Crime and Mystery Fiction.**)

The Honey Well (2003) is a mother–daughter story that makes Joan Crawford's behavior in *Mommie Dearest* seem only mildly disturbed. In this case, the mother profits materially from manipulating her daughter into a series of degrading situations. A novel in which suspense is genuinely generated from character rather than events, *The Honey Well* leads the reader to wonder, alternately, how much this mother will be capable of doing to her daughter and how much this daughter will be willing to acquiesce to.

Exploiting some of the conventions of the **romance novel**, *Distant Lover* (2004) centers on a woman whose long-deteriorating marriage has finally fallen apart. But when she retreats with her son to her father's home to get some perspective on her situation, she finds more perplexing issues rather than solace or resolution, and uncovers more questions than answers about who she is and what she wants from the rest of her life.

Resources: Paul D. Colford, "Publishers Find It Pays to Do Write Thing," *New York Daily News*, Dec. 11, 2000, p. 34; "A Conversation with Gloria Mallette," *Random House Adult Trade Group*, Aug. 2001, www.randomhouse.com/randomhouse/authors/results.pperl?authorid=18791; Gloria Mallette: *Distant Lover* (New York: Kensington, 2004); *The Honey Well* (New York: Kensington, 2003); *Promises to Keep* (New York: Villard, 2002); *Shades of Jade* (2000; New York: Villard, 2001); *Weeping Willows Dance* (New York: Gemini, 2001); *When We Practice to Deceive* (Holloway House, 1995); Tara McKelvey, "Resolute Writer Has It Made in the Shade," *USA Today*, Sept. 13, 2001, p. D7; Gerrie E. Summers, "Author Spotlight: Gloria Mallette," *Today's Black Woman*, Oct.–Nov. 2003, p. 68; "When Authors Speak . . . Gloria Mallette," *Booking Matters*, Nov. 2003, p. 11.

Martin Kich

Margetson, George Reginald (1877–?). Poet. Although Margetson is not recognized as a poet of great stature, he is among the few Black writers whose careers spanned the era before the **Harlem Renaissance.** These writers include **Fenton Johnson, Walter Everette Hawkins,** Lucien B. Watkins, Roscoe Conkling Jamison, and **Joseph Seamon Cotter, Jr.,** who "collectively" are of "high importance" (Brawley, 236). George Reginald Margetson was born in St. Kitts, British West Indies, in 1877. His writing was greatly influenced by his English education at Bethel Moravian School, from which he graduated with honors in 1895 (Kerlin, 110). Two years later, Margetson left St. Kitts and relocated to the United States. He married Elizabeth Matthews of Cambridge, Massachusetts, on November 1, 1905. Margetson supported his wife and several children by working as a sanitary engineer. He also found the time to give life to the memories of his native country and to express his thoughts and views in his poetry (Nuñez, 303).

Margetson wrote several volumes of poetry. They include *England in the West Indies* (1906), *Ethiopia's Flight: The Negro Question, or, The White Man's Fear* (1907), and *Songs of Life* (1910). He is also represented in the following anthologies: *The Book of American Negro Poetry* (1931), *Singers in the Dawn* (1934), *Negro Poets and Their Poems* (1923), and *An Anthology of Verse by American Negroes* (1968). He is best known for the 100-page poem *The Fledgling Bard and the Poetry Society* (1916). This is a poem about a young poet who "sets out to find the Poetry Society" (Johnson, 107). En route, he comments on life, politics, the "questions of interest to the negro" and various other musings (107). Many of his poems address current events, social conditions, politics, **World War I**, racism, art, literature, and religion. He often pulls inspiration from the "tropical and natural environments" of his native West Indies (Johnson, 108). Margetson characteristically wrote in the genteel style of the day used by both Black and White writers. His models were English poets from Spenser to Byron (Johnson, 110).

Resources: Benjamin Brawley, *The Negro Genius* (New York: Dodd, Mead, 1940); Robert E. Eleazer, comp., *Singers in the Dawn: A Brief Anthology of American Negro Poetry*, 5th ed. (Atlanta: Conference on Education and Race Relations, 1939); James Weldon Johnson, ed., *The Book of American Negro Poetry* (New York: Harcourt, Brace, 1922); Robert T. Kerlin, *Negro Poets and Their Poems* (Washington, DC: Associated Publishers, 1923); George Margetson: *The Fledgling Bard and the Poetry Society* (Boston: R. G. Badger, 1916); *Songs of Life* (1910; repr. Freeport, NY: Books for Libraries, 1972); Benjamin Nuñez, "George Reginald Margetson," in his *Dictionary of Afro-Latin American Civilization* (Westport, CT: Greenwood Press, 1980); Theressa Gunnels Rush, Carol Fairbanks Myers, and Esther Spring Arata, "George Reginald Margetson," in *Black American Writers Past and Present: A Biographical and Bibliographical Dictionary*, ed. Theressa Gunnels Rush, Carol Fairbanks Myers, and Esther Spring Arata (Metuchen, NJ: Scarecrow Press, 1975).

Gladys L. Knight

Marrant, John (1755–1791). Autobiographer and minister. John Marrant's *A Narrative of the Lord's Wonderful Dealings with John Marrant, a Black* (1785) is one of the earliest African American narratives. It records his Christian conversion, Indian captivity, and early ministry. The *Narrative* helped establish the African American literary tradition, and it has come to be considered an early precursor to **slave narratives**. A transatlantic figure of the late eighteenth century, Marrant was born a free Black in New York on June 15, 1755. He later moved to Charleston, South Carolina, and in 1769 or 1770, was converted to Christianity by Rev. George Whitefield. After leaving his family because of their religious indifference, Marrant was captured by the Cherokee tribe but then came to minister to them and other Native Americans of the area. In 1772 he returned to Charleston and established a church school before being pressed into the British Royal Navy during the Revolutionary War. After being discharged in 1782, he traveled to London, where he became an ordained Methodist minister in the chapel of Selina Hastings, Countess of Huntingdon, on May 15, 1785. Working with an amanuensis, Rev. William Aldridge, Marrant produced his *Narrative*, a widely popular spiritual **autobiography** and captivity narrative. In November 1785, Marrant moved to Birchtown, Nova Scotia, to minister among Black Loyalists and indigenous peoples. Enduring both financial and physical difficulties, he relocated to **Boston, Massachusetts**, in 1788. There he met **Prince Hall**, Grand Master of the African Lodges of the Honorable Society of Free and Accepted Masons of Boston. Eventually he became chaplain to this Black Masonic lodge. On the Festival of Saint John, Marrant delivered a sermon, later published as *A Sermon Preached on the 24th Day of June 1789*. In 1790, Marrant returned to London, where he published *A Journal of the Rev. John Marrant, from August the 18th, 1785, to the 16th of March 1790*, which continued his earlier autobiography and included his interaction with Hall. Marrant died in London on April 15, 1791, and is buried in Islington.

Resources: Primary Sources: John Marrant: *A Journal of the Rev. John Marrant, from August the 18th, 1785, to the 16th of March 1790* (London: J. Taylor, 1790); *A Narrative of the Lord's Wonderful Dealings with John Marrant, a Black (Now Going to Preach the Gospel in Nova Scotia) Born in New-York, in North-America. Taken Down from His Own Relation, Arranged, Corrected, and Published by the Rev. Mr. Aldridge* (London: Gilbert and Plummer, 1785); *A Sermon Preached on the 24th Day of June 1789* (Boston: Bible and Heat, 1789). **Secondary Sources:** William Andrews, *To Tell a Free Story* (Urbana: University of Illinois Press, 1986); Joanna Brooks, *American Lazarus* (Oxford: Oxford University Press, 2003); Vincent Carretta, ed., *Unchained Voices* (Lexington: University Press of Kentucky, 1996); Vincent Carretta and Philip Gould, eds., *Genius in Bondage* (Lexington: University Press of Kentucky, 2001); Angelo Costanzo, *Surprizing Narrative* (Westport, CT: Greenwood Press, 1987); Frances Smith Foster, *Witnessing Slavery* (Westport, CT: Greenwood Press, 1979); Sandra Gustafson, *Eloquence Is Power* (Chapel Hill: University of North Carolina Press, 2000); Sidney Kaplan and Emma Nogrady Kaplan, *The Black Presence in the Era of the American Revolution*, rev. ed. (Amherst: University of Massachusetts Press, 1989); James Levernier and Douglas Wilmes, eds., *American Writers Before 1800* (Westport, CT: Greenwood Press, 1983); Emmanuel Nelson, ed., *African American Autobiographers* (Westport, CT: Greenwood Press, 2002); Dorothy Porter, *Early Negro Writing* (Boston: Beacon Press, 1971); Adam Potkay and Sandra Burr, eds., *Black Atlantic Writers of the Eighteenth Century* (New York: St. Martin's, 1995); Rafia Zafar, *We Wear the Mask* (New York: Columbia University Press, 1997).

Katy L. Chiles

Marriage. Marriage has always been a central theme in literature, but it takes on a particular resonance in African American literature. Because slave marriages were not legally recognized, they were subject to the whims of slave masters; consequently, families were often torn apart. Thus, after emancipation, when the legal right to marry was granted to former slaves, many hurried to have their marriages legally recognized. As Claudia Tate has noted, the right to marry, in addition to the right to vote, was considered integral to attaining full U.S. citizenship. This view of marriage as emblematic of freedom is a popular theme in much African American literature in the later half of the nineteenth century, if not always a central theme. However, in the twentieth century, the institution of marriage and the bourgeois values it is often thought to embody came increasingly under attack, as is evident in some of the literature of the **Harlem Renaissance** but especially in the **realism** and naturalism of the 1940s and 1950s and the **Black Arts Movement** in the 1960s and 1970s. Critics note that recently some authors have begun to reclaim marriage, but by redefining the institution for their characters, they also reject many of the patriarchal values marriage represented in the Victorian era.

The fragility of family structure is a common theme in **slave narratives** and abolitionist literature (*see* **Abolitionist Movement**). **William Wells Brown** opens *Clotel* (1853), considered the first novel published by an African American, with a description of the effects of **slavery** upon marriage, asserting, "Marriage is, indeed, the first and most important institution of human existence—the foundation of all civilization and culture—the root of church and state" (47). Brown then proceeds to dramatize the damage that the absence of marriage rights has on slaves, even when slaves have comparatively well-intentioned owners. The only African American couple for whom there is hope in the novel, Clotel's daughter Mary and Henry Green, must live outside the United States.

Slave owners could also force slaves to marry according to their wishes. In *Incidents in the Life of a Slave Girl* (1861), **Harriet Ann Jacobs** recounts how Dr. Flint, her conniving owner, refuses to allow her to marry the man of her choice. Jacobs consequently sacrifices her fiancé, explaining, "Even if he could have obtained permission to marry me while I was a slave, the marriage would give him no power to protect me from my master. . . . And then, if we had children, I knew they must 'follow the condition of the mother'" (373–374). Thus, women were unable to remain "faithful" wives because they were subject to rape by their masters, and men were unable to protect wives and children. Jacobs ends her narrative with a curious twist of convention: "Reader, my story ends with freedom; not in the usual way, with marriage" (513), revealing her awareness of the conventional, nineteenth-century Anglo-American "marriage plot" but also emphasizing the denial of that plot and the freedom that plot embodies. Nonetheless, other slave narratives, such as **Olaudah Equiano**'s *The Interesting Narrative of the Life of Olaudah Equiano; or, Gustavus Vassa, the African* (1791) and **Frederick Douglass**'s *Narrative of the Life of Frederick Douglass* (1845), do end with a marriage. Although the wedding is not the focus of the culmination of these narratives, as it is in the marriage plot, the mention of the narrator's marriage after he or she has attained freedom seems a confirmation of that freedom.

Brown's *Clotel* is also known for popularizing the idea of the "tragic **mulatto**" (in this case, mulatta), which adds further complications to the depiction of marriage in African American literature, raising the issues of miscegenation, **passing**, and the debate between marrying within one's race and marrying outside it. In *Iola Leroy, or Shadows Uplifted* (1892), **Francis Ellen Watkins Harper** emphasizes the importance marriage plays in the "uplift" of the Black race in America. Iola, a mulatta, repeatedly refuses an offer of marriage from the White Dr. Gresham, whom she does admire, and in the end marries Dr. Latimer, a Black man, with whom Iola feels a much deeper connection, for her marriage is not just one of personal desire; it is a marriage to her heritage. **Charles Waddell Chesnutt**'s *The House Behind the Cedars* (1900) explores both the pressures to pass and the pitfalls in doing so, through the story of siblings John and Rena Walden. John successfully passes, going so far as to marry a White Southern woman, though he has had to cut himself off from his dark-skinned mother in order to do so. However, when John attempts to arrange a similar marriage for Rena, it fails because Rena does not completely cut herself off from her mother and her ethnicity is discovered. Chesnutt also illustrates the hierarchy of skin color within middle-class African American society in his short story "The Wife of His Youth" (1899). Ryder, the light-skinned leader of his city's "Blue Vein Society" is about to propose to a light-skinned woman when the dark-skinned wife of his youth suddenly appears and he, after some debate, acknowledges her, embracing his ethnicity. (*See* **Race Uplift Movement**.)

The depiction of marriage in the twentieth century changed significantly, with the rise of modernism and experimentalism in the Harlem Renaissance. These portrayals of marriage in African American literature also reveal a **gender** split that mirrors American literature in general. Male authors, such as **Jean Toomer** in *Cane* (1923), tended to focus on racism, African heritage, literary experimentation, and individual freedom, including freedom from the bonds of marriage, while female authors, such as **Jessie Redmon Fauset** in *Plum Bun* (1929) and **Nella Larsen** in *Quicksand* (1928) and *Passing* (1929), tended to write critiques of patriarchy and bourgeois values within marriage and the effects of racism on marriage. **Zora Neale Hurston**'s *Their Eyes Were Watching God* (1937) has come to epitomize this burgeoning feminist critique of marriage. Janie Crawford's three marriages encapsulate a feminist history of marriage: her first husband, Logan Killocks, is selected by her grandmother for financial security; her second husband, Joe Starks, a typical middle-class patriarch, becomes a financial success and a community and political leader but believes his beautiful wife should be a silent trophy; her last husband, Tea Cake, is much younger, and Janie marries him purely out of desire. Even this last marriage, however, is not ideal, and Janie's journey is not complete until she is comfortable in solitude.

This split between male and female authors is perhaps even more apparent in the realist and naturalist works of the 1940s and 1950s. **Richard Wright**'s *Native Son* (1940) and **Ralph Ellison**'s *Invisible Man* (1952), though traditionally considered opposing standards for the African American novel, both focus on masculine antihero plots in which depictions of marriage are notoriously absent. In contrast, **Ann Lane Petry**'s *The Street* (1946), while similarly brutal, illustrates the destruction of marriage by racism and poverty in mid-twentieth century **Harlem, New York**. Lutie and Jim Johnson get their marriage off to a good start; however, when Jim loses his job, due to the racist climate of 1940s New York, Lutie goes to work as a domestic, which destroys their marriage: "She'd cleaned another woman's house and looked after another woman's child while her own marriage went to pot; breaking up into so many little pieces it couldn't be put back together again, couldn't even be patched into a vague resemblance of its former self" (30).

Since the 1960s, the examination of marriage and its reflection of racism and patriarchy continues to be a popular topic, especially among women writers, such as **Alice Walker, Toni Morrison, Gloria Naylor, Dorothy West**, and **Terry McMillan**. Alice Walker's *The Color Purple* (1982) tells the story of Celie, who is abused by both her stepfather and her husband; it is not until she has a relationship with a woman, Shug Avery, that she develops the self-confidence to leave her husband and start a new life. By the end of the novel, however, Celie and her husband are somewhat reconciled in friendship, and Walker offers some redemption for the institution of marriage through the egalitarian marriage of Celie's son, Adam, and his African bride, Tashi. Following in Chesnutt's and Larsen's steps, in *The Wedding* (1995) West portrays the conflation of skin color and class in an African American resort town called the Oval, whose residents try to marry their way into higher and often "lighter" social strata. More recently, some male authors, such as **John Edgar Wideman** and the playwright **August Wilson**, have focused more on families in their work. Symbolically, **Charles R. Johnson**'s *The Middle Passage* (1990) fuses the archetypal masculine adventure story with the comedic novel by ending with the wedding of Rutherford Calhoun to Isadora Bailey, from whom he had run away at the beginning of the novel. Of their union, Rutherford says, "I wanted our futures blended, not our limbs, our histories perfectly twined for all time, not our flesh" (208). In many of these novels of the late twentieth century, critics have noted a move toward healing the relationships between African American men and women, redefining and redeeming the institution of marriage, though sometimes rejecting it altogether.

Resources: Primary Sources: William Wells Brown, *Clotel; or, the President's Daughter* (1853; repr. in *Three Classic African-American Novels*, ed. Henry Louis Gates, Jr. [New York: Vintage, 1990]); Charles Chesnutt: *The House Behind the Cedars* (1900; repr. New York: Penguin, 1993); *"The Wife of His Youth" and Other Stories* (1900; repr. Ann Arbor: University of Michigan Press, 1968); Frederick Douglass, *Narrative of the Life of Frederick Douglass, an African Slave* (1845; repr. in *The Classic Slave Narratives*, ed. Henry Louis Gates, Jr. [New York: Mentor, 1987]); Ralph Ellison,

Invisible Man (1952; repr. New York: Vintage, 1972); Olaudah Equiano, *The Interesting Life of Olaudah Equiano; or, Gustavus Vassa, the African* (1791; repr. in *The Classic Slave Narratives*, ed. Henry Louis Gates, Jr. [New York: Mentor, 1987]); Jessie Redmon Fauset, *Plum Bun* (1929; repr. Boston: Beacon, 1990); Francis E. W. Harper, *Iola Leroy, or Shadows Uplifted* (1892; repr. in *Three Classic African-American Novels*, ed. Henry Louis Gates, Jr. [New York: Vintage, 1990]); Zora Neale Hurston, *Their Eyes Were Watching God* (1937; repr. New York: HarperPerennial, 1990); Harriet Jacobs, *Incidents in the Life of a Slave Girl* (1861; repr. in *The Classic Slave Narratives*, ed. Henry Louis Gates, Jr. [New York: Mentor, 1987]); Charles R. Johnson, *Middle Passage* (New York: Atheneum, 1990); Nella Larsen, *Quicksand and Passing* (1928, 1929; repr. New Brunswick, NJ: Rutgers University Press, 1986); Ann Petry, *The Street* (1946; repr. Boston: Houghton Mifflin, 1974); Jean Toomer, *Cane* (1923; repr. New York: Norton, 1988); Alice Walker, *The Color Purple* (New York: Harcourt Brace Jovanovich, 1982); Dorothy West, *The Wedding* (New York: Doubleday, 1995); Richard Wright, *Native Son* (1940; repr. New York: HarperPerennial, 1998). **Secondary Sources:** Keith Clark, ed., *Contemporary Black Men's Fiction and Drama* (Urbana: University of Illinois Press, 2001); Ann duCille, *The Coupling Covention: Sex, Text, and Tradition in Black Women's Fiction* (New York: Oxford University Press, 1993); Sybille Kamme-Erkel, *Happily Ever After? Marriage and Its Rejection in Afro-American Novels* (New York: Peter Lang, 1988); Claudia Tate, *Domestic Allegories of Political Desire: The Black Heroine's Text at the Turn of the Century* (New York: Oxford University Press, 1992); Alfred Lee Wright, *Identity, Family, and Folklore in African American Literature* (New York: Garland, 1995).

Kimberly A. Freeman

Marshall, Paule (born 1929). Novelist, short story writer, essaysist, and professor. Marshall was born on April 9, 1929, in **Brooklyn, New York**, to Ada and Samuel Burke, both of whom had come from the Caribbean island of Barbados. Marshall's original given name was Valenza Pauline Burke. She grew up in a tightly knit Barbadian immigrant community, and her published work demonstrates the myriad influences and multiple points of view that her upbringing involved. Her work is informed by American immigrant, African American, Caribbean, Barbadian, and African points of view. Marshall's first novel, *Brown Girl, Brownstones* (1959) is considered by many black feminist critics to be a prime example of contemporary African American women's writing (*see* **Feminist/Black Feminist Literary Criticism**). Such critics take this view in part because of the novel's focus on Black womanhood rather than Black manhood and in part because "it portrayed black women's centrality within the context of a specifically black culture" (Gates and McKay, 2050). This centrality of Black women and Black culture continues to be a focus of Marshall's work. She followed her first novel with a collection of novellas titled *Soul Clap Hands and Sing* (1961). The short stories "Reena" and "To Da-Duh, in Memoriam" were published in the mid-1960s, and the novel *The Chosen Place, the Timeless People* appeared in 1969. In 1983 Marshall published the essay "The Making of a Writer: From the Poets in the Kitchen," in which she traced her passion for language and writing to listening to her mother and other Barbadian immigrant women talking after work. (The essay was an introduction to her collection *Reena and Other Stories*.) In the same year Marshall published *Praisesong for the Widow*. In 1992 Marshall published the novel *Daughters*, and the novel *The Fisher King* appeared in 2000.

Marshall received a degree in English from Brooklyn College in 1953. After graduation, she worked as a journalist for *Our World*, a small Black magazine, before devoting her attention to fiction. She married Kenneth Marshall, a psychologist, in 1950 and they had one son. Marshall divorced in 1963 and was remarried in 1970 to a Haitian businessman, Nourry Ménard. She has taught English and creative writing at several universities and colleges, including the University of California at Berkeley, the Iowa Writers Workshop, the University of Massachusetts at Boston, Columbia University, Yale University, and Virginia Commonwealth University. She has also received a number of awards, fellowships, and grants. These include a Guggenheim Fellowship in 1960 and a Ford Foundation Grant for Poets and Fiction Writers in 1964; NEA awards in 1967 and 1978; an American Book Award in 1984; and a John D. and Catherine T. MacArthur Fellowship in 1992.

Marshall's formal education reportedly included the assigned reading of only two African American writers—**Paul Laurence Dunbar** and **Richard Wright** ("The Making of a Writer"). It was in her self-directed informal education that she read African American writers such as **Ralph Ellison**, **Zora Neale Hurston**, **Dorothy West**, and **Gwendolyn Brooks**.

Among the themes found in Marshall's work are the ongoing impact of the African **diaspora** created by the slave trade, the effects of **colonialism**, the struggles of immigration, the pressures of assimilation, the implacability of American racism, the impact of American materialism, the importance of knowing one's history, and the difficulty of understanding identity amid multiple cultural affiliations. There are three main critical approaches to her work. The first claims Marshall as an African American writer whose novels define a fluid African American sensibility (Coser). The second emphasizes that she is an African American woman writer, whose work is decidedly feminist and also addresses the particular struggles of African American women in the United States (DeLammote). The third approach emphasizes Marshall's Caribbean heritage and her exploration of the impact of the historical diaspora from Africa (Hathaway). Perhaps the most accurate description of Marshall, one well supported by her novels, is that she encompasses all three experiences simultaneously rather than singularly.

Her first novel, *Brown Girl, Brownstones*, begins in 1939 and focuses on a Barbadian immigrant family in Brooklyn, New York. This novel, like much of Marshall's other work, has autobiographical details but remains a work of fiction. The Boyce family is made up of Deighton and Silla and their two daughters, Selina and Ina. Selina Boyce is the main character, and it is through Selina that Marshall argues indirectly for a cross-cultural fluency that is simultaneously American, Caribbean, and African. The family is troubled.

Deighton is perceived as something of a wastrel by his wife, more apt to daydream than to work. Silla, meanwhile, hires herself out as a day maid, a common job among Barbadian women. In her essay "The Making of a Writer: From the Poets in the Kitchen," Marshall describes this practice, as well as the goal of such hardworking women: to "buy house"—to save enough money to buy the brownstone they currently rent. Themes such as the pressures of assimilation, the constancy of American racism, and the difficulty of understanding identity amid multiple cultural affiliations are found in the novel, though it essentially explores the pressures experienced by a young girl becoming a young woman within an immigrant community.

Several critics, most notably Joyce Pettis, describe Marshall's work as exploring the fragmentation created in part by the often competing claims of identity—American, Caribbean, African—and the struggle to reconcile these claims into a sense of wholeness where all are present and significant. In *Praisesong for the Widow*, Avatara Johnson, a widow in her sixties, interrupts her Caribbean pleasure cruise because she suffers an emotional crisis. This crisis proves a positive one because Avey awakens to her deadened, white-washed, materialistic existence and finds her real self again on the island of Carriacou. She undergoes an emotional remembering of her past, particularly the unspoken bargain that she and her late husband made to be successful, no matter what the cost, in the racist and materialist atmosphere of the United States. On Carriacou, Avey is brought back to life by reconnecting with the whole of herself—her African roots, her childhood experiences with her Aunt Cuney on the Sea Island of Tatem, South Carolina, and her life in North White Plains, New York.

In many ways, the transformation of Avatara Johnson in *Praisesong for the Widow* proves a potent symbol of Marshall's work as a whole. In all her novels, short stories, and essays, Marshall demonstrates the complexity of an African American identity and embraces the multiple claims that culture and history make on that identity.

Resources: Primary Sources: Paule Marshall: *Brown Girl, Brownstones* (1959; repr. New York: Feminist Press, 1996); *The Chosen Place, the Timeless People* (1969; repr. New York: Vintage, 1992); *Daughters* (New York: Plume, 1992); *The Fisher King* (New York: Scribner's, 2000); *Merle: A Novella and Stories* (New York: Virago, 1985); *Praisesong for the Widow* (1983; repr. New York: Plume, 1992); *Reena and Other Stories* (Old Westbury, NY: Feminist Press, 1983), which includes the essay "The Making of a Writer: From the Poets in the Kitchen"; *Soul Clap Hands and Sing* (1961; repr. Washington, DC: Howard University Press, 1988). **Secondary Sources:** Stelamaris Coser, *Bridging the Americas: The Literature of Paule Marshall, Toni Morrison, and Gayl Jones* (Philadelphia: Temple University Press, 1995); Eugenia C. DeLamotte, *Places of Silence, Journeys of Freedom: The Fiction of Paule Marshall* (Philadelphia: University of Pennsylvania Press, 1998); Dorothy Hamer Denniston, *The Fiction of Paule Marshall: Reconstructions of History, Culture, and Gender* (Knoxville: University of Tennessee Press, 1995); Henry Louis Gates, Jr., and Nellie Y. McKay, eds., *The Norton Anthology of African American Literature* (New York: Norton, 1996); Heather Hathaway,

Caribbean Waves: Relocating Claude McKay and Paule Marshall (Bloomington: Indiana University Press, 1999); Joyce Pettis, *Toward Wholeness in Paule Marshall's Fiction* (Charlottesville: University Press of Virginia, 1995).

Rachael Barnett

Marxism. Political, economic, and social philosophy. The relationship between Marxism and African American literature was most extensive during the 1930s. That relationship has usually been described according to critical standards influenced to some degree by the cultural politics of the **Cold War**. Until the 1990s, when a wider variety of scholarly viewpoints arose, Marxism was conceptualized as an oppressive doctrine that constrained rather than liberated African American writers. Many important African American authors—including **Richard Wright, Claude McKay, Langston Hughes, Arna Bontemps, William Attaway, Willard Motley, Ann Lane Petry, Margaret Abigail Walker, Dorothy West**, and **Amiri Baraka** became interested, to varying degrees, in Marxism. Most critics chose not to focus on how Marxism may have positively influenced the work of such writers, but instead focused on how these and other writers drifted away from or expressed dissatisfaction with Marxist theory and the artistic dictates of the Communist Party.

The German philosopher Karl Marx claimed that societies had been structured to promote the interests of the economically dominant class. However, social structures are never static. Influenced by Hegelian thought, Marx argued that social structures were transient historic forms determined by the productive forces and tending toward a society without distinct social classes—a society that would be created through a proletarian revolution. Marxism conceives of literature as a social and material practice that is explicable only in relation to other social practices. In Marxist terms, history is seen as a field of struggle for different interests and forces, particularly struggles between social classes. Through the control of a society's economic production, the dominant classes dictate its cultural and intellectual output. Therefore, literature bears the mark of the class struggle. Yet the majority of Marxist criticism has been careful not to treat literature as a mere reflection of history, but has granted it autonomy from its social and historical contexts. In addition, Marxist literary scholars emphasize the importance of looking for the ideological significance of a given work not simply in its political content, but also in its narrative structures, generic conventions, characterization strategies, and modes of imagery.

Postwar literary scholars followed the guidelines set forth by political theorists such as Theodore Draper, Harvey Klehr, and Harold Cruse, who argued that American Marxism had become increasingly manipulated by and dependent on Moscow and Stalinism. As Mark Naison and William Maxwell have emphasized, manipulation, disillusionment, and betrayal are the three different phases through which the encounter between African Americans and Marxism pass, and Marxism's commitment to class struggle, which was difficult to reconcile with the lyricism and subtlety of the black **vernacular** tradition, is seen as especially problematic.

Because the prevailing critical climate of the Cold War years was extremely hostile to Marxism, critics tended to focus on the influence of **Black Nationalism** as the chief political factor in African American literature. In addition, critics and biographers stressed the elements of disaffection from Marxism in both the lives and the writing of African American authors. Readings of central texts in the African American **literary canon**, such as **Richard Wright**'s *Native Son* (1940) and **Ralph Ellison**'s *Invisible Man* (1952), often emphasize the sharp critique of Marxist theories in both books. The anticommunist message in, for example, Richard Wright's "I Tried to Be a Communist" (1950), *The Outsider* (1953), and *American Hunger* (1977), and **Claude McKay**'s *A Long Way from Home* (1937) and *Harlem: Negro Metropolis* (1940) have received wider attention than Wright's and McKay's efforts to combine African American heritage and a Marxist perspective in "Blueprint for Negro Writing" (1937) and *The Negroes in America* (1923), respectively.

The "witch hunts" that characterized **McCarthyism** also caused previously Marxist authors to downplay their radical activities. For example, in his first **autobiography**, *The Big Sea* (1940), Langston Hughes conceals all association with the proletarian literary movement of the 1930s. Nonetheless, he published numerous Marxist-influenced poems in the 1930s, and his remarkable first collection of short fiction, *The Ways of White Folks* (1934), transforms Marxist critiques into fiction in a variety of ways. Even after drifting away from Marxism, Hughes maintained his critique of the excesses and injustice of capitalism and **colonialism**, and he continued to argue implicitly and explicitly for the full economic and social citizenship of African Americans. Hughes appeared before Senator McCarthy's Permanent Subcommittee on Investigations on March 26, 1953, where he answered questions and read a brief statement. In the statement, he pointed to circumstances leading to his sympathies with socialist philosophies, and he explained how the "red flag" of the Soviet Union symbolized the possibility of freedom for oppressed peoples. He noted that one cause of his change in attitude toward the Soviet Union was its pact with Nazi Germany. He also noted that, nonetheless, the United States faced "many problems" (Ostrom, 203, 239–240). Hughes spoke only of his own political views and mentioned no other individuals or groups. His biographer, **Arnold Rampersad**, suggests that Hughes agreed to appear before the committee knowing he would "draw the disapproval, even the contempt, of the white left, but keep more or less intact the special place he had painstakingly carved out within the black community" (Rampersad, vol. 2, 219; Ostrom, 240). Given the complexity of Hughes's situation and political views and the danger that McCarthyism posed, Rampersad describes Hughes's statement as "a rhetorical tour de force" (219).

More recent scholarship has revised descriptions of the connection between Marxism and African American literature. Mark Solomon and Robin Kelley have produced studies that challenge the notion that the main vehicle for the dissemination of Marxism in America, the American Communist Party, was controlled by Moscow. Focusing specifically on African Americans, Solomon has argued that "more important than Comintern directives was the Party's life and work at the social and cultural grassroots where the material and spiritual realities of Communist lives were manifested in a thoroughly American context." On the issue of race, in particular, while the Comintern put pressure on American Communists to consider African American rights as a crucial goal, "the application of the theoretical precepts from Moscow soon was influenced by American realities. The Comintern did not order the imprisonment and the death sentences of the **Scottsboro Boys**. That cause and others—not orders from Moscow—became the most influential factors in the drawing Communists and their allies into a vortex of political struggle." (Langston Hughes was heavily involved in trying to support the Scottsboro Boys and published *Scottsboro Limited: Four Poems and a Play in Verse* in 1932.)

Anthony Dawahare has challenged the standard idea that writers with nationalist leanings wrote the most politically aware fiction, poetry, and prose of the day. He argues that the adoption of a Marxist worldview contributed more effectively to pressing forward the antiracist politics of African American writing than did a nationalist ideology. Nationalist approaches to political and cultural resistance insufficiently emphasized the capitalist foundation of modern racial discrimination, he argues. Conversely, Black writers who adopted a Marxist standpoint were able to offer sharp critiques of the capitalist system, Dawahare notes.

This newer appreciation of African American artists who relied on Marxism for their literary inspiration has been coupled with the awareness that the standard paradigm of manipulation, disillusionment, and betrayal is too simplistic. African Americans consciously and voluntarily sought in Marxism a theory that could shape their literary and political achievements. Furthermore, as William Maxwell contends, "the supposition that the meeting of black and white Reds [Marxists and/or Communists] remade only the black" is inadequate. Such an assumption denies any type of agency to Black intellectuals and their capacity to adapt Marxist theory to their own ends. White Marxists did not manipulate African Americans into viewing society through the lens of class struggle. For example, Black Marxists such as Claude McKay were influential in shaping the Black Belt Nation thesis that was approved by the Communist International in 1928. The thesis conceptualized the presence of African Americans in Southern states in nationalistic terms. It argues that African Americans formed a separate nation which was oppressed but showed vital cultural signs of resistance. That ideas like the Black Belt Nation thesis influenced American Marxist politics in the 1930s is "documentation that a radical **Harlem Renaissance** position found a second home in Moscow, where it stretched the intellectual borders of the **Black Atlantic** and rephrased Marxism's Negro Question in the earshot of a receptive Kremlin" (Maxwell, 93).

African American nationalism and Marxism are also starting to be linked rather than opposed in some literary analyses. Analyzing the relationship between Claude McKay and the proletarian writer and theorist par excellence Mike Gold, William Maxwell has concluded that "numerous fictions and

critical pieces by Gold suggest that his influential pronouncements on proletarian literature were formulated in conversation with Harlem's literary
renaissance" (123). Richard Wright, who has repeatedly been accused of
sacrificing African American folk culture to Marxist dogmas, tried in his
fiction and nonfiction prior to the 1950s to establish a dialectical relationship
between African American cultural heritage, Marxism, and **Modernism**. In
his essay "Blueprint for Negro Writing," Wright states that African American
writers should combine the best of their folk tradition with the techniques of
literary Modernism. He stresses that "nationalist spirit in Negro writing means
a nationalism carrying the highest possible pitch of social consciousness."
Wright is careful not to conflate the categories of **race** and class: the revolutionary and class consciousness of the writer "draws for its strength upon the
fluid lore of a great people, and moulds this lore with the concepts that move
and direct the forces of history today." African American artists will be helped
by the "Marxist conception of reality and society" to "learn to view the life of
a Negro living in the New York's **Harlem** or **Chicago**'s South Side with the
consciousness that one-sixth of the earth's surface belongs to the working
class." As Barbara Foley has argued, "The goal of working class revolution is thus
in no way contradictory to the fostering of a vital Negro nationalism.... In
Wright's dialectical formulation, nationalism would point the way to revolutionary class consciousness, be transformed and eventually be negated by the
higher level of consciousness to which it had given rise."

Marxism also influenced controversial radical African American intellectuals of the 1960s and 1970s, such as Amiri Baraka and **Angela Y. Davis**.
Embracing Marxism in the mid-1970s after abandoning Black Nationalism,
Baraka defined himself as a "Third World socialist." Since 1974, he has produced a number of Marxist poetry collections and plays, including *Hard Facts*
(1976), *Poetry for the Advanced* (1979), and *Heathens and Revolutionary Art:
Poems and Lecture* (1994). Baraka's fundamental aims did not change with his
ideological shift from race to class struggle, and his idea of poetry as didactic
remained an important part of his intellectual profile.

Davis, a radical feminist working for **gender** and racial equality, was repeatedly
ostracized during her university career because of her membership in the Communist Party and was persecuted by the CIA. Her Marxist conception of art is
clear in her idea that progressive art can help people to learn about the social
forces at work within society and the social character of their inner lives. In
addition, Davis argues that progressive art can lead people to social emancipation. Her previously strong popularity among African Americans was endangered
by her stance against Louis Farrakhan's 1995 Million Man March, which Davis
claimed would increase male chauvinism by excluding Black women.

Works by Claude McKay, Langston Hughes, Richard Wright, Harry Haywood (*Black Bolshevik*), Angela Davis, and others dramatize the interplay
within the African American consciousness between racial and political allegiances, and especially between African American political predicaments
and ideas advanced in Marxist theory.

Resources: Faith Berry, ed., *Good Morning, Revolution: Uncollected Social Protest Writings* [by Langston Hughes] (New York: L. Hill, 1973); Anthony Dawahare, *Nationalism, Marxism and African American Literature Between the Wars: A New Pandora's Box* (Jackson: University Press of Mississippi, 2003); Michael Denning, *The Cultural Front: The Laboring of American Culture in the Twentieth Century* (New York: Verso, 1998); Barbara Foley, *Radical Representations: Politics and Form in U.S. Proletarian Fiction, 1929–1941* (Durham, NC: Duke University Press, 1993); Laura Hapke, *Labor's Text: The Worker in American Fiction* (New Brunswick, NJ: Rutgers University Press, 2001); Harry Haywood, *Black Bolshevik: Autobiography of an Afro-American Communist* (Chicago: Liberator, 1978); Langston Hughes: *The Big Sea* (New York: Knopf, 1940); *Scottsboro Limited: Four Poems and a Play in Verse* (New York: Golden Stair Press, 1932); Robin D. G. Kelley, *Hammer and Hoe: Alabama Communists During the Great Depression* (Chapel Hill: University of North Carolina Press, 1990); William J. Maxwell, *New Negro, Old Left: African-American Writing and Communism Between the Wars* (New York: Columbia University Press, 1999); Claude McKay, *A Long Way from Home* (1937; repr. San Diego: Harcourt Brace & World, 1970); Bill V. Mullen, *Popular Fronts: Chicago and African-American Cultural Politics, 1935–1946* (Urbana: University of Illinois Press, 1999); Hans Ostrom, *A Langston Hughes Encyclopedia* (Westport, CT: Greenwood Press, 2002); Arnold Rampersad, *The Life of Langston Hughes*, 2 vols. (New York: Oxford University Press, 1986–1988); Alan Wald: *Exiles from a Future Time: The Forging of the Mid-Twentieth-Century Literary Left* (Chapel Hill: University of North Carolina Press, 2002); *Writing from the Left: New Essays on Radical Culture and Politics* (New York: Verso, 1994); Richard Wright, "A Blueprint for Negro Writing," *New Challenge* 2 (Fall 1937), 58–65.

Luca Prono

Mataka, Laini (born c. 1951). Poet. Born in **Baltimore, Maryland**, Mataka now lives in **Washington, D.C.**, where she participates in poetry readings and spoken word performances.

In 1971, under the name Wanda Robinson, Mataka recorded the first of two spoken word albums, *Black Ivory*, which was followed by *Me and Friend*. She took the name of her first album from the group Black Ivory, which often provided background music for her performances.

Mataka self-published *Black Rhythms for Fancy Dancers* in 1977. In 1988 she began her association with Black Classics Press in Baltimore with the publication of *Never as Strangers*. On the cover of Mataka's 1994 collection, *Restoring the Queen*, she proclaims herself a Pan Afrikanist [*sic*] and a Black Nationalist. Her poetry is concerned with politics and **race**, especially with their effect on Black women.

Mataka's most recent collection, *Being a Strong Black Woman Can Get U Killed* (2000), includes the poem of that title—the popularity of which is evidenced by its appearance on dozens of Internet sites, sometimes without crediting Mataka, a "theft" that Black Classics Press addresses on the cover of the collection. The publisher's blurb describes the collection as "a lament for strong Black women who carried the family in her belly, the community on her head, and the race on her back." Nikki Herd's review of *Being a Strong Black Woman* applauds Mataka's honest grappling with the ills of Black women, their relationships with their children, their men, and their community. But she also criticizes the poems for their wordiness and lack of universality. (*See* **Performance Poetry**.)

Resources: Nikki Herd, "Review of *Being a Strong Black Woman Can Get U Killed*," *Black Issues Book Review* 3, no. 3 (May/June 2001), 37; Laini Mataka: *Being a Strong Black Woman Can Get U Killed* (Baltimore: Black Classics, 2000); *Black Rhythms for Fancy Dancers* (Baltimore: self published, 1977); *Never as Strangers* (Baltimore: Black Classics, 1988); *Restoring the Queen* (Baltimore: Black Classics, 1994).

Patricia Kennedy Bostian

Matheus, John F. (1887–1983). Poet, playwright, and short story writer. Although John F. Matheus is generally regarded as a minor figure of the **Harlem Renaissance**, his works were highly regarded and are among the most technically polished ones published at that time.

John Frederick Matheus was born September 20, 1887, in Keyser, West Virginia. His father, John W. Matheus, was a bank messenger who did other jobs to support his family; his mother, Mary Susan Brown, was a housewife. As a young boy, Matheus moved with his parents and three brothers to Steubenville, Ohio. He was educated at Western Reserve University in Cleveland, where he earned a bachelor's degree in classics in 1910; in 1921, he earned the M.A. degree from Columbia University. He pursued further study at the Sorbonne and the University of Chicago. Matheus embarked on a career of university teaching in 1910, first teaching classics and foreign languages at Florida A&M College in Tallahassee. In 1922, he moved to West Virginia State College, where he was a professor of French until his retirement in 1953. After his retirement, he continued to teach at a number of historically black colleges and universities. He died in Tallahassee in 1983, at age ninety-five.

Matheus's best-known short story, "Fog," won first place in the 1925 **Opportunity** contest. Thematically, it melds with the best-foot-forward propaganda that many theorists during the Harlem Renaissance embraced. On a train ride across the foggy river from Ohio to West Virginia, a multicultural group of passengers is thrown together with their various racial, ethnic, and religious prejudices fully exposed. The Whites are en route to an evening meeting that aims to settle the issue of foreigners among them. Suddenly, the bridge supports shift, and all of the passengers are faced with impending death. However, they empty the coach and flee to safety on the Ohio side with a newly discovered common humanity that has replaced their former prejudices.

'Cruiter, Matheus's prize-winning play in the 1926 **Opportunity** contest, concerns another social phenomenon of the times, that of the early-twentieth-century migration of African Americans from **the South** to the North (*see* **Great Migration**). This play specifically addresses the recruitment of African Americans to work in Northern munitions factories during **World War I**. It also concerns the different opinions about freedom of the older and younger generations of African Americans.

Although Matheus wrote a number of relatively inconsequential poems, he was a prolific writer of short stories and plays, many of which appeared in the leading anthologies of the day, including *The New Negro* (1925), which was edited by **Alain Locke**; *Ebony and Topaz* (1927); *Plays of Negro Life* (1927); *Plays and Pageants from the Life of the Negro* (1930); and *The Negro Caravan* (1941). His works tended to explore social issues and simultaneously to insist upon the general humanity of African Americans. In 1955, he collaborated with Clarence Cameron White on *Ouanga: A Haitian Opera in Three Acts*.

Resources: Rita B. Dandridge, "John F. Matheus," in *The Oxford Companion to African American Literature*, ed. William Andrews, Frances Smith Foster, and Trudier Harris (New York: Oxford University Press, 1997), 483; Venetria K. Patton and Maureen Honey, *Double-Take: A Revisionist Harlem Renaissance Anthology* (New Brunswick, NJ: Rutgers University Press, 2001); Clarence Cameron White and John F. Matheus, *Ouanga: A Haitian Opera in Three Acts* (New York: S. Fox, 1955).

Warren J. Carson

Mathis, Sharon Bell (born 1937). Author of children's and young-adult literature. Born on February 26, 1937, in Atlantic City, New Jersey, Mathis grew up in the Bedford-Stuyvesant section of **Brooklyn, New York**. Encouraged by her mother, Mathis began writing and reading voraciously as a young child. She read her favorite books—**Richard Wright**'s *Black Boy*, Betty Smith's *A Tree Grows in Brooklyn*, and **Willard Motley**'s *Knock on Any Door*—repeatedly and wrote stories of her own. Encouraged by her teachers, Mathis shared many of her stories in class. She dreamed of becoming a professional writer. However, discouraged by those who pointed out that few African Americans were able to support themselves financially as writers, she put writing off for a few years, opting to turn her interests toward obtaining a college degree. Mathis graduated from Morgan State College in 1958 with a degree in sociology. Already married, she began working as an interviewer at the Children's Hospital in **Washington, D.C.**, and later as an elementary school teacher. But her desire to become a writer did not diminish.

By 1963, Mathis had begun to work diligently at developing her writing skills. Finally, in 1968 her first children's story was published in *Tan Confessions*, and in 1969, "The Fire Escape" was published in *News Explorer*. Also in 1969, Mathis became director of the children's literature division of the D.C. Black Writers Workshop. It was in this capacity that she met and encouraged the children's book author **Eloise Greenfield**. In 1970, two poems by Mathis, "Ladies Magazine" and "R.S.V.P.," were anthologized in *Night Comes Softly: Anthology of Black Female Voices* by **Nikki Giovanni**. Of the notable titles that would follow, *Teacup Full of Roses* (1972) and *Listen for the Fig Tree* (1974) were published for young adults; *Brooklyn Story* (1970), *Sidewalk Story* (1971), *Ray Charles* (1973), *The Hundred Penny Box* (1975), and *Cartwheels* (1977) are for younger readers. During the 1972–1973 school year, Mathis taught courses in creative writing and African American literature as writer-in-residence at Howard University. In 1975, she earned a master's degree in library science from Catholic University of America.

Most of Mathis's titles were penned during the 1970s, a time when there were very few positive depictions of African American children in literature. Through her realistic fiction for youth, Mathis has put forth a sincere commitment to providing literature for African American children that is both thought-provoking and culturally affirming. Her stories include references to African American culture that young people can be proud of, such as African American music, Kwanzaa, and the importance of extended family. She has won numerous honors for her work. Among them are the Council on Interracial Books for Children Prize in 1971 for *Sidewalk Story*; the Coretta Scott King Honor Book Award in 1973 for *Teacup Full of Roses*; the Coretta Scott King Award in 1974 for *Ray Charles*; and the Newbery Honor Book Award and the Boston Globe-Horn Book Honor Book Award, both in 1976, for *The Hundred Penny Box*. Mathis did not publish any books during the 1980s because she suffered from writer's block. In 1991, she published *Red Dog Blue Fly: Football Poems*, a collection of poems for young people about a football team, and in 1997, she published *Running Girl: The Diary of Ebonee Rose*, a series of diary entries that reveal the protagonist's love of running and her link to other phenomenal African American women athletes. Mathis's work, though written for all children, is especially significant for African American youth, urging them "to carry on" ("Ten Pennies," 437).

Resources: Frances Smith Foster, "Sharon Bell Mathis," in *Dictionary of Literary Biography*, vol. 33, *Afro-American Fiction Writers After 1955*, ed. Thadious M. Davis and Trudier Harris (Detroit: Gale, 1984), 170–173; Gwendolyn S. Jones, "Sharon Bell Mathis," in *Contemporary African American Novelists: A Bio-Bibliographical Critical Sourcebook*, ed. Emmanuel S. Nelson (Westport, CT: Greenwood Press, 1999), 305–308; Sharon Bell Mathis: *Something About the Author*, vol. 58, ed. Anne Commire (Detroit: Gale, 1990), 124–132; "Ten Pennies and Green Mold," *Horn Book*, Aug. 1976, 433–437.

KaaVonia Hinton-Johnson

Matthews, Victoria Earle (1861–1907). Social activist, writer, and orator. Born into **slavery** in Fort Valley, Georgia, one month after the **Civil War** began, Matthews dedicated her life to improving social conditions for African Americans, especially women. Her mother Caroline Smith, who had fled to New York to escape the sexual abuse of her master (Matthews's father), returned to Georgia in 1870 and regained custody of four of her nine children, including Matthews. The family settled in New York City in 1873; three years later, illness and financial hardship in the family forced Matthews to leave school to work as a domestic. Thereafter she educated herself through voracious reading and frequent attendance at lectures and cultural events. In 1879, she married William Matthews; they had one son, who died in 1895. Shortly after her marriage, Matthews began writing about her childhood for *Waverly* and other children's magazines. She went on to work as a freelance journalist for the *New York Times*, the *New York Herald*, and the *Brooklyn Eagle*. She was also a frequent contributor to leading Black periodicals, including the *National Leader*, *Detroit Plaindealer*, *Washington Bee*, *Richmond Planet*, *Boston Advocate*, *Cleveland Gazette*, *New York Globe*, and *New York Age*. By 1891, Matthews was acclaimed as the most popular woman journalist of her day. Her short story "Aunt Lindy: A Story Founded on Real Life" (1889), published as a single volume in 1893, depicts the dignity and generosity of spirit that allow a former slave to nurse her former master back to health when he is injured in a fire years after slavery has ended. Matthews's other extant works include at least two short stories, "Eugenia's Mistake: A Story" (1892) and "Zelika: A Story" (1892), a collection of **Booker T. Washington**'s speeches titled *Black Belt Diamonds* (1898), and three speeches.

In "The Value of Race Literature" (1895), Matthews defines race literature as "all the writings emanating from a distinct class—not necessarily race matter; but a general collection of what has been written by the men and women of that Race" in every discipline. She asserts the need for writing shaped by the particularities of the Black experience as a means of balancing out unfavorable depictions of African Americans, providing "an outlet for the unnaturally suppressed inner lives which our people have been compelled to lead," and increasing the overall cultural capital of the race. "The Awakening of the Afro-American Woman" (1897) charts the progress of Black Christian womanhood since the end of slavery and calls for reforms to aid in further growth, such as the repeal of laws against intermarriage (which she calls "the greatest demoralizing forces with which our womanhood has to contend") and Jim Crow laws, prison reform, and greater access to health care and child care. "Some of the Dangers Confronting Southern Girls in the North" (1898) exposes discriminatory hiring practices and prostitution schemes as impediments to successful migration. Matthews was vigorously involved in the Black **women's club** movement, including the Woman's Loyal Union of New York and Brooklyn and the National Association of Colored Women. She founded the White Rose Mission Industrial Association, which later became part of the Urban League, and the White Rose Traveler's Aid Society, both of which were designed to help women from the rural South make safe and successful transitions to the urban North. When Matthews died of tuberculosis on March 10, 1907, her obituary ran in the *New York Times* under the heading "Friend of the Negroes Dies."

Resources: Hallie Q. Brown, *Homespun Heroines and Other Women of Distinction* (New York: Oxford University Press, 1988); Shirley Wilson Logan, *We Are Coming: The Persuasive Discourse of Nineteenth-Century Black Women* (Carbondale: Southern Illinois University Press, 1999); Shirley Wilson Logan, ed., *With Pen and Voice: A Critical Anthology of Nineteenth-Century African-American Women* (Carbondale: Southern Illinois University Press, 1995); Cheryl Waites, "Victoria Earle Matthews: Residence and Reform," in *African American Leadership: An Empowerment Tradition in Social Welfare History*, ed. Iris B. Carlton-LaNey (Washington, DC: National Association of Social Workers Press, 2001).

April Gentry

Mayfield, Julian (1928–1984). Novelist, playwright, screenwriter, essayist, editor, and actor. Born in Greer, South Carolina, Mayfield served in the U.S. Army and attended Lincoln University. His subsequent professional life was a complex amalgam of careers.

From 1949 to 1954, Mayfield established himself as an actor. His first major role was in the Broadway staging of *Lost in the Stars,* Maxwell Anderson's and Kurt Weill's musical adaptation of *Cry, the Beloved Country,* Alan Paton's acclaimed novel about the entrenchment of the apartheid system in South Africa. Mayfield's stage experience led him to write one-act plays—*417, The Other Foot,* and *A World Full of Men*—that were produced in the early 1950s and attracted some notice. From 1954 to 1958, he served as editor in chief and theater reviewer for the *World Journal,* which he cofounded in Puerto Rico. He reworked *417* into his first novel, *The Hit* (1957), and after it proved successful, wrote two more novels over the next four years, *The Long Night* (1958) and *The Grand Parade* (1961).

In a major shift in his career, Mayfield next accepted an invitation to become communications aide to President Kwame Nkrumah of Ghana, and served in that capacity from 1962 to 1966. From 1964 to 1966, he also was the founding editor of the *African Review,* published in Accra, Ghana. In the 1967–1968 and 1970–1971 academic years, he taught at Cornell University. In between, in 1969–1970, he taught at New York University. In 1969, he wrote the screenplays for the films *Uptight!* and *The Hitch,* and he appeared as an actor in *Uptight!*

From 1971 to 1975, Mayfield again lived overseas, serving as an adviser to Prime Minister Forbes Burnham of Guyana. In 1973, he also was the editor of *New Nation International.* After spending the 1976–1977 academic year as a Fulbright–Hays Fellow lecturing in several European countries, Algeria, and Turkey, he spent a year as a visiting professor at the University of Maryland. Then, from 1978 until his death from heart failure in 1984, he was writer-in-residence at Howard University.

In his multifaceted career, Mayfield made many contributions to African American culture and to the development of African American studies as an academic discipline. Although he wrote more essays than work in any other genre, in literary terms Mayfield's reputation rests on his three novels and especially on his first. *The Hit* is a story of dogged hope in the midst of daily desperation and highlights the ways in which even instances of good luck can be turned into greater disappointment. It focuses on a **Harlem, New York**, numbers bettor who consistently plays the number 417. When he finally "hits" with the number, he discovers that the runner with whom he placed his bets has disappeared with his winnings. The novel was republished in British, French, and Czech editions. *The Long Night* and *The Grand Parade* (reprinted as *Nowhere Street*) present even grimmer depictions of families struggling to cope with poverty, crime, and the loss of dignity and hope.

Resources: Arthur P. Davis, *From the Dark Tower: Afro-American Writers (1900 to 1960)* (Washington, DC: Howard University Press, 1974), 198–203; Julian Mayfield:

The Grand Parade (New York: Vanguard, 1961); *The Hit* (New York: Vanguard, 1957); *The Long Night* (New York: Vanguard, 1958); Holly I. West, "The Goal of Julian Mayfield: Fusing Art and Politics," *Washington Post*, July 7, 1975, pp. B1 and B3.

Martin Kich

Mays, Benjamin Elijah (1894–1984). Autobiographer, religious writer, essayist, professor, and college president. Born the son of a sharecropper in South Carolina, Benjamin Mays grew up to become a respected academician, agitator for desegregation, and president of Morehouse College during some of that institution's most influential years, including those when **Martin Luther King, Jr.**, was a student there. In his **autobiography**, *Born to Rebel*, Mays recounts his father's advice to stay out of trouble with White people, advice whose wisdom he challenged in his lifelong response to racism.

After graduating from the High School Department of South Carolina State College in 1916, Mays completed his education at Bates College in Maine and the University of Chicago before returning in 1925 to South Carolina State, where he taught English. After a number of appointments with religious organizations, he became the Dean of the School of Religion at Howard in 1934. Two books that he wrote in the 1930s, *The Negro's Church* (1933, with Joseph W. Nicholson) and *The Negro's God as Reflected in His Literature* (1938), remain key works in the study of African American religious history. For the first of these, Mays surveyed more than 800 Black churches to document their problems, resources, achievements, and importance to the communities they served, presenting a scientifically accurate picture of Black churches. The latter focuses on the role of images of God in **sermons** and literature, particularly arguing that in Black literature religion is not so much compensatory for the hardships of racism, but rather has played a key role in developing a rationale for freedom.

From 1940 to 1967 Mays was the president of Morehouse College in **Atlanta, Georgia**, where his students included a generation of future political activists, such as **Julian Bond**, **Andrew Young**, and Martin Luther King, Jr. His autobiography, *Born to Rebel* (1971), uses his lifelong experiences to make a social critique about the necessity of confronting the limitations imposed by racism. He is not simply telling one man's story; beginning as he does with a scene of White mob violence, he uses his life to tell the story of African American responses to racism. In the 1970s Mays was an adviser to President Jimmy Carter before becoming President Emeritus of Morehouse in 1981. Also in 1981, he completed his autobiography with a second volume, *Lord, the People Have Driven Me On*. He died in Atlanta on March 28, 1984.

Resources: William L. Andrews, ed., *African American Autobiography* (Englewood Cliffs, NJ: Prentice-Hall, 1993); Lawrence Edward Carter, Sr., ed., *Walking Integrity: Benjamin Elijah Mays, Mentor to Martin Luther King Jr.* (Macon, GA: Mercer University Press, 1998); Benjamin E. Mays: *Born to Rebel: An Autobiography* (1971; repr. Athens: University of Georgia Press, 2002); *Lord, the People Have Driven Me On* (New York: Vantage, 1981); *The Negro's God as Reflected in His Literature* (1938; repr. New

York: Russell & Russell, 1968); Benjamin Mays and Joseph William Nicholson, *The Negro's Church* (1933; repr. New York: Arno, 1969).

Thomas J. Cassidy

Mays, Willie Howard, Jr. (born 1931). Professional baseball player and autobiographer. Willie Mays is known as the "Say Hey Kid" for the enthusiasm he displayed while playing the game; he is also known as one of the most complete professional baseball players, excelling in all phases of the game in three different decades (1951–1973). During his early days with the New York Giants, after playing at the Polo Grounds, he could be found playing a game of stickball in the streets with the kids in **Harlem, New York**.

Mays was born May 6, 1931, in Westfield (near Birmingham), Alabama. He began his career with the Birmingham Barons in the Negro Baseball Southern League. In 1951 he was signed by the New York Giants and joined recently racially integrated Major Leagues. Mays played for the New York Giants, remaining with the team when it moved west in 1958 and became the San Francisco Giants, and later playing for the New York Mets, wearing the number 24 throughout his career. He ended his professional career in 1973 after playing in the World Series with the New York Mets. He was elected to the Baseball Hall of Fame in 1979.

Mays's baseball record provides ample material for myriad stories, but the story told most often, the one known to diehard fans as simply "The Catch," has been told and retold in nonfiction, fiction, children's literature, and even in film, and memorialized in song. "The Catch"—considered one of the greatest defensive plays ever made in the game—was the spectacular over-the-shoulder catch that Mays made during the opening game of the 1954 World Series between the New York Giants and the Cleveland Indians. He caught a 450-foot blast hit by Vic Wertz, the Indians' first baseman. The Giants went on to win the game 5–2 and swept the series in four games. "The Catch" has become part of baseball's **folklore**. Wertz later said, "I just can't hit a ball any harder than that...I hit it so hard my mind just went black and I don't know what kind of pitch it was. I couldn't believe any man would ever haul it down."

Among the best-known books about this feat are *A Day in the Bleachers*, by Arnold Hano, and *Willie's Time: Baseball's Golden Age*, by Charles Einstein; the latter remains the only biography of a ballplayer to ever be a finalist for the Pulitzer Prize.

"There are only two authentic geniuses in the world," the legendary actress Tallulah Bankhead was purported to have said, "Willie Mays and Willie Shakespeare."

Resources: Frank Ardolino, "'Say Hey' Willie Mays: The 'Catch' in Sports Literature and Film," *Journal of Evolutionary Psychology* 21, no. 1–2 (Mar. 2000), 51–61; *The Baseball Index*, "Willie Mays Bibliography," www.baseballlibrary.com; Charles Einstein, *Willie's Time: Baseball's Golden Age* (1979; repr. Carbondale: Southern Illinois University Press, 2004); Arnold Hano, *A Day in the Bleachers* (1955; repr. New York: Da Capo Press, 1982); Willie Mays, as told to Charles Einstein, *My Life in and* *out of Baseball*, rev. ed. (New York: Dutton, 1972); Willie Mays, with Lou Sahadi, *Say Hey: The Autobiography of Willie Mays* (New York: Simon and Schuster, 1988); Joan Walsh, "Brilliant Careers: Willie Mays," *Salon*, July 13, 1999, www.salon.com.

Wilma Jean Emanuel Randle

McBride, James (born 1957). Journalist, memoirist, and novelist. McBride's education reflects the dual focus of his subsequent career. He attended the Oberlin Conservatory of Music, then he received a master's degree from the Columbia University School of Journalism. For almost a decade, he worked as a journalist with the *Boston Globe*, the *Washington Post*, and *People* magazine. Then he abandoned his journalistic career to compose and perform **jazz**. Eventually, however, while continuing his work as a musician, he returned to writing—first as a memoirist and then, on the heels of that success, as a novelist.

As a writer, McBride is best known for *The Color of Water: A Black Man's Tribute to His White Mother* (1996). Named a Notable Book of the Year by the American Library Association, this book also brought McBride the Anisfield–Wolf Award for Literary Excellence. Ruth McBride Jordan, McBride's mother, was born Rachel Shilsky in Poland, but when she was a young girl, her family emigrated to Virginia, where her father, who had been educated as a rabbi, opened a grocery. Her father was a racist and sexually abused her, and to escape him, McBride's mother ran away to New York City. There she met Andrew McBride, an African American minister. She changed her first name to Ruth, **passed** as a light-skinned African American, and helped him to establish a successful church while bearing their eight children. Andrew McBride died before the youngest of these children, James, was born. His mother remarried and bore four more children to her second husband, Hunter Jordan. *The Color of Water* developed from an article McBride had written almost a decade earlier. In the memoir, he alternates chapters presenting his mother's recollections about different periods and aspects of her life with chapters consisting of his own reflections on her life and her revelations about that life, on the degree to which he has been capable of understanding her experiences, and on the ways in which her experiences and his own have converged and diverged.

McBride's first novel, *Miracle at St. Anna* (2002), is based on an actual incident from **World War II**. It focuses on a small group African American soldiers serving in a segregated unit in Italy and explores their responses to a Nazi massacre of all but one young resident of an Italian village.

Resources: Ronald Kovach, "James McBride: Illuminating the Past—and Going Beyond It," *Writer*, June 2003, pp. 22–26; James McBride: *The Color of Water: A Black Man's Tribute to His White Mother* (New York: Riverhead, 1996); *Miracle at St. Anna* (New York: Riverhead, 2002).

Martin Kich

McCall, Nathan (born 1955). Journalist and autobiographer. McCall earned a B.A. from Norfolk State University; as a journalist, he has held positions at the *Newark Star-Ledger*, the *Atlanta Constitution*, and the *Washington Post*.

McCall gives voice to issues of concern to contemporary African American males. His adolescent and early adult life in Portsmouth, Virginia, was shaped by segregation, insecurity, frustration, paranoia, violent anger, unemployment, gang membership, teenage fatherhood, and incarceration. His ongoing struggle between making ethical decisions and giving in to peer pressure often resulted in his irrational thinking and engagement in indiscriminate criminal activity and violence in the streets. As a means of reflecting on and drawing attention to his irresponsibility and repeated encounters with racism and prejudice as they intersect with the contemporary plight of many young African American men, McCall wrote *Makes Me Wanna Holler: A Young Black Man in America* (1994), which chronicles his life's journey, including the main turning points. Detailed in his memoir is his explanation of the extent to which young Black men's perpetuation of negative stereotypes contributes to their own demise.

After having served three years in prison, the hardships McCall faced were balanced by personal accomplishments—the knowledge that, in returning to himself and the strength of his forebears, as well as in the basic values that make African Americans human, he understood himself and the world better. The political urgency that motivated McCall's debut work also appears in his 1997 collection of essays on race and politics, *What's Going On*. His work has inspired African American men to transform their lives by seeking to transcend mainstream society's misconceptions of African Americans through education, self-respect, and dignity.

For Nathan McCall, personal and artistic worlds can never be apolitical, and thus his future work will continue to illuminate those points that have always been central to his life: racism, oppression, injustice; young men on a collision course with history who nevertheless seek personal and political affirmations.

Resources: Nathan McCall, *Makes Me Wanna Holler: A Young Black Man in America* (New York: Random House, 1994); *What's Going On: Personal Essays* (New York: Random House, 1997).

Teresa Gilliams

McCarthyism (1950–1954). Political and social phenomenon. McCarthyism takes its name from Wisconsin Senator Joseph McCarthy. In reaction to the **Cold War** and in an attempt to exploit Americans' fears about the United States being infiltrated by Communists after **World War II**, McCarthy began to try to alarm Americans about the alleged presence of Communists in the federal government. In a speech given at Wheeling, West Virginia, on February 9, 1950, McCarthy claimed that the State Department was infested with Communists, subversives, and "fellow travelers"—people sympathetic to communism (Griffith). He and his supporters then set into motion almost five years of investigations of people, many of whom had had ties with the Communist Party or with other socialist groups in the 1920s and 1930s, especially during the Great Depression, but who had since repudiated communism or drifted away from socialist politics (Rovere). These investigations came to be known as witch hunts, a term which alludes to the Salem (Massachusetts) witch trials and the frenzy surrounding these trials in 1692. Investigations and hearings by the House Un-American Activities Committee (HUAC) and by the Senate Permanent Subcommittee on Investigations (which McCarthy chaired) in effect destroyed many careers, for after appearing before (or refusing to appear before) HUAC or the Permanent Subcommittee, individuals were blacklisted—unable to find employment, shunned by friends and associates, and so on. As a result, many lives were ruined. McCarthy and those working with him targeted individuals in government offices, universities and colleges, the entertainment industry, and arts groups. Herbert Block, a *Washington Post* cartoonist, was the first to coin the term "McCarthyism." He used it in a cartoon as a synonym for mudslinging (Griffith).

Many African American writers were caught in McCarthy's web of reckless investigations. Maxwell observes that "the gallery of black intellectuals variously affiliated with Communism in the 1920s and 1930s makes a fair who's who of African American writing from the same decades" (Maxwell, 2). Aided in part by the Works Progress Administration (WPA) and various subsidiary programs, such as the Federal Theater Project (FTP), the **Federal Writers' Project** (FWP), and the **Negro Units**, African American writers, especially in **Chicago, Illinois**, and New York City, flourished, and many of these writers found socialist or "leftist" politics appealing (Mullen and Smethurst). The Communist Party, publicizing racial issues and injustices such as the infamous **Scottsboro Boys** trial (1931) and promoting the improvement of the economic status of African Americans, encouraged African Americans to join the party at a time when Jim Crow laws were the rule. Some two decades later, African Americans who had been involved in leftist politics were likely targets of McCarthy's investigations. The racist element of McCarthyism can be inferred from **Mary Helen Washington**'s statement that "White people who were called before HUAC found themselves under suspicion for having black friends, or being in an interracial marriage, or for listening to black music—as if the mighty one drop of black blood could produce a communist" (Washington, 183). The list of writers investigated includes **Richard Wright** and **Ralph Ellison**. Both were charged by HUAC with subversion of American ideals, beliefs, and institutions. The Federal Bureau of Investigation (FBI), which often participated in investigations related to McCarthyism, amassed 119 pages on **Claude McKay**, 181 pages on Wright, and 559 pages on **Langston Hughes** (Maxwell; Mullen and Smethurst). Hughes appeared before the Permanent Subcommittee, provided a written statement, and answered questions, but he did not speak of other individuals (Ostrom). Other writers who came under scrutiny during the McCarthy era include **James Baldwin**, **Gwendolyn Brooks**, and **Alice Childress**. The FBI file on Baldwin runs well over 1,000 pages (Campbell). **Countee Cullen**, **Paul Robeson**, and **W.E.B. Du Bois** also were investigated. **Lorraine Hansberry**, **Robert Hayden**, **Chester Himes**, **Jean Toomer**, **Alain**

Locke, and **Dorothy West** were viewed as subversives, too (Maxwell; Mullen and Smethurst; Washington). The beginning of McCarthy's precipitous fall from power and popularity began when he investigated the U.S. Army (Rovere), but the effects and vivid memories of his investigations persisted, in part because many of his hearings were televised (Doherty). J. Edgar Hoover, Director of the FBI, never really abandoned his McCarthyistic fervor, and he continued to investigate almost anyone he viewed as subversive, including African American activists in the 1950s, 1960s, and 1970s. Among them were **James Baldwin**, **Martin Luther King, Jr.**, and members of the **Black Panther Party** (Powers). (*See* **Marxism**.)

Resources: James Campbell, *Talking at the Gates: A Life of James Baldwin* (New York: Viking, 1991); Michael Cooke, *Afro-American Literature in the Twentieth Century: The Achievement of Intimacy* (New Haven, CT: Yale University Press, 1984); Thomas Patrick Doherty, *Cold War, Cool Medium: Television, McCarthyism, and American Culture* (New York: Columbia University Press, 2003); Robert Griffith, *The Politics of Fear: Joseph McCarthy and the Senate* (Lexington: University Press of Kentucky, 1970); William J. Maxwell, *New Negro, Old Left: African American Writing and Communism Between the Wars* (New York: Columbia University Press, 1999); Bill Mullen and Sherry Lee Linkon, eds., *Radical Revisions: Rereading 1930s Culture* (Urbana: University of Illinois Press, 1996); Bill Mullen and James Smethurst, eds., *Left of the Color Line: Race, Radicalism, and Twentieth-Century Literature of the United States* (Chapel Hill: University of North Carolina Press, 2003); Hans Ostrom, "McCarthyism," in Ostrom's *A Langston Hughes Encyclopedia* (Westport, CT: Greenwood Press, 2002), 239–240; Richard Gid Powers, *Secrecy and Power: The Life of J. Edgar Hoover* (New York: Free Press, 1987); Richard H. Rovere, *Senator Joe McCarthy* (New York: Harcourt, Brace, 1959); Usha Shourie, *Black American Literature* (New Delhi, India: Cosmo Publications, 1985); Jessie Carnie Smith and Joseph Palmisano, eds., *The African American Almanac*, 8th ed. (Detroit: Gale, 2000); Mary Helen Washington, "Alice Childress, Lorraine Hansberry, and Claudia Jones: Black Women Write the Popular Front," in *Left of the Color Line: Race, Radicalism and Twentieth-Century Literature of the United States*, ed. Bill Mullen and James Smethurst (Chapel Hill: University of North Carolina Press, 2003).

Claudia Matherly Stolz

McCauley, Robbie (born 1947). Actor, performance artist, playwright, teacher, and director. Although active in many facets of contemporary theater production, McCauley is best known for her innovative solo and collaborative performance-based work, much of which documents race-related struggles throughout twentieth-century American history.

Born in Norfolk, Virginia, on July 14, 1947, McCauley spent most of her childhood and adolescence in **Washington, D.C.**, and Georgia. In the mid-1960s, she moved to New York City where she became involved in experimental and Black theater, acting in such venues as La Mama, Caffé Cino, the Negro Ensemble Company, the Public Theater, and the New Lafayette Theatre. As an actor, McCauley originated the role of Clara in **Adrienne**

Kennedy's *A Movie Star Has to Star in Black and White* (1976) and was featured in **Ed Bullins**'s *The Taking of Miss Janie* (1975) and **Ntozake Shange**'s *for colored girls who have considered suicide/when the rainbow is enuf* (1975).

In 1979, McCauley began creating her own performance work, initially in collaboration with the composer Ed Montgomery. Her first solo performance piece, *My Father and the Wars*, debuted in 1985 and was quickly followed by other works, including *Indian Blood* (1987), *Teeny Town* (a collaboration with Jessica Hagedorn and Laurie Carlos, 1988), *Persimmon Peel* (also with Hagedorn and Carlos, 1992), and *The Food Show* (1992). McCauley's most acclaimed work to date, *Sally's Rape* (1989), premiered at P.S. (Public School) 122 in New York City. The play, in which "the voices of [McCauley's] foremothers emerge to reveal the historical precedence for the use of rape as a tool of oppression" (Mahone, xxix), was awarded an Obie and a Bessie (Achievement in Performance) in 1992. *My Father and the Wars*, *Indian Blood*, and *Sally's Rape* are part of a series that McCauley has titled "Confessions of a Working Class Black Woman" and that depicts stories of her family's survival since the nineteenth century.

Throughout the 1990s, McCauley developed a series of site-specific performances based on texts from local witnesses. These performance works include *Mississippi Freedom* (early 1990s), about voting rights in Jackson, Mississippi; *Turf* (1996), about court-enforced busing and school desegregation in **Boston, Massachusetts**; *The Other Weapon* (1994), about law enforcement and the **Black Panther Party** in **Los Angeles, California**; and *The Buffalo Project* (1990), about the 1960s riots in Buffalo, New York.

McCauley's most recent performance work includes *love and race in the United States* (2003) and *Post-Traumatic Slave Disorder*, a collaboration with Kamal Sinclair Steele that McCauley directed at the New Federal Theatre. In 1998, McCauley's work was listed (alongside works by Igor Stravinsky, Pablo Picasso, and John Cage) as part of the *Village Voice*'s "51 (or so) Greatest Avant-Garde Moments."

In addition to her acting and performance work, McCauley is active in stage direction. Her list of directing credits includes Adrienne Kennedy's *Suzanne in Stages* at the Joseph Papp Public Theater; Aimee Cesair's *A Tempest* at UBU Repertory Theater; and Daniel Alexander Jones's *Bel Canto* at Abe Rybek's Theater Offensive in Boston.

McCauley is Associate Professor of Theater Arts at Emerson College.

Resources: Sydné Mahone, "Introduction," in *Moon Marked and Touched by Sun: Plays by African-American Women*, ed. Mahone (New York: Theatre Communications Group, 1994); Robbie McCauley: "Mother Worked," in *Out of Character: Rants, Raves, and Monologues from Today's Top Performance Artists*, ed. Mark Russell (New York: Bantam, 1997), 251–258; "Obsessing in Public: An Interview with Vivian Patraka," in *A Sourcebook of Feminist Theatre and Performance*, ed. Carol Martin (New York: Routledge, 1996), 205–238; "Sally's Rape," in *Moon Marked and Touched by Sun: Plays by African-American Women*, ed. Sydné Mahone (New York: Theatre Communications Group, 1994), 211–238; "Thoughts on My Career, *The Other Weapon*, and Other

Projects," in *Performance and Cultural Politics*, ed. Elin Diamond (New York: Routledge, 1996), 265–282; Robbie McCauley, Laurie Carlos, and Jessica Hagedorn, "Teeny Town," in *Out from Under: Texts by Women Performance Artists*, ed. Lenora Champagne (New York: Theatre Communications Group, 1990), 89–117.

Heath A. Diehl

McClellan, George Marion (1860–1934). Poet and short story writer. George Marion McClellan is known for his distinctive literary expression and philosophy. He was born in Belfast, Tennessee, on September 29, 1860. He attended Fisk University (B.A., 1885) in **Nashville, Tennessee**, and Hartford Theological Seminary (B.D., 1891). After marrying Mariah Augusta Rabb (1889), he returned to Fisk University (M.A., 1890). He supported his wife and two sons as a Congregational minister in Louisville, Kentucky (1887–1890), a financial agent (1892–1894), a teacher and a chaplain at the State Normal School in Alabama (1894–1896), and a pastor in **Memphis, Tennessee** (1897–1899). He taught Latin and English at Central Colored High School (1899–1911) and was a principal at Dunbar Public School in Louisville (1911–1919).

Like his contemporaries, McClellan based his poems and short stories on the experiences of Blacks in America, but he did not embrace changes in Black writing. In the 1890s, many Black writers began to create works that reflected the unique voice and history of Blacks (Bruce, 208). They explored **folklore**, utilized Black dialect, and concentrated on **realism** rather than an idealistic image of Black life.

In contrast, McClellan, like most Black writers prior to this paradigm change, followed a White literary tradition. He "used literature to portray a genteel black world that was culturally identical to that of whites" (Bruce, 208). McClellan's writing was "sentimental," "genteel," and "conservative" (207). He believed all Black writers should follow the same tradition. He did not like the use of Black dialect in writing and thought that Black writers were at a "disadvantage," because Blacks had no "strong traditions" or a "national life" other than **slavery** (208). Only rarely did McClellan stray from his literary ideal, as when he wrote about **conjuring** in "Annette," a short story in *Old Greenbottom Inn and Other Stories* (1906). Even then he continued to focus on the "genteel" aspects of the story and "made clear his own rejection of conjure as anything more than superstition" (209).

Other works by McClellan include *Poems* (1895), *Songs of a Southerner* (1896), "The Negro as Writer," in D.W. Culp's *Twentieth Century Negro Literature* (1902), and *The Path of Dreams* (1916).

Resources: Benjamin Brawley, *The Negro Genius: A New Appraisal of the Achievement of the American Negro in Literature and the Fine Arts* (New York: Dodd, Mead, 1937); Dickson D. Bruce, Jr., "George Marion McClellan," in *Dictionary of Literary Biography*, vol. 50: *Afro-American Writers Before the Harlem Renaissance* (Detroit: Gale, 1986), 206–212; Daniel Wallace Culp, ed., *Twentieth Century Negro Literature* (1902; repr. New York: Arno Press, 1969); Arthur P. Davis and Michael W. Peplow, *The New*

Negro Renaissance: An Anthology (New York: Holt, Rinehart & Winston, 1975); Richard A. Long and Eugenia W. Collier, *Afro-American Writing: An Anthology of Prose and Poetry*, vol. 1 (New York: New York University Press, 1972); George Marion McClellan: *Old Greenbottom Inn and Other Stories* (1906; repr. New York: AMS, 1975); *The Path of Dreams* (Louisville, KY: J. P. Morton, 1916); *Poems* (1895; repr. Freeport, NY: Books for Libraries Press, 1970); *Songs of a Southerner* (1896); Joan R. Sherman: *Invisible Poets: Afro-Americans of the Nineteenth Century* (Urbana: University of Illinois Press, 1974); "Tennessee's Black Poet: George Marion McClellan," *Tennessee Studies in Literature* 18 (1973), 147–162.

Gladys L. Knight

McCluskey, John Ashbery, Jr. (born 1944). Novelist, short story writer, educator, and editor. John McCluskey, Jr., is a talented yet often overlooked author. Noted for his piercing fiction, editing, and "wisdom, professionalism, balance, steadiness, family orientation, and strength," McCluskey has eluded the casual reader (Johnson and McCluskey). Born in Middletown, Ohio, in 1944, McCluskey learned the importance of family, history, and tradition. As a young man, he excelled at academics and sports, which led to his admission to Harvard on scholarship. At Harvard, he took his first creative writing course. After receiving his degree in 1966, McCluskey attended Stanford University, where he earned a master's degree and began work on his first novel, *Look What They Done to My Song* (1974). Touted as a "terse" and "poetic" story about immigrants "trying to make it by bootlegging, marrying doctors, preaching, pimping, singing the songs of soul and sex," McCluskey's first book met with quiet but steady success (Kilgore). Described as a "pilgrimage to self-understanding," the novel details the efforts of a young musician "to carry on **Malcolm X**'s message about the need for human beings to know and understand each other" through the sounds of his horn. Characterized as a "lonely, yet triumphant story" that "sings of justice, of love, of freedom, of survival," the novel "reflects deep insight into what our songs and our lives are all about" (Kilgore).

McCluskey has taught humanities, English, and Afro-American Studies at institutions including Miles College in Birmingham and Indiana University. Much of his work centers on the struggle to forge identity within chaos, and it focuses specifically upon the role of the Black male "in the workings of the national psyche" (Johnson and McCluskey). His second novel, *Mr. America's Last Season Blues*, chronicles the life of a failed sports star as he is forced to accept the mundane existence he fought so hard to escape. McCluskey's main character seeks to "be all things to all people in the black community" in an effort to regain not only his personal "identity, unity, and purpose," but also that of the society at large (Moorer). McCluskey's subjects range from adultery to drug use, from war to oral history, and from music to human understanding, as he strives to give his readers a glimpse of the "true and complex stories" that "must be told and retold" (Johnson and McCluskey).

Resources: Charles Johnson and John McCluskey, eds., "Preface" and "Introduction," in *Black Men Speaking*, ed. Charles Johnson and John McCluskey, Jr. (Bloomington: Indiana University Press, 1997), vii–xx; John C. Kilgore, "Books Noted: *Look What They Done to My Song*," *Black World* 24, no. 9 (1975), 51–52; John McCluskey, Jr.: *Look What They Done to My Song* (New York: Random House, 1974); *Mr. America's Last Season Blues* (Baton Rouge: Louisiana State University Press, 1983); Frank E. Moorer, "John A. McCluskey, Jr.," in *Dictionary of Literary Biography*, vol. 33, *Afro-American Fiction Writers After 1955* (Detroit: Gale, 1984).

Jessica Chapman

McDonald, Janet A. (born 1953). Young-adult novelist, essayist, memoirist, and journalist. McDonald's first major publication, *Project Girl* (1999), is a frank memoir that traces the profound psychological and cultural complexities of growing up African American. A writer of young-adult novels, McDonald creates characters who portray the intricate relationship between collective and individual African American identities. The fourth of seven children and the only one to receive a college education, she grew up in the crowded Brooklyn Farragut housing project in **Brooklyn, New York**, always surrounded by people but often mentally and emotionally isolated by her exceptional intelligence (she is a member of MENSA). After attending an upper-middle-class, mostly White public high school and Harlem Preparatory School in **Harlem, New York**, McDonald entered Vassar, where she majored in French literature and spent her junior year in **Paris, France**. She holds a Bachelor of Arts degree from Vassar (1977), a master's degree in journalism from Columbia University (1984), and a law degree from New York University (1986).

Following graduation from NYU, she practiced corporate law for several years, then went to France on a three-month American Bar Association exchange program. From 1991 to 1993 she lived in Paris, "trying (and failing) to write the Great American Novel." After a stint as Assistant Attorney General for the state of Washington (1993–1995), McDonald returned to Paris to practice law. Her international status as an author came with the publication of *Project Girl* (1999), a memoir based largely on entries from childhood journals. Publicly endorsed by Pulitzer Prize winner Frank McCourt, this bestseller was quickly followed by a "project girls" trilogy for young adults: *Spellbound* (2001); *Chill Wind* (2002), winner of the 2003 Coretta Scott King/John Steptoe New Talent Award; and *Twists and Turns* (2003). All three books received widespread literary commendations. *Spellbound* and *Chill Wind* have been translated into French as *Brooklyn Babies* (2003) and *Top Rondes* (2004), respectively. McDonald's fourth novel, *Brother Hood* (2004), initiated the author's plans for a "project boys" trilogy. Her short story, "Zebra Girl," appears in the anthology *Skin Deep* (2004).

According to McDonald, her objective as a writer is to "depict in an edgy, authentic, urban voice the challenges of inner city life without pandering to sensationalism, pessimism, and stereotypes." Her list of favorite authors includes

Jamaica Kincaid, Dostoevsky, Tolstoy, Kafka, Zola for his "grittiness," Nabokov for his "brilliance," Virginia Woolf for her "perspicacity," and Herman Hesse. McDonald's future goals include a second memoir as well as a series of legal thrillers and adult novels set in Paris. Her writing style is generally characterized as insightful, humorous, authentic, and engaging; and her tone, despite her often grim subject matter, is determinedly optimistic. In both her nonfiction and her fiction, McDonald repeatedly returns to the subject of the alien soul. Her thematic emphasis on the psychological needs of the African American individual functioning within a unique social milieu makes her writing both culturally informing and personally compelling. Ultimately, her works extend beyond the narrowly cultural to integrate the universally shared experience of "disconnection from others" with a hopeful vision of individual and collective healing. In addition to her major works, McDonald has written numerous articles and essays for national and international publications, and has published poetry in an avant-garde French journal, *Van Gogh's Ear*. She is also the publisher of *Project Boy*, by her brother Kevin McDonald, and a regular contributor to her official Web site, projectgirl.com.

Resources: Gillian Engberg, "Spotlight on Black History—*The Booklist* Interview: Janet McDonald," *The Booklist* 98 (2002), 1026–1027; Thomas E. Kennedy, "Up from Brooklyn: An Interview with Janet McDonald," *Literary Review* 44 (2001), 704–720; Janet McDonald: *Brother Hood* (New York: Farrar, Straus, and Giroux, 2004); *Chill Wind* (New York: Foster, 2002); "Double Life," *Literary Review* 45 (2002), 679–684; *Project Girl* (New York: Farrar, Straus, and Giroux, 1999); "Re: Your African-American Bibliography," e-mail to author (Oct. 10, 2004); *Spellbound* (New York: Foster, 2001); *Twists and Turns* (New York: Foster, 2003); "Zebra Girl," in *Skin Deep: A Collection of Stories About Racism*, ed. Tony Bradman (New York: Puffin-Penguin, 2004); "McDonald, Janet," *Contemporary Authors Online*, Gale Literary Databases, http://galenet.galegroup.com [Search: Janet McDonald].

Karen Sloan

McDowell, Deborah E. (born 1951). Literary and feminist critic, editor, and memoirist. McDowell has made significant contributions to the study of African American literature, especially to the study of African American women's writing. At the same time, she has helped to advance the acceptance of African American literature into the literary mainstream. Born in Bessemer, Alabama, McDowell grew up under segregation and experienced the **Civil Rights Movement** firsthand. She earned her bachelor's degree at the Tuskegee Institute (1972) and completed graduate studies in English at Purdue University (1972–1979). While serving as the founding and general editor of the Black Women Writers series published by Beacon Press (1985–1993), McDowell brought out new editions of **Jessie Redmon Fauset**'s novel *Plum Bun* (1929), **Nella Larsen**'s novels *Quicksand* (1928) and *Passing* (1929), and **Emma Dunham Kelley-Hawkins**'s *Four Girls at Cottage City* (1898). Through such projects, McDowell became a leader of those working to reclaim and revalue African American women's literature. McDowell is also well known for her collection of essays, *"The Changing Same": Black Women's Literature, Criticism, and Theory* (1995). The writing in this text spans fifteen years and thus provides a chronicle of changing concerns among Black academic feminists. Rather than advocating a single approach to Black women's literature, McDowell creates a dynamic model that includes commentary on her past essays and the use of multiple critical approaches. *"The Changing Same"* is also important in its insistence that Black women's viewpoints be included in academic discussions.

McDowell's work took a new form in *Leaving Pipe Shop: Memories of Kin* (1996), a bittersweet memoir of her childhood neighborhood that was sparked when McDowell returned home in order to consider participating in a class-action suit against the pipe shop where her father had worked. She explores the past with a sense of loss and longing, not only recognizing the importance of strong role models who taught her to value religion and education as sources of empowerment but also mourning the decline of the pipe shop neighborhood. Like her scholarly work, McDowell's memoir values and gives voice to the experiences of African American women, so that the everyday experiences she recounts provide a rich sense of local and cultural history without sentimentalizing or simplifying the past. McDowell edited *Slavery and the Literary Imagination* (1989) with **Arnold Rampersad**, became a period-editor for *The Norton Anthology of African American Literature* (1996), and, in 1999, brought out a new edition of the *Narrative of the Life of Frederick Douglass: An American Slave* (1845) for Oxford's World's Classics. She has taught at a number of colleges, held a Woodrow Wilson fellowship (1994–1995), and is currently a professor of American literature and African American Studies at the University of Virginia.

Resources: Deborah E. McDowell: *"The Changing Same": Black Women's Literature, Criticism, and Theory* (Bloomington: Indiana University Press, 1995); "Interview," *Critical Texts: A Review of Theory and Criticism* 6, no. 3 (1989), 13–29; *Leaving Pipe Shop: Memories of Kin* (New York: Scribner's, 1996).

Laurie McMillan

McElroy, Colleen (born 1935). Poet, fiction writer, and professor. A prolific author with an extensive educational résumé marked by many awards and fellowships, Colleen McElroy has emerged as one of the most prominent African American female authors of the twentieth century. She was born in **St. Louis, Missouri**. Her parents divorced when she was three, and her mother was remarried to Jesse O. Johnson, who was posted to St. Louis in the service of the U.S. Army. As an "army brat," McElroy traveled all over the world, living in Wyoming, Munich, Germany, and Kansas City, Missouri. The value of traveling, learned in her youth on military bases, remains with her today—she has been to Europe, South America, Southeast Asia, Africa, Japan, and Majorca—and is manifested in the thematic mission of her writing: "coming face-to-face with the new." McElroy attended the University of Maryland and Harris Teachers College before she received her B.S. degree at Kansas State

University in 1958. She did graduate work at University of Pittsburg (in Kansas) in speech and hearing, and later obtained an M.S. in neurological and language learning patterns from Kansas State University in 1963.

Originally, her career path led her toward a position as the chief speech clinician at the Rehabilitation Institute in Kansas City, where McElroy worked for three years. From there, she moved to the West Coast, where she attended a postgraduate program at Western Washington University and earned her Ph.D., with a dissertation on ethnolinguistic patterns of dialect differences and oral tradition, at the University of Washington at Seattle in 1973. She was immediately offered a position there as an assistant professor, and in 1983 she was the first Black woman promoted to full professor there. She is a professor of English and creative writing there today.

Strangely enough, considering her prominence, McElroy did not begin writing with serious intent until her thirties, while still married to the author David McElroy, and then only upon encouragement from such established poets such as Richard Hugo, Robert Huff, and Denise Levertov. She cites a rich lineage of African American poets as influences, including **Langston Hughes, Anne Spencer, Robert Hayden, Gwendolyn Brooks**, and **Margaret Abigail Walker**. The rugged landscape and wet weather of the Pacific Northwest have inspired many of her poems, including her first chapbook, *Mules Done Long Since Gone* (1973). Later books of poetry, such as *Winters Without Snow* (1979), a deeply personal reflection on her second divorce, and *Queen of the Ebony Isles* (1984), which won the National Book Award in the same year, emphasize issues of self, **race**, and **gender**, and particularly the experience of the African American woman, as Johnson notes in praise of her: "McElroy is clearly a feminist writer, meaning simply that as a black woman she writes from a center so strong, so self-confident, so sure of her place in the world that polemicism is replaced by wisdom, love, and a remarkably powerful poetic and prose line" (6).

Not surprisingly, given background in linguistics, much of McElroy's later poetry in *Bone Flames* (1987) and *What Madness Brought Me Here* (1990) reflects self-consciously on the insufficiency of language to communicate and the ways in which it constructs identity; yet Quashie sees her strength in the ways that "She foregrounds the process and function of poetry, personifying the poem as storyteller and narrating in simple language the beauty and bleakness of the people around her" (729). McElroy's recent memoirs, *A Long Way from St. Louie: Travel Memoirs* (1997) and *Travelling Music* (1998), reveal her love of travel, and its singularity as a way to experience one's individual and cultural identities as well as one's otherness.

Throughout her career, McElroy has been politically and intellectually active in fostering a community for writers, especially minorities, and educational opportunities for all students, participating on national and local committees ranging from the National Council of Teachers of English to the Washington State Commission for the Humanities to the United Black Artists Guild of Seattle. Some of her major awards for her writing include the

Breadloaf scholarship for fiction (1974), the National Endowment for the Arts fellowship in creative writing (1978, 1991), the Matrix Women of Achievement Award (1985), the Before Columbus American Book Award (1985), a Fulbright creative writing fellowship to Madagascar, which produced her 1999 lyrical exploration of Malagasy culture and myth: *Over the Lip of the World* (1990), Rockefeller Fellowship (1991), and the Jessie Ball DuPont Distinguished Black Scholar residency (1992).

McElroy has proved to be a highly versatile author, composing not only poetry, but fiction and memoirs as well as **drama**, from the choreopoem, *The Wild Gardens of the Loup Garou*, and a play about **Harriet Tubman**, *Follow the Drinking Gourd*, both written with **Ishmael Reed**, to scores of television screenplays. Johnson considers her to be "the best, most balanced black woman poet working today" (6).

Resources: Primary Sources: Colleen McElroy: *Blue Flames* (Middletown, CT: Wesleyan University Press, 1989); *Bone Flames* (Middletown, CT: Wesleyan University Press, 1987); *Driving Under the Cardboard Pines and Other Stories* (Berkeley, CA: Creative Arts, 1990); *Jesus and Fat Tuesday and Other Short Stories* (Berkeley, CA: Creative Arts, 1987); *Lie and Say You Love Me* (Seattle: Circinatum Press, 1988); *A Long Way from St. Louie: Travel Memoirs* (Minneapolis, MN: Coffee House Press, 1997); *Looking for a Country Under Its Original Name* (Seattle/Spokane: Blue Begonia Press, 1985); *The Mules Done Long Since Gone* (Seattle: Harrison-Madronna Press, 1973); *Music from Home: Selected Poems* (Carbondale: Southern Illinois University Press, 1976); *Over the Lip of the World: Among the Storytellers of Madagascar* (Seattle: University of Washington Press, 1999); *Queen of the Ebony Isles* (Middletown, CT: Wesleyan University Press, 1984); "Traveling with White People," in *When Race Becomes Real: Black and White Writers Confront Their Personal Histories*, ed. Bernestine Singley (Chicago: Lawrence Hill, 2002), 241–252; *Travelling Music* (Ashland, OR: Story Line Press, 1998); *What Madness Brought Me Here: New and Selected Poems, 1968–1988* (Hanover, NH: University Press of New England, 1990); *Winters Without Snow* (Berkeley, CA: I. Reed, 1979). **Secondary Sources:** *Contemporary Authors Online* (Detroit: Gale, 2001); Charles Johnson, "Whole Sight: Notes on New Black Fiction," *Callaloo*, Autumn 1984, 1–6; Kevin Everod Quashie, *New Bones: Contemporary Black Writers in America* (Upper Saddle River, NJ: Prentice-Hall, 2001), 716–730.

Alicia D. Williamson

McFadden, Bernice (born 1965). Novelist and short story writer. Bernice McFadden became serious about her writing in 1990. During a period of unemployment, she began to read widely, finding that the work of African American writers such as **Alice Walker**, **Zora Neale Hurston**, and **Nella Larsen** particularly spoke to her. Though previously unpublished, she began to consider how the short stories she was producing might develop into full-length works. McFadden's first novel, *Sugar*, was released in 2000 to wide critical acclaim. This work has been followed by four others: *The Warmest December* (2001), *This Bitter Earth* (2002), *Loving Donovan* (2003), and *Camilla's Roses* (2004). Her novels feature strong Black female characters who must face the realities of child abuse, alcoholism, prostitution, and ostracism from their communities. She frequently explores issues of redemption, self-love, and lost love.

Born and raised in **Brooklyn, New York**, Bernice McFadden attended New York University's Laboratory Institute of Merchandising for training as a fashion merchandiser and buyer. Though she took positions at Bloomingdale's and Itokin, and later pursued travel planning, she found these career paths lacking. She cites the time that she spent at Fordham University taking classes in history and literature as most crucial to her development as a professional writer. McFadden has received the American Library Association Black Caucus Fiction Honor Award (2000); the Go On Girl Book Club's Best New Author of the Year Award (2000); the Golden Pen Award—Best Mainstream Fiction (2001); the Golden Pen Best New Author Award (2002); and the Zora Neale Hurston Award for Creative Contribution to Literature (2002). She has been touted as a leading new voice in contemporary African American literature by such notable authors as **Terry McMillan** and **Toni Morrison**.

Resources: Bernice McFadden: Bernice L. McFadden home page, http://www .bernicemcfadden.com; *Camilla's Roses* (New York: Dutton, 2004); *Loving Donovan* (New York: Dutton, 2003); *Sugar* (New York: Dutton, 2000); *This Bitter Earth* (New York: Dutton, 2002); *The Warmest December* (New York: Dutton, 2001).

Michelle LaFrance

McKay, Claude (1889–1948). Poet, novelist, critic, and journalist. Throughout his life, Claude McKay was a man of many identities, some of them conflicting. Born to relatively well-off peasant parents in the small Jamaican village of Nairne Castle, he became a leading intellectual and writer, a world traveler, a Communist, and eventually a Catholic. While McKay has been criticized, both during his lifetime and after his death, for ideological inconsistency and opportunism, he is widely acknowledged to have been one of the foremost figures of the **Harlem Renaissance**, as well as a touchstone figure for the West Indian **Négritude** movement.

McKay was educated according to the conventional British model. He read British literature in school, and his father complemented this education by teaching him about the Ashanti, an African people, some of whom later settled in Jamaica. In 1911 McKay moved from his small village to the city of Kingston, where he encountered a larger White population and more racism. For a short time he took a job as a policeman, enforcing White colonial rule; he gave this up after coming to believe that he was serving as a tool of oppression against his fellow Blacks and natives.

McKay's first volumes of poetry were published while he was still a young man. In 1912, with the assistance of his friend and patron, the White English folklorist Walter Jekyll, McKay published *Songs from Jamaica* and *Constab Ballads*. The poems in these volumes were written in Jamaican dialect, which Jekyll encouraged McKay to develop as a literary voice. *Songs from Jamaica* shows an early sign of McKay's lifelong devotion to a rural, idyllic lifestyle, while *Constab Ballads* contrasts this peaceful, egalitarian life with the harsh, racist world he encountered in Kingston.

After the publication of his two volumes of poetry, McKay decided to study agriculture in the United States, at the Tuskegee Institute in Alabama. He later transferred to Kansas State College, then abandoned his studies completely in favor of a return to writing and a move to New York City. **Harlem, New York**, was fast becoming a thriving center of African American culture, and while McKay lived outside of its geographical perimeter, he was a key figure in the "**New Negro**" movement and the Harlem Renaissance. He took a position as editor of the radical Communist journal *The Liberator* and continued writing his own poetry. In 1919 *The Liberator* published McKay's poem "If We Must Die," which protested violence by White mobs against Black workers in major cities across the United States. The poem and the rallying cry it engendered propelled McKay to literary celebrity, alongside such writers as **Langston Hughes**, **Countee Cullen**, and **Zora Neale Hurston**.

Later in 1919 McKay traveled to England, where he worked on Sylvia Pankhurst's Communist newspaper, *The Workers' Dreadnought*. He continued to publish his poetry in magazines, and in 1920 published another book of poems, *Spring in New Hampshire and Other Poems*. He returned to New York in 1921, after Pankhurst was jailed for her publication, and the next year published an expansion of *Spring*, retitled *Harlem Shadows*. His work with *The Liberator* resumed, and he published both political journalism and protest poems about the conditions of African American life in the United States.

Spring in New Hampshire and *Harlem Shadows* secured McKay's position as a major writer of the Harlem Renaissance, but did not halt his involvement in politics. In 1922 he traveled to the Soviet Union to attend the Fourth Congress of the Third International as a special delegate–observer. McKay's commitment to communism was already waning at this point; for years he had criticized American and European Communists for their failure to address race politics, and his experience in Moscow confirmed his belief that formal communism would not make race a high priority. He stayed in the Soviet Union for several months as a special guest of the government, traveling, speaking, and writing for Soviet publications, but felt that his contributions were not taken seriously enough. He left the country in 1923, and later that year published the works he had written during this period in *The Negroes in America*.

Following his departure from the Soviet Union, McKay began a long period of international exile, during which he traveled in Europe and Africa. He also turned to writing fiction, which enabled him to shed some of the constrained tone that his poetry had taken. His first novel, *Home to Harlem*, was published in 1928. It concerned the lives of working-class migrant Blacks in Harlem, and emphasized a theme that McKay struck repeatedly in many of his writings: the inherent health, vitality, and dignity of Black people, contrasted with the enfeeblement of Whites corrupted by western European and American culture. *Home to Harlem* was criticized by some Black readers for its failure to present

Claude McKay, c. 1930. Courtesy of the Library of Congress.

socially stable, conventionally admirable Black characters, but it was a best-seller and was praised by many reviewers, including Langston Hughes.

McKay's second novel, *Banjo: A Story Without a Plot* was published in 1929, and set in Marseilles, France. The main characters are Black immigrants from the United States and the West Indies, who live on the margins of society and show both a primal zeal for life and a keen awareness of the social injustices they face. The novel was open to criticisms of stereotyping, but McKay's defenders saw it as continuing to develop an argument he had always favored; namely, that Blacks enjoy superior strength, **humor**, and fortitude because of their closeness to the natural world, while Whites have sacrificed these qualities in the drive for industrialization and urbanization.

Banjo was followed in 1932 by *Gingertown*, a collection of short stories set in both Harlem and Jamaica. McKay's final work, and the one in which he is deemed to have achieved his fullest creative powers, is the novel *Banana Bottom*, published in 1933. Set in Jamaica during the period of McKay's childhood, it concerns a young Jamaican woman who is raised partly in England, and who then returns to Jamaica as an adult. The rural, pastoral life she rediscovers in Jamaica is presented as vastly preferable to the stuffy, misguided morality of England.

Unfortunately, neither *Gingertown* nor *Banana Bottom* sold well, partly due to the financial crisis of the **Great Depression**. McKay found himself impoverished, and in 1934 had to return from Morocco to New York City. For several years he wrote for the New York **Federal Writers' Project**, and published a study titled *Harlem: Negro Metropolis* (1940). He also wrote and published a memoir, *A Long Way from Home* (1937). He became increasingly disillusioned with organized Leftism, and especially with the Communist Party. At the same time he criticized Black leaders and exhorted his fellow African Americans to take responsibility for their social and economic fates. As a result of these critiques, he became increasingly isolated from the Black community in his later years.

In 1944, suffering from ill health and poverty, McKay was baptized into the Roman Catholic Church in **Chicago, Illinois**. He had been an agnostic his entire life, and despite an early marriage was openly bisexual; his conversion was one more surprise in a life of contradictions. McKay may have tired of this tumult; in the final year of his life he wrote and published *My Green Hills of*

Jamaica (1979), a memoir longing for the peaceful, uncomplicated country of his youth. (*See* **Dialect Poetry; Marxism.**)

Resources: Primary Sources: Claude McKay: *Banana Bottom* (New York: Harper & Bros., 1933); *Banjo: A Story Without a Plot* (New York: Harper & Bros., 1929); *Complete Poems*, ed. William J. Maxwell (Urbana: University of Illinois Press, 2004); *Gingertown* (New York: Harper & Bros., 1932); *Home to Harlem* (New York: Harper & Bros., 1928); *A Long Way from Home* (1937; repr. New York: Harcourt Brace Jovanovich, 1970); *Trial by Lynching: Stories About Negro life in North America*, trans. Robert Winter, ed. A. L. McLeod (Mysore, India: Centre for Commonwealth Literature and Research, University of Mysore, 1977). **Secondary Sources:** Wayne F. Cooper, "Claude McKay, 1890–1948," in *African American Writers*, ed. Valerie Smith, Lea Baechler, and A. Walton Litz (New York: Collier, 1993); David Goldweber, "Home at Last," *Commonweal* 126, no. 15 (1999), 11–13; Heather Hathaway, *Caribbean Waves: Relocating Claude McKay and Paule Marshall* (Bloomington: Indiana University Press, 1999); Winston James: "Becoming the People's Poet: Claude McKay's Jamaican Years, 1889–1912," *Small Axe* 13 (2003), 17–45; "New Light on Claude McKay: A Controversy, a Document, and a Resolution," *Black Renaissance* 2, no. 2 (1999), 98–106; Wolfgang Karrer, "Black Modernism: The Early Poetry of Jean Toomer and Claude McKay," in *Jean Toomer and the Harlem Renaissance*, ed. Geneviève Fabre and Michel Feith (New Brunswick, NJ: Rutgers University Press, 2001); Sarala Krishnamurthy, "Claude McKay," in *African American Authors, 1745–1945*, ed. Emmanuel S. Nelson (Westport, CT: Greenwood Press, 2000); Diane Masiello, "McKay, Claude," in *African-American Writers: A Dictionary*, ed. Shari Dorantes Hatch and Michael R. Strickland (Santa Barbara, CA: ABC-CLIO, 2000); A. B. Christa Schwarz, "Claude McKay: 'Enfant Terrible' of the Negro Renaissance," in her *Gay Voices of the Harlem Renaissance* (Bloomington: Indiana University Press, 2003), 88–119; Tyrone Tillery, *Claude McKay: A Black Poet's Struggle for Identity* (Amherst: University of Massachusetts Press, 1992).

Karen Munro

McKay, Nellie Yvonne (born 1947). Literary critic, editor, and university professor. A native of New York City, McKay completed a Ph.D. in American literature at Harvard in 1977. At a time when few minority writers were studied at American universities, McKay wrote her dissertation on **Jean Toomer** and quickly became an influential force in the emerging discipline of African American Studies. In 1978 she joined the faculty of the University of Wisconsin at Madison (UM), where she put together the first curriculum in literature for the Department of Afro-American studies. She currently serves as Evjue-Bascom Professor of American and African-American Literature at UM.

As a critic, McKay has contributed significantly to the canonization of at least two major African American authors: Toomer, on whom she published the first full-length study (*Jean Toomer, Artist: A Study of His Literary Life and Work, 1894–1936* [1984]), and **Toni Morrison**, on whom she edited the first collection of essays (*Critical Essays on Toni Morrison* [1988]). Her most popular success has been *The Norton Anthology of African American Literature* (1996), which she edited with **Henry Louis Gates, Jr.** This important anthology sold nearly a million copies, was adopted at more than 1,275 colleges and universities worldwide, and was nominated for a 1997 Image Award from the National Association for the Advancement of Colored People (**NAACP**), an honor more commonly associated with the performing arts. A substantially revised second edition appeared in 2004.

In her more than twenty-five years as an African Americanist, McKay has done much to galvanize the field and bring it credibility in the academy. In an influential *PMLA* (*Publications of the Modern Language Association*) guest column (1998), she targeted three obstacles that have prevented the study of African American literature from earning the respect it deserves: "the insufficiency of the black PhD pipeline, the efforts to discourage white graduate students from exploring black literature, and untrained white scholars' undertaking of scholarship in black literature" (363). In her contribution to *Black Studies in the United States* (1990), she implored African American Studies programs to communicate and cooperate with one another in order "to think and plan seriously together for more consolidated and unified success" (29). Eleven years later, after black studies had grown significantly, McKay suggested to interviewer Donald E. Hall that the discipline needed to reach out to smaller ethnic literature programs that lack its resources, in order to ensure equitability in the field of minority studies (275).

Resources: Donald E. Hall, "A Love for the Life: An Interview with Nellie McKay," in *Professions: Conversations on the Future of Literary and Cultural Studies*, ed. Donald E. Hall (Urbana: University of Illinois Press, 2001), 264–276; Robert L. Harris, Jr., Darlene Clark Hine, and Nellie McKay, *Black Studies in the United States* (New York: Ford Foundation, 1990); Nellie Y. McKay, "Naming the Problem That Led to the Question 'Who Shall Teach African American Literature?'" *PMLA* 113 (1995), 359–369.

Clay Morton

McKinney-Whetstone, Diane (born 1953). Novelist. Diane McKinney-Whetstone's visibility and prominence as a major African American fiction writer and interpreter of the African American community and experience continue to evolve. Best known for her debut novel and national bestseller, *Tumbling* (1996), she reveals in her fiction a superb gift for language and storytelling. A native of **Philadelphia, Pennsylvania**, whose father served two terms as a Pennsylvania state senator, she grew up in a close-knit family with five sisters and one brother, attended public schools, and graduated from the University of Pennsylvania in 1975 with a bachelor's degree in English. The novels of McKinney-Whetstone offer insightful awareness of and informed responses to imposed cultural restraints on African Americans. All four of her novels—*Tumbling* (1996), *Tempest Rising* (1998), *Blues Dancing* (2000), and *Leaving Cecil Street* (2004)—are set in Philadelphia between the 1940s and the 1970s. They demonstrate her connection to working-class Philadelphians as they cope daily with changes in their work and personal lives. Political consciousness is forged into the plots of each of her novels, which evoke the joys of love and family; the pain of deception, loss, and separation; and a celebration of strength and perseverance. Her numerous awards include a Pennsylvania Council on the Arts grant, Discipline Winner in the Pew Fellowship in the Arts, the Zora Neale Hurston Society Award for creative contribution to literature, a citation from the Commonwealth of Pennsylvania for her portrayal of urban family life as presented in *Tumbling*, and Author of the Year Award from the national Go On Girl Book Club.

Resources: Dianne McKinney-Whetstone: *Blues Dancing* (New York: Morrow, 1999); *Leaving Cecil Street* (New York: Morrow, 2004); *Tempest Rising* (New York: Morrow, 1998); *Tumbling* (New York: Morrow, 1996).

Teresa Gilliams

McKissack, Patricia (born 1944). Author of over 100 titles for young readers, including picture books, information books, easy readers, historical fiction, and biographies. Born in Tennessee as Patricia L'Ann Carwell, McKissack comes from a family deeply rooted in the oral tradition, a tradition she credits with influencing her own storytelling. In fact, several of McKissack's earlier titles—*Flossie & the Fox* (1986), *Mirandy and Brother Wind* (1988), and *Nettie Jo's Friends* (1989)—were directly inspired by family storytellers. McKissack began writing while working as an English teacher in Missouri. Having difficulty locating biographies about her favorite poet, **Paul Laurence Dunbar**, to share with her students, McKissack wrote one. Since then, she and her husband, Fredrick, have committed themselves to creating literature for children that preserves American history and culture. A great deal of research—primary and secondary sources and interviews—helps make the McKissacks' historical fiction noteworthy. McKissack has written books about important historical figures (**Sojourner Truth, W.E.B. Du Bois, Booker T. Washington**, etc.), groups (Tuskegee Airmen, Negro Baseball League, Brotherhood of Sleeping Car Porters), and moments in history (**Civil War, Civil Rights Movement**). She has also written a number of series books, such as those authored with her husband in the Great African Americans series. She has published three books in the Dear America series: *A Picture of Freedom: The Diary of Clotee, a Slave Girl* (1997); *Color Me Dark: The Diary of Nellie Lee Love, the Great Migration North* (2000); and *Look to the Hills: The Diary of Lozette Moreau, a French Slave Girl* (2004).

With her husband, McKissack runs a company, All-Writing Services, which provides educational consulting services on multicultural literature. Much of her fiction accentuates personal experiences and elements of the African American literary tradition. Set in **the South**, many of McKissack's stories contain Southern dialect, folkloric aspects, and African American issues and concerns. For example, in *Goin' Someplace Special* (2001), McKissack uses a fictional story to convey reflections of her own experiences navigating Jim Crow laws enforced in the South. Similarly, her experiences during the Civil Rights Movement largely impact her books on the subject (*Martin Luther King,*

Jr.: Man of Peace [1991] and *The Civil Rights Movement in America from 1865 to the Present* [1987]). McKissack has a large number of award-winning titles to her credit: *Mirandy and Brother Wind* (1988; Caldecott Honor Book, 1989), *The Dark-Thirty: Southern Tales of the Supernatural* (1992; Newbery Honor Book and Coretta Scott King Award, 1993); *A Long Hard Journey: The Story of the Pullman Porter* (1989; Jane Addams Children's Book Award, Womens' International League for Peace and Freedom, and the Coretta Scott King Award); *Sojourner Truth: Ain't I a Woman?* (1992; Coretta Scott King Honor Award and Boston Globe-Horn Book Award, 1993). McKissack has done much to improve the quality and quantity of nonfiction and fiction titles about African American experiences in the United States.

Resources: "Fredrick L. and Patricia C. McKissack," *Children's Literature Review*, vol. 55, ed. Deborah J. Morad (Detroit: Gale, 1999), 98–121; Patricia McKissack, *Can You Imagine?* (Katonah, NY: Richard C. Owen, 1997).

KaaVonia Hinton-Johnson

McKnight, Reginald (born 1956). Novelist, short story writer, essayist, and editor. One of America's foremost writers, Reginald McKnight has thus far published seven books: two novels, three books of short stories, and two edited volumes. McKnight was born in Germany; his father was a U.S. Air Force sergeant, and his mother was a native of **Texas**. Because of living in a military family, McKnight had attended fifteen schools by the time he was sixteen years old, mainly in the West, near the Air Force bases at which his father was stationed. He also lived for a time in **the South** and attended a segregated school, all of which gave him a solid background for his writing, which often focuses on the complexities of race in the post–Civil Rights era. While McKnight's work often involves **race**, he doesn't consider himself to have any obvious agendas, preferring politics to take a backseat to story and characterization (Ashe).

Spending his college years in Colorado, McKnight attended Pike's Peak Community College and Colorado College before he receiving his master's degree in creative writing at the University of Denver in 1987. A turning point in his life as a writer came when he lived in Senegal for a year while in his early thirties. Isolated because he was halfway across the world from all his friends and family, and not knowing the Senegalese culture enough to feel at home, McKnight spent up to sixteen hours a day writing thousands of words. He later noted that almost all of the work he has created since then came out of that experience, and that it transformed both him and his writing.

McKnight is arguably best known for his book of short stories *White Boys* (1998) and for his novel *He Sleeps* (2001). *White Boys*, which deals primarily with characters who are alienated outsiders, is an examination of the nuances of **race** and the antagonisms that often result from interracial conflicts. *He Sleeps* focuses on the life of American anthropologist Bertrand Milworth, who studies urban legends in Senegal. His two other books of short stories are the prize-winning *Moustapha's Eclipse* (1988) and *The Kind of Light That Shines on*

Texas (1992); his other novel is *I Get on the Bus* (1990). His nonfiction works include *African American Wisdom* (1994) and *Wisdom of the African World* (1996), both collections of sayings and quotes; he has also published a number of essays and book reviews.

McKnight has won numerous awards for his writing, such as an NEA fellowship, an O. Henry Award, the Kenyon Review Award for Literary Excellence, the PEN Hemingway Special Citation, the Pushcart Prize, the Drue Heinze Literature Prize, a Thomas J. Watson Foundation fellowship, and a Whiting Writer's Award. Currently Hamilton Holmes Professor of Creative Writing at the University of Georgia, a post he has held since 2002, he has also taught at the University of Maryland, College Park, the University of Michigan, and Carnegie-Mellon University.

Resources: Primary Sources: Reginald McKnight: *African American Wisdom* (1994; repr. Novato, CA: New World Library, 2000); *He Sleeps* (New York: Henry Holt, 2001); *I Get on the Bus* (Boston: Little, Brown, 1990); *The Kind of Light That Shines on Texas: Stories* (Boston: Little, Brown, 1992); *Moustapha's Eclipse* (Pittsburgh, PA: University of Pittsburgh Press, 1988); *White Boys: Stories* (New York: Henry Holt, 1998); *Wisdom of the African World* (Novato, CA: New World Library, 1996). **Secondary Sources:** Bertram D. Ashe, "Under the Umbrella of Black Civilization: A Conversation with Reginald McKnight," *African American Review* 35, no. 3 (Fall 2001), 427–437; Laurie Champion, "Reginald McKnight," *Contemporary African-American Novelists: A Bio-Bibliographical Critical Sourcebook*, ed. Emmanuel S. Nelson (Westport, CT: Greenwood Press, 1999), 314–318.

Stephanie Gordon

McLarin, Kim (born c. 1964). Novelist and journalist. Born in **Memphis, Tennessee,** Kim McLarin is a graduate of Phillips Exeter Academy and Duke University. Educated as a journalist, she has reported for the *St. Petersburg Times,* the *Greensboro News-Record,* the Associated Press, the *Philadelphia Inquirer,* and the *New York Times.* Since establishing herself as a novelist, McLarin has held a visiting professorship in creative writing at Emerson University, and she has contributed articles and short stories to a variety of publications. Several of these shorter works have been anthologized.

McLarin's first novel, *Taming It Down* (1998), focuses on a twenty-eight-year-old African American woman named Hope Robinson. Although her mother works as a domestic, Robinson manages to earn scholarships to a prestigious prep school and to an Ivy League university. When she lands a job with a major Philadelphia newspaper, her dreams of a successful career in journalism seem within her grasp. But most of Hope's colleagues at the newspaper are White, and suspect that she has been hired less for her credentials than because of her race and gender. Entering into a relationship with a White editor exacerbates her sense that she is betraying her own aspirations. Even when Hope develops a subsequent relationship with an African American man, she is stung by his observations on the various ways in which she seems to have sold out. In effect, she is caught between what Blackness and Whiteness represent to her.

In McLarin's second novel, *Meeting of the Waters* (2001), Lee Page, an African American woman reporting on the riots in South Central Los Angeles, saves the life of Porter Stockman, a White reporter with a major Philadelphia newspaper. When Page later is hired by that newspaper, Stockman resolves to develop a relationship with her, but she has always been outspokenly critical of interracial relationships, and her own convictions, as well as the attitudes of her closest friends, conflict with her growing attraction to him.

McLarin has also coauthored *Growing Up X* (2002), the **autobiography** of Ilyasah Shabazz, the daughter of **Malcom X**.

Resources: Kim McLarin: *Meeting of the Waters* (New York: Morrow, 2001); *Taming It Down* (New York: Morrow, 1998); Eli Quinn, "Novel of Black and White on Big-City Newspaper," *Philadelphia Inquirer*, June 28, 1998, p. Q4; Ilyasah Shabazz and Kim McLarin, *Growing Up X* (New York: One World/Ballantine, 2002).

Martin Kich

McMillan, Terry (born 1951). Novelist, short story writer, and editor. McMillan is known for her character-driven novels, portrayals of contemporary African American life, and feisty, tough, African American heroines. Because of her unprecedented success and popularity, she has attracted an audience of diverse readers. She also has a distinctive talent for confronting universal themes such as romantic commitment, family obligations, and relationships between parent and children, especially mother and daughters, in ways that resonate in her readers' lives.

McMillan is the author of five novels: *A Day Late and A Dollar Short* (2001), *How Stella Got Her Groove Back* (1996), *Waiting to Exhale* (1992), *Disappearing Acts* (1989), and *Mama* (1987). She is also editor of *Breaking Ice: An Anthology of Contemporary African-American Fiction* (1990).

McMillan combines a keen sense of family dynamics, an ear for dialogue, and astute social observation to create a cast of characters that one critic calls "sassy, resilient, and full of life." Two of her books made the *New York Times* best-sellers list: *Waiting to Exhale* for thirty-eight weeks, and *How Stella Got Her Groove Back* for twenty-one weeks; she also cowrote the screenplays for both, which were made into successful movies. McMillan received a National Endowment for the Arts Award in 1988, and the Barnes and Noble Writers Award in 1999. She was Yaddo Colony Fellow in 1982, 1983, and 1985, and a MacDowell Colony Fellow in 1983. She has taught English at Stanford University, the University of Wyoming, and the University of Arizona at Tucson (McMillan, "Terry McMillan," 66).

McMillan's ability to draw on her own life experiences and evoke her own emotional truth in her novels is one important element of her tremendous popular appeal. McMillan sees her novels as a record of her own spiritual growth; consequently, her formal structure changes with each work. This distinctive approach to writing and her commercial success have caused some members of the literary establishment to dismiss her as a popular, rather than a serious and committed, fiction writer. However, while the establishment has dismissed Terry McMillan, her continued improvisation upon popular women's fiction genre-conventions to suit her own artistic ends is a measure of her talent and skill (Richards, 1). All in all, however, she has made important contributions as a teacher, scholar, and mentor to younger writers in addition to inspiring a new school of urban Black fiction.

McMillan was born October 18, 1951, in Port Huron, Michigan. She was the oldest of five children. Her parents, Edward Lewis McMillan and Madeline Washington Tillman, divorced in 1964. Three years later her father died of complications related to diabetes. According to Terry, her mother became a sustaining force in the lives of her children. She worked as a domestic worker, on an auto assembly line, and in a pickle factory to support her five children. McMillan remarks that "For an uneducated woman, she's probably one of the smartest women I'll ever meet in my life. She taught me how to think, that's what she did. And to let people know what you think. And if you don't have an opinion about something, get one, because you'll need it" (Richards, 2). Madeline Tillman not only worked to support her family but she instilled a strong sense of responsibility in her children early in their lives. While she was away at work, she expected them to keep the house neat and stay out of trouble. The McMillan children also did odd jobs so that they could contribute to the household budget.

Although she attended public schools in Port Huron, it wasn't until her job at the library that McMillan discovered African American writers. The works of **James Baldwin** were an important revelation to her because nothing in her experience had indicated that African Americans could write and publish books.

McMillan left Port Huron when she was seventeen. She moved to **Los Angeles, California**, where she worked as a typist for an insurance company by day and attended classes at night at Los Angeles City College. She enrolled in an African American literature class, her formal introduction to African American writers. **Zora Neale Hurston, Frederick Douglass**, and **Langston Hughes** are a few of the writers whose works she read during those early years. McMillan also enrolled in a literature class taught by the novelist, poet, and literary critic **Ishmael Reed**. She received a Bachelor of Science degree in journalism in 1979. After moving to New York City, she enrolled at Columbia University and earned a Master of Fine Arts degree in film.

Resources: Terry McMillan: *A Day Late and a Dollar Short* (New York: Viking, 2001); *Disappearing Acts* (New York: Viking, 1989); *How Stella Got Her Groove Back* (New York: Viking, 1996); *Mama* (Boston: Houghton Mifflin, 1987); "Publicizing Your Commercially-Published Novel," *Quarterly Black Review of Books*, May 31, 1994; "Terry McMillan," *The Writer* 114, no. 8 (Aug. 2001), 66; *Waiting to Exhale* (New York: Viking, 1992); Terry McMillan, ed., *Breaking Ice: An Anthology of Contemporary African-American Fiction* (New York: Penguin, 1990); Paulette Richards, *Terry McMillan: A Critical Companion* (Westport, CT: Greenwood Press, 1999).

John Greer Hall

McPherson, James Alan (born 1943). Novelist and short story writer. McPherson was born in Savannah, Georgia. His writing has brought him many of the highest accolades accorded any U.S. writer, the most significant being the Pulitzer Prize in 1978 for what is now his best-known collection of short stories, *Elbow Room* (1977). His other significant awards include a Guggenheim Fellowship in 1973 and a MacArthur Foundation Award in 1981. In 1995 McPherson was inducted into the American Academy of Arts and Sciences.

McPherson writes with clarity and precision about male and female African Americans as they grapple with racial indignities and oppression in the United States. His characters often discover larger dimensions within themselves as they attempt to cope with the struggles of racism, isolation, and love. Ultimately McPherson's focus is on affirming what is universal and human about his characters. Many of his stories grapple with issues of U.S. citizenship, and what it means for an African American citizen to live in this country.

McPherson grew up in the segregated **South** in a lower-class Black community and attended Morris Brown College, an historically Black college in Georgia funded by the African Methodist Episcopal Church. McPherson graduated in 1965, then attended Harvard Law School, from which he graduated in 1968. At Harvard became interested in studying the Fourteenth Amendment to the Constitution, which guaranteed former slaves legal equality under the law. His exploration of this amendment, in conjunction with his study of the landmark legal case of *Plessy v. Ferguson* (1896), led McPherson to arrive at his personal notion of what he believes actual citizenship should be. In his essay "On Becoming an American Writer," he argues that each citizen of the United States carries the main ideas of the culture within him or her, and, furthermore, that it is the obligation of each citizen to understand and support the blend of diverse races and cultures within the United States ("On Becoming an American Writer"). This thinking has led McPherson to claim, along with another African American writer, **Ralph Ellison**, that citizenship within the United States means to accept and live according to inherent contradictions in a society that represents the extremes in races, classes, genders, geographies, and lifestyles. In "Indivisible Man," an essay he wrote with Ralph Ellison, McPherson states: "I believe that if one can experience diversity, touch a variety of its people, laugh at its craziness, distill wisdom from its tragedies, and attempt to synthesize all this inside oneself without going crazy, one will have earned the right to call oneself 'citizen of the United States'" ("Indivisible Man").

Early in his career McPherson wrote short stories and essays for *The Atlantic*, which sponsored a short story contest that he won in 1965, and he received an M.F.A. from the prestigious Iowa Writers Workshop at the University of Iowa in 1969. That same year he published his first collection of short stories, *Hue and Cry*, which included a glowing endorsement by Ralph Ellison on the book jacket. This collection won the National Institute of Arts and Letters Award for Literature. Other publications include texts McPherson has edited, such as *Railroad: Trains and Train People in American Culture* and, more recently, *Fathering Daughters: Reflections by Men*. He published a collection of short stories, *Crabcakes*, in 1998, and personal essays in *A Region Not Home: Reflections from Exile*, in 2000. McPherson has taught English at the University of California-Santa Cruz and Harvard, and has lectured at Meiji and Chiba universities in Japan. He is currently teaching at the Iowa Writers Workshop.

McPherson came of age during the **Black Arts Movement**, but his writing has always moved beyond the specific political issues of his time. He claims Ralph Ellison and **Albert Murray** as his literary mentors, especially in terms of using elements of **folklore**, parable, and legend in his writing. McPherson's characters often discover myths that help them define the world and themselves, and his larger purpose is often about deepening a personal awareness in order to more fully accept oneself and others. Thus his characters often wage psychological battles in order to transcend the limits imposed by an oppressive society. He is especially known for the **realism** and clarity of his characters and dialogue

McPherson's writings have appeared in publications such as *The Iowa Review*, *The Atlantic Monthly*, the *New York Times Magazine*, *Esquire*, and *Newsday*, and his short stories have been chosen for literary collections such as *The O. Henry Prize Stories*, *The Best American Essays*, and *The Best American Short Stories*.

Resources: Ralph Ellison and James McPherson, "Indivisible Man," *The Atlantic Monthly*, Dec. 1970, 45–60; James McPherson: *Crabcakes* (New York: Simon and Schuster, 1998); *Elbow Room: Stories* (Boston: Little, Brown, 1977); *Hue and Cry: Short Stores* (Boston: Little, Brown, 1969); "On Becoming an American Writer," *The Atlantic Monthly*, Dec. 1978, 53–57; *A Region Not Home: Reflections from Exile* (New York: Simon and Schuster, 2000); James McPherson and DeWitt Henry, eds., *Fathering Daughters: Reflections by Men* (Boston: Beacon Press, 1998); James McPherson and Miller Williams, eds., *Railroad: Trains and Train People in American Culture* (New York: Random House, 1976).

Lin Knutson

Memphis, Tennessee. The area now occupied by Memphis, in Shelby County, Tennessee, was part of the Chickasaw nation's domain. The Spanish explorer De Soto and his men encountered the Chickasaws in this area as early as 1541. A treaty between the Chickasaws and the U.S. government signaled the Chickasaws' relinquishment of their claims on the land. Memphis was founded in 1819, under the leadership of John Overton, James Winchester, and a future president of the United States, Andrew Jackson. Situated on a bluff overlooking the Mississippi River in the southwest corner of Tennessee, the city had previously been the site of a military fort and, because of its proximity to the river, held great potential as a trading center, including as a center of the slave trade. In 1857 the Memphis–Charleston Railroad, upon its completion, linked Memphis to Atlantic ports, enhancing its power as a trading center. During the **Civil War**, Union troops occupied the city in the summer of 1862, and Memphis remained under federal control through the end of the war. In the late 1800s and early 1900s, Beale Street, first known as Beale Avenue, became a hub of Memphis's African American community, playing a crucial role in the development and popularizing of the **blues**, and later in the development of **jazz**, rhythm and blues, and rock and roll. (Sun Records is located in Memphis, as are Stax Records and Elvis Presley's home, Graceland.) In 1909, W. C. Handy composed "Memphis Blues," which was first titled "Boss Crump Blues," referring to a powerful politician of the era. "Memphis Blues" is often considered the first written blues composition. **Ida B. Wells-Barnett** lived in Memphis for a period and taught school there beginning in 1888. She also helped to establish and wrote for an African American newspaper, *The Free Speech and Headlight*, in which she published antilynching articles. She also kept a diary about her time in Memphis, and this was subsequently published, edited by Miriam DeCosta-Willis, a native of Memphis and a founder of the Memphis Black Writers' Workshop. The writer **Mary Church Terrell** was born in Memphis. The novelist **Richard Wright** spent time in Memphis as a young man before moving to **Chicago, Illinois**. The novelist **Arthur Rickydoc Flowers** is a native of Memphis, as are the playwright Levi Frazier and the feminist literary scholar Beverly Guy-Sheftall and the literary scholar **Hortense J. Spillers**. The writer **Gloria Wade-Gayles** is also from Memphis. A Black Writers and Film Festival is held annually in Memphis; it was begun in 1988. (*See* **Nashville, Tennessee**.)

Resources: Rob Bowman, "The Stax Sound: A Musicological Analysis," *Popular Music* 14, no. 3 (Oct. 1995), 285–320; Lynn Domina, "Ida B. Wells-Barnett (1862–1931)," in *African American Autobiographers: A Sourcebook*, ed. Emmanuel S. Nelson (Westport, CT: Greenwood Press, 2002), 373–378; Margaret McKee and Fred Chisenhall, *Beale Black & Blue: Life and Music on Black America's Main Street* (Baton Rouge: Louisiana State University Press, 1981); Earline J. Moore, "Remembering Black Writers Associated with Tennessee: A Representative Bibliography," http://www.utm.edu/~ejmoore/blackauthors/tennblack2.htm; Harry Oster, "The Afro-American Folktale in Memphis: Theme and Function," *Negro American Literature Forum* 3, no. 3 (Fall 1969), 83–87; Ida B. Wells-Barnett, *The Memphis Diary of Ida B. Wells*, ed. Miriam DeCosta-Willis (Boston: Beacon Press, 1995); Grace M. White, "Wright's Memphis," *New Letters: A Magazine of Fine Writing* 38, no. 2 (1971), 105–116; Juanita V. Williamson, *A Phonological and Morphological Study of the Speech of the Negro of Memphis, Tennessee* (University: University of Alabama Press, 1970).

Hans Ostrom

Menard, John Willis (1838–1893). Journalist and poet. John Willis Menard was a man of many political and literary achievements. He was born on April 3, 1838, to Black **Creole** parents. Menard received his education at an abolitionist school and attended Iberia College in Ohio until he could no longer afford to. His first major achievements included the speech *An Address to the Free Colored People of Illinois* (1860) and an appointment as a clerk in the U.S.

Department of the Interior during the **Civil War**. He was the first Black to occupy this position.

Menard moved to **New Orleans, Louisiana**, in 1865 to assist in the **Reconstruction** efforts. He worked as an inspector of customs and as Commissioner of Streets, and he also edited two **newspapers**, *The Free South* and *The Radical Standard*. By 1868, he was elected to represent Louisiana's Second Congressional District. He would have been the first African American in Congress, but the seat was given to a White man because it was allegedly "too early to admit a Negro to the U.S. Congress" (Purdy). Nevertheless, Menard became the first Black man to address Congress to contest the appointment. He was unable to persuade Congress to change the decision.

Undeterred by the turn of events, Menard continued to play an active role in politics and to pursue writing. By 1873, he was elected to serve in the state legislature. Once again, he was denied the position, but in 1877 George F. Drew "reappointed him as a justice of the peace" (Stone). Meanwhile, Menard edited the *Florida Sun*. He later edited the *Florida News* (also known as the *Island City News*), using the paper as a platform to advocate his views, particularly on Black equality, and became "the most influential black editor of the 1880s" (Stone). He also, in 1879, published his only volume of poetry, *Lays in Summer Lands*. It was reprinted in 2002. The themes in this volume include politics, nature, faith, and love. In 1885, Menard moved to Jacksonville, Florida, where he "battled for the rights and interests of blacks with the newspaper *Southern Leader*" (Stone).

Menard spent the last few years of his life in **Washington, D.C.**, as a clerk in the Census Office. He died on October 8, 1893.

Resources: John Mason Brewer, *Negro Legislators of Texas* (Dallas: Mathis, 1935); W.E.B. Du Bois, *Black Reconstruction* (New York: Harcourt, Brace, 1935); John Ficklen, *History of Reconstruction in Louisiana* (Baltimore: Johns Hopkins Press, 1910); Horace Greeley, "Letter," *National Anti-Slavery Standard*, Oct. 17, 1868, p. 1; Langston Hughes and Milton Meltzer, *A Pictorial History of the Negro in America*, new rev. ed. (New York: Crown, 1963); "John Willis Menard," *Biography Resource Center*, http://galenet.gale group.com/servlet/BioRC; Annjenette Sophie McFarlin, comp., *Black Congressional Reconstruction Orators and Their Orations, 1869–1879* (Metuchen, NJ: Scarecrow Press, 1976); Edith Menard: "John Willis Menard," *Negro History Bulletin* 28 (1964), 53–63; "John Willis Menard," *Negro History Bulletin* 31 (1968), 10–11; "Men of the Month," *The Crisis* 9 (1915), 117; John Willis Menard, *Lays in Summer Lands*, ed. Larry E. Rivers, Richard Mathews, and Canter Brown (1879; repr. Tampa, FL: University of Tampa Press, 2002); Gilbert Wesley Purdy, "The Reconstruction of John Willis Menard," review of *Lays in Summer Lands*, http://poetry.allinfo-about.com/features/menard.html; Spessard Stone, "John Willis Menard," http://freepages.geneaology.rootsweb.com/~crackerbarrel/Menard.html; Carter Woodson, ed., *Negro Orators and Their Orations* (Washington, DC: Associated Publishers, 1925).

Gladys L. Knight

Meriwether, Louise (born 1923). Activist, short fiction writer, essayist, biographer, and freelance writer. Louise Meriwether has written about the struggles involved in the African American journey with special insight into the **Great Depression** and the African American historical perspective. Born and raised in **New York City**, Meriwether received a B.A. from New York University and an M.A. in journalism in 1965 from the University of California at **Los Angeles**. She has pursued a variety of occupations, including freelance reporting, legal secretarial work, and real estate sales. Rita B. Dandridge notes that in order to facilitate her writing, Meriwether "limited herself to three years on any job she secured" (*DLB*, 183). Meriwether may also be credited as the first African American story analyst for Universal Studios. She became interested in writing biographical sketches in the 1960s and published several on noteworthy African Americans including Grace Bumbry, Audrey Boswell, Vaino Spenser, and Matthew Henson. In the latter half of the 1960s, Meriwether began publishing short stories and published three notable ones in succession: "Daddy Was a Number Runner" (1967), "A Happening in Barbados" (1968), and "The Thick End Is for Whipping" (1969).

Meriwether's involvement in the Watts Writers' Workshop and her work with the *Antioch Review* during this time helped to develop her writing and editing capabilities. Combining aspects of her three pervious short stories, Meriwether's first novel details the life of a young black girl growing up during the Depression. The story details the struggles of the main character and her family, describing their battles with economic ruin and racial prejudice. Titled *Daddy Was a Number Runner*, the novel, published in 1970, is considered to be Meriwether's most important work. In the next three years, Meriwether would publish three short books, intended for young audiences, on historical Black figures: *The Freedom Ship of Robert Smalls* (1971), *The Heart Man: Dr. Daniel Hale Williams* (1972), and *Don't Take the Bus on Monday: The Rosa Parks Story* (1973).

During these years of prolific writing, Meriwether was also involved with the Congress of Racial Equality and with the Deacons, an anti-Ku Klux Klan coalition. In 1967, she joined Vantile Whitfield to create the Black Anti-Defamation Association, and their work prevented Twentieth Century Fox from producing a movie based on William Styron's controversial book *The Confessions of* **Nat Turner**. Meriwether's efforts in this cause were noted by **Martin Luther King, Jr.,** shortly before his death. Many years later, Meriwether published her second major novel, *Fragments of the Ark* (1994), which describes the journey of a male slave during the **Civil War** and is based on the life of Robert Smalls. In 2000, Meriwether published *Shadow Dancing*, a novel about a complex female Black author. Meriwether has been most influential in her efforts to promote accuracy in the representation of African American history.

Resources: Rita B. Dandridge: "Meriwether, Louise," in *Afro-American Writers After 1955*, vol. 33 of *Dictionary of Literary Biography*, ed. Thadious M. Davis and Trudier Harris (Detroit: Gale, 1984), 182–186; "Meriwether, Louise," in *Black Women in America*, vol. 2, ed. Darlene Clark Hine (Brooklyn, NY: Carlson, 1993), 783–784; "Meriwether, Louise," in *The Oxford Companion to African American Literature*, ed. William L. Andrews et al.

(New York: Oxford University Press, 1997), 493–494; Louise Meriwether: *Daddy Was a Number Runner* (Englewood Cliffs, NJ: Prentice-Hall, 1970); *Don't Ride the Bus on Monday: The Rosa Parks Story* (Englewood Cliffs, NJ: Prentice-Hall, 1973); *Fragments of the Ark* (New York: Pocket Books, 1994); *The Freedom Ship of Robert Smalls* (Englewood Cliffs, NJ: Prentice-Hall, 1971); *The Heart Man: Dr. Daniel Hale Williams* (Englewood Cliffs, NJ: Prentice-Hall, 1972); *Shadow Dancing* (New York: One World, 2000).

Amanda Holt

Messenger, The (1917–1928). Magazine edited by **A. Philip Randolph** and Chandler Owen. *The Messenger* was one of a plethora of publications circulating in Black neighborhoods during the early decades of the twentieth century. It was one of five important magazines that were established in New York City during the **New Negro** era and that have been of continuing importance. And it is only one of a handful of valued early twentieth-century African American radical publications. The other New York publications were **The Crisis** (1910), **Opportunity** (1923), **Negro World** (1918), and *Crusader* (1918); among the radical publications the *Boston Guardian* newspaper (1901) was an early twentieth-century leader. All of these magazines were venues where prominent New Negro/**Harlem Renaissance** era writers would publish. *The Messenger* was a nationally circulated magazine, as were *The Crisis, Opportunity* and *Negro World*.

The editors of *The Messenger* published literary pieces in their first issue in 1917, as well as later literature by New Negro writers: **Walter Everette Hawkins**'s poetry; **Zora Neale Hurston**'s "The Eatonville Anthology"; **Langston Hughes**'s first published short stories as well as some of his poetry; **Countee Cullen**'s poetry; **Georgia Douglas Johnson**'s poetry; a short story by **Dorothy West**; and it reprinted **Claude McKay**'s "If We Must Die" as well as other poems by this poet. An anthology of literature published in *The Messenger* appeared in 2000. *The Messenger* was distinguished in its early days as a magazine that emphasized political ideas influenced by the Left; its publishers were Socialists who called for labor alliances across color lines and a class consciousness along with group consciousness among Black people (*see* **Marxism**).

In 1917, A. Philip Randolph and Chandler Owen were recruited to edit *Hotel Messenger*, a journal for the Headwaiters and Sidewaiters of Greater New York. As a result of differences between the labor union and the two men, the editing pair soon departed from the union's publication and published their own magazine. The first issue *The Messenger* appeared in November 1917. By September 1918, Owen had been drafted to serve in **World War I**. Both he and Randolph were conscientious objectors, but neither had declared his status by formal application to the draft board. Randolph's marriage to Lucille E. Green kept him from being drafted.

As a result of the political ideas that Owen and Randolph advocated in speeches and in *The Messenger*, both men were arrested in the spring of 1918 in Cleveland, Ohio, for treason, and the Postmaster General of the United States revoked the magazine's bulk rate postage status, which was not reinstated until 1921. The treason charges against the men were dropped because the judge believed the two Black men were lackeys who were incapable of producing the ideas that appeared in print under their names.

Chandler Owen was born to a financially comfortable family in Warrenton, North Carolina, in 1889. He earned his undergraduate degree from Virginia Union University, which was established for young Black men and was, then, well known for its students' independent thought and for their rejection of accommodationist ideas; social and economic accommodation was often associated with the writings and speeches of **Booker T. Washington**. Owen went on to attend Columbia University's program in social work and its law school. When he met A. Philip Randolph in New York in 1915, Randolph was a student at City College and had been working in a variety of low-paying jobs. Asa Philip Randolph was born in Crescent City, Florida, also in 1889. His father was a tailor as well as a minister in the African Methodist Episcopal Church; his mother took in sewing and laundry. Randolph earned a high school diploma from the Cookman Institute (later Bethune-Cookman College), another educational facility that was established for Black youths and that, like Virginia Union University, rejected accommodationist ideas.

By 1923, the radical politics that had previously been found in the pages of *The Messenger* had diminished. This year also found Chandler Owen living in Chicago, and by 1924 he had little to do with the magazine that he helped found. His name, however, remained on the masthead. In 1923, **George S. Schuyler**—who earlier had joined the Socialist Party in Syracuse, New York—was employed as office help. By 1924 Schuyler became managing editor of *The Messenger*, a position he held—except for a leave of absence to travel through **the South** in 1926—until the paper's demise in June 1928. Schuyler's column, "Shafts and Darts," which he started in 1923, was one of the highly regarded items in *The Messenger*. Also in 1923, **Theophilus Lewis** joined *The Messenger* as the theater critic. His essays provide some of the most perspicacious reviews of theatrical performances as well as of literature from the era. In 1925, Randolph began organizing the Brotherhood of Sleeping Car Porters, using the pages of *The Messenger* as the mouthpiece for this group.

During their early radical years, the editors of *The Messenger*, rather than establishing themselves as doctrinaire participants in any one particular script for radical change or as orthodox practitioners of a particular political ideology, instead operated from a position that advocated the most efficacious means and methods available for a complete transformation of the position of Black people in the United States. The stories that Randolph heard from his activist parents helped him see that direct and practical action was revolutionary, and more valuable than reading socialist theory and imposing those ideas on the lived reality of Black people in the United States. This approach might be viewed as cynical, yet perhaps would be more accurately described as radically pragmatic about the entrenched power of supremacist narratives in the United States during the early decades of the twentieth century. In its last years, however, *The Messenger* gained a reputation for being banal and insipid.

Wallace Thurman, who was managing editor for several months in 1926 and whose interest was in publishing great literature by Black writers, said that the politics of the *The Messenger* "reflected the policy of whoever paid off best at the time." Langston Hughes reported that that the politics of *The Messenger* was "God knows what" (Hughes, 233–234, 236). Even so, series and articles that appeared in *The Messenger*—including "An Analysis of Negro Patriotism" (August 1919), "These 'Colored' United States," (January 1923–September 1926), and "A New Crowd—A New Negro," a topic that consistently appeared from 1919 to 1927—are invaluable for a full and rich understanding of the New Negro and the literary, intellectual, political, and cultural discourses that were in operation at the time. Notwithstanding the shifting political positions found in *The Messenger* (which was marketed on its masthead variously as "The Only Radical Negro Magazine in America"; "A Journal of Scientific Radicalism"; "The World's Greatest Negro Monthly"; and, finally, "New Opinion of the New Negro"), the magazine's founders managed to make it a venue for important cultural and intellectual exchanges that early on refused to replicate for its primarily Black readership both the dominant discourse among New Negro intellectuals as well as the dominating discourse in the country.

Resources: Langston Hughes, *The Big Sea: An Autobiography* (1940; repr. New York: Thunder's Mouth Press, 1986); George Hutchinson, *The Harlem Renaissance in Black and White* (Cambridge, MA: Belknap Press, 1995); Abby Arthur Johnson and Ronald Maberry Johnson, *Propaganda and Aesthetics: The Literary Politics of Afro-American Magazines in the Twentieth Century* (Amherst: University of Massachusetts Press, 1979); Theodore Kornweibel, Jr., *No Crystal Stair: Black Life and The Messenger, 1917–1928* (Westport, CT: Greenwood Press, 1975); Tom Lutz and Susanna Ashton, eds., *These "Colored" United States: African American Essays from the 1920s* (New Brunswick, NJ: Rutgers University Press, 1996); Adam McKible, "Our(?) Country: Mapping 'These "Colored" United States' in The Messenger," in *The Black Press: New Literary and Historical Essays*, ed. Todd Vogel (New Brunswick, NJ: Rutgers University Press, 2001), 123–139; Sondra Kathryn Wilson, ed., *The Messenger Reader: Stories, Poetry, and Essays from The Messenger Magazine* (New York: Modern Library, 2000).

A. Yemisi Jimoh

Metaphor. Metaphor is a type of literary trope, or mode of expression, that implies or states a comparison, often by taking a word, phrase, or image from an accustomed context and using it unexpectedly. Later in this entry, for instance, an example from **Zora Neale Hurston** implies a comparison between words and coins, so that the image of money is taken from the conventional context of commerce and used unexpectedly in the context of language, enabling Hurston to illustrate an idea. Uses of metaphor in African American literature might be seen as evolving from two separate but related traditions of cultural expression: the ancient African oral tradition and the classical tradition of the West. Likewise, there are varying outlooks on the study of metaphor. Scholars and literary critics generally agree on the preeminence of metaphor in African

American culture, from its pervasive presence in **vernacular** forms such as **spirituals**, **blues** songs, and **folktales** to its refined and complex appearance in poetry and **novels**. Much more contention emerges in debates about metaphor and its relation to perception, reality, and truth.

The New Princeton Encyclopedia of Poetry and Poetics (Preminger et al.) defines metaphor as "a trope, or figurative expression, in which a word or phrase is shifted from its normal uses to a context where it evokes new meanings." Metaphor is generally considered the most important of the five principal tropes (the others are simile, metonymy, personification, and synecdoche). In order to distinguish metaphor from the other tropes, one may refer to **Zora Neale Hurston**'s examination of metaphor in her essay "Characteristics of Negro Expression" (1934). There, Hurston describes the Negro's words as "action words": the Negro's "interpretation of the English language is in terms of pictures. One act described in terms of another. Hence the rich metaphor and simile" (1019). This sort of metaphor she describes as "primitive": it is "easier to illustrate than it is to explain because action came before speech." Hurston herself uses a striking metaphor in order to explain metaphor: "Language is like money. In primitive communities actual goods, however bulky, are bartered for what one wants. This finally evolves into coin, the coin being not real wealth but a symbol of wealth. Still later even coin is abandoned for legal tender, and still later for checks in certain usages" (1019–1020).

Hurston's analogy ends there, but may be taken further. While the descriptions of language use that Hurston provides are decidedly anthropological (there are section headings such as "Will to Adorn," "Originality," and "Absence of the Concept of Privacy"), there are specific intersections between Hurston's categories and the explication of metaphor provided by Aristotle in his *Poetics*, produced some 300 years B.C.E. What is more, the numismatic (coinlike) character assigned to Negro language by Hurston is echoed, in **deconstruction** and poststructuralist theory, by Jacques Derrida in his essay "White Mythology." Hurston, Aristotle, Derrida, and others agree that there is a certain value assigned to language in general and to metaphor in particular, and the production of language by a specific culture or subculture gains value in relation to, or in barter with, the language cultures surrounding it.

Aristotle's definition of metaphor is largely considered to be foundational to contemporary understandings of how metaphors are constructed. It reads as follows: "A 'metaphor' is the application [to something] of a name belonging to something else, either (a) from the genus to the species, or (b) from the species to the genus, or (c) from a species to [another] species, or (d) according to analogy." As an example of (a), Aristotle gives " 'here stands my ship': for [the species] lying at anchor is a [part of the genus] standing." An example of (b) would be " 'truly has Odysseus done ten thousand deeds of worth': for [the species] 'ten thousand' is [part of the genus] 'many,' and Homer uses it here instead of 'a lot.' " An instance of metaphor that "moves" from "species to species" (c) is found in a phrase such as "[killing a man by] 'draining out his life with bronze,'" that is, with a weapon made of bronze. Each of these examples implies a logical relation that ties the terms together. And finally, by analogy is meant "when *b* is to *a* as *d* is to *c*; for [the poet then] will say *d* instead of *b*, or *b* instead of *d*" (Aristotle, 108).

We are given only two terms of the analogy, and to glean the meaning we must infer the missing terms. Aristotle suggests, then, that metaphors can be words, sentences, or even discourses. They can be simple or complex. They are a kind of naming that can also be vehicles for making meaning. And, importantly, they are at the foundation of specific sorts of language use in various genres of writing, such as poems, novels, and plays. Very important to our understanding of metaphor and its use in African American literature is that Aristotle points toward mimesis, or representation, as being foundational to metaphor, for in transferring the name of one thing to something else, there must be present some sort of recognition of the word that makes the transference work, that makes one word or image reflect another. In other words, metaphors make sense because they cause the reader or listener to recognize the similar within the dissimilar. Hence, metaphor itself may be understood as inherently paradoxical.

Now we may look a bit more closely at specific instances of metaphor as it appears in the literature.

Metaphor abounds in the vernacular tradition. Spirituals such as "Swing Low, Sweet Chariot" do not simply allude to the promise of home represented by lines referring to an afterlife in heaven, but they also suggest the metaphorical train of the **Underground Railroad**, which would carry the slave northward to earthly freedom. The song "Go Down, Moses" puts forward metaphors that consist in drawing an implicit comparison between the situation of the Jews in captivity and that of African slaves in bondage. Many scholars agree that the song is one of open protest, a melody that might have been sung only in the absence of White slaveholders and overseers.

Blues songs, which evolved from spirituals, are characterized by the well-known jazz and blues critic **Albert Murray** as double-voiced expressions of concerns and care. Their lyrics operate via metaphor, allusion, and innuendo. Witness the "How Long Blues," first recorded in 1928: "The brook runs into the river, the river runs into the sea/If I don't run into my baby, a train is going to run into me/How long, how long, how long?" Various elements of metaphor contribute to the figurative nature of language here: the repetition of words and themes; the play of orientational tropes (Lakoff and Johnson, 15) that capitalize on various uses of the prepositional phrase "run into"; and the echoing of the first line by the second. **Billie Holiday**'s "Fine and Mellow" (1939) employs metaphor more forthrightly: "Love is just like a faucet/It turns off and on/Love is just like a faucet/It turns off and on/Sometimes when you think it's on, baby/It has turned off and gone." We understand the explicit comparison between love and a faucet as a humorous metaphor employing ontological and somewhat personified descriptions of "love" and "faucet" because society understands "love" as a capricious human sentiment that we may hope to contain (through the controlling mechanism of the faucet), but can never quite manage to fix.

The literature of African America is no less ripe with metaphor than its oral tradition. Metaphor is seen in its earliest examples, beginning with the often discussed "trope of the talking book" in the narratives of **John Marrant** (*A Narrative of the Lord's Wonderful Dealings with John Marrant, a Black (Now Going to Preach the Gospel in Nova Scotia) Born in New-York, in North-America*, 1785) and **Olaudah Equiano** (*The Interesting Narrative of the Life of Olaudah Equiano, or Gustavus Vassa, the African. Written by Himself*, 1789) among others (Gates, 1988). **Paul Laurence Dunbar**'s "We Wear the Mask" (1895) foreshadows the "two-ness" of American existence expressed by a number of later writers: "We wear the mask that grins and lies/It hides our cheeks and shades our eyes/This debt we pay to human guile/With torn and bleeding hearts we smile/And mouth with myriad subtleties." The mask of which Dunbar speaks is akin to **W.E.B. Du Bois**'s metaphor of the "veil," which serves to hide and separate Blacks from the rest of American society: both metaphors are personified, and attest to social barriers that must be negotiated. Du Bois's figures of the "veil" and the "color-line," as well as his idea of "double consciousness" are developed at length and with eloquence in *The Souls of Black Folk* (1903). These are rivaled in importance only by **Ralph Ellison**'s metaphor of "invisibility" as presented in his 1952 novel *Invisible Man*. Dunbar's "mask that grins and lies" reminds of us the invisible man's determination to "yes 'em to death" with his false acquiescence. In a narrative that takes its shape from metaphor, Ellison begins *Invisible Man* with a trope: the novel's prologue is actually the introduction to the memoir of the narrator, who tells us that the "end is in the beginning." Ellison is one of a small number of African American writers who engage the concept of metaphor in critical essays (see "Twentieth-Century Fiction and the Black Mask of Humanity," written in 1946 and first published in 1953). Likening the underlying message of his novel to the quest for existential identity each American must undertake, Ellison underscores the idea of home as democracy and, by extension, democracy as love (see "Brave Words for a Startling Occasion"). For it is only by realizing the ideal of democracy that American citizens can live up to Ralph Waldo Emerson's (Ellison's namesake) call for politics as an expression of love. Ellison's concern is to give voice to a crisis of belonging or homelessness that culminates in a state of social invisibility and that is, itself, indicative of a crisis in democracy.

Toni Morrison extends the legacy of this metaphor in her novel *Paradise* (1998), which, as she explains in the critical essay "Home" (1997), attends to "seemingly impenetrable, race-inflected, race-clotted topics" (9). In framing the problematic of America's "racial house," Morrison points out that "the anxiety of belonging is entombed within the central metaphors in the discourse on . . . nationalism . . . and the fictions of sovereignty. . . . [T]hese figurations of nationhood and identity," she continues, "are frequently as raced themselves as the originating racial house that defined them. When they are not raced, they are . . . imaginary landscape, never inscape; Utopia, never home" (10–11).

The idea of **race** has been at the heart of many metaphorical constructions in African American literature, and African Americanists have debated the concept of race itself as metaphor. In his introduction to the highly influential collection *"Race," Writing, and Difference* (1986), **Henry Louis Gates, Jr.** insists that "[w]hen we speak of 'the white race' or 'the black race,'...we speak in biological misnomers and, more generally, in metaphors....Race has become a trope of ultimate, irreducible difference between cultures, linguistic groups, or adherents of specific belief systems which—more often than not—also have fundamentally opposed economic interests" (4–5). **Joyce A. Joyce**, in "The Black Canon: Reconstructing Black American Literary Criticism" (2000), takes issue with Gates's position, attributing his "denial of blackness" and "rejection of race" to his own "class orientation" (292). **Houston A. Baker, Jr.**, however, generally agrees with Gates, and proffers his own theory of **poststructuralism**. In "Belief, Theory, and Blues: Notes for a Post-Structuralist Criticism of Afro-American Literature" (1986), Baker calls "metaphor the ground...on which theory and belief meet" (224). Baker's poststructuralist approach rescues metaphor from the trash heap of Derridean deconstruction and poststructuralism, which degrade metaphor for its relation to symbolic uses of language that inhere in the Western power structure.

Resources: Aristotle, *Poetics*, in *The Norton Anthology of Theory and Criticism*, ed. Vincent Leitch (New York: Norton, 2001), 90–117; Houston A. Baker, Jr., "Belief, Theory, and Blues: Notes for a Post-Structuralist Criticism of Afro-American Literature," in *African American Literary Theory: A Reader*, ed. Winston Napier (New York: New York University Press, 2000), 224–241; Leroy Carr, "How Long Blues," *The Norton Anthology of African American Literature*, ed. Henry Louis Gates, Jr., and Nellie McKay (New York: Norton, 1996), 31; Jacques Derrida, "La mythologie blanche," in *Marges de la philosophie* (Paris: Éditions de Minuit, 1972), 249–324; W.E.B. Du Bois, *The Souls of Black Folk* (Chicago: McClurg, 1903), repr. in Du Bois's *Writings*, ed. Nathan Huggins (New York: Literary Classics of the United States, 1986), 357–547; Paul Laurence Dunbar, "We Wear the Mask," in *The Norton Anthology of African American Literature*, ed. Henry Louis Gates, Jr., and Nellie McKay (New York: Norton, 1996), 896; Ralph Ellison: "Brave Words for a Startling Occasion" and "Twentieth-Century Fiction and the Black Mask of Humanity," in his *Shadow and Act* (1964; repr. New York: Quality Paperback, 1994); *Invisible Man* (1953; repr. New York: Quality Paperback, 1994); Ralph Waldo Emerson, "Politics," in *Ralph Waldo Emerson: Essays and Lectures* (New York: Library of America, 1983); Olaudah Equiano, *The Interesting Narrative of the Life of Olaudah Equiano, or Gustavus Vassa, the African. Written by Himself*, ed. Werner Sollors (New York: Norton, 2001); Henry Louis Gates, Jr.: *The Signifying Monkey: A Theory of Afro-American Literary Criticism* (New York: Oxford University Press, 1988); "Writing 'Race' and the Difference It Makes," in *"Race," Writing, and Difference*, ed. Henry Louis Gates, Jr. (Chicago: University of Chicago Press, 1986); Billie Holliday, "Fine and Mellow," in *The Norton Anthology of African American Literature*, ed. Henry Louis Gates, Jr., and Nellie McKay (New York: Norton, 1996), 34; Zora Neale Hurston, "Characteristics of Negro Expression," *The Norton Anthology of African American Literature* ed. Henry Louis Gates, Jr., and Nellie McKay (New York: Norton, 1996), 1019–1032; Joyce

A. Joyce, "The Black Canon: Reconstructing Black American Literary Criticism," in *African American Literary Theory: A Reader*, ed. Winston Napier (New York: New York University Press, 2000), 290–297; George Lakoff and Mark Johnson, *Metaphors We Live By* (Chicago: University of Chicago Press, 1980); John Marrant, *A Narrative of the Lord's Wonderful Dealings with John Marrant, a Black (Now Going to Preach the Gospel in Nova Scotia) Born in New-York*, in *North-America* (1785), excerpted in *Black Atlantic Writers of the Eighteenth Century: Living the New Exodus in England and the Americas*, ed. Adam Potkay and Sandra Burr (New York: St. Martin's, 1995); Toni Morrison: "Home," in *The House That Race Built: Black Americans, U.S. Terrain*, ed. Wahneema Lubiano (New York: Pantheon, 1997); *Paradise* (New York: Random House, 1998); Albert Murray, *Stomping the Blues* (New York: McGraw-Hill, 1976); Alex Preminger, T.V.F. Brogan et al., eds., *The New Princeton Encyclopedia of Poetry and Poetics* (Princeton, NJ: Princeton University Press, 1993); Paul Ricoeur, *The Rule of Metaphor: Multi-Disciplinary Studies of the Creation of Meaning in Language*, trans. Robert Czerny (Toronto: University of Toronto Press, 1977).

Rebecka Rychelle Rutledge

Micheaux, Oscar (1884–1951). Homesteader, novelist, screenwriter, producer, and director. "Pioneer" best describes the industrious Micheaux. Known primarily as a pioneer of American film, Micheaux is also a unique, important voice in American literature. In the late nineteenth and early twentieth centuries, homesteaders in the Upper Midwest—specifically Minnesota and the Dakotas—were of European and Russian descent; few were African American. Like **Era Bell Thompson**'s *American Daughter*, Micheaux's two autobiographical novels—*The Conquest: The Story of a Negro Pioneer* (1913) and *The Homesteader* (1917)—recount his experiences as an African American homesteader on the northern Plains.

Micheaux grew up on a farm outside of Metropolis, Illinois, one of eleven children of freed slaves who moved from Kentucky to Illinois after the **Civil War**. His mother, Bell, an intensely religious woman, insisted that her children receive as much education as possible. In childhood, Micheaux proved himself precocious. His father, Swan, preferred Oscar to run the family's vegetable stand in town because of his business savvy: he sold more than any other family member. Early in childhood the young Micheaux was already a voracious reader. His favorite and most formative book was *Up from Slavery*, by **Booker T. Washington**. Washington's ideas, especially his insistence that African Americans seek out economic prosperity as a means of achieving equality, governed Micheaux's entrepreneurial spirit for the rest of his life.

Micheaux's grandmother and several uncles and aunts had been among the "exodusters," the 15,000 African Americans who poured into Kansas in 1878–1879 to homestead 160-acre farms. Their pioneering spirit inspired the restless Micheaux, who in 1900 left Metropolis for **Chicago, Illinois**, where he worked as a shoeshine boy and Pullman porter. In 1905 he purchased his own 180-acre homestead near Gregory, South Dakota. Here Micheaux began to write, publish, and market his novels.

In 1915, after a drought, Micheaux lost his homestead and moved to Sioux City, Iowa, where he started his own book supply business. That year, an African American film company, Lincoln Motion Picture Company, expressed interest in buying the rights to *The Homesteader*. Negotiations failed, so, in typical fashion, Micheaux financed and made the film himself in Chicago, becoming the first African American to make a feature-length film.

Micheaux wrote, directed, produced, and distributed forty-three feature films—twenty-seven silent and sixteen sound—and he was the first African American to make a "talkie" (sound feature), *The Exile* (1931). He invented the cross-cutting technique, among other film innovations. ("Cross-cutting" edits together two action sequences so that they appear to be occurring simultaneously.) Among other Black actors, **Paul Robeson** made his film debut in a Micheaux film, *Body and Soul* (1924). Micheaux was more a businessman than an artist or a social critic; thus many of his films were exploitative. They often included gratuitous sex scenes, such as they were then. Nonetheless, some of his films boldly address social problems related to **race**. *Within Our Gates* (1920), which features a **lynching**, is Micheaux's film response to D.W. Griffith's film *Birth of a Nation* (1915), and *Birthright* (1939) explores the trials of an African American attending Harvard University. Although most of his films are lost, Micheaux and his work continue to attract intense scholarly, cultural, and popular interest. The Library of Congress and the **John Hope Franklin** Collection of African-American Documentation contain the largest holdings of extant Micheaux films.

Resources: **Primary Sources:** *Books:* Oscar Michaeaux: *The Case of Mrs. Wingate* (1945; repr. New York: AMS, 1975); *The Conquest: the Story of a Negro Pioneer* (1913; repr. Lincoln: University of Nebraska Press, 1994); *The Forged Note: A Romance of the Darker Races* (Lincoln, NE: Western Book Supply, 1915); *The Homesteader: A Novel* (1917; repr. College Park MD: McGrath, 1969); *The Masquerade: A Historical Novel* (New York: Book Supply, 1947); *The Story of Dorothy Stanfield* (New York: Book Supply, 1946); *The Wind from Nowhere* (1941; repr. Freeport, NY: Books for Libraries Press, 1972). *Films:* Oscar Micheaux, dir.: *Birthright* (Micheaux Pictures, 1939); *Body and Soul* (Micheaux Pictures, 1925); *The Exile* (Micheaux Pictures, 1931); *Girl from Chicago* (Micheaux Pictures, 1932); *God's Stepchildren* (Micheaux Pictures, 1938); *Lem Hawkins' Confession* (Micheaux Pictures, 1935); *Lying Lips* (Micheaux Pictures, 1939); *Murder in Harlem* (Micheaux Pictures, 1935); *Ten Minutes to Live* (Micheaux Pictures, 1932); *Underworld* (Micheaux Pictures, 1937); *Veiled Aristocrats* (Micheaux Pictures, 1932); *Within Our Gates* (Micheaux Book and Film, 1920). **Secondary Sources:** Pearl Bowser, Jane Gaines, and Charles Musser, eds., *Oscar Micheaux and His Circle: African-American Filmmaking and Race Cinema of the Silent Era* (Bloomington: Indiana University Press, 2001); Pearl Bowser and Louise Spence, *Writing Himself into History: Oscar Micheaux, His Silent Films, and His Audiences* (New Brunswick, NJ: Rutgers University Press, 2000); Betti Carol, *Oscar Micheaux: A Biography* (Rapid City, SD: Dakota West Books, 1999); Jane M. Gaines, *Fire and Desire: Mixed-Race Movies in the Silent Era* (Chicago: University of Chicago Press, 2001); J. Ronald Green, *Straight Lick: The Cinema of Oscar Micheaux* (Bloomington: Indiana University Press, 2000); Joseph

A. Young, *Black Novelist as White Racist: The Myth of Black Inferiority in the Novels of Oscar Micheaux* (Westport, CT: Greenwood Press, 1989).

Kevin L. Cole

Middle Passage, The (c. 1540–1855). The Middle Passage was the route used to transport slaves from Africa across the Atlantic Ocean to the Americas. The Portuguese developed the passage during the 1540s to force Africans to immigrate to the New World to satisfy a labor shortage caused by Native Americans' refusal to submit to **slavery**. African slaves would be responsible for sowing cotton, indigo, and tobacco, and for rice and sugar production (Klein, 9). European slave traders used the Middle Passage to turn America into a center of affordable products by manipulating Black **labor**. The Middle Passage continues to be a major theme in African American literature, and African American texts are often vexed with the adverse cultural implications of being transported from Africa to America.

Various representations have surfaced about the Middle Passage. The historian Genevieve Fabre has insisted that the Middle Passage be studied through its nonverbal tradition. The principal nonverbal idiom is the slave ship dance that was "used to solicit intercession, to thwart wrath or punishment that human actions might have incurred, to flatter or appease" (Fabre, 33). Slaves would dance in order to communicate with one another, to escape surveillance, to warn when an overseer was approaching, and to establish a hierarchy among themselves. The slave ship dance consisted of bodily contortions representing the pain felt by Africans during their voyage to America.

The literary critics Maria Diedrich, **Henry Louis Gates, Jr.**, and Carl Pedersen have noted that a linear study of bondage would only reinforce Eurocentric interpretations that distort the Afro-American experience of slavery. The Middle Passage is therefore "not as clean a break between past and present but a special continuum between Africans and the Americas" (Diedrich et al., 8). The gap that the Middle Passage created has developed into a major metaphor of African American writing that has come to connote the cultural tear that slaves underwent when transported to America. John Henrik Clarke has argued that altering African history has been a traditional imperialist "moral justification for their rape, pillage, and destruction of African American cultural patterns and ways of life" (11). Clarke's statement implies that the Black Americans should efface White constructions of history, and that rewriting the true story of Africans' initiation into America is crucial to restoring African culture. (*See* **Afrocentricity; White.**)

Olaudah Equiano's *The Interesting Narrative of Olaudah Equiano, or Gustavas Vassa, the African, Written by Himself* (1813) presents the Middle Passage as a symbol of accepting White culture and commerce. Submitting to White culture is based on a double consciousness (*see* **W.E.B. Du Bois**) that separates slaver from slave, obliging Blacks to adopt a White Western mindset to gain power in a White-subjugated world. Equiano's approval of White culture compromises his Black identity because that acceptance is a direct admission of his inferior status to Whites. Submission to White practices is demonstrated through Equiano's use of the collective "we" pronoun. Throughout the narrative the reader repeatedly encounters passages where Equiano mentions that "[w]hen we had discharged our cargo here, and we loaded again, we left this fruitful land once more" (98) "[a]fter we had discharged our cargo there, we took in live cargo, as we called a cargo of slaves." The inclusive "we" pronoun is significant because Equiano refers to his fellow slaves using the same terminology as his enslavers do—that is, as live cargo without any further commentary, "clarifying his position, which is closer to the Whites" (Benito and Manzanas, 52) than to "his fellow slaves, who are referred to in the third person." The White market economy has obliged Equiano to tolerate slavery, to some degree, in order to sustain his livelihood.

Phillis Wheatley's "On Being Brought from Africa to America" (1773) considers the Middle Passage to be a route toward salvation and redemption. The slaves' "benighted souls" (2) shall soon enter a land that is modern and intellectual and that does not believe in "Pagan" (1) performances. Wheatley argues that the Middle Passage will encourage Africans to demonstrate their cognitive skills and negate the "scornful eye" (5) through which Whites have traditionally viewed Blacks. The nouns *Christian* (7) and *Negro* are italicized to equate Blacks and Whites. The supposition that Wheatley sets forward is that both races are intelligent, pious, and watched over by God. The journey from Africa to America has saved Blacks from a degenerate condition, thus allowing the possibility to live in harmony with Whites. Wheatley's expectation is that America will refine her race and sanction them aboard the "angelic train" to Heaven. Wheatley attempts to make herself one of the few writers to examine the "dual relation to the realities of the Middle Passage and to an African heritage" (Fabre, 34). Equiano's representation of the Middle Passage differs from Wheatley's because the latter appreciates America for the intellectual progress it will allow Blacks, while Equiano defines the Middle Passage as a mode of gaining monetary power.

Robert Hayden's portrayal of the Middle Passage depicts a rebellion and "redemptive occasion for the future" (McDowell and Spillers, 1489). Enslaved Africans will unite with American abolitionists and terminate slavery. The voyage to America is, according to Hayden, one of rejuvenation and rebirth. The tenor of Hayden's poem "Middle Passage" (1962) is that slaves would much rather die than enter continual oppression. Africans consider their "voyage through death/to life upon these shores" (6–7) to be a commencement into a country where slaves and abolitionists can combat forced servitude. The "tempestuous sea" (21) signifies the exploitation that slaves' work will encounter. Hayden purposely leaves a space between the adjective and noun to indicate a division from one's homeland and cultural origins. The Middle Passage consequently stands for a geographical space where unimaginable pain is much too powerful for any "word" to "take shape" (28). King Anthracite's "French parasol" (80) symbolizes a form of weak leadership that has conformed to White materialism, and the exploiting of one group to satisfy the egotistical needs of another. Upon their arrival in America, Africans will be greeted by figures such as John Quincy Adams, who will "speak with so much passion of the right/of chattel slaves to kill their lawful masters" (165–166). The masters are the lawful owners of the slaves because of Eurocentric race regulations, not because Whites are inherently superior to Blacks. Hayden believes that once Africans have crossed the Atlantic, their opinions of Whites will change due to abolitionists who are awaiting them to terminate slavery. What separates Hayden's representation of the Middle Passage from those of the above-cited authors is that Hayden seeks to end slavery through political action with the help of Whites.

Toni Morrison regards the Middle Passage to be an irredeemable break in Black history that can never be properly filled. The historical cleavage that the Middle Passage caused will continue to grow and haunt America. Claudine Raynaud has argued of Morrison's *Beloved* (1987) that "[i]n between the laconic notations, the textual blankness bears witness to the effort to find words that would translate the visions into language" (70). Morrison patterns her neo-slave narrative on Hayden's view that words can never truly express human bondage. The horrors of the Middle Passage are so atrocious that fictional characters must narrate them: "She told Sethe that her mother and Nan were together from the sea. Both were taken up many times by the sea. Both were taken up many times by the crew" (62). It is no coincidence that Morrison chooses Sethe, the slave mother who has murdered her child Beloved, to narrate her story. Sethe represents the maternal figure who has willingly killed her baby instead of having slavery continue to infect her family. Morrison's rendition of the Middle Passage is a novel one that uses poetics, diction, and metaphorical langue to transport ancestors of slaves to the point where their new existence commenced and their origins altered.

Charles R. Johnson's rendition of the Middle Passage presents a dualism between "[s]ubject and object, perceiver and perceived, self and other" (97–98). In *Middle Passage* (1990), Johnson's audience enters Rutherford Calhoun's journey toward the break in African America cultural roots that culminates into the understanding that there is no absolute past, present, or future. Fusing time in this fashion creates a literary tradition that "questions the structure of human literary identity by testing the capabilities of binary opposition, dualism and abstraction to create a meaning and experience" (Scott, 646). It is imperative that those who have either undergone slavery firsthand or have felt its repercussions write about bondage. Charles Johnson becomes the ideal interpreter of slavery because it has continued to affect his race to the present day. Rutherford Calhoun demonstrates how slavery has contracted time in African American culture by stating that "[i]n a way, I have no past. . . . When I look behind me, for my father, there is only emptiness" (160). Johnson's representation of the Middle Passage suggests that the repercussions of being brought from Africa to America have caused a break in Black American history and psychology.

Representations of the Middle Passage have maintained the barbarity of the slave trade through authors' use of gothic imagery. Volumes of African

American literature are filled with accounts of Africans plunging into the Atlantic Ocean, fearing that their situation is to worsen. The Middle Passage has proven to be the travel route that has caused more pain, death, and dissociation among Black Americans than any other. Its connotations persist into the twenty-first century. (*See* **Black Atlantic; Diaspora.**)

Resources: Primary Sources: Olaudah Equiano, "The Interesting Narrative of the Life of Olaudah Equiano, or Gustavus Vassa, the African. Written by Himself," in *The Classic Slave Narratives*, ed. Henry Louis Gates, Jr. (New York: Mentor, 1987), 1–182; Robert Hayden, "Middle Passage," in *The Norton Anthology of African American Literature*, ed. Henry Louis Gates, Jr., and Nellie Y. McKay (New York: Norton, 1996), 1501–1505; Charles Johnson, *Middle Passage* (New York: Plume, 1990); Toni Morrison, *Beloved* (New York: Plume, 1987); Phillis Wheatley, "On Being Brought from Africa to America," in *The Norton Anthology of African American Literature*, ed. Henry Louis Gates, Jr., and Nellie Y. McKay (New York: Norton, 1996), 171. **Secondary Sources:** Jesus Benito and Ana Manzanas, "The (De)-Construction of the 'Other' in *The Interesting Narrative of the Life of Olaudah Equiano*," in *Black Imagination and the Middle Passage*, ed. Maria Diedrich, Henry Louis Gates, Jr., and Carl Pedersen (New York: Oxford University Press, 1999), 47–56; John Henrik Clarke, "Reclaiming the Lost African Heritage," in *Black Fire: An Anthology of Afro-American Writing*, ed. Leroi Jones and Larry Neal (New York: Morrow, 1968), 11–18; Maria Diedrich, Henry Louis Gates, Jr., and Carl Pedersen, "The Middle Passage Between History and Fiction: Introductory Remarks," in *Black Imagination and the Middle Passage*, ed. Diedrich, Gates, and Pedersen (New York: Oxford University Press, 1999), 5–13; Genevieve Fabre, "The Slave Ship Dance," in *Black Imagination and the Middle Passage*, ed. Maria Diedrich, Henry Louis Gates, Jr., and Carl Pedersen (New York: Oxford University Press, 1999), 33–45; Herbert S. Klein, "The American Demand for Slaves and the Afro-American Patterns of Settlement," in his *The Middle Passage: Comparative Studies in the Atlantic Slave Trade* (Princeton, NJ: Princeton University Press, 1978), 2–22; Deborah McDowell and Hortense Spillers, "Robert Hayden," in *The Norton Anthology of African American Literature*, ed. Henry Louis Gates, Jr., and Nellie Y. McKay (New York: Norton, 1996), 1487–1489; Claudine Raynaud, "The Poetics of Abjection in *Beloved*," in *Black Imagination and the Middle Passage*, ed. Maria Diedrich, Henry Louis Gates, Jr., and Carl Pedersen (New York: Oxford University Press, 1999), 70–84; Daniel M. Scott, "Interrogating Identity: Appropriation and Transformation in *Middle Passage*," *African America Review* 29 (1995): 645–655.

Gerardo Del Guercio

Milestone Comics/Milestone Media (1992–present). Publisher of comic books. In 1992, Milestone Media, owned and operated by African Americans, was the first to develop a mainstream superhero comic-book line which was nationally distributed through special arrangement with DC Comics, allowing the principal creators to maintain creative control. The Milestone principals at its inception were writer-editor Dwayne McDuffie, artist and creative director Denys Cowan, president Derek Dingle, and Christopher Priest (then known as Jim Owsley) and Michael Davis, who both left the project early to pursue other ventures. The concern over accurate representations of African

Americans in comic books is something "that's been in the air for as long as I've been in the business," observes Dwayne McDuffie. "Anytime you'd have a couple of black guys get together and stand around in the hall, they'd start talking about what they couldn't do that they wanted to do" (Lander).

Milestone Media produced a total of nearly 250 issues of a number of titles that attempted to address issues that the creators felt were important. Within this framework, Milestone discussed issues of racism, capitalism, sexism, teen pregnancy, homophobia, anti-Semitism, abortion, drug abuse, and gang warfare in an unflinching yet compassionate style.

Although Milestone Media ceased regular production of comic books in 1997, it received several fan-based awards during that time as well as a number of Eisner nominations. Since 1997, there have been several new releases from Milestone, and the Milestone character "Static" is the basis for a cartoon currently airing on the Warner Brother's Network.

The central premise of all Milestone comics, set in the fictional Midwestern town of Dakota, is that a gang conflict referred to as the "Big Bang" was interrupted by police using an experimental tear gas on the crowd. It killed gang members and bystanders, and mutated those who survived, gifting them with super powers.

Milestone originally launched four comic book series. *Blood Syndicate*, by Ivan Velez, Jr., and Chriscross, provided a realistic look at the gang experience combined with the effects of the "Big Bang." The series included the death of a main character, a struggle for leadership, questioning of loyalty within the group, a crack-addicted member, and another member trying to hide his sexual orientation. In *Hardware*, by Dwayne McDuffie and Denys Cowan, the protagonist, Curtis Metcalf, is a young genius whose corporate father figure, Edwin Alva, shows him no respect and is, in fact, a major criminal. Metcalf creates armor and, acting as the vigilante Hardware, use it to take revenge on Alva. Metcalf contemplates issues of personal and business ethics. *Icon*, by Dwayne McDuffie and M.D. Bright, is the story of Augustus Freeman IV, an alien who crash-landed into slavery in 1839 and eventually became a conservative lawyer. Fifteen-year-old Raquel Ervin convinces him to become Icon, with herself, Rocket, as his sidekick. The series deals with various political issues. Most notably, Raquel is a highly intelligent, fiery young heroine who is pregnant and decides to have her baby, thus becoming the first single teenage mother superhero. *Static*, by Robert Washington III and John Paul Leon, tells the story of fifteen-year-old Virgil Hawkins, who gains electrical powers at the "Big Bang" and becomes "Static." Static deals with a crush on his best friend, Frieda, another friend running guns, the temptation to join with a villain named Holocaust, and many other issues.

Resources: Primary Sources: *Blood Syndicate*, issues 1–35 (Apr. 1993–Feb. 1996); *Deathwish*, issues 1–4 (Dec. 1994–Mar. 1995); *Hardware*, issues 1–50 (Apr. 1993–Apr. 1997); *Heroes*, issues 1–6 (May 1996–Nov. 1996); *Icon*, issues 1–42 (May 1993–Feb. 1997); *Icon: A Hero's Welcome*, volume 1, issue 1 (Jan. 1996), trade paperback; *Kobalt*, issues 1–16 (June 1994–Sept. 1995); *Long Hot Summer*, issues 1–3 (July 1995–Sept. 1995);

My Name Is Holocaust, issues 1–5 (May 1995–Sept. 1995); *9–11*, volume 2, issue 1 (Jan. 2002), graphic novel; *Shadow Cabinet*, issues 0–17 (Jan. 1994–Oct. 1995); *Static*, issues 1–45 (June 1993–Mar. 1997); *Static Shock*, televised cartoon (since Sept. 2000); *Static Shock! The Rebirth of the Cool*, issues 1–4 (Jan. 2001–Sept. 2001); *Static Shock! Trial by Fire* (Oct. 2000), trade paperback; *Steel*, issues 6, 7 (July 1994–Aug. 1994); *Superboy*, issues 6, 7 (July 1994–Aug. 1994); *Superman: The Man of Steel*, issues 35, 36 (July 1994–Aug. 1994); *Wise Son: The White Wolf*, issues 1–4 (Nov. 1996–Feb. 1997); *Worlds Collide*, issue 1 (July 1994); *Xombi*, issues 0–21 (Jan. 1994–Feb. 1996). **Secondary Sources:** Hafeez Amin, "Static on Your Set," *Just Comics & More*, http://frostbytei.com/jc/issues/1/page14.html; Jeffrey A. Brown, *Black Superheroes, Milestone Comics, and Their Fans* (Jackson: University Press of Mississippi, 2001); Les Daniels, *DC Comics: Sixty Years of the World's Favorite Comic Book Heroes* (New York: DC Comics, 1995); Randy Lander, "A Milestone Retrospective," 1999, www.psycomic.com.

Valerie Lynn Guyant

Miller, E. Ethelbert (born 1950). Poet, essayist, critic, educator, and cultural activist who believes that African American poetry is a bridge by which history and values are conveyed from one generation to the next, and that it preserves the cultural memory of a people (Williams). Miller has devoted his life and career to promoting the arts. As a writer who was deeply affected by the **Black Arts Movement**, he defines himself as a cultural worker and activist who emphasizes the relationship between art and politics. He also believes that it's important to place literature in a public forum. This is one of the reasons that he founded the Ascension Poetry Reading Series, one of the oldest literary series in **Washington, D.C.**, which provided opportunities for beginning and established poets to read their work for audiences. The series lasted from 1974 to 2000. During the same period, Miller was director of the African American Studies Resource Center at Howard University.

Miller edited several poetry anthologies, including the *Synergy D.C. Anthology* (with **Ahmos Zu-Bolton**, 1975), *Women Surviving Massacres and Men* (1977), *In Search of Color Everywhere* (1994), and *Beyond the Frontier: African American Poetry for the 21st Century* (2002). He is also author of eight volumes of poetry, the most recent being *How We Sleep on the Nights We Don't Make Love* (2004). *Fathering Words: The Making of an African American Writer* (2000) is Miller's memoir.

Eugene Ethelbert Miller was born in New York City on November 20, 1950, the youngest of three children. His father Egberto was a postal worker, and his mother, Enid, was a seamstress. Miller graduated from Howard University in 1972 with a B.A. in African American Studies. He is respected for his artistic integrity and his tireless encouragement of other writers.

Resources: E. Ethelbert Miller: *How We Sleep on the Nights We Don't Make Love* (Willimantic, CT: Curbstone Press, 2004); *Fathering Words: The Making of an African American Writer* (New York: St. Martin's, 2000); E. Ethelbert Miller, ed.: *In Search of Color Everywhere: A Collection of African American Poetry* (New York: Stewart, Tabori & Chang, 1994); *Where Are the Love Poems for Dictators?*, 2nd ed. (Greensboro, NC: Open

Hand Press, 2001); *Whispers, Secrets, and Promises* (Baltimore: Black Classic Press, 1998); Priscilla R. Ramsey, "E. Ethelbert Miller," in *Dictionary of Literary Biography*, vol. 41, *Afro-American Poets Since 1995*, ed. Trudier Harris and Thadious M. Davis (Detroit: Gale, 1985); Derek A. Williams, "E. Ethelbert Miller," in William L. Andrews, Francis Smith Foster, and Trudier Harris, eds., *The Oxford Companion to African American Literature* (New York: Oxford University Press, 1997), 499–500.

John Greer Hall

Miller, May (1899–1995). Actress, playwright, poet, editor, and teacher. Born and raised in **Washington, D.C.**, Miller was one of the pioneers in African American theater during the **Harlem Renaissance**. Her father, Kelly Miller, was a prominent professor of sociology, and Dean of Arts and Sciences at Howard University, which Miller attended after completing Paul Laurence Dunbar High School and studying with the poet **Angelina Weld Grimké** and the dramatist **Mary (Marrie) Powell Burrill**, who encouraged her to write plays. The prominent intellectuals **W.E.B. Du Bois, Carter G. Woodson, Alain Locke,** and **Booker T. Washington** also encouraged her to have a career in writing. At Howard, she collaborated with Locke, Montgomery Gregory, and others to create an African American **drama** movement on campus. With a group of artists, Miller struggled to write, direct, perform in, and produce quality performances.

During the 1920s, Miller became a close friend of the poet and playwright **Georgia Douglas Johnson** and an active member of her literary salon, the S Street Group, which offered support and encouragement to Miller and such other writers as **Alice Moore Dunbar-Nelson, Marita Bonner, Langston Hughes, Zora Neale Hurston, Anne Spencer, Jessie Redmon Fauset,** and **Jean Toomer.** For the next decade, Miller wrote nearly twenty one-act plays, including *The Bog Guide* (1925), which helped establish her in the Black cultural scene as the most prolific woman playwright of the Harlem Renaissance. Other plays include *Scratches* (1929), *Stragglers in the Dust* (1930), *Nails and Thorns* (1933), the historical plays *Harriet Tubman* and *Sojourner Truth* (1935), and her last play, *Freedom's Children on the March* (1943). With the playwright **Willis Richardson**, she edited the anthology *Negro History in Thirteen Plays* (1935). At this writing, Miller's plays have not been published in selected or collected form. From 1945 until her death in 1995, Miller devoted her life to writing poetry, producing seven volumes, and giving poetry readings for children in schools and in public presentations with other notable poets. Her *Collected Poems* appeared in 1989. As a pioneer and a leader, Miller will always be praised for her impact on the theater and African American culture.

Resources: Jeanne Marie A. Miller, "Georgia Douglas Johnson and May Miller: Forgotten Playwrights of the New Negro Renaissance," *College Language Association Journal* 33, no. 4 (1990), 349–366; May Miller: *The Clearing and Beyond* (Washington, DC: Charioteer Press, 1974); *Collected Poems* (Detroit: Lotus Press, 1989); *Dust of Uncertain Journey: Poems* (Detroit: Lotus Press, 1975); *Not That Far* (San Luis Obispo,

CA: Solo Press, 1973); Barbara Molette, "Black Women Playwrights," *Black World* 25 (April 1976), 28–34; Willis Richardson and May Miller, eds., *Negro History in Thirteen Plays* (Washington, DC: Associated Publishers, 1935); Yvonne Shafer, "May Miller (1899)," in *American Women Playwrights 1900–1950*, ed. Yvonne Shafer (New York: Peter Lang, 1997), 309–321; Winifred L. Stoeling, "May Miller," in *Dictionary of Literary Biography*, vol. 41, *Afro-American Poets Since 1955*, ed. Trudier Harris and Thadious M. Davis (Detroit: Gale, 1985), 241–247.

Loretta G. Woodard

Miller, R. Baxter (born 1948). Literary critic and theorist, editor, and professor. Miller is probably best known as a scholar and critic specializing in the work of **Langston Hughes**. He won an American Book Award in 1991 for *The Art and Imagination of Langston Hughes* (1989). He is also one of the leading critics working on contemporary and traditional African American literature. Miller's criticism draws on a variety of literary theories, including **multicultural theory** and **deconstruction**.

In addition to writing criticism, Miller has served as editor of *Black American Literature and Humanism* (1981). At this writing, he is Professor of English and the Director of the Institute for African American Studies at the University of Georgia in Athens. He is credited for expanding the scope of the Institute and increasing the enrollment in the program. The Institute issues the official publication of the **Langston Hughes Society**, the *Langston Hughes Review*, for which Miller serves as Executive Editor. Previously he was Professor of English and Director of the Black Literature Program at the University of Tennessee, Knoxville.

Miller attended North Carolina Central University, a historically black public university in Raleigh, from which he graduated magna cum laude with a Bachelor of Arts degree in 1970. He earned his Master of Arts from Brown University in 1972; his thesis was "No Crystal Stair: Imagery in Langston Hughes." Miller earned his Ph.D. at Brown in 1974 after completing the dissertation "Dark Magician: Shelley—Urbanity, Insanity, and Poetic Structure."

Two books by Miller—*The Art and Imagination of Langston Hughes* and *Langston Hughes and Gwendolyn Brooks: A Reference Guide*—have become standard works in African American literary studies. For the landmark multivolume *Collected Works of Langston Hughes*, Miller edited the volume of Hughes's **short fiction**.

Miller has received a number of awards for his scholarly work and criticism, including the American Book Award; the Phi Kappa Phi Love of Learning Award (2003); the Langston Hughes Prize: Scholar, Leader, and Steward (2001); regional designation awards for excellence and innovation in the humanities (with Will Holmes, John Inscoe, and Robert Pratt) from the Cultural Olympiad and Southern States Humanities Councils for "Black and White Perspectives on the American South" (1994); and the College Language Association Prize (1993).

Resources: Patricia L. Hill, Bernard Bell, Trudier Harris, William J. Harris, and R. Baxter Miller, eds., *The Riverside Anthology of African American Literary Tradition* (Boston: Houghton Mifflin, 1998); R. Baxter Miller: *The Art and Imagination of Langston Hughes* (Lexington: University Press of Kentucky, 1989); *Langston Hughes and Gwendolyn Brooks: A Reference Guide* (Boston: G. K. Hall, 1978); *The Short Stories*, vol. 15 of *The Collected Works of Langston Hughes*, Arnold Rampersad, gen. ed. (Columbia: University of Missouri Press, 2001); *Southern Trace in Black Critical Theory*, spec. iss. of *Xavier Review* 11 (1991); R. Baxter Miller, ed.: *Black American Literature and Humanism* (Lexington: University Press of Kentucky, 1981); *Black American Poets Between Worlds, 1940–1960* (Knoxville: University of Tennessee Press, 1986).

Iyabo F. Osiapem

Millican, Arthenia Jackson Bates (born 1920). Novelist, short story writer, literary critic, and professor. Millican follows in the tradition of **Zora Neale Hurston**, **Richard Wright**, **Ernest James Gaines**, and **Alice Walker**, whose fiction often dramatizes and interprets the lives of agrarian African Americans. A native of Sumter, South Carolina, and the daughter and granddaughter of Baptist ministers, Millican pursues themes in her writing that explore the tensions between good and evil, youth and age, Christianity and Islam, and the Black woman's positions in the home and in the church.

Millican launched her writing career with the publication of her first short story, "Christmastime," in the *Sumter Daily Item* when she was just sixteen years old and a student at Lincoln High School. She attended Morris College, from which she received a B.A. in English in 1941, and Atlanta University, from which she received the M.A. in English in 1948. There she met and took a class under **Langston Hughes**, who had come to Atlanta University in 1947 as a visiting professor of creative writing. Millican worked as a teacher first at Westside High School in Kershaw, South Carolina (1942–1945), then at Butler High School in Hartsville, South Carolina (1942–1943), during which time she wrote several short stories—"Down the Santee River Way," "Voyage End," "Tell Me," "When Will It Be"—that she self-published with Exposition Press in 1946. She became English Department Chair at Morris College (1947–1949) and then moved to Halifax, Virginia, where she taught at Mary Bethune High School (1949–1955) and married and divorced Noah Bates of South Boston, Virginia. Her Virginia sojourn inspired her to write "The Bottoms and Hills: Virginia Tales," an unpublished collection.

Millican left Virginia in 1955 to take a one-year appointment at Mississippi Valley State in Itta Bena, and then she taught at Southern University in Baton Rouge, Louisiana, where her colleagues included the poet **Pinkie Gordon Lane** and Charles H. Rowell, who penned the introduction to "The Bottoms and Hills" and launched *Callaloo: A Journal of African-American and African Arts and Letters*. During her tenure at Southern (1956–1974), Millican received her Ph.D. in American literature from Louisiana State University in 1969, the same year that she published *Seeds Beneath the Snow*, a collection of twelve vignettes of Southern Black folk. Reviewers praised the collection for its wit, message tales, and realistic portrayals. Ruby Dee and **Ossie Davis**, Black film stars, have presented dramatized sections from the collection on National Black Network radio.

In 1973, Millican published *The Deity Nodded*, an apprenticeship novel, chapter 51 of which is the same as "A Ceremony of Innocence," one of the short stories in *Seeds Beneath the Snow*. The novel was inspired by the conversion of Millican's younger sister, Catherine J. Rhodes, from Christianity to Islam in the 1960s. In 1974, Millican came to Virginia to teach at Norfolk State University, and she published *Such Things from the Valley* (1977), a collection of two short stories. She returned to Southern University in 1976, and retired from there in 1980.

Millican's literary reviews on the works of African American writers can be found in *CLA Journal*; her uncollected short stories are scattered in **Negro Digest**, *Black World*, *The Last Cookie*, and *Obsidian*. After the death of her second husband, Wilbert Millican, she returned to Sumter, where she still resides.

Resources: Rita B. Dandridge, "The Motherhood Myth: Black Women and Christianity in *The Deity Nodded*," *MELUS* 12 (Fall 1985), 13–22; Harry Lee Faggett, "Character Delineation Is Excellent," review of *Seeds Beneath the Snow*, *Advocate* (Baton Rouge, LA), Nov. 2, 1969; Edward W. Farrison, "Review of *Seeds Beneath the Snow*, by Arthenia J. Bates," *CLA Journal* 13, no. 2 (Mar. 1970), 325–327; John Oliver Killens and Jerry W. Ward, Jr., eds., *Black Southern Voices: An Anthology of Fiction, Poetry, Drama, Nonfiction, and Critical Essays* (New York: Meridan, 1992), 119–129; Arthenia Bates Millican: *The Deity Nodded* (Detroit: Harlo, 1973); *Seeds Beneath the Snow* (New York: Greenwich, 1969); *Such Things from the Valley* (Norfolk, VA: H. C. Young, 1977); Adimu Owusu, "The Development of Black Women: An Interview with Arthenia Bates-Millican," *Nuance* 1, no. 7 (Mar. 1982), 14–16; Bettye J. Parker, "Reflections: Arthenia Bates Millican," in *Sturdy Black Bridges: Visions of Black Women in Literature*, ed. Roseann P. Bell et al. (Garden City, NY: Anchor, 1979), 201–108.

Rita B. Dandridge

Milner, Ron (1938–2004). Playwright, essayist, and founder and director of Langston Hughes Theatre. Born in **Detroit, Michigan**, Ronald (Ron) Milner graduated from Northeastern High School and attended Highland Park Junior College, the Detroit Institute of Technology, and Columbia University. He grew up on Hastings Street, with Muslims on one corner, hustlers and pimps on another, winos on one, and Aretha Franklin singing from her father's church on the other. It was these experiences that became his source of inspiration. He told one interviewer, "The more I read in high school, the more I realized that some tremendous, phenomenal things were happening around me. What happened in a Faulkner novel happened four times a day on Hastings Street. I thought why should these crazy people Faulkner writes about seem more important than my mother or my father or the dude down the street. Only because they had someone to write about them. So I became a writer" (Cunningham, 202).

Driven to tell "his people's story," Milner combined his talents as a writer with the stories of his childhood, and created drama in which audiences recognized the genuine portrayal of their own stories. Milner's empathetic storytelling and his ability to reveal his characters' inner worth earned him the title "Playwright of the People" (Smitherman). Milner's main thrust is directed toward unifying the family and centers on basic moral principles.

Milner's first play was *Who's Got His Own*, a drama that focused on a family's struggles with the devastation of a death in the family. Some of Milner's other plays include *The Warning: A Theme for Linda, What the Wine-Sellers Buy*, and *Checkmates*. He also edited an important anthology of drama with **Woodie King, Jr.** Ron Milner died in Detroit of liver cancer on July 9, 2004. (*See* **Drama.**)

Resources: Beunyce Rayford Cunningham, "Ron Milner," in *Dictionary of Literary Biography*, vol. 38, *Afro-American writers After 1955: Dramatists and Prose Writers*, ed. Thadious M. Davis and Trudier Harris (Detroit: Gale, 1995), 201–207; Woodie King Jr., "Log of a Theater Hit," *Black World*, Apr. 1976, 21–27; Woodie King and Ron Milner, eds., *Black Drama Anthology* (New York: Columbia University Press, 1972); Ron Milner, *What the Wine-Sellers Buy Plus Three: Four Plays by Ron Milner*, ed. Amiri Baraka and Woodie King, Jr. (Detroit: Wayne State University Press, 2001); Geneva Smitherman, "Ron Milner, People's Playwright," *Black World*, Apr. 1976, 5–19.

John Greer Hall

Minstrelsy. In the medieval period, "minstrels" in Europe were traveling singers and lyric poets, and since then "minstrelsy" has referred to this category of entertainment. In the United States, however, especially in the nineteenth century, minstrelsy was closely linked to attitudes about **race**. Satisfying the sweeping desire for a uniquely American cultural institution after the War of 1812, "Negro" or "Ethiopian" minstrelsy became a popular and economically successful form of entertainment in the 1840s. It did so chiefly through the exploitation of prevailing stereotypes of African Americans. The "Black" figure presented on stage and delineated on the posters and handbills advertising minstrel shows was a grotesque and heartless burlesque of African Americans, most of whom were forced to inhabit an abject, powerless position in American society. Using greasepaint or burned cork to darken their skin, White minstrel performers enacted caricature-like portrayals of Blacks by grossly exaggerating what their White audiences perceived to be African American idiosyncrasies.

Physically, the African American of the minstrel tradition was represented in extreme, overstated proportion. Protruding eyeballs, excessively flat, wide noses, and elongated lower lips and feet were assumed to lampoon African Americans, to the delight of minstrel show audiences. Drawing on and manipulating common perceptions of Blacks, the minstrel entertainer depicted the African American as puerile, witless, immoral, and innately musical. In keeping with their cruel and unequivocally false characterizations of African Americans, minstrels used unwieldy **vernacular**, affected distorted inflections, and spoke in an embellished, sluggish drawl to render Blacks mentally inferior to Whites.

It is not coincidental that the minstrel show's popularity grew at a time when the American public became concerned about **slavery** and the status of African Americans. Although the songs and plantation stories performed from the African American point of view could be somewhat sensitive to the hardships that slaves endured, the minstrels were careful not to disparage the institution of slavery itself. They limited their portrayals to contented slaves and discontented freed slaves, and the shows' racist content emanated from the performers' interest in appeasing boisterous, outspoken audiences. If minstrel shows were somewhat ambivalent about the brutality and injustice of slavery at times, there is no doubt that they cast African Americans as being subordinate to Whites. In short, minstrelsy fulfilled the prophecy that African Americans were incapable of seizing the opportunities afforded them outside White supervision, Minstrelsy provided a medium through

A poster for one of the earlier minstrels, G. Swaine Buckley, the "Ethiopian Comedian." Courtesy of the Library of Congress.

which Whites could satiate their curiosity, could mollify their guilt, and could strengthen their weakening convictions about slavery.

Charles Matthews, an Englishman, was the first known White man to appropriate African American material for a staged show. Matthews's use of the song "Possum up a Gum Tree" in his 1822 performance, "A Trip to America," inspired black-faced White American performers such as Thomas D. Rice, John N. Smith, J. W. Sweeney, George Washington Dixon, Bob Farrell, and George Nicols to perform songs claimed to be of African American origin on stage, in circuses, and between acts of plays. Although the melodies of most of the songs were of British origin, the lyrics were largely motivated by American frontier lore. Dramas for and about the common man were fashioned out of the American public's desire for a brand of entertainment that could serve as a substitute for the folk culture that was lost once Americans migrated to urban centers en masse. Such dramas also satisfied the growing antiaristocratic, antiromantic, anti-European aesthetic sentiments of Americans in the nineteenth century. Fulfilling America's appetite for a popular culture that spoke to and for the common man, minstrelsy brought African Americans into the mainstream of American culture, but only as grotesque caricatures of themselves.

Stereotypical characters such as the cunning but moronic Jim Crow and the ludicrous coxcomb Zip Coon evolved out of the minstrel show tradition. As testament to how firmly fixed minstrelsy conventions became, even African Americans who performed as minstrels after the **Civil War** were expected to conform their acts to old expectations. Only gradually were they able to revise stereotypes and recast plantation caricatures as they attracted a large number of African Americans into theaters.

In 1843, troupes commenced their adherence to and expansion of the minstrel show's tripartite structure. Groups such as Dan Emmett's Virginia Minstrels would conventionally open with a blend of songs, dances, demeaning jokes, and riddles. These would then lead to set skits which would often include mock "**sermons**" or "stump speeches." The show would conclude with a staged production set in **the South**. One year after the first minstrel show was performed in 1843, the Ethiopian Serenaders, a blackface minstrel troupe of White performers, played the White House. This event not only signifies minstrelsy's wide, accelerated popularity, but also indicates the extent to which the caricatures it devised and perpetuated were accepted in America. Countering the widespread acceptance of these farcical images of Blacks on stage were the numerous denunciations of minstrelsy by African American writers.

In the entertainment industry, stereotypes from minstrelsy persisted well into the twentieth century. For example, **Bert Williams**, remembered as an enormously gifted, innovative comedian in vaudeville, nonetheless was expected to play to stereotypes and, ironically, even to wear blackface (Smith).

In the 1840s, **Frederick Douglass**'s editorial condemnations of minstrelsy appeared regularly in his newspaper, *The North Star*, and cutting revisions of minstrel lyrics appeared in **Martin R. Delaney**'s novel *Blake* (1861). Sardonic depictions of minstrelsy are also found in **Paul Laurence Dunbar**'s *The Sport of the Gods* (1902) and **Wallace Thurman**'s *The Blacker the Berry* (1929). Among later works that discredit the images upheld by blackface performances are **Zora Neale Hurston**'s "Characteristics of Negro Expression" (1934), **Ralph Ellison**'s "Change the Joke and Slip the Yoke" (1958), **Amiri Baraka**'s *Blues People* (1963), which Baraka published under his previous name, LeRoi Jones, and **George C. Wolfe**'s play *The Colored Museum* (1988).

Resources: Eric Lott, *Love and Theft: Blackface Minstrelsy and the American Working Class* (New York: Oxford University Press, 1993); William J. Mahar, *Behind the Burnt Cork Mask: Early Blackface Minstrelsy and Antebellum American Popular Culture* (Urbana: University of Illinois Press, 1999); Eric Ledell Smith, *Bert Williams: A Biography of the Pioneer Black Comedian* (Jefferson, NC: McFarland, 1992); Robert C. Toll, *Blacking Up: The Minstrel Show in Nineteenth-Century America* (New York: Oxford University Press, 1974); Carl Wittke, *Tambo and Bones: A History of the American Minstrel Stage* (Durham, NC: Duke University Press, 1930).

Alex Ambrozic

Misogyny. Term meaning the hatred of women. The most extreme form of misogyny is historically found in patriarchal (male-dominated) societies in which women are believed to be inferior. In an article on **Toni Morrison**'s novel *Sula*, Pessoni writes, "Patriarchal consciousness is oriented toward individuality, competition, personal acquisition—traits that are not necessarily harmful in themselves, but which become potentially fatal to the species when they are overvalued at the expense of feminine traits" (440). Within patriarchal societies, women are commonly thought of as wicked and unclean, and are placed in a submissive role in relation to their male counterparts. For women in a misogynistic society, marriage is tremendously difficult. Misogynistic males believe their wives are property. Therefore, the woman's role is similar to that of a slave or an indentured servant, in that she is to obey her husband (master) and endure the abuse inflicted upon her. This abuse often includes physical and emotional abuse, as well as legalized rape (Quale).

The patriarchal misogynistic society, as a whole, serves to fuel this hatred of women. For example, women are kept subservient to males through their lack of rights, including the right to vote, the right to work, and even the right to control their own bodies. Within a patriarchal misogynistic society, rape may be considered to be the female victim's fault, thereby adding to women's lack of personal security and legal status.

The theme of misogyny is evident in much African American literature, including **slave narratives**, which often show the degree to which misogyny was a part of the institution of **slavery**. The misogyny was exhibited not just by male slave masters but my the masters' wives. For example, in *Twelve Years a Slave* (1853), **Solomon Northup** gives readers a graphic view of misogyny as well as of the atrocities of slavery, especially in his account of the slave girl Patsey. Not only did her master, the abusive and misogynistic Mr. Epps, continuously harrass Patsey, but he also repeatedly raped and flogged her, and Epps's wife often encouraged Epps to abuse Patsey because she was jealous of her.

In the novel *Native Son*, by **Richard Wright**, the issue of misogyny is complicated and not easy to interpret. In "Spectacle and Event in *Native Son*," Jonathan Elmer describes Bigger Thomas, the main character of Wright's novel, as being "resentful towards whites, sullen, angry, ignorant, emotionally unstable, and depressed . . . capable of premeditated murder" (773). Bigger's mental and emotional state lead him to commit his first murder; he accidentally suffocates Mary Dalton, the daughter of a wealthy real estate magnate. In an effort to hide this accident, Bigger decapitates and incinerates Mary's body. The novel raises the question of the extent to which Bigger's attitude toward Mary and other women is determined by the fear and hatred of women—by a form of misogyny. Although readers of *Native Son* may feel compassion for Bigger because of the circumstances in which he found himself and the racist society he must negotiate, readers must also confront the horror of Bigger's murder of Mary Dalton and his murder, by bludgeoning, of his girlfriend Bessie. The novel invites readers to ponder the source of Bigger's attitudes toward White women, African American women, and women in general.

James Baldwin's novel *Another Country* (1962) touches on the theme of misogyny, especially in relation to complex modern American attitudes toward sexuality (including homosexuality), in relation to White males's attitudes toward African American women, and in African American males' attitudes toward White women. The novel depicts the variety of contexts in which misogyny may appear and the extent to which it may be masked.

Other works by African American authors that illustrate misogyny include **Maya Angelou**'s *I Know Why the Caged Bird Sings* (1969), **Alice Walker**'s *The Color Purple* (1982), and **Zora Neal Hurston**'s *Their Eyes Were Watching God* (1937). Toni Morrison explore the issue of misogyny in her novels *The Bluest Eye* (1970), *Sula* (1973), and *Beloved* (1987). In "The Black Person in Art: How Should S/He Be Portrayed," **Henry Louis Gates, Jr.**, asserts that Alice Walker and Toni Morrison "choose to write about the archetypal female experiences of incest, rape, and battering" (6). In writing about misogyny, that is, writers such as Walker and Morrison emphasize the abuse of women that is part of a patriarchal society, as well as the ways in which women have had to confront the abuse and try to overcome the obstacles of misogyny.

Resources: Katherine Anne Ackley, ed., *Misogyny in Literature: An Essay Collection* (New York: Garland, 1992); James Baldwin, *Another Country* (New York: Dial, 1962); Jonathan Elmer, "Spectacle and Event in Native Son," *American Literature* 70, no. 4 (Dec. 1998), 767–798; Henry Louis Gates, Jr., "The Black Person in Art: How Should S/He Be Portrayed?" *Black American Literature Forum* 21, no. 1/2 (Spring–Summer 1987), 3–24, 317–324; Zora Neale Hurston, *Their Eyes Were Watching God* (1937; repr. Urbana: University of Illinois Press, 1978); Toni Morrison: *Beloved* (1987; repr. New York: Knopf, 1990); *The Bluest Eye* (New York: Holt, Rinehart and Winston, 1970); *Sula* (New York: Knopf, 1974); Solomon Northup, *Twelve Years a Slave* (New York: Dover, 1970); Michele Pessoni, "'She Was Laughing at Their God:' Discovering the Goddess Within in *Sula*," *African American Review* 29, no. 3 (Autumn 1995), 439–451; G. Robina Quale, *A History of Marriage Systems* (Westport, CT: Greenwood Press, 1988); Alice Walker, *The Color Purple* (New York: Harcourt Brace Jovanovich, 1982); Richard Wright, *Native Son* (1940; repr. New York: Perennial Classics, 1998).

DaNean Pound

Mississippi Delta. The Mississippi Delta area has been a source of literary inspiration to generations of writers. The lower Mississippi River delta is an enduring theme in American and African American literature, and the source of great fiction and fancy, travel, history, and tales. Fictional and autobiographical interpretations of life throughout the Delta recall the sickness, adversity, wonder, and insight that Mississippi Delta life brought to many. These accounts are cultural classics: **Mark Twain** learning how to "read" the river; William Alexander Percy walking the levees, looking for "boils"; Lyle Saxon describing the "flotsam and jetsam, the riffraff of the world" who gathered above the barrooms of Gallatin Street in **New Orleans, Louisiana**; William Johnson, a freedman, detailing everyday life in antebellum Natchez; George Washington Cable's portrait of Louisiana Creoles; and John McPhee describing the near collapse of the Old River control structure during the 1973 flood (*Heritage Study*). There are also authors who grew up in the Mississippi Delta who chose to write about the Delta as well as other subjects. The Delta region is not central in their writings, but it contributes to the authors' outlook. For example, the early feminist author Kate Chopin of **St. Louis, Missouri**, and New Orleans, wrote of a married woman's "awakening" in a repressive household in New Orleans.

At the very heart of the Deep South, the Mississippi Delta is referred to as the "most southern place" by Cobb. The Deep South region is composed of a river artery flanked by five southern states: Louisiana, Mississippi, Arkansas, Tennessee, and Kentucky. The lower Mississippi Delta is one of the poorest areas in the United States. The region, throughout the years, has had high, sometimes extreme, levels of poverty as a result of sluggish economies and the legacy of the Jim Crow segregated South. The Delta region most often referred to in Southern literature is the area that encompasses ten counties in the state of Mississippi. This area stretches from just south of **Memphis, Tennessee**, to the Yazoo River plain west to Greenville, Mississippi, and south to Vicksburg, Mississippi.

Over time, the forbidding junglelike forests, swamps, and bayous gave way to fields of cash crops. In most parts of the Delta, the soil is rich, creating the largest cotton producing region in the United States. The soil was so rich that it supported the entire agricultural economy known as the Cotton Kingdom.

Music and the Mississippi Delta are synonymous; indeed, the Delta is the cradle of American music. Musical styles within the Delta region are diverse; it was here that the **blues**, Cajun music, **jazz**, and zydeco evolved. Best known around the world is the blues music of the lower Delta. Developed by people engaged in struggle, infused with spirit and speaking in dialect, the blues are rooted in African music and evolved from field hollers, the work songs of slaves that often carried deeply layered, coded messages. It is said that misery produces creativity and resiliency, and the blues is deeply rooted in the African American experience and the rural settings of the Mississippi and Arkansas deltas. The blues tell stories of frustrated love, broken homes, and other miseries of an oppressed and displaced people. The blues is a music of hardworking, exploited people, and this distinct, indigenous music was largely developed by musicians with no formal training but with an ear for the rhythms of their daily lives.

At the center of the myth and **folklore** concerning the region is the Mississippi River. The mighty river's name comes from the Algonquian word Meschasipi or Mesipi, which means "big river" or "great river." Mark Twain drew inspiration from the river and the delta region that permeates all of his work. The river is the focus of the *Adventures of Tom Sawyer* and *The Adventures of Huckleberry Finn*, as well as other short stories, poems, and literary works (Rust).

During the early 1800s, the region presented obstacles to settlers that seemed nearly impossible to overcome. It was sparsely populated and isolated from the territory around it. There are reported cases of typhoid fever and malaria, and severe weather conditions killed many of the crops. These obstacles added to the **myth**s of the hard life and the struggle to live in the region. Many early settlers remained isolated and developed their own culture, and used the Delta culture to paint a picture of life in the region that contrasted with life in other parts of **the South**.

The Mississippi Delta has a long, rich history from which literary legends sprang. Several authors use themes that center in the region. These writings tend to portray the Southern lifestyle's economic, social, racial, and cultural groups and their interactions. For example, Eudora Welty's *Delta Wedding* (1946) is set in the northwestern section of the Mississippi Delta from Vicksburg, Mississippi, to just south of Memphis, Tennessee. Welty depicts a Delta plantation in "Old South" style, complete with extended family, friends, African American servants, and field workers. Her stories of Southern family life bring to mind a Southern sense of place that is often associated with Southern writers' local color.

Other writers of this area include **Anne Moody**, an African American memoir writer. **Richard Wright** lived in the Delta region, and the extreme economic and race relations conditions had an impact on his writings. He depicted harsh truths about slavery, segregation, and racism, and his best-known work, *Native Son*, is set in a burgeoning African American community in Chicago, many of whose residents had migrated north from the lower Delta region (*Heritage Study*). Wright later moved to the North, and ultimately to **Paris, France**, but took the cultural influence of the Mississippi Delta with him. Some of Wright's literary works include *Uncle Tom's Children* (1938), *Native Son* (1940), *Black Boy* (1945), and *The Long Dream* (1958). Wright is one of the primary contributors to the understanding of the extensive enmeshment of the lives of Black and White Americans. The use of local color in his writings helps to define the region's racial and ethnic tensions and to set the stage for the understanding of the American **Civil Rights Movement**. Similar themes, such as **race**, economics, and sexual issues, can be found in other writers of the mid-twentieth century, such as **Margaret Abigail Walker**'s *Jubilee* (1966).

Other Delta-based or -inspired authors include Mississippi natives William Faulkner, who used the Delta as the setting for his intricate novels, and Willie Morris, who embodies the Southern tradition of back-porch storytelling. Cape Fear resident Thomas "Tennessee" Williams shared his perceptions of the colorful Delta characters he grew up with in rural Mississippi in his many plays. The historian Shelby Foote, of Greenville, Mississippi, enthralled readers with the personalities, ironies, and triumphs of the **Civil War**, and **Alex Haley** of Henning, Tennessee, poignantly depicted the struggles of African Americans in his works of historical fiction. Contemporary best-selling author John Grisham uses the rich heritage of the Delta as a palette for his popular suspense novels. As Greenville, Mississippi, resident Hodding

Carter noted in 1942, however, both the Mississippi River and the Southern Delta tradition remain elusive (*Heritage Study*). Many of the novels and short stories by **Ernest James Gaines** are set in the Mississippi Delta region.

The environment is another theme that dominates literature about the Delta region. The literary heritage of William Faulkner depicts images of the Delta as mystical and captivating, even during the flood season. According to Butler, "It is William Alexander Percy who so memorably describes in *Lanterns on the Levee* (1941) the charm of the land itself, the people, and walking the levee to watch for breaks in the dike during flood time" (506). Just as the lower Mississippi River provides nourishment for plants and animals, so the Delta region provides inspiration for the cultural life of people who live there. Its image is reflected literally, figuratively, spiritually, and musically in the rich lives and diverse expressions of its residents. (*See* **Nature**.)

Resources: Jerry H. Bryant, "Ernest J. Gaines: Change, Growth, and History," *Southern Review* 10 (Fall 1974), 851–864; Rebecca Butler, "Mississippi Delta," in *The Companion to Southern Literature*, ed. Joseph Flora and Lucinda MacKethan (Baton Rouge: Louisiana State University Press, 2002); *Heritage Study: Lower Mississippi Delta Region* (Washington: DC: U.S. Department of the Interior, 1998); Richard Rust, "Mississippi River," in *The Companion to Southern Literature*, ed. Joseph Flora and Lucinda H. MacKethan (Baton Rouge: Louisiana State University Press, 2002).

DeMond S. Miller

Mitchell, Loften (1919–2001). Playwright, theater historian, novelist, and social worker. Loften Mitchell's histories of the African American theater, *Black Drama: The Story of the American Negro in the Theatre* (1967) and *Voices of the Black Theatre* (1975), established him as a preeminent black theater historian. His stage plays, which frequently highlighted the impact of racism, voiced pride in the unique and distinctive aspects of African American culture(s).

Mitchell's enthusiasm for the theater began while he was a high school student in **Harlem, New York**. Frequently visiting the Lafayette, the Lincoln, and the Alhambra theaters, he observed the performances and professional lives of many pioneering Black vaudevillians. In the 1930s, he became an actor, performing and writing sketches with the Rose McClendon Players. Facing the hardships of a Black actor in a primarily White theatrical world, he began writing plays in order to provide better roles for Black actors and more honest representations of the Black experience and the impact of racism.

Mitchell briefly attended City College of New York, did social work in New York City, and later moved south to attend Talladega College in Alabama on a scholarship. In 1951, he completed an M.A. in playwriting at Columbia University. He was mentored at Columbia by Barrett H. Clark (writer and host of the popular 1940s radio program *Broadway Talks Back*) and John Gassner (who had taught Tennessee Williams, Arthur Miller, and William Inge). In 1969, Mitchell served as an adjunct professor of English at Long

Island University. In 1970, he was a lecturer at New York University. In 1971, he began teaching in the Department of Theater and the Department of Afro-American Studies at the State University of New York at Binghamton. He became a professor emeritus in 1985.

Though known primarily for his histories and his plays, Mitchell was amazingly prolific in nonfiction as well. He authored a collection of essays, *Harlem, My Harlem*, scripted several radio plays, and contributed to *The Oxford Companion to the Theatre* and *The Encyclopedia della spetta colo*. He also wrote for the **Amsterdam News**, **The Crisis**, *Freedomways*, **Negro Digest**, the *New York Times*, and *Theatre Arts Monthly*, and was the editor of the *Freedom Journal* of the **NAACP**. Mitchell received a Guggenheim fellowship, a Rockefeller Foundation grant, a Harlem Cultural Council special award, an award for playwriting from the Research Foundation at the State University of New York, and an award for outstanding theatrical pioneering from the Audience Development Committee. (*See* **Drama**.)

Resources: Phyllis Hartnoll, ed., *The Oxford Companion to the Theatre*, 4th ed. (New York: Oxford University Press, 1983); "Loften Mitchell" (obituary), *New York Times*, May 23, 2001, p. C19; Lofton Mitchell: *And the Walls Came Tumbling Down* (opera; music by Willard Roosevelt) (1976, unpublished); *Black Drama: The Story of the American Negro in the Theatre* (New York: Hawthorn, 1967); *Bubbling Brown Sugar* (musical; adapted from a concept by Rosetta LeNoire; music and lyrics by various artists) (1976); "Harlem My Harlem," *Black World* 20, no. 1 (1970), 91–97; *The Stubborn Old Lady Who Resisted Change* (New York: Emerson Hall, 1973); *Tell Pharaoh* (New York: Emerson Hall, 1970); *Voices of the Black Theatre* (Clifton, NJ: J. T. White, 1975).

Michelle LaFrance

Modernism (c. 1890–1940). Artistic and literary movement. This loosely defined movement of the late nineteenth to middle twentieth century understood itself as a break with tradition that prized the "new." Modernism can be discussed in terms of what it reacted against socially—the rise of industry and mass production, commodification, the loss of tradition, secularity—or in terms of what it celebrated aesthetically—abstraction, obscurity, fragments, difficulty, experimentation, the unique, genius. The figures usually associated with Modernism were Europeans and Americans. That African American writers of the period have been excluded from discussions of Modernism owes more to scholarly parochialism than to a lack of substantive aesthetic affiliations between Black and White artists in the Modernist period.

To the extent that Modernism's diverse aesthetic strains can be reduced to a single defining practice, Ezra Pound's famous dictum "Make it new" serves as well as any. Since Modernism's most prominent writers were Europeans and Americans in conversation with European traditions, Black writers and critics initially found little to value in its promotion of works that were difficult, highly learned, experimental, and abstract. Many White Modernists explored and lamented what they considered the decay of Western civilization—depicting "the modern" as fragmentary, alienating, urban, and materialistic—and offered the purities of art for art's sake (*l'art pour l'art*) as a remedy for a civilization that had reduced people to machinelike consumers and severed their ties with tradition, offering them only advertisements, mass-produced goods, and world war in return. The "Lost Generation" (a term attributed to Gertrude Stein), as the White American Modernists were known, sought to find themselves in art.

Though scholars have more often than not considered African American literature of the period *in contrast* to Modernism, they have found many connections between African American visuals arts and Modernism. Modernist abstraction's most prominent advocate in the visual arts, Clement Greenberg, argued that painting was the abstract medium par excellence, which may in part explain the apparently greater interaction of Modernist ideas and forms with African American cultural production—in the reduction of the human form to the silhouette, for example, in the work of Aaron Douglas, who was part of the **Harlem Renaissance**. The Modernist vogue for the "primitive"—a term of condescension—led many notable European painters and sculptors to draw on African or pseudo-African forms, lending these a kind of cultural legitimacy that Black artists were able to reappropriate as "folk" art forms. The faith that art offered a kind of secular salvation and an interest in folk, or untutored, art forms were significant points of commonality between White Modernists and those African American artists associated with the Harlem Renaissance: both groups believed in the salvific power of art, and both looked for inspiration to folk art, the supposedly greater authenticity of which distinguished it from the culture of mass production. Still, by paying little or no attention to Black artists of the period, the majority of Modernist critics have lent credence to the view that Modernism had nothing to do with African Americans.

The first work of African American literature widely understood to exhibit Modernist sensibilities is **Jean Toomer**'s *Cane* (1923), which catapulted Toomer, briefly, to the forefront of Black letters. Defying generic classification, *Cane* consists of poetry, short stories, and one dramatic piece that are unified through common themes, such as the rootedness of Black folk life in the rural South; the black migration to Northern cities such as **Washington, D.C.**, and **Chicago, Illinois**; and the rise of a Black middle class alienated from its rural Southern roots. The loss of tradition and religion as guiding lights animates much Modernist work, as it does *Cane*, but Toomer soon sought a remedy to this loss not in art but in the mysticism of the Russian George Gurdjieff, with whom the Modernist writer Katherine Mansfield was also associated. Toomer also rejected the notion that he was a "Negro" artist, insisting instead that he was racially "American." Neither Toomer's later mysticism nor his refusal to identify himself as **Negro** endeared him to critics. His personal involvement in Black letters was thus short-lived, but *Cane*'s influence on a generation of African American writers was immediate and profound.

Inspired by the publication of *Cane*, the Harlem Renaissance's inventor was, in a sense, the philosopher **Alain Locke**, who edited the groundbreaking anthology *The New Negro* (1925). In his foreword to that volume, Locke urged that "the **New Negro** must be seen in the perspective of a New World, and especially of a New America" (xxv). In his focus on the "new" and his faith in artists as a redeeming avant-garde, Locke exemplified major Modernist values. He highlighted the value he placed on the arts by foregrounding the work of creative writers and cultural commentators in the book's first and longer section, which was followed by a section of sociological works. "In art and letters, instead of being wholly caricatured," Locke wrote, the New Negro "is being seriously portrayed and painted" (9). Locke has since been criticized by some for his allegedly naïve faith in art's ability to transform society, but he was joined in this faith by many of the foremost thinkers of his day.

Present, too, in Locke's formulations is the value of folk culture. In introducing *The New Negro*, Locke wrote that "in the very heart of the folk-spirit are the essential forces" (xxv). Locke's validation of Black folk culture may at first glance seem surprising in so highly cultured and Europeanized a figure. On the contrary, though, folk forms constitute African America's most important and, indeed, quintessentially Modernist contribution to the cultural productions of the first half of the twentieth century. One need think only of the centrality of **jazz**—the originators of which were unschooled in the traditional sense—to what F. Scott Fitzgerald would label the Jazz Age, the 1920s, to begin to appreciate how integral African American folk culture was to the transatlantic movement we now call Modernism. As **Ralph Ellison** so aptly remarked, jazz is by definition both derivative from a folk tradition and dramatically new with each performance. Its artists remain for the most part local heroes, and it "finds its very life in an endless improvisation upon traditional materials" (*Shadow*, 234). Only recently have critics seriously begun to ask why "the Jazz Age" conjures images of White expatriate artists in Paris or Berlin but not of African American artists in **Harlem, New York**, or Kansas City, Missouri. (*See* **Johnson, James P[rice]**.)

Jazz and the other folk forms associated with Africans and African Americans were romantically understood by many white Modernists to be atavistic. For Euro-Americans disillusioned with modernity's sordid commercialization and cold mass production, the folk or "primitive" forms of Africa and African America offered what they, heirs of Jean-Jacques Rousseau, understood as noble authenticity and warm sensuousness. Thus, primitivism constitutes a major strain of Modernism. As such, it acted as a double-edged sword for those African American artists who worked under its aegis. On one hand, thanks to their association with the "primitivist" works of august European visual artists such as Man Ray and Pablo Picasso, "primitive" or folk forms were granted legitimacy as high art. On the other hand, such forms had the potential to consign African Americans to a lower stratum of humanity and facilitated Whites' condescension toward Black creativity. Today, the notions of African primitivity expressed in such works of Euro-American Modernism as Sigmund

Freud's treatise on theoretical psychology, *Totem and Taboo* (1918), and Eugene O'Neill's play *The Emperor Jones* (1921) are likely to strike readers as decidedly antique, even though they were part and parcel of the same trends that produced the Cubist cornerstone of Modernism, Picasso's *Demoiselles d'Avignon* (1907), as well as African American works such as Aaron Douglas's elegant illustrations for *The New Negro*; Richmond Barthé's astonishing sculpture *Feral Benga* (1935); and **Zora Neale Hurston**'s detailed ethnography of **Haiti**, *Tell My Horse* (1938).

In fact, the paintings of William H. Johnson and **Jacob Lawrence**—arguably the most significant African American visual art of the period—clearly draw on one variety of "folk" style, the faux-naïf, or "false naïve," so called because its practitioner is in fact an educated painter. Johnson spent much of the Harlem Renaissance abroad, studying from 1926 to 1929 in **Paris, France**. When he returned to Harlem, he encountered the work of Lawrence and developed, in Richard J. Powell's words, his "own distillation of European Post-Impressionism and African American folk culture" (Hayward Gallery, 92). His faux-naïf style is simple and apparently untutored, used to depict modern, urban scenes. Thus, while the style is folk, the Harlem depicted is one of rich and confusing urban immixture. As Paul Gilroy writes: "The city's growth created new Harlemites not only from the West Indies but from the South and other rural areas. That rich and volatile mixture yielded no pure, seamless, or spontaneous articulation of black America's world-historic, national spirit" (Hayward Gallery, 107). Johnson's work attempts to extract aesthetic order from Harlem's discontinuities. The faux-naïf style, in particular, offered Johnson a strategy for doing so, since it was not only amenable to depicting the lives of rural people newly urbanized but was also available as a respected, modern, European aesthetic.

Among the most interesting African Americans' commentaries on Modernism is **Richard Wright**'s reaction to Gertrude Stein's "Melanctha," the central story in her novel *Three Lives* (1909). The critic and poet Judy Grahn remarks that Stein's technique in this story centers the **mulatto** main character, Melanctha, in her own language rather than subordinating her Black dialect to the Standard English of a "superior" narrator (142–144). After Wright discovered Stein's novel, which he immediately admired, he was surprised to see her technique denounced by a Marxist critic as decadent. To test the validity of his own admiration of Stein's experimental technique, Wright read the story aloud to a group of "semi-literate Negro workers" in Chicago (Grahn, 144). The dockworkers responded enthusiastically to Stein's story, and Wright concluded that "the prose of Stein is but the repetitive contemporaneousness of our living speech woven into a grammarless form of narrative." Embracing Stein's "grammarless form," Grahn suggests, Wright found in Stein a powerful legitimation of Black speech's literary—and Modernist—authenticity. Stein's interest in the phenomenology of character clearly attracted Wright, who devoured the philosophical works of Sören Kierkegaard, Friedrich Nietzsche, and Edmund Husserl only to conclude that these giants of modern European philosophy taught him nothing that his experience as a Black American had not: that the individual is both formed by and alienated from community, that the "truer" perspective is the outsider's, that alienation is the norm rather than the exception; in short, that the modern condition is one of inescapable contradiction. Wright thus claimed African American experience as central to modernity, a position that many commentators since have promoted.

Despite Wright's immersion in the works and milieus of the Modernists, it was not until the arrival of **Ralph Ellison** that Black letters would find its greatest advocate and practitioner of Modernist values. In the essays collected in *Shadow and Act* (1964), Ellison claimed all of European literature for the African American writer, noting that whereas artists cannot choose their biological heritage, they can and do choose their artistic heritage. His 1952 novel *Invisible Man* exemplified Ellison's claims. Drawing at once on the most "advanced" Modernist themes, such as alienation, and on traditional folk material, the novel displays a dazzling, encyclopedic knowledge of Western culture, not to mention a formal elegance of language and plot that few other novels can match. Ellison's judgment of Hemingway, however, illustrates his critical stance toward Modernism. Though Hemingway exerted a strong influence on Ellison, Ellison argued that Hemingway's work was so emotionally and formally detached that it "conditions the reader to accept the less worthy values of society" (*Shadow*, 40). Ellison demanded that literature achieve exacting formal standards but also that it assume ethical responsibility. It was Ellison's view that too much Modernist literature abdicated its social responsibility in favor of an amoral formal experimentation. For Ellison, there was no contradiction in asserting "that the work of art is important in itself, that it is a social action in itself" (137).

Resources: Houston Baker, *Turning South Again: Re-thinking Modernism/Re-reading Booker T.* (Durham, NC: Duke University Press, 2001); Ralph Ellison: *Invisible Man* (New York: Random House, 1952); *Shadow and Act* (New York: Random House, 1964); Paul Gilroy, *The Black Atlantic: Modernity and Double Consciousness* (Cambridge, MA: Harvard University Press, 1993); Judy Grahn, *Really Reading Gertrude Stein* (Freedom, CA: Crossing Press, 1989); Hayward Gallery, *Rhapsodies in Black: Art of the Harlem Renaissance* (Berkeley: University of California Press, 1997); George Hutchinson, *The Harlem Renaissance in Black and White* (London: Oxford University Press, 1996); David Levering Lewis, *When Harlem Was in Vogue* (New York: Penguin, 1997); Alain Locke, ed., *The New Negro* (1925; repr. New York: Atheneum, 1992); Hans Ostrom: "The Ways of White Folks, Hughes, and Modernism," in his *Langston Hughes: A Study of the Short Fiction* (New York: Twayne, 1993), 5–8; "Modernism and Hughes," in his *A Langston Hughes Encyclopedia* (Westport, CT: Greenwood Press, 2002), 250–253; Jean Toomer, *Cane* (1923; repr. New York: Norton, 1988).

Douglas Steward

Mojo. A charm, amulet, or spell related to "hoodoo" or "**voodoo**"; traditional magical practices (*see also* **Conjuring**). The word is believed to be derived from the Yoruba word *mojuba* (I salute), used in prayers of supplication

(Major, 306). The term has been absorbed into mainstream culture, as can be seen in the name of a popular British **jazz** magazine, a trademarked cookie, and a tag phrase in the Austin Powers spy-spoof movies. It entered the **vernacular** by way of **blues** songs like "I got my mojo working," written by Preston Foster, performed in the 1950s by Ann Cole, and recorded as a signature hit song by Muddy Waters. In it the lover complains that even though he has his "mojo working," his girl does not return his feelings, and so he plans to go to Louisiana to get a "mojo hand." According to traditional **folklore**, this "mojo hand" is a charm bag, much like "fetish bags" in Native American cultures, containing a variety of ingredients designed to bring about specific results. So when a blues singer refers to a "mojo hand," he is alluding to a bag of hoodoo charms.

While double entendres undeniably are implied in "Take Your Hands Off My Mojo," recorded in 1932 by Leola B. Wilson and Wesley Wilson, the title refers primarily to the practice of stealing another's mojo bag in order to counteract a love spell. References to concealing one's mojo hand abound in blues songs of the 1920s and 1930s, most notably "Scarey Day Blues," recorded by, among others, Blind Willie McTell, which begins with the line "My good gal got a mojo, she's tryin' to keep it hid." One of the most frequently used components of such a luck-in-love packet is "John the Conqueror root," variously known as "John the Conqueroo" and "High John de Conquer" (*see* **John the Conqueror**). For example, in Willie Dixon's "Hootchie Cootchie Man," recorded by Muddy Waters for Chess Records in the 1940s and revived by Eric Clapton in the 1970s, the would-be lover has "a mojo" which includes "a John the Conqueror root," which he intends to use to attract women. Another Dixon song, "My John the Conquer Root," also recorded by Waters, refers to the John the Conqueror root, and that his luck "will never fail" when he rubs "my root." The recessed sexual connotations of the root's properties in blues songs were made explicit when Jim Morrison of The Doors sang with furtive intensity, "Mr. Mojo Risin'," imitating, and perhaps paying homage to, Muddy Waters's celebrated refrain "Got my mojo workin'." Moreover, Morrison's incantatory phrase, insofar as it is an anagram of his own name, recalls the immemorial magic of transposition to bring about a transformation.

Muddy Waters's influence on rock music was far-reaching indeed, even providing the Rolling Stones with their name from a song title recorded early in his career. And because he later toured with that band, a new generation of eager listeners was exposed to the blues style of **Chicago, Illinois**, that he did so much to create and promote. Waters is also a link to the past as well, specifically to the older folk music and African traditions and rhythms which he had learned as a child raised among sharecroppers in Rolling Fork, Mississippi. This music, in turn, carried within it remnants of earlier slave songs, replete with references to mojo and hoodoo. In this regard, then, and notwithstanding how the term came to be part of the Anglo-American rock music tradition, mojo continues to mean a mysterious, hidden power which, with the proper charm, can be drawn out to bring one the desired love, luck, or success that is missing in his life. **Nalo Hopkinson** published a volume titled *Mojo: Conjure Stories* (2003), and **Arthur Rickydoc Flowers** has written *Mojo Rising: Confessions of a 21st Century Conjureman* (2001).

Resources: Yvonne P. Chireau, *Black Magic: Religion and the African American Conjuring Tradition* (Berkeley: University of California Press, 2003); David Dalton, *Mr. Mojo Risin': Jim Morrison, the Last Holy Fool* (New York: St. Martin's, 1991); Arthur Flowers, *Mojo Rising: Confessions of a 21st Century Conjureman* (New York: Wanganegresse Press, 2001); James George Frazer, *The Golden Bough* (Oxford: Oxford University Press, 1998); Nalo Hopkinson, *Mojo: Conjure Stories* (New York: Warner Books, 2003); Harry Hyatt, *Hoodoo-Conjuration-Witchcraft-Rootwork*, 4 vols. (Hannibal, MO: Western Publishing, 1970–1978); Clarence Major, ed. *Juba to Jive: A Dictionary of African-American Slang* (New York: Penguin, 1994); Sandra B. Tooze, *Muddy Waters: The Mojo Man* (Toronto: ECW Press, 1997); Catherine Yronwode, *Hoodoo Herb and Root Magic* (Forestville, CA: Lucky Mojo Curio Co., 2002).

Bill Engel

Monk, Thelonious. *See* **Gillespie, Dizzy, Charlie Parker, and Thelonious Monk.**

Monroe, Mary (born 1951). Novelist and short story writer. As a novelist, Monroe has earned both critical and popular acclaim. She was born on December 12, 1951 in Toxely, Alabama, to Otis and Ocie Mae Nicholson. She married Joseph Monroe on January 19, 1969; they had two daughters, and were divorced in 1973. Monroe's writing career began when she wrote her first short story at age five. As a teen, she wrote short stories for confession magazines such as *Bronze Thrills*. She was later encouraged to write novels by **James Baldwin**, whom she met briefly before he died, and **Toni Morrison**, who encouraged Monroe to develop her own unique voice. Monroe's first novel, *The Upper Room* (1985), is a tale about Mama Ruby, who steals her best friend's baby and flees to Florida. The novel was inspired in part by the Audrey Hepburn film *The Unforgiven* (1960); it exhibits an African American folk style but also includes strange violence. Monroe's novels have an authentic ambiance reminiscent of the works of **Zora Neale Hurston** and an autobiographical undercurrent à la **Maya Angelou**'s *I Know Why the Caged Bird Sings* (1969). *The Upper Room* is filled with captivatingly quirky characters and lush settings that have become a trademark of Monroe's unique style.

Monroe's second novel, *God Don't Like Ugly* (2000), won critical acclaim and remained on the *Essence* best-seller list for six months. *Ugly* is a **coming-of-age** story about a young girl, Annette, who is repeatedly raped by her stepfather. When Annette meets and befriends Rhoda, she finds the strength to end her abuse. *God Don't Like Ugly* was followed by *Gonna Lay Down My Burdens* (2002), a dark **romance novel** whose captivating characters inhabit the reader's imagination with vitality and humor. In 2003, Monroe published *God Still Don't Like Ugly*, which continues the saga of Annette and Rhoda and their troubled friendship. Monroe's most recent novel, *Red Light Wives* (2004), is a rousing tale of six prostitutes and their pimp, Clyde.

Monroe's works frequently explore the nuances of friendship and how compelling events, including romance and murder, help shape and change her characters' relationships to one another. Monroe lives in Oakland, California, where she writes full time.

Resources: Hazel V. Carby, *Reconstructing Womanhood: The Emergence of the Afro-American Woman Novelist* (New York: Oxford University Press, 1987); Anne duCill, *The Coupling Convention: Sex, Text, and Tradition in Black Women's Fiction* (New York: Oxford University Press, 1993); Mary Monroe: *God Don't Like Ugly* (New York: Dafina, 2000); *God Still Don't Like Ugly* (New York: Dafina, 2003); *Gonna Lay Down My Burdens* (New York: Dafina, 2002); *Red Light Wives* (New York; Kensington, 2004); *The Upper Room* (1985; New York: Kensington, 2001).

Debbie Clare Olson

Monteilh, Marissa (born c. 1974). Novelist. A television news reporter and a commercial actress, Marissa Monteilh began hosting relationship seminars in **Los Angeles, California**. She was exposed to so many nuances in the relationships between men and women that she began to consider how she might share her growing appreciation for how emotionally and psychologically complex most romances actually are. Ultimately she decided to write novels in which she could synthesize what she had learned about relationships without being constrained by the details of any one relationship.

Monteilh self-published her first novel, *May December Souls*. The novel's protagonist is a thirty-nine-year-old African American woman named Mariah Pijeaux. The widow of a man who was her soul mate, she is currently involved in a physically exciting but otherwise unsatisfying relationship with a former pro basketball player. Monteilh makes direct use of her experience with relationship seminars when Mariah attends such a seminar and subsequently becomes involved with a twenty-one-year-old pro football player. Despite their age difference, they are emotionally very compatible, sharing, among other things, an inability to come to terms with their fathers. In the end, Mariah finds satisfaction in her professional life as well, restarting a career in broadcasting.

The novel received such good word-of-mouth notices that Monteilh secured contracts with Avon for the rerelease of *May December Souls* and for her next two novels. In a reversal of the use of her own experience in *May December Souls*, Monteilh first wrote *The Chocolate Ship* (2003), about a cruise ship catering *Love Boat* style to African Americans; she then became involved in organizing cruises that have used the novel as a focal point and a selling point.

Monteilh's third novel, *Hot Boyz* (2004), is a family chronicle about the lives of three brothers in a wealthy African American family in Los Angeles. Each of the brothers attempts to find an emotional satisfaction that matches his material prosperity and a kind of family life that satisfies his private yearnings as well as the social expectations that he has been conditioned, to some extent, to accept. The need that each of the brothers feels in his own way is represented in their mother's decline due to Alzheimer's disease.

Resources: Janine Gardner, "Review of *May December Souls*," *Black Issues Book Review* 4 (July/Aug. 2002), 38; Marissa Monteilh: *The Chocolate Ship* (New York: Avon, 2003); *Hot Boyz* (New York: Avon, 2004); *May December Souls* (New York: Avon, 2000); "Review of *May December Souls*," *Kirkus Reviews*, Feb. 1, 2002, pp. 132–133; Glenn Townes, "Review of *The Chocolate Ship*," *Black Issues Book Review* 5 (Jan./Feb. 2003), 35.

Martin Kich

Moody, Anne (born 1940). Autobiographer, short story writer, and political activist. Moody's *Coming of Age in Mississippi* (1968) ranks with **Harriet Jacobs**'s *Incidents in the Life of a Slave Girl* (1861) and **Maya Angelou**'s *I Know Why the Caged Bird Sings* (1969) as a poignant, enduring memoir of growing up African American. Born near Centreville, Mississippi, to sharecropper parents, Fred and Elmira Moody, Moody worked at an early age cleaning houses for White families. After graduating from high school in 1959, Moody attended Natchez Junior College and Tougaloo College. During her college years, she became active in the Congress of Racial Equality (CORE), the Student Non-Violent Coordinating Committee (SNCC), and the National Association for the Advancement of Colored People (**NAACP**). After graduating in 1964, Moody was appointed Cornell University's civil rights project coordinator. In 1967, Moody served as counsel for New York City's poverty program (1975). Today Moody lives a private life in New York City.

Coming of Age in Mississippi, detailing her family's poverty, her problematic relationship with her mother, and her extensive work in the **Civil Rights Movement,** offers a personal look at a culture undergoing radical social change during the 1960s. Outraged by the racially motivated murder of **Emmett Till** (1955), Moody began high school with a determination to fight White cruelty and oppression. As the Civil Rights Movement intensified, Moody participated in a luncheon-counter sit-in at Woolworth's in Jackson, Mississippi (May 1963) and in the 1963 March on Washington, where she heard Dr. **Martin Luther King**'s "I Have a Dream" address. After reflecting on that year's violence, the bombing of the Birmingham church and the murder of **Medgar Evers**, Jr., Moody ends her memoir on a pessimistic note, wondering if the American South will ever accept integration. Along with her pointed criticism of institutionalized racism, Moody censures Black tolerance of it. The **autobiography** won two awards: the Brotherhood Award from the National Council of Christians and Jews and Best Book of the Year Award from the National Library Association. In addition to her memoir, Moody published *Mr. Death: Four Stories* (1975).

Resources: William L. Andrews, "In Search of a Common Identity: The Self and the South in Four Mississippi Autobiographies," *Southern Review* 24, no. 1 (1998), 47–64; Rita B. Dandridge, *Black Women's Blues: A Literary Anthology* (New York: G. K. Hall,

1992); Nellie Y. McKay, "The Girls Who Became the Women: Childhood Memories in the Autobiographies of Harriet Jacobs, Mary Church Terrell, and Anne Moody," in *Tradition and the Talents of Women*, ed. Florence Howe (Urbana: University of Illinois Press, 1991), 106–124; Anne Moody: *Coming of Age in Mississippi* (New York: Dial, 1968); *Mr. Death: Four Stories* (New York: Harper & Row, 1975); Emmanuel S. Nelson, "Anne Moody," in *African American Autobiographers: A Sourcebook*, ed. Nelson (Westport, CT: Greenwood Press, 2002), 280–285.

Cheryl D. Bohde

Moore, Charles Michael (1948–2003). Playwright, director, and actor. Moore was an acclaimed playwright whose work dramatized a wide range of topics and conflicts. Born in Ypsilanti, Michigan, he graduated from Northwestern High School in Flint, Michigan, in 1966. After graduation, he enlisted in the U.S. Marines and served in the **Vietnam War**. After his three-year obligation, he was honorably discharged and enrolled in the University of Michigan at Flint. Always interested in theater and community, Moore became active in the McCree Theater in Flint and eventually became its first drama director in 1974. That same year, Moore won the Hopwood Award for Creative Writing from the University of Michigan for his play *One Nickel on This Wine*.

Moore continued his writing, winning the American College Theater Festival Playwriting Award for his play *And That's The Way It Was, Walter*. He eventually served as the Artistic Director of the McCree Theater between extended visits to New York. Moore moved to **Chicago, Illinois**, in mid-1970 and began a relationship with several theaters as a writer and director. He wrote plays performed at the Kuumba Workshop, the Lamont Zeno Theater, the Chicago Theater Company, Congo Square, and the eta Creative Arts Foundation, where he served as artist-in-residence for many years. This theater became an artistic base for Moore, and eta presented a number of his works, which he often directed. These works include *The Hooch*, his play about Black soldiers and the Vietnam conflict in 1986 and 1998, *Love's Light in Flight* in 1987 and 1989, and *SAY-RAH*, a play concerning the life of Madame C. J. Walker, an entrepreneur connected to the Harlem Renaissance. For *SAY-RAH*, he received two Joseph Jefferson nominations. Other works include *Tatum Family Blues* and *Father and Son Night*. Moore originated the role of the blind man in the Chicago Black Ensemble's *Muddy Waters: The Hoochie Coochie Man*, the story of the **blues** artist, and he received the Black Theater Alliance Award for Best Actor for that role in 1996. He worked with the Mexican Fine Arts Center Museum and traveled to Vera Cruz, Mexico, to explore the Afro-Mestizo culture and heritage in 1997. Moore also worked as an artist in public schools through the Urban Gateway programs in Chicago. He appeared in the films *One Week* and *Love Relations*, and acted in Congo Square's production of *The Piano Lesson*. He died of a heart attack. Moore was inducted posthumously into the Hall of Fame of Literary Writers at the **Gwendolyn Brooks** Center at Chicago State University on October 30, 2003. (*See* **Drama**.)

Resources: *Charles Michael Moore Memorial Program* (Chicago: Chicago State University, 2003) (anonymously written program for a memorial service); Woodie

King, Jr., ed., *The National Black Drama Anthology* (New York: Applause Books, 1995); Robert Simonson, "Playwright, Actor and Director, Charles Michael Moore Is Dead at 54," *Playbill*, Sept. 30, 2003, http://www.web.playbill.com/news/article/81905.html.

Joan F. McCarty

Moore, Jessica Care (born 1971). Poet, singer-songwriter, and publisher. Moore's mother was originally from the United Kingdom, and her father, from Alabama. Moore grew up in **Detroit, Michigan**, where she established credentials as a contributor to both print publications and television productions. She then relocated to **Brooklyn, New York**, where she founded Moore Black Press, publishing her own work as well as that of such authors as Sharrif Simmons and Saul Williams. More recently, she has resided in **Harlem, New York**, and in **Atlanta, Georgia**. She has traveled widely throughout the United States and Europe to perform as a singer and a poet.

In addition to her literary pursuits, Moore has performed as a singer-songwriter, most often with a rock/**hip-hop** band called Detroit Read. In fact, it is somewhat difficult to separate Moore's development as a musical performer and lyricist from her development as a "spoken-word" or **"performance" poet**. She won the *Showtime at the Apollo* competition for five consecutive weeks, and she has made featured appearances on the HBO series *Russell Simmons Presents: Def Poetry Jam*. (*See* **Simmons, Russell**.)

Moore's collections of poems have included *The Words Don't Fit in My Mouth* (1997) and *The Alphabet versus the Ghetto* (2002). Unlike many spoken-word poems, Moore's stand up well on the page. Her sense of line and stanza is often superb. The poems contain much wit, irony, and wry observation, and they thereby avoid triteness in image, wordplay, and theme. Typically, they synthesize references to familiar locations, characters, and tableaux within the urban milieu and display an energetic resourcefulness with colloquial language. Although Moore is clearly a **feminist** and a political progressive, her poems are more energized than overwhelmed by her sense of cause.

Moore has written one-woman stage plays in which she has performed. These have included *There Are No Asylums for the Real Crazy Women*, in which she portrays the decline into madness of T. S. Eliot's wife, Vivienne; *Alpha Phobia*, in which she portrays a poet who begins to believe that the alphabet is trying to kill her; *Born to Sing Mama 3*; and *The Revolutions in the Ladies Room*. She has also performed in films, playing one of the leads in the independent film *His/Herstory*.

A selection of Moore' work has been chosen for inclusion in **Kevin Powell's** *Step into a World: A Global Anthology of the New Black Literature* (2000), as well as in the anthologies *Abandon Automobile* (2001), *Bum Rush the Page: A Def Poetry Jam* (2001), *Listen Up!* (1999), and *Role Call* (2002). Her poems and other work have appeared in such periodicals as *African Voices, BE, Blaze, Bomb, Essence, Good News*, the *Metro Times, Mosaic*, the *New York Times, Rap Pages, Savoy, Source, Stress Source*, and *Vibe*.

Resources: Winston Majette, "Jessica Moore and AIDS," *New York Amsterdam News*, Sept. 7, 1996, p. 23; Michael Marriott, "From Rap's Rhythms, a Retooling of Poetry," *New York Times*, Sept. 29, 1996, p. 1; Carrie Mason-Draffen, "Jessica Care Moore," *Essence* 31 (Oct. 2000), 104–106; Jessica Care Moore: *The Alphabet versus the Ghetto* (New York: Moore Black Press, 2002); *The Words Don't Fit in My Mouth* (New York: Moore Black Press, 1997); Gwendolyn Osborne, "Moore Black Press," *Black Issues Book Review* 3 (May/June 2001), 39; "Publishers Briefly: Moore Black Press," *Publishers Weekly*, May 1, 2000, p. 17; Yusef Salaam, "Spoken Word Message—Gotta Have Park," *New York Amsterdam News*, Aug. 19, 1999, p. 31.

Martin Kich

Moore, Lenard D. (born 1958). Poet, community activist, literary critic, and teacher. Born in Jacksonville, North Carolina, as a child Lenard D. Moore loved to listen to his grandfather tell stories, and was encouraged in his literary aspirations by both parents. Captivated by language from his earliest years, Moore wrote poems and stories in high school. While in the U.S. Army (1978–1981), he wrote and sent poems to his future wife, Lynn, with whom he had a daughter, Maiisha, also a published poet. Moore received a B.A. from Shaw University and an M.A. from North Carolina A&T State University. Since they first met in 1993, **Jerry W. Ward, Jr.**, has encouraged Moore as a poet. **Eugene B. Redmond** has been another important mentor.

In 1992, Moore founded and became the Executive Director of the Carolina African American Writers' Collective (CAAWC). The group was formed because of the experiences of its early members (including Beverly Fields Burnette and Janice W. Hodges), who felt alienated and misunderstood in predominantly White writing workshops. The CAAWC was designed to provide an empathetic and supportive environment for African American writers, based on Moore's belief that "any ethnic group would have some things that are culturally specific to their community which might be reflected in the structure and function of the literary and cultural organizations" (Laryea). Under Moore's directorship, many CAAWC members—such as Evie Shockley, L. Teresa Church, Gina Streaty, Patricia A. Johnson, and Mendi Lewis Obadike—have amassed an impressive array of publications and awards.

Moore's gifts as a poet draw heavily on his rural upbringing, focusing on **nature** as a dominant theme. His use of Japanese forms has helped to open conceptions of what African American poetry consists of by drawing correspondences between two seemingly disparate cultures. His tanka and **haiku**, which meld African American imagery and experience with the classical Japanese forms, characteristically stress verbal compression, appreciation for nature, and the importance of familiar detail and vivid imagery. Moore's level of achievement in these forms has earned him the Haiku Museum of Tokyo Award (1983, 1994, 2003), the only African American to be so honored. Other awards include two Pushcart Prize nominations, a Cave Canem fellowship (1998–2000), the Margaret Walker Creative Writing Award (1997), and the Shaw University Alumni Achievement Award (2000). Moore has written three poetry collections: *The Open Eye* (1985), *Forever Home* (1992), and *Desert Storm: A Brief History* (1993). He and Eugene B. Redmond also collaborated on a chapbook of poems and photos about the Million Man March, *Gathering at the Crossroads* (2003). His poetry and critical writings have appeared in numerous anthologies and magazines, including *Agni*, *African American Review*, *Callaloo*, and *The Norton Haiku Anthology*. Moore currently teaches at Shaw University.

Resources: Guy Davenport, "Lenard Moore," in *The Hunter Gracchus and Other Papers on Literature and Art* (Washington, DC: Counterpoint, 1996), 176–179; Doris Lucas Laryea, "The Open Eye of Lenard Duane Moore: An Interview," *Obsidian II: Black Literature in Review* 11, no. 1&2 (1996), 159–184; Lenard D. Moore: *Desert Storm: A Brief History* (San Diego: Los Hombres Press, 1993); *Forever Home* (Laurinburg: St. Andrews College Press, 1992); *The Open Eye* (Raleigh: North Carolina Haiku Society Press, 1985); Lenard D. Moore and Eugene B. Redmond, *Gathering at the Crossroads* (Winchester, VA: Red Moon Press, 2003); Lauri Ramey, "Report from Part I: The Carolina African American Writers' Collective," *BMa: The Sonia Sanchez Literary Review* 5, no. 1 (1999), 5–24.

Lauri Ramey

Moore, Opal (born 1953). Poet, fiction writer, and critic of **children's literature**. After receiving her M.A. and M.F.A. from the University of Iowa, Moore moved to Richmond, Virginia, where she became part of a group of women scholars, The Wintergreen Women, who recognized the need for women to form supportive communities around creativity in writing. She joined the English Department faculty at Spelman College in 1997. She admits that she had become discouraged as a writer; however, the women-centered environment of Spelman gave her new insight to write, and clarified her work's focus on women's lives. Her interest in the vulnerability versus capability of women is reflected in her collection of poetry, *Lot's Daughters*.

At this writing, Moore is working on a new collection of poems, *Children of the Middle Passage*, in conjunction with portraits of disappeared children created by Dr. Arturo Lindsay of Spelman's Art Department. Moore noted that writing creatively points out what you do not know. Visiting the Door of No Return in West Africa gave Moore emotional input for her poems. She was able to get a more concrete sense of what going into **slavery** may have been like for sons and daughters of Africa. Moore, inspired by her visit to a women's museum in Senegal, found a poster that told the story of a community of women who sacrificed themselves by setting their houses on fire. Their mass suicide, the purpose of which was to avoid going into slavery, was for Moore an example of women not submitting to oppression. One child, who is selected not to die, must pass the story on to the men once they return home. Moore's poem "A Lullaby for the Children of the Ship" depicts the mother of the middle passage children as their country, Africa. Moore's lullaby is for those children who never belonged to anyone, and whose feet never touched the ground.

Resource: Opal Moore, *Lot's Daughters* (Chicago: Third World Press, 2003).

Kelli Randall

Morrison, Toni (born 1931). Novelist, nonfiction writer, editor, and professor. Born Chloe Anthony Wofford in Lorain, Ohio, Morrison took the risk of abandoning a successful career in publishing to become a full-time novelist. It was a risk that paid off. She has become the most prominent American novelist of her time, and she won the Nobel Prize for Literature in 1993. She is the first African American to earn this prestigious award. She is also the recipient of the National Book Critics' Circle Award for *Song of Solomon* (1977) and the Pulitzer Prize for *Beloved* (1987), two novels that have become contemporary classics. She has been Robert F. Goheen Professor at Princeton University since 1988.

Morrison studied literature at Howard University, then earned an M.A. at Cornell University in 1955. She taught English at Texas Southern University for the next two years, then returned to teach at Howard, where she met and married a Jamaican architect named Harold Morrison. The marriage produced two sons but only lasted a few years. In 1964 she left her teaching post and divorced her husband. The recurrence of the subject of motherhood and the motif of flight in Morrison's work are arguably connected to this period of her life.

Morrison began as a textbook editor for Random House in New York City and soon became a senior editor there while beginning work on her first novel, *The Bluest Eye* (1970). Part of her legacy at Random House was to bring into prominence the writings of African American writers, notably **Toni Cade Bambara** and **Angela Y. Davis**, and her 1992 book, *Playing in the Dark: Whiteness and the Literary Imagination*, details her reflections on the "validity or vulnerability of a certain set of assumptions conventionally accepted among literary historians and critics and circulated as 'knowledge.' This knowledge holds that traditional, canonical American literature is free of, uninformed, and unshaped by the four-hundred-year-old presence of, first, Africans and then African-Americans in the United States" (*Playing*, 4–5). To say nothing of Morrison's influence on other writers, the power of her fiction alone has gone a long way toward reshaping the American **literary canon** as well as deepening the meaning of historical memory as it affects fiction. She began her Nobel Prize lecture with the following belief: "Narrative has never been merely entertainment for me. It is, I believe, one of the principal ways in which we absorb knowledge" (Nobel, 7). The knowledge one absorbs through Morrison's fiction is often unpleasant and frequently disturbing, but that is precisely her strength: to illuminate the darkest corners of personal and cultural history and to demonstrate how such illumination can lead to catharsis and growth.

Morrison's first novel, *The Bluest Eye*, begins with a meditation on infertility, on marigold seeds that will not grow, and on a perversion of fertility: the character Pecola Breedlove is carrying her father's child. The structure of the novel is based on the four seasons, beginning in the dying season of autumn and ending in summer, the season of ripeness. The novel's structure would seem to imply a cycle, but there is little hope for rebirth. Pecola is powerless to preserve her innocence or to shelter herself from violence; a character named Junior kills a cat and blames it on Pecola, and her father rapes her. These are not the only instances of physical or emotional abuse in the novel: a lodger named Mr. Henry molests Freida, the narrator Claudia's sister, for instance, and the schoolchildren are constantly taunting each other. In many ways the novel traces the difficult journey from innocence into something more evil than mere experience. Young girls who cannot correctly pronounce "menstruating," let alone cope with its meaning, are sexually initiated by older men.

The stark change from a child's sensibility to an adult's is signaled by the repeated quotation of the language of a childhood primer in which Dick and Jane laugh and play in their perfect suburban existence with the love and support of their parents. The language of the Dick and Jane primer runs throughout the novel, and Morrison crushes the words together to show how the rote memorization of such books can embed their messages into the minds of those who read them. In this case, a model of perfection provides a stark contrast to the disturbing events of the novel, and Pecola's desire for blue eyes is linked to a specifically White form of beauty. The irony of the novel is that Pecola, deranged or perhaps insane, believes she has the bluest eyes of all at the end of the novel even though she has been cast out by her entire society. Young Black girls pay a terrible price for their loss of innocence in the novel, but Pecola is too damaged to realize that she has paid the price.

Critics have viewed Pecola as a scapegoat or a victim of the troubled consciousness of her community. Philip Page believes that the narrator, Claudia, is aware of how she and the rest of the community have used Pecola: "Claudia realizes that she and everyone else defined themselves by scapegoating Pecola, the other" (58). Although readers will likely not be sympathetic to Pecola's father, Cholly, we are given access to the events from the past that turned him into the sexual predator he becomes. He turns his tragic experience outward, victimizing his daughter to alleviate some of his own suffering.

The members of the community in Morrison's second novel, *Sula* (1973), also need an outlet for their anguish, and they pour their troubles into a ritual called National Suicide Day, but they also dump their anguish onto the title character, Sula Peace. If innocence is stolen in *The Bluest Eye*, then it is outright murdered in *Sula*. Sula's grandmother Eva, for instance, burns her own son alive, and Sula throws young Chicken Little into the river, where he drowns. Just as National Suicide Day is a way for the community to face its fears of death and inadequacy, so these ritual murders are attempts to get rid of these fears.

Though Sula and Pecola are both dumping grounds for their communities, they are not the same type of character: Sula is a brash, defiant woman who follows her own rules and would never dream of being influenced by such a clichéd version of beauty as blue eyes. Sula is the creator of her own story. It is Nel, the less adventurous protagonist of the story, who is in danger of absorbing a dominant worldview; in fact, she tries to alter her nose in pursuit of a White standard of beauty before she meets Sula. The densely packed novel is about the dissolution of Nel's and Sula's relationship, anticipating a theme that recurs in Morrison's fiction: friendships and love relationships are difficult to sustain when one person is a nonconformist and other is a joiner. The residents of the Bottom—the ironic name of the community in *Sula*—are a powerful force because they have been given so little. Yet the residents' tendency to judge Sula and her mother for their sexual promiscuity weakens the community and indirectly leads to their destruction. Strong, independent women like Sula live on as powerful forces in nature: even after her death, Sula's memory continues to haunt Nel and causes her to regret the fact that she rejected her best friend.

The ironic suicide of so many members of the community at the end of *Sula* and the dissolution of the friendship between Sula and Nel both anticipate the themes of Morrison's next novel, *Song of Solomon*. Morrison's emphasis on history becomes even more pronounced in this novel: the context for *Sula* was partially the aftermath of **World War I**; the context for *Song of Solomon* is the struggle of the **Civil Rights Movement** in the 1960s. Yet the novel has often been praised less for its historical context than for its rendering of mythology in a contemporary context. Milkman Dead's quest for selfhood leads him to trace his personal history through a children's playground chant. His quest is to fly, something the suicidal insurance agent Robert Smith fails to do in the novel's opening scene, yet something that Milkman's legendary ancestors were able to do.

Morrison's first two novels contain an implicit critique of **White** standards of beauty and of the hypocritical adherence to conventional morality as a means of ostracizing a member of the community. *Song of Solomon* similarly critiques excessive materialism and selfishness, both espoused by Milkman's parents, Ruth and Macon Dead. Ruth gives Milkman his unwanted name by nursing him too long, and Macon gives Milkman his twisted set of values by encouraging him to "own things. . . . Then you'll own yourself and other people too" (*Song*, 55). Milkman's aunt Pilate and his friend

Toni Morrison, 1977. Courtesy of the Library of Congress.

1123

Guitar attempt, in very different ways, to rescue Milkman from the poisoned atmosphere of his home and to send him on a journey to discover who he is or could become. Guitar represents the political consciousness of the 1950s and early 1960s. Outraged by the murder of **Emmett Till** and by the insensitivity of a White mill owner after his father's death, Guitar seeks to avenge his race by joining a group, called the Seven Days, who are committed to murder a White person for every Black person who dies. He tries to awaken a similar animosity in Milkman, who has lived most of his life in self-gratifying bliss. Milkman cannot accept his friend's race-motivated, murderous rage; he gravitates toward the sensibility of Pilate, who guides him into a personal journey to connect him with his past. Through it all, Milkman's life is threatened by those he loves most: his cousin Hagar and his friend Guitar. "Everybody wants the life of a black man" (*Song*, 222), Guitar tells him, and the novel's ambiguous conclusion indicates that the challenge of forging a meaningful life is worth the risk of losing it.

It is clear that Morrison is challenging the mythology of **folklore** and fairy tales in her first three novels, and in that sense her fourth novel, *Tar Baby* (1981), continues the themes of the first three. Nevertheless, it has received less critical attention than most of her other novels: critics seem unprepared to cope with *Tar Baby*'s blunt critique. Set on a Caribbean island, in Paris, and in the United States, this novel takes on postcolonial themes of domination and oppression with a deep consideration of global marketing as the context for the particular conflicts on the island. In this sense it grows out of the greed and materialism associated with Macon Dead in *Song of Solomon*. Yet here White characters, not just their values, are brought into contact with Black characters. Jadine Childs is a version of Milkman and Pecola, someone who has been removed from the context of her racial background and who has sought a White version of beauty and security. Just as Milkman needs someone like Guitar to lift him out of his complacency, so Jadine needs Son, and although she initially disdains him for representing the opposite of what she considers "civilization," she develops a new consciousness as she grows to love him.

The fact that the relationship between Son and Jadine does not last should not be a surprise, for Morrison's novels nearly all end with separation and loss; yet the protagonists still benefit from the intense love they have felt. Son arrives almost mystically on the island to awaken Jadine; in Morrison's fifth and most celebrated novel, *Beloved*, the title character arrives from beyond the grave to awaken something similar in Sethe. All of her novels up to this time feature characters who do not truly love themselves in the context of their racial and personal history, and Sethe is no exception. She has murdered her daughter in order to save her from a life of **slavery**, and her guilt over this act has caused her to loathe herself, and thus to be paralyzed, or to lead nothing better than a dead life. Beloved comes back from the grave to teach her to love again, and thus to embrace life, which is, as Pilate asserted in *Song of Solomon*, "precious."

Beloved is inspired partially by the true story of Margaret Garner, a slave caught in the process of escaping who murdered one of her children because she believed death preferable to slavery. Sethe has similarly killed the child named Beloved, and part of Morrison's genius in this novel is that she is able to imagine the pain that someone like Margaret Garner must have suffered to arrive at such an awful decision. Sethe was systematically dehumanized, as all slaves were, not only in physical ways—beatings and rape—but also in emotional ways, as she is the subject of a lesson imparted by Schoolteacher, a pseudoscientist who uses Sethe's body to argue for the inferiority of African Americans. Her murdering Beloved cannot be completely forgiven, but it can be better understood through the process of what she calls "rememory"—the attempt to make oneself whole through the reconstruction of the past. Her inability to love her daughter, Denver, or her lover, Paul D., is related to her inability to love herself, or her tendency to blame herself for her awful act without sufficiently blaming the institution of slavery that drove her to it.

Beloved is powerful because of its depth of emotion, but also because Morrison has perfected her oblique method of narration, including a consistent shift in perspective, a disruption of linear chronology, and attention to gaps or unspoken spaces between known events. Her thematic treatment of love, death, and memory is highly developed here, and the relationship between narrative and piecing together the past initiated in *Song of Solomon* is what makes the novel so enduring. One of the final sentences in the novel is "This is not a story to pass on" (*Beloved*, 275), suggesting that stories that are lodged somewhere in personal or historical memory do not die. The novel's tremendous weight and importance are evident throughout, and many critics and literary historians consider it one of the greatest works of American fiction.

The three novels Morrison has published since *Beloved* have gained widespread respect, but not the same degree of critical attention. *Jazz* (1992), like *Sula* and *Beloved*, is situated in history and focuses on a female pariah. All three of these novels involve murder and memory, as well as the haunting presence of the past. The novel is less coherent than *Beloved*; Morrison seeks to challenge the reader in the way that technically advanced jazz music challenges the listener. There are motifs that recur, even a central story line involving Joe, the murdered Dorcas, and the woman named Violet who slashes the face of Dorcas's corpse at her funeral. Some of Morrison's familiar themes are contained in this story line, and the reader is encouraged to understand the intention behind Violet's act of scarification that recalls Sethe's murder of Beloved. More interesting than the novel's bewildering plot, though, is the way its narrator mimics jazz in print, calling to mind again the distinction between an oral or performed history and written or official history.

Morrison's next novel, *Paradise* (1998) is a similar whirlwind of narration whose plot is less fascinating in some ways than the way it is told. Her single published short story, "Recitatif" (1994), demonstrates the division between the two main characters, Twyla and Roberta, who were best friends in school but who grew apart partially because they become increasingly aware of their different racial backgrounds. We know that one character is White and one is Black, but it is never clear which is which. Morrison does something similar in *Paradise*, in which we know that one of the girls at the convent is White—we even know from the first sentence that "They shoot the white girl first." Yet we are never sure which girl is White. The implication in both of these works is that racial discrimination is real and divisive, but also that the relationship between individual identity and racial identity is confusing, regardless of perspective. Morrison also forces the reader to question his or her own racial stereotypes. *Paradise* tells the story of a convent, a place where women can exist free from the pressures of contemporary society, on the margins of an all-Black town in **Oklahoma**. The town of Ruby developed from a town called Haven in the late nineteenth century, the purpose of which was to provide a safe, segregated place for Blacks to flourish as they moved west following **Reconstruction**. The violence that opens the novel and the irony of the title suggest that such notions of exclusion are not the best response to a long history of oppression. Indeed, the founders of Haven are known as the "8-rocks," which sounds like the next step after the Seven Days, the racially motivated revenge killers in *Song of Solomon*.

The title of Morrison's most recent novel, *Love* (2003), is every bit as ironic as *Paradise*. At the very least, Morrison is trying to get her readers to reassess the meaning of notions such as love and paradise, which are too often confused with pleasantry. Love can be a violent force in Morrison's fiction, and it has the power to kill. This novel is another attempt to come to terms with the destructive or murderous passion that is part of love. Many of the motifs of this novel are familiar to Morrison's readers. At the novel's center is Bill Cosey, a wealthy patriarch who returns as a ghost to Junior and as a memory to Christine and Heed. These three women live in the same house, yet it is no convent, as in *Paradise*. Much animosity and jealousy center on the disputed fact of Bill Cosey's will, and we learn deep into the novel of Cosey's pedophilia, recalling Cholly Breedlove's rape of Pecola in *The Bluest Eye* and Ruth's nursing of Milkman in *Song of Solomon*: this type of love is selfish and destructive, and we see the gang rape in *Love* as well as Junior's perverse seductions of the young Romen in the same light. Sex in this world is too often an act of power and not often enough an act of love. As usual, Morrison challenges her readers to think of what growth might be possible in such a barren landscape.

Morrison's landscapes are the product of a superb literary imagination focused intently on the legacy of post–**Civil War** history. And yet it would be reductive to regard her writing as historical or realistic fiction. Her novels are often fantastic, steeped in a rich knowledge of folklore and mythology, and her meaning is never obvious. More than anything, her command of language and her narrative innovation, no less than her subject matter, have earned Morrison the reputation as an author who will endure the fluctuations of literary history.

Resources: Sture Allén, ed., *Nobel Lectures, Literature 1991–1995* (Singapore: World Scientific Publishing, 1997), 47–53; Patrick Bryce Bjork, *The Novels of Toni Morrison: The Search for Self and Place Within the Community* (New York: Peter Lang, 1992);

Harold Bloom, ed., *Toni Morrison* (Broomall, PA: Chelsea House, 2000); Henry Louis Gates, Jr., and Anthony Appiah, eds., *Toni Morrison: Critical Perspectives Past and Present* (New York: Amistad, 1993); Carol Kolmerten, Stephen M. Ross, and Judith Bryant Wittenberg, eds., *Unflinching Gaze: Morrison and Faulkner Re-envisioned* (Jackson: University Press of Mississippi, 1997); Nellie McKay, comp., *Critical Essays on Toni Morrison* (Boston: G. K. Hall, 1988); Philip Page, *Dangerous Freedom: Fusion and Fragmentation in Toni Morrison's Novels* (Jackson: University Press of Mississippi, 1995); Nancy J. Peterson, ed., *Toni Morrison: Critical and Theoretical Approaches* (Baltimore: Johns Hopkins University Press, 1997); Wilfred D. Samuels and Clenora Hudson-Weems, *Toni Morrison* (Boston: Twayne, 1990); Valerie Smith, ed., *New Essays on Song of Solomon* (Cambridge: Cambridge University Press, 1995); Danille Taylor-Guthrie, ed., *Conversations with Toni Morrison* (Jackson: University Press of Mississippi, 1994).

D. Quentin Miller

Mosley, Walter (born 1952). Novelist. Mosley is an accomplished writer in the **science fiction** and mystery genres. He has also published several works of nonfiction and literary fiction. Mosley has said that he wants to tell the story of the Black man's life in America, using as many literary styles as possible (Wilson, 19). He was born January 12, 1952, in **Los Angeles, California**, to Leroy Mosley, an African American, and Ella Mosley, a Jewish American whose family was from eastern Europe; his parents were not officially married until a few years after his birth, because even though interracial marriage was legal, the couple was not able to receive a marriage license (Wilson, 2). This did not bother them, though, and as Mosley has said, people who were disturbed by his parents' marriage or his own racial identity had no effect on him, since what others thought "didn't have anything to do with me" (Whetstone, 108).

Mosley attended public schools in Los Angeles and was mentored by several excellent teachers. He went east to attend Goddard College, but was more interested in "hitchhiking across the country" than in attending class (Wilson, 7). He dropped out, but later earned a degree in political science from Johnson State University. Throughout the late 1970s and early 1980s, Mosley lived in **Boston, Massachusetts**, and New York City, working as a computer programmer and consultant. When he read *The Color Purple*, by **Alice Walker**, his creativity came to life. He had been an avid reader, but Walker wrote in a style and language that especially reached out to him, and he decided to try to write (Wilson, 7). Bored at work one day, he crafted a sentence—"On hot sticky days in southern Louisiana the fire ants swarmed"—and was pleased enough with the result that he continued with the notion of becoming a writer (Whetstone, 110).

After several years of taking classes in creative writing at City College of the City University of New York, Mosley broke through when his instructor, Frederic Tuten, passed one of Mosley's works to his own agent (Wilson, 7). That manuscript was published shortly thereafter as *Devil in a Blue Dress* (1990), which was nominated for several "best first crime novel" awards

(Wilson, 8). Success came quickly, including words of praise and recognition in 1992 from President Bill Clinton (Whetstone, 110), but Mosley has amusedly reported that during that same time, when a new editorial staff took over at *Callaloo*, he received a rejection letter for a story that he had submitted—and that they had published—a year earlier (Wilson, 8).

The series of detective novels featuring Easy Rawlins, which was launched with *Devil in a Blue Dress*, represents the majority of Mosley's writing, with eight books in the series so far. *Devil in a Blue Dress* was made into a motion picture in 1995. Starring Denzel Washington as Rawlins, the film had limited commercial success but received critical acclaim. In the series, Rawlins is a World War II veteran who lives in Los Angeles. He works as a school maintenance supervisor and also owns several buildings, although that is not widely known. He is seen as someone other African Americans can trust, and he becomes involved in a number of cases as an amateur detective. With each case, Rawlins "confront(s) the ambiguous boundaries between right and wrong," dealing with ethical dilemmas (Knotts, 352). Along with being excellent hard-boiled crime novels, the Rawlins series offers strong, captivating portrayals of postwar Los Angeles.

Mosley has begun two new mystery series, featuring Socrates Fortlow and Fearless Jones. Fortlow is a convict who moves to Los Angeles after serving his time in the Midwest, and sets about living a new life. The tone of this series is more philosophical and less action-oriented, with Fortlow becoming involved in cases to help his new friends and neighbors. Fearless Jones, along with his friend Paris Minton, solves mysteries in another series set in 1950s Los Angeles.

Mosley has produced works of science fiction—*Blue Light* (1998) and *Futureland* (2001)—as well as two works of general fiction. *RL's Dream* (1995), which tells of a friendship between an elderly African American man who once played with Robert Johnson and his young White female neighbor, is steeped in the history of the **blues**, and *The Man in My Basement* (2004) is a work of psychological suspense. Throughout the 1990s, Mosley published a number of stories in various journals and magazines and was nominated for several awards, winning the Shamus Award in 1990 and a Grammy for best liner notes in 2002 (for the complete recordings of Richard Pryor). Mosley has published several works of nonfiction, including a post-9/11 memoir dealing with politics, **race**, and war, and he edited a volume titled *Black Genius*, which included lectures from a series he initiated. Mosley was New York University's Africana Studies Institute's first artist-in-residence, and after that appointment ended, he continued organizing the speaker series (www.waltermosley.com). He also worked with the City University of New York to establish a unique certificate program in publishing (www.waltermosley.com). Mosley's extensive, excellent writing in many fictional genres, as well as his nonfiction works and service to academia, belie his contention that his life is not "very interesting in any kind of major way" (Whetstone, 110). (*See* **Crime and Mystery Fiction**.)

Resources: Primary Sources: Walter Mosley: *Always Outnumbered, Always Outgunned* (New York: Norton, 1998); *Bad Boy Brawly Brown* (Boston: Little, Brown,

2002); *Black Betty* (New York: Norton, 1994); *Blue Light* (Boston: Little, Brown, 1998); *Devil in a Blue Dress* (New York: Norton, 1990), also available on video, dir. Carl Franklin (Columbia/Tristar, 1995); *Fear Itself* (Boston: Little, Brown, 2003); *Fearless Jones* (Boston: Little, Brown, 2001); *Futureland* (New York: Warner Books, 2001); *Gone Fishin'* (Baltimore: Black Classic Press, 1997); *A Little Yellow Dog* (New York: Norton, 1996); *The Man in My Basement* (Boston: Little, Brown, 2004); *RL's Dream* (New York: Norton, 1995); *A Red Death* (New York: Norton, 1991); *Six Easy Pieces* (New York: Atria, 2003); *Walkin' the Dog* (Boston: Little, Brown, 1999); *What Next: A Memoir Toward World Peace* (Baltimore: Black Classic Press, 2003); *White Butterfly* (New York: Norton, 1992); *Workin' on the Chain Gang: Shaking off the Dead Hand of History* (New York: Ballantine, 2000). **Secondary Sources:** Kristina L. Knotts, "Walter Mosley," in *Contemporary African American Novelists*, ed. Emmanuel S. Nelson (Westport, CT: Greenwood Press, 1999), 350–354; *Walter Mosley: Meet Walter*, Time Warner Books, 2003, www.waltermosley.com; Muriel Whetstone, "The Mystery of Walter Mosley," *Ebony*, Dec. 1995, pp. 106–112; Charles E. Wilson, *Walter Mosley: A Critical Companion* (Westport, CT: Greenwood Press, 2003).

Elizabeth Blakesley Lindsay

Moss, Thylias (born 1954). Poet and playwright. The critic Edward B. Germain characterizes Moss's poems as being "rooted in the fourth quarter of the twentieth century, and all of the period's effects are here, its sounds, its materialism, its distrust of logic and government, its agonizing awareness of **race**, femininity, and sexuality." The style of Moss's poetry works to serve the voice of the poetry; thus, she utilizes loosely broken lines and enjambments (Germain, 247). **Akasha Hull** notes that Moss's poetry distrusts cultural norms that predominate in society. These poems suggest that "The only redemption here is the seeing, not the vision (Bloom, 1995, 135).

Born in Cleveland, Ohio, Moss is the only child of Calvin Theodore and Florida Missouri Gaiter Brasier. Her original given name was Thylias Rebecca Brasier. Her parents were from **the South** and established a warm, encouraging environment for her childhood (*Tale of a Blue-Sky Dress*). In 1973 she married John Moss, whom she had met when she was sixteen. Because of her experience with racism at Syracuse University (1971–1973), Moss withdrew from her classes. However, she went on to earn her B.A. from Oberlin College (1981) and her M.A. from the University of New Hampshire (1983). Her awards include the annual Dewar's Profiles Performance Artist Award, a MacArthur fellowship, a Guggenheim fellowship, a Witter Bynner Award, and a Whiting Award (Bloom, 1995, 132). Professor of English at the University of Michigan, she lives in Ann Arbor with her husband and two sons.

In her review of *At Redbones* (1990), Joyce Peseroff notes that Moss blends the sacred and the profane. "Vicious Circles in the Trenches" and "The Eyelid's Struggle" illustrate the tension between the female body and the male nature of organized religion. She focuses on the lives of children, after her difficult childhood at the hands of a bully. Joel Brouwer, reviewing *Last Chance for the Tarzan Holler* (1998), comments on the long lines that Moss uses, sometimes twenty or thirty syllables. Citing "A Shoe in the Road," he notes that her poems begin slowly, picking up steam as they draw in associations and images, especially contemporary issues and identity within social strife. In an interview with **Jerry W. Ward, Jr.**, **Alvin Aubert** suggests Moss is "among those southern writers who treat the life in the south by using details which have not been treated overmuch" (Ervin, 283). This insight confirms Braxton's and McLaughlin's observation that Moss possesses "a freshness of style, sensitivity, and language; a boldness of subject and stance; and a newness of treatment imbued with exciting promise" (198–199).

Moss's contemporaries **Rita Dove** and **Gwendolyn Brooks** cover some of the same ground that one finds in Moss's writing, specifically the effect of the American challenges of racism and sexism as they impact women's lives. Craig Werner suggests that Moss more consciously delves into "the musical mainstream of African-American culture," citing such musical forms as **gospel**, Motown, house, **blues** (see also **Blues Poetry**), **rap**, **reggae**, **jazz**, funk, and **hip-hop** as influencing her poetic rhythms (299).

Resources: Primary Sources: Thylias Moss: At Redbones (Cleveland, OH: Cleveland State University Poetry Center, 1990); The Dolls in the Basement (play produced at New England Theater Conference, 1984); Hosiery Seams on a Bowlegged Woman (Cleveland, OH: Cleveland State University Poetry Center, 1983); I Want to Be (New York: Dial, 1993), children's book; Last Chance for the Tarzan Holler (New York: Persea, 1998); Pyramid of Bone (Charlottesville: University Press of Virginia, 1989); Rainbow Remnants in Rock Bottom Ghetto Sky (New York: Persea, 1991); Small Congregations: New and Selected Poems (Hopewell, NJ: Ecco, 1993); Somewhere Else Right Now (New York: Dial, 1998), children's book; Tale of a Sky-Blue Dress (New York: Bard, 1998), autobiography; Talking to Myself (play produced at Durham, NH, 1984). **Secondary Sources:** Harold Bloom, The American Religion (New York: Simon and Schuster, 1992); Harold Bloom, ed., Contemporary Black American Poets and Dramatists (New York: Chelsea House, 1995); Joanne M. Braxton and Andrée Nicola McLaughlin, eds., Wild Women in the Whirlwind (New Brunswick, NJ: Rutgers University Press, 1990); Joel Brouwer, "Last Chance for the Tarzan Holler: Review," Boston Review (Oct./Nov. 1998), www.bostonreview.net; Hazel Arnett Ervin, ed., African American Literary Criticism, 1773 to 2000 (New York: Twayne, 1999); Edward B. Germain, "MOSS, Thylias (Rebecca)," in Contemporary Women Poets, ed. Pamela L. Shelton (Detroit: St. James, 1998); Joyce Peserof, "Book Review: At Redbones," Ploughshares, Spring 1991, http://www.pshares.org/issues/articlef.cfm?prmArticleID=3089; Eve Silberman, "About Thylias Moss: A Poet of Many Voices and a Spellbinding Delivery," Michigan Today, http://www.umich.edu/newsinfo/MT/95Oct95/mt8095.html; Craig Hansen Werner, Playing the Changes (Urbana: University of Illinois Press, 1994).

Martha Modena Vertreace-Doody

Mossell, Gertrude Bustill (1855–1948). Journalist, nonfiction writer, and political activist. Mossell is best known as a journalist who first gained national attention when she wrote a newspaper column called "The Woman's Department" for the African American newspaper The Freeman, but she was also extremely active in the suffragist movement and in feminist issues generally, with a special interest in African American women's concerns. Her book *The Work of the Afro-American Woman* (1894) urges African American women to pursue careers and otherwise become full participants in the society and economy of the United States. Somewhat ironically, she published the book as "Mrs. N.F. Mossell," using the initials of her husband, Dr. Nathan Francis Mossell, a prominent physician who helped to found the Frederick Douglass Memorial Hospital.

Mossell was born in **Philadelphia, Pennsylvania**, and named Gertrude E. H. Bustill. The Bustills were free Blacks who were Quakers (but later became Presbyterians) and part of a well-established Black middle class in Philadelphia. The famous American singer, actor, athlete, and activist **Paul Robeson** was Mossell's cousin.

Before becoming a journalist, Mossell briefly pursued a teaching career, but journalism seems to have been her true vocation; she wrote for a wide range of both Black and White **newspapers**, including the *Indianapolis Freeman*, the *Philadelphia Echo*, the *Indianapolis World*, *Women's Era*, the *Philadelphia Times*, and the *Philadelphia Inquirer*. She also wrote for the *Ladies' Home Journal*. Mossell urged African American newspaper owners and managers to distribute their product by means of newsboys, in a system similar to that of the Associated Press. Ultimately the idea became a reality with the creation of the Associated Negro Press. The original edition of *The Work of the Afro-America Woman* is considered extremely valuable, valued at $2,500 in 2002 (Juvelis). Photographs of Mossell and her children are in the photography collection of the Center for African American History at Temple University in Philadelphia. (*See* **Feminism/Black Feminism**.)

Resources: Patricia Juvelis, ad for *The Work of the Afro-American Woman*, in online catalogue, http://juvelisbooks.com/fall02-4.html; Mrs. N. F. [Gertrude Bustill] Mossell, *The Work of the Afro-American Woman* (Philadelphia: George S. Ferguson, 1894; repr. New York: Oxford University Press, 1988); Rodger Streitmatter, *Raising Her Voice: African-American Women Journalists Who Changed History* (Lexington: University Press of Kentucky, 1994); Marcia Williams, ed., *In Search of Our Sisters' Garden* (London: X Press, 2003).

Hans Ostrom

Motley, Willard (1909–1965). Novelist. Motley's life, literary fame, and political allegiances became increasingly obscure after the publication of his first novel, *Knock on Any Door* (1947), the immediate success of which briefly made Motley one of the most controversial and best-known African American writers. The book was in its third printing five days after its publication, and remained on the *New York Times* best-seller list for nearly a year. Approximately 350,000 copies of the novel were sold in just two years (Abbott). *Omnibook* and *Look* popularized the novel, and Hollywood star Humphrey Bogart chose it as the basis of the first movie of his independent production company (Abbott). The novel featured an Italian American juvenile delinquent as its protagonist.

It received rave reviews in major literary publications, including as *The Saturday Review*, *Harper's*, and *The New Republic*. Motley was listed as a prominent member of the Chicago "school" of literary naturalism, along with **Richard Wright** and James T. Farrell. In 1949 the magazine *Color* published an article declaring Motley one of "America's Top Negro Authors."

Born in **Chicago, Illinois**, into a middle-class African American family in which he did not feel at ease, Motley completed Englewood High School in 1929 and then traveled throughout the United States, holding a variety of jobs, including working for the Works Progress Administration. He also served time in jail (Fleming, 1978). Before the publication of *Knock on Any Door*, Motley had published short stories and nonfiction in travel and outdoor magazines; one of these was *The Ohio Motorist* (Fleming, 1978). However, Motley also published work in radical periodicals, including the **Chicago Defender** and the short-lived *Hull House Magazine*. *Knock on Any Door* took seven years to write, in part because of Motley's detailed research of slum life in Chicago, and because publishing houses were put off by the length of the novel (the original manuscript totaled 1,951 pages), by its sexual scenes, and by its social realism.

Knock on Any Door charts the increasing corruption of the former altar boy Nick Romano when, because of economic reversals, his parents are forced to move from Denver to a slum in Chicago. As the novel chronicles Nick's transition from innocent youth to criminal and eventually to murderer, Motley documents the failure of social institutions to help him. The critics Robert Fleming and **Clarence Major** have tried to dilute Motley's political commitment and allegiance to the Left and, as Alan Wald suggests, perhaps even to the Communist Party (*see* **Marxism**). Major views Motley as "a conventional writer and a conservative person" (ix). Fleming characterizes Motley as an incarnation of the all-American, Horatio Alger myth of going from "rags to riches." Far from celebrating America as the land of opportunity either in his biography or his fiction, however, Motley describes the gang not as an aberration far removed from American civilization but as the very incarnation of ruthless American values. Tellingly, the only characters willing to help Nick are themselves confined to the margins of American society or are dissatisfied with it: the reformer Grant Holloway and the homosexual Owen, who may represent Motley himself (Wald).

Motley was never able to repeat the commercial and critical success of *Knock on Any Door*. His three subsequent novels were *We Fished All Night* (1951), which concerns the effects of **World War II** on the lives of three Chicagoans; *Let No Man Write My Epitaph* (1958), a sequel to *Knock on Any Door*; and *Let Noon Be Fair* (1966), which concerns the exploitation of a Mexican fishing village by Americans. In the 1950s, Motley moved to Mexico, where he died in 1965.

Resources: Craig S. Abbott, "Versions of a Best-Seller: Motley's *Knock on Any Door*," *Papers of the Bibliographical Society of America* 81 (1987), 175–185; Robert E. Fleming: "Introduction," in *Knock on Any Door* by Willard Motley (De Kalb:

Northern Illinois University Press, 1989); *Willard Motley* (Baston: G. K. Hall, 1998); Clarence Major, "Foreword," in *The Diaries of Willard Motley*, ed. Jerome Klinkowitz (Ames: Iowa State University Press, 1979), vii–x; William J. Maxwell, *New Negro, Old Left: African-American Writing and Communism Between the Wars* (New York: Columbia University Press, 1999); Willard Motley, *Knock on Any Door* (New York: Appleton-Century, 1947); *Let No Man Write My Epitaph* (New York: Random House, 1958); *Let Noon Be Fair: A Novel* (New York: Putnam, 1966); *We Fished All Night* (New York: Appleton-Century-Crofts, 1951); Alan Wald, "American Writers on the Left," in *The Gay and Lesbian Literary Heritage*, ed. Claude J. Summers (New York: Henry Holt, 1995).

Luca Prono

Mowry, Jess (born 1960). Novelist and short story writer. Born in Mississippi, Jess Mowry has lived for most of his life in Oakland, California. For years, he was homeless, living out of a junked bus and earning what money he could by collecting cans to sell to recycling centers. Although he had had no instruction in writing and very limited formal education, Mowry scraped together enough money to buy a secondhand typewriter and began to write stories taken from his experiences on the streets.

Mowry's stories are unusual because they are written not only about young people but also for young people. While dealing directly with many of the grittiest and most heart-rending realities of urban life, the stories open up, rather than assault, their young readers' sensibilities. For his first book, *Rats in the Trees* (1990), a collection of short stories, Mowry received the PEN Oakland Josephine Miles Award. His first novel, *Children of the Night* (1991), received limited attention, but his second, *Way Past Cool* (1992), has become something of a cult classic of young-adult literature. It details with considerable subtlety the attitudes of boys in their early teens whose identities have already been largely defined by the gangs in their neighborhoods. In 2000, it was adapted to film by Adam Davidson.

Mowry's subsequent novels have included *Six out Seven* (1993), *Ghost Train* (1996), and *Babylon Boyz* (1997). The last has come closest to generating the buzz that surrounded *Way Past Cool*. It focuses on three boys in an Oakland neighborhood whose dreams of escape are as necessary as they are improbable. (*See* **San Francisco Bay Area, California**.)

Resources: Jess Mowry: *Babylon Boyz* (New York: Simon and Schuster, 1997); *Ghost Train* (New York: Henry Holt, 1996); *Rats in the Trees* (Santa Barbara, CA: John Daniel, 1990); *Six Out of Seven* (New York: Farrar, Straus, and Giroux, 1993); *Way Past Cool* (New York: Farrar, Straus, and Giroux, 1992); Geoff Nicholson, "Mean Streetz and Lost Boyz," *Washington Post Book World*, Nov. 2, 1993, p. E2; "Wordsmiths: Contemporary Black Male Writers," *Ebony Man*, Nov. 1993, 54–55.

Martin Kich

Mulatto. No longer in standard use due to its derogatory origins and connotations, the term "mulatto" derives from the Spanish and Portuguese *mulatto*, meaning both "a person of mixed race" and "a small mule" (a mule is the sterile offspring of a donkey and a horse). In the United States, "mulatto" originated from the distinct historical context of African American **slavery** and referred to a person with one White and one Black parent, though it came to be used as a term to label anyone of mixed **race**. During the mid-nineteenth century, with frequent miscegenation resulting in a growing mulatto population and slavery in jeopardy as a system to segregate the races, the pseudoscience of eugenics helped support the legal definitions surrounding race by deploying blood quantum laws to determine a person's racial status into subcategories such as "mulatto" (one-half Black blood) "quadroon" (one-quarter) "octoroon" (one-eighth), and so on. Though this "one-drop" rule had been culturally accepted since the beginnings of slavery, it now officially declared anyone with "one drop" of Black blood legally Black.

In the context of these rigid definitions that equated being Black with slavery and being **White** with freedom, a significant population of light-skinned mulattoes posed as Whites in order to escape the confines of slavery. African American **slave narratives** attest to the frequency of this racial "**passing**" of mulattoes, including **William and Ellen Craft**'s *Running a Thousand Miles for Freedom* (1860), which chronicles their escape from slavery by Ellen posing as an invalid White male slave owner and her husband, William, as an attending slave. Hiram Mattison's *Louisa Picquet, the Octoroon: A Tale of Southern Slave Life* (1861) shows how Louisa's status as a mulatto sets her apart from the other slaves, with both negative and positive impacts, but eventually helps in her escape.

Especially popular both before and after the **Civil War** was the figure of the "tragic mulatto" that appeared in sentimental novels written by both White authors and the earliest African American fiction writers. *Clotel* (1853) by **William Wells Brown**, *Our Nig* by **Harriet E. Wilson** (1859), and the recently recovered *The Bondwoman's Narrative* by **Hannah Crafts** (185?) all loosely support the "tragic mulatto" character: a light-skinned mulatto, usually female, who has matured into a refined, educated, and beautiful young woman ignorant of her racial heritage is thrust back into the shadows of slavery as her "tainted" blood is revealed. Her marriage to a dashing White suitor is ruined because of her exposed racial secret and the tragic mulatto is abandoned or dies, often by suicide, at the end of her narrative.

Such domestic melodramas of romance and scandal were consumed by a liberal White audience, mostly women, who were curious to observe the plights of slavery and eager to support the **abolitionist movement** by sympathizing with a mulatto character they could in some ways relate to, because she looked White and was fully functional in a White world. Though recognizing the strategic abolitionist agenda of African American authors who deployed this tragic mulatto character, some critics dismiss such novels as catering to a White audience and ultimately resulting in the reaffirming and exalting of the virtues of Whiteness and femininity, including beauty, piety, chastity, and loyalty, at the expense of rejecting or degrading the Black female body. Others have reclaimed them, alongside such later works as **Frances E. W. Harper**'s *Iola Leroy*

(1892) and **Pauline Elizabeth Hopkins**'s *Contending Forces* (1900), to stress the authors' manipulation of conventional characters and storylines in order to present empowered black female characters inhabiting explicitly public and political spaces during slavery and **Reconstruction**.

The status of the mulatto was especially impacted by the historical 1896 court case of *Plessy v. Ferguson* that supported the "separate but equal" clause to the Constitution and legalized racial segregation. With the color line now legally and spatially drawn, racial segregation forced mixed-race people to choose between "passing" as Whites in order to gain the rights and privileges they would otherwise be denied (often at the cost of being accused of betraying the race) or claiming a Black identity and embracing their racial heritage. Many writers of the **Harlem Renaissance** explicitly revisited the tragic mulatto character in order to reveal the inequalities of legal segregation, paying particular attention to the relationships among **race**, class, **gender**, and sexuality. Both **Walter White**'s *Flight* (1926) and **Jessie Redmon Fauset**'s *Plum Bun* (1929) depict women who eventually return to their African American communities after experiencing life on the other side of the color line. **Countee Cullen**'s poem "Two Who Crossed a Line" (1925) is divided into two sections, "She Crosses" and "He Crosses," to highlight the gendered complexities of racial passing. **Nella Larsen**'s *Passing* (1929) presents a mulatto character who, after daring to cross the color line and marry a White man to better her life, tragically dies at the novel's end. Such texts underscore how African American writers were aware of the consequences for women who trespassed on a patriarchal as well as racist social order. *Passing* also highlights the relationship between racial passing and sexuality in a society where sexual transgressions and lesbianism were considered taboo.

Other works of the Harlem Renaissance that foreground the mulatto figure to reveal the complex practical, economic, and often survivalist reasons for African Americans to choose to pass include **Jean Toomer**'s *Cane* (1923), Nella Larsen's *Quicksand* (1928), and **Langston Hughes**'s play *Mulatto: A Tragedy of the Deep South* (1935). Hughes's short story "Father and Son," which uses the same plot and characters as in *Mulatto*, appeared in his collection *The Ways of White Folks* (1934) (Ostrom, 14–17, 55–57, 92). The story "Passing" also appeared in this collection. The poetry of **Joseph Seamon Cotter, Jr.** ("The Mulatto to His Critics"), Countee Cullen ("Near White"), Langston Hughes ("Mulatto" and "Cross"), **Georgia Douglas Johnson** ("The Octoroon" and "Cosmopolite"), and **Claude McKay** ("The Mulatto" and "Near-White") address similar themes. The frequency of which the mulatto character appeared in African American literature during this era attests to how common passing was for people of mixed race and how writers attempted to reveal the hypocritical and discriminatory racism of Jim Crow segregation through this literary figure.

James Weldon Johnson's *The Autobiography of an Ex-Colored Man* (originally published in 1912 and republished with greater success in 1927) deliberately confuses and challenges the unjust line between a "true" African American identity and an "impostor" white one because though the anonymous narrator confesses that he is a Black man passing in a White world who has "sold [his] birthright for a mess of pottage" (362), the reader is left wondering if this is all part of the narrator's (or Johnson's) "practical joke on society" (274). The "failure" of Johnson's ambivalent narrator is less his own than the failure of society's oversimplified divisions between the two races. The later surrealist plays of **Adrienne Kennedy**, including *Funny House of a Negro* (1962) and *A Movie Star Has to Star in Black and White* (1976) also challenge the fixed and static notions of race that the former mulatto character was trapped between, and instead present more performative aspects of identity that allow for negotiations and fluidities. Though no longer as prevalent a figure in African American literature since desegregation and the gains of the **Civil Rights Movement**, the mulatto character's significance lies in its ability to both reveal the historically changing meaning of race in U.S. history and to show how writers of literature have played a crucial role in its making and unmaking in an effort to challenge racism and other systems of oppression.

Resources: Primary Sources: William Wells Brown, *Clotel; or, The President's Daughter* (New York: Dover, 2004); Charles Chesnutt, *The House Behind the Cedars* (Athens: University of Georgia Press, 1988); William and Ellen Craft, *Running a Thousand Miles for Freedom* (Athens: University of Georgia Press, 1999); Hannah Crafts, *The Bondwoman's Narrative*, ed. Henry Louis Gates, Jr. (New York: Warner Books, 2002); Jessie Fauset, *Plum Bun: A Novel Without a Moral* (Boston: Pandora Press, 1985); Frances E. W. Harper, *Iola Leroy; or, Shadows Uplifted* (Boston: Beacon Press, 1987); Pauline Hopkins, *Contending Forces* (New York: Oxford University Press, 1988); Langston Hughes: *Five Plays* (Bloomington: Indiana University Press, 1963); *The Ways of White Folks* (New York: Knopf, 1934); James Weldon Johnson, *The Selected Writings of James Weldon Johnson*, ed. Sandra K. Wilson, vol. 2 (New York: Oxford University Press, 1995); Adrienne Kennedy, *The Adrienne Kennedy Reader* (Minneapolis: University of Minnesota Press, 2001); Nella Larsen, *The Complete Fiction of Nella Larsen*, ed. Charles R. Larson (New York: Anchor, 2001); Hiram Mattison, *Louisa Picquet, the Octoroon: A Tale of Southern Slave Life* (New York: The Author, 1861); Werner Sollors, ed., *An Anthology of Interracial Literature: Black–White Contacts in the Old World and the New* (New York: New York University Press, 2004); Jean Toomer, *Cane* (New York: Liveright, 1993); Harriet Wilson, *Our Nig* (New York: Random House, 1983); Walter F. White, *Flight* (Baton Rouge: Louisiana State University Press, 1998). **Secondary Sources:** Hazel Carby, *Reconstructing Womanhood: The Emergence of the Afro-American Woman Novelist* (New York: Oxford University Press, 1987); Barbara Christian, *Black Women Novelists: The Development of a Tradition, 1892–1976* (Westport, CT: Greenwood Press, 1980); Elaine Ginsberg ed., *Passing and the Fictions of Identity* (Durham, NC: Duke University Press, 1996); Deborah McDowell, *"The Changing Same": Black Women's Literature, Criticism, and Theory* (Bloomington: Indiana University Press, 1995); Hans Ostrom, *Langston Hughes: A Study of the Short Fiction* (New York: Twayne, 1993); Claudia Tate, *Domestic Allegories of Political Desire: The Black Heroine's Text at the Turn of the Century* (New York: Oxford University Press, 1992).

Hee-Jung Joo

Mullen, Harryette (born 1954). Poet, critic, and professor. Mullen's critical and creative writings are dedicated to the significance and varieties of Black cultural expression, especially texts that have not usually been included in the representative canon of Black literature. Mullen was born in Florence, Alabama, and grew up in Fort Worth, **Texas**, the daughter of a schoolteacher. Mullen earned her B.A. from the University of Texas at Austin, and her Ph.D. in literature at the University of California, Santa Cruz. She is the author of six books of poetry.

Tree Tall Woman (1981), her first collection, is what Mullen characterizes as a more obvious engagement with the canon of African American literature. *Trimmings* (1991) and *S*PeRM**K*T* (1992) mark Mullen's deeper exploration of the formal and thematic concerns of such innovative women poets as Gertrude Stein as well as her investment in what many term "language poetry." Her fourth book, the book-length poem *Muse & Drudge* (1996), is Mullen's effort to merge the formally innovative with recognizably "Black" thematic concerns. While Mullen was writing this and her previous two books, her critical work began to emphasize the false split that occurs between the idea of experimental writing on the one hand and Black literature on the other. Interviews upon the release of *Muse & Drudge* take up this tension as well. In 2002, she published a collection of her older, out of print poetry in *Blues Baby* and her latest poetry collection, *Sleeping with the Dictionary*. Her most critically acclaimed publication to date, *Dictionary* brought Mullen to national attention with her nomination for the National Book Award for poetry. Her poems have been published in numerous journals, including **Callaloo**, *Antioch Review*, **Hambone** (edited by **Nathaniel Mackey**), *Black Renaissance*, and the *Voice Literary Supplement*, as well as anthologies including *Moving Borders: Three Decades of Innovative Writing by Women* and *The Jazz Poetry Anthology*.

Awards for Mullen's creative writing include the Gertrude Stein Award in Innovative American Poetry. Mullen has published scholarly writing in *Callaloo*, *Meridians*, and *MELUS*. She identifies her writing as formally innovative poetry. She also consciously attempts to bridge a gap between White and Black poetry audiences, and her work is often compared with the poetics of the Modernist writer Gertrude Stein; it also draws from a long genealogy of Black women's writing. Her critical writing emphasizes **race**, **gender**, and class in multicultural American literature and often focuses on the construction of language, especially that between orality and textuality. She currently teaches African American literature, poetry, and creative writing at the University of California at **Los Angeles**.

Resources: Primary Sources: Harryette Mullen: *Blues Baby* (Lewisburg, PA: Bucknell University Press, 2002); *Muse & Drudge* (Philadelphia: Singing Horse Press, 1996); "Poetry and Identity," *West Coast Line* 30, no. 19 (Spring 1996), 85–89; *Sleeping with the Dictionary* (Berkeley: University of California Press, 2002); *S*PeRM**K*T* (Philadelphia: Singing Horse Press, 1992); "Telegraphs from a Distracted Sibyl," *American Book Review* 17, no. 4 (Apr./May 1996), 1; *Tree Tall Woman* (Galveston, TX: Energy Earth

Communications, 1981); *Trimmings* (New York: Tender Buttons, 1991). **Secondary Sources:** Academy of American Poets, "Harryette Mullen," www.poets.org/poets; Calvin Bedient, "The Solo Mysterioso Blues: An Interview with Harryette Mullen," *Callaloo* 19, no. 3 (1996), 651–669; Electronic Poetry Center, "Harryette Mullen," Wings.buffalo.edu/epc/authors/mullen; Sascha Feinstein and Yusef Komunyakaa, editors, *Jazz Poetry Anthology*, vol. 1 (Bloomington: Indiana University Press, 1991); Farah Griffin, Michael Magee, and Kristen Gallagher, "A Conversation with Harryette Mullen," COMBO #1, Summer 1998; Barbara Henning, "An Interview with Harryette Mullen," http://www.poetryproject.com/newsletter/mullen.html; Mary Margaret Sloan, ed., *Moving Borders: Three Decades of Innovative Writing by Women* (Jersey City, NJ: Talisman House, 1998).

Samantha Pinto

Multicultural Theory. Scholarly and pedagogical idea with roots in the Civil Rights era. Multicultural theory encompasses an array of overlapping definitions that challenge homogeneous conceptions of national culture. One of the many outcomes of the intellectual, educational, and social investment in multicultural theory since the 1960s has been increased support for the study of African American literature, along with many other formerly silenced literary traditions.

One can identify at least three related assumptions that buttress the claims of multicultural theory. First, it has become economically, socially, and politically beneficial to develop a better understanding of the many perspectives of the world's diverse peoples. Second, dominant Euro-American intellectual traditions have placed the upper-class White Western heterosexual man as the central actor in history. Third, while interactions between different cultures often breed violence and hatred, there are also inherent possibilities for hope, understanding, and solidarity.

Defining multicultural theory has been a challenge for many scholars. As Ella Shohat and Robert Stam aptly state regarding the fluidity of the notion of multicultural theory: "The concept... is polysemically open to various interpretations and subject to diverse political force-fields; it has become an empty signifier onto which diverse groups project their hopes and fears" (47). In other words, the term itself has been appropriated for a whole host of interests. While scholars and teachers have been the primary users of multicultural theory, politicians, psychologists, physicians, attorneys, diplomats, and others all have recourse to its central ideas.

The theory, while not a single dominant way of thinking in and of itself, generally posits that understanding the cultural differences among the world's communities is crucial to any attempt at critically thinking about people and their diverse frames of reference, because people with different traditions and different histories have crucially different ways of conceptualizing their experiences. If our aim is to envision a more inclusive, democratic, and harmonious society, these different ways of knowing the world need to be understood in great detail, both as distinct cultural traditions that stand alone and in their dynamic interactions with each other. While there are many contradictions in the ways different people experience the world, these contradictions can potentially be managed through finely honed understanding.

In order to ground the debate over what multicultural theory is and how it can be used, a turn to its ideologically charged historical origins is appropriate. The theory has its roots in America's long and tumultuous **Civil Rights Movement**, in which a series of crucial events that occurred with stunning near-simultaneity. One involved the rise of global decolonization movements, particularly in nations of Africa and Southeast Asia, which forged their politics of self-determination against the wrongful misrepresentation of local desires by the colonizing West. From 1945 through the mid-1960s, dozens of new nations were formed whose claims to self-governance centered on unique communal identities that had been oppressed by Western "universalist" economic and political interests. Intellectuals such as C.L.R. James, Aimé Césaire, Frantz Fanon, and others gave shape to these adamant anticolonial pursuits.

In the U.S. context in particular, under pressure from a wide-ranging array of American communities, Congress passed major federal legislation, including the Civil Rights Act (1964) and the Voting Rights Act (1965), which mandated unencumbered access, regardless of **race**, ethnicity, or religion, to the benefits of American citizenship. Discrimination based on racial and cultural differences in the workplace, in schools, in housing opportunities, in polling places, and elsewhere was explicitly made illegal. This legislation followed in the footsteps of the groundbreaking Supreme Court rulings in *Brown v. Board of Education* (1954), two cases argued by **NAACP** attorney (and future Supreme Court justice) Thurgood Marshall, which pledged the desegregation of educational institutions. After decades of enforcing tight national borders and limited access to immigration, in 1965 the U.S. government also initiated a major overhaul of immigration law, expanding exponentially the number of people entering the country every year.

The late 1960s also saw a broadening of access to colleges and universities through systemic reforms such as **affirmative action** and the GI Bill, radically changing the composition of student populations. "Minorities"—including African Americans, Asian Americans, Hispanics, Chicanos, Native Americans, and other non-Europeans—entered college classrooms in extraordinary numbers. This tumultuous moment simultaneously saw activist organizations and driven leaders—including the NAACP, the Nation of Islam, the **Black Panthers Party**, La Raza, and American Indian movements, as well as **Martin Luther King, Jr., Angela Y. Davis, Malcolm X, Stokely Carmichael, Huey P. Newton**, and the faculty at schools such as San Francisco State University—putting pressure on schools, workplaces, and the government to reform their Eurocentric practices. And while activism around racial and ethnic difference flowered, so too did interventions in regard to sexuality and **gender**, challenging heterosexual and masculine norms of behavior.

These developments spurred initiatives to study nondominant cultures and sparked what became widely known in the United States in the 1980s and early 1990s as the "culture wars." In this post-Civil Rights moment, multicultural theory began to fracture into different camps, all fiercely contesting each other's central assumptions. One relatively conservative mode of using multicultural theory was to identify the ways in which these nondominant cultures were of, at most, peripheral importance and to include them in educational curricula, scholarly research, and elsewhere only to supplement or bolster a superior Eurocentric canon of ideas. Harold Bloom's early work on the development of the so-called Western canon is a groundbreaking articulation of this approach. A more moderate approach was simply to highlight the primacy of the liberal democratic ideas in the nation's founding documents by claiming that the very structure of American democracy was meant to withstand the incorporation and assimilation of many cultural differences. The most radical and arguably the most challenging approach to the dominant notion of national identity claimed that any national culture needs to be understood as having been produced through continual struggles between culturally distinct groups. From the landing of Christopher Columbus in 1492 to the arrival of the *Mayflower* in 1620 and the simultaneous displacement and near-destruction of America's indigenous peoples, to the forced migrations of the transatlantic slave trade and the expropriation of Chinese and Mexican labor, violent struggle around cultural difference lay at the nation's heart. Prominent intellectuals developing and popularizing this approach include **bell hooks**, **Ishmael Reed**, and Ronald Takaki. The backlash to such an approach from the likes of Nathan Glazer and Lynne Cheney produced exclusionary "nativist" claims that deified the authors of the nation's founding documents, made recourse to a stable canon of great books, and saw any addition of a multiperspectival approach, let alone one that highlighted struggles, as a threat to the very core of the nation's identity.

As an example, one could trace at least two very different kinds of multicultural curricula for the study of African American history and culture. The first, based on the moderate liberal-democratic inclusion model, takes as its point of departure Black History Month and describes the transatlantic slave trade as at most an unfortunate turn in Southern history. Abraham Lincoln's Emancipation Proclamation (1863) is celebrated, as is the *Brown* ruling; such a history would likely conclude with the "I Have a Dream" speech by Martin Luther King, Jr. at the March on Washington (1963). The second curriculum, based on the more radical model, traces America's history as a history of Black people's struggles in a nation structured around White privilege. Key literary figures come from a much longer time span and include such writers as **Phillis Wheatley**, **Harriet Jacobs**, **Frederick Douglass**, **Ida B. Wells-Barnett**, **Booker T. Washington**, **W. E. B. Du Bois**, **Jean Toomer**, **Claude McKay**, **Zora Neal Hurston**, **Langston Hughes**, **Richard Wright**, **Ralph Ellison**, **James Baldwin**, **Maya Angelou**, **Toni Morrison**, and **Alice Walker**, as well as musicians, politicians, activists, and scholars. Instead of presuming both the nation's inclusive coherence and the coherence of African American culture, this model clarifies the many fractures and contradictions deeply embedded in both.

Generally speaking, by the late 1990s and into the first years of the twenty-first century, the culture wars in one sense had become muted, with multicultural theory widely accepted as a central component to one's education in the United States, though often through the use of the first, inclusivist model. Alternative histories are increasingly included in elementary, middle, and high school curricula, filling out the story of American struggles with difference. In the academic world, departments of Ethnic Studies, Asian American Studies, African American Studies, and Chicano Studies assure the continued inclusion of cultural history in undergraduate education, and English literature departments have expanded the kinds of texts being taught and studied to include a range of writers of color. In another sense, though, the culture wars continue to rage, having shifted to such issues as abortion rights, gay marriage, and interracial adoption. While public debates around the usefulness and importance of multicultural theory have subsided, the critical pressure put on any notion of homogeneous culture or a universally shared national identity remains.

Resources: John Arthur and Amy Shapiro, eds., *Campus Wars: Multiculturalism and the Politics of Difference* (Boulder, CO: Westview, 1995); James A. Banks and Cherry A. McGee Banks, eds., *Handbook of Research on Multicultural Education* (San Francisco: Jossey-Bass, 2004); Paul Gilroy, *Against Race: Imagining Political Culture Beyond the Color Line* (Cambridge, MA: Belknap, 2000); Avery Gordon and Christopher Newfield, eds., *Mapping Multiculturalism* (Minneapolis: University of Minnesota Press, 1996); David Hollinger, *Postethnic America: Beyond Multiculturalism* (New York: Basic Books, 1995); bell hooks, *Teaching to Transgress: Education as the Practice of Freedom* (New York: Routledge, 1994); Will Kymlicka, *Multicultural Citizenship: A Liberal Theory of Minority Rights* (New York: Oxford University Press, 1996); Toni Morrison, *Playing in the Dark: Whiteness in the Literary Imagination* (Cambridge, MA: Harvard University Press, 1992); Michael Omi and Howard Winant, *Racial Formation in the United States: From the 1960s to the 1990s*, 2nd ed. (New York: Routledge, 1994); Ishmael Reed, ed., *From Totems to Hip-Hop: A Multicultural Anthology of Poetry Across the Americas, 1900–2002* (New York: Thunder's Mouth Press, 2003); Lillian S. Robinson, *In the Canon's Mouth: Dispatches from the Culture Wars* (Bloomington: Indiana University Press, 1997); Ella Shohat and Robert Stam, *Unthinking Eurocentrism: Multiculturalism and the Media* (New York: Routledge, 1994); Ronald Takaki, *A Different Mirror: A History of Multicultural America* (Boston: Little, Brown, 1993); Cornel West, *Race Matters* (New York: Vintage, 1994).

Keith Feldman

Murray, Albert (born 1916). Novelist, cultural critic, and poet. Beginning with the essay collection *The Omni-Americans* (1970), released when he was fifty-four, Murray has been exceedingly prolific. He has published twelve books in total, including fiction, poetry, essays, memoir, and **jazz** history and criticism. Murray was born in 1916 in Nokomis, Alabama, and raised in that small town on the outskirts of Mobile. In 1935, he began college at the Tuskegee Institute, where he began a decadeslong friendship with **Ralph Ellison**. Murray graduated in 1939 and, after a year at the University of Michigan, returned to Tuskegee in 1940 to teach literature and composition. During **World War II**, he enlisted in the Air Force, and served until 1946. In 1948, he received an M.A. from New York University then returned to active military duty in the Korean War. Murray retired from the Air Force as a major in 1962 and began to devote himself to writing full-time.

Though perhaps less widely known than Ellison, Murray is an equally forceful voice in articulating the irrefutable place of African Americans within any definition of American identity or culture. Throughout his celebrated essays and novels, he suggests in diverse ways how the Black subject is the "omni-American," speaking always, in Ellison's words, on the lower frequencies for a collective American "you." Moreover, Murray's work, in all its varied forms, is notable for its ongoing exploration and celebration of African American **vernacular** expressivity. His fiction, for example, revels in the semantic possibilities of African American spoken English, and imbues narrative with the rhythms and structural play of jazz. In his essays, Murray argues for the vitality of African American culture. For Murray, Black American culture counters persistent myths of Black victimhood, and articulates unfailing resilience in the face of American racism. Beyond the printed page, Murray has been an influential figure on the contemporary jazz scene, as one of the founding artistic directors of New York's prestigious Jazz at Lincoln Center program.

Resources: **Primary Sources:** Albert Murray: *The Blue Devils of Nada: A Contemporary American Approach to Aesthetic Statement* (New York: Pantheon, 1996); *Conjugations and Reiterations* (New York: Pantheon, 2001); *From the Briarpatch File: On Context, Procedure, and American Identity* (New York: Pantheon, 2001); *The Hero and the Blues* (Columbia: University of Missouri Press, 1973); *The Omni-Americans: New Perspectives on Black Experience and American Culture* (New York: Outerbridge and Dienstfrey, 1970); *The Seven League Boots* (New York: Pantheon, 1995); *South to a Very Old Place* (New York: McGraw-Hill, 1971); *The Spyglass Tree* (New York: Pantheon, 1991); *Stomping the Blues* (New York: McGraw-Hill, 1976); *Train Whistle Guitar* (New York: McGraw-Hill, 1974); Albert Murray with Count Basie, *Good Morning Blues: The Autobiography of Count Basie* (New York: Random House, 1985); Albert Murray and Ralph Ellison, *Trading Twelves: The Selected Letters of Ralph Ellison and Albert Murray*, ed. Albert Murray and John F. Callahan (New York: Modern Library, 2000). **Secondary Sources:** Warren Carson, "Albert Murray: Literary Reconstruction of the Vernacular Community," *African American Review* 27, no. 2 (1993), 287–295; Henry Louis Gates, Jr., "King of Cats," *The New Yorker*, April 8, 1996, pp. 70–81; John Gennari, "Slumming in High Places: Albert Murray's Intercontinental Ballistics," *Brilliant Corners* 1, no. 1 (1996), 59–67; Carolyn M. Jones, "Race and Intimacy: Albert Murray's *South to a Very Old Place*," in *South to a New Place: Region, Literature, Culture*, ed. Suzanne W. Jones and Sharon Monteith (Baton Rouge: Louisiana State University Press, 2002), 58–75; Wolfgang Karrer, "Nostalgia, Amnesia, and Grandmothers: The Uses of Memory in Albert Murray, Sabine Ulibarri, Paula Gunn Allen, and Alice Walker," in *Memory, Narrative, and Identity: New Essays in Ethnic American Literatures,* ed. Amritjit Singh, Joseph T. Skerrett, Jr., and Robert E. Hogan (Boston: Northeastern University Press, 1994), 128–144; Roberta S. Maguire, ed., *Conversations with Albert Murray* (Jackson: University Press of Mississippi, 1997); Sanford Pinsker: "Albert Murray: The Black Intellectuals' Maverick Patriarch," *Virginia Quarterly Review* 72, no. 4 (1996), 678–684; "'The Blue-Steel, Rawhide, Patent-Leather Implications of Fairy Tales': A Conversation with Albert Murray," *Georgia Review* 51, no. 2 (1997), 205–221; Charles H. Rowell, "'An All-Purpose, All-American Literary Intellectual': An Interview with Albert Murray," *Callaloo* 20, no. 2 (1997), 399–414; Tony Scherman, "The Omni-American," *American Heritage* 47, no. 5 (1996), 68–77.

Michael Borshuk

Murray, Pauli (1910–1985). Poet, novelist, lawyer, and Episcopal priest. The first Black woman to be ordained an Episcopal priest in the United States, Pauli Murray was an accomplished attorney, poet, and novelist, as well as an author of civil rights legal literature. Born in **Baltimore, Maryland**, and raised in Durham, North Carolina, by her aunt and maternal grandparents, she graduated with honors in 1933 from Hunter College in New York City. After she was denied admission to law school at the University of North Carolina at Chapel Hill and Harvard University because of her **race** and **gender**, respectively, Murray's **NAACP**-supported campaign received national publicity. During the 1930s and 1940s, Murray worked with the National Urban League, the Works Progress Administration, and the Workers Defense League; participated in sit-ins to integrate lunch counters in the national capital; and was arrested and jailed in Virginia for refusing to sit on a broken seat at the back of a bus. Her novel *Angel of the Desert* appeared in serial form in the *Carolina Times*.

Murray went on to earn the LL.B. from Howard University in 1944, the LL.M. from the Boalt Hall School of Law at the University of California at Berkeley in 1945, and in 1965 was the first black person to be awarded the JS.D. by Yale Law School. During this time, she was a civil rights lawyer, a professor at Brandeis University, Vice President of Benedict College, and Deputy Attorney General of California. In 1943, Murray published two influential essays on civil rights, "Negroes Are Fed Up" in *Common Sense*, and her thoughts on the **race riot** in **Harlem, New York**, in the *New York Call*, a Socialist newspaper. She was named "Woman of the Year" by *Mademoiselle* in 1947. One of Murray's most important literary contributions to the **Civil Rights Movement** was her book *States' Laws on Race and Color* (1950), which Thurgood Marshall described as "the Bible for civil rights lawyers."

In 1956, Murray published a biography of her grandparents, *Proud Shoes: The Story of an American Family*, which highlighted their struggles with racial prejudice and **slavery**. This literary turn toward autobiography was a lived transition for Murray, and in 1960, she traveled to Africa, teaching at the Ghana School of Law in Accra, hoping to explore the cultural roots of her ancestors. Upon her return, President John F. Kennedy appointed Murray to the President's Commission on the Status of Women (PCSW) Committee on

Civil and Political Rights, where she distinguished herself by linking the Civil Rights Movement to the women's rights movement's federal quest for equity. Murray was the primary author of the 1963 PCSW report, which alerted governors to review state laws and policies regarding women, creating similar commissions on the state level. Continuing to link civil rights and women's rights, in 1964 Murray published the influential legal article "Jane Crow and the Law: Sex Discrimination and Title VII" in the *George Washington Law Review*, and cofounded the National Organization for Women (NOW) in 1966, serving as coauthor of the statement of purpose for NOW. Murray also joined the Equality Committee of the ACLU, where she revised the ACLU's policies on gender discrimination. In 1970, Murray published a prize-winning volume of poetry on race relations, *Dark Testament and Other Poems*.

Murray increasingly saw religion as a location where links might be forged between the movements of White women and Black people. At the age of sixty-two, Murray entered the General Theological Seminary in New York City, and in 1977 was ordained as an Episcopal priest. She first celebrated the Eucharist at the Chapel of the Cross in Chapel Hill, North Carolina, where her grandmother had been baptized as a slave. Pauli Murray died of cancer on July 1, 1985, in **Pittsburgh, Pennsylvania**. Her **autobiography**, *Song in a Weary Throat: An American Pilgrimage*, was published posthumously in 1987.

Resources: Primary Sources: Pauli Murray: *Dark Testament and Others Poems* (Norwalk, CT: Silvermine Press, 1970); *Human Rights U.S.A.: 1948–1966* (Cincinnati, OH: Service Center, Board of Missions, Methodist Church, 1967); *Pauli Murray: The Autobiography of a Black Activist, Feminist, Lawyer, Priest, and Poet* (Knoxville: University of Tennessee Press, 1989), originally published as *Song in a Weary Throat* (New York: Harper & Row, 1987); *Proud Shoes: The Story of an American Family* (New York: Harper, 1956); Pauli Murray, ed. and comp., *States' Laws on Race and Color* (1950; repr. Athens: University of Georgia Press, 1997). **Secondary Sources:** Elly Haney, "Pauli Murray: Acting and Remembering," *Journal of Feminist Studies in Religion* 4 (Fall 1988), 75–79; Suzanne R. Hiatt, "Pauli Murray: May Her Song Be Heard at Last," *Journal of Feminist Studies in Religion* 4 (Fall 1988), 69–73; Jean M. Humez, "Pauli Murray's Histories of Loyalty and Revolt," *Black American Literature Forum* 24 (Summer 1990), 315–335; Casey Miller, "Pauli Murray," *Ms* 8, no. 9 (Mar. 1980); Darlene O'Dell, *Sites of Southern Memory: The Autobiographies of Katharine Du Pre Lumpkin, Lillian Smith, and Pauli Murray* (Charlottesville: University Press of Virginia, 2001); Pat Williams, "The Struggle to Belong," *The New York Times Biographical Service* 18 (Mar. 1987), 282–284.

Stephen Butler Murray

Musical Theater. African American musical theater includes popular stage shows involving Black composers, lyricists, and performers; it combines spoken scenes, acting, music, comedy, and dance. African American musical theater has its origins in the decades after the **Civil War**. Arguably it reached its apex during the **Harlem Renaissance**, when productions began to move away from older theatrical and musical conventions toward a new understanding of Black popular performance.

The roots of the African American musical reach back to the African continent. Music and dance were central to African religious rituals and tribal celebrations. They survived the Middle Passage and were transformed and adapted to the new environment once the slaves arrived in America. In the 1840s and 1850s, African American culture became a prominent subject on the popular stage; White performers in blackface makeup (burned cork) impersonated figures from Black life in burlesque presentations that ranged from overt racism to admiring parody (*see* **Minstrelsy**).

With the market for mass entertainment growing after the Civil War, job opportunities for Black musicians, dancers, comedians, and actors increased. Black performers, though often forced, ironically, to wear blackface, sought to portray minstrel characters in their own way. Many saw this as a chance to hone their talents and tone down the more racist elements of the shows. Early Black musicals, like minstrel shows, featured a combination of music, comedy, burlesque skits, and thematically unconnected songs. These musicals retained minstrel techniques such as exaggeration and burlesque, something White audiences and critics preferred to more realistic portrayals of African Americans. Many Black audiences, however, discerned double meanings in the stage action at a time when humor and music were the only mechanisms allowing Black Americans to face White audiences in a public forum.

Since interest in music and Black theater came to fruition at about the same time, traveling shows and local theaters soon combined music and comedic/dramatic skits, thereby seeking to secure maximum commercial viability for such emerging entertainers as Tom Fletcher and Sam Lucas. The earliest Black musicals (before one could speak of a fully formed genre) were the Hyers Sisters' performances in *Out of the Wilderness* (written by Joseph Bradford), *Colored Aristocracy*, *Out of Bondage*, and *The Underground Railroad* (all by **Pauline Elizabeth Hopkins**). Performed in the 1870s and 1880s, they showcased **spirituals**, popular songs, and dances.

While *The Creole Show* (1890), *The Octoroons* (1895), *Black Patti's Troubadours* (1896), and *Oriental America* (1896) were devised by White impresarios and basically followed the episodic structure of the minstrel shows, Bob Cole and Billy Johnson's *A Trip to Coontown* (1898) premiered as the first Black musical play that presented a full plot ("book musical"). *Coontown* was also the first Black show produced and performed exclusively by African Americans. Alex Rogers, J. A. Shipp, and Will Marion Cook's *In Dahomey* (1902), Rogers and **Bert Williams**'s *Abyssinia* (1905), and Cole and J. Rosamond Johnson's *The Red Moon* (1909) soon followed. Staging their musical comedy *Clorindy, or the Origin of the Cakewalk* at Ed Rice's Casino Theatre Roof Garden in 1898 (the first time a Black musical was performed on Broadway), the poet **Paul Laurence Dunbar** and the composer Will Marion Cook added another important production to the roster of nineteenth-century shows.

Between 1890 and 1915, approximately thirty shows were produced in the Black neighborhoods of New York and on Broadway (Riis, xxi). Though the majority of them did not differ substantially from the White shows produced in this period (all featured **ragtime** music), Thomas Riis emphasizes important elements introduced to the American popular stage by African American composers and performers. Besides the effect of Black actors supplanting Whites in blackface, shows such as *Clorindy* highlighted Ernest Hogan's energetic dancing to the Dunbar-penned "Who Dat Say Chicken in Dis Crowd." *In Dahomey, Abyssinia,* and *Bandanna Land* (1907) displayed the comedic and dancing genius of George Walker and Bert Williams, a popular comedy team known for their cakewalk. Walker and Williams also appeared in *The Policy Players* (1899), *The Sons of Ham* (1900), and several other shows.

Early Black musicals had a fairly narrow corpus of themes. *In Dahomey, Abyssinia, An African Prince* (1920), and *Bamboula* (1921) satirized the **Back to Africa movement**, and *The Cannibal King* (1900), *Jes' Lak White Fo'ks* (1901), and *Brown Sugar* (1927) dealt with the position of African Americans in a society controlled by Whites. *Bandanna Land, Who's Stealing?* (1918), *Africana* (1922), *Liza* (1922), *Come Along Mandy* (1924), and *Lucky Sambo* (1925) all contained sweet- and fast-talking dandies, much to the dismay of **W.E.B. Du Bois** and other Harlem Renaissance intellectuals. For many black theatergoers, however, dandies, coons, and gamblers (the latter appeared in *The Man from 'Bam* [1906], *They're Off* [1919], and *The Chocolate Dandies* [1924]) were not necessarily regarded as stereotypes. Instead, most African American viewers probably enjoyed the burlesque and comic qualities embodied by these exaggerated figures drawn mostly from Black working-class life. Additional themes included love relationships, ethnic stereotypes, and nostalgic images of the Old South. Though hardly the source of overt serious criticism, the musicals changed the perception of Black stock figures. Though Dunbar and other Black writers capitalized on the popularity of stereotypical "coon" imagery, their versions of watermelon- and chicken-eating characters were less vicious than the racial caricatures of contemporary White writers.

Many scholars see the hit show *Shuffle Along* (1921), by Flournoy Miller, Aubrey Lyles (book), Noble Sissle (lyrics), and composer Eubie Blake, as the musical that announced the arrival of the "Jazz Age." *Shuffle Along* combined a story about two criminal-minded politicians trying to manipulate the result of their mayoral campaigns with an appealing love story. The show was a great success, running at the Sixty-third Street Theater in New York and on Broadway throughout the 1920s. Songs such as "Love Will Find a Way" and "I'm Just Wild About Harry," with outstanding performances by **Josephine Baker**, Adelaide Hall, and **Paul Robeson**, depicted serious love relationships between African American characters, an innovation that broke with the established stage image of Blacks as comic figures.

Runnin' Wild (1923) and *Hot Chocolates* (1929) also rank as highlights of the 1920s. The first was written by Miller and Lyles (music by **James P. Johnson**) and introduced the Charleston, the dance that dominated the "Roaring Twenties." The latter spotlighted music by Fats Waller (lyrics and story by Andy Razaf and Harry Brooks) and showcased the impressive skills of a rising star on the jazz trumpet: Louis Armstrong's renditions of "Ain't Misbehavin'" quickly attained a legendary reputation. These shows enabled African American composers and lyricists to address all-American audiences—*Shuffle Along* was the beginning of desegregation on Broadway—and to write in a variety of musical styles. Stardom and permanent employment were more immediate benefits for Black performers, even though the majority of venues and production companies continued to be owned by White (often Jewish) businessmen.

Musicals such as *Shuffle Along*, *Runnin' Wild*, and *Hot Chocolates* point to a central conflict over the role and course of Black musical theater in the Harlem Renaissance and in the political struggles of African Americans more generally. The theater scholar Samuel Hay emphasizes **Alain Locke**'s vision of a musical theater that would portray realistic characters and themes taken from the everyday lives of America's Black population. Locke favored a theater that would draw from the rich Black cultural tradition and invent characters and situations speaking to the basic humanity of Black Americans. Locke imagined the elevation of Black folk music by melding it with the sophistication of the European concert tradition. While envisioning a similar musical fusion, Du Bois advocated a theater that would express indignation over minstrel and coon imagery as well as denounce publicly the daily violence and discrimination against African Americans.

The Black musical during the Harlem Renaissance only partially followed Locke's and Du Bois's visions. Most shows demonstrated a more or less stringent allegiance to humorous stock figures or avoided political commentary altogether. The significance of 1920s Black musical theater, thus, lay not so much in advocating progressive thought, which Locke, Du Bois, **James Weldon Johnson**, and others did more effectively. Instead, Black musicals worked toward social change by allowing Black composers to experiment in a variety of musical styles, by providing employment for many Black performers and writers, and by creating a large audience—Black and White—for Black entertainment. The shows not only increased the visibility of Black performers and made them fixtures of the American popular stage; they also expressed a sense of self-empowerment that put into practice what Locke had announced in the introduction to his *New Negro* anthology (1925).

In the 1930s, the **Great Depression** took its toll on Black musical theater. Although the number of Black shows initially increased early in the decade because of cheap production costs, most of them folded quickly. By mid-decade, African Americans began to be featured in major roles in theatrical productions by such Jewish Americans as George and Ira Gershwin, Jerome Kern, and Oscar Hammerstein II. George Gershwin's folk opera *Porgy and Bess* (1935), Kern/Hammerstein's *Showboat* (1927), and Hammerstein's *Carmen Jones* (1943) dramatized ethnic conflicts in American culture through the portrayal of Black life and characters. *Porgy and Bess*, in particular, drew on Black folk music for its musical score.

In the period between the 1940s and 1960, African American musicals continued to be produced, but television and movies attained greater cultural prominence. Films such as *Cabin in the Sky* (1943), *Stormy Weather* (1943), and *New Orleans* (1947) featured several famous Black performers. **Ethel Waters**, Louis Armstrong, **Billie Holiday**, and Bill "Bojangles" Robinson made the best of their narrowly scripted roles. A few musicals, however, did appear between 1940 and 1963, most significantly *St. Louis Woman* (1946), by **Arna Bontemps**, Harold Arlen, and **Countee Cullen**, and **Langston Hughes**'s *Simply Heavenly* (1957), *Black Nativity* (1961), and *Tambourines to Glory* (1963).

Black musical theater up to 1957 had displayed scarce interest in overt political advocacy and social commentary. According to Hay, the more than 700 musical comedies produced in the years between Cole and Johnson's *Coontown* and Hughes's *Simply Heavenly* (1957) "show almost no evidence of social consciousness" (32). Considering the racist climate of the first half of the twentieth century, this comes as no surprise. Only with the **Civil Rights Movement** strengthening in the 1960s did African American musical theater become more willing to tackle social and political issues overtly (still to a lesser degree than the nonmusical theater of **Ed Bullins**, **Alice Childress**, **Amiri Baraka**, **James Baldwin**, and **Ntozake Shange**). White audiences fond of Black musicals had long been unwilling to accept open criticism of American race relations, and while **Richard Wright** was able to sustain an audience despite the radical nature of *Native Son* (1940), the fact that musicals were traditionally considered entertainment and were geared toward a mainstream audience prevented such outspokenness.

Hay divides the Black musical theater beginning in the late 1950s into five subgroups: social, historical, personality, romantic, and sacred/gospel (50–55). The social musical balances the traditional privileging of music and dance over content by avoiding simplified plots and superficial treatment of serious issues. Sex, violence, and drug addiction play a role in Runako Jahi's *A Place to Be Me* (1989), Michael Mathews's *Momma Don't* (1990), and Karmyn Lott's *Stop and Think* (1989), and Micki Grant raises issues of race and social environment in *Don't Bother Me I Can't Cope* (1972). Richard Wesley's *The Dream Team* (1989) tackles desegregation; Ron Stewart/Neal Tate's *Sambo* (1969), *Purlie* (1970), by **Ossie Davis**, Philip Rose, Peter Udell, and Gary Geld, **Melvin Van Peebles**'s *Ain't Supposed to Die a Natural Death* (1971) and *Don't Play Us Cheap!* (1972), as well as the 1973 Broadway version of **Lorraine Hansberry**'s *A Raisin in the Sun* also comment on social problems such as urban crime and suburban racial segregation.

The romantic musicals of recent years are distinguished from earlier shows by their inclusion of socioeconomic conditions as a central element of the love plot. In James M. Brown's *Count Your Blessings* (1990), the romantic relationship between an imprisoned **rap** artist and a young female lawyer goes beyond a simple love story in its incorporation of class issues. *Once on This Island*, by Lynn Ahrens (1990), explores racial conflicts on a Caribbean island, where differences in socioeconomic class, instead of tragic fate, are responsible for separating the peasant girl and the son of an affluent **mulatto** landowner.

Since the 1970s, historical musicals have become increasingly popular. Some of the shows restaged musicals from the 1920s and 1930s. **Loften Mitchell**'s *Bubbling Brown Sugar* (1976; concept by Rosetta LeNoire) and *Black Broadway* (1980), by Honi Coles and Bobby Short, featured actors and musicians from the bygone era, such as Avon Long, Joseph Attles, and Josephine Premice in *Bubbling Brown Sugar*, Edith Wilson from *Plantation Revue* (1922), and Elizabeth Welch from *Runnin' Wild*. In Vernel Bagneris's *One Mo' Time* (1979), conflicts between Black performers and White theater owners, unmentionable in the 1920s, were restored to the historical record.

Personality musicals can be divided into mostly uncritical and more balanced tributes to great African American historical figures. Ashton Springer's *Eubie!* (1978) celebrated Eubie Blake; **Duke Ellington** received a similar treatment in Donald McKayle's *Sophisticated Ladies* (1981) and Julian Swain's *Mood Indigo* (1981), both of which used original music either by Ellington or by other Black artists (Fats Waller, Ma Rainey, **Bessie Smith**). Elmo-Terry Morgan's *The Song of Sheba* (1988) presented the lives of great female **blues** and **jazz** singers (Bessie Smith, Billie Holliday, Dinah Washington, Lena Horne). With Vincent D. Smith's *Williams and Walker* (1986), recounting Bert Williams's and George Walker's lives, the personality musical took on greater analytical depth. Later works, such as Josh Greenfield's *I Have a Dream* (1989) and Clarence Cuthbertson and George Broderick's *Faith Journey* (1994; both about **Martin Luther King, Jr.**), Queen Esther Marrow's *Truly Blessed* (1989; about Mahalia Jackson), Reenie Upchurch's *Yesterdays* (1990; about Billie Holliday), and **George C. Wolfe**'s *Jelly's Last Jam* (1992; about Jelly Roll Morton) presented more complex views of their subjects: *Jelly's Last Jam*, for instance, criticizes Morton's denial of his Black ancestry.

The sacred/**gospel** musical begins with Langston Hughes's *Black Nativity* and *Tambourines to Glory* and continues the rich African American tradition of religious expression in music and literature. **Vinnette Carroll's** *Trumpets of the Lord* (1963) adapted James Weldon Johnson's folk sermon *God's Trombones* (1927), and Carroll's *Your Arms Too Short to Box with God* (1976) is based on the book of Matthew. Due to the ongoing popularity of gospel music, the sacred/gospel musical is enjoying continued success, inspiring such plays as **Ron Milner**'s *Don't Get God Started* (1987) and Vy Higgerson's *Mama I Want to Sing, Part I* (1982), *Let the Music Play Gospel* (1989), and *Mama I Want to Sing, Part II* (1990).

Following current literary and musical scholarship, three musicals from the 1990s took a new historicist approach to Black musical theater: George C. Wolfe's *Bring in 'Da Noise Bring in 'Da Funk* (1996) retells African American history through tap dance; *A Brief History of White Music* (1996) features songs with Black musical roots but written or popularized by White performers; and *It Ain't Nothin' but the Blues* (1999) presents a chronology of Black music by embedding songs within their specific historical contexts. Wolfe also produced *Harlem Song* at Harlem's Apollo Theatre in 2002.

1149

Resources: Harry J. Elam, Jr., and David Krasner, eds., *African American Performance and Theater History: A Critical Reader* (New York: Oxford University Press, 2001); Samuel A. Floyd, Jr., "Music in the Harlem Renaissance: An Overview," in *Black Music in the Harlem Renaissance: A Collection of Essays*, ed. Floyd (Knoxville: University of Tennessee Press, 1993), 1–27; John Graziano: "Black Musical Theater and the Harlem Renaissance Movement," in *Black Music in the Harlem Renaissance*, ed. Samuel A. Floyd, Jr. (Knoxville: University of Tennessee Press, 1993), 87–110; "Images of African Americans: African-American Musical Theatre, *Show Boat* and *Porgy and Bess*," in *The Cambridge Companion to the Musical*, ed. William A. Everett and Paul R. Laird (Cambridge: Cambridge University Press, 2002), 63–76; Samuel A. Hay, *African American Theatre: An Historical and Critical Analysis* (Cambridge: Cambridge University Press, 1994); John Bush Jones, *Our Musicals, Ourselves: A Social History of the American Musical Theatre* (Hanover, NH: Brandeis University Press, 2003); Glenn Loney, ed., *Musical Theatre in America: Papers and Proceedings of the Conference on the Musical Theatre in America* (Westport, CT: Greenwood Press, 1984); Hans Ostrom, *A Langston Hughes Encyclopedia* (Westport, CT: Greenwood Press, 2002); Thomas L. Riis, *Just Before Jazz: Black Musical Theater in New York, 1890–1915* (Washington, DC: Smithsonian Institution Press, 1989); Allen Woll, *Black Musical Theater: From Coontown to Dreamgirls* (Baton Rouge: Louisiana State University Press, 1989).

Daniel T. Stein

Myers, Walter Dean (born 1937). Young-adult novelist and poet. Myers is best known for his award-winning novels portraying African American teenagers, specifically boys, in positive ways. Myers was born August 12, 1937, in West Virginia. After his mother died when he was three years old, and he and two of his sisters moved in with foster parents and eventually went to **Harlem, New York**. Because of an early speech impediment, a teacher suggested that Myers read things that he had written out loud, and he quickly discovered that he enjoyed writing. His family, like many other poor blue-collar families, did not always encourage his talents because they could not see any potential for turning that talent into an ability to support himself (Bishop).

After a series of jobs and minor publications, Myers came to a realization similar to that experienced by fellow children's writer **Ezra Jack Keats**—that minority children were either neglected in children's literature or used only as background in books written for children and young adults. In 1969, Myers published *Where Does the Day Go?*, a picture book featuring children from various ethnic backgrounds. The book won the Council on Interracial Books competition for Best Children's Picture Book.

His writing career progressed quickly. After completing several children's books, including *The Dancers* (1972), which was named the Book of the Year by the Child Study Association of America, and informational works such as *The World of Work: A Guide to Choosing a Career* (1975), Myers began writing for young adults, producing works featuring African American teens growing up in Harlem. In addition to his realistic urban novels, Myers regularly contributes to the "My Name is America" historical fiction series; his titles include *The Journal of Joshua Loper: A Black Cowboy* (1999), *The Journal of Scott Pendleton Collins: A World War II Soldier* (1999), and *The Journal of Biddy Owens, the Negro Leagues* (2001).

Myers' also has written historical fiction such as *The Glory Field* (1994), fables such as *The Golden Serpent* (1980), and numerous nonfiction works for young adults, including those about **Muhammad Ali** and **Malcolm X**. He also has written several books of poetry, including the award-winning *Harlem: A Poem* (1997), which, along with *blues journey* (2001), was illustrated by his son, Christopher Myers. Myers's books have won numerous awards, including multiple Coretta Scott King Awards (1989, 1997, and 2000) and the prestigious Newbery Award twice (1989 and 1993).

The realistic books of Walter Dean Myers depict characters with whom most young readers can easily identify yet are not stereotypical. His storylines consist of the gritty reality of growing up today and all the pressures associated with being a teenager, such as teen pregnancy, gangs, and drugs. Within these stories, Myers describes the positive aspects of life, including the way in which family and community ties help each character cope with daily pressures and provide ways of overcoming hardship. The candid portrayals in *Hoops* (1981), *Scorpions* (1988), and *Somewhere in the Darkness* (1992) illustrate Myers's comprehension of and ability to represent the cross-cultural world that minority children live in today.

Resources: Primary Sources: Walter Dean Myers: *Bad Boy: A Memoir* (New York: HarperCollins, 2001); *blues journey* (New York: Holiday House, 2001); *The Dancers* (New York: Parents Magazine Press, 1972); *The Glory Field* (New York: Scholastic, 1994); *The Golden Serpent* (New York: Viking, 1980); *The Greatest: Muhammad Ali* (New York: Scholastic, 2001); *Harlem: A Poem* (New York: Scholastic, 1997); *Hoops* (New York: Delacorte, 1981); *The Journal of Biddy Owens, the Negro Leagues* (New York: Scholastic, 2001); *The Journal of Joshua Loper: A Black Cowboy* (New York: Scholastic, 1999); *The Journal of Scott Pendleton Collins: A World War II Soldier* (New York: Scholastic, 1999); *Malcolm X: A Fire Burning Brightly* (New York: HarperCollins, 2000); *Malcolm X: By Any Means Necessary* (New York: Scholastic, 1993); *Scorpions* (New York: Harper & Row, 1988); *Somewhere in the Darkness* (New York: Scholastic, 1992); *Where Does the Day Go?* (New York: Parents' Magazine Press, 1969); *The World of Work: A Guide to Choosing a Career* (Indianapolis, IN: Bobbs-Merrill, 1975). **Secondary Sources:** Rudine Sims Bishop, *Presenting Walter Dean Myers* (Boston: Twayne, 1990); Cormen Subryan, "Walter Dean Myers," in *Dictionary of Literary Biography*, vol. 33, *Afro-American Fiction Writers After 1955*, ed. Thadious M. Davis and Trudier Harris (Detroit: Gale, 1984), 199–202; "Walter Dean Myers," in *Something About the Author*, vol. 71, ed. Diane Telgen (Detroit: Gale, 1993), 133–137.

Susie Scifres Kuilan

Mystery Fiction. *See* **Crime and Mystery Fiction.**

Myth. A myth is a primitive "wonder story" that embodies the beliefs and values of the culture that created it. Most of the characters in it are supernatural or legendary. Often myths explain, according to their cultural worldview, how the universe came to be, how life has been in the past, and, by suggestion, how it ought to be. Cultures develop, in part, around their own original myths or core stories, which lend themselves to expansion and retelling. Newer myths are continually added to the existing body of stories or "mythos," all pieces generally arranged in a coherent system. The common use of the term "myth" for false, fictitious, or imaginary matter should be separated from its application to mythology, literature, and the like.

The veracity of the mythical narrative is seldom debated; it is generally considered sacred and thus integral to its religious faith, or at least figuratively "true." The content of a myth can be symbolic or metaphorical—"the big picture moments of a culture" projected, as Joseph Campbell says, on a large screen. The authorship of myths is communal, and the task of compiling all the stories can be the charge of an epic bard who voices "the public dreams" of a people as Homer does in *The Iliad* and *The Odyssey* or as Vyasa does in the *Mahabharata*, the largest epic in the world. In other words, myths grow out of an oral story-preserving and storytelling tradition, and they may later be written down or turned into visual art. (*See* **Epic Poetry/The Long Poem.**)

The human inner world, as psychologists would argue, has a deep, primitive need for heroes who dare to face the fears inherent in life and death. Of greater gravity is the human spiritual character, which feels the need to transcend itself. Myths address humans as spiritual beings rather than as *Homo sapiens*. Thus heroic models of every culture often operate in or interact with the supernatural. Their successes illustrate the inspirational principles of the culture. Their misfortunes evoke universal empathy and serve as object lessons or subjects of lofty philosophical commentary.

Regardless of geographical differences, myths of the world contain archetypal correspondences. An archetype is a cherished original theme or experiential pattern that inspires future representations or copies, embodied in such stock characters as the hero, the alter ego, the **trickster**, the warrior, the wanderer, the orphan, the martyr, the clever person who defeats the physically strong person, the fatal woman (*femme fatale*), the scapegoat, the altruist, and so on. Archetypal narratives come with common motifs such as the search for adventure, the quest for treasure, prophecy and fulfillment, mental or spiritual transformation, or battling and overcoming evil, to name a few. Comparative analysis of myths and mythology gives scholars reasons to think that the commonalities in mythical stories may have sprung from a single point of origin of the human family where it also should have received an "original revelation." The eventual transmittal of that revelation imaginably occurred with frequent alterations, each culture still taking pride in how the received story shaped its beliefs and ways. Scholars including Otto Rank and Joseph Campbell have traced the commonality of myths across cultures, from Asia to Africa to the Mediterranean to Europe. Certain stories or themes are basic to all myths. Creation, personified good and evil, the loss of innocence or grace, the great flood, and the cycles of time are some of them.

The "Creator" in many global narratives appears in a figure of mystic plurality, often in a triune godhead. Each member of the triad has specific attributes and functions. In the Bantu tradition, creation is the work of a three-in-one unity consisting of Nzame, Mbere, and Nkwa; the Nzeme part creates the world and life in it. The three also create Fam (the human) in their image to rule the earth. Astar, Beher and Mahrem form the triad of Ethiopia, Astar being first in rank. Menerva (predecessor of the Roman goddess Minerva), Tinia and Uni make up the Etruscan triad. The Hindu gods Brahma (the Creator), Vishnu (the Preserver), and Shiva (the Destroyer) proceeded from the world-egg deposited by the Supreme First Cause. "The Fire Children," a West African creation tale, has the first man and woman making children out of clay, and it features a "sky god" (Maddern and Lessac).

Similar to the legend, but more modest in scope, is the **folktale**, a short story with local color and traditional beliefs and customs. More realistic, the folktale is quasi-historical, is related as "fact," and usually is linked to everyday experience. In the anthology *Afro-American Folktales*, for example, Abrahams categorizes folktales in terms of theme: "How the World Got Put Together That Way," "Minding Somebody Else's Business," "Trickery," "Cleverness vs. Strength," and so on. The folktales can be interpreted, then, as smaller versions of myths; like myths, they emerge from an oral tradition; they may include features of the supernatural; and they are often used to explain a phenomenon or to encourage or discourage certain behavior.

Myths set the values of life and standards of conduct for a culture. In the Greek Oedipus myth, for instance, parricide and incest, though committed unwittingly, bring about desolation in the land. The Oracle of Delphi wants the murderer found and the land purged of the curse. Oedipus' and Creon's mocking of the prophet foreshadows the fall of each. Antigone, Oedipus' daughter, defies Creon's decree not to bury the body of her despised brother Polynices' because of her duty to the world of the dead. **Robert Farris Thompson** discusses the extent to which African Yoruba culture values creativity and "the power to make things happen," and he demonstrates how aspects of West African mythology were transferred to and absorbed by African American culture.

Two challenges faced by African American writers is that their ancestors were uprooted from African mythological traditions and that the mythologies available to these writers belonged to a cultural tradition that was in many cases hostile—that had, after all, supported the enslavement of African Americans. To some degree, then, from the beginning, African American writers were in the position of having to make sense of a fragmented mythological inheritance, a position all writers are in now because of living in a global culture, wherein innumerable mythic traditions coexist. Further, African American writers had to try to recover an African mythological past that had been erased or had been transmitted circuitously in Afro-Caribbean and African American oral traditions. **Arthur A. Schomburg** put it succinctly: "The American Negro must remake his past in order to make his future"

(Gates and McKay, 937). Of course, African Americans and African American writers have participated in the tradition of a Judeo-Christian worldview but have reshaped it, beginning with **spirituals** and **gospel music**. **Slave narratives** often combined aspects of a Judeo-Christian "mythos" with the specific circumstances of slavery and escape from it. Folktales, **ballads**, and **folklore** produced legendary narratives and figures with mythic qualities, including **John Henry**, **John the Conqueror**, and Brer Rabbit.

Attempts to recover or re-create an African past appear throughout African American literature. For example, one of **Frances E. W. Harper**'s earliest poems is "Ethiopia" (Gates and McKay, 408); **Paul Laurence Dunbar** wrote "Ode to Ethiopia"; and **Gwendolyn Bennett** evokes an imagined African past in "Heritage" (Gates and McKay, 884; 1226). **Marcus Garvey** took this impulse much further and argued that African Americans should literally return to Africa (*see* **Back-to-Africa Movement**). **Countee Cullen** expresses the complications and difficulties inherent in being positioned between different cultures in his poem "Heritage," which opens with the nonrhetorical question "What is Africa to me [?]" (Gates and McKay, 1311). **Langston Hughes** recovers a spirit of African culture in "Danse Africaine" (Gates and McKay, 1255).

Numerous writers have recast Judeo-Christian narratives. In the poem "The Creation," **James Weldon Johnson** retells the Judeo-Christian Genesis story (or creation myth); **Fenton Johnson** writes "My God In Heaven Said to Me"; and **Anne Spencer** retells an Old Testament narrative in "Before the Feast of Shushan" (Gates and McKay, 926, 946). In the gospel song-play *Black Nativity*, Langston Hughes dramatizes the story of a Black Jesus, Joseph, and Mary (Ostrom, 42–43).

Melvin B. Tolson approaches the folk hero John Henry as a mythic figure in "The Birth of John Henry" (Gates and McKay, 1357), and **Sterling A. Brown** transports the Greek myth of Odysseus to a contemporary African American wanderer in "Odyssey of Big Boy" (Gates and McKay, 1210). In his first novel, *Go Tell It On the Mountain* (1953), **James Baldwin** places his young **Harlem, New York**, protagonist, John Grimes, squarely in a Judeo-Christian context of maturation, sin, and redemption. In his nonfiction book *The Fire Next Time* (1963), Baldwin frames the catastrophe of American race relations and racism in terms of Judeo-Christian apocalypse and the story of Noah in the Old Testament. In the novel *Linden Hills* (1985), **Gloria Naylor** uses Dante's symbolism in writing about African American suburbia as a kind of Hell.

In the novel *Invisible Man* (1952), **Ralph Ellison** arguably creates a quasi-mythic figure who symbolizes the African American condition of "invisibility," of living in a culture that deliberately does not recognize the full humanity of African Americans.

The **Black Arts Movement** of the 1960s and 1970s urged writers and other artists to be much more critical of an Anglo-European cultural and mythological heritage. Some writers, for example, renamed themselves in order to shed, literally and figuratively, a Anglo-European heritage; LeRoi Jones changed his name to **Amiri Baraka**, and Don L. Lee changed his name to **Haki R. Madhubuti**, for instance. The Black Arts Movement coincided and in some cases established connections with the rise of the **Nation of Islam** and with other **Black Nationalist** movements.

Traditions of myth provide literature with an inexhaustible reservoir of images, plots, themes, and motifs, but for African American writers, the mythological heritage is arguably more various and more complicated.

Resources: D. L. Ashliman, ed. and trans., *Folklore and Mythology: Electronic Texts*, University of Pittsburgh, 1996–2004, http://www.pitt.edu/~dash/folktexts.html; Thomas Bulfinch, *Bulfinch's Mythology* (New York: Random House, 1998); Joseph Campbell, *The Hero with a Thousand Faces* (Princeton, NJ: Princeton University Press, 1968); Arthur Cotterell, *A Dictionary of World Mythology* (New York: Oxford University Press, 1990); Eric Csapo, *Theories of Mythology* (Oxford: Blackwell Publishing, 2005); Walter Evans, ed., *The Humanities Handbook*, 7th ed. (Augusta, GA: Augusta University, 1995), http://www.aug.edu/langlitcom/humanitiesHBK/handbook_htm/index.html; Pierre Grimal, *Dictionary of Classical Mythology* (New York: Penguin, 1991); Henry Louis Gates, Jr., and Nellie Y. McKay, eds., *The Norton Anthology of African American Literature* (New York: W.W. Norton, 1996); Hesiod, *Theogony: Works and Days*, trans. M. L. West (New York: Oxford University Press, 1999); Michael F. Lindemans, ed., *Encyclopedia Mythica* (1999), http://www.pantheon.org/mythica/articles/z/zeus.html; Eric Maddern and Frané Lessac, *The Fire Children: A West African Creation Tale* (New York: Penguin, 1999); Hans Ostrom, *A Langston Hughes Encyclopedia* (Westport, CT: Greenwood Press, 2002); Otto Rank, "The Myth of the Birth of the Hero," in *In Quest of the Hero* (Princeton, NJ: Princeton University Press, 1990); Robert Farris Thompson, *Flash of the Spirit: African and Afro-American Art and Philosophy* (New York: Penguin, 1984).

Varghese Mathai

N

NAACP (National Association for the Advancement of Colored People).
The beginnings of the NAACP are to be found in a three-day conference held
from July 11 through 13 in Fort Erie, Canada, in 1904. The twenty-nine
attendees, all Black intellectuals, were gathered there by the activist **W.E.B.
Du Bois** to organize what would be known as the Niagara Movement. Its
purpose was to achieve the complete abolition of all forms of racial discrimination and, somewhat ironically, the segregation of schools. Also on the
agenda were the increased election of Blacks to political office and the enforcement of Black voting rights in America. Among the other notable Blacks
present at the conference who became part of its five-year existence as an
activist body were John Hope, J. Max Barber, and William Monroe Trotter.
Perhaps because of its insistence on educational segregation, the Niagara
Movement did not gain popular acceptance, and so its membership and their
goals dissolved, and revived in the new movement for Black rights organized
as the NAACP.

The National Association for the Advancement of Colored People was
founded in New York City on February 12, 1909, heralded by the publication
of "The Call." (The year 1909 was also the centennial of Abraham Lincoln's
birth.) This announcement urged all leaders to abolish racially biased legislation and to take up the Black cause in America by enforcing the Thirteenth,
Fourteenth, and Fifteenth amendments to the Constitution. Published in
Black newspapers across the United States, "The Call" recruited members
into the new social and political body whose national office was located in
New York City. The initial board of directors for the NAACP was entirely
composed of Whites, including the organization's first president, Moorfield

Storey, an attorney. W.E.B. Du Bois, the only Black initially named to an important position in the organization, was made publicity director and, by extension, editor of the NAACP's official journal, *The Crisis*. After the initial "call" for other progressives to join the racial struggle, the NAACP held its first official conference in New York on May 31, 1909, with more than 300 Blacks and Whites in attendance. Once the NAACP became relatively established, its board of directors became increasingly composed of Blacks; by 1934, most board members were Black, and this trend has continued to the present time.

Among the most notable successes of the new body was its highly organized protest against Woodrow Wilson's segregation of the federal government (1913) and against D.W. Griffith's film *Birth of a Nation* (1915), in which Blacks were portrayed as lazy, violent, and ignorant. Through the NAACP's rigorous advertising campaign, the racist film was banned or at least not viewed in many cities around the country. This first use of organized protest against the film and the Ku Klux Klan it glorified set a precedent of success that inspired the organization to move quickly and loudly against any and all misrepresentations of Black people and culture. These two protests forced NAACP organizers to recognize the body's growing power, and in 1917, they chose to use this power as a lever to force the federal government to allow Blacks to be commissioned as officers in **World War I**. This success led to the commission of 600 Black officers and the registration of 700,000 Blacks for the draft.

Perhaps because of its early emphasis on local organizing practices and rigorous recruitment, the NAACP's membership grew quickly, as did its number of branch offices across the United States. By 1919, the NAACP had more than 300 branch offices and 90,000 members. The year 1919 was also noteworthy in the NAACP for its publication of its investigative report, *Thirty Years of Lynching in the United States*. Although the organization had spoken out against **lynching** as early as 1917, with this report the NAACP took up the antilynching cause first emphasized by **Ida B. Wells-Barnett** in earnest, and although the organization never successfully forced antilynching legislation to be passed on a federal or state level, its persistent protest against lynching is credited with its decrease and eventual cessation. Equipping all its branches with a flag hung outside each time "A Black Man Was Lynched Today," the NAACP once again demonstrated the power of collective dissent as President Woodrow Wilson spoke out publicly against lynching.

Even as the NAACP was still fighting against lynch mobs and hostility against Blacks on a more general level, it also began to turn its attention to the unequal access to education, housing, health care, and public transportation that Blacks had historically received. In a series of court cases and legislation involving the unconstitutionality of discrimination in these areas so crucial to civil rights, the NAACP won a string of victories in state and federal courts, as well as in Congress. Notable among them were *Buchanen v. Worley* (housing districts could not be forced on Blacks, 1917), admission of

Black students to the University of Maryland (1935), *Morgan v. Virginia* (Supreme Court recognized that states cannot segregate interstate public transport by bus or train, 1946), discrimination in federal government offices banned (1948), *Brown v. Board of Education* ("separate but equal" struck down in favor of desegregation, 1954), and the Civil Rights Act (1964). Thurgood Marshall, later the first African American Supreme Court Justice, played a crucial role in the NAACP's legal activity and its Legal Defense Fund (Ostrom, 266).

As the **Civil Rights Movement** gathered momentum in the late 1950s and early 1960s, the NAACP discussed the role it would play in these important

Poster supporting the NAACP, 1941. Courtesy of the Library of Congress.

times. Resolute in its use of state and federal courtrooms to battle racism and discrimination, the body kept itself as a whole out of the often fractious and dangerous social battles being waged on the streets of **the South**. This did not prevent individual members from engaging in nonviolent protests, however, and in 1960, the NAACP's Youth Council began a series of lunch counter "sit-ins" around the South, resulting in the desegregation of more than sixty department store eateries. In addition to these nonviolent protests, NAACP members organized widespread civil rights rallies. As a result of the rallies' success, the NAACP named its first field director to oversee the legal and safety concerns of these peaceful protests. Tragically, the field director and highly successful organizer **Medgar Evers** was shot outside his home in 1963, just five months before the assassination of John F. Kennedy.

As the civil rights war evolved, the NAACP did as well, eventually turning its attention to Black participation in self-government through voting. Lobbying for voting sites in high schools, the NAACP persuaded twenty-four states to set up such sites by 1979. Concentration on the Black vote would continue through the 1980s, as the NAACP obtained extension of the Voting Rights Act (1981) and as it registered record numbers of Black voters (500,000 in 1982 alone). In tandem with its persistent efforts in the 1980s to increase political participation among the Black community, the NAACP also brought global attention to apartheid in South Africa by rallying in New York City (1989) and by encouraging a boycott of that nation by all people of color. By 1993, the antiapartheid movement was successful, and in 1994, South Africa held its first all-race elections.

Since then, the NAACP has focused on the appointment of racially sensitive Supreme Court justices, on preventing economic hardship in the Black community, on promoting higher education among Blacks and other people of color, and on providing alternatives to gang affiliation and violent behavior for Black youths. Still thriving, still with much work to do, the NAACP continues to be a viable social, economic, legal, and political force in and for the Black community in the United States. Although the organization's earliest and most direct connections to American literature are certainly the editor of The Crisis, W.E.B. Du Bois (The Souls of Black Folk), and the poet and lyricist **James Weldon Johnson** ("Lift Every Voice and Sing"), the NAACP is also closely linked to Black arts and literature through its nearly forty-year distribution of Image awards to Black cultural personages, including the poet **Nikki Giovanni** (Quilting the Black Eyed Pea) in 2002. **Walter White** was affiliated with the organization for many years, and **Langston Hughes** wrote a history of the NAACP, as well as a poem about the organization first published in The Crisis in June 1941 (Ostrom). **Jessie Redmon Fauset** was an editor for The Crisis as well as for a children's magazine affiliated with the NAACP, *The Brownies' Book*.

Resources: Langston Hughes, Fight for Freedom: The Story of the NAACP (New York: Berkeley Books, 1962); Kenneth Janken, White: The Biography of Walter White, Mr. NAACP (New York: New Press, 2003); Gilbert Jonas, Freedom's Sword: The

NAACP and the Struggle Against Racism in America, 1909–1969 (New York: Routledge, 2005); Charles Flint Kellogg, NAACP: A History of the National Association of Colored People (Baltimore: Johns Hopkins Press, 1967); Hans Ostrom, A Langston Hughes Encyclopedia (Westport, CT: Greenwood Press, 2002), 266–267; Mary White Ovington, Black and White Sat Down Together: The Reminiscences of an NAACP Founder (New York: Feminist Press, 1996); Barbara Ross, J. E. Springarn and the Rise of the NAACP, 1911–1939 (New York: Atheneum, 1972); Mark Tushnet, The NAACP's Legal Strategy Against Segregated Education, 1925–1950 (Chapel Hill: University of North Carolina Press, 1987); Carolyn Wedin, Inheritors of the Spirit: Mary White Ovington and the Founding of the NAACP (New York: Wiley, 1998).

Deirdre Ray

Nadir (1877–1915). A name given to the grim era between the end of **Reconstruction** and **World War I**. The term "nadir" (one definition of which is "lowest point") was first applied to this period by the historian Rayford W. Logan, designating it as the lowest point in postemancipation African American history. The period of Reconstruction after the **Civil War** had been relatively hopeful, with public facilities and institutions in **the South** open to African Americans for the first time, and some Black men elected to political offices. After federal troops were withdrawn from the South in 1877, however, the federal government abandoned the project of social equality for African Americans. In the years that followed, the rights of Black people shrank dramatically. In addition to political disenfranchisement, they were subject to "Jim Crow" segregation, which forced them to use public facilities entirely separate from those for White people. This system was widely practiced, and eventually was sanctioned by the federal government in the Supreme Court case *Plessy v. Ferguson* (1896). Most disturbingly, thousands of **lynching**s, gruesome public acts of torture and murder, were recorded during this era. Lynchings were carried out by White mobs not only to punish individuals, but also to control the entire Black community with terror. In response, African Americans organized politically, forming groups such as the National Association of Colored Women (1895), the National Association for the Advancement of Colored People (**NAACP**) (1909), and the National Urban League (1911).

An equally important form of resistance was the unprecedented proliferation of literature by African Americans in this era. This included not only explicitly antiracist political tracts such as **Ida B. Wells-Barnett**'s widely influential *Southern Horrors: Lynch Law in All Its Forms* (1892), **essays** such as those collected in *The Souls of Black Folk* by **W.E.B. Du Bois** (1903), and **Booker T. Washington**'s **autobiography**, *Up from Slavery* (1901), but also numerous volumes of significant imaginative literature. **Paul Laurence Dunbar**, the most prominent poet of the nadir, gained a national reputation when his second collection, *Majors and Minors* (1895), was lauded in *Harper's Weekly* by the magazine's editor, William Dean Howells. **Charles Waddell Chesnutt**, a novelist, essayist, and author of "local color" short stories, was the first African American to be published in the *Atlantic Monthly*. Following two collections of stories, Chesnutt published his two most successful novels, *The House Behind the Cedars* (1900) and *The Marrow of Tradition* (1901), cementing his position as one of the most important writers in the African American tradition. Among the most impressive achievements of this time were contributions to politics and literature by African American women, leading the author **Frances E. W. Harper** to declare that the 1890s was the brink of a "Woman's era." In addition to political treatises, including **Anna Julia Haywood Cooper**'s *A Voice from the South* (1892), African American women produced numerous successful novels, including Harper's *Iola Leroy* (1892) and **Pauline Elizabeth Hopkins**'s *Contending Forces* (1900). Though these works are most often characterized as bourgeois domestic novels, in contrast to the racial protest style of some male novelists, African American women of this period should be credited with writing novels representing a wide range of political concerns, from **feminism** to Christian evangelism to **Black Nationalism**. (*See* **Novel**.)

Resources: Primary Sources: Charles W. Chesnutt, *Stories, Novels, and Essays* (New York: Library of America, 2002); Anna Julia Cooper, *A Voice from the South* (New York: Oxford University Press, 1988); W.E.B. Du Bois, *The Souls of Black Folk* (1903; repr. New York: Modern Library, 1996); Paul Laurence Dunbar, *The Collected Poetry of Paul Laurence Dunbar*, ed. Joanne Braxton (Charlottesville: University Press of Virginia, 1993); Frances E. W. Harper, *Iola Leroy; or, Shadows Uplifted* (New York: Oxford University Press, 1988); Pauline E. Hopkins, *Contending Forces: A Novel Illustrative of Negro Life North and South* (New York: Oxford University Press, 1988); Booker T. Washington, *Up from Slavery* (New York: Penguin, 1986); Ida B. Wells-Barnett, *Southern Horrors and Other Writings: The Anti-lynching Campaign of Ida B. Wells, 1892–1900*, ed. Jaqueline Jones Royster (Boston: Bedford, 1997). **Secondary Sources:** Dickson D. Bruce, *Black American Writing from the Nadir: The Evolution of a Literary Tradition, 1877–1915* (Baton Rouge: Louisiana State University Press, 1989); Hazel Carby, *Reconstructing Womanhood: The Emergence of the Afro-American Woman Novelist* (New York: Oxford University Press, 1987); Rayford W. Logan, *The Negro in American Life and Thought: The Nadir, 1877–1901* (New York: Dial Press, 1954).

Holly A. Jackson

Naming. Naming patterns in African American literature reflect the naming history of African Americans as it has developed over some three centuries. Several traditional naming practices of West Africa (the birth place of most of the early slaves in America) are still apparent in African American life as well as in the literature that has grown from this existence.

Traditional West African naming practices represent the idea that names literally define the people who hold them. In one sense, a name in traditional West Africa might give very detailed information about conditions of birth: the day, the time of day, place, physical condition, appearance, whether the birth was a multiple birth, and so on. A contemporary example of this kind of naming in African American liteature is the character Copper in **Ernest**

James Gaines's short story "Bloodline." He is the son of a White man and a Black woman, and is thought to be the color of copper.

Often names indicate the hopes that the parents have for their children's futures. In fact, one generation of the Day family in **Gloria Naylor**'s *Mama Day* attempts to introduce peace and hope to the family by naming two of their children Peace and Hope. Names sometimes represent events important to the familial or group history. Since names served as a conduit of oral history, they were extremely important to West African culture.

Many of the West African naming practices survived the slave trade from Africa to America. Although most of the names in America were not recognizably African, the name constructions followed some of the patterns of traditional West African names. In particular, slaves, especially those living on isolated coastal islands, maintained the practice of naming children for the day on which they were born. In African American literature, the significance of day names appears, for example, in *Mama Day*, which is set on a coastal island. In this novel, Sapphira, an enslaved woman, gives her children the last name Day. In doing so, she maintains the West African naming tradition, although not overtly so. **Toni Morrison** recalls the importance of day names in her novel *Song of Solomon*, in which a secret group of avengers is called the Seven Days.

As their ancestors did, many enslaved African Americans had birth names that were so intimate that those other than family members and close friends were unaware of the names. This, too, is a pattern that appears in African American literature. In *Song of Solomon*, Toni Morrison writes: "Under the recorded names were other names, just as 'Macon Dead,' recorded for all time in some dusty file, hid from view the real names of people, places, and things. Names that had meaning. No wonder Pilate put hers in her ear. When you know your name, you should hang on to it, for unless it is noted down and remembered, it will die when you do" (23). In this passage, Morrison highlights the contrast between orality and literacy; the name, once a strictly oral conduit of family information in Africa, must be written down in America in order for it to live on.

Also, as their ancestors had done, enslaved African Americans named each other beyond the birth event to chronicle life changes or major events. Although birth names are usually a matter of official record in African American literature, as in African American life in general, often the community bestows names to recognize an event or a characteristic of a person. For instance, the community and the readers of *Song of Solomon* come to know the main character as Milkman, not Macon Dead, Jr., his birth name. When Milkman is five years old, a neighbor looks through a Dead family window to see that Macon, Jr., is still breast-feeding. Thus, he acquires the name Milkman. In *Mama Day*, Miranda Day is a midwife who has delivered so many babies and nurtured the community that she acquires the name Mama Day. And when Janie in **Zora Neale Hurston**'s novel *Their Eyes Were Watching God*, asks Tea Cake about his name, he answers that his mother named him Vergible Woods, making the distinction between his birth name and the name that he acquired at some later point in life.

The uniquely American component of African naming strategies is that names come to represent freedom among African Americans, especially those who were enslaved or who were active in the political protests of the 1960s and 1970s during the **Black Power** movement. The **slave narratives** by **Frederick Douglass, Harriet Ann Jacobs**, and others chronicle the approach to naming in the life of those enslaved and newly freed. These authors wrote of assuming the master's name when they were slaves but discarding it upon their freedom from **slavery**. Since most slave narrative authors had escaped from slavery, the changing of their names was as much a survival tactic as an important declaration of freedom. However, for the slaves who escaped and for those African Americans who were declared free from slavery by the Thirteenth Amendment (1865), the choice to change names was also to define themselves as free people. A people who had essentially no liberties in the system of slavery now had the freedom to choose who they wanted to be. The first step toward making a new life was defining self in a name. In *Narrative of William W. Brown, a Fugitive Slave*, **William Wells Brown** considers the changing of his name to be one of his first acts after escaping slavery: "What would be my occupation, was a subject of much anxiety to me, and the next thing what should be my name?" (96). During his years as a slave, Brown's name had been changed from William to Sandford because a relative of his master was also named William, and he had come to live with the master's family. This forced renaming was a point of much contention for Brown. About seeking physical and emotional freedom from slavery, Brown observes: "So I was not only hunting for my liberty, but also hunting for a name" (97).

Demonstrating that this valorizing of the name was common among freed persons, **Booker T. Washington** comments in his autobiography, *Up from Slavery*: "In some way a feeling got among the coloured [sic] people that it was far from proper for them to bear the surname of their former owners, and a great many of them took other surnames. This was one of the first signs of freedom" (102). In the novel *Beloved*, Toni Morrison's Stamp Paid names himself once he obtains his freedom from slavery.

The concept of naming oneself resurfaced as a symbol of freedom during the **Black Arts Movement** in literature that correlated with the Black Power movement of the 1960s and 1970s. Ernest James Gaines's Robert X character in *In My Father's House* is the talk of the town when he arrives in search of his estranged father. The residents are leery of him primarily because of what his name represents. Virginia, the woman who owns the boardinghouse where Robert X stays, can't remember what group goes by the last name "X"—"She couldn't remember now whether it was the Black Panthers or the Black Muslims" (3). When talking to Virginia, another character says, "One of them, hanh? Well, you got something on your hands now" (79). **Malcolm X**, a Black Muslim and a noted activist during the 1950s and 1960s, had the birth name of Malcolm Little. He was also known as Malik El-Shabazz after he converted to Islam. The act of renaming himself was an effort to divest himself of the slave master's name that may have been Little.

Gayl Jones's *Corregidora* is about Ursa Corregidora's familial hatred for the slave master who was named Corregidora and who sexually abused Ursa's great-grandmother and grandmother. This hatred is passed down from generation to generation. Kiswana Brown, a character in Gloria Naylor's *The Women of Brewster Place* and *Linden Hills*, rebels against what she perceives as the social conformity and associated material success of her parents' generation to redefine herself and her connection to the Black community. She changes her name from Melanie to Kiswana, a Swahili name.

Biblical names are prevalent in African American literature as well. The two Dead sisters in *Song of Solomon* are named First Corinthians and Magdelene. Milkman's aunt is named Pilate for the Roman magistrate who sentenced Jesus to death by crucifixion. Her father, who had wanted a biblical name, pointed to the Bible and settled on the name Pilate for his daughter. Gloria Naylor's *Bailey's Café* is replete with biblical names. In this case, the novelist uses the names to aid in a feminist revision of the Bible.

Often, African American authors deliver other messages in their characters' names. Writing for the **Chicago Defender** newspaper, Langston Hughes created a character named Jesse B. Semple, later changed to Jesse B. Simple, who commented on subjects from economics to love in a way that common readers could understand; thus his name. Also, he was deceptively simple, and in the tales featuring him, he often outsmarts the supposedly more sophisticated character, Boyd. In Hughes's eighteen poems featuring Madam Alberta K. Johnson, the character insists upon being called "Madam," and in the poem "Madam and the Census Man," Madam argues with the government official about her name.

In **Richard Wright**'s *Native Son*, Bigger Thomas is the embodiment of Black angst in the first half of the twentieth century. The unspoken pressure from White America on his actions is "bigger" than he, a Black man from an urban tenement. Even the two murders that he commits are more than the murders of two women. They represent the tremendous weight of White oppression on a Black man of Richard Wright's time.

In addition to craftily naming their characters, African American writers often assign place names that speak with cultural specificity. For instance, the Bottom in Toni Morrison's *Sula* is where the Black residents in Medallion, Ohio, live, a great irony since the Bottom is located in the hills. The land was compensation to a slave. The White farmer who gave him the land said that when God looks down, he sees that land as bottom land—"the best land there is" (5). The land is not suitable for planting, but the residents take "small consolation that every day they could literally look down on the white folks" (5).

The emphasis on naming is apparent in the names of many African American authors who have changed their names to further define themselves. The poet LeRoi Jones changed his name to **Imamu Amiri Baraka**, and the writer Don L. Lee changed his name to **Haki R. Madhubuti**. The source of

Toni Cade Bambara's last name is unclear, but she did add Bambara herself. **Ntozake Shange**, author of the well-known work *for colored girls who have considered suicide/when the rainbow is enuf*, was formerly known as Paulette Williams. In Xhosa, the Zulu language, her name means "she who comes with her own things" and "she who walks like a lion." The Nobel laureate Toni Morrison changed her name from Chloe Anthony Wofford Morrison. The noted scholar and essayist **bell hooks** was named Gloria Watkins at her birth. The Marguerite Johnson of the autobiography *I Know Why the Caged Bird Sings* is better known to the world as **Maya Angelou**.

Resources: William Wells Brown, *Narrative of William W. Brown, a Fugitive Slave* (London: Addison-Wesley, 1969); Ernest J. Gaines, *In My Father's House* (New York: Knopf, 1978); Donna Akiba Sullivan Harper, *Not So Simple: The "Simple" Stories by Langston Hughes* (Columbia: University of Missouri Press, 1995); Langston Hughes: *The Best of Simple* (New York: Hill and Wang, 1961); *The Collected Poems of Langston Hughes*, ed. Arnold Rampersad (New York: Vintage Classics, 1995); Toni Morrison, *Song of Solomon* (New York: Plume, 1987); Booker T. Washington, *Up from Slavery* (Boston: A. L. Burt, 1901).

Sharese Terrell Willis

Narrative Poetry. Narrative poetry tells a story in a verse form that usually employs regular meter, regular rhyme, or both meter and rhyme. It is among the oldest types of poetry and is strongly rooted in oral traditions and in performance. This is just as true of the ancient Greek epic tales of *The Iliad* and *The Odyssey* and the **ballad**s of the Scottish borderland as it is of a large category of African American poetry. It is thus fitting that the earliest known poem by an African American author, **Lucy Terry**'s "Bars Fight" (1755), is a simple narrative poem, establishing in its opening lines the date—August 25, 1746—of an Indian attack in Massachusetts, and then recounting the fates of eight individuals during that attack. Subsequent narrative poems by African American writers cover a broad range of themes and frequently record specifically Black experiences in the United States.

James Weldon Johnson's poems collected in *God's Trombones* (1927) tell stories in verse and frequently adopt the conventions of the **sermon**. "The Creation" retells the creation story of Genesis in a manner that includes idiomatic expressions (such as "I'll make me a world") and develops distinctively Southern imagery, as in the lines "Blacker than a hundred midnights/Down in a cypress swamp." The poem presents God as not just a voice but a fully embodied craftsman who shapes the planets and the human form with his skilled hands and whose whole body—including his feet, his eyes, and even the saliva produced in his mouth—plays a role in this **myth** of origins. A second poem in Johnson's collection, "Go Down Death, a Funeral Sermon," similarly draws on the storytelling traditions of the Black church and depicts a woman who has lived and worked long and hard being led to heaven by Death.

Other important narrative poems dating back to the early twentieth century are far more secular in nature, and include the "toasts" collected and analyzed in Roger D. Abrahams' groundbreaking study, *Deep Down in the Jungle . . . : Negro Narrative Folklore from the Streets of Philadelphia*, first published in 1964 and reissued in heavily revised form in 1970. Abrahams defines these toasts as "openly heroic, wildly imaginative, coercive, often violent stories and epic poems manufactured and performed by the young men" (p. 6) in his urban Black community. The patterns and performances of this particular subgenre of African American narrative poetry, including the boast and the verbal contest, has been linked by some scholars to cultural practices in Africa. Today, this tradition is perhaps most clearly manifested in the United States in the lyrics of **rap** music, in which modern (anti)heroes frequently engage in bragging and signifying, and often express a readiness for verbal contests or physical violence. Toasts such as those studied by Abrahams, as is often true of contemporary rap lyrics, have been regarded by many observers as obscene. Thus, if written down at all, they were often presented in bowdlerized form. For example, there are multiple twentieth-century versions of the exploits of Shine, a Black man working on the *Titanic* who is kept alive when disaster strikes only by his strong sense of self-preservation. The version of this narrative poem presented by **Langston Hughes** and **Arna Bontemps** in *The Book of Negro Folklore* (1958) has none of the sexually explicit offers and curse words found in the performed versions recorded and transcribed by Abrahams for his study almost a decade later. Other famous and anonymous toasts dating back to the early twentieth century include "Stackolee" and "The Signifying Monkey." The latter, which presents the monkey as an African American **trickster** figure, functions as a central text in **Henry Louis Gates**'s study *The Signifying Monkey* (1988); here, Gates sets out to develop a new theoretical discourse—one "generated from within the black tradition itself, autonomously" (p. xx)—for analyzing African American literature.

African American poets have also written significant examples of narrative poetry that follow European models. Langston Hughes works within the tradition of dramatic poetry in a series of poems using dialogue to tell a story; these include "Ballad of the Landlord" (1940, 1955), "Madam and the Rent Man" (1943), and "Madam and the Phone Bill" (1949). Hughes published numerous ballads, including twenty-five with "ballad" in the title, and he published eighteen "Madam" poems (Ostrom, 19–20; 229–230). Although **Countee Cullen**'s poetry tends to be lyrical in nature, he also has at least one notable example of narrative poetry, "Incident" (1925), written in the standard form of the ballad, with four-line stanzas alternating between four and three stresses per line. One of the most notable examples of this ballad form is **Dudley Randall**'s "Ballad of Birmingham" (1965), which uses the narrative function of the ballad to dramatic effect. The poem recounts the tragic impact of a Black church bombing in Birmingham, Alabama, in 1963. James Sullivan (1997) offers an insightful analysis of the relation between Randall's poem and the tradition up through the nineteenth century of printing inexpensively illustrated sheets of narrative poetry that recount recent sensational events in ballad form.

One of the most interesting developments in Black narrative poetry in the twentieth century is the reworking of popular songs or versified tales that have their origins within the African American literary tradition. **Sterling A. Brown**'s "Frankie and Johnny" (1932) takes up the ballad of the same name, a story retold for White audiences again and again in later decades to the extent that its likely Black origins have been all but erased. Brown makes a number of significant changes in his retelling of the tale: he establishes a clear racial difference between the title characters and introduces brutal imagery and ironic language. The most significant change, however, is in the poem's ending: rather than being shot by his jealous lover, Johnny is lynched for having sexual relations with a White woman. (Brown also wrote the narrative poem "The Odyssey of Big Boy".) Other modern retellings of Black narrative poetry include **Melvin B. Tolson**'s "The Birth of John Henry" (1965), which has its source in the anonymous ballads that relate a contest between the Black folk hero and a steel-driving machine developed to replace him, and **Ishmael Reed**'s "Railroad Bill, a Conjure Man" (1972), a modern and compelling revisioning of the traditional "Railroad Bill"; both versions present a folk (anti)hero who is **John Henry**'s opposite in almost every way.

In recent years, narrative poems have been incorporated as key elements in longer works by African American writers. Examples include **Toni Morrison**'s *Song of Solomon* (1977) and **Colson Whitehead**'s *John Henry Days* (2001). In Morrison's novel, the main character, Milkman, gradually realizes that the story rhymes in a children's game have preserved his own family's forgotten history, just as other songs throughout the novel play important communal and restorative functions. The ballad "John Henry" has a similarly fundamental but far more ironic function in Whitehead's novel. *John Henry Days* presents a young Black writer sent to cover the ceremony surrounding the first annual John Henry Days, a festival honoring the steel-driving folk hero, and establishes a series of connections or disconnections between the industrial and information ages. This reappearance of versified Black folk tales in modern poetry, and even in recent prose fiction, attests to narrative poetry's continuing cultural significance and its ability to influence multiple forms of literary expression. (*See* **Folklore; Folktales**.)

Resources: Roger D. Abrahams, *Deep Down in the Jungle . . . : Negro Narrative Poetry from the Streets of Philadelphia*, rev. ed. (Chicago: Aldine, 1970); Sterling Brown, "Frankie and Johnny" and "The Odyssey of Big Boy," in *The Portable Harlem Renaissance Reader*, ed. David Levering Lewis (New York: Viking, 1994), 229–232; Henry Louis Gates, Jr., *The Signifying Monkey: A Theory of Afro-American Literary Criticism* (New York: Oxford University Press, 1988); Langston Hughes and Arna Bontemps, eds., *The Book of Negro Folklore* (New York: Dodd, Mead, 1958); Toni Morrison, *Song of Solomon* (New York: Knopf, 1977); Hans Ostrom, *A Langston Hughes Encyclopedia* (Westport, CT: Greenwood Press, 2002); Alex Preminger, Frank J. Warnke, and O. B. Hardison, eds., *Princeton Encyclopedia of Poetry and Poetics*, enl. ed. (Princeton, NJ: Princeton University Press, 1974); Arnold Rampersad, ed., *The Collected Poems of Langston Hughes* (New York: Vintage Classics, 1995); James

D. Sullivan, *On the Walls and in the Streets: American Poetry Broadsides from the 1960s* (Urbana: University of Illinois Press, 1997); Melvin B. Tolson, *"Harlem Gallery" and Other Poems of Melvin B. Tolson*, ed. Raymond Nelson (Charlottesville: University Press of Virginia, 1999); Colson Whitehead, *John Henry Days* (New York: Doubleday, 2001).

James B. Kelley

Nashville, Tennessee. Shaded by magnolia trees and surrounded by craggy outcrops of limestone, Nashville rests among the gently sloping hills of middle Tennessee. It is a city of nicknames: Music City, USA, the Buckle of the Bible Belt, the Athens of the South. It is a city of cultural variety: only a few miles separate Music City Row, the nexus of the country music industry and home of Elvis Presley's gold piano, from Vanderbilt University and an exact replica of the Greek Parthenon. It is a city of firsts: the Ku Klux Klan held its first meeting there in 1866, the same year Fisk University was founded, one of the first institutions to educate the newly freed slaves.

As of this writing, about 570,000 people live within the metro Nashville area, which was settled by Whites on Christmas Day, 1779, but had been inhabited by American Indians in 8000 B.C.E. and later by Mississippian culture American Indians from around 1000 to 1400 C.E. Originally called Fort Nashborough, after Francis Nash, a general in the Revolutionary War, the settlement became Nashville in 1784, Tennessee became a state in 1796, and Nashville became its capital in 1843. The frontier area prospered as the northernmost stop on the Natchez Trace, a trail beginning in Mississippi, and as a center of cotton, tobacco, livestock, and grain trade; nevertheless, only 345 people lived there in 1800, of whom 154 were Black, some free but most enslaved (Goodstein, 74). As the village grew into a city and more families arrived looking for new opportunities, more slaves were brought in to help change the surrounding farmland into large, prosperous plantations. Some Blacks and Whites worshipped together in churches, chiefly Methodist, that had sprung up alongside the stores and other buildings. As opposed to the North, however, where discrete African American Protestant sects could form, African Americans in **the South** were usually not allowed to worship away from watchful eyes of Whites. Prevented from learning to read and write during the antebellum period (1780–1861), African Americans therefore channeled their creativity into oral media.

In fact, singing and storytelling stand as the earliest examples of African American literature in the young United States generally and Nashville particularly. **Spirituals** and **folktales**—many concerning the **trickster** figure commonly found in African stories—spread from farm to farm. In 1935 **Zora Neale Hurston** published several fables as *Mules and Men*, arguably the first collection of African American **folklore** gathered by an African American. Whether sung or told, these allegorical works fostered community, as in the lines "Talk about me much as you please,/Chillun, talk about me much as you please," from "I Been Rebuked and I Been Scorned." Some works encouraged optimism, as reflected in the line "I ain't got long to stay here," from the song

"Steal Away." Some works were religious in nature, as reflected in the lines, "Tell old Pharaoh,/Let my people go," from the song "Go Down, Moses."

Although the formation of independent African American churches, primarily Baptist and Methodist, indicates a more progressive interracial association, nonetheless, the city itself purchased sixty slaves in 1830–1831 for civic work (Lovett, 20). Similarly, in the mid-1800s, Nashville considered numerous proposals for all-Black schools, but by 1856 city law contained a statute that imposed a $50 fine on any White teacher found educating Blacks (Goodstein, 152). With regard to literary and quasi-literary documents from this period in Nashville, only a few letters written by Susanna Carter, a slave at Belle Meade Plantation, have survived.

Shortly before the decisive **Civil War** battle of Shiloh in the spring of 1862, Union troops captured Nashville to use it as a base from which to launch campaigns into the Deep South; the battle of Shiloh occurred about nine miles from Savannah, Tennessee. The last major Confederate offensive of the Civil War was the battle of Nashville in 1864. Most of the social and political gains achieved locally during the Union occupation, as well as nationally through the Emancipation Proclamation (1863) and the Thirteenth Amendment (1865), were almost immediately revoked in the violent, impoverished environment that characterized the Black experience during **Reconstruction** and the early years of the period of segregation known as Jim Crow (1870–1950). Terrorized by Whites, confined to slums by low wages coupled with little opportunity for advancement, and losing friends and family to the **Great Migration**, African Americans in and around Nashville nevertheless developed a strong literary culture from 1865 forward. The "Letter to the Union Convention, 1865," signed by fifty-nine prominent Black citizens of Nashville, joined the chorus of published entreaties urging the government to legally abolish slavery. Soon thereafter, William B. Scott began the first Black newspaper in Nashville, the *Nashville Colored Tennessean* (1865–1866). Believing that Blacks should issue their own theological materials, Richard Henry Boyd founded the first Black religious publishing house, the National Baptist Publishing Board, in 1896, which continues to print approximately 14 million copies of works annually. In 1924 the Board published the play *Because He Lives: A Drama of Resurrection*, by the Nashville native Willa Ann Hadley Townsend (Moore).

Boyd also founded *The Globe*, a newspaper in circulation from 1905 to 1960. He founded it originally to publicize African Americans' boycott of streetcars in Nashville (1905–1907) in reaction to city-mandated segregation of such services as transportation. Boyd's son, Henry Allen Boyd, eventually inherited control of *The Globe*; he and other leaders used its editorial pages to propose civic improvements, including the state-funded creation of an African American college, the Tennessee Agricultural and Institutional State Normal School, in 1912. This institution became Tennessee State University in 1968. Then it absorbed the University of Tennessee at Nashville in 1979 after a lengthy legal battle. This was the first time a predominately Black school took over a predominantly White school.

The founding of Fisk School (later University) in 1866 stands as Nashville's most significant contribution to African American literature. Fisk's original purpose was twofold: to provide a free education from primary through secondary grades and to train its graduates as Christian teachers capable of establishing schools elsewhere. Five months after opening, close to 1,000 students, the youngest seven and the oldest seventy, attended regularly (Richardson, 7). In 1867 Fisk School became Fisk University, charging a fee for its services. By 1871 the school faced a financial crisis; it formed the Fisk Jubilee Singers, who toured the nation, singing popular music and encores of "slave songs," and helping to raise money for the university. The Singers' success not only raised several thousand dollars but also probably rescued traditional spirituals from potential obscurity. The Jubilee Singers have remained a fixture at Fisk.

Among notable Fisk graduates are the historian **John Hope Franklin** (graduated 1935), the novelist **Frank Yerby** (M.A., 1938), the novelist **Julius Lester** (graduated 1960), the poet Helen Quigless (graduated 1966), and the poet **Nikki Giovanni** (graduated 1967), who was active in the campus chapter of the Student Nonviolent Coordinating Committee (SNCC). The novelist **Nella Larsen** and the playwright **Joseph Seamon Cotter, Jr.**, both attended Fisk around 1910, but neither graduated. Distinguished teachers at Fisk include the philosopher **Alain Locke** (1927–1928), the poet **Sterling A. Brown** (1928–1929), the novelist **James Weldon Johnson** (1930–1934), the **Harlem Renaissance** painter Aaron Douglas (1944–1966), and the poet **Robert Hayden** (1946–1968). **John Oliver Killens** was writer-in-residence from 1965 to 1968, and **Arna Bontemps** served as head librarian from 1943 to 1966. Fisk's first black President, the sociologist **Charles Spurgeon Johnson**, created the Race Relations Institute in 1944; past leaders of the three-week conference include the Supreme Court justice Thurgood Marshall and the writer **Countee Cullen**. Spurgeon also arranged for the donation of the Alfred Stieglitz Collection to Fisk. A negative response at Fisk to an early version of his autobiography in 1943 was among the factors that led **Richard Wright** to rework the text into *Black Boy* (1945). The Fisk University Library owns a first edition of *Poems on Various Subjects* (1773) by **Phillis Wheatley**, as well as correspondence from **Langston Hughes**, who described a visit there (c. 1931) in his first autobiography, *The Big Sea* (1940): "For the first time I stood before a large audience of my own people, reading my poems, and I was thrilled, because they seemed to like those poems—poems in which I had tried to capture some of the dreams and heartaches that all Negroes know."

Literary Nashville, however, reflected the schism between the White and Black communities in the early and mid-twentieth century. The first public library exclusively for African Americans, the Negro Branch of the Carnegie Library, opened in 1916. Across town at Vanderbilt University, only a few years before Hughes's visit, a group of writers had organized as the Fugitives in

1922. The group included Allen Tate, John Crowe Ransom, Donald David-son, and Robert Penn Warren. One of their purposes was to try to preserve an idyllic, distinctly Southern way of life in the face of encroaching modernity. Though not overtly racist, the writers idealized a society that itself had been undeniably so, since much White culture had developed in the leisure time permitted by the exploitation of Black labor.

Over a forty-year period (1911–1951), no African Americans were elected to the city council, partly because a poll tax prevented lower- and middle-class Blacks from voting. Segregation and its "separate-but-equal" doctrine, legally sanctioned by *Plessy v. Ferguson* (1896), distorted every aspect of Southern life until the historic rulings in *Brown v. Board of Education* (1954) and Nashville's *Kelley v. Board of Education* (1955) forced the integration of public schools in 1957 and helped create the **Civil Rights Movement**. The success of the lunch counter sit-ins in Greensboro, North Carolina, encouraged James Lawson, a student at Vanderbilt's Divinity School and cofounder of SNCC with **Martin Luther King, Jr.**, to organize similarly successful sit-ins at Nashville's lunch counters and bus terminals in 1960. Disagreements within the Civil Rights Movement in the late 1960s pervaded the Fisk Writers' Conferences in 1966 and 1967. Longing for a markedly Black aesthetic, **Melvin B. Tolson** derided Robert Hayden's use of traditional poetic forms and accused him of being apolitical. Picking up on the "black power" tenor of the time, as well as on Tolson's tone, some students began calling Hayden "Oreo," driving him to abandon his professorship at Fisk for one at the University of Michigan (Conniff, 488). **Gwendolyn Brooks**, in contrast, found her exposure at Fisk to the **Black Arts Movement** and the activism of **Amiri Barka** so transforming that she later divided her work into "pre-1967" and "post-1967."

Other writers with roots in Nashville include the civil rights activist **Julian Bond** and the poet **Sarah Webster Fabio** (Moore). Emily Bernard, a scholar specializing in American and African American Studies, including the Har-lem Renaissance, was born in Nashville. She edited the correspondence be-tween Langston Hughes and **Carl Van Vechten**.

Since 1982, Tennessee State University and the Metropolitan Historical Commission have sponsored an annual conference on African American culture and history. **Patricia McKissack**, a Newbery Award-winning author of children's and young-adult books, resides in Nashville, and the journalist **Afi-Odelia E. Scruggs** describes her trip there to reconnect with her family in *Claiming Kin* (2002). Each summer the journal **Callaloo** sponsors writing workshops at Fisk. Every February, Vanderbilt's Bishop Joseph Johnson Black Cultural Center hosts public lectures and programs in honor of Black History Month.

Resources: Edward L. Ayers and Bradley C. Mittendorf, eds., *The Oxford Book of the American South* (New York: Oxford University Press, 1997); Emily Bernard, ed., *Remember Me to Harlem: The Letters of Langston Hughes and Carl Van Vechten, 1925–1964* (New York: Knopf, 2001); J. A. Bryant Jr., *Twentieth-Century Southern Literature* (Lexington: University Press of Kentucky, 1997); Brian Conniff, "Answering 'The

Waste Land': Robert Hayden and the Rise of the African American Poetic Sequence, *African American Review* 33, no. 3 (Autumn 1999): 487–506; Anita Shafer Goodstein, *Nashville 1780–1860: From Frontier to City* (Gainesville: University of Florida Press, 1989); Langston Hughes, *The Big Sea* (New York: Knopf, 1940); John Oliver Killens and Jerry W. Ward, Jr., eds., *Black Southern Voices* (New York: Meridian, 1992); Bobby L. Lovett, *The African-American History of Nashville, Tennessee, 1780–1930: Elites and Dilemmas* (Fayetteville: University of Arkansas Press, 1999); Earlene J. Moore, "Remembering Black Writers Associated with Tennessee: A Representative Bibliography," Library, University of Tennessee, Memphis, http://www.utm.edu/departments/acadpro/library/information_pages/tennblack2.htm; Joe M. Richardson, *A History of Fisk University, 1865–1946* (University: University of Alabama Press, 1980); Charles Reagan Wilson and William Ferris, eds., *Encyclopedia of Southern Culture* (Chapel Hill: University of North Carolina Press, 1989).

Jessica Allen

Nation of Islam. The Nation of Islam, a religious and political organization, developed out of several black nationalist organizations in the early decades of the twentieth century (*see* **Black Nationalism**). Among these precursors is one group of particular note: Drew Ali's Moorish Science Temple of America, established in 1913. Drew believed that by following the precepts of the Muslims, African Americans, who, he preached, were truly descendants of the Muslim faith, would be free of racial oppression. By following the Christian faith of their enslavers, Drew argued, they were participants in their own downfall.

Wallace Fard Mohammad (also known as Wali Fard) was another primary shaper of the Nation of Islam movement. A door-to-door salesman, Fard used his charismatic personality to win over followers to the movement he called the Lost-Found Nation of Islam. Instead of focusing on the five pillars of Islam, the heart of Muslim belief, he created a mythology revolving around the claim that African Americans were all descended from a tribe called Shabazz, a superior race of beings. Whites were created by an evil scientist and are therefore not human. His birthplace has never been verified, but Fard and many of his followers believed that he was born in Mecca, and he led them to believe he was an incarnation of Allah. Fard immigrated to the United States and established a mosque in **Detroit, Michigan**, in 1931.

Although Fard established the movement, it was developed by Elijah Muhammad (originally named Elijah Poole), who succeeded Fard after his disappearance in 1934. It was under Muhammad's leadership that the Nation of Islam became most associated with racial uplift. He believed, as Drew had, that the Christian religion was designed to enslave and oppress Blacks, especially men, and that by throwing off the yoke of Christianity, Black men could take their place as the true leaders of the world. White people were referred to as a race of devils who were responsible for all the evils of the African American community. By joining together to fight crime and drug addiction, African Americans could find economic independence.

While serving a prison sentence, Malcolm Little, later known as **Malcolm X**, was strongly influenced by the Nation of Islam and became a major spokesperson for the movement after his release, preaching black supremacy. After a pilgrimage to Mecca, Malcolm X modified his views and leaned more toward mainstream Islamic principles, shedding his more extreme anti-White stances. Three Nation of Islam members were arrested for his assassination in 1965. Indirectly, the Black nationalist views of the Nation of Islam contributed to the social and political ferment during the period of the **Black Arts Movement** in the 1960s and early 1970s.

Muhammad's son, Wallace Muhammad (Warith Deen), was installed as his father's successor in 1975. Although he was suspended from the movement for his dissident views, he eventually returned to the Nation of Islam, renaming it the World Community of Al-Islam in 1985, and publicly repudiating his father's racist and Black separatist views. Wallace worked toward the group's assimilation with the worldwide Islamic community.

However, under the leadership of Louis Farrakhan, the Nation of Islam continues as an organization that holds to its founding precepts. Farrakhan moved the Nation of Islam headquarters to New York to continue the work of Fard and to promote his Black separatist views. The movement continues to fight for Black independence from White oppression and for complete segregation of the races. Farrakhan calls for Black men to take responsibility for themselves and to band together to forge independence. The Million Man March on **Washington, D.C.**, in 1995 has been the crowning achievement of the Nation of Islam, but has been criticized as an example of the organization's refusal to allow women any recognition or ability to work toward the goals of Black economic independence.

Orthodox Islam continues to reject the principles of the Nation of Islam, which are disseminated through *The Final Call*, the organization's official newspaper. Islam particularly rejects racism, for the Koran teaches that God created all men to be equal. Islam also rejects the Nation of Islam's belief that Wali Fard was a human incarnation of God, and that Elijah Muhammad was a prophet.

Resources: Martha F. Lee, *The Nation of Islam: An American Millennarian Movement* (Syracuse, NY: Syracuse University Press, 1996); Elijah Muhammad, *History of the Nation of Islam* (Atlanta: Secretarius Memps Publications, 1994); Steven Tsoukalas, *The Nation of Islam: Understanding the "Black Muslims"* (Phillipsburg, NJ: P & R, 2001); Vibert L. White, *Inside the Nation of Islam: A Historical and Personal Testimony by a Black Muslim* (Gainesville: University of Florida Press, 2001).

Patricia Kennedy Bostian

Nature. From early **folktales** to contemporary environmental prose, nature has figured prominently in African American literature. It plays a role in essentially two ways that cannot be clearly separated: as a metaphor for a range of political, aesthetic, spiritual, and erotic concerns, and as actual physical presence with which people interact in various ways. While the metaphorical dimensions have been studied widely, critics are only beginning to explore the environmental implications of human–nature interactions in the African American imagination. As important forerunners of this shift, **Melvin Dixon** (1987) emphasized the role of wilderness, underground, and mountaintop as spatial metaphors that link African American identity to geography, Vera Norwood (1993) traced the development from rupture to positive identification with nature in a chapter on Black women writers, and Rachel Stein (1997) discussed links between nature and resistance against racism and sexism in works of **Zora Neale Hurston** and **Alice Walker**. More recently, ecocriticism, the ecologically informed study of literature and the environment, has started to ask vital new questions (for example, how African American texts challenge dominant notions of nature as pristine wilderness or idyllic pastoral landscape), promising fresh insights into the ways in which the natural world factors in the African American imagination.

In general, the development of African American literary views of nature parallels the larger shifts in the history of Blacks and Black literature in the United States, but it has two major distinguishing characteristics regarding the role of nature as physical presence. First, the significance of nature as living system has *increased* throughout the history of African American literature, even though the struggle for Black freedom and equality has long deemed serious literary interest in the natural environment as apolitical, even opportunistic. Second, many texts address a prevailing *tension* between an affirmative relationship with the environment, expressed in a deeply felt connection with nature and the possibility of life in accordance with it, and a critical, skeptical distance toward American landscapes as sites of fear and apprehension that carry traumatic memories of racist oppression.

In African American texts from the colonial and early national periods, meditations about nature formed an integral part of the larger cultural endeavor to use literature in countering assumptions of Black inferiority at the basis of the slaveholding ideology. **Phillis Wheatley**'s neoclassical *Poems on Various Subjects* (1773), for example, contains reflections about nature's beauty that echo religiously motivated expressions of sentiment in European and Euro-American texts of the day, pastoral scenes that gain a subversive significance as they promote the Black poet's intellectual assertion of Self. Her observations of natural phenomena, as in "An Hymn to the Morning," "An Hymn to the Evening," and "Ode to Neptune," also tell of a pervasive interest in and familiarity with the natural landscapes of the New World. The knowledge of the land implied in her poems does not seem to differ from eighteenth-century White ways of singing nature, but the cultural expression of this knowledge forms a basis for later, more explicit African American claims on the land itself.

Nature also figures prominently in African American folktales, especially the popular Brer Rabbit stories. The allegorical tales about the (animal) protagonist outwitting his physically superior (animal) antagonists, which primarily celebrate African American subversive wit, are based on a deep familiarity with the natural world. Moreover, many scenes contain subliminal messages of environmental knowledge and responsibility—for example, the animal figures communally clear the ground for planting corn, or learn how (not to) use a well—and can be read as early expressions of African American environmental sensibilities. Both in the stylized rhymes of Wheatley's hymns and in African American folktales, references to nature remain largely figurative, yet their symbolic import also carries with it early Black knowledge of and care for the continent's actual geographies.

In the pre–**Civil War** era, African American literary perspectives on nature were directly linked to the national struggle against **slavery**. In nineteenth-century **slave narratives**, in particular, nature is a distinctive thematic element that structures the movement from slavery to freedom—both spiritually, as the protagonists critically review the condition of slavery by way of natural metaphors, and physically, through the movement from a Southern plantation through a kaleidoscope of regional geographies to Northern territories. One of the most prominent examples of nature's powerful presence is **Henry Walton Bibb**'s *Narrative of the Life and Adventures of Henry Bibb* (1849); less frequent references to nature can be found in **Frederick Douglass**'s *Narrative of the Life of Frederick Douglass* (1845) and in **Harriet Ann Jacobs**'s *Incidents in the Life of a Slave Girl* (1861).

On a metaphorical level, all of the above slave narratives turn the protagonist's experiences into a "test of the wilderness" during which control of land and language affirms Black selfhood (Dixon, 20). Also, slave narratives challenge White idealizations of **the South** as an idyllic garden by opposing the horrors of the plantation to the harmonies and spiritual truths found in nature, as in Bibb's text: "I thought of the fishes of the water, the fowls of the air, the wild beasts of the forests, all appeared to be free, to go where they pleased, and I was an unhappy slave" (72). In their references to animals, they also counter the stigmatization of Blacks as subhuman "beasts" by applying animal imagery to Whites. Bibb's protagonist claims: "[A]mong slaveholders and slave hunters, to me it was like a person entering a wilderness among wolves and vipers" (98), and the fugitive in Jacobs's narrative symbolically links her experiences in Southern swamps to the sexual abuse faced by female slaves: "[E]ven those large, venomous snakes were less dreadful to my imagination than the white men in that community called civilized" (91). Bibb's protagonist also identifies himself with individual animals—"Oh, that I had the wings of a dove, that I might soar away to where there is no slavery" (72)—a partial identification on the slave's own premises designed to formulate alternative codes of ethics.

In conjunction with these symbolic levels, the slave narratives of Bibb, Jacobs, and Douglass also reflect upon "nature as such" and specifically African American relationships to the land. The narrators' critique of the slaveholding economy includes references to enforced **labor** in the fields and woods, small-scale gardening in the slave quarters, and religious meetings in the forests, all of which highlight the slaves' paradoxical ties to a land which they are forced to cultivate and know intimately, but cannot own. In Bibb and Jacobs, close-ups on African American relationships to nature on the plantation are followed by accounts of dramatic escapes into the surrounding woods, swamps, and rivers, addressing the conflicted position of Blacks vis-à-vis America's natural world as a space that both protects the fugitive and threatens his or her survival. Douglass, whose actual flight takes a different route, still imagines this paradigmatic scene as a potential scenario of failure, further emphasizing its significance in the African American literary imagination: "We were stung by scorpions, chased by wild beasts, bitten by snakes, and finally . . .—after swimming rivers, encountering wild beasts, sleeping in the woods, suffering hunger and nakedness—we were overtaken by our pursuers" (57). Douglass's narrative is also particularly strong in its anti-pastoralism, moving from oppressive rural to liberating urban spaces (Butler).

Considering their primarily political purpose, slave narratives pay remarkable attention to nature in its own right. Apart from serving as a complex metaphor and as a stage for Black protagonists' quest for freedom and subjectivity, the environment has a tangible presence in these texts, as a space to which people relate in historically specific ways, and even as an agent that hinders or promotes the fugitives' deliverance. Yet the political context prevents slave narratives from taking a more detailed look at the environment, from expressing a fully fledged sense of place, and from imagining alternative ways of relating to the land.

The period between the Civil War and the **Harlem Renaissance**—when former slaves, legally free to own land, were promised "forty acres and a mule," but were soon forced into the sharecropping system—did not bring significant new developments in African American literary visions of nature. Postbellum slave narratives continue to critically examine human interaction with nature on the plantation and to retrace the move from rural South to urban North. Also, some of **Charles Waddell Chesnutt**'s stories, such as "The Goophered Grapevine" (1887), value nature as a space that provides "conjure" stories as well as economic sustenance. In poetry, lesser-known writers work within traditional forms and themes; **William Stanley Braithwaite**, for example, muses about the effect of the seasons on New England's landscapes, and **Albery Allson Whitman**'s *The Rape of Florida* (1884) and other long poems deal with lost pastoral worlds and the superiority of primeval nature.

When the Harlem Renaissance emerged around 1920, the upsurge of African American creativity also brought new positions vis-à-vis the American continent. In particular, the mass migration of Blacks from the segregated South to Northern industrial centers, together with a self-conscious literary interest in thematic and aesthetic innovation, opened new possibilities for reconsidering traditional views of the land. Nature may not have been a major theme of the **New Negro** movement, but it was more closely linked to the central concerns of African American literature than before—particularly in two classical texts of the era, **Jean Toomer**'s *Cane* (1923) and Zora Neale Hurston's *Their Eyes Were Watching God* (1937).

Toomer's *Cane* moves from scenes of Black folk life in rural Georgia to the urban North and back to the South, exploring how the natural environment and human culture influence one another in different regions. In the dynamic geography of this multigenre text, natural metaphors figure prominently: the title suggests the rootedness of Black culture in Southern landscapes; black women's "natural" beauty is equated with the land, particularly the lush, exotic Southern flora (Kutzinski); and the text's evocations of mythical Southern territories can be read as an exploration of Black consciousness at the beginning of the twentieth century. At the same time, *Cane* is rich with details of Georgia's "plowed lands" and sawmills, with (failed) harvests ("November Cotton Flower"), and memories of "red soil and sweet-gum tree,/ So scant of grass, so profligate of pines" ("Song of the Son"), creating not only politically but also environmentally significant subtexts. Especially the blurred lines between rural and urban spaces, human and natural agency, wild and cultivated landscapes suggest an implicit critique of dominant visions of human mastery and control. Vera M. Kutzinski has argued that "*Cane* is not a mythical celebration of landscape as repository of shared cultural values and . . . racial essences but in fact a criticism of the folk romanticization so pervasive among early twentieth-century American intellectuals" (164); similarly, the history of enforced Black labor and the constant threat of White violence in these topographies undercut any attempt at celebrating a supposed Black rootedness in this "white-man's land," or at reclaiming an unspoiled affinity with nature, even as the text takes account of Black peasants' lives and the land's complex history.

Their Eyes Were Watching God (1937) in many ways marks the opposite pole of literary reformulations of nature during the Renaissance. The protagonist, Janie, moves from central Florida farther south, into the "wild" Everglades, embracing Black folk life and its earth-centeredness as authentic source of Black culture. Here, natural phenomena serve as metaphors for Janie's erotic longing (in an extended revelation under a blooming tree) for the role of Black women ("De nigger woman is de mule uh de world"; 14), Black placelessness ("us colored folks is branches without roots"; 15), Black class differences ("he's de wind and we's de grass"; 46), and the necessity to acknowledge superior forces (through a hurricane and a deadly bite of a rabid dog). From an ecological perspective, Janie's growing self-realization is also a movement away from her grandmother's memories of racist and sexist violence in the "wilderness" (echoing the role of nature in slave narratives) and toward a life in and with nature of the muck, fishing, hunting, and harvesting. Her ability to understand "nature's language" suggests a certain green humility and empathy; her defense of an overworked mule constitutes an example of environmental ethics; and her observations of the land grow increasingly environmentally perceptive ("Ground so rich that half a mile of it would have fertilized a Kansas wheat field"; 123); the disastrous end of her time in the Everglades is due to Tea Cake's decision to disregard the signs of nature. Hurston, based on her knowledge of nature's role in **voodoo** (Stein), celebrates the ability of Blacks to move beyond the experience of profound geographical displacement and to turn American places into personally meaningful, valuable locales. Nature plays a similar role in many of Hurston's short stories, her **autobiography**, her collections of **folklore**, and her other Florida novels.

In the poetry of this period, a small but important group of works combines expressions of racial pride with a fresh look at America's topographies. From **Langston Hughes**'s "The Negro Speaks of Rivers," "Earth Song," and "Our Land" to **Countee Cullen**'s "Heritage" and "To John Keats, Poet, at Spring Time," from **Alice Moore Dunbar Nelson**'s "April is on the Way" to **Helene Johnson**'s "Invocation," these poems merge political vision with an interest in particular landscapes, genteel sensibilities with the history of placelessness, and the longing for spiritual immersion in nature with oppressive memories of racist violence.

The decades following the Harlem Renaissance were dominated by racial **protest literature** and a focus on urban life that did not sustain literary explorations of nature. Characteristically, the protagonist of **Richard Wright**'s *Native Son* (1940) is confined in a Chicago tenement, and his initial fight against a rat constitutes one of the text's few reference to "nature," in ways that question common views of the environment as a benign system located in rural areas. When Wright does explore the role of unbuilt, largely uncultivated landscapes, the desire of Blacks to relate to nature on their own terms is often brutally checked by outbursts of racist violence in Southern fields and woodlands. In the story "Big Boy Leaves Home" (1936), the innocent swim of several Black boys is interrupted by a White woman, leading to the accidental killing of a White man and the **lynching** of one of the boys. Big Boy's flight into the "wilderness," where he has to defend his hiding place by killing a snake and a dog, revives patterns of nature's double role in slave narratives, yet the fact that he has to witness the death of his friend emphasizes a negative, pessimistic view of African American relationships to the land (Dixon, 60). However, in the thousands of **haikus** Wright wrote, fascination with nature's harmonies and attention to its many small phenomena figure prominently, suggesting that nature was more than a minor theme in his work. Underscoring the conflicting attitudes of African Americans to nature in this era, **Eldridge Cleaver**'s radical essay "The Land Question and Black Liberation" (1968) argues that slavery has invested Blacks with a lasting hatred of the land, so that they "measure their own value according to the number of degrees they are away from the soil" (58), and calls Black men to arm themselves and wrest land from White America.

Since the 1970s, the works of Alice Walker and **Toni Morrison** have marked the emergence of a new kind of ecologically sensitive African American literature. After the height of the **Civil Rights Movement** and its primary concern with Black–White relationships, African American literature turned more toward life inside Black communities. This also led to fresh explorations of the interplay between class, **gender**, and nature, and to bold reevaluations of the troubled history of Black ties to the land. Questioning old binaries and recognizing the complex, paradoxical character of this relationship, many texts now arrive at an affirmative, often environmentally informed, stance vis-à-vis the natural world.

In many of her novels, poems, and essays, Alice Walker explores nature's potential to inspire respectful human–nonhuman relationships; acknowledging Zora Neale Hurston's influence on her work, she especially emphasizes the role of Black women as mediators in the process. In *The Third Life of Grange Copeland* (1970), the sharecropping system drives three generations of Black men in a poor Georgia family to cruelties against women and the land, while their wives, sisters, and aunts struggle to establish lasting connections with nature, often through gardening. In *The Color Purple* (1982), Walker focuses on the lives of landowning Southern Blacks, using "landscape imagery to depict passage from the bruise to the beauty of purple in one woman's journey to song and self-possession" (Dixon, 104); in one scene, the protagonist, Celie, imaginatively turns into a tree to protect herself from her husband's abuse. Celie's development, after being sold to her husband together with a cow and forced to work in the fields, is also linked directly to nature through her abiding affection for gardens and her growing awareness of nature's beauty, which promote her healing. *The Temple of My Familiar* (1989), in its mythic rewriting of a large web of family histories, links interpersonal relationships to healthy ecosystems and "every individual to the ecological web" (Murphy, 55–56); Patrick Murphy has read the book as based on "the spiritualist wing of ecological feminism" (55). *Now Is the Time to Open Your Heart* (2004) is the most explicit expression of Walker's spiritual eco-womanism: a Black writer, through repeated river journeys (including one into the Amazon rain forest) and encounters with shamans and ancient medicines, feels what is wrong with modern civilization and finds a deep, physical and spiritual, relationship with "mother earth."

Walker's poetry, too, has become increasingly explicit about the universal need to develop human–nature relationships of mutuality, empathy, and care. Her collection *Her Blue Body Everything We Know: Earthling Poems: 1965–1990* (1991) reveals this development, and in her *Absolute Trust in the Goodness of the Earth* (2003), the celebration of earth's beauty and of women in relation to nature are her central concerns. Several of Walker's essays are also environmentally oriented. Her classic "In Search of Our Mothers' Gardens" (1974), for example, commemorates her mother and generations of unknown Black women who express their creativity through gardening, artists of nature and survival. In 1988, Walker pulled together her most ecologically concerned texts in *Living by the Word*, addressing the junctions between racism, sexism, and environmental destruction, and urging readers to transcend homocentric, utilitarian views of nature: "I set out on a journey to find my old planet.... I saw, however, that it cannot tolerate much longer the unwanted ways of humans that batter it so unmercifully, and I spent many hours and days considering how it must be possible to exist, for the good of all, in what I believe is a new age of heightened global consciousness" (xx).

The novels of Toni Morrison both contrast and connect past and present, Black and White perceptions of the environment. Her work has been noted for the blend of African environmental symbolism with American views of nature, and for its attention to Midwestern places. **Barbara Christian** has identified "the relationship between her characters' belief system and their views of Nature" as a particular theme of Morrison (65), and Wallace and Armbruster have discussed her emphasis on particular sensibilities of African Americans due to the history of subjugation they share with nature (213). *The Bluest Eye* (1970) is about a displaced Southern Black family in rural Loraine, Ohio, where the people fail to relate to each other and their environment, indicated by "unyielding" gardens and the abuse of humans and animals; *Sula* (1974) tells the story of a rural Black community's disintegration due to its dislocation; and *Tar Baby* (1981) explores one Black character's concern for the ruthlessly abused nature in the Caribbean in conjunction with the perspective of the natural world itself, lamenting its destruction (Wallace and Armbruster 211–212). In *Paradise* (1998), the descendants of freedmen fail to overcome the history of geographical displacement because of their controlling frontier mentality, which turns even gardening into "garden wars"; feeling threatened by women who live self-sufficiently among corn fields, their aggression against them is also motivated by greed for land, and directed against a form of life which is not dominated by visions of ownership and mastery.

In *Song of Solomon* (1977) and *Beloved* (1987), the significance of the natural environment is even more pronounced, in ways that foreground the impossibility to judge and to articulate a resolution concerning African Americans' conflicted views of nature. As *Song of Solomon's* protagonist, Milkman, moves to Virginia's mountains to search for his father's gold, he moves away from his father's sense of owning nature: he finds the history of his ancestors' productive relationship with their land, Black folklore (his grandfather flew like a bird to escape slavery), and "his place" on earth ("like his legs were stalks, tree trunks, a part of his body that extends down down down into the rock and soil," 281). He begins to understand nature and nature's voice as did his ancestors (who were, however, murdered by Whites), suggesting the potential to relate to the land without culminating in naïve optimism. *Beloved*, too, mediates between the history of racist violence embodied by Southern nature, and its transformative powers. The supposed "savagery" of Blacks is literally and symbolically inscribed onto the protagonist's body when being brutally whipped carves Sethe's back into a "tree," yet when Paul D. later "reads" the "tree" on her back, he acknowledges its history and turns it into a object of loving care. Sethe manages to escape from slavery only by "savagely" killing her daughter, yet her "wild" subversive power is recognized by herself and others who describe her as "snatching up her children . . . like a hawk on the wing" (Armbruster and Wallace). Paul D., during his escapes, struggles not to love "a land that was not his," in vivid phrases that express the love for the land he is trying to negate. Morrison uses literary strategies about nature that have been established in African American literature, starting from slave narratives, and makes them contemporary to her time, both in terms of literary form and in terms of rereading history.

Other recent works that explore African American perspectives of nature include **Toni Cade Bambara**'s *Gorilla, My Love* (1972), *The Sea Birds Are Still Alive* (1977), and *The Salt Eaters* (1980), which merge spiritual and revolutionary, traditional African and futuristic perspectives with environmental concerns; **Gloria Naylor**'s *Mama Day* (1988), about a community on a Southern island where a matriarch embodies the ancient, intimate Black knowledge of the land; **Octavia E. Butler**'s science fiction, which links critical perspectives on human slavery to dystopian visions of ecological destruction; **Eddy L. Harris**'s *Mississippi Solo* (1988) and *South of Haunted Dreams: A Ride Through Slavery's Old Back Yard* (1993), blending exploration narrative and nature writing traditions; **Dori Sanders**'s *Her Own Place* (1993), about a landowning Southern Black woman between **World War II** and the 1960s; the poetry of **Nikki Giovanni**, especially her classic "Winter Poem" and her "environmental piece" *Blues: For All The Changes* (1999); and **bell hooks**'s essays "Touching the Earth" (1993) and "Earthbound: On Solid Ground" (2002), which urge reclaiming Black spiritual and physical relationships to nature and their healing potentials. In contemporary African American literature, the interplay between a deep appreciation of the natural environment and the difficulties of relating to a sphere that has been intimately linked to the history of Black oppression still constitutes an important driving force. Yet in a time of global environmental crisis, African American texts have also become more directly concerned with ecological issues, constituting an important part not only of American literature about nature, but also of the growing body of American environmental literature.

Resources: Primary Sources: Henry Bibb, *Narrative of the Life and Adventures of Henry Bibb, An American Slave, Written by Himself* (1849), in *Puttin' on Ole Massa: The Slave Narratives of Henry Bibb, William Wells Brown, and Solomon Northup*, ed. Gilbert Osofsky (New York: Harper & Row, 1969), 51–171; Eldridge Cleaver, "The Land Question and Black Liberation," in *Eldridge Cleaver: Post-Prison Writings and Speeches*, ed. Robert Scheer (New York: Random House, 1967), 57–58; Frederick Douglass, *Narrative of the Life of Frederick Douglass, an American Slave, Written by Himself* (1845; repr. New York: Norton, 1997); Zora Neale Hurston, *Their Eyes Were Watching God* (New York: Perennial, 1990); Harriet Jacobs, *Incidents in the Life of a Slave Girl*, ed. Nellie Y. McKay and Frances Smith Foster (New York: Norton, 2001); Toni Morrison, *Song of Solomon* (New York: Knopf, 1977); Jean Toomer, *Cane*, ed. Darwin T. Turner (New York: Norton, 1988); Alice Walker, *Living by the Word: Selected Writings, 1973–1987* (New York: Harcourt Brace Jovanovich, 1988). **Secondary Sources:** Wes Berry, "Toni Morrison's Revisionary 'Nature Writing': *Song of Solomon* and the Blasted Pastoral," in *South to a New Place: Region, Literature, Culture*, ed. Suzanne W. Jones and Sharon Monteith (Baton Rouge: Louisiana State University Press, 2002), 147–164; Alan Brown, " 'De Beast' Within: The Role of Nature in *Jonah's Gourd Vine*," in *Zora in Florida*, ed. Steve Glassman and Kathryn Lee Seidel (Orlando: University of Central

Florida Press, 1991), 76–85; Robert Butler, "The City as Liberating Space in *Life and Times of Frederick Douglass*," in *The City in African-American Literature*, ed. Yoshinobu Hakutani and Butler (Madison, NJ: Fairleigh Dickinson University Press, 1995), 21–36; Barbara Christian, "Community and Nature: The Novels of Toni Morrison," *Journal of Ethnic Studies* 7, no. 4 (1980), 65–78; Melvin Dixon, *Ride out the Wilderness: Geography and Identity in Afro-American Literature* (Urbana: University of Illinois Press, 1987); Vera M. Kutzinski, "Unseasonal Flowers: Nature and History in Placido and Jean Toomer," *Yale Journal of Criticism* 3, no. 2 (1990), 153–179; Sylvia Mayer, ed., *Restoring the Connection to the Natural World: Essays on the African American Environmental Imagination* (Münster: LIT, 2003); Patrick D. Murphy, *Literature, Nature, and Other. Ecofeminist Critiques* (Albany: State University of New York Press, 1995); Vera Norwood, *Made from This Earth: American Women and Nature* (Chapel Hill: University of North Carolina Press, 1993); Rachel Stein, *Shifting the Ground: American Women Writers' Revision of Nature, Gender, and Race* (Charlottesville: University Press of Virginia, 1997); Kathleen R. Wallace and Karla Armbruster, "The Novels of Toni Morrison: 'Wild Wilderness Where There Was None,'" in *Beyond Nature Writing: Expanding the Boundaries of Ecocriticism*, ed. Karla Armbruster and Kathleen R. Wallace (Charlottesville: University Press of Virginia, 2001), 211–230.

Christine Gerhardt

Naylor, Gloria (born 1950). Novelist, playwright, and professor. Naylor is among the more highly regarded American novelists of the late twentieth and early twenty-first centuries. She was born in New York City to Southern parents, Roosevelt and Alberta McAlpin Naylor, who had moved north from Mississippi to secure better opportunities for their children. Naylor's mother was an avid reader who had been refused use of the public library in **the South** under the racist policies of segregation. Naylor received a B.A. in English from Brooklyn College of the City University of New York in 1981. Her writing career developed in the midst of her education. Naylor's first novel, *The Women of Brewster Place*, was published in 1982. Her second novel, *Linden Hills*, published in 1985, was the creative thesis in her M.A. program at Yale University; she completed the M.A. in 1983. Naylor's subsequent novels are *Mama Day* (1988) and *Bailey's Café* (1992). These four novels were conceived by Naylor as a quartet, and although they are not necessarily sequential in either chronology or plot, the novels do connect to each other in the shared characters and, most important, in the nuanced, varied, and rich characterization of African Americans and their experiences in the United States, a nation that is often hostile to them.

Naylor's novels include a number of African American men as significant characters, but the focus is on the experiences of African American women. In this regard, Naylor's writing is influenced by African American women writers who rose to prominence in the 1970s, including **Alice Walker** and **Toni Morrison**, who in turn were influenced by both a popular rediscovery of the **Harlem Renaissance** and by literature and theory from the **Black Arts Movement** of the 1960s.

Although Naylor grew up in the North, her work has been identified as "inherently southern" because of how she pays "careful attention to the details of her characters' lives and in the painstaking meticulousness with which she draws the places where those fictional characters dwell" (Whitt, 5).

Naylor's novels draw upon a variety of literary traditions, including African American literature, **folktales** and the oral tradition, and classics of English and world literature. Some of the authors and texts that have influenced her work, as evidenced by allusions in the works, include **Jean Toomer**'s *Cane*, **Toni Morrison**'s *The Bluest Eye*, the poetry of **Langston Hughes**, **Charles Waddell Chesnutt**'s *The Conjure Woman*, the folktales collected by **Zora Neale Hurston**, the Bible, Chaucer's *The Canterbury Tales*, Shakespeare's *The Tempest* and *A Midsummer Night's Dream*, and Dante's *Inferno*.

Her first novel, *The Women of Brewster Place*, is made up of seven stories concerning seven different African American women, all of whom live on the same dead-end street in an unnamed Northern city. Naylor begins her novel with an excerpt from Langston Hughes's poem "Harlem" and frames the novel as the answer to his question "What happens to a dream deferred?" ("Harlem" is part of Hughes's longer work, *Montage of a Dream Deferred* [1951]). The stories told are of dreams long deferred, of lives marked by poverty, struggle, and violence. The women who make up Brewster Place are Mattie Michael, Cora Lee, Ceil, Etta Mae Johnson, Kiswana Browne, Lorraine, and Theresa. The arrest and flight of Mattie's only son, an illegitimate child, forces her to sell her house and move to Brewster Place. Cora Lee has too many children, all of whom run wild. Ceil's young child dies tragically. Etta Mae is a former "kept woman," grown too old to be kept. Kiswana is a privileged girl attempting to give back to the community. Lorraine and Theresa are a lesbian couple who have been harassed from place to place, finally ending up at Brewster Place. Brewster Place is the end of the line for these characters and all the other residents. The novel culminates in the rape of Lorraine and in the literal and symbolic destruction of the brick wall that has shut off Brewster Place from the city and has separated the residents from success and fulfillment in life. *The Women of Brewster Place* was made into a television movie in 1989 and starred **Oprah Winfrey**.

The structure of Naylor's second novel, *Linden Hills*, to some degree mirrors the structure of Dante's *Inferno*. Luther Nedeed, the founder of Linden Hills, a wealthy Black subdivision in an unnamed city, established Linden Hills in 1820 on a hillside unwanted by Whites. The physical layout of Linden Hills corresponds to the circles of Dante's hell, and those who live there are understood to have made a deal with the devil.

The novel is linked to *The Women of Brewster Place* by the characters Kiswana Brown and Theresa (Lorraine's partner), who escaped from Linden Hills to Brewster Place. The wife of the fifth and current Luther Nedeed is Willa Prescott. Willa is the grandniece of Miranda Day, Mama Day of Naylor's later novel of the same name. Luther Nedeed has her locked in the basement because he deems their newborn son an abomination for having skin color that is too light. Their son dies during her imprisonment, and the action switches between Willa's grieving and the experiences of Willie and Lester, two young men who travel the "circles" of Linden Hills doing odd jobs. The novel argues that the residents of Linden Hills are damned because they have accepted the racist and materialist doctrine of the United States—one that claims Whiteness is superior to Blackness and money is everything.

Naylor's third novel, Mama Day, is set in the fictional Sea Island of Willow Springs, an island situated between but unclaimed by either South Carolina or Georgia. It is magical place. This magic is felt by all the residents and is traced to Sapphira Wade, the powerful and mysterious ancestress of the island, of whom Miranda Day, the Mama Day of the title, is a direct descendant and thus has inherited her power. The narrative structure of Mama Day is one of Naylor's most complicated. The novel opens with three pages of documents that include a hand-drawn map of the island, a genealogy chart of the Day family naming Sapphira Wade as the sole origin of the family, and the bill of sale for Sapphira Wade to Bascombe Wade. Bascombe Wade was the original owner of Willow Springs, but it was deeded to the residents of the island so long ago that no one can remember exactly when. All three of these documents provide the reader with information that the characters of the novel lack. Indeed, the name and identity of Sapphira Wade is unknown to the residents of Willow Springs, at least to the parts of their minds that use words. The legends of the island tell of Sapphira's power to wrest freedom for herself and all the slaves of Bascombe Wade. The novel then opens in the second person ("you") and exhorts the reader to listen. The story is told in flashback and is framed as a conversation between Ophelia, Mama Day's grandniece, and Ophelia's husband, George. It is a dramatic story with grand themes of enduring love, unshakable faith, and worthy sacrifice, and is arguably Naylor's most optimistic novel.

The action of Naylor's fourth novel, Bailey's Café, is centered on the café and its surrounding neighborhood. "Bailey" and his wife Nadine run the café, and the novel itself is made up of stories concerning the inhabitants of and visitors to the neighborhood. In addition to the café, there is a boardinghouse (or bordello) run by Eve and a pawnshop run by Gabriel. There are seven stories of abuse and oppression experienced by women who visit the café or live at Eve's. One of the women is Sadie, who is turned into a prostitute and sterilized at age thirteen by her mother. Esther, another character, is twelve when she is sold (or "married" off) by her brother to his employer, who sexually abuses and punishes her in the basement. The adult Esther lives in Eve's basement, where she has sex with men. The character Mary is traumatized by her father's overzealous protection of her beauty and chastity and, having internalized shame and guilt, she gouges her face. She, too, works at Eve's. The character Jesse Bell is a heroin addict, harassed because she is a lesbian. Eve takes Mariam in because she is fourteen and pregnant, apparently by an immaculate conception. Mariam's child is George of Mama Day. In this novel Naylor emphasizes music, with **blues** and **jazz** songs as a recurrent motif informing, for instance, the titles of chapters. *Bailey's Café* was adapted into a stage play and performed in Hartford, Connecticut, in 1994.

Naylor's next novel, *The Men of Brewster Place*, can be understood as an answer to criticism leveled at her and other contemporary African American women writers that positive Black male characters are missing from their work. Naylor revisits Brewster Place, this time telling the stories of seven men, most of whom are characters from her previous novel: Ben the janitor; Mattie's son, Basil; Etta Mae's seducer, Moreland T. Woods; the gang leader C. C. Baker; Ciel's husband, Eugene; the silent Brother Jerome; and Kiswana's boyfriend, Abshu. Their stories also tell of the loneliness, the despair, and the oppression these men endure. Abshu emerges from the ruins of these stories as the only one with hope for a better future.

Like many other contemporary novelists, Naylor not only writes but also teaches and lectures. Among the universities where she has taught are New York University, Princeton, the University of Pennsylvania, Boston University, Brandeis, Cornell, and the University of Kent in Canterbury, England. She received an American Book Award in 1983, a National Endowment for the Arts fellowship in 1985, and a Guggenheim fellowship in 1988. Naylor established One Way Productions in 1990, a multimedia production company. She is currently at work on a novel that is reportedly a further exploration of Sapphira Wade of *Mama Day*. (*See* **Conjuring**; **Feminism**.)

Resources: Primary Sources: Gloria Naylor: *Bailey's Café* (New York: Harcourt Brace Jovanovich, 1992); *Linden Hills* (1985; repr. New York: Penguin, 1995); *Mama Day* (1988; repr. New York: Vintage, 1989); *The Men of Brewster Place* (New York: Hyperion, 1998); *The Women of Brewster Place* (1982; repr. New York: Penguin, 1983). **Secondary Sources:** Sharon Felton and Michelle C. Loris, eds., *The Critical Response to Gloria Naylor* (Westport, CT: Greenwood Press, 1997); Henry Louis Gates, Jr., and K. A. Appiah eds., *Gloria Naylor: Critical Perspectives Past and Present* (New York: Amistad, 1993); Margot Anne Kelly, ed., *Gloria Naylor's Early Novels* (Gainesville: University of Florida Press, 1999); Shirley A. Stave ed., *Gloria Naylor: Strategy and Technique, Magic and Myth* (Newark: University of Delaware Press, 2001); Margaret Earley Whitt, *Understanding Gloria Naylor* (Columbia: University of South Carolina Press, 1997).

Rachael Barnett

Neal, Larry (1937–1981). Playwright, poet, essayist, editor, folklorist, and filmmaker. Larry Neal was a major figure in the development of the **Black Arts Movement** (BAM). According to the writers of *The African-American Odyssey*, "the formal beginning of the movement was the founding in 1965, of the Black Arts Repertory Theater" (547). The founders of the **Black Arts Repertory Theatre** were LeRoi Jones (later **Amiri Baraka**), Larry Neal, and **Askia M. Touré**. The theater brought "plays, concerts, and poetry readings right on the streets of Harlem" (Henderson). The theater was closed due to internal conflicts among its members, a lack of funding, and opposition from what Neal referred to as "the Establishment," or mainstream culture

(Henderson). Despite this setback, numerous other theaters sprouted all across the country. Larry Neal, like many of his contemporaries, gave definition to this movement, such as the following, from *African-American Odyssey* (547):

> The Black Arts Movement is radically opposed to any concept of the artist that alienates him from his community. Black Art is the aesthetic and spiritual sister of the Black Power concept. As such, it envisions an art that speaks directly to the needs and aspirations of Black Americans. In order to perform this task, the Black Arts Movement proposes a radical reordering of the western cultural aesthetic.

Larry Neal was born in **Atlanta, Georgia**, and raised in **Philadelphia, Pennsylvania**. After graduating from a Roman Catholic high school, he studied history and English at Lincoln University in Pennsylvania. While in graduate school at the University of Pennsylvania, Neal "gained an appreciation for all aspects of black life, such as **folktales**, **slang**, and street chants, and used them as sources of artistic expression" (Henderson). He received his master's degree in 1963. He taught creative writing at various universities, including Yale University, from the early 1960s to the mid-1970s. For a brief period, he was also copywriter for John Wiley and Sons. In the 1960s, he served as the educational director of the **Black Panther Party**. From 1976 to 1979, he was executive director of the Columbia Commission on the Arts and Humanities. This agency "made grants to artists and organizations that encouraged the development of the arts in black communities, including the Elma Louis School of Fine Arts in Roxbury, Massachusetts" (*ChickenBones*).

The back cover of *Black Magic*, featuring Larry Neal and LeRoi Jones, 1968. Yale Collection of American Literature, Beinecke Rare Book and Manuscript Library.

Neal's literary achievements, all centered in BAM philosophy, consisted of articles, essays, plays, anthologies, poetry, and more. From 1964 to 1966, he wrote for *The Liberator*, and later became its arts editor. *The Liberator* was "a progressive journal of that time" (*ChickenBones*). Neal's articles included interviews with writers, artists, and musicians, as well as reports on Black activities and events. Neal wrote articles for other journals as well, including *Black Theater Magazine*, **Ebony**, **Negro Digest**, and **Journal of Black Poetry**. With Baraka and **A. B. Spellman**,

Neal founded *Cricket*, "a publication devoted to African-American music, which espoused a black nationalistic philosophy" and "served as a vehicle through which black writers attempted to define black art forms and aesthetics" (*ChickenBones*). The fundamental belief of BAM was that "[African American] perception was different from that of the white American majority" (*Chicken-Bones*). *Cricket* published only three issues.

Neal also produced several of Baraka's plays, including *Jello* (1970) and *Dutchman* (1964). He himself wrote the plays *The Glorious Monster in the Bell of the Horn* (1976) and *In an Upstate Motel: A Morality Play* (1980). In 1968, Neal and Baraka edited *Black Fire: An Anthology of Afro-American Writing*. It is considered one "of the most definitive works on the Black Arts Movement," and included a host of writers, among them James Boggs, **Ed Bullins**, **Sonia Sanchez**, **Stokley Carmichael**, John Henrik Clarke, **Harold Cruse**, **Henry Dumas**, and **Hoyt Fuller** (Henderson). Neal wrote many essays on various topics pertinent to the black experience, and on writers and artists such as **Ralph Ellison**, **Zora Neale Hurston**, and **Charlie Parker** (*see* **Gillespie, Dizzy, Charlie Parker, and Thelonious Monk**). He also wrote critical essays "on social issues, aesthetic theory, literary topics, and other subjects" (Engelhardt, 529). He wrote the introductions to Hurston's *Jonah's Gourd Vine* (1971) and *Dust Tracks on a Road* (1971).

Neal's first book of poetry, *Black Boogaloo* (1969), "focuses on discovering the historical moment when Africans lost their connection with their gods and ancestors, thereby losing themselves" (*ChickenBones*). His second book of poetry, *Hoodoo Hollerin' Bebop Ghosts* (1974), "explores black folk culture and figures, especially black liberation and Shine" (*ChickenBones*). In 1981, Larry Neal died of a massive heart attack, leaving behind an immense body of work that has greatly impacted the African American literary tradition.

Resources: Imamu Amiri Baraka: *Dutchman and the Slave: Two Plays* (New York: Morrow, 1964); *Jello* (Chicago: Third World Press, 1970); Elizabeth Sanders Delwiche Engelhardt, "Larry Neal," in *The Oxford Companion to African American Literature*, ed. William L. Andrews, Frances Smith Foster, and Trudier Harris (New York: Oxford University Press, 1997), 529–530; William J. Harris, "Black Aesthetic," in *The Oxford Companion to African American Literature*, ed. William L. Andrews, Frances Smith Foster, and Trudier Harris (New York: Oxford University Press, 1997); *Biography Resource Center*, Info2go, Tacoma Public Library, Tacoma, WA, http://galenet.galegroup.com/servlet/BioRC; Ashyia Henderson, "Larry Neal," in *Contemporary Black Biography*, vol. 38, ed. Ashyia Henderson (Detroit: Gale, 2003); Darlene Clark Hine, William C. Hine, and Stanley Harrold, *The African-American Odyssey* (Upper Saddle River, NJ: Prentice-Hall, 2000); Zora Neale Hurston: *Dust Tracks on a Road: An Autobiography* (Philadelphia: Lippincott, 1971); *Jonah's Gourd Vine* (Philadelphia: Lippincott, 1971); LeRoi Jones and Larry Neal, eds., *Black Fire: An Anthology of Afro-American Writing* (New York: Morrow, 1968); "Larry Neal," *ChickenBones: A Journal*, http://www.nathanielturner.com/larryneal.htm; Larry Neal: *Black Boogaloo; Notes on Black Liberation* (San Francisco: Journal of Black Poetry Press, 1969); *Hoodoo Hollerin' Bebop Ghosts* (Washington, DC: Howard University Press, 1974); *Visions of a*

Liberated Future: Black Arts Movement Writings (New York: Thunder's Mouth Press, 1989).

Gladys L. Knight

Neely, Barbara (born 1941). Mystery novelist. Barbara Neely is best known as the creator of Blanche White, the feisty protagonist in a series of mystery novels. A very dark-skinned domestic worker strapped with an improbable name, Blanche White stands out from other female detectives because she is Black, middle-aged, and overweight. She's also frankly sexual. Neely uses the insightful, outspoken Blanche as much to comment on social issues as to solve whatever mystery is the focus of the plot.

Four novels feature Neely's popular protagonist: *Blanche on the Lam* (1992), *Blanche Among the Talented Tenth* (1994); *Blanche Cleans Up* (1998), and *Blanche Passes Go* (2000) (*see* **Talented Tenth**). Each book examines social issues that are root causes of the problems confronting Blanche, a woman incensed at the ways of the world but who has not allowed her anger to settle into bitterness. Blanche also has a rich sense of humor, a deeply satisfying spiritual life, great love for the two children she is raising, and a keen interest in affirming her sexuality. Her strong, outspoken personality accounts for much of the appeal of Neely's books.

Blanche's debut came in *Blanche on the Lam*, which won the Agatha, Macavity, and Anthony awards, which honor excellent writing in the mystery novel genre. The story opens with Blanche in court for bouncing a check, not for the first time. When the panic-stricken woman flees rather than go to jail, she hides in the one place she thinks the law won't look for her—in the kitchen of a wealthy White family in need of a replacement cook-domestic worker. But Blanche soon realizes this family has dangerous secrets she must unravel if she is to stay safe. Her search for answers is accompanied by many pointed observations about White employer/Black "help" relationships, which she sees as shaped by racism and classism continued from historic master/slave times. Her analysis of how power relationships respond to race and class is complicated, however, when she sees the White family treating a young mentally challenged relative in much the same way they treat her.

In appearance and occupation Blanche fits the "mammy" stereotype. But Neely's portrayal of her protagonist as intelligent, assertive, witty, and courageous dispels any temptation to think of Blanche as a "mammy"; moreover, Neely uses Blanche to undercut the assumptions behind this pervasive African American stereotype while making clear the emotional resilience it takes for women like Blanche to retain dignity, self-esteem, and confidence in a culture so invested in believing this negative image.

In each subsequent Blanche novel, Neely examines a new social issue. *Blanche Among the Talented Tenth* looks at the color hierarchy among African Americans. The dark-skinned Blanche feels the weight of this prejudice when she spends time at an exclusive resort frequented by wealthy, light-skinned African Americans. This novel also stresses Blanche's sexuality, her Africa-influenced

1189

spirituality, and the difficulties of raising two children as a single parent. The third book in the series, *Blanche Cleans Up*, looks at issues facing parents of teens, especially teen pregnancy, as well as political corruption and homophobia. In the fourth book, *Blanche Passes Go*, Neely writes about violence against women. Blanche's involvement with a victim of domestic violence eventually leads her to a greater understanding of how she was—and still is—affected by a rape she suffered years earlier.

Neely's compulsion to respond outspokenly to social injustices was evident long before she created Blanche. After growing up in Lebanon, Pennsylvania, she moved in 1971 to **Philadelphia, Pennsylvania**, where her commitment to social activism led her to work for the Philadelphia Tutorial Project on a range of inner-city issues, including housing. She continued to pursue this interest in graduate school at the University of Pittsburgh, where she earned a master's degree in urban studies. After graduation, Neely worked for the Pennsylvania Department of Corrections, where she helped to set up and run, despite much community resistance, a suburban facility for formerly incarcerated women. Later she moved to Raleigh, North Carolina, a city whose name inspired her fictional Farleigh. Here she wrote for *Southern Exposure* and produced radio programming for the African News Service. Later contributions to social activism include work with Women for Economic Justice and Women of Color for Reproductive Freedom. Neely currently lives in Jamaica Plain, Massachusetts, part of **Boston**.

Neely's first work of fiction was a story published by *Essence* in 1981; *Blanche on the Lam* (1992), was her first novel-length work and initiated her into a small group of African American detective fiction writers, the most famous of whom is **Walter Mosley**. Neely's significance comes from her use of Blanche to add a distinctively feminist voice to African American mystery writing and from her commitment to use the mystery genre to explore social problems, many of which are racial. (*See* **Crime and Mystery Fiction.**)

Resources: Frankie Y. Bailey, "*Blanche on the Lam*, or the Invisible Woman Speaks," in *Diversity and Detective Fiction*, ed. Kathleen Gregory Klein (Bowling Green, OH: Bowling Green State University Popular Press, 1999), 186–204; Barbara Neely: *Blanche Among the Talented Tenth* (New York: St. Martin's, 1994); *Blanche Cleans Up* (New York: Viking, 1998); *Blanche on the Lam* (New York: St. Martin's, 1992); *Blanche Passes Go* (New York: Penguin, 2000); "Barbara Neely," *Voices from the Gaps*, ed. Tiya Miles, University of Minnesota, 2002, http://voices.cla.umn.edu/newsite/authors/NEELYbarbara.htm; Doris Witt, "Detecting Bodies: Barbara Neely's Domestic Sleuth and the Trope of the (In)Visible Woman," in *Recovering the Black Female Body: Self-Representations by African American Women*, ed. Michael Bennett and Venessa D. Dickerson (New Brunswick, NJ: Rutgers University Press, 2001), 165–194.

Grace McEntee

Neff, Heather (born 1958). Novelist, critic, and professor. Neff was born in Akron, Ohio, and grew up in **Detroit, Michigan**, where she graduated from high school in 1975. She earned a B.A. in English from the University of Michigan in 1978. From 1983 to 1990 she lived in Switzerland, working as a corporate trainer for such companies as Swissair and Shell Oil, but also studying at the universities of Basel and Zurich; from the latter she received a doctorate in literature in 1990 (personal home page). Since 1993 Neff has taught literature and directed multicultural programs at Eastern Michigan University. She is the author of two novels, *Blackgammon* and *Wisdom*, and of a critical study about protest as expressed in African American poetry. She has also published poems and short stories in magazines and has written critical essays about **James Baldwin** and **Audre Lorde**.

Resources: Heather Neff: *Blackgammon* (New York: One World/Ballantine, 2000); personal home page, http://www.emich.edu/public/english/literature/neff.html; *Redemption Songs: The Voice of Protest in Poetry of Afro-Americans* (Berne: Franke Verlag, 1990); *Wisdom* (New York: Ballantine, 2002).

Hans Ostrom

Négritude (c. 1930–1960). The concept of Négritude arose in France and concerns the formulation of a cultural identity based on the **diaspora** of African peoples. It served as an organized response to European **colonialism** and post-colonialist domination of peoples of color worldwide. Négritude embraces a range of cultural expressions, including literature and visual arts, that focus on African traditions which have spread beyond Africa. It respects "Blackness" and lauds its virtues.

Aimé Césaire is credited with inventing the term "Négritude," which springs from the French word *negre*, meaning "black"; "Negro"; or even the epithet "nigger," depending on the context. Césaire perceived "Négritude" to connote pride in African heritage. He had gone to France from his native Martinique, a French colony, to study. However, it was Léopold Senghor who gave the term Négritude wide usage and application.

Even before Négritude became a movement, the concept of Black pride was known and championed elsewhere in the African diaspora. For instance, early in the twentieth century **Martin R. Delany** and **W.E.B. Du Bois**, in their writing and activism, urged Blacks throughout the world to be proud of their heritage and not settle for less than full acceptance in the world community. Also, the **Harlem Renaissance** served as a cultural reawakening for African Americans in the United States. Writers of the Harlem Renaissance such as **Langston Hughes**, **Claude McKay**, **Jesse Redmon Fauset**, and **Countee Cullen** were some of those whose publications had been translated and read by the founders of Négritude. Even before the Harlem Renaissance, **James Weldon Johnson** had written the song, "Lift Ev'ry Voice and Sing," and declared it the Negro national anthem (1900). Also in the political arena, **Marcus Garvey** had launched his **Back-to-Africa Movement**, which emphasized Black pride.

By the end of **World War II**, a new spirit was emerging among the Black French-speaking intelligentsia in France. This spirit gave momentum to the

Négritude movement. Joining Césaire in the founding of the Négritude movement were Léopold Sédar Senghor from Senegal and Frantz Fanon from Martinique. The three, who met while living in France during the 1930s, are recognized "fathers" of Négritude.

Léopold Senghor was a prolific writer and respected politician. Later he became president of the Republic of Senegal. In 1948 he edited an anthology of poetry that articulated the voices of francophone Africans, *Anthologie de la Nouvelle Poésie Nègre et Malgache*. He developed the concept of a "black personality" and advocated, philosophically, the existence of a "black soul." The renowned French philosopher Jean-Paul Sartre wrote the preface to his book. Sartre's philosophy on color was a guiding force in shaping the direction of Négritude. He supported the movement, and his stature among French intellectuals gave further validity to Négritude.

Aimé Césaire left France to return home to the Caribbean in 1939. From 1941 to 1945 he, his wife, Suzanne Roussy-Césaire, René Menil, Luci Thesée, and Aristide Maugée edited a journal called *Tropique*. This publication continued to perpetuate the concept of Négritude and to show the cultural commonalities that existed in the African diaspora. After the journal ceased publication, Césaire continued to pursue a successful writing career and entered local politics.

The other founder of the Négritude movement was Frantz Fanon. Originally from Martinique, he studied in France and was a student of Césaire. However, the teacher and student were not always in agreement about the philosophic direction of Négritude. Fanon was a psychiatrist who left France for Algeria during the period when that French colony was struggling for independence from France. His book *Black Skin, White Masks* (1952) contributed to the increasing dialogue on Négritude. He established the first psychiatric clinic on the African continent and was very active in the Algerian liberation movement. He edited a magazine, *Moudjahid*, in Tunisia and wrote another major work, *The Wretched of the Earth* (1961).

Léon-Gontran Damas, whose early works contributed to defining Négritude, was born in French Guiana. He published a book of poems, with a Négritude theme, titled *Pigments*, a year before Senghor's anthology was released. Some other well-known writers who contributed to the literature of Négritude were Ousmane Sembene, David Diop, and Cheikh Hamadou Kane. Perhaps the publication that popularized Négritude most widely throughout France, Africa, the African diaspora, and points beyond was a sophisticated journal titled *Présence Africaine*. Founded by Alioune Diop, from Senegal, it served as an eloquent mouthpiece for Négritude. Supported by Jean-Paul Sartre, Albert Camus, Aimé Césaire and many others, it was circulated globally. Published in **Paris, France**, it was printed in French and English. *Présence Africaine* sponsored a conference in Paris, at the Sorbonne (1956), and in Rome (1959) for the express purpose of bringing together Black scholars from around the African diaspora to celebrate their strengths and similarities. Perhaps the biggest gathering of peoples of African descent, sponsored by *Présence Africaine*, was the First World Festival of Negro Arts held in Dakar, Senegal (1956). This was an assembly of approximately 2,000 blacks from all over the world. It celebrated and showcased the broad spectrum of literary and other artistic expressions from throughout the African diaspora. The media described it as the single greatest event in Senegal's cultural life. By the 1960s the world was changing. The colonialism of the past was ending and Négritude became laden with ideological and political distractions. It is undeniable that the impact of Négritude was significant. It greatly influenced liberation movements in Africa as well as the **Civil Rights Movement**, the **Black Power** movement, and other radical movements in the United States.

Resources: Sylvia Washington Bâ, *Concept of Negritude in the Poetry of Léopold Sédar Sénghor* (Princeton, NJ: Princeton University Press, 1973); Aimé Césaire, *Lyric and Dramatic Poetry 1946–82*, trans. Clayton Eshleman and Annette Smith (Charlottesville: University Press of Virginia, 1990); Frantz Fanon: *Black Skin, White Masks* (1952; repr. New York: Grove Press, 1967); "Reciprocal Bases of National Culture and the Fight for Freedom," Speech, Congress of Black African Writers, 1959, http://www.marxists.org/referencesubject/philosophy/works/fanon.htm; *The Wretched of the Earth*, trans. by Constance Farrington (1961; repr. New York: Grove Press, 1963); Langston Hughes, ed., *Poems from Black Africa* (Bloomington: Indiana University Press 1963); Arnold A. James, *Modernism and Negritude: The Poetry and Poetics of Aimé Césaire* (Cambridge, MA: Harvard University Press, 1981); Thomas Melone, *De la Négritude dans la Littérature Négro-Africaine* (Paris: Présence Africaine 1962); Léopold Sédar Senghor, *Anthologie de la Nouvelle Poésie Nègre et Malgache de langue Française . . . Précédée de Orphée Noir par Jean-Paul Sartre* (Paris: Presses Universitaires de France, 1948).

Betty W. Nyangoni

Negro. Derived from Latin *nigrum* (n) and *niger* (adj), both meaning the color black, the noun "negro" entered the English lexicon through Spanish and Portuguese. Richard Eden's *Decades of the New World* (1555) shows its first English use for African people of dark skin. The King James Version of the Bible gives the name Symeon the Niger in Acts 13.1 unaltered from Jerome's Vulgate (382), signifying his color. John Rolle's cargo note (1619) about "20 and odd Negers" brought to Virigina connects the word in known history to North America. Variations of the term, such as *negar*, *neger* and *nigar*, *niggar*, or *niggor*, evolved over the next two centuries. *The House of Names* site shows a coat of arms of Carlo Negri di Piera Santa, a bishop of Ferrara, Italy, in 929. The city records of Ferrara reportedly contain other names, such as Negri, Negris, Negro, Nigra, Negrelli, Negrello, Negrotto, and Negroni.

Negroid and *negroloid*, in traceable use since 1859, are anthropological labels for dark-skinned people groups of the sub-Saharan or tropical regions. Until the Renaissance, "Moor" and "Ethiopian," both from the Greek, synonymously identified continental Africans. These labels are based on what are now anthropologically and scientifically outmoded classifications of different races, such as Caucasian, Oriental, and Negroid.

According to *Harper's Weekly*, June 2, 1906, **Booker T. Washington** preferred "negro," in lowercase for the individual and in uppercase for the race, a practice formalized in the 1930 *New York Times Stylebook* for the next three decades. The Negro History Week that **Carter G. Woodson** established in 1926 kept the "Negro" until 1976, when the annual event was changed to Black History Month. Consistent with the formal use of the term, the 1960 Spingarn Medal cited **Langston Hughes** as "the Poet Laureate of the Negro race."

The **Civil Rights Movement** of the 1960s helped replace the term "Negro" with "Black," which had been pejorative until then. Within another two decades, "Black" was replaced by "Afro-American," and then "African American," as a more accurately descriptive ethnonym, one that was based neither on inaccurate anthropology nor on alleged skin color.

An unwelcome by-product of the mutations to the term "negro" has been the derisive **slang** "nigger," or the "N-word." Randall Kennedy, in his *Nigger: The Strange Career of a Troublesome Word* (2002), notes that in the 1700s *niger* was suitable for "dignified argumentation," as seen in Samuel Sewall's denunciation of **slavery**, *The Selling of Joseph*. However, by the late 1830s, *niger* or *neger* had turned into *nigger*, "a familiar and influential insult." The word continued to appear in the work of many authors—Conrad, **Mark Twain**, Dickens, Joyce, and Faulkner among them—none spared of its undying controversy.

Essentially all phrases with "nigger" convey prejudice, bigotry, derision, or even hatred. Examples: to nigger (to ruin) or niggerish (unappreciated quality), "negrolatry" (unpopular admiration), "nigger-heaven" (segregated balcony), "nigger-rich" (flamboyant), "nigger-stick" (police baton), "nigger-luck" (undeserved). "Nigger-breaker," "nigger-dealer," or "nigger-killer" recall past oppression. Jews in the United States have been referred to as "white niggers," the Arabs as "sand niggers," and some Oriental groups as "yellow niggers." As a term of hate crime, its use is forbidden by a 1992 U.S. House Resolution. Randall Kennedy has documented "23 Supreme Court decisions, 524 federal appellate court documents, 1,010 federal district trial decisions and 2,414 state court cases that involve the N-Word." In response to a 1997 **NAACP** protest, Merriam-Webster has agreed to revise its entry "Nigger" to be "no longer synonymous with African Americans" (Pilgrim and Middleton).

"Nigger" also has a complicated duality in its status. While the word is deeply offensive when used by Whites, some African Americans draw on the inherent tension created by the word as a means of endearment or empowerment. **Dick Gregory**'s *Nigger: An Autobiography* (1964), H. Rap Brown's *Die Nigger Die* (1969), Richard Pryor's *Bicentennial Nigger* (1976), and **Tupac Shakur**'s "Strictly 4 My N.I.G.G.A.Z" exploit the "taboo" word, to reverse its power to hurt, a view shared by Langston Hughes. The movies *Pulp Fiction* (1994) and *Jackie Brown* (1997) present the harsh use of "nigger" as "a symbol of hipness and street authenticity" (Pilgrim and Middleton). The comedians Chris Rock and Dave Chappelle routinely use the word.

In a formal sense, both "Negro" and "Black" are still in use, as in United Negro College Fund, Black Women in the Academy, National Society of Black Engineers, and so on.

The word "niggard" has no linguistic connection with any of the N-words.

Resources: Jamie Glazov, "The N-Word, Randall Kennedy, and the Complexity of Meaning," *FrontpageMagazine.com*, May 2002, http://www.frontpagemag.com/Articles; Randall Kennedy, *Nigger: The Strange Career of a Troublesome Word* (New York: Pantheon, 2002); *Oxford English Dictionary* online, http://dictionary.oed.com.ezproxy.ups.edu; Kim Pearson, "Nigger," *Rhetoric of Race*, http://kpearson.faculty.tcnj.edu/Dictionary/nigger.htm; David Pilgrim and Phillip Middleton, "Nigger and Caricatures," Jim Crow Museum of Racist Memorabilia, September 2001, http://www.ferris.edu/news/jimcrow/caricature/.

Varghese Mathai

Negro Digest (1942–1951, 1961–1970). Periodical. John H. Johnson used his mother's new furniture as collateral for a $500 business loan to launch his first publishing venture, *Negro Digest*, in November 1942. In the inaugural issue, Johnson explained that the monthly magazine intended to give a "complete survey of current Negro life and thought...dedicated to the development of interracial understanding and the promotion of national unity" (Johnson and Bennett, 122). The magazine's format and design were patterned after *Reader's Digest*, but with a marked difference. It reprinted selected articles by and about African Americans from Black and White magazines, newspapers, books, and reports. It also developed original sections. Within eight months, 50,000 copies a month were sold across the nation (Johnson and Bennett, 128). Johnson's publication resonated with the African American middle class seeking information about the Black community during a time when "there was an almost total White-out on positive Black news in White-oriented media" (Johnson and Bennett, 113). The magazine also provided an outlet for personal expression about the complexities of life in Black America. Moderate in tone, *Negro Digest* reflected a broad perspective on racial issues. One of the magazine's regular features, "If I Were a Negro," invited Whites to answer some difficult questions about race. Among the contributors were Pearl Buck, Orson Welles, Edward G. Robinson, and Eleanor Roosevelt (Hall, 192). Other well-known figures whose work appeared in *Negro Digest* include **Richard Wright**, Erskine Caldwell, H. L. Mencken, Carl Sandburg, **Zora Neale Hurston**, **Langston Hughes**, and Adam Clayton Powell (Daniel 262).

When Johnson launched the picture magazine **Ebony** in 1945, it became a runaway success and went from 25,000 to nearly half a million copies in circulation, quickly surpassing the circulation of *Negro Digest* (Johnson and Bennett, 173). Johnson decided to discontinue the *Digest* in November 1951, although he revived it almost ten years later in June 1961. Among Johnson's reasons for reprising the magazine was his concern that the "talented young Negro writer does not always find a ready outlet for his creative efforts" (Hall,

195). **Hoyt Fuller**, an experienced journalist and former contributor to *Ebony*, served as managing editor until his resignation in 1968. Over a period of years, he changed the focus of *Negro Digest* from its existing format to "a comprehensive publication of critical analysis and literary expression . . . [making it] the most widely read Black literary magazine in this country" (Semmes, xii). A cadre of African American writers contributed an impressive range of fiction, drama, and poetry. Fuller himself wrote an influential column, "Perspectives," which covered literary events and developments in African American literature. Through forums and surveys, he engaged readers in a wide-ranging cultural debate about **Afrocentricity**, Black literary criticism, and black aesthetics. Fuller also sponsored literary contests under the auspices of the journal. Described as revolutionary, the journal adopted a more politically activist stance than the first *Negro Digest*. It emerged as a leading voice for the "growing coalescence between political and artistic activism . . . [fostering] a conflict between followers of the Imamu Amiri Baraka wing of black artists and such established black writers as Ralph Ellison" (Daniel, 264).

To reflect the changing times, changing terminology, and the extended Pan-African scope of the periodical, *Negro Digest* became *Black World* in May 1970. During the declining years of the **Black Arts Movement**, its circulation decreased from 100,000 to 15,000 (Johnson and Bennett, 189). In 1976 the second iteration of *Negro Digest* ceased publication once again. *Negro Digest/ Black World* serves as a valuable historical record of the African American cultural renaissance in the 1960s and 1970s. According to one writer, "As an outlet for African-American literary production and a shaper of taste, it remains unsurpassed" (Hall 189). (*See* **Magazines, Literary.**)

Resources: Walter C. Daniel, *Black Journals of the United States* (Westport, CT: Greenwood Press, 1982); James C. Hall, "On Sale at Your Favorite Newsstand: *Negro Digest/Black World* and the 1960s," in *The Black Press: New Literary and Historical Essays*, ed. Todd Vogel (New Brunswick, NJ: Rutgers University Press, 2001); Abby Arthur Johnson and Ronald Maberry Johnson, *Propaganda and Aesthetics: The Literary Politics of Afro-American Magazines in the Twentieth Century* (Amherst: University of Massachusetts Press, 1979); John H. Johnson and Lerone Bennett, Jr., *Succeeding Against the Odds* (New York: Amistad, 1992); Clovis E. Semmes, comp., *Roots of Afrocentric Thought: A Reference Guide to Negro Digest/Black World, 1961–1976* (Westport, CT: Greenwood Press, 1998); Robert E. Wolseley, *The Black Press, U.S.A*, 2nd ed. (Ames: Iowa State University Press, 1990).

Lori Ricigliano

Negro Units, Federal Theatre Project (1935–1939). Government-sponsored theatrical organization employing African Americans during the **Great Depression**. A branch of the Federal Theatre Project (FTP), sixteen Negro Units were established in an effort both to employ and to train African American theatre artists in their respective fields and to reflect the needs of the large number of poor, predominantly African American communities that peppered the major cities of the United States. (*See* **Federal Writers' Project.**)

Though the origins of the Negro Units are debated, it is generally agreed that the African American actress Rose McClendon brought the idea of a "New Negro Theatre" to the attention of the FTP's national director, Hallie Flanagan. She proposed a theater that would use a "selection of plays that deal with Negroes, with Negro problems, with phases of Negro life, faithfully presented and accurately delineated" (McClendon, 10).

The first and most active Negro Unit (initially directed by John Houseman and a young Orson Welles) was founded in **Harlem, New York** (1935). It quickly began a series of popular productions including a "**voodoo**" *Macbeth* (adapted by Welles in 1935), the violent **labor** drama *Turpentine* (1936), and **W.E.B. Du Bois**'s drama of slave rebellion, *Haiti* (1938). The **Chicago, Illinois**, Negro Unit made history with the immensely popular *Swing Mikado* (1938), a "swung" version of Gilbert and Sullivan's *The Mikado*, and Theodore Ward's *Big White Fog* (1938) posed vital political and social questions. Similar themes characterized the productions of Negro Units in **Boston, Massachusetts**, Seattle, Washington, **Los Angeles, California**, and

Poster for Federal Theatre Project Negro Unit presentation of *Noah*, New York, c. 1939. Courtesy of the Library of Congress.

many other cities, as African American playwrights wrote and adapted plays for African American performers and audiences.

In spite of the Negro Units' popular successes, the most enduring contribution of these theater companies was to establish high quality, legitimate drama written, performed, and produced by African Americans. African American playwrights such as **Theodore Ward**, **Frank Wilson**, **Theodore Browne**, and **Hughes Allison** wrote pieces that reshaped the public perception of African American stereotypes. It was through these experiences that African American theater professionals for the first time gained admittance to unions, received training and experience, and established a national sense of community and camaraderie among African Americans throughout the performing arts.

Resources: E. Quita Craig, *Black Drama of the Federal Theatre Era* (Amherst: University of Massachusetts Press, 1980); Jane S. DeHart, *The Federal Theatre, 1935–1939: Plays, Relief, and Politics* (Princeton, NJ: Princeton University Press, 1967);

Hallie Flanagan, *Arena* (New York: Duell, Sloan and Pearce, 1940); Rena Fraden, *Blueprints for a Black Federal Theatre, 1935–1939* (New York: Cambridge University Press, 1994); Glenda E. Gill, *White Grease Paint on Black Performers: A Study of the Federal Theatre, 1935–1939* (New York: Peter Lang, 1988); http://memory.loc.gov/ammem/fedtp/fthome.html; Edith J. R. Isaacs, *The Negro in the American Theatre* (New York: Theatre Arts, 1947; repr. 1968); Rose McClendon, "As to a New Negro Stage," *New York Times*, June 30, 1935, p. 10; Loften Mitchell, *Black Drama: The Story of the American Negro in the Theatre* (New York: Hawthorn, 1967); "The New Deal Stage: Selections from the Federal Theatre Project, 1935–1939," American Memory Special Collections, Music Division, Federal Theatre Project Collection, Library of Congress; John O'Connor and Lorraine Brown, eds., *Free, Adult, Uncensored: The Living History of the Federal Theatre Project* (Washington, DC: New Republic Books, 1978); Research Center for the Federal Theatre Project, George Mason University, *Breaking the Barriers: Blacks of the Federal Theatre Project*, 7 VHS videocassettes (1978).

Elizabeth A. Osborne

Negro World (1918–1933). Newspaper. Founded by Jamaican-born **Marcus Garvey** in August 1918, *Negro World* was the official news organ of the Universal Negro Improvement Association (UNIA), whose purpose was to "promote the destruction of **colonialism** and the political unification of African peoples everywhere" (Schomburg, 69). The paper's masthead bore the organization's motto, "One Aim, One God, One Destiny," and under it was the phrase "A Newspaper Devoted Solely to the Interests of the Negro Race" (Cronon, 46). It was regarded as "one of the most remarkable journalistic ventures ever attempted by a Negro in the United States" (Cronon, 45). The writer and poet **Claude McKay**, who was often a critic of the Garvey movement, once wrote that it was "the best edited colored weekly in New York" (Fax, 90). Still, others were critical and asserted that *Negro World* was the "'bulletin of the Imperial Blizzard' or the *weakly* organ of Admiral Garvey's African Navy" (Cronon, 48–49).

On the front page of each issue, Garvey wrote a lengthy editorial addressed to "'Fellowmen of the Negro Race' and signed, 'Your obedient servant, Marcus Garvey, President General,'" with Garvey's large signature reproduced at the bottom (Digby-Junger, 269). The editorials were wide-ranging and reflected Garvey's nationalistic philosophy. The remaining pages covered current events from around the world, activities of the various branches of the UNIA, African history, and news of African Americans. Among its contributors were **Zora Neal Hurston**, **Arthur A. Schomburg**, William H. Ferris, and **Eric Walrond** (People & Events). A favorite feature was "Bruce Grit's Column," contributed by the journalist John E. Bruce, who was active in the UNIA and wrote about everyday topics. "Poetry for the People" was devoted to works by readers who were admirers of Garvey. An arts section featured art, fashion, and theater stories, and ministers contributed library notes and sermons (Digby-Junger, 270).

Garvey's second wife, Amy Jacques Garvey, introduced a women's page, "Our Women and What They Think," during her tenure as associate editor from 1924 to1927. She encouraged women to share their ideas, whether in the form of news, articles, poems, or other writings. She led the way by contributing nearly 200 editorials in which she expressed her views on **Black Nationalism** and **feminism** (Taylor, 108–109).

Negro World enjoyed a wide circulation which has been variously estimated from 50,000 to 200,000 copies during the height of its popularity (Wolseley, 67). According to Robert Brisbane in *The Negro Vanguard*, "By 1919 *Negro World* had become the most widely read Negro weekly in America, if not in the world" (Fax, 92). Its broad distribution reached the entire United States, as well as Africa and the Caribbean. In an effort to make the paper more accessible to non-English readers, sections were published in French and Spanish. Fearful of its radical ideology, several colonial governments banned the publication for its nationalistic and anticolonial content (Carnegie, 60).

Many of the paper's pages were filled with advertisements for products ranging from medicines to blood purifiers and mail order handguns (Digby-Junger 271). However, Garvey opposed endorsing products that demeaned Blacks. It was *Negro World*'s policy to refuse advertisements for skin lighteners and hair straightening compounds, notwithstanding their importance as a major source of advertising income for black newspapers (Fax, 90–91).

The last issue of *Negro World* appeared in 1933, although there have been a few attempts by Garvey followers to revive it. James R. Stewart published a magazine in 1942 called the *New Negro World*, but it lasted only a few months. Three years later, the *Voice of Freedom* appeared with the approval of Garvey's widow. It ceased publication after a few issues (Cronon, 49). On the Web, there is an online magazine based on *Negro World*. It features the writings of Marcus Garvey, opinion pieces, a section called "The People's Poetry," and a link to the official Web site of the Universal Negro Improvement Association and African Communities League. (*See* **Back-to-Africa Movement; Newspapers, African American.**)

Resources: Charles V. Carnegie, "Garvey and the Black Transnation," *Small Axe* 5 (March 1999), 48–71; Edmund David Cronon, *Black Moses: The Story of Marcus Garvey and the Universal Negro Improvement Association* (Madison: University of Wisconsin Press, 1955); Richard Digby-Junger, "*The Guardian*, *Messenger*, and *Negro World*: The Early 20th-Century Black Radical Press," *Howard Journal of Communications* 9 (1998), 263–282; W. F. Elkins, "Marcus Garvey: The *Negro World* and the British West Indies, 1919–1920," *Science & Society* 14, no. 2 (1972), 43–77; Elton C. Fax, *Garvey: The Story of a Pioneer Black Nationalist* (New York: Dodd, Mead, 1972); Mark D. Matthews, " 'Our Women and What They Think,' Amy Jacques Garvey and the Negro World," *Black Scholar* 10, no. 8–9 (1979), 2–13; *Negro World*, UNIA-ACL, http://www.negroworld.com; "People & Events: The *Negro World*," PBS American Experience (2000), www.pbs.org/wgbh/amex/garvey/peopleevents/e_negroworld.html; Schomberg Center for Research in Black Culture, "Universal Negro Improvement Association (UNIA)," *The New York Public Library African American Desk Reference* (New York: Wiley, 1999); Ula Y. Taylor, " 'Negro Women Are Great Thinkers as Well as Doers': Amy Jacques-Garvey and Community Feminism in the United

States, 1924–1927," *Journal of Women's History* 12, no. 2 (2000), 104–126; Robert E. Wolseley, *The Black Press, U.S.A.*, 2nd ed. (Ames: Iowa State University Press, 1990).

Lori Ricigliano

Nell, William Cooper (1816–1874). Historian, journalist, and activist. Nell's decades of reform journalism and authorship of one of the most important early histories of African Americans, as well as his consistent support of other African American writers and artists, made him an important figure on the antebellum African American literary landscape even though he is primarily recognized today for his ties to William Lloyd Garrison and the **Abolitionist Movement**.

Born in **Boston, Massachusetts**, to William G. and Louisa Nell, community activists and neighbors of the abolitionist **David Walker**, Nell was introduced early to three issues that would shape much of his life: education, activism, and racial discrimination. Nell completed his schooling at the top of his class at the African Meeting House's Smith School in 1829. However, because of his race, he was denied the municipal recognition accorded other excellent students. This experience led him to study law with William Bowditch (though he never practiced) and, in 1840, to begin a fifteen-year campaign to integrate Boston's schools.

The year 1840 also marked Nell's rise to direct *The Liberator*'s Negro Employment Office after nine years of performing various and sundry duties for the paper and its editor, William Lloyd Garrison. In addition to, in essence, acting as Garrison's assistant (and, sometimes, stand-in), Nell exercised his own voice as a lecturer, delegate to various Black conventions, founder of the Freedom Association (designed to aid fugitive slaves), leader of several literary societies, and civic activist. And, known for both his keen insight and his wit, he wrote letters, articles, and editorials that appeared not only in *The Liberator* but also in many other abolitionist periodicals of the day.

In 1848, Nell moved to Rochester, New York, to help **Frederick Douglass** begin publishing *The North Star*, but left the paper and returned to Boston when Douglass and Garrison publicly split. (While often painted as a firm Garrisonian, though, Nell shared some views—including a sense of political activism—with Douglass; he ran unsuccessfully for the Massachusetts legislature as a Free Soil candidate in 1850.) His dedication to the abolitionist press was unfailing; in addition to writing and editing, he acted as a subscription agent for a number of periodicals and regularly chastised abolitionists who did not financially support those periodicals.

Nell's work in the antislavery press up to 1850, when illness forced him to curtail his activism, would in itself be worth note as a contribution to African American literature. But the 1850s saw the publication of a range of texts on African Americans and the American Revolution—including the pamphlet *Services of Colored Americans in the Wars of 1776 and 1812* (1851) and culminating in his book *Colored Patriots of the American Revolution* (1855).

Historians of African Americans since then have been deeply influenced by Nell's approach, which relied on both documentary evidence and oral history. The book also contributed to Nell's ongoing fight for racial equality and led, in part, to his organization, on March 5, 1858, of the first of seven annual Crispus Attucks Day celebrations.

This sense of connecting African Americans' writing to community work—especially work designed to educate and to fight racial discrimination—guided his life and brought Nell to the aid of a generation of African American writers and artists. In addition to Douglass, he was instrumental in helping **Harriet Jacobs, Frank J. Webb, Mary Webb**, and a score of others recognized as important voices by contemporary critics. (His private letters have also become central to contemporary historians' understanding these writers, antebellum Black Boston, and abolitionism.)

Nell's recovery and return to activist work was marked by new contributions to most major abolitionist periodicals and renewed petitioning to the Massachusetts legislature—arguing, for example, for a monument to Crispus Attucks, an African American killed in the Revolutionary War. At this time he also wrote more pamphlets, including *Property Qualification or No Property Qualification: A Few Facts from the Record of Patriotic Services of the Colored Men of New York, During the Wars of 1776 and 1812* (1860), which was issued by the early Black publisher Thomas Hamilton. Some historians have also suggested he was the driving force behind the pamphlet *The Loyalty and Devotion of Colored Americans in the Revolution and War of 1812* (1861), which is generally attributed to Garrison.

In 1861, Nell was appointed a U.S. postal clerk—the first African American appointed to such a position—but this did not stop his writing. His work in later issues of *The Liberator* is especially poignant. He also continued working for social change, and often focused this work through the activities of the Union Progressive Association, which he helped found.

In April 1869, Nell married Frances Ann Ames, the daughter of the successful Black barber Philip O. Ames of Nashua, New Hampshire, who was more than two decades his junior. The couple had two sons. At his death, he was reportedly writing a history of Black troops in the **Civil War**.

Resources: Robert P. Smith, "William Cooper Nell: Crusading Black Abolitionist," *Journal of Negro History* 55 (1970), 182–199; Dorothy Porter Wesley, "Integration versus Separation: William Cooper Nell's Role in the Struggle for Equality," in *Courage and Conscience: Black and White Abolitionists in Boston*, ed. Donald M. Jacobs (Bloomington: Indiana University Press, 1993), 207–224.

Eric Gardner

Nelson, Annie Greene (1902–1993). Novelist. With *After the Storm* (1942), Annie Greene Nelson became the first Black woman in South Carolina to publish a novel. Two more novels followed: *The Dawn Appears* (1944) and *Don't Walk on My Dreams* (1961). Each novel characterizes local folk life as it focuses on Black dialect, a theme central to African American literature. Her characters live in close-knit Black communities located on South Carolina plantations during the first half of the twentieth century. Like her contemporary **Zora Neale Hurston**, Nelson neither portrays victims nor writes protest novels. Instead, her characters span social statuses, mostly teachers and preachers, and they demonstrate a range of emotions and considerable psychological depth. Much like the **slave narratives** of nineteenth-century Black women, Nelson's novels depict a heroine in a three-generation family relationship. The eldest of thirteen children, Nelson was born in Cartersville, South Carolina, on December 5, 1902. She grew up on the Parrotts' plantation in Darlington County, South Carolina; studied for two years at Benedict College in Columbia, South Carolina; and completed her education at Voorhees College in Denmark, South Carolina, earning degrees in nursing and education in 1923, the year she married Edward Nelson. She died in December 1993.

Resources: Idella Bodie, *South Carolina Women* (Orangeburg, SC: Sandlapper, 1990); Reginald V. Bruster, "Rooted in the Body: Architectonics in Black Women's Literature," Ph.D. diss., Indiana University of Pennsylvania, 1999 (Dissertation Abstracts International no. AAT 9936346); Annie Greene Nelson: *After the Storm* (Spartanburg, SC: Reprint Company, 1976); *The Dawn Appears* (Spartanburg, SC: Reprint Company, 1976); *Don't Walk on My Dreams* (Spartanburg, SC: Reprint Company, 1976); Jessie Carney Smith, ed., *Notable Black American Women*, vol. 1 (Detroit: Gale, 1992).

Reginald Bruster

Nelson, Jill (born 1952). Journalist, novelist, and political activist. In her writing, Nelson offers candid explorations of middle-class African American life. In particular, these explorations consider the situations facing professional African American women. Born and raised in New York City, Nelson holds a B.A. from the City College of New York and an M.A. from the Columbia School of Journalism. She was a staff writer at the *Washington Post Magazine* from its inception in 1986 until 1990; she was subsequently named **Washington, D.C.**, journalist of the year. Her memoir, *Volunteer Slavery: My Authentic Negro Experience* (1993), which described her experience at the *Post*, was a national best-seller and won an American Book Award. In it, Nelson writes of stereotyping and tokenism in the media, describing her critical participation in corporate life as walking a "thin line between Uncle Tomming and Mau-Mauing" (10). Her second work of autobiographical nonfiction, *Straight, No Chaser: How I Became a Grown-Up Black Woman* (1997), recounts the challenges and solidarities that she found as an ambitious middle-class Black woman, offering at once wry reflections and impassioned indictments of current inequities linked to **race** and **gender**. Her novel *Sexual Healing* (2003) portrays the social circles of professional women of color, representing what **Henry Louis Gates, Jr.,** called "a profound paradigm shift in the discussion of sexual relations between black men and women." Nelson's work has appeared in the *New York Times*, the *Chicago Tribune*, the *Village*

Voice, the *New York Review of Books, USA Today, The Nation, Essence, Ms., Salon.com,* and *MSNBC.com;* she has also taught journalism at the City College of New York. Nelson is currently at work on a second novel and a third memoir about the Black community on Martha's Vineyard.

Resources: Henry Louis Gates, Jr., "Advertisement," in *Sexual Healing,* by Jill Nelson (Chicago: Agate, 2003); Beverly Guy-Sheftall, "Review of *Straight No Chaser,*" *New York Times Book Review,* Dec. 21, 1997, pp. 20–21; Jill Nelson: *Police Brutality: An Anthology* (New York: Norton, 2000); *Sexual Healing* (Chicago: Agate, 2003); *Straight, No Chaser: How I Became a Grown-Up Black Woman* (New York: Putnam, 1999); *Volunteer Slavery: My Authentic Negro Experience* (New York: Penguin, 1994); Emily Toth, "Review of *Sexual Healing,*" *Women's Review of Books* 20, no. 12 (Sept. 2003), 9.

Alex Feerst

Nelson, Marilyn (born 1946). Poet, biographer, and editor. Born in Cleveland, Ohio, Marilyn Nelson followed her father, Melvin M. Nelson, a U.S. Air Force officer, from military base to military base, along with her sister and her brother. According to her short autobiographical essay in *Contemporary Authors,* her early memories include pride in her father's profession as a pilot and her mother's skill at telling stories of their family's heritage. In 1969, the Lutheran Campus Ministry program at Cornell University hired Nelson as a lay associate, in which position she worked for a year. She married a German graduate student she met at the University of Pennsylvania, Erdmann F. Waniek, in 1970 (CA). For two years after her marriage, she was a professor at Lane Community College in Eugene, Oregon, and at Reed College. In 1973, she and her husband moved to Denmark, where she taught as well. After later becoming an English professor in Minnesota, at St. Olaf's College, Nelson published her first volume of poetry, *For the Body,* in 1978. She divorced Waniek the following year (and married Roger R. Wilkenfield), but continued to publish under the name Waniek until 1996, when she began to publish under the name Marilyn Nelson.

Nelson's many awards include the Kent, the National Endowment for the Arts, the Fulbright teaching, the Guggenheim, and the Contemplative Practices fellowships; the *Boston Globe* and the Flora Stieglitz Straus awards for nonfiction; the Poet's Prize; and two Pushcart Prizes. In addition to *For the Body,* Nelson's poetry collections include *Mama's Promises* (1985), *The Homeplace* (1995), *Magnificat* (1994), and *Fields of Praise: New and Selected Poems* (1997). In 2001, Nelson used poetry to tell the story of George Washington Carver's life in *Carver: A Life in Poems,* for which she won the Coretta Scott King Honor, the Flora Steigletz Straus, and the Newbery awards. Nelson's poetry collections include poems for children, especially poems which charmingly depict the details of family life. But her poetry evokes the spiritual as well. She writes of *Mama's Promises,* "I'd hoped [the collection] would be read as a book of black feminist theology . . . [celebrating] myself, my mother, and other mothers . . . but also the Divine Mother, the feminine face of God" (2).

Nelson's poetry receives rave reviews; she is known for her skill in handling both narrative and lyric forms. According to *Contemporary Authors*, Nelson "evokes complex visions of life through a simple style, colloquial language, and functional allusions that often carry charming humor and ironic power" (3). In the *New Bones* anthology, Kevin Everod Quashie says, "What [Nelson's] poetry challenges the reader to do is something that the poetry allows her own self to do—to name and claim the triumphant and sweet and bitter that is our lives. Her work is always prayerful, never superficial, and invitingly well-crafted" (960).

Resources: Marilyn Nelson: *Fields of Praise: New and Selected Poems* (Baton Rouge: Louisiana State University Press, 1997); *Carver: A Life in Poems* (Asheville, NC: Front Street, 2001); "Marilyn Nelson," *Contemporary Authors* Database, Literary Resource Center, Author Resource Pages, http://galenet.galegroup.com/contemporary/authors/; Kevin E. Quashie, et al. *New Bones: Contemporary Black Writers in America* (Upper Saddle River, NJ: Prentice-Hall, 2001); Marilyn Waniek: *For the Body* (Baton Rouge: Louisiana State University Press, 1978); *The Homeplace* (Baton Rouge: Louisiana State University Press, 1990); *Magnificat* (Baton Rouge: Louisiana State University Press, 1994); *Mama's Promises* (Baton Rouge: Louisiana State University Press, 1985).

Jacqueline A. Blackwell

New Criticism (1930–1970). New Criticism was a literary movement that gained popularity from the 1930s through the 1960s. It promoted a close, analytical reading of a text, focusing on the intrinsic value of a work of literature and a work itself as an independent source of meaning. The time period between 1930 and 1970 was one of great social upheaval and change. New Criticism was, in part, a response to new forms of mass literature and literacy, competition for tuition dollars with the sciences, and an increased enrollment in college by students who were newly financially able to attend through the G.I. Bill. To some degree, New Criticism developed in opposition to biographical criticism, wherein a literary work was judged as a reflection of the author's life.

New Criticism was classified as a type of formalism—studying the form and structure of artistic or literary works. It was seen as an objective approach to poetry and literature. New Criticism wanted to discuss the part of literature that made it *literary*—its formal characteristics. New Critics examined these formal characteristics using close reading. This method of analysis involved the reader looking at individual words, syntax, symbolism, plot, foreshadowing, irony, paradox, metaphor, and the structure of a work. The New Critics believed that their job was to help the general audience appreciate the technique and form of a given literary work.

New Criticism treated literary works as having an objective and independent existence. In other words, texts possessed meaning in and of themselves, and analyses emphasized intrinsic meaning over extrinsic meaning. Unlike previous literary movements, New Criticism removed the author from the analysis of a text. This distancing was necessary so that the biography and history of an author could not influence the reading of a text. New Critics coined the term "intentional fallacy"—the mistake of attempting to understand the author's intentions when interpreting a literary work, because doing so violated the autonomy of the work. Once a work escaped the author's hands, it also escaped his influence and became the intellectual property of the audience. When a work was published, its meaning was irrevocably fixed, regardless of the author's feelings about that meaning or the historical circumstances surrounding the work's creation.

In treating a text as independent entity, New Critics also removed the influence of the reader from the analysis of a text. They sought to avoid the affective fallacy—the mistake of equating a work with its emotional effects upon the audience, a practice which would compromise a work's inherent meaning, according to the rationale of New Criticism. In many ways, New Criticism made it difficult to analyze texts from the perspective of Black literary criticism, which was marked with the sense that Black writing is born out of a sociological, political, ideological, and cultural situation marked by oppression and marginalization. Black literary criticism also emphasized that criticism is inevitably ideological and political, defining Black creative works as complex cultural products. In New Criticism, these factors were rendered irrelevant because historical context was deemphasized.

Organic unity was also important to New Critics. The idea of organic unity was that all elements of a good literary work are interdependent and create a whole emotional or intellectual effect. If any one part of the art is removed—whether it be a character, an action, a speech, a description or an authorial observation—the entire work is diminished. The idea also suggested that the growth or development of a piece of good literature—from its beginning to its end—occurred naturally, according to a certain sequence. That sequence could be chronological, logical, or otherwise step-by-step in some productive manner. Since every part contributes to the whole organism of the piece of literature, this concept further encouraged a close and comprehensive attention to its details.

New Critics used several other principles to interpret a text. These included tension, irony, ambiguity, and paradox. Tension was the interplay of conflicting elements within a text that made the organic unity of a work possible and gave shape to the work's central themes. Irony represented contradictions or incongruities within a text—when a character and the reader (or two characters within a work) viewed a particular situation from opposing perspectives with one knowing/understanding more than the other. For New Critics, recognizing irony was integral to articulating the oppositional elements that contributed to the complex organic unity of a work as a whole. The principle of ambiguity defined the existence of several possible meanings, including conflicting attitudes or feelings. New Critics did not necessarily consider ambiguity a weakness. Instead, ambiguity was seen as a virtue of the text because it reflected another layer of richness or complexity of meaning in a work (Empson). Finally, New Critics looked for paradoxes, or seemingly contradictory statements that could nonetheless prove true.

New Criticism valued poetry over other creative forms of expression. Poetry was viewed as the purest expression of the literary values of New Criticism. Poetry was also held in high esteem because it represented a creative form in which language is used in uncommon ways to produce more complex relations among words that are literary than those found in the **vernacular**. Among the poets most analyzed by New Critics was T. S. Eliot, a prominent American poet with a unique poetic style. As a critic himself, Eliot was drawn to precise and concrete language, and he became an influential part of the New Criticism movement. Despite the New Critics' preoccupation with poetry, the New Criticism approach was taken with fiction, drama, essays, and other literary forms.

Aside from T. S. Eliot, the two most significant figures in the New Criticism movement were John Crowe Ransom and Cleanth Brooks. Ransom published his first book of poetry, *Poems About God,* in 1919. Within the next eight years, he released two other volumes—*Chills and Fever* (1924) and *Two Gentlemen in Bonds* (1927). Throughout his career he was more interested in philosophy than in poetry or literature, and his later endeavors in literary criticism became his claim to fame. Between 1939 and 1959, he taught at Kenyon College and served as editor of the prestigious *Kenyon Review.* In 1941, he published a book of essays titled *New Criticism,* for which the New Criticism was named. Though he grew skeptical of New Criticism, his impact on the movement was indelible. Ransom's student Cleanth Brooks became another luminary in the world of New Criticism. With the poet, novelist, and professor Robert Penn Warren, he wrote the textbook *Understanding Poetry* (1938), an enormously influential book that brought techniques of New Criticism into innumerable college classrooms. In 1947, Brooks published his most famous book of criticism, *The Well Wrought Urn,* and moved to Yale, where he became a professor emeritus of rhetoric thirteen years later. Though he wrote several critical studies on William Faulkner, Brooks was most widely known as the epitome of a New Critic: his ideas, critical studies, and textbooks embodied everything that New Criticism represented.

In a literary twist of irony, New Criticism was not without its own critics. Some in the world of literary criticism felt that the close reading and emphasis on technique and structure were incompatible with literary forms other than poetry. These detractors also believed that New Criticism ignored diversity and asserted that the context of a literary work was just as important as the work itself. This critique of New Criticism was particularly relevant to the New Critical approach to Black literature. Ultimately, many believed that the values the New Critics espoused were not universal, but were based upon their own histories and perspectives—the very things New Critics sought to omit from their analyses of literary works.

Resources: Cleanth Brooks, *The Well Wrought Urn: Studies in the Structure of Poetry* (New York: Harcourt Brace, 1947); Cleanth Brooks and Robert Penn Warren,

Understanding Poetry: An Anthology for College Students (New York: Henry Holt, 1938); T. S. Eliot: *Collected Poems, 1909–1962* (New York: Harcourt, Brace and World, 1963); *The Sacred Wood: Essays on Poetry and Criticism* (New York: Knopf, 1930); William Empson, *Seven Types of Ambiguity* (London: Chatto and Windus, 1930); Mark Jancovich, *The Cultural Politics of the New Criticism* (New York: Cambridge University Press, 1993); John Crowe Ransom, *The New Criticism* (Norfolk, CT: New Directions, 1941); William Spurlin and Michael Fischer, eds., *The New Criticism and Contemporary Literary Theory* (New York: Garland, 1995); W. K., Wimsatt, Jr., *The Verbal Icon: Studies in the Meaning of Poetry by W.K. Wimsatt, Jr., and Two Preliminary Essays Written in Collaboration with Monroe C. Beardsley* (Lexington: University Press of Kentucky, 1954); Thomas Daniel Young, ed., *The New Criticism and After* (Charlottesville: University Press of Virginia, 1976).

Roxane Gay

New Negro (1920s). The term "New Negro" came to identify a young generation of African Americans who, ideally, would be educated in prestigious universities in America and Europe, and who would naturally constitute the intellectual and artistic leadership of "the race" as they personified the positive and progressive values of the middle class to which they belonged. More practically, less ideally, the term stood for the incipient attitude of the educated African American middle class, which had evolved in the years leading up to **World War I**. The New Negro was mainly characterized by self-assertion and self-articulation, and therefore replaced the racist stereotype of the "Old Negro." This stereotype included passivity, accommodation, and lack of education. The new attitude symbolized by the image of the New Negro also sprang from changes that the **Great Migration** and, especially, African Americans' involvement in World War I (Du Bois, "Returning Soldiers"). The attitude was linked to racial pride, which had been enhanced, in part, by African American troops' patriotic behavior during the war (Lewis). Cary D. Wintz defines this new attitude as follows: "the belief that large numbers of black Americans had become proud of their race, self-reliant, and assimilated to American middle-class values, and that they were demanding their rights as American citizens" (31). The New Negro was supposed to be a self-assured, well-educated, politically progressive, and urban new generation of African Americans in the 1920s.

Originally, the term was widely employed at the end of the nineteenth century with different meanings, ranging from the idea of "self-help" to the protest against any type of discrimination, even including the first references to Pan-Africanism. Although some critics date the term differently, **Henry Louis Gates, Jr.**, argues, in "The Trope of a New Negro and the Reconstruction of the Image of the Black" (1988), that the term was first used in 1745 by a British newspaper to designate slaves coming from Africa. This use is quite ironic if we take into account African Americans' zeal to "reconstruct" their public image precisely by means of the term under discussion.

Nevertheless, later the term was specifically associated with the intellectual and cultural milieu of the 1920s, especially after the publication of *The New*

Negro, a landmark anthology edited by **Alain Locke** in 1925 that acquired the character of a foundational manifesto. Growing out of a special edition of **Survey Graphic** titled "Harlem—Mecca of the New Negro," published in March 1925, this book is a collection of essays and primary works by some of the most influential artistic and intellectual voices of the **Harlem Renaissance**. As a whole, it reflected the wide range of the movement's artistic expression, but also its manifold contradictions and controversies. Its main objective is delineated by Locke in the introduction: "This volume aims to document the New Negro culturally and socially—to register the transformations of the inner and the outer life of the Negro in America that have so significantly taken place in the last few years" (xxv). Thanks to this momentous anthology, the concept of the New Negro would remain closely linked to the Harlem Renaissance as its most visible icon.

To account for the importance of this timely publication, the text can be read as an extension of ideas put forward by **W.E.B. Du Bois**. For instance, it promoted the idea that African Americans might achieve social equality with White Americans through advacement in the arts. Rampersad confirms this link in the introduction to the 1992 edition: "*The New Negro* was the first literary attempt to revise the collective portrait of black America painted by him [Du Bois] in his own epochal collection *The Souls of Black Folk* in 1903" (xiv). Du Bois's privileged position is clearly revealed in his essay "The Negro Mind Reaches Out," which closes the volume and demonstrates the enormous influence of *Souls* on Locke's anthology. Du Bois's essay discusses progress of the African American community in the first three decades of the twentieth century and some two decades after the publication of *The Souls of Black Folk*.

Du Bois's influence is also noticeable in Locke's adaptation of two of his key ideas in the text: the **Talented Tenth** and double consciousness. For instance, when Locke declares, "the more intelligent and representative elements of the two race groups have at so many points got quite out of vital touch with one another" (9), he clearly alludes to Du Bois's notion of the Talented Tenth—the best educated, most socially engaged 10 percent of African Americans whom Du Bois and others believed would lead all African Americans. Indeed, Locke echoes Du Bois's view that the intellectual parity between the two races and the cooperation between their intellectual minorities would be to ways to overcome racism in the United States. Locke places all his hopes for a better future in that new generation, and he considers artistic and literary expression to be its best vehicle to achieve the desired aims. One implication of Locke's and Du Bois's ideas is that the New Negro would be part of the Talented Tenth.

Du Bois's concept of double consciousness is evident in Locke's anthology. In the *Souls of Black Folk*, Du Bois had described the predicament whereby African Americans must, like all humans, be conscious of themselves as individuals but must, because of their unique position in American society, also be conscious of themselves as Black people; therefore, they are almost constantly "doubly conscious."

In *The New Negro*, Locke writes of an "outer" and an "inner life," described, respectively, by Locke as "the ideals of American institutions and democracy" and "the development of a more positive self-respect and self-reliance . . . the rise from social disillusionment to race pride" (10). Indeed, most of the contributions of the volume negotiate between the allegiance to the Euro-centric value system and the overriding imperative to manifest the new attitude of racial pride. For example, the famous poem by **Langston Hughes**, "I Too," celebrates the sense of belonging to American society with the suggestive line "I, too, am America" (145), which also echoes Walt Whitman. Similarly, Melville J. Herskovits's essay "The Negro's Americanism," pictures **Harlem, New York**, as "a typical American community" (354), the social and cultural organizations of which, in Herskovits's view, are similar to those found in any other American community.

On the other hand, *The New Negro* also stresses the distinctiveness of African American culture: "that there should have developed a distinctively Negro art in America was natural and inevitable" (19). Locke regarded this "Negro art" as a cultural project that would demonstrate the creativity of the Black race. But even this notion of creativity is complicated and seems to include an element of double consciousness, especially with respect to the cultural legacy of Africa. The origins of African American culture art comprise a "treasury of folk lore which the American Negro inherited from his African forefathers" (238). At the same time, Locke takes pains to distinguish between African and African Amerian culture: "Music and poetry, and to an extent the dance, have been the predominant arts of the American Negro. This is an emphasis quite different from that of the African cultures, where the plastic and craft arts predominate" (254). In other words, Locke and others may have felt ambivalent toward the value and influence of African culture. In any event, the ambitions that Locke, Du Bois, and others had for African American art, including literature, are connected to the concept of the New Negro, an imagined ideal African American characterized by education, refinement, economic wherewithal, and a willingness to lead African Americans forward.

Resources: William W. Cook, "The New Negro Renaissance," in *A Companion to Twentieth-Century Poetry*, ed. Neil Roberts (Oxford: Blackwell, 2001), 138–152; W.E. B. Du Bois: "Returning Soldiers," in *The Portable Harlem Renaissance Reader*, ed. David Levering Lewis (New York: Viking, 1994), 3–5; *The Souls of Black Folk: Essays and Sketches* (Chicago, A. C. McClurg, 1903); Henry Louis Gates, Jr., "The Trope of a New Negro and the Reconstruction of the Image of the Black," *Representations* 24 (Fall 1988), 129–155; Nathan Irvin Huggins, ed., *Voices from the Harlem Renaissance* (New York: Oxford University Press, 1994); David Levering Lewis, *When Harlem Was in Vogue* (New York: Knopf, 1981); Alain Locke, *The New Negro. Voices of the Harlem Renaissance* (1925; repr. New York: Atheneum, 1992); Richard A. Long, "The Genesis of Locke's *The New Negro*," *Black World* 25, no. 4 (1976), 14–20; Cary D. Wintz, *Black Culture and the Harlem Renaissance* (Houston: Rice University Press, 1988).

Mar Gallego

New Negro, The (1925). A collection of fiction, poetry, drama, music, essays, and artwork, *The New Negro* is heralded as the first definitive publication of the **Harlem Renaissance**, a period of burgeoning Black artistic expression. It was edited by **Alain Locke**, a Howard University professor of philosophy.

The New Negro was conceived in 1924 when Paul Kellogg, founder and editor of **Survey Graphic**, the leading journal in social work at the time, commissioned Locke to guest edit an issue that would capture the spirit of the period. Locke's efforts resulted in a special March 1925 edition (vol. 6, no. 6) titled "Harlem: Mecca of the New Negro." Often referred to as "the Harlem number," the sixty-six-page *Survey Graphic* issue surpassed previous sales of the journal; the first printing of 30,000 copies sold out, and Kellogg was compelled to run a second printing of 12,000. Benefactors such as "Albert C. Barnes, George Foster Peabody, and Professor [Joel] and Mrs. [Amy] Springarn," contributed to the journal's peak in sales, purchasing up to 1,000 copies each (at 50 cents per copy) and distributing them free to interested parties, including "a wide sector of Black students and organizations" (Long, 16). Publishers Albert and Charles Boni were so impressed with the journal's success that they asked Locke to expand the Harlem number into a book-length publication, which appeared in December 1925 as *The New Negro*.

Locke's anthology was predated in publication by William Pickens's book, also entitled *The New Negro* (1916), suggesting that the public was familiar with the phrase "**New Negro**" at least a decade prior to Locke's use of it (Long, 15). The collection was also preceded by **James Weldon Johnson**'s *The Book of American Negro Poetry* (1922), which included work by some of the key figures featured in the subsequent anthology. In addition, two pivotal magazines, **Opportunity: A Journal of Negro Life** (of the Urban League) and **The Crisis** (of the **NAACP**), publicized the period's increase in artistic activity by sponsoring contests and facilitating publishing opportunities for up-and-coming Black poets and writers. With its artistic layout and breadth of coverage, however, *The New Negro* anthology surpassed its predecessors in influence.

From the outset, *The New Negro*'s artistic design captured the attention of its readers. Filled with the African and Cubist-inspired "decorations" of the Bavarian artist Winold Reiss, who had previously provided most of the illustrations for the *Survey Graphic* Harlem number, the anthology also included eleven Aaron Douglas drawings and designs that celebrated the Negro's beauty and rich heritage. W.V. Ruckterschell's "Young Negro," Miguel Covarrubias' drawing "Blues Singer," as well as reprints of title pages from **slave narratives** (compliments of the **Arthur A. Schomberg** collection) and photos of tribal masks and sculptures (from the Barnes collection and other museums) rounded out *The New Negro*'s historical tribute through the visual arts, making Locke's pronouncement of the Negro community's "renewed self-respect and self-dependence" quite evident to all (4).

The anthology was divided into two sections: "Part I: The Negro Renaissance" and "Part II: The New Negro in a New World." These sections were followed by an extensive bibliography, "A Select List of Negro-Americana and Africana," which was considered "the most comprehensive to appear since [W.E.B.] Dubois' [bibliography], published by Atlanta University early in the century" (Long, 19).

"Part I: The Negro Renaissance" sought not only to define what Locke termed a "metamorphosis" or "spiritual emancipation" of the Negro but also to chronicle the strides made in art, literature, and music toward that emancipation (3–4). For instance, in his essay "Negro Art and America," Albert C. Barnes asserted the Negro's artistry through poetry and the **spirituals**, and **William Stanley Braithwaite** chronicled the portrayal of Blacks in American literature, beginning with the Black and unknown bards and culminating with **Jean Toomer**'s *Cane*. Arthur A. Schomburg and others acknowledged slave narratives, commentaries, and folk literature, providing a tribute to the ancestry of the African American literary tradition.

Prominent in this first section were **Langston Hughes**, who provided several poems, and Alain Locke, who set the tone of the anthology with "The New Negro" and other essays, including "Negro Youth Speaks," an introduction to the young authors, poets, and playwrights represented in the anthology.

"Part II: The New Negro in a New World" began with Paul Kellogg's examination of the pioneering among Blacks, such as northward migration (which he equated with westward expansion) and the break with "Nordic conventions" found in Winold Reiss's artistic portrayal of Negroes (277). **Charles Spurgeon Johnson** contributed an essay on a "new type of Negro . . . a city Negro" (285), and other contributors offered analyses of various centers of Black culture (**Harlem, New York**), industry (Durham, North Carolina), and education (Howard, Hampton, and Tuskeegee), while W. A. Domingo shared insight on a growing segment of the Black population: the "foreign-born Negro population" (342).

In addition to recognizing the distinguishable aspects of Negroes and their culture, the second section of the anthology pointed out various arenas in which Blacks are similar to their White counterparts. Melville Herskovits addressed similar organizations, professions, and businesses found in Black and White communities, while Walter White focused on talent, specifically performer **Paul Robeson**'s artistic ability to make his audiences forget the color of his skin. Also in Part II, Elise Johnson McDougald contributed a discussion of the challenges as well as the contributions of Black women, and **W.E.B. Du Bois** provided the final essay: a reexamination of his previous assertion (most profoundly made in his 1903 treatise, *The Souls of Black Folk*) that "[t]he problem of the twentieth century is the problem of the color line" (385).

Even decades later, *The New Negro* continues to serve as a leading source on a definitive era in African American literary history. In the words of the Harlem Renaissance scholar Cary Wintz, "[t]he most significant accomplishment of both *The New Negro* and [its forerunner] *The Survey Graphic* issue was that they identified and publicized the literary developments of the Harlem Renaissance and for the first time made this work easily available to the reading public" (*Black Culture*, 82).

Resources: Aberjhani and Sandra L. West, *Encyclopedia of the Harlem Renaissance* (New York: Facts on File, 2003); Victor A. Kramer and Robert A. Russ, eds., *Harlem Renaissance Re-examined*, rev. and enl. ed. (New York: Whitston, 1997); David Levering Lewis, *When Harlem Was in Vogue* (1981; repr. New York: Penguin, 1997); Alain Locke, *The New Negro* (1925; New York: Simon and Schuster, 1997); Richard Long, "The Genesis of Locke's *The New Negro*," *Black World* 25, no. 4 (1976), 15–20; Arnold Rampersad, "Introduction," in *The New Negro* (New York: Simon and Schuster, 1997); Steven Watson, *The Harlem Renaissance: Hub of African-American Culture, 1920–1930* (New York: Pantheon, 1995); Cary D. Wintz, *Black Culture and the Harlem Renaissance* (Houston: Rice University Press, 1988); Cary D. Wintz, ed.: *The Critics and the Harlem Renaissance* (New York: Garland, 1996); *The Politics and Aesthetics of "New Negro Literature"* (New York: Garland, 1996).

Veronica Adams Yon

New Orleans, Louisiana. New Orleans (pop. 484,674) is one of the largest and most diverse cities in the southern United States. Located on the banks of the Mississippi River, it has a thriving African American community that helps to define the city's rich cultural heritage. The city's world-renowned French Quarter, an area filled with music clubs, restaurants, and risqué nightlife, is considered one of the most distinctive areas in the country and is a popular tourist destination for people throughout the world.

New Orleans became the capital of the French colony of Louisiana in 1722, and it soon established itself as a significant port city. The French then transferred Louisiana to Spain under the Treaty of Fontainebleu (1762), later confirmed by the Treaty of Paris (1763). The city passed back to the French before the United State took control of it after the Louisiana Purchase in 1803. In 1815, Major General Andrew Jackson defeated the British army in New Orleans as an aftermath to the War of 1812. Jackson Square, a city landmark, honors him for his victory.

The French influence on New Orleans is significant. It was the dominant force in the city's culture until the late nineteenth century. **Creole** language, food, and music became synonymous with open-minded lifestyles, and the city is now known for its acceptance and celebration of diversity and multiculturalism. Mardi Gras, French for Shrove Tuesday or "fat Tuesday," is perhaps the best-known festival in the United States. Elaborate floats, street musicians, and revealing costumes are all part of the annual event.

Although the French influence on New Orleans culture is important, the African American contribution is incalculable. After the Louisiana Purchase and until the **Civil War** was over, New Orleans became infamous as a major slave trade port. As the United States continued to split over the issue of **slavery** in the nineteenth century, plantation owners in the environs of New Orleans exploited slaves to grow cotton, which was then shipped on the Mississippi River. American democracy arrived in New Orleans just as the cotton gin made the country the largest slave center in the world (Carter et al., 81). This painful legacy remains an important aspect of the city's cultural and political life.

After New Orleans fell to Union Admiral David G. Farragut during the Civil War, the city suffered through the end of the steamboat era and re-created itself as an economic powerhouse in industry, shipping, and tourism. But this would take several years, for New Orleans merchants paid heavily for their support of Southern independence (Capers, 154).

It would take decades after the Civil War before African Americans were fully involved in the city's economic successes, though some former slaves in New Orleans were employed in highly skilled occupations and were able to use those skills immediately to raise their standard of living. Violence against African Americans in New Orleans was rampant after the war. The New Orleans race riot in July 1866 resulted in the deaths of thirty-six Black residents who were killed by Whites.

The African American contribution to New Orleans culture is immeasurable. African Americans are credited with creating **jazz** music in the late nineteenth century, and the city is still known for its famous jazz clubs. Considered the first jazz musician in the country, New Orleans's Buddy Bolden formed a band in the mid-1890s (Jackson, 279). Bolden's music later influenced Louis Armstrong, the famous twentieth-century jazz cornet player, who began his career in the city, playing on street corners as a child to help support his mother. Armstrong later became one of the most admired jazz musicians in American history.

Voodoo and **folklore** are also important parts of New Orleans's history. Using a mixture of Jamaican and Catholic spiritual customs, New Orleans's voodoo practitioners still enrich the city's cultural life. African American visual artists also are at the forefront of cultural life. The New Orleans African American Museum of Art, Culture, and History remains a significant part of its artistic life.

The African American contribution to New Orleans's literary life also has a long and rich history. L'Union, the first African American newspaper in the United States, was founded in New Orleans in 1862. Two years later, it was sold. Under new ownership, it became the La Tribune de la Nouvelle Orléans (New Orleans Tribune), and it served as a major political voice for Black residents of the city until it closed in 1869.

The African American writer and New Orleans resident **Alice Moore Dunbar-Nelson** began publishing short stories and poems in the 1890s. Her work deals with racial and women's issues. She was a field organizer for the women's suffrage movement. Her books, which include Violets and Other Tales (1895) and The Goodness of St. Rocque and Other Stories (1899), also deal with the cultural identity of New Orleans.

Marcus Bruce Christian was head of the black writers' component of the **Federal Writers' Project** in Louisiana from the 1930s until the early 1940s. He later taught at the University of New Orleans. Much of his work deals with the Black experience in twentieth-century New Orleans.

New Orleans writer and editor **Thomas Covington Dent** published two books of poetry, Magnolia Street (1976) and Blue Lights and River Songs (1982). Dent also wrote the play Ritual Murder, which was produced in the 1970s.

The Levee at Canal Street, New Orleans, Louisiana, c. 1900. Yale Collection of Western Americana, Beinecke Rare Book and Manuscript Library.

Born in New Orleans and raised in the New York area, Anatole Broyard, an African American writer for *The New Times*, was later a subject in the book *Thirteen Ways of Looking at a Black Man*, by **Henry Louis Gates, Jr.** (1997). The book looks at Broyard's career and life in the mid-twentieth century.

The African American writer **Bob Kaufman** was a major voice among the **Beat** poets and writers in the 1950s and 1960s. His work challenges the country's power structure with its critiques of capitalism and racial issues. Known also for his ascetic lifestyle, Kaufman took a vow of silence after witnessing the assassination of President John F. Kennedy. It is reported the vow of silence lasted until the end of the **Vietnam War** (Charters, 327). Kaufman's work includes *Solitudes Crowded with Loneliness* (1965), *The Ancient Rain: Poems 1956–1978* (1981), *Abomunist Manifesto* (1959), *Second April* (1959), *Does the Secret Mind Whisper?* (1960) and *Golden Sardine* (1967). (*See* **Nkombo**; **Salaam, Kalamu ya.**)

Resources: Gerald M. Capers, *Occupied City: New Orleans Under the Federals, 1862–1865* (Lexington: University Press of Kentucky, 1965); Hodding Carter, William Ransom Hogan, John. W. Lawrence, and Betty Werlein Carter, eds., *The Past as Prelude: New Orleans 1719–1968* (New Orleans: Tulane University Press, 1968); Ann Charters, ed., *The Portable Beat Reader* (New York: Penguin, 1992); Leonard Huber, *New Orleans: A Pictorial History* (New York: American Legacy Press, 1981); Joy Jackson, *New Orleans in the Gilded Age* (Baton Rouge: Louisiana State University

Press, 1969); Stuart M. Lynn, *New Orleans* (New York: Hastings House, 1949): Sheila Smith McKoy, "Alice Dunbar-Nelson," in *The Works of Alice Dunbar-Nelson*, vol. 2, ed. Gloria T. Hull (New York: Oxford University Press, 1988); "Tom Dent: A New Orleans Writer," *The Black Collegian Online*, June 1998, http://www.black-collegian .com/african/dent9.shtml; *U.S. Census 2000* (New Orleans), http://www.new-orleans .la.us/population.asp.

Kurt Hochenauer

New York City. *See* **Brooklyn, New York**; **Harlem, New York**; **Harlem Renaissance**.

Newsome, Effie Lee (1885–1979). Children's author, poet, and fiction writer. Newsome primarily wrote children's poems and occasional fables and tales during the **Harlem Renaissance**. The daughter of graduates of Wilberforce University in Ohio, Newsome was academically trained at Wilberforce University, Oberlin, the Academy of Fine Arts, and the University of Pennsylvania. She first published poems in *The Brownies' Book*, a periodical for children supported by **W.E.B. Du Bois** and edited by **Jessie Redmon Fauset**. Beginning in the 1920s, she wrote a regular children's column, "The Little Page," in *The Crisis* magazine, another publication supported by Du Bois and the **NAACP**. The most recent and most inclusive collection of her poetry is *Wonders: The Best Children's Poems of Effie Lee Newsome*.

Newsome's alliance with Du Bois was important in the promotion of the Harlem Renaissance's artistic mission of disproving misconceptions about Blacks and presenting a more realistic portrayal of the Black experience. Both Du Bois and Newsome recognized the impact issues of representation had on children. Du Bois documented scandals involving inheritance rights for Black children, life-threatening conditions for children denied access to hospitals, and injustices in public education. Perhaps more insidious was the representation of Black children in popular culture from the postbellum era to the first twenty years of the twentieth century. African American children in cartoons, stories, nursery rhymes, and advertisements were depicted as dirty, partially clad, often pursued by alligators (thus encouraging the deaths of Black children), wild, uncivilized, foolish creatures who needed and desired the paternal control of White society.

Newsome's most anthologized poem is "To a Brown Boy," which first appeared in *The Crisis*. It makes clear that to be brown is to be strong, as exemplified in mountains, trees, lions, eagles. The poem exemplifies Newsome's style and illustrates her attention to reaffirming a child's sense of beauty, identity, and empowerment. In response to the overt and covert racist attitudes toward Black children, Newsome embraced the aims of the Black aesthetic and artistically wrote poems that would reinforce the child's self-image, affirm the Black child's understanding of beauty, expand a young person's understanding of the natural world, reinforce a child's Christian theology, encourage children to playfully and imaginatively embrace their world, introduce Black children to their African heritage, and, most important, help African American children acknowledge and respond to the political and personal racial assaults of their current environment.

Resource: Effie Lee Newsome, *Wonders: The Best Children's Poems of Effie Lee Newsome*, comp. Rudine Sims Bishop (Honesdale, PA: Boyds Mills Press, 1999).

Judith Musser

Newspapers, African American. African American newspapers, also known as "the Black press," have been both a political and a literary force in the United States for over 150 years.

Vigorously proclaiming the right of men to be free of taxation without representation, the Founding Fathers unanimously exhorted their position to King George III of England that **colonialism** was no longer the "rule" but the "exception." Unfortunately, by the time the new nation had come to this conclusion, **slavery** had become the unofficial law of the land. The Founding Fathers had decided America would hold the truth to be self-evident that freedom and liberty did not apply to people of African descent but was the province of Whites only.

Free African Americans at the time of the Revolutionary War petitioned the new governing body led by Thomas Jefferson, George Washington, James Madison, Benjamin Franklin, and Alexander Hamilton to acknowledge their rights as "free" citizens and end the savage institution of slavery. Their cries for justice fell on deaf ears. In 1791 **Benjamin Banneker**, a free African American of much prominence and intellect, reminded Jefferson in a letter of the Constitution and the words he (Jefferson) used so powerfully and convincingly: "all men are created equal and endowed by their Creator with certain inalienable rights." The letter implies Banneker's disappointment with Jefferson's determination to perpetuate the institution of slavery in the new republic: "But sir how pitiful it is to reflect, that although you were so fully concerned of the benevolence of the Father of Mankind and his equal and impartial distribution of these rights and privileges which hath conferred upon them, that you should at the same time counteract his mercies" (160). African Americans could not rely on the good faith efforts of White leaders.

Undeterred in their pursuit of justice, the free African Americans above the Mason Dixon Line were determined to seize the attention of the United States and demand liberty for all people or justice for none; the seeds of the Black press were thereby planted.

On March 16, 1827, the first Black newspaper, *Freedom's Journal*, debuted on the national scene. It was founded by John Russwurm just one year after his graduation from Bowdoin College, to give African Americans their own voice in print. The motto for *Freedom's Journal* was "Righteousness Exalteth a Nation." In partnership with his longtime friend **Samuel Cornish**, Russwurm launched responses to White voices exhorting pro-slavery agendas.

Other nineteenth-century African American newspapers included *The Colored American*, *The National Watchman*, and *The Mystery*, all of which were headquartered in New York state, with the exception of *The Mystery*, which

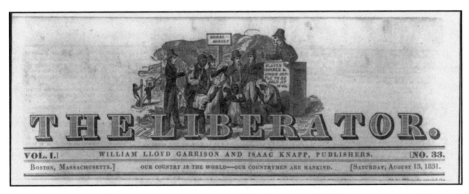

Masthead for the African American newspaper *The Liberator*, 1831. Courtesy of the Library of Congress.

was published in **Pittsburgh, Pennsylvania**, beginning in 1843. In these newspapers, educated Black men such as Russwurm and Cornish could openly voice their opinions in the company of affluent White liberals in the North who shared abolitionist views. Abolitionists, including William Lloyd Garrison, joined the chorus to end slavery. Soon Garrison published his own newspaper, *The Liberator*, to express antislavery sentiments (*see* **Abolitionist Movement**).

Those nascent years of the black press were fraught with economic realities inherent in the publishing business. African Americans, when faced with either buying a newspaper or feeding a family, chose family. Literate African Americans with disposable income were not numerous enough to sustain a Black newspaper enterprise fully, leading to financial challenges endemic to the world of publishing. Although many Black publishing companies had to close their doors after having swung them open so widely in the beginning, events would soon give the Black press a much needed shot in the arm. The fact that a nation would go to war over disparate treatment of African Americans and dismantle the foundations of slavery gave the Black press needed ammunition to increase its readership and encourage the recruitment of blacks to fight in a war for the elimination human bondage; the **Civil War** created a financial lifeline for the Black press.

On September 27, 1862, just five days after the Emancipation Proclamation was signed by Abraham Lincoln, *L'Union*, the first African American general circulation newspaper in **the South**, was published (Simmons). Unlike its predecessors in the North, vociferously lamenting the profanity of slavery, *L'Union* employed carefully presented strategies for freed African Americans to survive in a Southern society hostile to their newfound freedom: "We inaugurate today a new era in the destiny of the south to further the cause of the rights of man and humanity" (Simmons, 14). *L'Union* at first published in French. The **Creole** population in Louisiana, descendants of French settlers, used their native language to launch their publication, thereby attracting very little attention to a very feisty Black newspaper.

The Civil War period was the breeding ground for over 110 African American newspapers (Brooks). Many Black publications folded in haste. Chased by bloodthirsty White mobs angered by the exposure of their unlawful activities, Black editors barely escaped with their lives. If his publication carried stories about **lynching** or Ku Klux Klan cross burnings, for example, the Black editor published at his peril.

The removal of federal troops by President Rutherford B. Hayes precipitated one of most dangerous periods in American history, not only for African Americans but also for the Black press. "African American editors in the south adopted a self-imposed 'muzzle' policy toward racial issues. Lynching was ignored, lawlessness was void of mention in most black newspapers, but anti-white black militias against white violence sprang up, clashing often with white would-be lynching" (Simmons, 164).

From the inception of *Freedom's Journal* 1827 to the Emancipation Proclamation of 1863, nearly forty-two African American newspapers hoisted their banners to protest slavery. Undaunted by government claims of sedition, some Black editors refused to curb their militant reporting to avert threats of closing their publications. This spirit of determination carried through into the twentieth century.

One of the most important Black newspapers of the twentieth century was the **Chicago Defender**, founded in 1905 by Robert S. Abbott (Suggs). By 1910 it was read by one tenth of Chicago's Black population, and by 1920 it had gained a national readership (Walker). The **Baltimore Afro-American**, the **Pittsburgh Courier**, and the **Amsterdam News** were among the Black newspapers that, like the *Defender*, generated both a local and a national readership. These newspapers not only reported on events important to African Americans but also published poems and short stories. **Langston Hughes** published numerous poems in the *Chicago Defender*, the *Baltimore Afro-American*, and the *Amsterdam News* over his career, and he covered the Spanish Civil War for the *Afro-American* (Ostrom). For the *Chicago Defender*, Hughes began a weekly column, "Here to Yonder," in 1942, and continued writing it for twenty-three years. The column gave birth to Hughes's humorous tales about the fictional Jesse B. Simple. The tales were subsequently reprinted in several books (Harper).

During the period of the **Civil Rights Movement**, the Black press pursued a broad five-point agenda, advocating "1) Equal voting rights in every section of the country, 2) Equal access to all public accommodation, 3) Equal opportunity in employment, 4) Equal and unsegregated education, 5) Equal opportunity to make a home anywhere within one's means" (Simmons, 93).

Young African Americans and White students from the North engaged throughout **the South** in a massive voting rights campaign. The *Defender*, the *Jackson Advocate*, and the *Pittsburgh Courier* avidly reported on the events of this undertaking. With reporting skills honed over time, African American reporters were able to extract more details than their White colleagues from African Americans living in South on conditions of their disenfranchisement.

The *Pittsburgh Courier* began its coverage of sit-ins (nonviolent protests) in the South on February 13, 1961: "The event was so unnewsworthy at the time, the beginning of the sit-ins appeared on page four among other race interest stories" (Simmons, 97). In order to alert other African Americans to the significance of this public action, the *Courier* ran the story with a picture on the front page suggesting "the protest had spread from Raleigh, North Carolina, South Carolina, on its way to Virginia, Tennessee and Florida" (Simmons, 97).

The black Press was born out of the anguish, frustration, and disappointment of African American people who wanted nothing more than to be considered contributors and recipients of the American bounty they helped to produce the early days of American life. African American newspapers continue to serve a vital social role. As Charles Simmons observes, " Educators have come to learn that repetition is the key to retention. But it can be also said that high visibility is another key to retention. Those black editors, indeed, did have high visibility. Their high visibility occurred during inauspicious times in the history of United States" (165).

Resources: Benjamin Banneker, "Letters & Essays," in *Anthology of African American Literary Tradition* (Boston: Houghton Mifflin, 1998); Maxwell R. Brooks, *The Negro Press Re-Examined* (Boston: Christopher Publishing House, 1959); John Hope Franklin and Alfred Moss, Jr., *From Slavery to Freedom: A History of African Americans*, 8th ed. (Boston: McGraw-Hill, 2000); W. George Gore, *Negro Journalism* (Greencastle, IN, 1922); Donna Akiba Sullivan Harper, *Not So Simple: The "Simple" Stories by Langston Hughes* (Columbia: University of Missouri Press, 1995); Hans Ostrom, *A Langston Hughes Encyclopedia* (Westport, CT: Greenwood Press, 2002), 25–28, 72–73, 298–301; Charles A. Simmons, *The African American Press* (Jefferson, NC: McFarland, 1998); Henry Lewis Suggs, ed., *The Black Press in the Middle West, 1865–1985* (Westport, CT: Greenwood Press, 1996); Juliet E. K. Walker, "The Promised Land: The *Chicago Defender* and the Black Press in Illinois, 1862–1979," in *The Black Press in the Middle West, 1865–1985*, ed. Henry L. Suggs (Westport, CT: Greenwood Press, 1996).

Robert H. Miller

Newton, Huey Percy (1942–1989). Political activist, political party leader, and writer. Newton is best known for his cofounding of the **Black Panther Party** in 1966, as well as his numerous philosophical and scientific papers and political books. Much of his writing explains, in pragmatic terms, ideas from classical philosophy and theories of African American intellectualism, but it is also alert to the daily experiences of working-class people and those living in poverty.

After growing up in Oakland, California, Newton graduated from high school functionally illiterate, but he learned how to read by listening to records of Vincent Price reading poetry and then trying to read the corresponding poems to see how the words looked. Soon, Newton was attending Merritt College intermittently, ultimately earning an Associate of Arts degree, as well as studying law at Oakland City College and San Francisco Law School. He earned his Ph.D. in 1980, in the history of consciousness, from the University of California at Santa Cruz.

Although Newton was tried and convicted in 1967 of voluntary manslaughter for killing a policeman, he was later granted three new trials, which all ended in mistrials, and was cleared of the charges in 1971. At about the same time, he directed the Black Panthers to a more nonviolent strategy that focused on community services to African Americans. He fled to Cuba in 1974 to avoid being arrested for drug-related charges, returned three years later, and was tried but not convicted. In 1989, Newton was shot to death in Oakland.

Literary critics such as Tom Orloff of the *San Francisco Chronicle* and **Stanley Crouch**, and author Hugh Pearson, have labeled Newton as a "thug," a "criminal," and a "hoodlum," respectively. However, former Black Panther Party member Donald Cox wrote, "For some of us, Huey represented the equivalent of the Messiah.... A cult of his personality was created. Huey was elevated to the status of the gods, and his every word became gospel" (Cleaver and Katsiaficas, 121).

Like many activists, Newton was a complex figure. His radical political and literary activism prompted both conservatives and liberals alike to paint Newton as either savior or devil, concentrating on his misdeeds or romanticizing his revolutionary rhetoric. Newton's literary works were influenced by **W.E.B. Du Bois**, **James Baldwin**, **Frederick Douglass**, Frantz Fanon, **Malcolm X**, Mao Tse-Tung, Karl Marx, Emile Durkheim, and Che Guevara. His tone is more balanced than that of many of the other activists of his time; his writing often considered both structures in society and personal responsibility as keys to the elimination of racism.

A poster featuring Huey Newton supporting the Black Panther Party, c. 1972. Courtesy of the Library of Congress.

Integral to Newton's literary legacy is his synthesis of racial analysis with that of philosophy, merging theories of Malcolm X and Karl Marx, or those of Franz Fanon and Thomas Hobbes. This prowess is highlighted in the work of Judson L. Jefferies, *Huey P. Newton: The Radical Theorist* (2002). Jeffries shows the connection between Newton's use of the Durkheimian theory of "Reactionary Suicide" and the ideas of Dostoyevsky on poverty and beggary in *Crime and Punishment*. Further, Jeffries analyzes Newton's papers and speeches with regard to Nietzsche and psychological warfare; to Bakunin's fatalistic view of revolutionaries; to Plato's "cave" analogy; and to Marx's theories on existence and social consciousness.

Newton's **autobiography** (*Revolutionary Suicide*, 1973) is strikingly similar to *The Autobiography of Malcolm X* (1965) and epitomizes a well crafted narrative of human enlightenment and possibility. Newton's four other published books are *To Die for the People* (1972), *In Search of Common Ground* (1973), *War Against the Panthers* (1996), and *Insights and Poems* (1975). These books emphasize his shift from **Black Nationalism** into a synthesis called "intercommunalism," in which Newton prophetically claimed that there would be a collapse of the nation-state within the global economy, which would then forge a universal brotherhood. Newton's ostentation, public image, and zeal came to represent the spirit of the 1960s and 1970s. Yet what best can be concluded of Newton's literary and intellectual contributions is that he centered his writings on a thin line between postmodernist and essentialist viewpoints, ultimately distinguishing humanity as possessing the agency to amend socialization processes but also as a body that is inherently optimistic, cooperative, and divine. (*See* **San Francisco Bay Area, California**.)

Resources: Kathleen Cleaver and George Katsiaficas, eds., *Liberation, Imagination, and the Black Panther Party: A New Look at the Panthers and Their Legacy* (New York: Routledge, 2001); Judson L. Jeffries, *Huey P. Newton: The Radical Theorist* (Jackson: University Press of Mississippi, 2002); Malcolm X with Alex Haley, *The Autobiography of Malcolm X* (1965; New York: Ballantine, 1992); Huey P. Newton: *Revolutionary Suicide* (1973; New York: Writers and Readers, 1995); *To Die for the People*, ed. Toni Morrison (1972; New York: Writers and Readers, 1999); *War Against the Panthers: A Study of Repression in America* (New York: Writers and Readers, 1996); Huey P. Newton and Erik H. Erikson, *In Search of Common Ground* (New York: Norton, 1973); Huey P. Newton and Ericka Huggins, *Insights and Poems* (San Francisco: City Lights, 1975); Dr. Huey P. Newton Foundation, Inc. Collection, M864, Department of Special Collections, Stanford University Libraries.

Matthew W. Hughey

Newton, Lionel (born 1961). Novelist. In his two works of fiction, *Getting Right with God* (1994) and *Things to Be Lost* (1995), Newton provides a distinct perspective of the young adult African American male growing up in suburban Long Island, New York, at the end of the twentieth century. Newton is the son of Seventh-Day Adventist missionaries who lived in the United States and Africa. When he was sixteen years old, his family moved to Copiague, Long Island, where he later graduated from the College at Old Westbury.

In *Getting Right with God*, Newton explores family dynamics, friendships, and religion. The protagonist, Lucas Martin, struggles between the desire to be righteous and the temptations presented by his friends. His father, a widower, encourages some of Lucas's behavior by drinking with him. When his father remarries, his new wife provides structure for both father and son and becomes the catalyst for change in the Martin household.

Things to Be Lost tells the story of a family's downfall. Again themes of growing up and religion are explored, in addition to the effects of violence and adultery on a family. The story begins with the son, as an adult, telling about the day he committed a violent act against his disabled father at his father's behest. Each family member is, in some negative way, affected by the father's recent disability and his ultimate death. Newton's novels contribute to African American literature by broadening the portrayal of African American males growing up in the modern-day United States.

Resources: Dan Bogey, "Review of *Getting Right with God*, by Lionel Newton," *Library Journal* 15 (Dec. 1993), 176; Thomas Calvin, "With Roots in Copiague, a Stern View of L.I.," *New York Times*, July 3, 1994, p. 15; Lionel Newton: *Getting Right with God* (New York: Dutton, 1994); *Things to Be Lost* (New York: Dutton, 1995); Erika Taylor, "Review of *Things to Be Lost*, by Lionel Newton," *Los Angeles Times*, June 4, 1995, p. 6.

Heather L. Althoff

Nichols, Nichelle (born 1933). Actor and writer. Nichols is best known for having portrayed Lieutenant Uhura in the television series *Star Trek* in the late 1960s and in feature films based upon the series. She was born in Robbins, Illinois, the daughter of a civic leader and factory worker, Earl Nichols, and a homemaker, Lishia Mae (Parks) Nichols. In 1994, Nichols published her **autobiography**, *Beyond Uhura: Star Trek and Other Memories*, which was well received by *Star Trek* fans. It included Nichols's remembrances of racial discrimination from her childhood and throughout her adult years and discusses the positive reaction that she received for her kiss with William Shatner during *Star Trek*, the first interracial kiss televised in the United States. Nichols's second work, *Saturn's Child*, is a **science fiction** novel in which the main character, Saturna, is based upon a childhood "alter ego [who carries] all that I understood from the teachings of my mother and father." *Saturna's Quest* is a sequel to *Saturn's Child*. Written with Jim Meechan, it explores the secret of Saturna's birth, which has the potential to destroy her father's kingdom. Nichols uses the science fiction genre to discuss issues of race relations across planets. Nichols earned a position working with the National Space Institute and the National Aeronautics and Space Administration (NASA), through her paper "New Opportunities for the Humanization of Space." She spent a number of years raising awareness of the space program among minorities, resulting in a number of women and minorities entering the program.

Resources: Nichelle Nichols: *Beyond Uhura, Star Trek and Other Memories* (New York: Putnam, 1994); *Down to Earth* (Los Angeles: Koch Entertainment, 2004), Audio CD; official Website, http://www.uhura.com; *Saturn's Child* (New York: Putnam, 1995), with Margaret Wander Bonanno; *Saturn's Quest* (Los Angeles: Planet X, 2002), with Jim Meechan; "Nichelle Nichols Talks to SciFiPulse About Charting Literary Frontiers and More," February 15, 2002, http://www.scifipulse.com.

Valerie Lynn Guyant

Njeri, Itabari (born 1955). Journalist, memoirist, essayist, and cultural critic. Itabari Njeri's was born Jill Stacey Moreland, the daughter of Marc Marion Moreland, a historian trained at the University of Toronto with Marxist and classical leanings, and Vivien Dacre Lord Moreland Reynolds, a nurse with experience as a hospital administrator. Njeri grew up in New York, where she was often shuffled among members of her close-knit Caribbean American family. The diversity of her West Indian background—she describes her heritage as an amalgam of African, East Indian, Amer-Indian, English, and French—has played a forceful role in her cultural and social criticism, which might succinctly be described as autobiographical critique. Horrific episodes from her family history, such as her grandfather's murder by a White Southerner who, to this day, has gone unprosecuted for the crime, spur her to delve into America's collective past in a manner that forces the unresolved schisms of the author's, and presumably the reader's, own present to the surface. The implications of Njeri's intimate revelations are, first and foremost, that if such divisions and tensions reside in her own psyche, then, arguably, hers is a story that can be read at the level of national allegory. America's collective consciousness suffers from a latent psychosis, she argues, and this disease stems from the history of **slavery** and racism that still haunts the United States, the ignorance and disavowal of which conditions the current state of racial relations in the country.

Njeri's first book is *Every Goodbye Ain't Gone: Family Portraits and Personal Escapades* (1990). Winner of the American Book Award, the collection of vignettes may be seen as something of a cautionary tale narrated with humor and vulnerability. She writes in the prelude that the family portraits that make up the book, depicting characters so unfamiliar to the average American reader that one might mistake them as fictional, are nonetheless the literal truth. Njeri herself is the "great-great-great-granddaughter of a notorious, rum-running English pirate named Sam Lord—his castle [is] now a resort in Barbados" (7). Her father, who "felt himself to be an intellectual giant boxed in by mental midgets" (67), is depicted as the tragic template of Harold Cruse's "Afro-American intellectual in crisis" (6). Her mother, Vivien, who suffered abuse at the hands of Njeri's father, is the subject of the chapter titled "Bag Lady." Sketches of a tough-talking grandmother (who utters the lines "Every shut eye ain't sleep. Every goodbye ain't gone."), an alabaster-complexioned "moll" aunt (the girlfriend of a gangster in her "salad days"), and a cousin, Jeffrey, who could be Ricky Nelson's (of *Ozzie and Harriet* television fame) twin are among the more interesting portraits. What each of Njeri's stories seems to say to us is that in multiracial America, where economic and social disparities are smoothed over with multicultural platitudes, and where an obstinately blind collective eye looks resolutely away from its painful past, **race** is not all that it appears to be. And racial inequalities operate on something more complicated than a binary opposition between Black and White, or White and "other." For, as Njeri insists in her preface, her diverse family *is* America: "So institutionalized is the ignorance of our history

[American history], our culture, our everyday existence, that often we do not even know ourselves" (7).

It is this history that Njeri determines to examine in her second book, aptly titled *The Last Plantation: Color, Conflict, and Identity. Reflections of a New World Black* (1997). In many ways, this book is a continuation of *Every Goodbye*. Njeri here repeats a number of the stories and quips first encountered in her 1990 collection. The dilemma of her cousin Jeffrey and the psychic horrors that ensue from her investigation of her grandfather's murder are among the narratives retold. But Njeri deliberately seeks to break new ground in this text by examining the conundrum of African American double consciousness, famously postulated by **W.E.B. Du Bois** in his landmark book *The Souls of Black Folk* (1903). Du Bois describes the dilemma not as the ceiling of African American identity but as the floor, as a state the collective Black consciousness should be able to overcome once the America Du Bois describes as "conglomerate" comes to full awareness of its history and of the racial and economic conditions that perpetuate systemic racism.

Njeri finds these conditions not simply present in contemporary society, but aggressively so. She is less concerned with the transnational implications of White racism and Western imperialism that subtend Du Bois's prophecy that "The problem of the twentieth century is the problem of the color-line, the relation of the darker to the lighter races of men in Asia and Africa, in America and the islands of the sea" (*Souls*, 372). Her immediate concern is to consider more closely the binary structure of American racism. Njeri is drawn to issues of colorism and multiracial/multiethnic identity, which she addressed in a number of her pieces appearing in the *Los Angeles Times* during the 1990s. *The Last Plantation* chronicles her analysis of the Latasha Harlins murder trial. She also uses this occasion of "Black-Korean" conflict in Los Angeles, which took place less than two weeks after the savage beating of Rodney King by Los Angeles police, to examine "the antagonism between a new generation of so-called multiracial people of partial African descent and the traditionally defined Black American population, which [sees] multiracial people as seeking a separate status from Blacks to gain preferred treatment in American life" (128).

Njeri holds a bachelor's degree in communications from Boston University and a master's degree in journalism from Columbia University. She is currently a doctoral student in the American Civilization program at Harvard University. In addition to winning the 1990 American Book Award and many fellowships, she was a finalist for the 1997 Pulitzer Prize for her work on race and **Black nationalism**. She has reported for the *Miami Herald* as well as the *Los Angeles Times*. Njeri currently divides her time between Lakeland, Florida, where her mother resides, and **Brooklyn, New York**, and is at this writing completing her first novel, titled *The Secret Life of Fred Astaire*.

Resources: Itabari Njeri: *Every Goodbye Ain't Gone: Family Portraits and Personal Escapades* (New York: Times Books, 1990); "A Ham, a Violin, and Ohhh Those Psychic Blues," in *The Farrakhan Factor: African-American Writers on Leadership, Nationhood, and Minister Louis Farrakhan*, ed. Amy Alexander (New York: Grove Press,

1998); *The Last Plantation: Color, Conflict, and Identity. Reflections of a New World Black* (Boston: Houghton Mifflin, 1997); "Sushi and Grits: Ethnic Identity and Conflict in a Newly Multicultural America," in *Lure and Loathing: Essays on Race, Identity, and the Ambivalence of Assimilation*, ed. Gerald L. Early (New York: Penguin 1993); Hans Ostrom, "Essays Illuminate Cultural Journey" (profile of Njeri and review of *Every Goodbye Ain't Gone*), *Soundlife* (Sunday supp.), *Morning News Tribune* (Tacoma, WA), Feb. 10, 1991, p. 9.

Rebecka Rychelle Rutledge

Nkombo (1968–1974). Literary magazine. The **New Orleans, Louisiana,**–based literary magazine *Nkombo*, began publication in December 1968, and it is considered an important magazine in the **Black Arts Movement**. The magazine sprang from the **Free Southern Theater** Company (FST), an acting-writing community-based group that performed dramatic literature about the issues facing Blacks in **the South** and in America in the late 1960s. Originally titled *Echoes from the Gumbo*, this publication was unlike the **black nationalist** or civil rights publications such as **Black Dialogue** or **Journal of Black Poetry**. This publication, in the spirit of reaching the masses, was designed as a cookbook. The editors **Thomas Covington Dent** and Vallery Ferdinand (who later changed his name to **Kalamu ya Salaam**) were influenced by the rich culinary traditions of New Orleans. Thus the first issue featured an introduction be Ferdinand/Salaam titled "Food for Thought," the table of contents was titled "Recipe," and the four sections were titled "Meat and Seafoods," "Seasonings," "Spices," and "Miscellaneous Ingredients." *Nkombo* was named for the food the maroons created out of necessity to survive in the wilderness, as Salaam explained in his 1980 booklet, *Our Women Keep Our Skies from Falling*.

Yet within these titles that would catch the eye of everyday people were the words of such great writers as LeRoi Jones (**Amiri Baraka**), **James Baldwin**, and Robert De Coy. It captured the reader with its connecting titles and held the reader there with Black revolutionary poetry, prose, and essays. Many of the local poets featured focused on the **Creole** lifestyle or referred specifically to New Orleans but also included larger-scale issues such as economics, civil rights, and oppression. These allusions to familiar places and problems connected readers with the writers and, thus, connected the Black community. The second issue was devoted solely to poetry in which writers became voices for their people; poets in and from the kitchen. The publication continued until December 1969, publishing four issues before Dent and Ferdinand/Salaam took a fifteen-month hiatus.

During this hiatus the publication underwent many changes. No longer a small, community-based publication, *Nkombo* was now funded partially by a grant from the Coordinating Council of Literary Magazines. The FST no longer supported the magazine; it was managed by a small group of New Orleans writers, BLKARTSOUTH, who sought to expand to the entire Deep South rather than remain a exclusively New Orleans publication. They changed the initial culinary theme that Dent and Ferdinand/Salaam focused on and used as a connecting mechanism with the community. The seventh and eighth issues, published June 1971 and August 1972, respectively, included writers from Georgia, **Texas**, Mississippi, Florida, and New Orleans. Additional affiliations with such groups as the Southern Black Cultural Alliance, a community theater federation, expanded the scope of the magazine. The magazine had changed, but it had accomplished what its editors had set out to do: it made something happen in the arts in New Orleans and in the South.

The primary goal of *Nkombo* was to bring a sense of self to the Black community through art and writing. In 1974, the final issue of *Nkombo* was published. The publication spanned five years and produced nine issues, making a difference in the literary landscape of New Orleans and the Deep South. In January 1975, a newer version of the magazine, *Nkombo: A Quarterly Journal of Neo-Afrikan/American Culture* began publication, but it was not as well received as its cookbook-style predecessor. *Nkombo* nonetheless remains a significant, although often overlooked, part of the Black Arts Movement.

Resources: Addison Gayle, *The Black Aesthetic* (New York: Doubleday, 1971); Jerry Ward, "Southern Black Aesthetics: The Case of *Nkombo* Magazine," *Mississippi Quarterly* 44 (Spring 1991), 143–150.

Judith Strathearn

NOMMO (1969–1976). Literary magazine. NOMMO was the publishing entity of the Organization of Black American Culture (**OBAC**) Writer's Workshop, founded in **Chicago, Illinois**, in 1967. Writers' Workshop 1987 President **Sandra Jackson-Opoku** stated that "*Nommo* is of Bantu origin and means the magical power of the word to make material change" (Jackson-Opoku, xiii). And material change it did make; advancing the Afrocentric **Black Arts Movement**, NOMMO published the Workshop's poets, who celebrated the beauty of Blackness and brought poetry and the arts to the community. In essays, NOMMO writers sought to describe a new Black aesthetic; OBAC member and leader Don L. Lee (**Haki R. Madhubuti**) described Black poetry in 1968 as poetry "written for/to/about & around the lives/ spiritactions/humanism & total existence of blackpeople . . . the concrete rather than the abstract . . . art for people's sake; black language or Afro-american language" (Lee, 13). Publishing OBAC writers such as Lee, Jackson-Opoku, **Sterling Plumpp**, and **Carolyn M. Rodgers**, NOMMO was originally planned as a quarterly, but was published irregularly from 1969, when it was started with an Illinois Arts Council grant, until it officially ceased publication in 1976. As OBAC founder **Hoyt Fuller** remembers, after the second NOMMO issue, in the first year of publication, "it became evident that OBAC was suffering from the same afflictions which inevitably bedevil voluntary groups—apathy, exhaustion, other-directedness. Furthermore, the flame of the revolution burned very low everywhere, and it was apparent that new blood and new outlooks would have to be added" (Fuller, 19).

Another OBAC periodical, *Cumbaya*, briefly replaced NOMMO in the 1980s. The end of periodical publication was not, however, the end of

Nommo publishing. In 1987, the Writers' Workshop's OBAhouse celebrated OBAC's twentieth anniversary by publishing a substantial anthology of work from OBAC Writer's Workshop members: *NOMMO: A Literary Legacy of Black Chicago (1967–1987)*, edited by Carole A. Parks. Combining previously published work with unpublished material and pieces written for the collection, *NOMMO: A Literary Legacy* provided a definitive view of the organization and its writers, from the 1967 founding of the Writer's Workshop through its 1987 celebration of OBAC as the only continuously operating and oldest Black arts organization in the United States. *NOMMO's* opening essays, mainly written by OBAC founders or early and important members, provided background on OBAC history, tradition, ideology, the Black aesthetic, and Black poetics. Two extensive poetry sections (1967–1976 and 1977–1987) dominate the *NOMMO* celebration volume—as poetry should, since most of the OBAC writers have been primarily poets—and represent work from organization founders to relative newcomers and unpublished poets. Guest contributors filled a section "Remembering Hoyt W. Fuller," commemorating the life and support of the organization leader and founder, Hoyt W. Fuller.

A second, slimmer NOMMO anthology appeared from OBAhouse in 1990: *Nommo 2: Remembering Ourselves Whole*. Described as "An OBAC Anthology of Contemporary Black Writing," this collection also commemorated the passing of a Black leader and was dedicated to the **Texas** legislator George "Mickey" Leland. *NOMMO 2* is expressly thematic and includes both OBAC and non-OBAC writers on the subject of memory, with slightly more than half the anthology devoted to poetry.

Resources: Hoyt W. Fuller, "Foreword to *NOMMO*," in *NOMMO*, ed. Parks, pp. 17–20; Sandra Jackson-Opoku, "Preface," in *NOMMO*, ed. Parks, pp. xiii–xiv; Don L. Lee (Haki R. Madhubuti), "Black Poetics/for the Many to Come," in *NOMMO*, ed. Parks, pp. 13–14; *NOMMO 2: Remembering Ourselves Whole* (Chicago: OBAhouse, 1990); Carole A. Parks, ed., *NOMMO: A Literary Legacy of Black Chicago (1967–1987)* (Chicago: OBAhouse, 1987).

Carol Klimick Cyganowski

Northup, Solomon (1808–1863). Abolitionist, violinist, carpenter, and autobiographer. Northup was born free in Minerva, New York, to Mintus Northup and a mother whose name and history are unknown. His father, a property owner and independent farmer, provided Solomon and his brother, Joseph, with a formal education at a time when Blacks, for the most part, had almost no access to formal education and were illiterate. There is little information regarding Northup's early life, but most researchers agree that he learned carpentry, reading, and writing while living on his family's farm (Andrews; Worley). He married Anne Hampton at age twenty-one and fathered three children. At thirty-three, Northup was offered a job as a musician with a traveling circus. Before embarking on this venture, he had procured "free papers," which established his status as a free man. Shortly after accepting the job, however, he arrived in **Washington, D.C.** and was kidnapped by Merrill Brown and Abram Hamilton, his alleged employers, who sold him into **slavery**. During his enslavement, Northup encountered the institution's cruelty and barbarism. His experiences as a slave ranged from violent encounters, in which he was beaten severely when he "asserted, aloud and boldly, that [he] was a freeman" (Northup, 183), to witnessing the results of sexual abuse against slave women. With help from an attorney, Henry B. Northup, a relative of his father's former master, Solomon regained his freedom in 1853. Although he later identified his kidnappers, Hamilton and Brown were not successfully prosecuted as kidnappers.

Northup's narrative, *Twelve Years a Slave* (1853), is significant to African American literature for several key reasons. First, the text gives a chronological account of Northup's kidnapping, enslavement, and escape. Second, it provides a description of slavery in Louisiana from the perspective of a free Black, important not only because Northup was free but also because accounts of slavery in Louisiana are rare. Additionally, Northup's **autobiography** offers a view inside the complexities of sexual abuse within a slave community. His reporting contributes to African American literature an evaluation of the consequences Black women faced when they were forced to live as concubines. Finally, his descriptions and appraisals of Blacks based on color complexion is an early African American literary work revealing how the thorny subjects of **race** and skin color were understood in Northrup's era. Although able to compose his narrative in its entirety, Northup chose to dictate his history to David Wilson. However, being literate allowed Northup to revise and edit Wilson's drafts.

Northup's narrative was widely accepted and profitable for him at the time of its publication, demonstrating that there was a market for African American literature before emancipation. However, the text fell into obscurity after its nineteenth-century popularity. As an anthologized work, it regained notice after about 1980. Northup's descendents continue to live in New York, and they celebrate his birth annually. On July 19, 1999, the mayor of Saratoga Springs, New York, proclaimed the date as Solomon Northup Day and placed a historical marker in Northup's name at Congress and Broadway to commemorate his life (Sweeney). (*See* **Slave Narrative**.)

Resources: William L. Andrews, *To Tell a Free Story: The First Century of Afro-American Autobiography, 1760–1865* (Urbana: University of Illinois Press, 1986); Charles T. Davis and Henry Louis Gates, Jr., eds., *The Slave's Narrative* (New York: Oxford University Press, 1985); Robert B. Stepto, *From Behind the Veil: A Study of Afro-American Narrative*, 2nd ed. (Urbana: University of Illinois Press, 1991); John E. Sweeney, "Solomon Northup Day: A Celebration of Freedom," in *Local Legacies* (New York: Library of Congress Bicentennial Committee, 2000), 102–109; Yuval Taylor, ed., *I Was Born a Slave: An Anthology of Classic Slave Narratives*, 2 vols. (Chicago: Lawrence Hill, 1999); Sam Worley, "Solomon Northup and the Sly Philosophy of the Slave Pen," *Callaloo* 20, no. 1 (Winter 1997), 245–259.

Ellesia Ann Blaque

Novel. A long form of narrative fiction. Typically, the novel has focused on the realistic depiction of the specificity of individuals' lives, but it is an open form; therefore, novels may also use surrealistic techniques, elements of fantasy, or stream-of-consciousness. Novels may be written in such long-established categories as **crime and mystery fiction** and **science fiction**, and one highly popular contemporary category is the **romance novel**. The **epistolary novel** is a form many novelists have used for over 200 years. **Coming-of-age fiction**, also known as the *Bildungsroman*, constitutes a looser but nonetheless important category of the novel, one focused on the experiences described (how individuals mature in societies) rather than conventions of form.

The history of the African American novel can be usefully, if somewhat artificially, discussed in terms of several periods: antebellum; **Reconstruction** and its aftermath; the **Harlem Renaissance**; the era of the **Civil Rights Movement**; the **Black Arts Movement**; and post-1970. Conventions and traditions of the novel, however, cut across these periods. Throughout this history, which spans roughly 200 years, the African American novel has proved to be intimately connected to social changes, devoted to the analysis of the various life conditions African Americans and others experience, and engaged in the kinds of promotion of interests and ideas that storytelling uniquely enables. Novels by African American authors have been central to many Americans' understanding of the pursuit of liberty in this country.

The fictional form that we now think of as the novel has many global lineages. The most prominent strains of the American novel have their roots in the English narratives that Ian Watt examines in his classic work *The Rise of the Novel*, as well as in other European narratives from the seventeenth and eighteenth centuries. Early English novels include *Pamela* (1740–1741) and *Clarissa* (1747–1748), by Samuel Richardson, and *Tom Jones* (1749), by Henry Fielding. However, the Spanish novel *Don Quixote*, by Miguel de Cervantes, was first published in 1605 and was available in English translations after 1612. Women authors, including Frances Burney, Maria Edgeworth, and Jane Austen, contributed to the genre almost from the beginning. Throughout its history, the African American novel has drawn not just on the European and American traditions of the novel, but also on the **folklore** that Africans brought to America.

The novel is a particularly difficult artistic form to define, since it has come in so many different shapes, sizes, and styles. Most typically, the novel focuses on the specificity of a fictional individual's life, shaping some period of that life into a prose narrative with a plot—a chain of causally connected events. The individual, moreover, is more often than not a person of modest or low, rather than noble, station. That is, from the beginning the novel turned toward examining the lives of middle-class and working-class men and women.

However, many exceptions exist to every conceivable element that one might propose as a convention of the novel. As Watt suggests, "the poverty of the novel's formal conventions would seem to be the price it must pay for its realism" (13). Notably, Watt elevates **realism** as the one convention that may trump all others. It is important to note that "realism" in this context does not mean "just like the world we actually live in"; instead, it denotes the detailed depiction of a lifelike world, one that may diverge significantly from what we see in our own world, and one that is, after all, made of words.

The African American novel has its most immediate and nourishing roots in **slave narratives**. Indeed, slave narratives were sometimes accused by **slavery**'s proponents and apologists of being fictions. Slave narratives depicted the lives of men and women who had endured and escaped slavery to tell their tales. The testimonial value of these narratives should be emphasized; they were used by former slaves and abolitionists to show African Americans' humanity and intelligence and, by contrast, the inhumanity and brutality of slavery. The most famous of these narratives—those by **Olaudah Equiano, Frederick Douglass, William Wells Brown**, and **Harriet Jacobs**—were written during slavery, but thousands more were recorded after its end. In giving narrative shape and sensual detail to the experiences and psychologies of former slaves, the narratives together constitute a dramatic historical record, a major indictment of the country's failure to live up to the ideals of its Constitution, and a rich tradition of African American storytelling.

Several conventions of the slave narrative influenced African American fiction, and the narratives' detailed, realistic, sometimes lengthy depictions of individuals' lives easily lent themselves to the novel. In fact, the influence was mutual. As Valerie Smith notes in her introduction to Harriet Jacobs's *Incidents in the Life of a Slave Girl* (1861), Jacobs drew on the conventions of the sentimental novel in order to tell a story of sexual vulnerability, a story that slave narratives by men offered her no way to tell (Jacobs, xxxi). Middle-class White women sympathetic to abolition and familiar with the sentimental novel were a primary audience for Jacobs's narrative. The sentimental novel's conventions, melded with those of the slave narrative, appealed to such women. Several novels were published during the antebellum period. The first of these was William Wells Brown's *Clotel; or, The President's Daughter*, published in England in 1853. The novel tells the story of Thomas Jefferson's much-rumored slave mistress and her daughter by Jefferson after he sold them. Because of its depiction of women in peril and its tragic end, Brown's novel, like Jacobs's slave narrative, owes something to the conventions of the sentimental and seduction novels. Other novels from the antebellum period include **Martin R. Delany**'s *Blake* (1859) and **Harriet E. Wilson**'s *Our Nig* (1859).

When slavery ended after the **Civil War**, novels continued the social work that slave narratives had begun. During this period, **the South** was first occupied by federal troops that enforced the end of slavery and ensured some progress in Southern Blacks' lives. Then, in 1877, the troops withdrew, allowing Southern states to institute Jim Crow laws that did much to reverse the gains that African Americans had made. In fact, the period of **Reconstruction** is the period in which the first Ku Klux Klan was active. (The second Klan was formed in 1915.)

Two novels may serve as examples of the trend over these years in modes of depicting America in Black novels. The first of these is **Frances E. W. Harper**'s *Iola Leroy; or, Shadows Uplifted* (1892). Bridging the antebellum and postwar periods, Harper began her career as an abolitionist lecturer and drew in her novel on antebellum writers' model of literary moral purpose, exemplified most famously in **Harriet Beecher Stowe**'s *Uncle Tom's Cabin* (1852), the novel that Abraham Lincoln only half-jokingly referred to as the book that "made" the Civil War. Like Stowe's, Harper's reputation as an artist was not recognized by scholars of literature until recently. This lack of recognition derived largely from a dual prejudice in literary scholarship on the novel: with few exceptions, neither popular nor political works were considered eligible for the **literary canon**. *Iola Leroy* plays on the reader's heart strings: when its heroine, living as a White woman, discovers that she is partially Black, she is enslaved and deprived of her inheritance by a villainous relative. By contrast with the heroine of a novel like *Clotel*, however, Iola is not a tragic figure, and this marks an important distinction. In the sentimental novel, a White heroine who has been thrown on her own resources but protected her virtue would end up married; in the seduction novel, any woman whose virtue has been compromised would end tragically. Iola receives a marriage proposal from a White doctor who knows about her race, but Harper does not allow her character the sentimental resolution. Instead, as with other novels of racial uplift that characterize the postwar era, *Iola Leroy* affirms the heroine's racial identity and devotes her to the advancement of the race. Iola leads a productive life as a teacher and race advocate; she becomes a "race" woman. In this respect, she epitomizes the novel, which does not scruple to interrupt its narrative with didactic passages that impress on the reader the importance and greater social relevance of events.

To a considerable degree, **James Weldon Johnson**'s *The Autobiography of an Ex-Colored Man* (1912) undermined the "uplift" novel's emphasis on racial identity and literary moral purpose. In a sense it separated literature from the imperative to inspire African Americans to greater heights and to persuade Whites of their worth. *The Autobiography*'s protagonist-narrator is born to a White father and a light-skinned Black mother. Raised in Connecticut as White, the narrator quickly displays a great facility with music and decides to go to a Black school in the South after he learns of his heritage. Having lost all his money, the narrator takes up menial employment and discovers a love of **ragtime** music. Eventually, he tours Europe thanks to the support of a White patron. (Although there are only hints in the novel, some critics have interpreted the relationship between the two men as romantic, a noteworthy early same-sex relationship in African American fiction.) Significantly, the narrator develops a compelling amalgam of classical European and ragtime music. Such an amalgam was in fact Johnson's own goal for literature: a blend of black **vernacular** and "standard" language.

After some time, the narrator resolves to break with his patron and returns to the South and the roots of African American music, convinced that he is allowing his talent for African American musical forms to go to waste. In the South again, the narrator witnesses a **lynching**, which profoundly disturbs him. His reaction is not so much fear or anger, however; it is shame. The narrator is ashamed to be a member of a race that could with impunity be treated more cruelly than animals. Therefore, he resolves to pass as White and returns to New York City, where he enters the business world and builds a family (*see* **Passing**). The novel closes with stunning psychological ambiguity, throwing into question the decision to pass. The narrator describes having heard **Booker T. Washington** speak, stealing the show from the other speakers through conviction and moral purpose. While the narrator expresses an urgent desire that his children never be branded as Black, the narrator also feels a sense of "longing for [his] mother's people" (210). Hearing Washington speak, the narrator recounts: "I feel small and selfish. I am an ordinarily successful white man who has made a little money. [Race leaders] are men who are making history and a race. . . . I cannot repress the thought that, after all, I have chosen the lesser part, that I have sold my birthright for a mess of pottage" (211).

Whereas Harper's protagonist, upon discovering that she is Black, takes up the task of racial uplift in the face of personal hardship, Johnson's narrator flees into the White world to escape his sense of shame. Harper's message was clearly more uplifting and urged readers, Black and White alike, to applaud African Americans' hard work if not to take it up themselves. But the tide was turning against the programmatic uplift novel, and Johnson's deft, subtle, psychological realism was the new wave (*see* **Race Uplift Movement**). Thus Johnson's novel, which was republished in 1927, attracted much more attention than Harper's during the Harlem Renaissance. African American literature was moving toward refined literary styles that innovatively blended standard and African American language, fearlessly explored moral ambiguity, and developed realistic portrayals of Black America. *The Autobiography*'s realism was reinforced by the fact that it was first published anonymously, purporting to protect the identity of its passing narrator. Other important novels published during Reconstruction and its aftermath include **Sutton E. Griggs**'s *Imperium in Imperio* (1899), **Pauline Elizabeth Hopkins**'s *Magazine Novels*, and **Charles Waddell Chesnutt**'s *House Behind the Cedars* (1900). Novels such as these trace the ground separating Harper's and Chestnutt's literary visions and foreshadow developments to come in the African American novel. Whereas Griggs's novel anticipated developments of the 1940s and 1960s, when highly politicized and confrontational aesthetics were developed, Hopkins's novels drew on "the strategies and formulas of the sensational fiction of dime novels and magazines" (Carby, 145). Chesnutt's novel tells another version of the tragic **mulatto** story, in which the protagonist is able to live neither in the Black world nor in the White one and dies as a result; its heroine achieves a greater moral complexity than *Clotel*'s but does not undertake the work of racial uplift that *Iola Leroy*'s does.

The dramatic changes that took place in the African American novel during the period loosely designated as the Harlem Renaissance may be measured in part by the fact that one of its major inspirations, **Jean Toomer**'s *Cane* (1923), bore little resemblance to a conventional novel but was instead a highly innovative, stylish novel-in-stories that also included poetry. Toomer's own term for his aesthetic was "poetic realism," which cast his work in contrast to the sentimental and romantic works of the antebellum and post-Civil War authors (Rusch). *Cane* does not have a unifying plot. Instead, it is a lyrical blend of poems, short stories, and one dramatic piece. In Bernard W. Bell's words, it is "an incantational collection of thematically related writings" (97). The book explores themes such as African Americans' rootedness in a rural past and their rapid urbanization, the rise of a Black middle class, and a mystical vision of sexuality. Toomer's experimental forms, which placed an unprecedented premium on the aesthetic possibilities for Black literature, immediately struck readers as the herald of a new literary era. Though previous African American authors had, to be sure, developed distinctive styles and voices, authors of the Harlem Renaissance excelled at putting the mark of their individual style on their works as they experimented with fictional and poetic forms. As a result, it becomes more difficult to generalize about novelistic production during this period.

It is clear, however, that a sense of "newness" marks the period, as **Alain Locke**'s volume *The New Negro* (1925) announced. In the opening essay of that volume, Locke declared a rupture with past modes of representation, especially those that drew on popular forms such as the sentimental novel that relied on stock characters: "In art and letters, instead of being wholly caricatured, [the **New Negro**] is being seriously portrayed and painted" (9). This new, serious representation was as interested in ambiguity, irony, and difficulty as antebellum and post-Civil War literature had been in clear, effective, and popular means of communicating messages about slavery and racial uplift. Following the work of Toomer and Johnson, Harlem Renaissance novels by men typically participate in a realistic aesthetic. Like Toomer, **Claude McKay** represented rural Black folk as rooted and stable, and their urban counterparts as struggling to adapt to materialism and industrialization; his *Home to Harlem* (1928) aroused controversy for its apparently primitivist view of Black rural origins. *Not Without Laughter* (1930), by **Langston Hughes**, is a coming-of-age novel set in the Midwest and counterbalances McKay's primitivist view of Black rural America. Arna Bontemps's work of **historical fiction**, *Black Thunder* (1936), like *Imperium in Imperio*, is a revolutionary tale, but Bontemps draws on an actual slave revolt, and the novel's debt to slave narratives is apparent. The title of **Wallace Thurman**'s *The Blacker the Berry* (1929) ironically refers to the folk saying, "The blacker the berry, the sweeter the juice." Far from living out this saying, the novel's female protagonist encounters constant discrimination because of her dark skin and internalizes others' negative attitudes about her complexion.

A number of women novelists emerged during the Harlem Renaissance. **Zora Neale Hurston**, for instance, devoted herself not only to the fictional representation of strong, independent women who feared neither men nor their own sexuality, but also to the anthropological study of African American and Haitian life, study that informed her portrayal of the Black South. Whereas depictions of women, often passing mulattoes, had been tightly constrained by the traditions of the sentimental and seduction novels, Hurston's *Their Eyes Were Watching God* (1937) tells the story of a Black woman at the center of several Black communities in Florida, describing these with the care of an anthropological eye. Hurston's protagonist survives first an abusive marriage and then a passionate affair with a younger man whom she must shoot after he contracts rabies. The novel closes as it opens, with the woman telling her story to a friend. Similarly ambitious in opening new possibilities for representing women were **Jessie Redmon Fauset** and **Nella Larsen**. Bell has called Hurston's work "folk romance," contrasting it with Fauset's and Larsen's, which he names "genteel realism." Like Hurston, Fauset and Larsen were concerned to address the limitations put on women, though the women are not always successful in overcoming such hurdles and are especially unsuccessful in Larsen's work. Unlike Hurston's, their settings were middle-class and urban. Fauset's *There Is Confusion* (1924) reverses tradition and attributes the mulatto's problems to his White blood. Fauset's *Plum Bun* (1929) is an intricate, somewhat underappreciated novel of passing set in **Philadelphia, Pennsylvania**, and New York City. The Black woman narrator of Larsen's *Passing* (1929) subtly reveals a lesbian attraction to a woman who is passing, an attraction that ends in the other woman's death, perhaps at the hands of the narrator.

The Harlem Renaissance set new standards of literary quality for Black literature and produced an astonishing number of enduring novels in a relatively short period. In some cases the success of the Harlem Renaissance has had the effect of obscuring the careers of writers whose work was in a popular mode or that otherwise violated the expectations of readers.

Chester Himes, for instance, wrote a number of significant detective and prison novels that show America's seamier side (*see* **Crime and Mystery Fiction**; **Prison Literature**). His first novels present a tragic vision of how racism determines Black men's lives. *Cast the First Stone* (1952) was published in bowdlerized form because it did not conform to the hard-boiled template that was expected of Himes and because of its depiction of situational homosexuality and tenderness among men in prison; republished in Himes's original form as *Yesterday Will Make You Cry* (1998), the novel focuses on a White convict who struggles unsuccessfully to overcome his grim circumstances. In his promotion of a deterministic vision, Himes was in step with the most prominent Black writer of the 1930s and 1940s, **Richard Wright**. Wright's "Blueprint for Negro Writing" (1937), one of the most influential literary manifestos of the twentieth century, represented a return of the repressed propaganda tradition in Black letters, demanding a sociological focus on the confrontation between Black and White cultures and a rejection of modes of representation that might entertain rather than instruct. Whereas it could be argued that many Harlem Renaissance writers were concerned primarily with aesthetic quality, Wright viewed their works as compromised by White patronage and middle-class values. Partly because of the influence of Wright's protest novel, brilliant work by women such as Hurston, whose novels did not conform to the model, were eclipsed for decades, only to be rediscovered in the 1970s. Wright's model is epitomized by *Native Son* (1940), in which the accidents of circumstance drive the protagonist, Bigger Thomas, to a tragic end. There is little to endear Bigger to the reader, and the novel's mechanistic plot clearly dooms him from the outset. However, after he is sentenced to death for murder, Bigger comes to a kind of psychological closure, understanding how his environment has determined who he is.

As the Civil Rights Movement began, Wright's preeminence as a novelist found challengers in **James Baldwin** and **Ralph Ellison**, both of whom appeared to reject Wright's didacticism and determinism. A former protégé of Wright's, Ralph Ellison seemed to be more interested in the aesthetics of the novel than in producing **protest literature**. Arguably, however, the plot of *Invisible Man* (1952) is nearly as deterministic as Wright's. Nonetheless, the style and structure of the novel are extraordinary and original. Its unnamed narrator eventually comes to understand that he has a "socially responsible role to play" (Ellison, 581). At of the end of the novel, he has yet to undertake such a role.

Baldwin's work launched additional challenges to Wright's preeminence. Perhaps his most admired novel, *Go Tell It on the Mountain* (1953) thoroughly eschewed Wright's sociological Black-White conflict in favor of a nuanced psychological exploration rendered in richly literary language that owed equal parts to the Black church and to Henry James. For Baldwin, the novel was an exercise in coming to terms with his sexuality and his relationships with his father and the church. Its protagonist finds a kind of secular salvation in suffering, and Baldwin would return to this theme frequently. Baldwin's modern adaptation of the Black church's oral traditions is perhaps his most enduring stylistic contribution to African American literature. *Giovanni's Room* (1956), set mainly in Paris, tells the story of a White American man who falls in love with an Italian man but ultimately is unable to love anyone. With *Another Country* (1962), which is set in New York City and concerns interracial relationships, among other things, Baldwin earned both critical and popular acclaim. His reputation as an essayist probably still overshadows his reputation as a novelist, and his later works of fiction are arguably as protest-oriented as Richard Wright's work.

As the Civil Rights Movement continued into the 1960s, the **Black Arts Movement** promoted an aesthetic to complement the greater militancy of the **Black Power** Movement. Reasserting politics as the most important dimension of literary production, some members of the movement rejected figures such as Ellison and Baldwin as assimilationists whose work was too invested in European literary models. Because their forms lent themselves to performance, poetry and drama are more characteristic of the Black Arts Movement's literary activism. However, novelists such as John Williams in *The Man Who Cried I Am* (1967), did represent African Americans successfully countering discrimination with strategic anger. The nonlinear narrative of Williams's novel underscores the historical determination of both collective and individual destinies. Other novelists of the period, such as **Margaret Abigail Walker** in *Jubilee* (1966) and **Ernest James Gaines** in *The Autobiography of Miss Jane Pittman* (1971), included clear critiques of racism in their work while maintaining a focus on the individual voice and psychology. Walker's novel, which was based on the life of her grandmother, and Gaines's, which is told in the voice of a 110-year old ex-slave, returned once again to the tradition of the slave narrative. Other supporters of the Black Arts Movement, such as **John Edgar Wideman** in *A Glance Away* (1967), did not strictly adhere to the movement's exclusive focus on African American politics.

The publication of **Alice Walker**'s *The Third Life of Grange Copeland* and **Toni Morrison**'s *The Bluest Eye* in 1970 marked a revival of interest in Black women's literature. Thanks to Morrison's position as a senior editor at Random House for a number of years and recovery work such as Walker's on Hurston, new novels by Black women and the republication of relatively unread works from previous decades permanently transformed the field of the African American novel. This transformation was not simply a restoration of **gender** parity; on the contrary, women novelists such as Morrison espoused an approach to storytelling that rejected anything like Wright's protest novel, which had usually foregrounded male characters and focused exclusively on Black communities in conflict with White communities. Instead, women novelists have encouraged fictional portrayals of Black families' and communities' interiors, leaving aside the violence of interracial conflict. Moreover, these novelists have confronted problems within the Black community, including spousal abuse, drawing criticism from those who prefer that art promote a positive, empowering image of African Americans. For instance, Morrison explores Black family dynamics, some of them dysfunctional, and Black women's internalization of White beauty standards in *The Bluest Eye*; in this exploration, her novel was anticipated by **Gwendolyn Brooks**'s *Maud Martha* (1953), a novel about an ordinary Black woman that was long eclipsed by fiction about men with extraordinary experiences. The epistolary novel *The Color Purple* (1982), which also concerns issues of gender and women's self-determination, is Alice Walker's most critically acclaimed work. Other significant women novelists include **Toni Cade Bambara, Gayl Jones, Paule Marshall, Terry McMillan,** and **Gloria Naylor**. Jones's *Eva's Man* (1976) provoked controversy over its explicit sex and violence and excited readers with its experimental narrative style, which took the form of an unreliable female narrator. The novel's depiction of sexuality is bleak and violent; its protagonist is sent to prison after she kills and castrates a lover. It closes with the woman's cellmate making love to her, the novel's only moment of possible redemption.

Naylor's *The Women of Brewster Place* (1982), *Linden Hills* (1985), and *Mama Day* (1988) are subtle, inventive narratives that explore women's issues, questions of identity, and conflicts within both the African American working class and middle class. McMillan's novel *Waiting to Exhale* (1992) was critically acclaimed and also enormously popular; it was adapted to the screen, as were Walker's *The Color Purple* and Morrison's *Beloved*.

Today the African American novel is richly informed by a variety of traditions and is breaking new ground in innovative forms and in genres such as science fiction, to which **Samuel R. Delany** in *Dhalgren* (1974) and **Octavia E. Butler** in *Patternmaster* (1976) have made important contributions. For both Delany and Butler, race remains a concern, but the conventions of science fiction allow them to address race in less literal and more conceptually creative ways than the traditional novel might. **Walter Mosley** and **Barbara Neely**, among others, have contributed original novels to the crime fiction genre. Writers such as **James Earl Hardy, E. Lynn Harris, Randall Garrett Kenan**, and **Ann Allen Shockley** have expanded the possibilities for gay and lesbian representation in the Black novel, ground that was first broken by James Baldwin and Nella Larsen (*see* **Gay Literature; Lesbian Literature**). In 1993 Toni Morrison became the first African American to win the Nobel Prize for Literature. Finally, the popular success of works by Baldwin, Walker, Morrison, McMillan, and Harris, among others, has meant that the African American novel now reaches a much larger audience than ever before without sacrificing any of its commitment to the representing African American experiences (Graham).

Resources: Primary Sources: James Baldwin, *Early Novels and Stories: Go Tell It on the Mountain, Giovanni's Room, Another Country, Going to Meet the Man* (New York: Library of America, 1998); Arna Bontemps, *Black Thunder* (1936; repr. Boston: Beacon, 1997); William Wells Brown, *Clotel; or, The President's Daughter: A Narrative of Slave Life in the United States* (1853; repr. New York: Collier, 1970); Octavia Butler, *Patternmaster* (New York: Warner, 1976); Charles W. Chesnutt, *The House Behind the Cedars* (1900; repr. New York: Collier, 1969); Martin Delany, *Blake; or, The Huts of America* (1859; repr. Boston: Beacon, 1970); Samuel R. Delany, *Dhalgren* (1974; repr. Hanover, NH: Wesleyan University Press, 1996); Ralph Ellison, *Invisible Man* (New York: Vintage, 1952); Ernest Gaines, *The Autobiography of Miss Jane Pittman* (1971; repr. New York: Bantam, 1982); Sutton Griggs, *Imperium in Imperio: A Study of the Negro Race Problem* (1899; repr. Miami: Mnemosyne, 1969); Frances E. W. Harper, *Iola Leroy; or, Shadows Uplifted* (1892; repr. Boston: Beacon, 1987); Chester Himes: *Cotton Comes to Harlem* (New York: Putnam, 1965); *If He Hollers, Let Him Go* (New York: Doubleday, 1946); *Yesterday Will Make You Cry* (1953; repr. New York: Norton, 1998); Pauline E. Hopkins, *The Magazine Novels of Pauline E. Hopkins* (New York: Oxford University Press, 1988); Langston Hughes, *Not Without Laughter* (1930; repr. New York: Scribner's, 1995); Zora Neale Hurston, *Their Eyes Were Watching God* (Philadelphia: Lippincott, 1937); Harriet A. Jacobs, *Incidents in the Life of a Slave Girl, Written by Herself* (New York: Oxford University Press, 1988); James Weldon Johnson, *The Autobiography of an Ex-Colored Man* (1912; repr. New York: Vintage, 1927); Nella Larsen, *Quicksand and Passing* (2 novels), ed. Deborah E. McDowell (New Brunswick, NJ: Rutgers University Press, 1986); Alain Locke, ed., *The New Negro* (1925; repr. New York: Atheneum, 1992); Claude McKay, *Home to Harlem*

(1928; repr. Boston: Northeastern University Press, 1987); Toni Morrison: *Beloved* (New York: Knopf, 1987); *The Bluest Eye* (New York: Plume, 1970); Gloria Naylor: *Linden Hills* (New York: Penguin, 1985); *Mama Day* (New York: Vintage, 1993); *The Women of Brewster Place* (New York: Penguin, 1982); Wallace Thurman, *The Blacker the Berry* (1929; repr. New York: Collier, 1970); Jean Toomer, *Cane* (1923; repr. New York: Norton, 1988); Alice Walker, *The Color Purple* (New York: Harcourt Brace Jovanovich, 1982); *The Third Life of Grange Copeland* (New York: Pocket, 1970); Margaret Walker, *Jubilee* (Boston: Houghton Mifflin, 1966); John Williams, *The Man Who Cried I Am* (Boston: Little, Brown, 1967); Harriet E. Wilson, *Our Nig; or, Sketches from the Life of a Free Black, in a Two-Story White House, North, Showing That Slavery's Shadows Fall Even There* (1859; repr. New York: Vintage, 1983); Richard Wright, *Early Works: Lawd Today!, Uncle Tom's Children, Native Son* (New York: Library of American, 1991). **Secondary Sources:** Bernard W. Bell, *The Afro-American Novel and Its Tradition* (Amherst: University of Massachusetts Press, 1987); Robert Bone, *The Negro Novel in America* (New Haven, CT: Yale University Press, 1958); Hazel V. Carby, *Reconstructing Womanhood: The Emergence of the Afro-American Woman Novelist* (New York: Oxford Universty Press, 1987); Barbara Christian, *Black Women Novelists: The Development of a Tradition, 1892–1976* (Westport, CT: Greenwood Press, 1980); Maryemma Graham, ed., *Cambridge Companion to the African American Novel* (Cambridge: Cambridge University Press, 2004); Frederik L. Rusch, "Form, Fuction, and Creative Tension in *Cane*: Jean Toomer and the Need for the Avant-Garde," *MELUS* 17, no. 4 (Winter 1991–1992), 15–28; Robert B. Stepto, *From Behind the Veil: A Study of Afro-American Narrative*, 2nd ed. (Urbana: University of Illinois Press, 1991); Ian Watt, *The Rise of the Novel: Studies in Defoe, Richardson, and Fielding* (Berkeley: University of California Press, 1957).

Douglas Steward

Nugent, Richard Bruce (1906–1987). Writer and artist. Nugent is often referred to as little more than an eyewitness to the **Harlem Renaissance**, yet he played a far more significant role, contributing to the movement as a prolific writer and artist. In **Washington, D.C.**, where he was born on July 2, 1906, Nugent became a member of **Georgia Douglas Johnson**'s artistic circle and befriended **Langston Hughes**. After settling in New York City in 1925, he was initiated into the Harlem Renaissance's inner circle and contributed his African-themed short story "Sahdji" to what was to become the "bible" of the Harlem Renaissance—**Alain Locke**'s famous collection of Renaissance writing, *The New Negro* (1925).

While this could have been the starting point of a successful career involving critical appraisal and awards, Nugent opted for the bohemian life. Unusual for a Renaissance member, he displayed great interest in the contemporary White avant-garde and regularly visited Greenwich Village. His open display of homosexual interests contributed to his special position within the movement: Nugent could be described as having embraced a "queer" identity. As one of the youngest Renaissance members, he delighted in playing the part of the extravagant bohemian and was famous for his informal way of dressing and his outrageous manners. Befitting this bohemian lifestyle, Nugent always lacked financial stability. He depended on friends' generosity and spent some of the Harlem Renaissance years on the floor of **Wallace Thurman**'s residence at 267 West 136th Street—which Thurman and others dubbed "Niggeratti Manor," a pun on literati—and was well known for outrageous partying (Lewis).

Nugent's creative process seemed to seemed to fit his chaotic environment: He wrote on paper bags and toilet paper, and occasionally, as was the case with the poem "Shadow"—eventually published in *Opportunity* in 1925—his work had to be retrieved from the trash can where it had been discarded, mistaken for garbage. Many of Nugent's artistic creations were similarly endangered because he often lost, destroyed, or gave away his drawings. This, however, does not mean that his contributions to the Harlem Renaissance were negligible. Apart from "Sahdji" and a number of poems, Nugent's fame during the Harlem Renaissance rested on his extraordinary stream-of-consciousness tale "Smoke, Lilies and Jade," the first openly homoerotic story published by an African American, which appeared in the highly provocative magazine *Fire!!* (1926).

In Nugent's work, **race** often plays only an incidental role because his focus was on aesthetics. Appropriately, he favored a decadent style as established by artists such as Aubrey Beardsley, to which he added African motifs. His range of literary subject material was wide, reaching from African themes to his late 1920s Bible stories, the undated Japanese-themed novel *Geisha Man*, and *Gentleman Jigger* (n.d.), Nugent's autobiographical account of the Harlem Renaissance. Since Nugent frequently featured male same-sex attraction in his works, few of his creations were published during the Harlem Renaissance.

Nugent's contribution to African American culture went far beyond the creation of literature and works of art. For instance, he proved himself a talented actor in *Porgy* (1927–1930) and was involved in the Negro Ballet Company in the late 1940s. In 1952, Nugent married Grace Marr, who died in 1969. In the early 1970s, Nugent was discovered as an expert on the Harlem Renaissance and, in the early 1980s, as a source of information on gay history. A film clip featuring him is used in the stylish quasi-documentary film by Issac Julien, *Looking for Langston* (1989). He died of congestive heart failure on May 27, 1987. In 2002, a collection of Nugent's works was published, finally enabling an appropriate appreciation of this artist and writer whose multifaceted literary and artistic heritage had been unknown to the public for decades. (*See* **Gay Literature**; **Queer Theory**.)

Resources: Primary Sources: Richard Bruce (pseudonym of Nugent): "Cavalier," in *Caroling Dusk: An Anthology of Verse by Negro Poets*, ed. Countee Cullen (New York: Harper & Bros., 1927), 205–206; "The Dark Tower," *Opportunity* Oct. 1927, pp. 305–306; "Sahdji," in *The New Negro*, ed. Alain Locke (New York: Boni, 1925), 113–114; "Sahdji: An African Ballet," in *Plays of Negro Life: A Sourcebook of Native American Drama*, ed. Alain Locke (New York: Harper & Bros., 1927), 387–400; "Shadow," *Opportunity*, Oct. 1925, p. 296; "Smoke, Lilies and Jade," *Fire!!* 1 (1926), 33–39;

"What Price Glory in Uncle Tom's Cabin," *Harlem*, Nov. 1928, pp. 25–26; Jean Blackwell Hutson, interview with Richard Bruce Nugent, videotape (Apr. 14, 1982), Schomburg Center for Research in Black Culture, New York City; Richard Bruce Nugent: "'. . . and More Gently Still': A Myth," *Trend: A Quarterly of the Seven Arts* 1 (1932), 53–54; *Gay Rebel of the Harlem Renaissance: Selections from the Work of Richard Bruce Nugent*, ed. Thomas H. Wirth (Durham, NC: Duke University Press, 2002); "Lighting FIRE!!," insert to *Fire!!* (1926; Metuchen, NJ: Fire!!, 1982); "Marshall's: A Portrait," *Phylon* 5 (1944), 316–318; "My Love," *Palms*, Oct. 1926, p. 20; Richard Bruce Nugent Papers, private collection of Thomas H. Wirth, Elizabeth, NJ; Thomas H. Wirth, interviews with Richard Bruce Nugent, tape recordings (June 19, 1983– Sept. 5, 1983), collections of Thomas H. Wirth, Elizabeth, NJ, and Schomburg Center for Research in Black Culture, New York City. **Secondary Sources:** Michael L. Cobb, "Insolent Racing, Rough Narrative: The Harlem Renaissance's Impolite Queers," *Callaloo* 23 (2000), 328–351; Rodney Evans, dir., *Brother to Brother* (Miasma, 2003); Eric Garber, "Richard Bruce Nugent," in *Afro-American Writers from the Harlem Renaissance to 1940*, ed. Trudier Harris and Thadious Davis (Detroit: Gale, 1987), 213–221; James V. Hatch, "An Interview with Bruce Nugent—Actor, Artist, Writer, Dancer," *Artists and Influences* 1 (1982), 81–104; Isaac Julien, dir., *Looking for Langston* (New York: Waterbearer Films, 1992); Jeff Kisseloff, *You Must Remember This: An Oral History of Manhattan from the 1890s to World War II* (San Diego: Harcourt Brace Jovanovich, 1989); David Levering Lewis, *When Harlem was in Vogue* (New York: Knopf, 1981); A. B. Christa Schwarz, *Gay Voices of the Harlem Renaissance* (Bloomington: Indiana University Press, 2003); Seth Clark Silberman: "Lighting the Harlem Renaissance aFire!!: Embodying Richard Bruce Nugent's Bohemian Politic," in *The Greatest Taboo: Homosexuality in Black Communities*, ed. Delroy Constantine-Simms (Los Angeles: Alyson, 2001), 254–273; "Looking for Richard Bruce Nugent and Wallace Henry Thurman: Reclaiming Black Male Same-Sexualities in the New Negro Movement," *In Process* 1 (1996), 53–73; Charles Michael Smith, "Bruce Nugent: Bohemian of the Harlem Renaissance," in *In the Life: A Black Gay Anthology*, ed. Joseph Beam (Boston: Alyson, 1986), 209–220; Thomas H. Wirth: "FIRE!! in Retrospect," insert to *Fire!!* (1926; Metuchen, NJ: Fire!!, 1982); "Introduction," in *Gay Rebel of the Harlem Renaissance: Selections from the Work of Richard Bruce Nugent*, ed. Thomas H. Wirth (Durham, NC: Duke University Press, 2002), 1–61.

A. B. Christa Schwarz

Núñez, Elizabeth (born c. 1950). Novelist, editor, and educator. Elizabeth Núñez, best known for her critically acclaimed novels, was born in Cocorite, Trinidad. When she was seven years old, her short story won a local newspaper's tiny tot contest, and she decided that she wanted to be a novelist. Núñez completed secondary school at St. Joseph's Convent in Port of Spain; she received a B.A. (1967) from Marian College in Wisconsin and an M.A. (1971) and a Ph.D. (1977) from New York University. In 1972, Núñez joined the faculty at Medgar Evers College of the City University of New York, where she is a CUNY Distinguished Professor of English. A former fellow at the Yaddo and MacDowell colonies and the Paden Institute, she founded the

National Black Writers Conference with **John O. Killens** in 1986; served as the conference's director from 1986 to 2000; was executive producer of *Black Writers in America*, a television series hosted by **Ossie Davis**; was a member of a committee commissioned by President Clinton to review the Public Programs Division of the National Endowment for the Humanities; and was a member of the White House Roundtable on Women's Initiatives and Outreach.

Núñez is the author of five novels: *When Rocks Dance* (1987); *Beyond the Limbo Silence* (1998), which received the Independent Press Award for Multicultural Fiction; *Bruised Hibiscus* (2000), which won an American Book Award; *Discretion* (2003); and *Grace* (2003). She edited a collection of essays, *Defining Ourselves: Black Writers in the 1990s* (1999), with Brenda M. Greene. Núñez's writing has appeared in publications including *Black Scholar*, *Essence*, the *New York Times Book Review*, and the *Philadelphia Inquirer*. She received an honorary Doctorate in Humane Letters from Marian College in 1999 and has garnered additional awards for her contributions to the arts and education.

Resources: "Elizabeth Núñez," *African American Literature Book Club*, http://aalbc .com/authors/elizabet.htm; Elizabeth Núñez: *Beyond the Limbo Silence* (Seattle, WA: Seal Press, 1998); *Bruised Hibiscus* (Seattle, WA: Seal Press, 2000); *Discretion* (New York: One World/Ballantine, 2003); *Grace* (New York: One World, 2003); *When Rocks Dance* (New York: Ballantine, 1987); Elizabeth Núñez and Brenda M. Greene, eds., *Defining Ourselves: Black Writers in the 90s* (New York: Peter Lang, 1999).

Linda M. Carter

Nuyorican Poets Café. Miguel Algarín and Miguel Piñero opened the Nuyorican Poets Café on Manhattan's Lower East Side in 1975, when poetry gatherings at Algarín's apartment became too crowded. A performance space for poetry, live music, and theater, the café first concentrated on the Nuyorican (New York Puerto Rican) experience, and participants, including Puerto Rican immigrants Pedro Pietro and **Piri Thomas**, performed autobiographical narratives about immigrant life in New York City and about immigrants' disillusionment with the American Dream. The café thrived during the mid-1970s, drawing attention to Nuyorican writing, including Piñero's award-winning play *Short Eyes* and the anthlology *Nuyorican Poetry*, which Algarín and Piñero edited. Nuyorican poetry, written in a wide range of styles, makes extensive use of code-switching, mixing English and Spanish. Code-switching had been used before as a linguistic tool, but the Chicano writer Alurista is generally credited with popularizing it in the 1960s. Later, Nuyorican poets employed code-switching as a method for establishing a middle ground between the United States and Puerto Rico. Many of these poets based their poems on street **slang** and rhythm, which contributed to their fluid approach to language.

Tackling themes of homosexuality, drugs, and disaffection with the mainstream, the first wave of Nuyorican writers followed in the footsteps of the **Beats** a decade before, some of whom frequented the café. Allen Ginsberg and

William Burroughs were often sighted at the café, as was **Amiri Baraka**. After moving in 1980, the café closed its doors in 1983. Five years later, Piñero died from drug and alcohol use at the age of forty. Soon after, Algarín and the poet Bob Holman reopened the café as a memorial to their friend. Algarín, who has taught Shakespeare at Rutgers University for two decades, has enlarged the definition of "Nuyorican" to encompass a multicultural mind-set—he has even claimed that Shakespeare was a Nuyorican. The café in its latest incarnation has become inclusive of all races, bound together as a community by the performative, *trovador* aspect of their writing and by their intense language play. The poets often self-identify as a vanguard, bringing a new poetic language to the masses via performance, MTV, and other popular media. Rather than celebrating art for art's sake, the Nuyorican poets find an almost Marxist use value to their poetry; it is polemical, the voice of the disaffected. Several notable contemporary poets have read at the café, including the late Pedro Pietro, Piri Thomas, Rudolfo Anaya, Maggie Estep, and **Paul Beatty**, as have many first-time performers and beginning writers. *Aloud: Voices from the Nuyorican Poets Café*, edited by Algarín and Holman, won the American Book Award in 1994. Algarín, with Lois Griffith, also edited *Action: The Nuyorican Poets Café Theater Festival* (1997). The café's Friday night slams are still held each week at the East 3rd Street location and are broadcast in **San Francisco, California, Chicago, Illinois**, and Tokyo, Japan. (*See* **Perdomo, Willie.**)

Resources: Miguel Algarín, *Love Is Hard Work: Memorias de Loisaida* (New York: Scribner's, 1997); Miguel Algarín, and Lois Griffith, *Action: The Nuyorican Poets Café Theater Festival* (New York: Simon and Schuster, 1997); Miguel Algarín, Bob Holman, and Nicole Blackman, *Aloud: Voices from the Nuyorican Poets Café* (New York: Owl Books, 1994); Miguel Algarín and Miguel Piñero, *Nuyorican Poetry: An Anthology of Puerto Rican Words and Feelings* (New York: Morrow, 1975); Carmen Delores Hernández, *Puerto Rican Voices in English: Interviews with Writers* (Westport, CT: Praeger, 1997); Bob Holman, *Bob Holman's The Collect Call of the Wild* (New York: Henry Holt, 1995); Nuyorican Poets Café Web page, http://www.nuyorican.org/; Miguel Piñero: *Short Eyes: A Play* (New York: Hill and Wang, 1975); *The Sun Always Shines for the Cool; A Midnight Moon at the Greasy Spoon; Eulogy for a Small Time Thief* (Houston, TX: Arte Público Press, 1984).

Ryan Chapman